ENVIRONMENTAL HEALTH STANDARDS IN HOUSING

AUSTRALIA AND NEW ZEALAND
The Law Book Company Ltd.
Sydney : Melbourne : Perth

CANADA AND U.S.A.
The Carswell Company Ltd.
Agincourt, Ontario

INDIA
N. M. Tripathi Private Ltd.
Bombay
and
Eastern Law House
Calcutta and Delhi
M.P.P. House
Bangalore

ISRAEL
Steimatzky's Agency Ltd.
Jerusalem : Tel-Aviv : Haifa

MALAYSIA : SINGAPORE : BRUNEI
Malayan Law Journal (Pte.) Ltd.
Singapore and Kuala Lumpur

ENVIRONMENTAL HEALTH STANDARDS IN HOUSING

by

David Ormandy, F.R.S.H., *Associate Fellow, Legal Research Institute, University of Warwick.*

and

Roger Burridge, *Barrister, Lecturer in Law, University of Warwick.*

In association with the Institution of Environmental Health Officers. Foreword by Terry Brunt, Chair of the Housing Committee

LONDON
SWEET & MAXWELL
1988

Published in 1988 by
Sweet & Maxwell Limited of
11 New Fetter Lane London
Computerset by Promenade Graphics Ltd., Cheltenham
Printed by Butler and Tanner Ltd., Frome, Somerset.

British Library Cataloguing in Publication Data
Ormandy, David
  Environmental health standards in housing.
  1. Great Britain. Housing. Public health aspects. Law
  I. Title   II. Burridge, Roger
  344.104'63635

ISBN 0–421–36550–1

All rights reserved.
No part of this publication may be
reproduced or transmitted, in any form or
by any means, electronic, mechanical, photocopying,
recording or otherwise, or stored in any
retrieval system of any nature, without the
written permission of the copyright holder
and the publisher, application for which shall be
made to the publisher.

©
D. Ormandy and R. Burridge
1988

FOREWORD

The conditions under which people live have been the direct concern of the environmental health officer for over one hundred years.

As conditions and standards of both old and new housing continue to deteriorate, the environmental health officers and housing practitioners face the growing and difficult task of reversing the spiral of decline.

Changing tenure patterns, smaller households, increases in the number of elderly owner/occupiers, escalating disrepair costs, the increased use of hostels, "bedsit" accommodation and growing homelessness, all point to the need for the environmental health profession to be more diligent in its efforts to prevent ill health. Environment health officers must ensure that conditions that prevailed in the earlier part of this century do not return to our towns and cities.

There is growing evidence that our housing continues to wear out faster than it is being renewed. Very largely because our generation is servicing three different generations of housing decay at once; Victorian, inter-war and 1960s housing.

Present and proposed housing legislation, heralded as the "Housing Revolution" will only add increased complexities to the law and practice of environmental health and housing, presenting new challenges to environmental health officers.

There is an ever growing demand for guidance through the complexities of this law and its interpretation.

Here is a practical book, written out of research and experience in work in housing.

It aims at being a guide for people involved in ensuring standards in housing are maintained and health is not threatened by relaxation of laws or changing attitudes.

Well set out, the book is easy reading, extremely practical, a complete reference, written by the practitioners for the practitioners in housing today.

As Chairman of the Institution's Housing Committee, I commend this book to all involved in housing, for inclusion in departmental libraries and as a constant companion to those striving to maintain better standards in housing today.

T. J. Brunt, F.I.E.H., M.B.I.M.,
Chairman of Housing Committee
Institute of Environmental Health Officers

PREFACE

This work is concerned with the practical application of housing standards to individual houses. It is primarily intended for local authority officers, and deals with the means by which the authority, through its environmental health department, can satisfy the powers and duties relating to individual dwellings and houses which are imposed on the authority by Parliament. It is therefore orientated towards the practical steps necessary to enforce the standards and emulates the earlier contribution of Swift's *Housing Administration*. It provides in a single volume information and details on the inspection of houses, the identification of sources of dampness, the assessment of housing conditions, the standards and their interpretation, and the procedures for the enforcement or implementation of those standards.

The presentation of the book reflects the process of diagnosing and treating substandard housing. For this reason the various separate legal norms and their procedures for enforcement are not set out sequentially. Instead, after explaining the duties and responsibilities of local authorities in relation to individual houses, the practice and purpose of inspecting the fabric of a house is discussed.

This physical appraisal of the building is the basis for the application of any legal standard. The book concerns itself next with a description of the legal norms and the circumstances in which each will apply, before setting out the enforcement procedures of each of the standards.

The legal standards which are the subject of this work are to be found in the Public Health and Housing Acts. Guidance in the interpretation of standards is contained in the decisions of the courts and in memoranda and circulars distributed by the Department of the Environment. But beyond these published blueprints operates a complex practice informed by professional training, accumulated experience and the requirements of the individual local authority which employs environmental health officers.

The Introduction acknowledges many of these influences on an officer's discretionary application of the various standards and the book recognises that the professional training and development of environmental health officers espouses an ethos directed towards protecting the health of occupiers by preserving or replacing the housing stock. Where relevant the text includes references to documents and statements from professional bodies articulating the wider concerns of the profession. An officer may resort to the guidance provided by such principles on those occasions when statutes and the pronouncements of the courts appear inadequate.

PREFACE

The book is the result of discussions and debates with many of those, too numerous to acknowledge personally, who are active in the enforcement of housing standards. Special mention must be made of the contributions and support of members of the Health and Housing Group; Stephen Battersby; Ann Stewart and other colleagues at the Law School, University of Warwick; and the Nuffield Foundation, since the book was largely conceived during a research project the authors were conducting into the work of environmental health officers. Thanks are due to the controller of Her Majesty's Stationery Office for permission to reproduce short extracts from various Crown copyright publications.

Environmental health officers are in the forefront of the effort to maintain adequate housing standards and this book is intended to be of assistance to them, as well as to those housing managers, lawyers and students who have an interest in the condition of housing. In an area in which there is much complex law and a correspondingly intricate practice, the analysis and interpretation may not meet with the agreement of all. The authors would appreciate comments, criticisms and suggestions, which can be made to them at the Law School, University of Warwick, Coventry CV4 7AL.

The law of housing standards is rapidly developing and requires further reform. At the time of writing a number of changes to housing legislation have been proposed. Where possible such changes are discussed. The book represents the state of the law on April 1, 1988.

March 26, 1988 David Ormandy
University of Warwick Roger Burridge

CONTENTS

	Page
Foreword	v
Preface	vii
Table of Cases	xiii
Table of Statutes	xx
Table of Statutory Instruments	xxx
Introduction	xxxiii

	Para.
1. The Duties and Powers of Local Government	
Definition of local authorities and local housing authorities	1.02
General duties of local housing authorities	1.05
Delegation of authorities' functions	1.11
Powers of entry, warrants and obstruction	1.15
2. Inspections and Surveys	
Principles of inspection and assessment of dwellings	2.02
Guidelines on healthful housing	2.05
Health effects of housing conditions	2.12
Effects of defects	2.23
Inspection of individual dwellings	2.40
Monitoring structural movement	2.69
Non-traditional house construction	2.71
Specifications of works	2.88
House condition surveys	2.89
3. Housing Standards	
Introduction	3.02
Statutory nuisances	3.08
Fitness for human habitation	3.19
Substantial disrepair	3.47
Interference with personal comfort	3.54
Standard amenities	3.60
4. Authentication and Service of Notices	
Informal notices	4.02
Authentication of orders, notices, demands, etc.	4.04

Service of notices, demands, etc. 4.11
Identification of persons to be served with orders and
   notices 4.17

5. Enforcement of the Standards
Action to deal with statutory nuisances 5.02
Action to deal with houses unfit for human habitation 5.65
Action to deal with houses in substantial disrepair and in
   disrepair which interferes with personal comfort 5.170
Houses lacking standard amenities 5.202

6. Houses in Multiple Occupation
Definition of "house in multiple occupation" 6.02
Fitness for multiple occupation 6.18
Management of houses in multiple occupation 6.29
Means of escape in case of fire 6.57
Action to deal with houses unfit for multiple occupation 6.64
Management orders 6.92
Prosecution for offences under management regulations 6.102
Notices to require works to make good neglect 6.104
Action to ensure adequate means of escape from fire 6.112
Enforcement of notices 6.132
Reconnection or maintenance of services 6.142
Control orders 6.147

7. Overcrowding
Historical background and introduction 7.02
Standards applicable to all dwellings 7.07
Definitions 7.14
Offences 7.20
Information 7.31
Enforcement of overcrowing provisions 7.39
Overcrowding in houses in multiple occupation 7.48
Procedure for abating or preventing overcrowding in
   houses in multiple occupation 7.52
Miscellaneous overcrowding provisions 7.67

8. Dampness
Definition of "dampness" 8.03
Direct physical damage from dampness 8.07
Threats to health resulting from dampness 8.20
Sources of dampness 8.34
Measurement for dampness in the fabric 8.84
Measurements for relative humidity and condensation 8.95

Sampling possible mould growth	8.97
Investigation of sources of dampness	8.103
Investigation of condensation	8.108

9. Other Matters: Evidence, Council Houses, Compensation
Evidence	9.02
Procedure for sub-standard council houses	9.18
Obligations to occupiers displaced	9.23

Page

Appendix 1
Example Inspection Reports 323

Appendix 2
Example Specifications 333

Appendix 3
Characteristics of Sources of Dampness 346

Appendix 4
Some Reference Material and Addresses 349

Index 353

TABLE OF CASES

Annicola Investments Ltd. v. Minister of Housing and Local Government [1968] 1 Q.B. 631; [1966] 2 W.L.R. 1204; 130 J.P. 163; 110 S.J. 447; [1965] 3 All E.R. 850; 64 L.G.R. 387 3–30
Anspach v. Chalton Steam Shipping Co. Ltd. [1955] 2 Q.B. 21; [1955] 2 W.L.R. 601; 99 S.J. 203; *sub nom.* Anspatch v. Charlton Steam Shipping Co. Ltd. [1955] 1 All E.R. 693, C.A. 7.15
Arieli v. Duke of Westminster (1983) 269 E.G. 535; (1984) 24 R.V.R. 45, C.A. 5–85, 5–119, 5–161, 5–187, 5–245
Associated Provincial Picture Houses v. Wednesbury Corp. [1948] 1 K.B. 223; [1948] L.J.R. 190; 177 L.T. 641; 63 T.L.R. 623; 112 J.P. 55; 92 S.J. 26; [1947] 2 All E.R. 60; 45 L.G.R. 635, C.A.; affirming [1947] L.J.R. 678 .... 5–173, 5–208, 5–233, 5–263
Att.-Gen. v. Mutual Tontine Westminster Chambers Association Ltd. (1876) 1 Ex.D. 469 3–29
Att.-Gen. (Gambia) v. Pierre Sarr N'Jie [1961] A.C. 617; [1961] 2 W.L.R. 845; 105 S.J. 421; [1961] 2 All E.R. 504, P.C. 6–103

Bacon v. Grimsby Corp. [1950] 1 K.B. 272; 65 T.L.R. 709; 113 J.P. 539; 93 S.J. 742; [1949] 2 All E.R. 875; 48 L.G.R. 42, C.A. 5–71, 5–75
Bacup Corp. v. Smith (1890) 44 Ch.D. 359 .... 5–13, 5–78
Bainbridge, South Shields (D'Arcy Street) Compulsory Purchase Order 1937, *Re* [1939] 1 K.B. 500 3–30
Barber v. Shah (1985) 17 H.L.R. 584, D.C. 5–126
Barney, *Re*; Harrison v. Barney [1984]·3 Ch. 562 .... 5–13, 5–78
Bennet v. Preston Borough Council, unrep., *Environmental Health*, April 1983 .... 3–16, 3–59
Berg v. Trafford Borough Council (1988) 20 H.L.R. 47 .... 6–09, 6–73A, 6–108, 6–122, 6–123
Betts v. Penge Urban District Council [1942] 2 K.B. 154 3–15
Bird v. Lord Greville (1844) C. & E. 317 3–23
Birmingham District Council v. Kelly and Others (1985) 17 H.L.R. 572, D.C. 3–14, 3–16, 5–07, 5–17
—— v. McMahon and Others (1987) 17 H.L.R. 452, D.C. 3–11
Bottomley v. Harrison 116 J.P. 113; 96 S.J. 90; [1952] 1 All E.R. 368, D.C. 5–13, 5–78
Bowditch v. Wakefield Local Board (1871) L.R. 6 Q.B. 567 .... 5–13, 5–78
Bradley v. Chorley Borough Council (1985) 17 H.L.R. 305; (1985) 83 L.G.R. 623; (1985) 275 E.G. 801, C.A. 5–71
Bristol Corp. v. Sinnot [1918] 1 Ch. 62 5–18
Brown v. Minister of Housing and Local Government [1953] 1 W.L.R. 1370; 118 J.P. 143; 97 S.J. 797; [1953] 2 All E.R. 1385; 4 P. & C.R. 111; *sub nom.* Wandsworth Borough Council (Sutherland Grove) Compulsory Purchase Order, *Re*, Brown v. Minister of Housing and Local Government, 52 L.G.R. 34 .... 5–82, 5–105, 5–185
Buswell v. Goodwin [1971] 1 W.L.R. 92; (1970) 115 S.J. 77; [1971] 1 All E.R. 418; 22 P. & C.R. 162; 69 L.G.R. 201, C.A. 7–24
Butler, Camberwell (Wingfield Mews) No. 2 Clearance Order 1936, *Re* [1939] 1 K.B. 570 .... 3–29, 3–30

TABLE OF CASES

Canterbury City Council v. Bern (1982) 44 P. & C.R. 178; [1981] J.P.L. 749,
D.C. 5–81, 5–96, 5–183, 5–197, 5–210, 5–225, 5–234, 5–240, 6–67, 6–115
Celcrest Properties Ltd. v. Hastings Borough Council, unrep., Ch.D., October 29,
1979 5–59
Chester v. Powell (1885) 52 L.T.(N.S.) 722 3–23
Church of Our Lady of Hal v. Camden London Borough Council (1980) 255 E.G.
991; (1980) 40 P. & C.R. 472, C.A. 5–81, 5–183
City of Westminster v. Mavroghenis (1984) 11 H.L.R. 56, D.C. 6–102
Cochrane v. Chanctonbury Rural District Council, 115 J.P. 17; [1950] 2 All E.R.
1134, C.A. 5–89
Cocks v. Thanet District Council [1983] A.C. 286; [1982] 3 W.L.R. 1121; (1982) 126
S.J. 820; [1982] 3 All E.R. 1135; (1983) 81 L.G.R. 81; (1984) 24 R.V.R. 31,
H.L. 5–86, 5–189
Cohen v. West Ham Corp. [1933] Ch. 814 .... 5–81, 5–183, 5–210, 5–225, 5–234, 5–240
Cole v. Harris [1945] K.B. 474 7–15
Coleman v. Dorchester Rural District Council (1935) 2 L.J.C.C.R. 113 5–109
Coventry City Council v. Cartwright [1975] 1 W.L.R. 845; 119 S.J. 235; [1975] 2 All
E.R. 99; 73 L.G.R. 218, D.C. 3–16
—— v. Doyle [1981] 1 W.L.R. 1325; [1981] 2 All E.R. 184; [1981] J.P.L. 666, D.C. .. 5–37
Critchell v. Lambeth Borough Council [1957] 2 Q.B. 535; [1957] 3 W.L.R. 108; 121
J.P. 374; 101 S.J. 515; [1957] 2 All E.R. 417; 55 L.G.R. 339, C.A. 3–28
Curl v. Angelo [1948] L.J.R. 1756; 92 S.J. 513; [1948] 2 All E.R. 189, C.A. 7–15

Daly v. Elstree Rural District Council, 64 T.L.R. 318; 112 J.P. 316; 92 S.J. 335;
[1948] 2 All E.R. 13, C.A. 3–42
De Rothschild v. Wing Rural District Council [1967] 1 W.L.R. 470; 131 J.P. 241; 111
S.J. 176; [1967] 1 All E.R. 597; 65 L.G.R. 203, C.A. 5–249
Dinefwr Borough Council v. Jones (1987) 19 H.L.R. 445, C.A. 3–04
Dover District Council v. Farrar (1982) 2 H.L.R. 32, D.C. 3–16, 5–07
Dudlow Estates v. Sefton Metropolitan Borough Council (1978) 3 H.L.R. 91; (1979)
249 E.G. 1271; [1979] J.P.L. 385, C.A. 5–71
Duke of Bedford v. Dawson (1875) L.R. 20 Eq. 353 3–29
Dunster v. Hollis [1918] 2 K.B. 795 3–23

Elliott v. Brighton Borough Council (1981) 79 L.G.R. 506; (1980) 258 E.G.
441; [1981] J.P.L. 504, C.A.; reversing June 16, 1979, Brighton County
Ct. 5–85, 5–86, 5–94, 5–188, 5–189, 5–196, 5–223, 5–238, 5–265
Ellis Copp & Co. v. Richmond-upon-Thames London Borough Council (1978) 3
H.L.R. 55; (1976) 245 E.G. 931; [1978] J.P.L. 619, C.A. 3–36, 5–71

F.F.F. Estates Ltd. v. Hackney London Borough Council [1981] Q.B. 503; [1980] 3
W.L.R. 909; (1980) 124 S.J. 593; [1981] 1 All E.R. 32; (1980) 4 P. & C.R. 54;
[1981] J.P.L. 34, C.A. 5–71
Fletcher v. Ikeston Corp. (1931) 96 J.P. 7 .... 5–109, 5–212, 5–236
Fulham Vestry v. London City Council [1897] 2 Q.B. 76 3–13

Glasgow Corp. v. Anderson (1970) S.L.T. 225, Ct. of Session 9–29
Glossop Corp. v. Cooper (1913) 136 L.T.N. 90 .... 5–13, 5–78
Goodrich v. Paisner [1957] A.C. 65; [1956] 2 W.L.R. 1053; 100 S.J. 341; [1956] 2 All
E.R. 176, H.L.; reversing sub nom. Paisner v. Goodrich [1955] 2 Q.B. 353;
[1955] 2 W.L.R. 1071; 99 S.J. 353; [1955] 2 All E.R. 330, C.A. 7–15
Gould v. Times Square Estates Ltd., unrep., September 1975 L.A.G. Bull. 247 3–10
Graddage v. Haringey London Borough Council [1975] 1 W.L.R. 241; (1974) 118
S.J. 775; [1975] 1 All E.R. 224; (1974) 29 P. & C.R. 441 .... 4–10, 5–85,
5–188, 5–248

TABLE OF CASES

Greater London Council v. Holmes [1986] Q.B. 989; [1986] 2 W.L.R. 628; (1985) S.J. 300; [1986] 1 All E.R. 739; (1985) 277 E.G. 641; (1985) 18 H.L.R. 131; (1985) 26 R.V.R. 98; [1986] J.P.L. 822; (1986) 83 L.S.Gaz. 1479, C.A.; reversing [1984] 1 W.L.R. 1307; (1984) 128 S.J. 815; [1984] 2 All E.R. 743; [1985] L.G.R. 354; (1984) 17 H.L.R. 31; (1984) 256 P.L.C.R. 39; (1985) 82 L.S.Gaz. 118 .... 9–26, 9–34
—— v. Tower Hamlets London Borough (1984) 15 H.L.R. 54, D.C. 3–13, 3–16

Hackney London Borough v. Ezedinma [1981] 3 All E.R. 438, D.C. 6–14, 6–85, 7–53
Hall v. Manchester Corp. [1915] L.J.Ch. 732 3–21
Hammersmith London Borough Council v. Magnum Automated Products Ltd. [1978] 1 W.L.R. 50; [1977] 1 All E.R. 401; (1977) 76 L.G.R. 159; 121 S.J. 529; [1978] J.P.L. 106, C.A. 5–57
Harrington v. Croydon Corp. [1968] 1 Q.B. 856; [1968] 2 W.L.R. 67; 111 S.J. 740; [1967] 3 All E.R. 929; 65 L.G.R. 95, C.A. 5–71, 5–74, 5–246
Harris v. Hickman [1904] 1 K.B. 563 4–03
Hart v. Windsor (1844) 12 M. & W. 68 3–03
Havant and Waterloo Urban District Council Compulsory Purchase Order (No. 4), Watson's Application, Re [1951] 2 K.B. 779; [1951] 2 T.L.R. 503; 95 S.J. 578; 2 P. & C.R. 131; 49 L.G.R. 738; sub nom. Watson v. Minister of Local Government and Planning, 115 J.P. 519; [1951] 2 All E.R. 664 .... 1–06, 7–41
Hayward v. Marshall, Winchester v. Sharp [1952] 2 Q.B. 89; [1952] 1 T.L.R. 779; 96 S.J. 196; [1952] 1 All E.R. 663, C.A. 7–15
Hillbank Properties v. Hackney London Borough Council [1978] Q.B. 998; [1978] 3 W.L.R. 260; (1978) 122 S.J. 401; [1978] 3 All E.R. 343; (1978) 37 P. & C.R. 218; (1978) 76 L.G.R. 677; (1978) 247 E.G. 807; [1978] J.P.L. 615, C.A. 3–52, 5–71, 5–74, 5–173, 5–177
Hillingdon London Borough Council v. Cutler [1968] 1 Q.B. 124; [1967] 3 W.L.R. 246; 65 L.G.R. 535; sub nom. Hillingdon Corp. v. Cutler (1967) 111 S.J. 275; sub nom. London Borough of Hillingdon v. Cutler 131 J.P. 361; [1967] 2 All E.R. 361, C.A. 5–115, 5–135
Hinchcliffe v. Sheldon [1955] 1 W.L.R. 1207; 120 J.P. 13; 99 S.J. 797; [1955] 3 All E.R. 406, D.C. 1–17, 1–42
Holborn and Frascati v. London County Council (1916) 80 J.P. 225 .... 5–91, 5–194
Holm v. Kensington Borough Council [1968] 1 Q.B. 646; [1967] 2 W.L.R. 1164; 131 J.P. 250; 110 S.J. 888; [1967] 1 All E.R. 289, C.A. 6–04
Honig v. Lewisham Borough Council, unrep. (1958) 122 J.P.J. 302 .... 5–85, 5–119, 5–161, 5–187, 5–245

Inworth Property Co. Ltd. v. Southwark London Borough Council (1977) P. & C.R. 186; (1977) 121 S.J. 16; (1977) 3 H.L.R. 67; (1977) 76 L.G.R. 263; [1978] J.P.L. 175; (1977) 245 E.G. 935, C.A. 5–71

James v. Coleman [1949] E.G.D. 122 7–15
—— v. James, unrep. [1952] C.L.Y. 2948 7–15
Johnson v. Duke of Westminster (1984) 17 H.L.R. 136 .... 5–85, 5–119, 5–161, 5–187, 5–245
—— v. Leicester Corp. [1934] 1 K.B. 638 5–111
Jones v. Green [1925] 1 K.B. 659 3–21

Keeves v. Dean [1924] 1 K.B. 685 .... 5–82, 5–185
Kenny v. Kingston upon Thames Royal London Borough Council (1985) 17 H.L.R. 344; [1986] J.P.L. 352; (1985) 274 E.G. 395, C.A. 5–71, 5–73, 5–74, 5–177
Kensington Borough Council v. Allen [1926] 1 K.B. 576 5–12
Kimsey v. Barnet London Borough Council (1976) 3 H.L.R. 45 .... 5–71, 5–165
Kingston-upon-Hull District Council v. University of Hull, unrep., August 1979 L.A.G. Bull. 191 6–116
Kyffin v. Simmons (1903) 67 J.P. 227 .... 6–04, 6–05

TABLE OF CASES

Lambeth London Borough Council v. Stubbs (1980) 255 E.G. 789; [1980] J.P.L. 517; (1980) 70 L.G.R. 650, D.C. 3–10, 5–39

Legg v. Leominster District Council, unrep., C.A., December 16, 1985 ..... 5–73, 5–119, 5–140, 5–161

Leslie Maurice & Co. Ltd. v. Willesden Corp. [1953] 2 Q.B. 1; [1953] 2 W.L.R. 892; 117 J.P. 239; 97 S.J. 298; [1953] 1 All E.R. 1014; 51 L.G.R. 334, C.A. 5–87, 5–122, 5–142, 5–163, 5–189

London Borough of Hillingdon v. Cutler. *See* Hillingdon London Borough Council v. Cutler.

London Housing and Commercial Properties Ltd. v. Cowan [1977] Q.B. 148; [1976] 3 W.L.R. 115; 120 S.J. 383; [1976] 2 All E.R. 385; (1976) 31 P. & C.R. 387, D.C. 5–71

Luganda v. Service Hotels Ltd. [1969] 2 Ch. 209; [1969] 2 W.L.R. 1056; [1969] 2 All E.R. 692; 20 P. & C.R. 337, C.A.; affirming 113 S.J. 165 3–30

Lurcott v. Wakely & Wheeler [1911] 1 K.B. 905 5–205

McCarrick v. Liverpool Corp. [1947] A.C. 219; [1947] L.J.R. 56; 176 L.T. 11; 62 T.L.R. 730; 111 J.P. 6; 91 S.J. 41; [1946] 2 All E.R. 646, H.L. 3–23

McGillivray v. Stephenson [1950] 1 All E.R. 142; [1950] W.N. 209; 48 L.G.R. 409, D.C. 5–43

McGreal v. Wake (1984) 128 S.J. 116; (1984) 13 H.L.R. 107; (1984) 81 L.S.Gaz. 739; (1984) 269 E.G. 1254, C.A. 3–04, 5–71, 5–92, 5–195

McPhail v. Islington Borough Council [1970] 2 Q.B. 197; [1970] 2 W.L.R. 583; (1969) 68 L.G.R. 145; 21 P. & C.R. 121; *sub nom.* McPhail v. London Borough of Islington [1970] 1 All E.R. 1004, C.A. 6–25

Malton Urban Sanitary Authority v. Malton Farmers Manure Co. (1879) 4 Ex.D. 302 3–16

Marela v. Machorowski [1953] 1 Q.B. 565; [1953] 2 W.L.R. 831; 117 J.P. 220; 97 S.J. 280; [1953] 1 All E.R. 960, C.A. 5–125

Martin v. Downham Rural District Council (1953) 51 L.G.R. 430, C.A. 5–134

Meade v. Haringey London Borough Council [1979] 1 W.L.R. 637; [1979] I.C.R. 494; (1979) 123 S.J. 216; [1979] 2 All E.R. 1016; (1979) 77 L.G.R. 577, C.A. 1–10, 5–252

Metropolitan Asylum District Managers v. Hill (1881) 6 App.Cas. 193 3–13

Metropolitan Properties v. Barder [1968] 1 W.L.R. 286; (1967) 112 S.J. 15; [1968] 1 All E.R. 536; 19 P. & C.R. 304, C.A. 7–15

Minford Properties v. Hammersmith London Borough Council (1978) 247 E.G. 561, D.C. 6–11

Morgan v. Liverpool Corp. [1927] 2 K.B. 131 3–21

National Coal Board v. Thorne [1976] 1 W.L.R. 543; 120 S.J. 234; (1976) 74 L.G.R. 429, D.C. 3–17, 3–57

Neale v. Del Soto [1945] K.B. 144 7–15

Newey v. Liverpool County Council (1982) 14 H.L.R. 73 9–32

Northern Ireland Trailers v. County Borough of Preston [1972] 1 W.L.R. 203; (1971) 116 S.J. 100; *sub nom.* Northern Ireland Trailers v. County Borough of Preston [1972] 1 All E.R. 260, D.C. 5–26, 5–46

Nottingham City District Council v. Newton; Nottingham Friendship Housing Association v. Newton [1974] 1 W.L.R. 923; 118 S.J. 462; *sub nom.* Nottingham Corp. v. Newton; Nottingham Friendship Housing Association v. Newton [1974] 2 All E.R. 760; 72 L.G.R. 535, D.C. 5–04, 5–17, 5–18, 5–25, 5–42, 5–167

Okereke v. Brent London Borough Council [1967] 1 Q.B. 42; [1966] 2 W.L.R. 169; 130 J.P. 126; 109 S.J. 956; [1966] 1 All E.R. 150; 64 L.G.R. 72, C.A. 6–04, 6–05, 6–08

Padfield v. Minister of Agriculture [1968] A.C. 997; [1968] 2 W.L.R. 924; 112 S.J. 171; [1968] 1 All E.R. 694, H.L. 5–173, 5–208, 5–233, 5–263

TABLE OF CASES

Patel v. Godal unrep. [1979] C.L.Y. 1620 7–15
—— v. Methab (1981) 5 H.L.R. 80 .... 5–31, 9–06, 9–10
Pearlman v. Keepers & Governors of Harrow School [1979] Q.B. 56; [1978] 3 W.L.R. 736; [1979] 1 All E.R. 365; (1978) 38 P. & C.R. 136; (1978) 247 E.G. 1173; [1978] J.P.L. 829, C.A. 5–252
Peaty v. Field [1971] 1 W.L.R. 387; 115 S.J. 77; [1971] 2 All E.R. 895; 69 L.G.R. 164, D.C. 5–23
Phillips v. Newham London Borough Council (1982) 43 P. & C.R. 54; (1981) 3 H.L.R. 136, C.A. 5–71
Plymouth Corp. v. Hurrell [1968] 1 Q.B. 455; [1967] 3 W.L.R. 1289; (1967) 111 S.J. 498; 65 L.G.R. 543; sub nom. Plymouth City Corp. v. Hurrell 131 J.P. 479; [1967] 3 All E.R. 354, C.A. 4–10
Pocklington v. Melksham Urban District Council [1964] 2 Q.B. 673; [1964] 3 W.L.R. 233; 128 J.P. 503; 108 S.J. 403; [1964] 2 All E.R. 862; 62 L.G.R. 427, C.A. 5–121
Pollway Nominees v. Croydon London Borough Council [1986] 3 W.L.R. 277; (1986) 130 S.J. 574; [1986] 2 All E.R. 849; (1986) 18 H.L.R. 443; (1986) 280 E.G. 87; (1986) 136 New L.J. 703; (1986) 83 L.S.Gaz. 2654; [1987] J.P.L. 121, H.L.; affirming [1986] Ch. 198; [1985] 3 W.L.R. 564; (1985) 129 S.J. 590; [1985] 3 All E.R. 24; (1985) 83 L.G.R. 770; (1985) 17 H.L.R. 503; (1985) L.S.Gaz. 2997, C.A.; affirming (1984) 128 S.J. 630; (1984) 16 H.L.R. 41; [1985] L.G.R. 79; (1985) 49 P. & C. 97 .... 3–30, 5–77, 5–85, 5–188, 5–248
Premier Garage Co. v. Ilkeston Corp. (1933) 97 J.P. 786 3–30
Proudfoot v. Hart (1890) 25 Q.B.D. 42 3–53

Quick v. Taff-Ely Borough Council [1986] Q.B. 809; [1985] 3 W.L.R. 981; (1985) 129 S.J. 685; [1985] 3 All E.R. 321; (1985) 18 H.L.R. 66; (1985) 276 E.G. 452; (1985) 135 New L.J. 848, C.A. 3–38
Quiltotex Co. v. Minister of Housing and Local Government [1966] 1 Q.B. 704; [1965] 3 W.L.R. 801; 109 S.J. 393; 18 P. & C.R. 50; 63 L.G.R. 332; sub nom. Quillotex Co. v. Minister of Housing and Local Government [1965] 2 All E.R. 913 .... 3–28, 3–30

R. v. Birmingham J.J., ex p. Guppy, The Times, October 8, 1987 .... 5–23A
—— v. Bros (1901) 66 J.P. 54 5–26
—— v. Camden London Borough Council, ex p. Comyn Ching & Co. (London) Ltd. (1984) 47 P. & C.R. 1417; [1984] J.P.L. 661 5–205
—— v. ——, ex p. Rowton (Camden Town) Ltd. [1984] L.G.R. 614 3–30
—— v. Cardiff City Council, ex p. Cross (1983) 81 L.G.R. 105; [1983] J.P.L. 245, C.A.; (1983) 45 P. & C.R. 156; [1981] J.P.L. 748; (1982) 1 H.L.R. 54 .... 1–12, 5–69, 5–82, 5–106, 5–182, 6–158, 9–18
—— v. Cumberland Justices, ex p. Trimble (1877) 41 J.P. 454 5–48
—— v. Ealing London Borough Council, ex p. Richardson (1982) 4 H.L.R. 125; [1983] J.P.L. 533; (1983) 265 E.G. 691; [1983] M.L.R. 125, C.A. ... 5–71, 5–119, 5–140, 5–161
—— v. Epsom and Ewell Corp., ex p. R.B. Property Investments (Eastern) [1964] 1 W.L.R. 1060; 128 J.P. 478; 108 S.J. 521; [1964] 2 All E.R. 832; 62 L.G.R. 498, D.C. 5–124
—— v. Fenney Stratford Justices, ex p. Watney Mann (Midlands) Ltd. [1976] 1 W.L.R. 1101; 120 S.J. 201; [1976] 2 All E.R. 888, D.C. 5–16, 5–43
—— v. Hackney London Borough Council, ex p. Teepee Estates (1956) Ltd. (1967) 19 P. & C.R. 87; sub nom. Teepee Estates (1956) v. London Borough of Hackney (1967) 204 E.G. 1201, D.C. 5–86, 5–189
—— v. Islington London Borough Council, ex p. Casale (1985) 18 H.L.R. 146 9–34
—— v. Kerrier District Council, ex p. Guppys (Bridport) Ltd. (No. 1) (1976) 120 S.J. 646; (1976) 32 P. & C.R. 411; [1977] L.G.R. 129; (1976) 242 E.G. 955, C.A. 3–66, 5–66, 5–68, 5–80, 5–95, 5–104
—— v. —— (No. 2) (1985) 17 H.L.R. 426 6–12
—— v. Lambeth Borough Council, ex p. Clayhope Properties Ltd. (1987) 283 E.G. 739; (1987) 19 H.L.R. 426, C.A. 3–30, 3–32, 6–09

TABLE OF CASES

R. v. Maldon District, *ex p.* Fisher (1986) 18 H.L.R. 197 5–73
—— v. Nottingham Quarter Sessions, *ex p.* Harlow [1952] 2 Q.B. 601; [1952] 1 T.L.R. 1546; 116 J.P. 397; 96 S.J. 413; [1952] 2 All E.R. 78; 50 L.G.R. 447, D.C. 5–85, 5–119, 5–140, 5–148, 5–161, 5–187
—— v. Parlby (1889) 22 Q.B.D. 525 3–16
—— v. Secretary of State for the Environment, *ex p.* Hillingdon London Borough Council [1986] 1 W.L.R. 807; (1986) 130 S.J. 481; [1986] 2 All E.R. 273; (1986) 83 L.S.Gaz. 2331, C.A.; affirming [1986] 1 W.L.R. 192; (1986) 130 S.J. 89; [1986] 1 All E.R. 810; (1986) 52 P. & C.R. 409; [1986] J.P.L. 363; (1986) 83 L.S.Gaz. 525; (1986) 136 New L.J. 16, D.C. 1–12
—— v. ——, *ex p.* Kensington and Chelsea Royal Borough (1987) 19 H.L.R. 161 6–151
—— v. Silverlock [1984] 2 Q.B. 76 ..... 9–08, 9–11
—— v. Southwark London Borough, *ex p.* Lewis Levy Ltd. (1983) 8 H.L.R. 1; [1984] J.P.L. 105; (1983) 267 E.G. 1041 ..... 5–86, 5–189, 6–151, 6–162
—— v. Wheatley (1885) 16 Q.B.D. 34 5–43
Reed v. Hastings Corp. (1964) 108 S.J. 480; (1964) 62 L.G.R. 588; 190 E.G. 961, C.A. 6–08
Riddell v. Spear (1879) 43 J.P. 317 5–07
Rhymney Iron Co. v. Gellingner District Council [1971] 1 K.B. 589 5–06
Roberton v. King [1901] 2 K.B. 265 3–30
Ross and Leicester Corp., *Re* (1932) 96 J.P. 459 3–30
Ryall v. Cubitt Heath [1922] 1 K.B. 275 ..... 5–81, 5–184

Saddleworth Urban District Council v. Aggregate and Sand Ltd. (1970) 114 S.J. 931; 69 L.G.R. 103, D.C. 5–48
Salford City Council v. McNally [1976] A.C. 379; [1975] 3 W.L.R. 87; 119 S.J. 475; [1975] 2 All E.R. 860; 73 L.G.R. 408, H.L.; affirming [1975] 1 W.L.R. 365; (1974) 119 S.J. 151; [1975] 1 All E.R. 597; (1974) 73 L.G.R. 151, D.C. 3–09, 3–15, 3–17, 5–04, 5–41, 5–167
Sarson v. Roberts [1895] 2 Q.B. 395 3–23
Scarborough Corp. v. Scarborough Sanitary Authority (1876) 1 Ex.D. 344 5–48
Sharpe v. Nicholls (1945) 147 E.G. 177 7–15
Sidebotham, *ex p.* (1880) 14 Ch.D. 458 ..... 5–85, 5–119, 5–140, 5–148, 5–161, 5–187
Silbers v. Southwark London Borough Council (1977) 122 S.J. 128; (1977) 76 L.G.R. 421, C.A. 3–30, 6–10, 6–11, 6–14
Simmons v. Pizzey [1979] A.C. 37; [1977] 3 W.L.R. 1; (1977) 121 S.J. 424; [1977] 2 All E.R. 432; (1977) 75 L.G.R. 583; (1977) 36 P. & C.R. 36, H.L. 6–13
Smith v. East Elloe Rural District Council [1956] A.C. 736; [1956] 2 W.L.R. 888; 120 J.P. 263; 100 S.J. 282; [1956] 1 All E.R. 855; 54 L.G.R. 233; 6 P. & C.R. 102, H.L.; varying [1955] 1 W.L.R. 380; 119 J.P. 325; 99 S.J. 235; [1955] 2 All E.R. 19; 5 P. & C.R. 148; 53 L.G.R. 299, C.A. 5–252
—— v. Marrable (1843) 11 M. & W. 5 ..... 3–03, 3–23
South Shields Compulsory Purchase Order 1937, *Re* [1939] 1 All E.R. 419 3–30
Stanton v. Southwick [1920] 2 K.B. 642 3–23
Stewart v. Chapman [1951] 2 K.B. 792; [1951] 2 T.L.R. 640; 115 J.P. 473; 95 S.J. 641; [1951] 2 All E.R. 613; 49 L.G.R. 816, D.C. 5–85, 5–119, 5–140, 5–161, 5–187, 5–210, 5–234, 5–245
Stidworthy v. Brixham Urban District Council (1935) 2 L.J.C.C.R. 41 5–109
Stroud v. Bradbury 96 S.J. 397; [1952] W.N. 306; 116 J.P. 386; [1952] 2 All E.R. 76; 50 L.G.R. 452, D.C. 1–17
Summers v. Salford Corp. [1943] A.C. 283 ..... 3–21, 3–22

Tennant v. London County Council (1957) 121 J.P. 428; 55 L.G.R. 421, C.A. 4–10
Thomas v. Nokes (1894) 58 J.P. 672 5–18
Thompson v. Arkell (1949) 99 L.J. 597 3–23
—— v. Gibbon (1841) 7 M. & W. 456 5–06
—— v. Hawse (1895) 59 J.P. 580 4–03
Tottenham London Borough v. Williamson (1893) 57 J.P. 614 5–13
Truman, Banbury, Buxton & Co. Ltd. v. Kerslake (1894) 2 Q.B. 774 ..... 5–12, 5–78

TABLE OF CASES

Trustees of the Waltham Abbey Baptist Church v. Stevens (1950) E.G. 294 7–15

Victoria Square Property Co. v. Southwark London Borough Council [1978] 1 W.L.R. 463; (1977) 121 S.J. 816; (1978) 2 All E.R. 281; (1977) 76 L.G.R. 349; (1977) 34 P. & C.R. 275; [1978] J.P.L. 243; (1977) 247 E.G. 989, C.A. 5–87, 5–100, 5–102, 5–166

Wandsworth London Borough v. Winder [1985] A.C. 461; [1984] 3 W.L.R. 1254; (1984) 128 S.J. 838; [1984] 3 All E.R. 976; (1984) 83 L.G.R. 143; (1984) 17 H.L.R. 106; (1985) 135 New L.J. 381; (1985) 82 L.S.Gaz. 201, H.L.; affirming [1984] 3 W.L.R. 563; (1984) 128 S.J. 384; [1984] 3 All E.R. 83; (1984) 82 L.G.R. 509; (1984) 15 H.L.R. 1; (1984) 81 L.S.Gaz. 1684, C.A. 5–86, 5–189
Wareham and Dale Ltd. v. Fyffe (1910) 74 J.P. 249 5–11
Warwick Rural District Council v. Miller-Mead [1962] Ch. 441; [1962] 2 W.L.R. 284; 126 J.P. 143; [1982] 1 All E.R. 212; 60 L.G.R. 29; *sub nom.* Warwick Rural District Council v. Miller Read, 105 S.J. 1124, C.A.; affirming [1961] Ch. 590; [1961] 3 W.L.R. 737; 125 J.P. 640; [1961] 3 All E.R. 542; 59 L.G.R. 436; *sub nom.* Warwick Rural District Council v. Miller Mead, 105 S.J. 707; *sub nom.* Miller Mead v. Warwick Rural District Council [1962] 1 W.L.R. 424 5–57
Watson v. Minister of Local Government and Planning. *See* Havant and Waterloo Urban District Council Compulsory Purchase Order (No. 4), Watson's Application, *Re*.
Weatheritt v. Cantley [1901] 2 K.B. 285 6–04
West Ham Corp. v. Benabo [1934] 2 K.B. 253 .... 5–99, 5–201, 5–269
—— v. Thomas [1908] 73 J.P. 65 4–13
Whatling v. Rees (1914) 84 L.J.K.B. 1122 5–17
—— v. —— (1940) 79 J.P. 209 5–43
Wigan Corp. v. Hartley, unrep. [1963] C.L.Y. 1664 5–135
Wilson v. Finch Hatton 2 Ex.D. 336 3–23
Winters v. Dance [1948] W.N. 317; [1949] L.J.R. 165; 64 T.L.R. 609; 92 S.J. 425 7–15
Wright v. Howell (1947) 92 S.J. 26 7–15
Wyse v. Secretary of State for the Environment and Another [1984] J.P.L. 256 3–46

Zaitzeff v. Olmi (1952) 102 L.J. 416; 160 E.G. 154, County Ct. 7–15
Zbytniewski v. Broughton [1956] 2 Q.B. 673; [1956] 3 W.L.R. 630; 100 S.J. 631; [1956] 3 All E.R. 348, C.A. 7–17, 7–24

TABLE OF STATUTES

1868	Artisans and Labourers Dwellings Act (31 & 32 Vict. c. 130)	3–19	1936	Public Health Act—*cont.* s. 94—*cont.*	
1875	Public Health Act (38 & 39 Vict. c. 55)	7–03		(2)	3–20, 5–37, 5–43, 9–24
	s. 4	5–12		(3)	5–34, 5–40
	s. 90	6–03		(6)	5–27
	s. 91	7–03		s. 95 (1)	5–47
1890	Housing of the Working Classes (51 & 54 Vict. 70)—			(2)	5–49
	s. 12	3–19		s. 96	5–38, 5–52
1909	Housing, Town Planning etc. Act (9 Edw. 7, c. 44)—			(2)	5–53
				s. 97 (1)	5–56
	s. 14	3–19		(2)	5–56
	s. 15	3–19		(3)	5–56
1925	Trustee Act (15 & 16 Geo. 5, c. 19)—			s. 98	5–08
				s. 99	9–22
	s. 63	5–136		s. 100	5–57
	Law of Property Act (15 & 16 Geo. 5, c. 20)	5–54, 5–64, 5–98, 5–200, 5–268, 6–138, 6–166, 6–193		s. 189	5–60
				s. 268 (2)	7–67
				(*a*)	7–03
				s. 270	7–68
1930	Housing Act (20 & 21 Geo. 5, c. 39)—			s. 283 (1)	4–05
				(2)	4–04
	s. 37	7–19		s. 284 (1)	4–08
1935	Housing Act (25 & 26 Geo. 5, c. 40)	7–19		(2)	4–10
				s. 285	4–11, 4–16
	ss. 1–12	7–04		s. 287	1–35
	Sched. 1	7–04		(1)	1–36
1936	Public Health Act (25 & 26 Geo. 5, c. 49)	3–08, 3–16, 3–17, 3–23, 3–57, 5–27, 7–03		(2)	1–38
				(3)	1–37, 1–39
				(4)	1–37, 1–39
				s. 288	1–35, 1–41
	Pt. III	3–08, 3–31, 5–04, 5–05, 5–57, 5–59, 5–63, 5–67, 5–94, 5–171, 5–196, 7–67		s. 289	1–40, 5–48
				s. 291 (1)	5–52, 5–54
				(2)	5–52
	Pt. IX	6–14		(3)	5–52
	s. 1	1–04		(4)	5–54
	s. 6	1–04		s. 293	5–52, 5–157
	s. 26	5–59		s. 294	5–53
	s. 91	1–08, 2–89, 5–03		s. 296	5–47
	s. 92 (1)	3–09		s. 297	1–41, 5–47
	(*a*)	3–09, 5–48, 5–59, 5–61, 5–167, 9–24		s. 300 (1)	1–40
				s. 301	5–41, 5–46
	(*c*)	3–16, 5–48		s. 328	5–04
	s. 93	5–04, 5–05, 5–07, 5–09, 5–14, 5–31, 5–61		s. 343	3–10, 3–16, 5–10, 5–78, 5–79
				Housing Act (26 Geo. 5 & 1 Edw. 8, c. 51)—	
	ss. 93–98	5–59			
	s. 94	5–42		s. 2	3–19
	(1)	5–25, 5–26		s. 36	6–03

xx

TABLE OF STATUTES

1936–1969	Public Health Acts	1–04, 1–08, 1–10, 1–35, 1–40, 1–41, 2–89, 5–45, 5–78, 6–151, 6–169
1947	Town and Country Planning Act (10 & 11 Geo. 6, c. 51)—	
	s. 29	5–62
1948	National Assistance Act (11 & 12 Geo. 6, c. 29)—	
	s. 29	9–30
	Agricultural Wages Act (11 & 12 Geo. 6, c. 47)—	
	s. 17 (1)	5–175, 5–205
1954	Housing Repairs and Rents Act (2 & 3 Eliz. 2, c. 53)—	
	s. 9	3–19, 3–24, 3–45
	s. 12	7–48
	Landlord and Tenant Act (2 & 3 Eliz. 2, c. 56)—	
	s. 10	3–27
1957	Housing Act (5 & 6 Eliz. 2, c. 56)	9–20, 9–21
	Pt. II	3–30
	Pt. III	3–30
	s. 4	3–27, 6–18
	(1) (*d*)–(*h*)	6–18, 6–19
	ss. 9–16	3–49
	s. 9 (1)	1–12, 9–18
	(1A)	3–49, 5–77, 5–173, 6–09
	(1B)	3–56
	s. 16 (1)	1–12, 9–18
	s. 36	6–18, 6–19
	s. 39 (2)	3–30
	s. 90	6–08
	s. 191 (4)	7–13
1961	Land Compensation Act (9 & 10 Eliz. 2, c. 33)	5–262
	s. 31	5–262
	Public Health Act (9 & 10 Eliz. 2, c. 64)—	
	s. 32 (1)	3–44
	Housing Act (9 & 10 Eliz. 2, c. 65)—	
	s. 12	6–03
	s. 13	6–29, 6–95
	(3)	6–95
	s. 15	3–30, 6–08, 6–12, 6–19
	s. 16	6–12
	s. 19	3–30, 6–13, 6–19
	s. 23 (9)	6–18
	s. 32	9–19
1962	Recorded Delivery Service Act (10 & 11 Eliz. 2, c. 27)—	
	s. 1	4–12
1963	London Government Act (c. 33)—	
	s. 40 (2)	1–04
1964	Housing Act (c. 56)—	
	s. 73	3–30
	(1)	6–10
1965	Compulsory Purchase Act (c. 56)	5–262
	s. 11	6–196
1967	Leasehold Reform Act (c. 88)—	
	s. 3	5–205
1968	Rent Act (c. 23)	3–30
1969	Public Health (Recurring Nuisances) Act (c. 25) ...	3–08
	s. 1	5–21
	(1)	5–22, 5–31
	(3)	5–23
	(4)	5–23
	s. 2	5–43
	(1)	5–25
	(2)	5–27, 5–37
	s. 3	1–04, 5–49, 5–56
	(1)	5–38, 5–47
	(2)	5–34, 5–40
	Housing Act (c. 33)	6–03, 6–04, 6–06
	s. 58	6–03
	s. 59	6–04
	s. 71	3–24, 3–39
	s. 72	3–49
	s. 89	6–17
	Sched. 8, para. 29	6–17
1971	Fire Precautions Act (c. 40)	6–130, 6–131
	Town and Country Planning Act (c. 78)—	
	s. 54	5–132, 5–134
	s. 192	9–27
1972	Defective Premises Act (c. 35)	3–04
	s. 4	3–03
	Local Government Act (c. 70)—	
	s. 101 (1)	1–11
	(2)	1–13
	(3)	1–13
	(5)	1–14
	s. 193	4–07
	s. 222	5–58
	s. 231	4–15
	s. 233	4–11, 4–18, 5–153
	Sched. 14, para. 1	1–04
	Sched. 22	4–07
	Sched. 29	4–08
1973	Land Compensation Act (c. 26)	5–45, 6–131
	Pt. III	5–45, 5–73, 5–113, 5–117, 5–121, 5–138, 5–145, 5–160, 5–169, 6–129, 7–21

xxi

TABLE OF STATUTES

1973	Land Compensation Act— cont.	
	s. 29	5–113
	(1)	9–37
	(a)	9–34
	(b)	9–34
	(c)	9–34
	(d)	9–34
	(2)	9–35
	(b)	9–35
	(3)	9–34
	(3A)	9–34
	(4)	9–35
	(7)	5–113
	(7A)	9–26, 9–28, 9–34
	(9)	9–34
	s. 30(1)	9–36
	(2)	9–36
	s. 32(1)	9–36
	(2)	9–36
	(3)	9–35
	(5)	9–35
	s. 37	5–113
	(1)	9–28, 9–31
	(a)	9–32
	(2) (b)	9–32
	(c)	9–32
	(3)	9–32
	(9)	9–28
	s. 38(1)(a)	9–29
	(b)	9–30
	(2)	9–30
	(3)	9–30
	(4)	9–30
	s. 39	5–45, 5–113
	(1)	9–25
	(a)	9–26
	(b)	9–26
	(c)	9–26
	(2)	9–27
	(3)	9–27
	(5)	9–27
	(6)	9–27
	(6A)	9–26
	(7)	9–26
	(8)	9–26
	(9)	9–26
	s. 42	9–26
	Powers of Criminal Courts Act (c. 62)—	
	s. 35	9–38
1974	Control of Pollution Act (c. 40)	5–23A
	Housing Act (c. 44)—	
	s. 56	6–17
	s. 125(1)	9–19
	s. 129	6–12
	s. 130	9–26, 9–27, 9–34, 9–37
	Sched. 6, Pt. I	6–17

1974	Housing Act—cont.	
	Sched. 13	9–26, 9–27, 9–34, 9–37
	Housing (Scotland) Act (c. 45)	3–46A
1975	Housing Rents and Subsidies Act (c. 6)—	
	Sched. 5	9–34
1976	Local Government (Miscellaneous Provisions) Act (c. 57)	6–142
	s. 16	4–18, 5–06 5–104, 5–117, 5–131, 5–132, 5–138, 5–153, 5–160, 5–211, 5–224, 5–235, 5–239
	s. 33(1)	6–143
	(2)	6–144
	(4)	6–145, 6–146
	(5)	6–143
1976	Rent (Agriculture) Act (c. 80)	5–175, 7–51
1977	Rent Act (c. 42)	5–45, 5–71, 5–113, 5–125, 5–145, 5–169, 5–175, 6–129, 6–131, 6–155, 7–51, 9–25
	s. 19	5–175
	s. 101	7–21, 7–24, 7–45
	s. 156	9–34
	Sched. 23	9–34
	Housing (Homeless Persons) Act (c. 48)	9–14
1978	Interpretation Act (c. 30)—	
	s. 12	1–10
1980	Magistrates' Courts Act (c. 43)—	
	s. 1	5–26
	s. 2	5–26
	Housing Act (c. 51)—	
	s. 146	7–48
	s. 149	3–56
	Local Government Planning and Land Act (c. 65)—	
	s. 114	9–36
1981	Acquisition of Land Act (c. 67)	5–262
1982	Local Government (Miscellaneous Provisions) Act (c. 30)—	
	s. 26	3–09
	ss. 29–32	5–152
	s. 29(2)	5–153
	(3)	5–153
	(4)	5–152
	(7)	5–153
	(8)	5–153
	(9)	5–153
	(10)	5–156
	(13)	5–157
	s. 30	5–158

TABLE OF STATUTES

1982 Local Government (Miscellaneous Provisions) Act—*cont.*
- s. 31 (1) 5–154
- (2) 5–154
- (3) 5–154
- (4) 5–154
- (5) 5–155
- (7) 5–154, 5–155

Criminal Justice Act (c. 48)—
- s. 37 .... 1–17, 1–41, 4–19, 5–37, 5–47, 5–112, 5–126, 5–144, 6–84, 6–91, 6–96, 6–102, 6–129, 6–139, 6–181, 7–20, 7–25, 7–34, 7–35, 7–38, 7–63

1984 Public Health (Control of Disease) Act (c. 22) 7–09
- s. 49 7–68

Registered Homes Act (c. 23) 6–25

Building Act (c. 55) 1–04, 1–08, 1–41, 9–19
- s. 72 6–130
- s. 76 .... 3–08, 5–59, 5–67, 5–94, 5–171, 5–196
  - (1) 5–61
  - (2) 5–61, 5–63
  - (3) 5–61
  - (4) 5–63
  - (5) 5–63
  - (6) 5–62
  - (7) 5–60
- s. 92 (1) 4–05
  - (2) 4–04
- s. 93 4–09
  - (2) 4–10
- s. 94 4–11
- s. 95 1–35
  - (1) 1–36
  - (3) 1–38
- s. 96 .... 1–37, 1–39
- s. 98 1–40
- s. 103 1–40
- s. 107 5–64
- s. 126 .... 1–04, 5–79

1985 Housing Act (c. 68) 1–02, 1–03, 1–05, 1–10, 1–15, 1–36, 2–89, 3–05, 3–19, 3–27, 3–32, 3–33, 3–48, 3–55, 3–57, 3–62, 3–63, 4–04, 4–07, 5–44, 5–67, 5–70, 5–78, 5–86, 5–135, 5–145, 5–167, 5–189, 5–249, 6–02, 6–03, 6–08, 6–151, 6–158, 6–169, 7–02, 7–19, 7–34, 9–19, 9–25
- Pt. II 5–262, 6–155, 6–194
- Pt. III .. 5–45, 7–21, 9–14, 9–24
- Pt. VI . 1–05, 1–16, 1–30, 3–30, 3–49, 5–92, 5–195

1985 Housing Act—*cont.*
- Pt. VII 1–18, 1–32, 5–82, 5–105, 5–126, 9–23
- Pt. VIII 1–05, 1–18, 5–203, 5–223, 5–229
- Pt. IX . 1–05, 1–20, 3–30, 5–60, 5–129, 6–128, 6–129
- Pt. X ... 1–07, 1–26, 3–05, 6–28, 6–79, 7–04, 7–14, 7–43
- Pt. XI . 1–05, 1–22, 1–33, 1–34, 4–14, 6–08, 7–68
- Pt. XII 6–14, 6–130
- Pt. XIV 5–74, 5–258, 5–260
- Pt. XV 5–67, 5–109, 5–218, 5–227, 5–243, 5–258, 5–264
- Pt. XVII 5–103, 5–262
- s. 1 1–03
- s. 8 .... 1–06, 7–41
- s. 17 6–194
- s. 23 7–68
  - (3) 7–09
- s. 90 7–48
- s. 189 ...... 1–12, 1–29, 3–27, 5–68, 5–70, 5–71, 5–95, 5–170, 6–58, 9–18
  - (1) 5–80
  - (2) 5–108
    - (a) 5–80
    - (b) 5–80
  - (3) 5–82, 5–104
  - (4) 5–81, 5–88
- s. 190 ...... 1–29, 5–60, 5–94, 6–58
  - (1) (a) 3–47, 5–77, 5–173, 5–180, 6–09
  - (b) 3–54, 5–174, 5–180
  - (2) 5–183
  - (3) 5–185
  - (4) 5–184, 5–191
- s. 191 .... 5–75, 5–93, 5–98, 5–176, 5–196, 5–201
- ss. 191–208 5–170
- s. 191 (1) 5–85, 5–187
  - (2) 5–87, 5–93, 5–100, 5–190, 5–196
  - (3) . 5–87, 5–89, 5–100, 5–104
  - (4) . 5–88, 5–93, 5–191, 5–196
    - (a) 5–88, 5–191
    - (b) 5–88, 5–191
- s. 192 .... 5–87, 5–89, 5–100
  - (2) 5–101
  - (3) 5–101
  - (4) 5–102
- s. 193 ..... 5–74, 5–93, 5–94, 5–196
- ss. 193–205 .... 5–89, 5–192
- s. 194 1–29
  - (1) 5–96
  - (2) 1–29, 5–96, 5–197
- s. 195 ...... 1–29, 1–30, 5–97, 5–198
  - (2) 1–31, 5–97, 5–198

TABLE OF STATUTES

1985 Housing Act—*cont.*
    s. 196 .... 1–29, 1–31
    s. 197 1–16
        (1) 1–16
    s. 198 ...... 1–16, 1–17, 1–29, 5–96,
                                        5–197
    s. 199 .... 5–90, 5–193
        (2) 5–90, 5–193
        (3) 5–90, 5–193
        (4) 5–90, 5–193
    s. 200 (1) 5–91, 5–194
        (2) 5–91, 5–194
        (3) 5–91, 5–194
        (4) 5–91, 5–194
        (6) 5–91, 5–194
    s. 201 (1) 5–91, 5–194
        (2) 5–194
    s. 202 ... 5–96, 5–82, 5–185, 5–197
    s. 203 (1) 5–92, 5–195
        (2) 5–92, 5–195
        (3) 5–92, 5–195
    s. 204 .... 5–66, 5–80
    s. 205 .... 3–27, 3–48, 3–55
        (*a*) 3–32
        (*b*) 3–33
    s. 206 .... 5–70, 5–71, 5–177
    s. 207 .... 3–27, 3–30, 5–69,
                        5–79, 5–175, 5–181
    s. 209 .... 3–63, 5–206, 5–209,
                      5–223, 5–230, 5–238
    s. 210 5–203
        (1) 5–209
        (2) 5–209, 5–223, 5–247
    s. 211 .. 1–19, 5–237, 5–253, 9–26,
                                    9–34
        (1) 5–213, 5–216
        (2) 5–216
        (3) 5–82, 5–105
            (*a*) 5–215, 5–216
            (*b*) 5–216
        (4) 5–217, 5–221
            (*a*) 5–216
        (6) 5–217
    s. 212 . 1–27, 5–203, 5–238, 5–263
        (1) 5–229
        (2) 5–229
        (3) 5–230, 5–232, 5–234
        (4) 5–231, 5–237, 5–242
    s. 213 .... 5–82, 5–105
        (1) 5–210, 5–234
        (2) 5–211, 5–235
        (3) 5–212, 5–236
        (4) 5–212, 5–236
    s. 214 .... 5–253, 5–263, 9–26
    ss. 214–216 1–19
    s. 214 (1) (*a*) 5–222
          (*b*) 5–221
        (2) 5–223
          (*d*) 5–247

1985 Housing Act—*cont.*
    s. 214—*cont.*
        (3) (*a*) 5–222
          (*b*) 5–221
        (4) 5–224
        (5) 5–224
    s. 215 .... 5–253, 5–263, 9–26
        (1) 5–238, 5–239
        (2) 5–238
          (*e*) 5–247
        (3) 5–239
        (4) 5–241
    s. 216 (1) 5–225, 5–240
        (*c*) . 5–225, 5–240, 5–252,
                                      5–266
        (2) 5–225, 5–240, 5–251
        (3) 5–225, 5–240
    s. 217 .... 5–214, 5–255, 5–269
        (1) 5–226, 5–241, 5–245,
                                      5–252
        (2) 5–246
        (3) (*a*) 5–247
          (*b*) 5–247
        (4) 5–249
          (*a*) 5–249
          (*b*) 5–249
          (*c*) 5–249
        (5) 5–249
        (6) 5–249
    s. 218 5–264
        (1) 5–226, 5–241, 5–252
        (2) 5–252
        (3) 5–252
        (4) 5–252
    s. 219 .... 5–228, 5–244
    s. 220 .... 5–249, 5–264
        (1) 5–264
        (2) 5–264
        (4) 5–264, 5–267
    s. 221 1–32
        (2) 1–32
    s. 222 .... 1–18, 1–32
    s. 223 .... 1–18, 1–32
    s. 224 .... 1–32, 5–253, 5–261
        (1) 1–27
        (2) 1–28
        (4) 5–254
    s. 225 (1) 5–261
        (2) 5–261
    s. 226 .... 5–211, 5–235
    s. 227 5–233
        (1) 5–262
        (2) 5–262
        (3) 5–262
    s. 228 5–264
        (1) 5–258
        (2) 5–258
        (3) 5–258
        (4) (*a*) 5–258

TABLE OF STATUTES

1985	Housing Act—*cont.*		1985	Housing Act—*cont.*	
	s. 228—*cont.*			s. 267	5–116, 5–129, 5–132, 5–134, 5–137
	(4)—*cont.*				
	(b)	5–258		(1)	5–124
	(5)	5–259		(2)	5–140
	(6)	5–259		(3)	5–137
	(7)	5–260		ss. 267–275	5–150
	s. 229 (1)	5–256		s. 268	5–117, 5–138, 5–150
	(2)	5–256		(1)	5–132, 5–160
	(3)	5–256		(2)	5–118, 5–122, 5–123, 5–139, 5–143, 5–160, 5–164
	(4)	5–256		s. 269	5–75, 5–114, 5–122, 5–143
	(6)	5–256		(1)	5–119, 5–140, 5–161
	s. 230	5–256		(2)	5–119, 5–140
	s. 232	5–207, 5–230		(3)	5–121, 5–142, 5–163
	(1)	5–207		(4)	5–121, 5–142, 5–163
	(2)	5–207		(5)	5–121, 5–142, 5–163
	(3)	5–207		(6)	5–122, 5–123, 5–143, 5–164, 5–165
	(4)	5–207		(b)	5–122, 5–143, 5–164
	s. 233	5–227		s. 270	5–116
	s. 234	3–64, 3–65, 5–206, 5–216, 5–230, 5–238		(1)	5–124
	s. 235	5–205, 5–215, 5–223, 5–238, 9–23		(2)	5–125
				(3)	5–125, 5–169
	s. 236	5–205, 5–224, 5–229		(4)	5–125
	(2)	5–175		(5)	5–126
	s. 237	3–61, 5–205, 5–206		s. 271	5–134
	s. 239	5–203, 5–219, 5–227, 5–242		s. 272 (1)	5–136
	s. 241	5–219, 5–227, 5–242		(2) (a)	5–136
	s. 250	5–220, 5–227, 5–242		(b)	5–136
	s. 251	5–220, 5–227, 5–242		(3)	5–136
	s. 253	5–203		(4)	5–136
	s. 258	5–220, 5–227, 5–242		(6)	5–136
	s. 260	1–18		s. 273	5–127, 5–129, 5–132
	s. 261	5–18		(2) (b)	5–127
	s. 264	3–27, 5–95, 5–121, 5–142, 5–159, 5–163, 9–23		(3)	5–127
				(4)	5–128, 5–129
	ss. 264–282	5–68, 5–89, 5–95, 6–158		s. 274	5–134
				(1)	5–129
	ss. 264–288	3–31		(b)	5–129
	s. 264 (1)	1–12, 5–104, 5–167, 9–18		(2)	5–129
				(3)	5–129
	(2)	5–108, 5–109		(4)	5–129
	(3)	5–107		(5)	5–129
	(4)	5–110, 5–121, 5–142, 5–163		s. 275	5–134
				(1)	5–131
	(b)	5–71, 9–23		(2)	5–131
	(5)	5–113, 5–121, 5–142, 5–163		s. 276	5–169
				s. 277	5–144, 5–148
	(6)	5–112, 5–121, 5–142, 5–163		s. 278	6–129
				(1)	5–147
	(7)	3–27, 3–33		(2)	5–148
	s. 265	1–20, 5–71, 5–115, 5–150, 5–159, 9–23, 9–26, 9–34		(3)	5–148
				s. 279 (1)	5–150
	(1)	5–115		(2)	5–150
	s. 266	1–20, 5–115, 5–150, 5–151		(3)	5–150
				s. 280	5–151, 5–159
	(a)	3–32, 5–159		s. 282	5–115, 5–151, 5–159
	(b)	5–159		ss. 283–288	9–26, 9–34

xxv

TABLE OF STATUTES

1985	Housing Act—*cont.*	
	s. 284	1–20
	s. 289	5–246
	ss. 289–298	5–04
	s. 299 (5)	5–257
	s. 300 (1)	5–159
	(2)	5–160
	(*a*)	5–160
	(*b*)	5–160, 5–161, 5–163, 5–164, 5–165
	(3)	5–165
	(4)	5–159
	(5)	5–159
	s. 302	5–69
	(*b*)	5–168
	(*c*)	5–167
	s. 303	5–132, 5–134
	s. 304	5–134, 5–150
	(1)	5–115, 5–159
	(2)	5–132
	(3)	5–133
	ss. 308–311	5–80, 5–104
	s. 308 (3) (*a*)	5–66, 5–80, 5–104
	s. 319	1–20
	(1)	1–20
	s. 320	1–20
	s. 321	5–70, 5–71
	s. 322	5–79, 5–104, 5–117, 5–125, 5–131, 5–132, 5–138, 5–145, 5–160
	s. 324	7–08
	ss. 324–331	7–33, 7–34
	s. 325 (1)	7–09
	(2)	7–09
	(*a*)	7–17
	(*b*)	7–15
	s. 326 (1)	7–11
	(2)	2–44, 7–11
	(*a*)	7–17
	(*b*)	7–15
	(3)	2–57, 7–12
	(4)	7–13
	s. 327 (1)	7–20
	(3)	7–20
	s. 328 (1)	7–22
	(2)	7–22
	(3)	7–22
	s. 329	7–22
	s. 330	7–27
	(2)	7–27
	(3)	7–27
	(4)	7–28
	(5)	7–27
	(6)	7–29
	s. 331 (1)	7–23
	(2)	7–23
	(*c*)	9–24
	(3)	7–25
	s. 332 (1)	7–33

1985	Housing Act—*cont.*	
	s. 332—*cont.*	
	(2)	7–34
	(3)	2–57, 7–36
	s. 333 (1)	7–38
	(2)	7–38
	(3)	7–38
	s. 334	1–07
	(1)	7–39, 7–40
	(2)	7–40
	s. 335 (1)	7–37
	(2)	7–37
	s. 336	7–35
	s. 337	1–26
	s. 338 (1)	7–44, 9–24
	(2)	7–45
	(3)	7–45
	s. 339 (1)	7–43
	(2)	7–26
	(*a*)	7–43
	(*b*)	7–43
	s. 340	1–26
	s. 341	1–26
	s. 342	7–18, 9–25
	s. 343	7–15, 7–16
	s. 345	3–65, 6–02, 6–25
	s. 346 (6)	1–23
	s. 352	3–30, 3–44, 3–65, 6–08, 6–12, 6–15, 6–19, 6–58, 6–71, 6–132, 6–139, 6–150, 6–169, 6–170, 6–184
	(1)	6–24, 6–65, 6–79, 6–82
	(2)	1–23, 6–15
	(*a*)	6–64
	(*b*)	6–64, 6–82
	(3)	6–68
	(4)	6–66, 6–67, 6–73
	(5)	6–70, 6–71
	(6)	3–61, 6–15, 6–64, 6–78
	s. 353	6–72
	(1)	6–72
	(2)	6–73
	(*e*)	6–67
	(3)	6–73
	(4)	6–75
	(5)	6–74
	s. 354	3–30, 6–13, 6–15, 6–64, 6–70, 6–75, 6–150
	ss. 354–357	6–19, 6–27, 6–150, 6–184, 7–02, 7–50
	s. 354 (1)	6–78
	(2)	6–82
	(*b*)	6–78
	(3)	6–80, 6–81
	(4)	6–83
	(5)	6–78
	(6)	6–78, 6–82
	(7)	6–78, 6–82
	s. 355 (1)	6–84

TABLE OF STATUTES

1985 Housing Act—*cont.*
  s. 355—*cont.*
    (2) 6–84
  s. 356 6–90
    (2) 6–91
  s. 357 (1) 6–87
    (2) 6–88
    (3) 6–89
  s. 358 6–08
  ss. 358–364 .... 6–79, 7–48
  s. 358 (1) 7–52, 7–55
    (2) 7–53, 7–54
    (3) 7–58
    (4) 1–23, 7–63
  s. 359 (1) 7–56
    (2) 7–57, 7–61
  s. 360 (1) 7–57
    (2) 7–09, 7–59
  s. 361 (1) 7–57, 7–60
    (2) 7–59
  s. 362 (1) 7–65
    (2) (*a*) 7–65
       (*b*) 7–65
  s. 363 (1) 7–64
    (2) 7–66
    (3) 7–66
  s. 364 7–62
    (2) 7–63
  s. 365 .... 6–132, 6–139
  ss. 365–368 6–151
  s. 365 (1) 6–112
    (2) 6–113
    (3) 6–112
  s. 366 .... 6–12, 6–121, 6–127,
                      6–163, 6–184
    (1) (*b*) 6–127
    (2) 6–114, 6–118, 6–120
    (3) 6–115, 6–117, 6–121,
                               6–123
  s. 367 (1) 6–120
    (2) 6–121
    (3) 6–121
    (4) 6–124
  s. 368 ..... 6–129, 9–23, 9–26, 9–34
    (1) 6–127
    (2) 6–128, 6–129
    (3) 1–23, 6–129
    (4) 6–128, 6–129
    (5) 6–129
    (6) 6–129
  s. 369 .... 6–95, 6–103
  ss. 369–373 6–17
  s. 369 (5) 1–23, 6–96, 6–102
  s. 370 .... 6–30, 6–150, 6–184
  ss. 370–372 .... 6–58, 9–14
  s. 370 (1) 6–93
    (2) 6–94
    (3) 6–51, 6–94
    (4) 6–97

1985 Housing Act—*cont.*
  s. 370—*cont.*
    (5) 6–94
  s. 371 .... 6–97, 6–150
    (1) 6–99
    (2) 6–100
    (3) 6–97, 6–100
    (4) 6–97
  s. 372 .... 6–104, 6–108, 6–132,
                   6–139, 6–150, 6–184
    (1) 6–105
      (*b*) 6–104
    (2) 6–105
    (3) 6–105, 6–108
    (4) 6–107
  s. 373 6–150
    (1) 6–108
    (2) 6–105, 6–108
    (3) 6–108
    (4) 6–109
  s. 374 .... 3–61, 6–16, 6–17
    (2) 3–61, 6–17
  s. 375 (1) 6–132, 6–134
    (2) 6–76, 6–110, 6–125
    (3) 6–135
  s. 376 (1) 1–23, 6–132, 6–139,
                               6–141
    (2) 1–23, 6–139, 6–141
    (4) 6–141
    (5) 6–132, 6–139
  s. 377 .... 1–33, 6–135
    (1) 1–34
    (2) 1–33
    (3) 1–33
  s. 379 3–30
    (1) 6–10, 6–150
    (2) 6–154
    (3) 6–153
  s. 380 6–152
  s. 381 6–186
    (1) (*b*) 6–155
      (*c*) 6–155
    (2) 6–155
    (4) 6–158
    (5) 6–152
    (6) 6–155
  s. 382 6–155
    (3) 6–155
    (4) 6–155
    (5) 6–158
  s. 383 (1) 6–159
    (2) 6–159
    (3) 6–159
    (4) 6–159
    (5) 6–159
  s. 384 6–175
    (1) 6–160, 6–161
    (2) 6–160
    (3) 6–160

TABLE OF STATUTES

1985	Housing Act—*cont.*	
	s. 384—*cont.*	
	(4)	6–161
	s. 385(1)(a)	6–158
	(b)	6–158
	(c)	6–157
	(2)	6–157
	s. 386	6–169, 6–195
	(1)	6–172
	(2)	6–174, 6–175, 6–176, 6–177
	(3)	6–170
	s. 387(1)	6–180
	(2)	6–180
	(3)	6–180
	(4)	6–181
	(5)	6–181
	s. 388	6–159
	s. 389(1)	6–179
	(2)	6–179
	(3)	6–179
	s. 390(1)	6–178
	(2)	6–182
	s. 391(1)	6–156
	(2)	6–156
	(3)	6–156
	(4)	6–156
	(5)	6–156
	s. 392(1)	6–191
	(2)	6–183
	(3)	6–183
	(4)	6–183
	(5)	6–184
	s. 393(1)(a)	6–185
	(b)	6–185
	(2)	6–186
	(3)	6–187
	(4)	6–188, 6–189, 6–190
	s. 394	6–191, 6–193, 6–194, 6–195, 6–196, 6–197, 6–198
	s. 395(1)	1–22
	s. 396	1–23, 6–180
	s. 397	1–24
	(3)	1–25
	(4)	1–25
	(5)	1–25
	s. 398	6–153, 7–51
	(6)	6–105
	s. 399	6–08, 6–76, 6–110, 6–125
	s. 406	7–09, 7–68
	s. 465(1)	5–264
	(2)	5–264
	ss. 467–473	5–209
	ss. 474–482	5–208, 5–209
	s. 477	5–218, 5–227, 2–243
	ss. 483–490	5–209, 6–02
	s. 486(1)(b)	6–119
	ss. 491–498	5–209

1985	Housing Act—*cont.*	
	ss. 494	5–84, 5–171, 5–173, 5–186
	s. 508	3–60, 3–62, 5–206, 5–229, 6–17
	s. 525	3–61, 6–02, 6–12
	s. 583	6–196
	s. 585(1)	5–165
	(3)	5–165
	s. 590	5–130, 5–149
	s. 604	3–20, 3–24, 3–35, 3–38, 3–45, 3–46A, 3–47, 3–59, 3–64, 5–44, 5–60, 5–66, 5–70, 5–151, 5–167, 6–18
	(1)	3–26
	s. 605	1–05, 2–89, 5–173, 7–41
	(2)	1–05
	s. 613	6–140
	s. 614	1–16, 1–19, 1–20, 1–22, 1–26, 4–04
	s. 617	4–11
	(1)	4–14
	(2)	4–14
	s. 622	7–51
	Sched. 10	5–74, 5–90, 5–98, 5–193, 5–199, 5–268, 6–136
	para. 6	5–86, 5–98, 5–189, 5–201, 5–266, 5–269
	para. 7	5–98, 5–200, 5–268, 6–138
	para. 8	6–137
	Sched. 13, Pt. I	6–169
	Pt. II	6–179
	para. 2(3)	6–171
	para. 3(1)	6–174
	(2)	6–176, 6–177
	(4)	6–175
	para. 4	6–178
	para. 5	6–173
	para. 6	6–173
	para. 15	6–156, 6–191
	para. 16	6–193
	(5)	6–193
	(6)	6–183
	para. 17(2)	6–163
	(3)	6–164
	(4)	6–164
	(5)	6–164
	para. 18	6–165
	para. 19	6–166
	para. 20(1)	6–168
	(2)	6–167
	para. 21(2)	6–188
	(3)	6–188
	(4)	6–189
	(5)	6–190
	(6)	6–190
	para. 22	6–194
	para. 23	6–195

TABLE OF STATUTES

1985 Housing Act—*cont.*
    Sched. 13, Pt. II—*cont.*
        para. 24 6–196
        para. 25(1) 6–197
            (2) 6–197
            (3) 6–197
            (4) 6–197
            (5) 6–197
        para. 26 6–198
    Sched. 22, para. 4(2) 5–108
    Sched. 23 .... 5–130, 5–149, 5–165
    Sched. 24 .... 5–130, 5–149, 5–165
    Housing Associations Act (c. 69) 9–28, 9–34
    Landlord and Tenant Act (c. 70) 3–04, 3–19, 7–34
        ss. 1–7 4–14
        s. 4 7–32
            (3) 7–32
        s. 5 7–33
        s. 7(1) 7–34
        s. 8 .... 3–03, 5–167
        s. 10 .... 3–03, 3–24, 5–92

1985 Landlord and Tenant Act—*cont.*
    s. 11 .... 3–03, 3–04, 5–07, 5–17, 5–92, 5–136, 5–185, 5–195, 9–19, 9–22
    s. 17(1) 9–19
    s. 34 7–43
    Housing (Consequential Provisions) Act (c. 71)—
        s. 2 .... 1–16, 1–19, 1–20, 1–22, 1–26, 3–64, 4–04, 5–80, 5–104, 5–116, 5–124, 5–127, 5–131, 5–132, 5–137, 5–151, 5–160, 5–183, 5–210, 5–225, 5–229, 5–234, 5–240, 6–29, 6–95, 6–158, 7–13, 7–18, 7–23, 7–27, 7–28, 7–33, 7–37, 7–44, 7–46
    Sched. 2, para. 23 .... 9–26, 9–28, 9–34

1986 Housing and Planning Act (c. 63)—
    Sched. 5, para. 10 5–77

TABLE OF STATUTORY INSTRUMENTS

1878 Canal Boat Regulations (as amended by S.R. & O. 1925 No. 843)—
    reg. 8 7–09
1878–1931 Canal Boat Regulations (S.R. & O. 1925 No. 843–S.R. & O. 1931 No. 444) 7–68
1937 Housing Act (Overcrowding and Miscellaneous Forms) Regulations (S.R. & O. 1937 No. 80) 7–13
    Form A 7–13
    Form B 7–37
    Form C 7–23, 7–46
    Form D 7–44
    Form E 7–27
    Form F 7–28
    Form G 7–18
    Form H 7–18
    Sched., Pt. I 7–33
1962 Housing (Management of Houses in Multiple Occupation) Regulations (S.I. 1962 No. 668) 6–29, 6–92, 6–95, 6–158
    reg. 2 6–32
    reg. 3 .... 6–31, 6–33
    reg. 4 6–36
    reg. 5 6–37
    reg. 6 6–38
    reg. 7 6–39
    (2) 6–39
    (3) 6–39
    reg. 8 6–40
    (1) 6–40, 6–41
    (3) 6–41
    (4) 6–41
    reg. 9 6–42
    reg. 10 6–43
    reg. 11 6–44
    reg. 12 6–45
    reg. 13 6–46
    reg. 14 .... 6–48, 6–105
    reg. 15 6–50
    reg. 16 6–55
    reg. 17 6–103
    reg. 18 6–105

1962 Housing (Management of Houses in Multiple Occupation) Regulations—*cont.*
    reg. 18—*cont.*
    (1) 6–51
    (2) 6–52
    (3) 6–53
    (4) 6–54
    (5) 6–49
    reg. 19 .... 6–34, 6–56
1965 Rules of the Supreme Court (S.I. 1965 No. 1776)—
    Ord. 59, r. 19 .... 5–88, 5–122, 5–143, 5–164, 5–191, 5–252, 7–65
1972 Housing (Prescribed Forms) Regulations (S.I. 1972 No. 228) 1–19, 1–20, 1–22, 1–26, 4–04
    Form No. 1 ..... 1–16, 1–36, 5–96, 5–197
    Form No. 2A 5–80
    Form No. 2B 5–183
    Form No. 2C 5–183
    Form No. 3 5–132
    Form No. 6 5–104
    Form No. 7 5–116
    Form No. 8 5–127
    Form No. 9 5–127
    Form No. 10 5–124
    Form No. 11 5–160
    Form No. 12 5–104
    Form No. 13 5–151
    Form No. 14 .... 5–131, 5–137
    Form No. 34 6–127
    Form No. 35 6–94
    Form No. 36 6–105
    Form No. 37 6–66
    Form No. 38 6–114
    Form No. 39 6–80
    Form No. 40 6–82
    Form No. 41 6–87
    Form No. 42 6–91
    Form No. 49 .... 6–68, 6–107, 6–118
    Form No. 50 6–152
    Form No. 51 6–153
    Form No. 52 5–210
    Form No. 53 5–229

TABLE OF STATUTORY INSTRUMENTS

1972 Housing (Prescribed Forms) Regulations—*cont.*
Form No. 54 5–234
Form No. 57 5–240
1974 Housing (Prescribed Forms) (Amendment) Regulations (S.I. 1974 No. 1511) 4–04, 5–80
1975 Housing (Prescribed Forms) (Amendment) Regulations (S.I. 1975 No. 500) 4–04, 5–80
1981 Housing (Prescribed Forms) (Amendment) Regulations (S.I. 1981 No. 1347) 4–04, 5–80, 6–114, 6–127

1981 Housing (Means of Escape from Fire in Houses in Multiple Occupation) Order (S.I. 1981 No. 1576) 6–113
County Court Rules (S.I. 1981 No. 1687 (L. 20)—
Ord. 11 5–136
1982 Housing (Payments for Well Maintained Houses) Order (S.I. 1982 No. 1112) 9–38
1985 Building Regulations (S.I. 1985 No. 1065) 3–05, 8–76
Building (Inner London) Regulations (S.I. 1985 No. 1936) 3–05

INTRODUCTION

Housing conditions in the United Kingdom are not controlled by the application of a detailed code of housing regulations specifying the minimum acceptable standard of each component part of the structure. Such an approach is adopted in the Building Regulations for the control of houses as they are built and in the Housing Codes adopted by many states in the U.S.A., but unacceptable housing conditions in England and Wales are the subject of broad statutory norms, which are now contained in the Housing Act 1985 and the Public Health Act 1936. These norms allow for considerable variation both in their interpretation, and in their selective application by those entrusted with their enforcement. An exposition of statutes elucidated by the decisions of the courts will frequently provide an inadequate explanation of the law.

Beyond the written law recorded in statutes and casebooks lies a legal practice, part profession, part tradition. The enforcement of housing standards thus involves more than the application of a narrow legal rule to the structure of a house. The influences are varied and include the dictates of the local housing stock, policy considerations of the employing authority, and the amount of subsidy available.[1] Since the law is not specific and precise about the matters which shall form the basis for their decisions, environmental health officers must look elsewhere for guidance. To a great extent this comes from the past practices of other environmental health officers. It is inculcated in training and reinforced by colleagues in practice. It is rarely articulated and lies in the evolution of the standards themselves and the development of the environmental health profession.

Thus the implementation of housing standards includes an awareness of their origins, and the authority that accompanies the expertise of those enforcing the standards is founded in the history of the profession. The following review of the development of the standards and the profession precedes a brief discussion of the role of discretion in the control of housing conditions.

The origins of housing standards

The roots of present day controls are to be found in the Industrial Revolution which brought a rush from the rural areas to the towns and cities. By 1830 the urban labouring population far out-numbered the agricultural labourers, during a period when there was also a dramatic increase in the population. Housing was needed for the crowds of urban

[1] See p. xliv.

newcomers, and the shortage was met by cheaply and hastily erected buildings, cramped onto any available land in and around the towns and new industrial centres.[2] There were no local authorities, and there was no central government control of building. The results were badly planned areas of housing, built of inadequate materials and to inadequate standards, without sufficient amenities, facilities and sanitation, and filled with overcrowded households.

The unrest which these conditions provoked was part of wider movements sweeping the country in the 1830s, particularly the agitation for the ten hour day and the activities of the Chartists. Concern for housing in particular was prompted by a fear of cholera and typhoid. Encouraged by the dramatic spread of epidemics which seemed to emanate from the crowded rookeries and tenemented quarters of the new towns and cities, a Royal Commission was established in 1832 to inquire into the administration and operation of the Poor Laws. Their First Report (in 1834) recommended the appointment of permanent officials based at local level (Relieving Officers), and the establishment of a central Poor Law Board.

The secretary appointed to this Board was Edwin Chadwick, a barrister and an assistant commissioner to the Royal Commission. He had also been a journalist, and it was while preparing an article on Life Assurance in 1828 that he conceived his "Sanitary Idea,"[3] which became the inspiration for the public health and housing legislation. The arguments employed by the Victorian reformers in support of the Sanitary Idea were couched in terms of the threat that epidemics posed for the middle classes when the contagions escaped from the slums and the economic good sense of reducing the "burthens" that paupers and the destitute became on the parish.[4] Such concern led to the qualified acceptance that the state had a duty to its citizens to protect them from health hazards arising out of bad living conditions, even if that meant interfering with the property rights of individual owners.

The Sanitary Idea combined at least two theories — that diseases were caused and transmitted by miasma, and that the poor were a "bad" life insurance risk as they did not live as long as others. The miasma theory, soon to be discredited, provided a good argument for the removal of materials which were likely to cause smells. Although there was some truth in the notion that where there were smells there was disease, there was much more truth, just as there is today, in the high morbidity and mortality rates of the poor and those inadequately housed.[5]

---

[2] See generally John Burnett, *A Social History of Housing 1815–1970* (1978) Chap. 3.
[3] S. E. Finer, *The Life and Times of Sir Edwin Chadwick* (1952) Chap. IV, p. 154.
[4] *Ibid.* p. 155.
[5] D. S. Byrne *et al.*, *Housing and Health, The Relationship between Housing Conditions and the Health of Council Tenants* (1986) Gower.

INTRODUCTION

A direct relationship between disease and the physical environment was first clearly identified in the fourth Annual Report of the Poor Law Board (in 1838). It was followed by the famous inquiry by the Poor Law Commissioners, *Report on the Sanitary Conditions of the Labouring Population of Great Britain*, published in 1842. Acknowledged to be largely the work of Chadwick, it was the inspiration for most of the legislative activity in housing for the next three decades. The main thrust of this legislation was the identification and removal of statutory nuisances.

The recommendations of the Poor Law Commissioners were enacted in the Nuisances Removal and Diseases Prevention Act 1846 which introduced a procedure for two medical practitioners to make a written complaint of the existence of a nuisance to the justices. The filthy and unwholesome condition of any dwelling house was a matter of complaint as a "nuisance likely to promote or increase disease."[6] If the existence of the nuisance was proved, the justices could order "the cleansing, whitewashing or purifying"[7] of any building or otherwise order the abatement of the nuisance.

The nuisance procedure was restricted to the cleaning or disinfestation of houses. It echoed the concern of Chadwick and his co-workers who had been interested in housing tangentially — "as places where overcrowding transmitted disease, or where the lack of water and sanitation discouraged cleanliness and modesty."[8] The Artisans and Labourers Dwellings Act 1868 gave far broader powers to local authorities to achieve the improvement or eradication of substandard housing; it required local authorities to deal with "any premises . . . in a Condition or State dangerous to Health so as to be unfit for Human Habitation."[9] The owner of such a property was to be served with a copy of the local authority's report and had an opportunity to object to any remedy suggested by the authority.

Such a remedy might include structural alterations or improvements and could include the demolition of the premises. The 1868 Act is the basis for the present procedure for dealing with unfitness and is significant for the link it made with danger to health.

Housing versus public health standards

The Artisans and Labourers Dwellings Act 1868 marks the beginning of legislative intervention in the housing market, although it was to be many years before local government was established on a firm enough

---

[6] Nuisance Removal and Diseases Prevention Act 1846, para. II.
[7] *Ibid.*
[8] John Burnett, *A Social History of Housing 1815–1970* (1978) p. 54.
[9] Artisans and Labourers Dwellings Act 1868, s.5.

basis for the effective implementation of the public health or the housing legislation. After 1868 the two branches of the law affecting housing standards developed separately.

The sanitary approach to nuisances was refined in the Public Health Act 1875 which was the principal Act until a series of amendments were consolidated in the Public Health Act 1936. Inherent in the notion of statutory nuisance lies a concept of health hazard, the source of which is essentially dirt, sewage and putrefaction.[10] If reflects the short horizons of nineteenth century science and their theories of miasma. The recommended remedies were cleanliness, sanitation and morality. In most important respects the nuisance procedures in force today are a reenactment of the 1846 Act and are inappropriate for dealing with many twentieth century hazards.

The statutory nuisance provisions of the Public Health Acts provided the major tool for local authorities dealing with basic housing disrepair and unsatisfactory living conditions for many years, although they tended to be used to achieve patch-repairs rather than comprehensive refurbishment. This preference for the statutory nuisance procedure continued until the mid 1970s. One factor influencing the change of preference was the Divisional Court decision in *N.C.B.* v. *Thorne*,[11] which appears to have been generally misunderstood. Another factor was that the use of the Housing Act procedures made available grant-aid toward the cost of the works. This, together with the promotion of grants generally, rendered the statutory nuisance provisions a secondary tool of most authorities.

However, the statutory nuisance provisions remained one of the few legal procedures available to individuals attempting to persuade their landlord to carry out remedial works (by way of section 99). This use of the provisions continued to bring the standard before the courts, and it became clear that more comprehensive remedial works could be required under the statutory nuisance provisions than had previously been thought (*e.g.*, works of thermal insulation, the provision of space heating and higher standards of repair works).

The housing legislation on the other hand underwent considerable change. It developed initially as a recognition that some properties were beyond salvation and should be pulled down to make way for better. The provisions relating to housing had been consolidated and extended in 1890 by the Housing of the Working Classes Act which remained the principal Act until 1925. By then the shortage of housing after the first world war and the needs of rapidly expanding transport systems, required the clearance of housing for planning purposes alone.

---

[10] See Lord Widgery in *Coventry City Council* v. *Cartwright* [1975] 1 W.L.R. 845 and para. 3.16, below.
[11] [1976] 1 W.L.R. 543. (For comments on this case, see para. 3.17.)

INTRODUCTION

The inter-war years saw the development of two distinct policies in relation to housing — the clearance of areas to make way for new roads, railways and fresh housing, and individual action to deal with insanitary houses. The latter concern was reflected in the publication of a *Manual on Unfit Houses and Unhealthy Areas*[12] which recommended the adoption of a standard of fitness and distinguished between remedying unfitness and improvement.

The housing shortage after 1945 precipitated a national effort on building new houses, but in the same period the repair and improvement of the older houses was encouraged by the introduction of grant-aid. In 1954, the first National Standard of Fitness was introduced, and this standard has remained (with only minor amendment) as the main yardstick to determine whether action is necessary by local authorities.

Although the basic standards have remained largely unaltered since the 1950s, the overall policies relating to housing have altered considerably. As the more grossly insanitary houses have been demolished, or the enthusiasm increased for clearing the large expanses that the states of the 1960s required, standards have probably fluctuated to accomodate these fresh objectives. For example, some houses which may have been declared unfit and demolished 30 years ago, might not today be so classified in time when there is more emphasis upon rehabilitation. The 1976 and 1981 House Condition Surveys showed that by far the most serious problem was disrepair of the fabric, and it was based on these findings that subsequent efforts have been directed towards ensuring the repair of houses.

Recently the Government has proposed adopting a more rigid approach to the basic standard determining those homes which are below the "fitness" standard.[13] The proposed standard calls for a house to be evaluated item by item. It will only fall below the fitness standard if it is clearly deficient in respect of any specified item and the notion of a standard that is applied on a cumulative basis is discarded.[14] Such an approach is undoubtedly more objective than the current process of assessing housing, but it does not follow that such a move will lead to an overall improvement in the national condition of housing. Whether or not such a change is progressive or not will depend upon the individual items that comprise the new standard and the resources allocated to its enforcement.

Houses in multiple occupation

Whilst there have been fluctuating demands upon the legal processes for dealing with individual houses, peculiar difficulties arose in houses in

---

[12] Ministry of Health (1919).
[13] *Home Improvement: the Government's Proposals*, DoE (1987) H.M.S.O.
[14] See below, para. 3.46.

INTRODUCTION

multiple occupation which warrant separate discussion. It is in such houses that some of the most serious problems are concentrated and the standards to be applied to them are in contrast or addition to the treatment of individual dwellings.[15]

Recent housing and welfare policies have led to an increasing number of the single unemployed and aged living in small flats and bedsits. It was recently estimated that 80 per cent. of all houses in multiple occupation have inadequate means of escape from fire, and that the possibility of death from fire in such houses is eight to ten times the average for singly occupied houses.[16] Since 1976 there has been a growing campaign for stronger action by local authorities to deal with unsatisfactory conditions in houses in multiple occupation. A number of local authorities have found it necessary to set up specialist sections to monitor such premises and take action where necessary.

Houses in multiple occupation have always been recognised as a problem and singled out for special attention in the legislation. The Public Health Acts contained general provisions to deal with any premises likely to affect health or cause a nuisance and included specific provisions for dealing with "common lodging houses."[17] As the complexity of the problems became more apparent, the legislation itself became more complex and the provisions for multi-occupied houses were incorporated into the Housing Acts. Chapter 6 of this work discusses the various standards and procedures for the regulation of conditions in houses occupied by more than one household.

The origins of housing legislation and the legislative response to new social problems explains to some extent the present array of standards. The practice of enforcement also requires an understanding of the evolution of the profession and the development of local government.

The development of the profession

The appointment of sanitary policemen and an authoritative body to control their activities in each locality was part of the political struggle for centralised control of the economy. Their ultimate success was dependent upon the formation of an effective structure of local government[18] to which the emergence of an environmental health occupation is inextricably linked. The tension that arose between the need for greater supervision of the economy and the property interests that operated in local parishes was another facet of the battles over the working day in

---

[15] See Chap. 6.
[16] Association of Metropolitan Authorities, *Multiple Occupation: Time for Action* (1987) A.M.A.
[17] See, *e.g.*, Public Health Act 1875, ss.77 *et seq.*, and now see Housing Act 1985, Pt. xi.
[18] See generally Sir Ivor Jennings, *Principles of Local Government* (1931) Chap. II.

INTRODUCTION

the factory and the costs of administering the new Poor Laws.[19] The housing responsibilities of the early officials were considerably hampered by the power of local property owners, since public health affected the pockets of the middle classes.[20]

The sanitary reformers were confronted with the problem that public health required a system of local enforcement and central supervision. The cost of such a system would inevitably meet resistance from ratepayers and the vested interests threatened by the imposition of drainage and sanitation such as the private water companies and large landlords. Chadwick's blueprint for reform was a semi-autonomous central body and local boards to supervise local Inspectors.[21] The Public Health Act 1848 introduced a rudimentary public health system and established a General Board of Health which could appoint superintending inspectors to inquire into and report on local conditions. The Act also provided for the setting up of local Boards of Health who had the power to appoint inspectors of nuisances. The office of inspector of nuisances is thus one of the oldest offices in the public health service.[22]

The landlords and factory owners whose activities the inspectors aspired to control were prominent in the nascent local government structures. Opposition to the reforms was vigorous and the General Board of Health was not granted the wide powers necessary. Where inspectors were appointed they were vulnerable to obstruction and interference. Throughout the remainder of the last century, the struggle continued to establish on the one hand an effective structure of administration and on the other a competent and adequately trained and salaried body of enforcers.

The vehicle for administrative control ceased to be the local Boards of Health. In its Report on Public Health in 1871, the Royal Sanitary Commission criticised the unnecessary proliferation of locally based authorities, and recommended that there "should be one local authority for all public health purposes in every place, so that no area should be without such an authority or have more than one," and also that every such local authority should have "at least one inspector of nuisances." The framework of modern local government was laid the following year when the Local Government Board was established, and England and Wales (except London) was divided into Urban and Rural Sanitary Districts. In 1875 the Public Health Act required each urban authority to appoint the two officials who had become the spearhead of public health policy — inspectors of nuisances and medical officers of health.

[19] See generally S. E. Finer, *The Life and Times of Sir Edwin Chadwick* (1952) Book 2, p. 39.
[20] *Ibid.* Book 3, Chap. 5, p. 180.
[21] *Ibid.* Book 7, Chap. 5, p. 319.
[22] Memorandum in Evidence to the Royal Commission on Local Government (1929) by the Sanitary Inspectors Association, Part XIII, Minute 37, 4688, p. 2338.

INTRODUCTION

The 1875 Act required that a medical officer of health must be a "legally qualified" medical practitioner. No qualifications, however, were stipulated for the inspectors. Unlike the "learned" professions,[23] there was no existing occupation or trade which monopolised the knowledge and skills required to regulate sanitation. The enforcer's job required the mixed disciplines of the medical and engineering professions. The administration of an efficient public health system demanded skilled and accredited officials and a body capable of representing them.

This emerged in 1876 with the establishment of the Sanitary Institute, which began training and examining inspectors a year later. The inspectors themselves recognised the need to consolidate their influence if only because some authorities were rejecting central government help with the salaries of inspectors and appointing unqualified persons in order to maintain local control over appointments. The wages of inspectors and medical officers of health were clearly an unacceptable burden on some local budgets.[24] Inspectors had combined locally to protect their interests and in 1883 the Association of Public Sanitary Inspectors was formed from these local initiatives. In September 1891, the Association became incorporated, and soon changed its name to the Sanitary Inspectors' Association. At this time it had a membership of around 300. There were separate North Western and Midland and South Wales associations.

Once established, and possibly because the job required the enhanced power that accompanies formal training and examined credentials, the new profession was granted statutory authority and a national system of accreditation. The Sanitary Inspectors Examination Board was first established in February 1899. In 1910[25] the Local Government Board published the terms of appointment, tenure, duties and salaries of medical officers of health and inspectors of nuisances. The job security of inspectors and medical officers of health was assured by the provision that once appointed, they would continue to hold office from year to year until death, resignation, insanity or removal by the Local Government Board, with or without the agreement of the local council. This security of tenure was necessary to protect inspectors because "the execution of their statutory duties had brought them into conflict with interested members of their own authority."[26]

In 1921 the title of inspector of nuisances was changed to sanitary inspector. The self respect of the profession was acute at this time and

[23] Magali Sarfatti Larson, *The Rise of Professionalism: A Sociological Analysis* (1979).
[24] Memorandum in Evidence to the Royal Commission on Local Government (1929) by the Sanitary Inspections Association, Minute 37,555, p. 2343.
[25] Sanitary Officers (Outside London) Order 1910 (S.R. & O. 1910).
[26] Memorandum in Evidence to the Royal Commission on Local Government (1929) by the Sanitary Inspectors Assocations, para. 20, p. 2340.

the Sanitary Inspector's Association was strenuously attempting to put its members on an equal footing with the other professions with whom they rubbed shoulders. Appearances were crucial, and a uniform which may have been appropriate "in the earlier days of public health administration when attention was mainly directed to enforcing penalties for breach of legislative ordinances"[27] was not the guise of the professional man:

> "In the course of their duties Sanitary Inspectors are often called into consultation with engineers, architects and other professional men, and their standing as executive officers is undoubtedly diminished and their influence correspondingly lessened if compelled to wear a distinctive uniform".[28]

A further complication facing sanitary inspectors in their efforts to establish themselves as autonomous experts came from the medical officer of health. In 1926 the inspectors were placed under the general direction of the medical officers. This was regarded as diminution in their status and was the subject of some annoyance to the Sanitary Inspector's Association.[29] Nevertheless it was a situation that continued for another 50 years.

In 1951 the new Minister of Local Government and Planning (later re-designated the Ministry of Housing and Local Government) was made responsible for all non-medical aspects of public health as well as local government. The Minister of Health, however, continued to have overall control of sanitary inspectors and medical officers of health.

The inspector's title was again changed in 1956 (by a Private Member's Bill), this time to public health inspector, a title which remained until 1974, when references to public health inspector were removed from any legislation and the term environmental health officer become the generally adopted title. In the reorganisation that occurred in 1974 responsibility for public health enforcement remained with local government. The medical officer of health (with new title) together with the clinical health functions were transferred to the reorganised National Health Service. A link was retained between the authorities on environmental health matters.

The removal of the medical officers of health from their supervisory responsibilities over public health inspectors, had been promoted by the Association of Public Health Inspectors since 1966. It had been argued that the public health inspector was now highly trained and equipped to deal with the complexity of public health work, and the role of the

---

[27] Memorandum in Evidence to the Royal Commission on Local Government (1929) para. 44, p. 2346.
[28] *Ibid*. para. 29, p. 2342.
[29] *Ibid*. para. 33, p. 2343.

medical officer in this field had declined. Ironically, however, at the same time the statutory obligation on local authorities to appoint a public health inspector, which had been in the legislation since 1855, was abolished.

In some respects the formal severing of the link between environmental health officers and the medical profession can be seen as a further readjustment of the professional role. The emphasis upon health has arguably been reduced and the role of the officer as local governnment employee (rather than as independent professional) has been enhanced. Similarly the abolition of the duty upon each authority to appoint an officer with environmental health qualifications represents a diminution of their status. It is interesting that this reassessment has taken place at a time when there is renewed interest in the relationship between substandard housing and the health of occupiers.[30]

The role of profession

The concept of profession is elusive and has in recent years been the subject of debate.[31] These studies have emphasised both the self interest of professions and their broader social functions. The professional status of environmental health officers and their precedessors has been advantageous to both local and central government. Thus their job security and accreditation can be seen as part of the process of containing the power of property owners, before a strong system of local government was established. Furthermore the mechanism of using broad statutory standards as the basis for legal control requires a trained body of experts and the professional status of environmental health officers has recently been recognised by royal charter. In recent years they have been the officials upon whose judgment local authority mandatory grants are distributed and without their decisions a bureaucratic system to apportion the subsidy might have been necessary.

The discretion underlying the decisions of environmental health officers is discussed further below. Frequently in court and elsewhere, however, they rely upon their status as a qualified member of the profession; their expertise is the justification for their opinion. In common with other professions that expertise is based upon a number of vague, and seldom articulated principles and ideals. Amongst the environmental health profession, for example, the vestiges of the Sanitary Idea,[32] or a

---

[30] See the various books on hypothermia, crowding and dampness referred to in this work; the papers from "Unhealthy Housing: a Diagnosis," Conference at the University of Warwick, December 1986, I.E.H.O., and M. Whitehead, *The Health Divide: Inequalities in Health in the 1980s* (1987).

[31] T. J. Johnson, *Professions and Power* (1972); R. Dingwall and P. Lewis, *The Sociology of the Professions: Doctors, Lawyers and Others* (1983); and also Larson, *The Rise of Professionalism: A Sociological Analysis* (1979) pp. 83 *et seq*.

[32] See p. xxxiv.

less tangible successor which has developed into an ideology of public health, are evident. It manifests itself frequently in the conversations of environmental health officers[33] and is the background to much discussion in the pages of their professional journals.[34] It appears in the lobbying activities of the Institution of Environmental Health Officers which reflect a concern to protect the well-being of occupiers of buildings and to control the power of owners.

Some of the aspirations of professional bodies are more specific and are recorded in a charter or reflected in their publications. In this country there is no formal code of professional guidance for the implementation of housing standards nor is there a record of any general professional objectives. In the United States, however, the American Public Health Association in 1939 published *Basic Principles of Healthful Housing*[35] and the European Regional Office of the World Health Organisation have prepared draft guidelines on basic hygiene for housing.[36] These works, along with the various Ministerial Circulars and local policy statements, can inform an officer's interpretation of the discretionary standards which underpin housing policy in England and Wales. On those occasions when an officer may feel the need for a professional justification of a decision, they provide a convenient record of the underlying principles.

Since most of the decisions of a local authority officer in this field will not be the subject of judicial supervision, the notion of a professional standard inculcated into an officer's behaviour is an important safeguard against the potential abuse of discretion. At those times when the behests of local politicians or the strictures of a depleted housing budget suggest the exercise of discretion in a manner than runs counter to the perceived purposes of the Public Health and Housing legislation, officers may have little alternative but to rely upon their professional instincts to resist.

Discretionary justice

The notion of a range of housing standards to be selectively applied to individual structures is one aspect of the wide discretionary powers of environmental health officers. In applying any chosen norm to a particular

---

[33] R. Burridge, "The Discrete Setting of Housing Standards", unpublished paper at W. G. Hart Workshop, Institute of Advanced Legal Studies, London, June 1987.
[34] See *e.g.*, Caney and Kliger, "Environmental Health: Professional Competence and its Assessment" in *Environmental Health*, November 1983 and the articles and correspondence on the issue of the Institution of Environmental Health Officers' proposals for an Assessment of Professional Competence in *Environmental Health News*, June 12, and July 3, 10 and 17, 1987.
[35] American Public Health Association (1939), and see para. 2–07 below.
[36] Ray Ranson (ed.) *Basic Housing Hygiene Guidelines*, Paper at Workshop on Housing Hygiene and Environmental Health Problems in Urban Fringes, WHO Ankara, 1985.

INTRODUCTION

building an officer exercises an element of discretion at three moments in the enforcement process: in finding the facts on which the decision is to be based in formulating or interpreting the standard to be applied; and in the application of the standard to those facts.[37]

The recognition that there is a significant element of discretion in the identification and selection of facts upon which any housing action (or inaction) is based emphasises the importance of the house inspection. Law books generally concentrate upon the rules of law and often ignore the practices which formulate and define legal action. The dedication of a considerable section of this book to the inspection of buildings and the writing of reports is directed towards the importance of this process of defining and selecting the facts to which the statutory norms may subsequently be applied.

The second moment of discretion arises in the interpretation of a standard. The definition and implementation of housing standards are heavily influenced by the strictures of local housing subsidy, the pattern of housing tenure in the locality, and the quality of the housing stock. In complex areas like housing renovation, discretionary standards enable decisions to be made that are sensitive to these local circumstances, or individual needs; they facilitate effective action to be taken without recourse to an intricate set of narrow regulations; and they are less prone to expensive challenges in the courts.

The significance of housing standards for housing subsidy arises through the distribution of mandatory and discretionary grants which are determined by reference to the standards set out in the Housing Act 1985. This book does not deal with the range of grants available, but their presence effectively ensures that many of the decisions of local authority officers will not be challenged in the courts since those who are regulated (private landlords and housing associations) derive benefit from the enforcement. Non-compliance on the other hand results in their losing any entitlement to grant aid. Thus as an enforcement agency, environmental health departments enjoy a peculiar advantage in their housing function. The carrot of grant aid is a more potent weapon that the stick of authoritative coercion. In this respect the control of housing standards by environmental health officers can be seen as part of a wider debate on the nature of discretion and regulation, of which much has been written recently.[38]

---

[37] D. J. Galligan, *Discretionary Powers: A Legal Study of Official Discretion* (1986) Chap. 1, p. 9.
[38] Bridget Hutter, *The Reasonable Arm of the Law? The Enforcement Procedures of Environmental Health Officers* (1988); D. J. Galligan, *Discretionary Powers: A Legal Study of Official Discretion* (see n. 37 above); K. Hawkins, *Environment and Enforcement: Regulation and the Social Definition of Pollution* (1984); G. M. Richardson *et al.*, *Policing Pollution: A Study of Regulation and Enforcement* (1983).

INTRODUCTION

A major thrust of this debate has been the concern that discretionary justice is vulnerable to administrative abuse.[39] It encourages inequitable decisions between individual cases and is open to undue influence from the executive, be it local or central government. It is secret and vests power in those who exercise it. It also means that only rarely will the courts be called upon to scrutinise an officer's interpretation of the normative standards.[40] Whether or not this continues in the light of recent proposals[41] to means-test grants, and to introduce a new fitness standard, remains to be seen. Arguably both of these measures will influence a re-emergence of the need for more formal enforcement. This could include the introduction of new offences to deal with recalcitrant or stubborn landlords.[42]

A broad standard such as the unfitness standard might be expected to be subjected to considerable latitude in interpretation nationally over the years, as well as differences in local interpretation amongst different authorities.[43] There is nothing sinister in the differential application of housing standards once it is appreciated that such regional variations may exist, and that a house which is unfit in Maidenhead might not be declared unfit in Maesteg.[44] It illustrates, however, the importance of establishing a clear concept of each standard so that any variations are reduced to the minimum that local enforcement requires. This book is directed towards the quest for clarification of the standards and more uniform patterns of enforcement.

---

[39] See, *e.g.*, M. Adler and S. Asquith (eds.), *Discretion and Welfare* (1981); R. A. Kagan, *Regulatory Justice* (1978), Russell Sage; and J. L. Mashaw, *Bureaucratic Justice: Managing Social Security Claims* (1983).
[40] R. Burridge, "The Discrete Setting of Housing Standards" (see above n. 33).
[41] *Home Improvement: the Government's Proposals*, DoE (1987) H.M.S.O.
[42] Announcement by William Waldegrave, Minister for Housing, reported in *Inside Housing*, March 18, 1988.
[43] The broad discretionary standard is evidently to be found in other spheres of the environmental health officer's job, see Hutter, *The Reasonable Arm of the Law?* (1988) Chap. 3, p. 60.
[44] See R. Burridge, "The Role of Discretion in the Formulation of Housing Standards", Paper given at the Conference on Unhealthy Housing: Prevention and Remedies, Warwick University, December (1987) I.E.H.O.

CHAPTER 1

THE DUTIES AND POWERS OF LOCAL GOVERNMENT

1. Definitions of local authorities and local housing authorities	1.01 1.02
2. General duties of authorities	1.05
3. Delegation of authorities' functions	1.11
4. Powers of entry, etc.	1.15

1. DEFINITION OF LOCAL AUTHORITIES AND LOCAL HOUSING AUTHORITIES

The Housing Act 1985 refers to "local housing authorities," while the Public Health Acts and the Building Act 1984 refer to "local authorities." The definition of these terms, and the pursuant duties and responsibilities vary, and are considered separately in the following section. **1.02**

The Housing Act 1985 defines a "local housing authority" as the district council, London borough council or the Common Council for the City of London.[1] **1.03**

The Public Health Acts 1936 to 1969 and the Building Act 1984 define a "local authority" as the district council, the London borough council or the Common Council for the City of London.[2] The Public Health Act 1936 enables two or more local authorities to establish a joint board to carry out certain functions, provided that the consent of the Secretary of State for the Environment is obtained.[3] **1.04**

2. GENERAL DUTIES OF LOCAL HOUSING AUTHORITIES

Housing Act 1985
It is the duty of every local housing authority to ensure that their district is inspected from time to time[4] so as to determine what action they should take in performance of their functions under the Act,[5] **1.05**

---

[1] Housing Act 1985, s.1.
[2] Public Health Act 1936, s.1 as amended by Local Government Act 1972, para. 1, Sched. 14; London Government Act 1963, s.40(2); Public Health (Recurring Nuisance) Act 1969, s.3, and Building Act 1984, s.126.
[3] Public Health Act 1936, s.6.
[4] See para. 1.10.
[5] Housing Act 1985, s.605.

specifically in relation to repair notices,[6] area improvement,[7] slum clearance[8] and houses in multiple occupation.[9]

In carrying out this general duty, local housing authorities are required to comply with any directions given by the Secretary of State[10] and must keep such records and supply such information as the Secretary of State may specify. Various circulars have been issued in the past, which comment on this duty. However, the directions are not detailed, but include suggestions that they should carry out sample surveys[11] and advice on the collection and recording of information. The most recent Circular recommends that such surveys should be carried out on a regular basis.[12]

1.06 Every local housing authority is also required to consider the housing conditions in their district[13] with respect to the provision of further housing accommodation, and for that purpose to review any information, including that brought to light as a result of inspections and surveys.[14]

1.07 In addition, when a local housing authority considers that it is necessary to prepare a report on overcrowding[15] in their district or a part of it, then the authority must cause an inspection of their district (or the part) to be made and submit the report to the Secretary of State.[16] The report should include details of the new dwellings required to ensure the abatement of any such overcrowding. An inspection and report can be demanded by the Secretary of State.[17]

Public Health Acts 1936 to 1969 and Building Act 1984

1.08 Every local authority is required to ensure that their district is inspected from time to time,[18] and is under a specific duty to look for matters required to be dealt with as statutory nuisances.[19]

---

[6] Housing Act 1985, Pt. VI.
[7] Ibid. Pt. VIII.
[8] Ibid. Pt. IX.
[9] Ibid. Pt. XI.
[10] Ibid. s.605(2).
[11] Ministry of Housing and Local Government Circular No. 63/69 (W.O. No. 62/69), August 20, 1969, in particular paras. 5 and 11. The requirements were confirmed by paras. 14 and 15 of Ministry of Housing and Local Government Circular No. 67/69 (W.O. No. 66/69).
[12] DoE Circular No. 10/71 (W.O. No. 20/71), March 29, 1971, in particular para. 5.
[13] *Re Havant & Waterloo Urban District Council Compulsory Purchase Order (No. 4)* [1951] 2 K.B. 779, which held that the needs of the district was not confined to the needs of those at present living in the district.
[14] Housing Act 1985, s.8.
[15] Ibid. Pt. X. See also Chap. 7.
[16] Ibid. s.334.
[17] Ibid. s.334(1).
[18] See para. 1.10.
[19] Public Health Act 1936, s.91.

There are other specific duties in relation to individual dwellings **1.09**
which arise when the authority becomes aware that those dwellings fail
to satisfy certain standards. These specific duties are dealt with in relation to the enforcement procedures in respect of those standards.[20]

"From time to time"

The phrase "from time to time" appears in both the Public Health **1.10**
and the Housing Acts in relation to the surveying and inspection of the
district.[21] The phrase is vague, but it would seem clear that total inaction
could be held to be *ultra vires*,[22] and that the duty must be exercised as
the occasion requires (*i.e.*, a single inspection of the district cannot be
said to have satisfied the duty).[23] It is also clear that taking a merely
reactive role—only reacting to complaints from members of the public—would not satisfy the duty, and that a positive role is required.

3. Delegation of Authorities' Functions

To ensure the effective discharge of its function, a local authority or **1.11**
local housing authority is empowered[24] to "make arrangements"
enabling any of the following to act in the name of that local authority:

(a) a committee of that local authority;
(b) a sub-committee of that local authority;
(c) an officer of that local authority; or
(d) another local authority.

The term "committee" has been held to have its ordinary meaning, **1.12**
and cannot consist of one person.[25] The effect of making such arrangements is that the committee, sub-committee, officer or other local authority may act in the name of the delegating authority. A local authority
cannot take legal action or enforcement procedures in respect of a house
solely owned and managed by itself,[26] and similarly neither can a delegate of that authority take such action, even though the management of
the house has been delegated to another committee, or officer.

---

[20] See Chap. 5, paras. 5.04 and 5.25.
[21] See paras. 1.05 and 1.08.
[22] *Mead v. Haringey London Borough Council* [1979] 1 W.L.R. 637.
[23] Interpretation Act 1978, s.12.
[24] Local Government Act 1972, s.101(1).
[25] In *R. v. Secretary of State for the Environment, ex p. Hillingdon London Borough Council* [1986] 1 W.L.R. 192 the Divisional Court stated that enforcement notices issued by the chairman of the Planning Committee, authorised to act in the name of the Committee, were *ultra vires*.
[26] *R. v. Cardiff City Council, ex p. Cross* (1982) 1 H.L.R. 54 (confirmed by the Court of Appeal, [1981] J.P.L. 749) that a local authority could not take action under s.9(1) or s.16(1) of the Housing Act 1957 [now s.189 and s.264(1) respectively of the Housing Act 1985] in respect of a house owned and managed solely by that local authority.

1.13 Where an authority has delegated functions to a committee, that committee may (unless the local authority have stated otherwise) pass the authorisation to a sub-committee or an officer of that local authority.[27] Similarly, a sub-committee may pass the authorisation to an officer of that local authority.

Where an authority has made arrangements with another authority, then (subject to the terms of the arrangements) that other authority may delegate the functions to a committee, sub-committee or officer of that other authority, and the committee or sub-committee may again pass on the authorisation.[28]

1.14 Two or more authorities may arrange to discharge their functions jointly, and the power to make arrangements (as set out above) apply to them together as it applies to a single authority.[29]

4. Powers of Entry, Warrants and Obstruction

Housing Act 1985

1.15 Local housing authorities are given specific powers of entry relating to the application and enforcement of standards. These powers are to be found in the following sections of the Housing Act 1985:

(a) Repair notices—sections 197–198;
(b) Improvement notices—sections 222–223;
(c) Area improvement—sections 260–261;
(d) Slum clearance—sections 319–320;
(e) Overcrowding—sections 340–341;
(f) House in multiple occupation—sections 395–397;
(g) Common lodging houses—sections 411–412;
(h) Compulsory purchase and land compensation—sections 600–601.

For the purposes of this work, it is intended to concentrate on the powers of entry in relation to the provisions applicable to individual premises and in particular those dealing with repair, improvement, slum clearance, houses in multiple occupation and overcrowding.

It should be noted that the provisions vary, and are described separately to avoid confusion. Authorisation in respect of the relevant provision is necessary in each case—although it may be that such authorisation could be given in anticipation of the need.

---

[27] Local Government Act 1972, s.101(2).
[28] *Ibid.* s.101(3).
[29] *Ibid.* s.101(5).

POWERS OF ENTRY, WARRANTS AND OBSTRUCTION

Powers of entry of authorised officers

Repair notices—sections 197 to 198. A representative of the local housing authority or of the Secretary of State who is authorised in writing by the authority (or the Secretary of State) is given a power to enter premises.[30] 1.16

This power of entry is available at any reasonable time, after giving 24 hours notice in writing to the occupier, and to the owner (if known). The notice must be in the form prescribed,[31] and the particular purpose(s) for which entry is required must be stated.

The purposes for which the power of entry is given are:

(a) to survey and examine in order to decide whether any powers under Part VI of the 1985 Act should be exercised;
(b) to examine after the service of a repair notice under sections 189 or 190 of the Act; or
(c) to survey and examine premises the authority has been authorised to purchase compulsorily under Part VI of the 1985 Act.[32]

It is an offence[33] to obstruct a person attempting to exercise this power of entry (carrying a penalty, on conviction, of a fine not exceeding level 2 on the standard scale[34]). However, if there is no proper authorisation,[35] then the obstruction will not be an offence, and the entry may be unlawful and a trespass. 1.17

Improvement notices—sections 222 to 223. There is no general power to enter a building to determine whether action should be taken under Part VII of the 1985 Act. However, this should not present difficulties since an officer may enter at the invitation of a tenant who intends to make representations. 1.18

When the local housing authority has declared a housing action area or general improvement area,[36] there is a separate power of entry.[37] However, this power of entry is restricted to purposes related specifically to area improvement and not for the purposes of survey and examination to determine whether an improvement notice should be served.

---

[30] Housing Act 1985, s.197.
[31] *Ibid.* s.614. See Form No. 1, Housing (Prescribed Forms) Regulations 1972 (S.I. 1972 No. 228) as amended, retained in force by Housing (Consequential Provisions) Act 1985, s.2.
[32] Housing Act 1985, s.197(1).
[33] *Ibid.* s.198. Obstruction may be merely making difficulties for the officer—see *Hinchcliffe v. Sheldon* [1955] 1 W.L.R. 1207.
[34] Criminal Justice Act 1982, s.37.
[35] *Stroud v. Bradbury* [1952] 2 All E.R. 76.
[36] 1985 Act, Pt. VIII.
[37] Housing Act 1985, ss.260–261.

THE DUTIES AND POWERS OF LOCAL GOVERNMENT

1.19 Although there is no power to enter associated with provisional notices, once an improvement notice[38] has been served or an undertaking[39] accepted there is a power to enter to carry out a survey and examination to determine whether the requirements of—

(a) an improvement notice have been complied with; or
(b) an undertaking accepted have been complied with.

This power of entry may be exercised at any reasonable time, after giving 24 hours notice in writing to the occupier, and to the owner (if known). The notice must be in the form prescribed.[40]

Obstruction of an officer may be an offence. (See para. 1.17.)

1.20 **Slum clearance—sections 319 to 320.** Properties which are being considered for clearance under Part IX of the 1985 Act may be entered by duly authorised officers[41] for the following purposes[42]:

(a) to survey and examine in order to determine whether any powers under Part IX of the Act should be exercised in respect of the premises;
(b) to survey and examine premises subject to a demolition, closing or obstructive building order[43]; or
(c) to survey or value premises which the authority has been authorised to purchase compulsorily under Part IX of the Act.

It should be noted that there is no specific power of entry where an undertaking[44] has been accepted.

The power of entry may be exercised at any reasonable time, after giving 24 hours notice in writing to the occupier, and to the owner (if known). The notice must be in the form prescribed.[45]

Obstruction of an officer may be an offence. (See para. 1.17.)

1.21 **Houses in multiple occupation.** There are three categories of powers of entry in respect of houses in multiple occupation. In the first two cases, the representative of the local housing authority can authorise entry of an officer. The third category is entry authorised by a warrant issued by a magistrate.

---

[38] Housing Act 1985, ss.214–216.
[39] *Ibid.* s.211.
[40] *Ibid.* s.614. See Housing (Prescribed Forms) Regulations 1972 (S.I. 1972 No. 228) as amended, retained in force by Housing (Consequential Provisions) Act 1985, s.2.
[41] Housing Act 1985, s.319.
[42] *Ibid.* s.319(1).
[43] *Ibid.* ss.265, 266 or 284 respectively.
[44] *Ibid.* s.265.
[45] *Ibid.* s.614. See Housing (Prescribed Forms) Regulations 1972 (S.I. 1972 No. 228) as amended, retained in force by Housing (Consequential Provisions) Act 1985, s.2.

POWERS OF ENTRY, WARRANTS AND OBSTRUCTION

(1) A general right of entry is available at any reasonable time to officers authorised to enter by the local housing authority. The written authority must state the particular purposes for which entry is required. Entry may be exercised after giving 24 hours notice in writing (in the form prescribed[46]) to the occupier, and to the owner (if known).

Entry may only be authorised for the carrying out of a survey and examination in order to determine whether any powers under Part XI of the 1985 Act should be exercised.[47] It seems therefore, that this power may be exercised by officers who suspect that a house is in multiple occupation and wish to investigate further. It should not be invoked on a random basis, but any indication that a building is being used as a house in multiple occupation such as its size, the number of door bells, the coming and going of a number of persons may be sufficient to justify exercise of the power. In all circumstances it is advisable to inform the local police station prior to attempting to obtain entry. If entry is challenged subsequently it would be necessary to show that there was evidence sufficient to amount to a reasonable suspicion that the house was in multiple occupation.

(2) A more specific power of entry is available, without the need for any prior notice to determine whether an offence has been committed in respect of the following:

    (a) failure to comply with a provision of a registration scheme[48];
    (b) failure to comply with a direction[49];
    (c) contravention of an overcrowding notice[50];
    (d) contravention of an undertaking not to use a part of the building because of inadequate means of escape in case of fire[51];
    (e) contravention of the management regulations[52]; or
    (f) failure to comply with a notice requiring works.[53]

Obstruction of an officer exercising this power of entry may be an offence.[54] (See para. 1.17.)

(3) In addition to these two powers of entry, where it is shown to the satisfaction of a Justice of the Peace that entry into particular premises is required for survey and examination or to determine whether an offence

---

[46] Housing Act 1985, s.614. See Housing (Prescribed Forms) Regulations 1972 (S.I. 1972 No. 228) as amended, retained in force by Housing (Consequential Provisions) Act 1985, s.2.
[47] Housing Act 1985, s.395(1).
[48] Ibid. s.346(6).
[49] Ibid. s.352(2).
[50] Ibid. s.358(4).
[51] Ibid. s.368(3).
[52] Ibid. s.369(5).
[53] Ibid. s.376(1) or (2).
[54] Ibid. s.396.

has been committed, the Justice may issue a warrant authorising an officer of the local housing authority to enter the premises.[55]

The Justice of the Peace is required to be satisfied that:

(a) entry has been refused after giving 24 hours notice of intention to enter or that entry is necessary for survey and examination to determine whether an offence has been committed in respect of those matters listed in (2) above; or

(b) an application to the occupier or owner for entry would defeat the object of the entry.

1.25 The power of entry granted by a warrant includes the power to enter by force, if need be, and may be exercised by the person authorised alone or with any other person (*e.g.* police officer and carpenter).[56] If the house entered is unoccupied, or occupiers are temporarily absent, the house must be left as effectually secured against trespassers as it was found.[57]

A warrant remains in force until the purpose for which entry is required has been satisfied.[58]

1.26 **Overcrowding—sections 337 and 340 to 341.** A representative of the local housing authority who is authorised in writing by the authority is given power to enter premises:

(a) for the purpose of measuring rooms of a dwelling to determine the permitted number of that dwelling[59]; and

(b) for the general purpose of survey and examination to decide whether any powers under Part X of the 1985 Act should be exercised.[60]

These powers of entry are available at all reasonable times, provided that 24 hours notice in writing has been given to the occupier and to the owner (if known). The notice must be in the form prescribed,[61] and must state the particular purpose for which entry is required.

Obstruction of a person attempting to exercise either of these powers may be an offence[62] carrying a penalty on conviction of a fine not exceeding level 2 on the standard scale. (See para. 1.17 on obstruction generally.)

---

[55] Housing Act 1985, s.397.
[56] *Ibid.* s.397(3).
[57] *Ibid.* s.397(4).
[58] *Ibid.* s.397(5).
[59] *Ibid.* s.337.
[60] *Ibid.* s.340.
[61] *Ibid.* s.614. See Housing (Prescribed Forms) Regulations 1972 (S.I. 1972 No. 228) as amended, retained in force by Housing (Consequential Provisions) Act 1985, s.2.
[62] *Ibid.* s.341.

Powers of entry of other persons

1.27 A right of entry is given to the person having control of premises where the occupying tenant has requested[63] the local housing authority to consider exercising its compulsory improvement powers. This power of entry is specifically for the purposes of enabling the person having control to survey and examine the premises with a view to providing any of the standard amenities and, where appropriate, putting it into good repair.[64]

1.28 Once an improvement notice has become operative, the person having control has a right to take any reasonable steps necessary for the purpose of complying with that notice. Where a local housing authority has entered into an agreement to carry out the works on behalf of the person having control, then this right is transferred to the authority.[65]

Power of entry to carry out works

1.29 **Repair notices—sections 194 to 196.** Where a repair notice[66] has not been complied with, and a local housing authority intends to carry out work, it may give written notice of that intention to the person having control of the house and, if it thinks fit, to any owner.

It is deemed to be an offence of obstruction[67] if, at any time after seven days after the service of such notice and while there is any workman or contractor employed by the authority carrying out works in the house, an addressee of the notice (or any workman or contractor employed by that person) enters the house for the purpose of carrying out works.[68] However, there is no offence if it is shown that the works were urgently necessary to remove danger to the occupants of the house.[69]

1.30 If, after receiving notice of the intended action, an occupier, owner, or person having control of premises prevents any officer, agent or workman of the local housing authority from carrying into effect any of the provisions of Part VI of the 1985 Act relating to the premises, then a magistrates' court may require that person to permit the authority to do what is necessary.[70]

Similarly, in circumstances where an occupier prevents an owner or a person having control of premises (or their representative) from carrying out any works required by the notice then a magistrates' court may require that person to permit the applicant to do what is necessary.[70]

---

[63] Housing Act 1985, s.212.
[64] *Ibid.* s.224(1).
[65] *Ibid.* s.224(2).
[66] *Ibid.* ss.189–190.
[67] *Ibid.* under s.198.
[68] *Ibid.* s.194.
[69] *Ibid.* s.194(2).
[70] *Ibid.* s.195.

THE DUTIES AND POWERS OF LOCAL GOVERNMENT

Failure to comply with the court order is an offence, with a maximum penalty on conviction of a fine not exceeding £20 for each day on which the offence continues.[71]

1.31 An owner may apply to a magistrates' court for an order permitting that person to carry out works specified in a repair notice. This may be necessary where the owner's interests may be prejudiced by the default of another owner.

Prior to the application for such an order, notice must be given to the local housing authority.

The court may empower the applying owner, and, if the court so decides, any other owner, to forthwith enter the premises and carry out the works within a specified period.[72]

1.32 Improvement notices—sections 221 and 224. If, after receiving an improvement notice or a copy of such a notice,

> (a) an occupier prevents an owner or a person having control of premises (or their representative) from carrying into effect any of the provisions of Part VII of the 1985 Act relating to the premises, or
>
> (b) an occupier, owner, or person having control of premises prevents any officer, agent or workman of the local housing authority from carrying into effect any of the provisions of Part VII of the 1985 Act relating to the premises,

a magistrates' court may, by order, require that person to permit the applicant to do what is necessary.[73]

Failure to comply with the court order is an offence, with a maximum penalty on conviction of a fine not exceeding £20 for each day on which the offence continues.[74]

1.33 Houses in multiple occupation—section 377. If, after receiving notice of the intended action, either:

> (a) an occupier prevents an owner (or representative) from carrying into effect any of the provisions of Part XI of the 1985 Act relating to houses in multiple occupation; or
>
> (b) an owner or occupier prevents any officer, agent or workman of the local housing authority from carrying into effect any of the provisions of Part XI of the Act,

a county court may order that person to permit the applicant to do what is necessary.[75]

---

[71] Housing Act 1985, s.195(2).
[72] Ibid. s.196.
[73] Ibid. s.221.
[74] Ibid. s.221(2).
[75] Ibid. s.377(2).

Failure to comply with the court order is an offence, with a maximum penalty, on conviction, of a fine not exceeding level 3 on the standard scale, and a further fine of £20 for every day (or part of a day) on which the offence continues.[76]

1.34 Where the person on whom a notice under Part XI of the Act was served is not in a position to carry out the specified steps required by the notice (perhaps because the consent of some other person(s) having an estate or interest in the house cannot be obtained) then the county court may give that consent to the applicant.[77]

Public Health Acts 1936 to 1969 and Building Act 1984

1.35 The provisions relating to powers of entry and warrants under these Acts are virtually the same, and are dealt with here together. The provisions for the Public Health Acts 1936 to 1969 are given in sections 287–288 of the 1936 Act, and in sections 95–96 of the Building Act 1984.

Powers of entry of local authority officers

1.36 An authorised officer has a right to enter any premises for the purposes specified, at all reasonable hours after giving 24 hours notice of intention.[78] The officer must be able to produce an authenticated document giving authority for entry. The purposes for which the right of entry is given are:

(a) ascertaining whether there is, or has been, any contravention of any of the provisions of the Acts;
(b) ascertaining whether circumstances exist which require action under the Acts by the local authority;
(c) the taking of any action or the carrying out of any works authorised or required by the Acts or by an order made under the Acts; or
(d) generally, for the performance of any functions of the local authority under the Acts.[79]

1.37 An authorised officer may take such other persons as may be necessary and may use force to gain entry, provided that, if the premises are unoccupied, they are left as effectively secured against trespassers as they were found.[80] Such other persons could include a police officer and carpenters, and in any event the local police station should be notified of the attempted entry.

---

[76] Housing Act 1985, s.377(3).
[77] *Ibid.* s.377(1).
[78] There is no prescribed format for the notice of intention, but it is suggested that the general format given in respect of the powers of entry under the Housing Act 1985 should be followed with appropriate amendments; *i.e.* Form No. 1 Housing (Prescribed Forms) Regulations 1972 (S.I. 1972 No. 228).
[79] 1936 Act, s.287(1); 1984 Act, s.95(1).
[80] *Ibid.* s.287(3) and (4); 1984 Act, s.96.

In circumstances where it is anticipated that force will be required, it is advisable to apply to the local magistrates' court for a warrant.

Warrants

1.38 A local authority may apply to a Justice of the Peace for a warrant to empower an authorised officer to enter onto premises. Before issuing the warrant the Justice of the Peace must be satisfied that the authority has reasonable grounds for requiring entry and that:

(a) access is likely to be refused;
(b) the premises are unoccupied (temporarily or permanently);
(c) access is urgently required; or
(d) notice of entry has been served and entry has been refused or that notice of entry would defeat the object of gaining entry.[81]

1.39 A warrant remains effective until the purpose for which it was given has been satisfied. As with the general power of entry, an authorised officer may take such other persons as may be necessary and may use force to gain entry, provided that, if the premises are unoccupied, they are left as effectively secured against trespassers as they were found.[82]

Power of entry of owners

1.40 Where an occupier of premises prevents the owner from carrying out works required under the Public Health Acts, the owner may apply to the magistrates' court for an order requiring the occupier to permit the execution of the works.[83]

Obstruction

1.41 It is an offence[84] to wilfully obstruct anyone carrying out duties under the Public Health or Building Acts, or acting under the authority of a warrant issued under those Acts.

The maximum penalty, on conviction, in respect of an offence of obstruction under the Public Health Acts is a fine not exceeding level 1 on the standard scale.[85] In addition, the Public Health Acts empower the court to impose a daily penalty not exceeding £20, for each day on which the offence continues after conviction. The court is also empowered to fix a reasonable time to stop the obstruction, and order the daily penalty to take effect if it continues after that time.[86]

There is no specific offence of obstruction created by the Building Act 1984.

---

[81] 1936 Act, s.287(2); 1984 Act, s.95(3).
[82] *Ibid.* s.287(3) and (4); 1984 Act, s.96.
[83] *Ibid.* s.289 (complaint made under s.300(1)); 1984 Act, s.98 (complaint made under s.103).
[84] *Ibid.* s.288.
[85] Criminal Justice Act 1982, s.37.
[86] 1936 Act, s.297.

Obstruction can be making it more difficult than it should be for the person to carry out their duties.[87] However, if there is no proper authorisation, then the obstruction will not be an offence, and the entry may be unlawful and a trespass.

1.42

[87] *Hinchcliffe* v. *Sheldon* [1955] 1 W.L.R. 1207.

CHAPTER 2

INSPECTIONS AND SURVEYS

2.01
1. Principles of inspection and assessment of dwellings   2.02
2. Guidelines on healthful housing   2.05
3. Health effects of housing conditions   2.12
4. Effects of defects   2.23
5. Inspection of individual dwellings   2.40
6. Monitoring structural movement   2.69
7. Non-traditional housing   2.71
8. Specifications of works   2.88
9. House condition surveys   2.89

1. PRINCIPLES OF INSPECTION AND ASSESSMENT OF DWELLINGS

Introduction

2.02 The inspection and assessment of housing conditions should be based on the use of the structure, and the effects or possible effects of any of the conditions and defects. In public health terms, the principle behind the assessment of a dwelling is to determine whether the basic physiological and psychological requirements for human life and comfort are satisfied. Any statutory standard will be influenced by many outside factors (including political and sociological attitudes, practical and historical considerations, and economics) and is dependent upon the efforts and efficiency of those empowered to enforce them. The legal housing standards are in essence, discretionary, and their interpretation is dependent on the training and experience of individual officers. This expertise, or professionalism, provides the basis for any implementation of the statutory standards. The public health principles underlying the housing function are directed towards an assessment of whether the structure and facilities enable the building to be used as a dwelling. If there is any defect, or deficiency, the effect on the occupiers and the use of the dwelling should be assessed. To be able to carry out the inspection and assessment it is necessary to fully appreciate the principal functions to be expected of a dwelling.

2.03 The principle from which any inspection should start is that a "building" is a structure which should have been designed, constructed (or converted) and maintained so as to satisfy the purpose for which it was intended to be used, or for which it is being used; a "house" or "dwelling" is a building (or a part of a building) which was intended to be used, or is being used, for human habitation. As such, a house or dwelling must be capable of satisfying the basic and fundamental needs for human existence at the very least, and more properly for the everyday life of a household. A house or dwelling must provide shelter, space and facilities for the occupants.

A "home" is the social, cultural and economic structure established by the occupants of a house. The physical attributes of a "home" will vary considerably. It will depend on the age and size of the household, and on the attitude, priorities and expectations of the household and the finances available. It will be very different for a household which includes young children compared to one which consists solely of relatively old and retired adults, and for a household with a regular and reasonable income compared to one which relies on State benefits.

The home established by the occupiers can have very different affects on the conditions. There may be members of one household at the dwelling throughout each day, maintaining some heat input, and generating moisture, while in another household members are absent throughout each day, and only minimal moisture is generated. One household may be able to afford to run the space heating system at a high level, while another (without adequate finances) may not be able to provide the same level of heat input. The structure should be capable of being occupied and used as a dwelling by households across the spectrum of life-styles; it should be able to cope with relatively low levels of heat input and relatively high moisture emissions without problems arising. If it is only capable of being occupied by a household which can afford to maintain high heat levels, and minimum moisture emissions, the dwelling cannot be said to be capable of satisfying the basic and fundamental needs for human life, and will interfere with efforts to establish a home.

In addition, the priorities and expectations of the household will determine the internal decoration and the general domestic and household equipment within the dwelling. One household may want, and be able (physically and financially), to redecorate on a frequent basis, while another may give decoration a low priority or may not be able to afford to decorate very often. Frequent redecoration will hide the effects of defects, and may obscure the seriousness of any defects and deficiencies.

An inspecting officer should assess the condition of the dwelling both in terms of its suitability for occupation by any household across the spectrum of possible life-styles, and in terms of the household occupying it at the time of the inspection. For example, the assessment should not be made in terms of the needs and demands of an employed young single male (who will be absent from the dwelling during working hours, and may place little demands on facilities), but having regard to the needs and demands of a household which includes children below school age (where there will be considerably more washing of clothes, preparation of meals, and where play and recreation will take place in or around the dwelling).

2.04 As suggested by Elliot,[1] the "first environment for a child is its home—the family shelter and immediate surroundings. The health of human beings has always been influenced by where and how they live. People have always made homes of some kind for their families because human babies cannot survive without continuous care for the first few years. They need to be fed, protected from the cold and from extreme heat, kept clean and watched over as they learn to crawl, walk, feed themselves, play and explore, gradually moving towards an independent existence." "The home therefore plays a significant part in all aspects of child health. Improvements in child care in most developed countries are clearly connected with the advent of more hygienic living conditions: improved water supplies, sanitation and general public health measures. These have played at least as great a part as the provision of curative medical services."

2. GUIDELINES ON HEALTHFUL HOUSING

2.05 The recognition of the relationship between health and housing provided the main impetus for the introduction of sanitary legislation, which formed the roots of the present Public Health and Housing Acts. Edwin Chadwick developed his "sanitary idea" during 1828, based on arguments that the poor were a bad life insurance risk as they had a shorter life expectancy than others.[2]

Around the early 1800s, disease was thought to be caused and transmitted by miasma, *i.e.* that infections were carried in the air by smells. While this was mistaken in fact, it was a reasonably successful basis for action—where there were smells there was usually disease; remove the causes of the smells and the incidence of disease dropped. Based on this approach, rubbish collection, housing ventilation, running water and drainage were provided and the improvement of housing conditions began.

2.06 Although the need for healthful housing has long been recognised, there have been few attempts to provide comprehensive guidelines which could provide the basis for both the assessment of housing and the setting of standards. Prepared in 1939, the American Public Health Association's "Basic Principles of Healthful Housing" is still a useful background to housing assessment.

---

[1] Elliot, K., "Home Conditions and Child Health" R.U.D. Network (Dec. 1986) No. 2, World Health Organisation, p. 2.
[2] See "On the Means of Insurance etc." Westminster Review (April 1828).

GUIDELINES ON HEALTHFUL HOUSING

"Basic principles of healthful housing"[3]

The introduction to the 1939 second edition of the A.P.H.A. stated: "Together with food and clothing, shelter is a fundamental need of human existence. No housing program can be sound unless the shelter it provides is healthful." 2.07

The report set out 30 basic principles and discussed the specific requirements relating to each and the methods of attaining them. The 30 principles are set out below. 2.08

Section A—Fundamental physiological needs

1. Maintenance of a thermal environment which will avoid undue heat loss from the human body.
2. Maintenance of a thermal environment which will permit adequate heat loss from the human body.
3. Provision of an atmosphere of reasonable chemical purity.
4. Provision of adequate daylight illumination and avoidance of undue daylight glare.
5. Provision for admission of direct sunlight.
6. Provision of adequate artificial illumination and avoidance of glare.
7. Protection against excessive noise.
8. Provision of adequate space for exercise and for the play of children.

Section B—Fundamental psychological needs

9. Provision of adequate privacy for the individual.
10. Provision of opportunities for normal family life.
11. Provision for opportunities for normal community life.
12. Provision of facilities which make possible the performance of the tasks of the household without undue physical and mental fatigue.
13. Provision of facilities for maintenance of cleanliness of the dwelling and of the person.
14. Provision of possibilities for aesthetic satisfaction in the home and its surroundings.
15. Concordance with the prevailing social standards of the local community.

Section C—Protection against contagion

16. Provision of a water supply of safe sanitary quality, available to the dwelling.

---
[3] A.P.H.A., 1790 Broadway, New York, 19 N.Y. Available from U.M.I., 30–32 Mortimer Street, London W1.

17. Protection of the water supply system against pollution within the dwelling.
18. Provision of toilet facilities of such character as to minimise the danger of transmitting disease.
19. Protection against sewage contamination of the interior surfaces of the dwelling.
20. Avoidance of insanitary conditions in the vicinity of the dwelling.
21. Exclusion from the dwelling of vermin which may play a part in the transmission of disease.
22. Provision of facilities for keeping milk and food undecomposed.
23. Provision of sufficient space in sleeping-rooms to minimise the danger of contact infection.

Section D—Protection against accidents

24. Erection of the dwelling with such materials and methods of construction as to minimise danger of accidents due to collapse of any part of the structure.
25. Control of conditions likely to cause fires or to promote their spread.
26. Provision of adequate facilities for escape in case of fire.
27. Protection against danger of electrical shocks and burns.
28. Protection against gas poisoning.
29. Protection against falls and other mechanical injuries in the home.
30. Protection of the neighbourhood against the hazards of automobile traffic.

2.09 This is a comprehensive consideration of the health related aspects of housing conditions, and other approaches have tended to be less comprehensive. In the assessment of new non-traditional methods of house construction in 1944,[4] the following basic technical considerations were given:

(a) Strength and stability;
(b) Moisture penetration and condensation;
(c) Thermal insulation;
(d) Sound insulation;
(e) Fire hazard;
(f) Maintenance and durability; and
(g) Vermin infestation.

[4] "Post-War Building Studies No. 1—House Construction" (1944) H.M.S.O., p. 9.

At the time of writing, the World Health Organisation, is considering 2.10
Basic Housing Hygiene Guidelines.[5] This is based on the definition of
the World Health Organisation Regional Office for Europe for "healthful housing" as:

> "a human habitation that is structurally sound and relatively free from accidental injury hazards, provides sufficient space for all normal household activities for all members of the family, has readily and easily available an adequate supply of potable and palatable water, has a sanitary means of collection, storage and disposal of all liquid and solid wastes, is provided with appropriate installed facilities for personal and household hygiene and cleanliness, is sufficiently weatherproof and watertight, provides proper protection from the elements, especially for those persons who may be particularly susceptible, for physical and/or physiological reasons to these potentially adverse environmental conditions, provides a hygrothermal indoor environment which is healthful and comfortable, is free from excessive noise from both interior and exterior sources of the structure, has natural and artificial means of illumination that are safe and adequate in quality and quantity for the fulfilment of all normal household activities and functions, is free from toxic and/or noxious odours, chemicals and other air contaminants or pollutants, has adequate but not excessive microbial and thermal characteristics, provides sufficient but not excessive solar radiation, provides adequate protection from insects and rodents which may be reservoirs and/or vectors of disease agents, and is served by the necessary and/or desirable health, welfare, social, educational, cultural and protective community services and facilities."

The sentiments behind these principles and statements look beyond 2.11
the narrow enforcement role of the environmental health officer towards an involvement in the continuing improvement of housing conditions. This objective, it is suggested, requires an emphasis upon education and a collective effort to improve statutory standards.

3. HEALTH EFFECTS OF HOUSING CONDITIONS

The importance of the relationship between poor housing and health is 2.12
once again being recognised, and it is now well established that bad housing can have an insidious deleterious affect on occupiers.[6] Studies

---

[5] Ed. Ranson R.P. (provisional edition, 1985).
[6] *Inequalities in Health,* Report of a Research Working Group, chaired by Sir Douglas Black (1980) D.H.S.S., *Inequalities in Health: The Black Report* (1982). *The Health Divide: Inequalities in Health in the 1980's* (1987) Health Education Council. Papers presented at "Unhealthy Housing: A Diagnosis" (Dec. 1986) University of Warwick.

comparing the general health of occupiers from areas of "bad" housing with the general health of those from areas of "good" housing, allowing for other factors, have clearly shown that those from areas of "bad" housing suffer poorer health, have more long-standing illnesses and more symptoms of depression than those from "good" housing.[7] The physical and mental health of households with young children is adversely affected almost in direct relationship to the height of the dwelling occupied above ground.[8] The spread of Legionella within a high-rise block appears to have been related to the design and construction.[9]

Studies into the effects of rehousing indicate that transfer from areas of unsatisfactory housing to areas of better housing does improve health.[10] Child health and development have been shown to be affected by housing conditions.[11]

Studies have also shown that while other social factors will affect health (*e.g.* age, unemployment, income and work experience), even when these variables are taken into account, unsatisfactory housing conditions will have a detrimental affect on health.

Some of the possible effects are obvious, others not so. A brief summary of some of the effects is given below.

2.13 It has long been accepted that some diseases are spread by contaminated water. Although mains water in England and Wales is purified and treated, there are houses which are served by private water supplies (wells and bore-holes). Such private supplies can be contaminated by human or farm sewage. Even where houses are connected to main supplies of water, that water can become contaminated within the dwelling.

Water which has a relatively high acidity can dissolve heavy metals used for water pipes. Lead and copper can become absorbed into the water and ingested by the users. Uncovered water storage tanks can be polluted by birds and small animals (both by their droppings and by their dead bodies decomposing in the tanks) and by insects.

---

[7] Byrne et al, "Housing and Health: the relationship between housing conditions and the health of council tenants" (1986) Gower; Burt W.O. "Poverty, Housing and Health" (1945) 2 Med J. Aust. 167–173; "Council Housing: is it bad for your health?" (1985) 21 Rad Comm Med 15–20.

[8] Fanning, "Families in Flats" (1967) 4 B.M.J. 382–386. Hird J.B. "Vertical living: health aspects" (1967) 87 R.S.H.J. 171–172.

[9] McEwan D. "Legionnaires Disease in a Tower Block"—paper presented at "Unhealthy Housing: A Diagnosis" (Dec. 1986) University of Warwick.

[10] Robinson, "Slum clearance pays off" (1955) 14 Nat. Mun. Review 461–465; Wilner et al, "The housing environment and family life" (1962) Baltimore John Hopkins Med. School; Saltos et al, "Hypersensitivity pneumonitis in a mouldy house" (1982) 2 Med. J. Aust. 244–246.

[11] Wedge & Prosser, *Born to Fail?* (1973); Davie, Butler & Goldstien, *From Birth to Seven* (1972); Wedge & Essen, *Children in Adversity* (1982).

HEALTH EFFECTS OF HOUSING CONDITIONS

Defective electric wiring can lead to shocks and to fires. Defective gas pipework can allow gas to escape and to asphyxiate occupants or cause explosions.

2.14

Physical injuries can result from poor design of houses, including ill defined changes in floor levels (small steps in a long ill lighted passage, or steps immediately outside a door), and from steep and winding staircases. Injuries can also result from disrepair, the sudden collapse of rotted floor timbers or the snapping of sash cords. Over 11,000 children attend hospital each year as a result of falls within the home while playing, and another 11,000 as a result of other physical injuries received within the home (including burning, electrical accidents and explosions).[12]

2.15

Dampness will reduce the ambient air temperature within a house, both by taking up heat during evaporation and by reducing the thermal insulation capabilities of the fabric. Dampness can be the direct result of disrepair allowing rain to penetrate through the structure to affect the living area, or defects which enable moisture to rise by capillary action from the ground, or by an imbalance in the provision for heating and ventilation and the thermal insulation resulting in high relative humidity or condensation. Dampness in the house (from whatever source) has been directly and indirectly related to respiratory and allergic conditions. The house dust mite population (present in even the cleanest home) will dramatically increase in damp conditions, and such mites are potent allergens.[13] Mould spores can germinate and grow where there is actual dampness and where the relative humidity levels remain above 70 per cent. for most of the time. The increased levels of air-borne spores in mould infected dwellings can cause allergic reactions and can sensitise previously non-allergic persons.[14]

2.16

(Dampness, its effects on health and on the fabric of dwellings, and its investigation are considered in more detail in Chapter 8.)

As with any kitchen and food preparation area, the design, layout, state of repair and facilities provided in the domestic kitchen must be such that cleanliness and hygiene can be easily and readily maintained so that food can be safely prepared. Similarly, the design, layout, state of repair and facilities provided in bathrooms and W.C. compartments must be such that cleanliness and hygiene can be easily and readily maintained to enable personal hygiene to be maintained and to reduce the possibility of the spread of disease. In such areas, wall and floor

2.17

---

[12] "Home Accident Surveillance System Report of 1984 Data" (1985) Dept. of Trade and Industry, Page M.; *Child Safety and Housing* (1986).

[13] Cunnington & Gregory, "Mites in Bedroom Air" (1968) 212 Nature 1271–1272; Cunnington, "Allergy to Mites in House Dust and the Domestic Environment" (1980) R.S.H.J. 229–230; Maunsell *et al*, "Mites and House Dust Allergy in Bronchial Asthma" (1968) Lancet 1267–1270.

[14] "Mould Fungal Spores" (1985) I.E.H.O. Prof. Practice Series Vol. 1, Chap. II.

INSPECTIONS AND SURVEYS

surfaces must be capable of being easily and thoroughly cleaned. The dwelling as a whole, and the kitchen and bathroom areas in particular, should be designed and constructed and maintained so as to limit access and harbourage for insects and other pests which might be a nuisance or spread disease.[15]

2.18   In addition to preventing high relative humidity levels and condensation, the provision for space heating and the thermal insulation of the structure will affect the thermal environment within the dwelling. Low temperature levels can result in hypothermia, particularly in the elderly and very young children whose body thermo-regulatory system is not fully effective.[16]

2.19   The provision for ventilation should allow adequate, but not excessive air changes (*i.e.* between 0.5 and 1.0 air changes per hour for the dwelling as a whole), both for biological an hygienic purposes. In addition, extra ventilation will be necessary to those areas where high moisture generating activities occur (*i.e.* the kitchen and the bathroom).[17]

2.20   Natural lighting is preferable both for aesthetic and hygienic purposes. The ultra-violet radiation of sunlight has sterilising properties which can benefit a dwelling generally and kitchen, bathroom and W.C. areas particularly. Artificial lighting is necessary throughout the dwelling for winter periods and to ensure safe passage throughout the dwelling, and to enable domestic tasks to be carried out safely.

2.21   Noise can affect mental health and can cause physical injury. Noise which causes a nuisance can be sufficient to disturb sleep and concentration and result in both mental and physical illness. A dwelling should be constructed so as to insulate the occupants from excessive noise from the external environment and from adjacent buildings.[18]

2.22   The design and layout of residential areas and of the interior of dwellings can affect the psychological and physiological well-being of occupants.[19]

---

[15] B.R.E. Digest 238.
[16] Collins K.J., *Hypothermia—the facts* (1983); Boardman B., "Seasonal Mortality and Cold Homes"—paper presented at "Unhealthy Housing: A Diagnosis" (Dec. 1986) University of Warwick, Collins K.J.; "The Health of the Elderly in Low Indoor Temperatures"—paper presented at "Unhealthy Housing: A Diagnosis" (Dec. 1986) University of Warwick.
[17] Loudon A.G., "The effects of ventilation and building design factors on the risk of condensation and mould growth in dwellings." (1971) B.R.E. Current Paper 31/71. See also—Turiel I., *Indoor Air Quality and Human Health* (1985).
[18] "Noise—Final Report" (1963) H.M.S.O.; Atherton R.P., "Effects of Noise on Occupiers"—paper presented at "Unhealthy Housing: A Diagnosis" (Dec. 1986) University of Warwick.
[19] Lawrence R.J., "Pyschological and Physiological Effects of Dwelling Design"—paper presented at "Unhealthy Housing: A Diagnosis" (Dec. 1986) University of Warwick; Gabe & Williams, "Women, Housing and Mental Health"—paper presented at "Unhealthy Housing: A Diagnosis." Coleman A., *Utopia on Trial*. Hilary Shipman 1985. Freeman H.L. (ed.), *Mental Health and the Environment* (1984).

4. Effects of Defects

Any defect should be considered in relation to its possible effect, and **2.23** not in terms of the cost of remedial works necessary. A defect which may involve minor work and little cost can have a serious affect on health. Its effect both on the function of that particular part and of the dwelling and on the overall health of the occupants should be considered. Examples of this approach are given below.

Foundations are intended to provide the support necessary for the **2.24** whole structure, and should take into account the geological conditions in the area and the intended function of the structure.

Failure of the foundations can result in settlement and fractures of other parts of the structure, or the complete collapse of the structure. If settlement has occurred it may have caused damage to damp proof courses and membranes, fractures to walls (particularly at window and door openings) which may allow moisture penetration, and it may affect the support given to floors and to the roof.

The external walls provide support for the floors and roof, and give **2.25** weather protection, thermal and sound insulation, and should be so constructed as to limit the spread of fire.

Open-jointed or soft and perished brickwork will allow moisture to penetrate easily through to affect the living space.

Render is a means of providing a water-proof finish to the external face of a wall, and is particularly important where the wall is constructed of porous material (*e.g.* "no-fines" concrete). Hair-line cracking of the protective render will cause water to be drawn into the wall structure by capillary action. Once behind the render the water cannot escape outwards and can only drain down or dry out through the interior surface finishes. The presence of moisture within the structure of the wall will reduce the thermal insulation capabilities of the wall.

Most materials used for the construction of walls will draw water from the ground by capillary action, and it is necessary to provide an impervious barrier (the damp proof course) to prevent rising dampness affecting the structure and the living space. Broken or damaged damp proof courses (particularly in older buildings, where the damp proof course may be of brittle materials such as slates or dense engineering bricks) will allow moisture to pass. Dampness can by-pass a damp proof course externally by the bridging provided by soil or render, by bridging within the cavity of a cavity wall provided by mortar droppings or other debris, and internally by solid floors where the damp proof membrane to the floor fails to connect with the damp proof course in the walls.

The weakest point in any wall is at door and window openings. Above the opening there must be a lintel to support the wall above and spread the load to either side of the opening. The joint between the reveals to

INSPECTIONS AND SURVEYS

the opening and the door/window frame must be tight and weather-proof. Window sills must be sloped to drain the water running off the window glazing away from the window frame, and must be provided with a drip or throating (a groove on the under-side) to break the adhesion of the water so that it drips off the sill rather than running into the wall structure. Inadequate weather-proofing to the joints between door and window frames and the wall will allow water to penetrate both into timber and the living space. Cracked sills will allow moisture into the structure and the living space.

2.26 Roofs must be constructed so as to be able to support not only their own weight but the additional loads imposed by winds and accumulations of snow. They must provide protection from the weather and provide thermal and sound insulation.

Cracked, loose or missing tiles or slates will allow water to penetrate into the building. Sagging roof timbers suggest that the roof timbers are defective, perhaps as a result of being of inadequate strength, or fungal or insect attack.

Generally, flat roofs require more maintenance than pitched roofs, and, because they are less easily checked, any deterioration may go unobserved. Felt or asphalt covered roofs should be provided with some protection from solar heat (usually in the form of reflective chippings) to limit expansion and contraction which will increase the rate of deterioration. Uneven flat roof coverings will retain water again increasing the rate of deterioration.

Where the roof covering is penetrated by a chimney stack or vent pipe the joint must be water-tight. Ill fitting flashings or fillets will allow moisture to penetrate into the structure.

Defective brickwork or render to a chimney stack will allow moisture into the structure of the stack, and (unless there is an effective damp proof course) into the main structure.

2.27 Eavesgutters are intended to collect the rain water draining off the roof and carry it safely to rain water fall pipes. The fall pipes should carry that water safely to a drainage inlet or soakaway.

A blocked, distorted, or leaking eavesgutter will not safely carry away the water, and may discharge it onto a wall in such quantities as to cause damage and penetration through the wall. A blocked or leaking rain water fall pipe will have a similar effect.

2.28 There should be safe and unhampered access to the dwelling from public footpaths, and safe and unhampered access to any amenity space for clothes drying and for play and recreation, and to any outbuildings associated with the dwelling. Paths and yards should be laid so as to be self-draining, and to avoid ponding of surface water.

Uneven, cracked and holed yards and paths will interfere with the safe passage of the occupiers and will collect surface water.

EFFECTS OF DEFECTS

2.29 Waste water from baths, wash hand basins and sinks, and sewage from W.C. basins must be safely and hygienically carried from the facility out of the dwelling and discharged properly and safely into the sewerage system. Waste pipes should discharge directly into a drainage inlet without splashing, or be connected directly into the system. There should be water seals (or traps) to W.C. basins, to waste pipes and to drainage inlets (gullies) to prevent foul air and rats from the sewerage system escaping. There should be ventilation of the system to avoid the water seals being broken or emptied, and such ventilation should be at a point where the foul air will not create nuisance.

Leaking waste pipes and drains will allow foul water to escape causing dampness and smells and the risk of spread of infections. Cracked and broken cement dishing around gullies will retain foul water causing smells, and may allow the water to soak into the structure.

2.30 External doors provide for access into and out of the dwelling, but also complete the weather protection, privacy and security provided by the structure. To ensure adequate weather protection, the door should fit closely to the frame and stop and be held closed by the door lock. Ill fitting doors with badly adjusted locks will allow draughts and water penetration. Defective locks and handles will mean that the door cannot be readily opened and securely closed.

2.31 Floors must be capable of providing support for the furniture and occupants, and should provide a safe and even surface for easy passage. In kitchens, bathrooms and W.C. compartments the floor should be impervious and smooth and capable of being hygienically maintained.

Springy, sloping or uneven suspended timber floors suggest that the joists or wall-plates are defective and require checking to avoid sudden collapse. Loose boarding can cause occupants to trip.

2.32 Internal walls divide the building into separate rooms and areas, enabling different activities to be carried out in each room; give privacy to individual members of the household, and enable personal and household tasks to be carried out in proper conditions in private and without interference to other occupants. The walls should provide some thermal and sound insulation, enabling different parts to be heated to different temperatures, and limiting noise nuisances within the dwelling. The walls also limit the spread of fire within the dwelling.

Internal surfaces of all walls should be smooth and even so that they can be easily decorated and easily maintained clean. This is particularly important in the kitchen, bathroom and W.C. compartment where hygiene should be easily maintained. (Wall plaster and ceramic wall tiles are not mere decorative finishes, but provide the smooth and even, and in the case of tiles the impervious, finish necessary.)

Damp affected plaster will not remain properly decorated and cannot be easily maintained clean and hygienic. Cracked and loose plaster, and cracked and broken tiles, are difficult to clean and will provide harbourage for dirt and insect pests.

Skirting boards seal the joint between the wall surface and the floor (bridging and protecting the gap between plaster and the floor surface).

2.33 Internal doors allow for access between different parts of the dwelling, and when closed complete the separation provided by the internal walls. Doors complete the privacy, prevent draughts, and, particularly kitchen and living room doors, help limit the spread of fire through the dwelling. To be effective, the doors when closed should be close-fitting to the frame and stop, and should be provided with the necessary door locks and handles to ensure that they are held close-fitting and are capable of being readily opened and closed.

Ill-fitting doors with gaps greater than 8mm will allow draughts and allow smoke and flames to pass.

2.34 Ceilings provide the vertical separation within the dwelling, separating one floor from another and the top floor from any roof void. They should provide sound and thermal insulation, limit the spread of fire within the room and between floors, and should have a smooth and even surface capable of being easily decorated and maintained clean.

Cracked and holed ceilings are difficult to clean and decorate, provide harbourage for dirt and insect pests, do not provide effective insulation, and may allow fire to pass through.

2.35 Windows provide natural lighting to the interior of the dwelling, enable occupants to view the outside environment, and provide for a means of natural ventilation. They also complete the structure and exterior, providing weather protection and some sound and thermal insulation.

Opening lights should be capable of being opened and securely closed, and when closed should be close-fitting against the frame to prevent draughts and water penetration. Defective putty or glazing beads mean that the glass is not held tight to the frame, may allow water penetration and mean that the glass cannot be properly cleaned without a risk of it being displaced from the frame. Cracked or holed glazing may allow draughts and water to penetrate, and cannot be properly cleaned.

Facilities

2.36 (*a*) *Kitchens*

Sinks are used for the preparation of food, for the cleansing of cooking and eating equipment and utensils, for washing of clothes and for personal washing. The material of the sink, and the internal surface in particular, should be smooth and impervious and capable of being easily maintained clean and hygienic. The sink should be close-fitting to adjacent wall surfaces, with the joints water-tight to ensure splashed water runs safely back into the sink. It should be properly connected to a trapped waste-pipe capable of safely carrying the waste water out of the dwelling and into the drainage system, and provided with a supply of water above. A chipped and worn glazed sink is insanitary and unhygienic; it will retain waste water and enable organisms to breed and infect fresh water.

Draining boards should be smooth and impervious, securely fitted and self-draining into the sink. Drainers should be close-fitting to adjacent wall surfaces and to the sink, with the joints water-tight to ensure water runs back into the sink.

Food preparation surfaces should be smooth and impervious and capable of being easily maintained clean and hygienic. Joints between the preparation surface and adjacent walls should be water-tight.

Food storage cupboards should be capable of being thoroughly cleaned, and should be provided with close-fitting doors capable of being readily opened and closed. They should be designed and maintained so as to prevent access for pests.

There should be facilities for the cooking of food. These facilities should be of adequate size for the intended household, and should be properly and safely designed. In the case of cooking facilities fuelled by gas, proper consideration should be given to the provision of adequate ventilation to provide sufficient air for the combustion, and for the removal of the waste products of combustion, and the burners should be properly maintained to ensure the completed combustion.

There should be sufficient space for the installation of clothes washing and clothes drying equipment and facilities, either within the kitchen area or a utility room. There should be readily available supplies of water, and provision for the disposal of the waste water. There should be space or facilities for the drying of clothes during cold and wet weather; for example, a properly designed cabinet with provision for heating, or space for the installation of a tumble dryer. The provision for drying clothes should include means of ventilation to remove moisture laden air quickly and safely out of the dwelling—extractor fans, or ventilation of the clothes drying cabinet to the external air, or a vent for connection to the ducting from a tumble drier.

(b) Bathrooms and W.C. compartments 2.37

Baths, showers and wash hand basins are used for personal washing. The internal surfaces should be smooth and impervious and capable of being easily kept clean and hygienic. They should be close-fitting to adjacent wall surfaces, with the joints water-tight to ensure splashed water runs safely back into the facility. Baths and showers should be securely fitted to ensure that they are capable of supporting their own and the occupant's weight, and a wash basin should be securely fitted to ensure that it can support the weight of an occupant leaning on it. The facility should be properly connected to a trapped waste-pipe which can safely carry the discharged water out of the dwelling into the drainage system, and provided with supplies of water.

W.C. basins should have a smooth and impervious surface and be self-cleansing. They should be connected to a properly working flushing cistern provided with a supply of water, and also properly connected to a drain capable of safely carrying the waste out of the dwelling and into the drainage system. The basin should be provided with a water seal to prevent foul air escape from the system. It should be securely fixed and capable of carrying the weight of occupants, and should be provided with a seat. Any cistern, basin, pipe or drain should not leak water or sewage.

2.38 *(c) Space heating*

There should be provision for the space heating of the dwelling. This provision should be of an appropriate type having regard to the design and construction of the dwelling, and the materials used in the construction, and the position of the dwelling. Such provision should be designed following the recommendations of British Standard BS5449.

A solid fuel heating system requires adequate storage provision for the fuel, and means of disposal for the waste ash. Such systems require more attention from the occupiers than systems using other fuels, particularly as they are less easily started and stopped. A system fuelled by oil also requires adequate storage provision.

Open fires are a relatively inefficient means of space heating compared to other forms. An open fire will be at best only around 40–50 per cent. efficient (with 50–60 per cent. of the heat being wasted), a modern high efficiency solid fuel boiler will be up to 75–80 per cent. efficient. Gas fires and gas fired boilers will be 75–85 per cent. efficient, and electric heaters will be up to 100 per cent. efficient.

In addition to the type of provision for space heating the distribution of the heat is important. Radiators sited under window openings will reduce draught and provide greater comfort. A forced warm-air system will reduce the risk of stagnant air pockets in room corners, while high temperature radiant heaters will leave parts of rooms cold and relatively unheated even though occupants are warm and comfortable.

Electric socket outlets and gas points are not provision for space heating, but sources of energy or fuel which may be used for different types of space heating facilities.

2.39 *(d) Ventilation*

There should be proper and effective provision for ventilation of the dwelling.

Natural ventilation should be properly provided to avoid draughts and excessive heat loss during winter periods. In kitchens and bathrooms it is preferable that ventilation is provided by mechanical means. This will ensure that moisture laden air is quickly and safely taken out of the dwelling close to points such as cookers and sinks where high levels of water vapour are generated.

(Ventilation for clothes drying is important, and is dealt with at para. 2.36.)

5. Inspection of Individual Dwellings

2.40 The general aim in carrying out any inspection of an individual dwelling is to collect information on the design, construction, layout, state of repair, facilities and deficiencies. This will enable the condition to be compared to the various housing standards and a decision to be made as to the appropriate enforcement action (if any) to be taken. Although in some cases the inspection begins with a particular enforcement procedure in mind (*e.g.* for the purposes of assessment within a possible clearance area) it may emerge that other action should be taken to deal with urgent unsatisfactory conditions and public health problems in the short-term.

Before discussing the inspection procedure, there are legal and practical constraints to be considered.

Legal considerations

2.41 The best practice is to begin an inspection with as few preconceptions of the outcome as possible. Each standard should be applied having regard to its legal status (*i.e.* whether it is a mandatory standard like statutory nuisance and fitness for human habitation, or a discretionary standard). Consideration should also be given to the remedy and procedure associated with each standard, and the appropriateness of those remedies and procedures having regard to the needs of the occupiers and the area and prospective life of the property.

It should also be remembered that any action taken will affect the rights and privileges of several people. The action may result in the removal of conditions which have been a threat to the health of the occupiers, and the provision of facilities which will improve the living condition of the occupiers, or it may result in occupiers being displaced from their home. Action may mean that an owner or landlord is forced to carry out works which involve considerable expense, or trigger grant-aid. The information collected during an inspection may be the basis of a decision as to whether an owner receives the market value for the dwelling or just the site value.

Action (or sometimes inaction) taken by an authority is open to challenge in a court or at a public inquiry. As the action taken in the name of the authority will be based on the information collected during an inspection, it is important that the inspection is carried out methodically, accurately and thoroughly. Any report based on the inspection should provide an accurate picture of the dwelling and its condition to anyone reading it, and should enable the inspector to answer questions about the dwelling and condition at the time of the inspection even if challenged several months after.

Practical considerations

2.42   While the inspection should be as thorough and accurate as possible, there are several restrictions on the officer. It will be carried out without detailed information as to the materials used in construction and the type of construction and alterations that may have been carried out since the original construction. It may be carried out without distructive investigations which might be the only means of properly identifying the actual cause or source of a defect, and without being able to remove all the furniture, furnishings and fittings. It may be a cold and wet day in winter, or a warm and dry day in summer; clearly the weather on the particular day and the days prior to the inspection, and the time of year can have a dramatic affect on the conditions in the dwelling. These factors should be taken into account both during the inspection, and in any report and assessment of the condition.

Inspection forms

2.43   It is important to remember the purpose for carrying out an inspection. In dealing with housing conditions and repairs, the purpose is not primarily for the collection of statistics. Inspection forms, while providing standardisation of the information collected and being useful aide-memoires, should not distract the inspector from collecting all the necessary or available information. Many inspection forms were originally designed with traditional terraced houses in mind, and are unsuitable for modern houses, particularly those constructed by non-traditional or system methods.

Any inspection form used should be capable of use in a variety of circumstances (*i.e.* house inspection in clearance areas, individual house inspections and houses in multiple occupation) and be capable of use in respect of a wide range of types of houses (*e.g.* traditional terraced houses, pre-cast reinforced concrete houses, timber-framed houses and "mobile homes").

2.44   In all inspections the following basic information should be recorded:

Address;
Date of inspection;
Outline description;

No. of households;
Details of owner, landlord and/or agent;
Name of tenant(s);
Date tenancy commenced;
Name, age and sex of members of household;
Equivalent number of household (1985 Act, s.326(2));
Permitted number as given in the rent book; and
Rent and rates.

2.45 A plan of the layout of the dwelling, and photographs of at least the front and rear elevations are useful. An inspection form should allow sufficient space for the information, and should enable the inspector to assess the condition after full details have been collected, and to give an indication of the appropriate action to be taken.

2.46 In the case of a house in multiple occupation it will be necessary to collect the basic information in respect of each separately let part of the house, but an overall assessment of the structure should be made to determine whether the house is unfit for human habitation or a statutory nuisance. In the case of dampness additional investigations may be necessary to attempt to identify the main source.

Description of the dwelling, etc.

2.47 Any description of the dwelling should be brief but clear, bearing in mind the purpose of the report. It should include the type of dwelling and an estimate of when it was originally constructed (and, if appropriate, when converted or rehabilitated), the number of storeys should be stated. Where there is a basement or attic, it is probably clearer to give the number of other storeys and then state "plus basement" or "plus attic." The direction faced by the front of the dwelling should be noted.

For example, "This is a two storey plus basement, terraced dwelling of traditional construction. It is estimated it was originally built around the 1900s, and appears to have been rehabilitated about ten years ago. There is a single storey bay to the front elevation, and a two storey back addition and single storey rear extension to the back addition. The front main wall of the dwelling faces approximately North-West."

2.48 A description of the site can also be useful, particularly where the site may affect the condition of the dwelling. If the site itself is high and exposed, and the site steeply sloping so that walls of the dwelling are particularly exposed to the weather, this will mean that the weatherproofing of the exposed walls is of particular importance.

2.49 There should be a description of the construction of the main parts of the structure, followed by any additions and extensions. In some cases the method and materials used in construction will be obvious, while in others it will not. The roof should be described as pitched, flat, lean-to,

INSPECTIONS AND SURVEYS

etc., and details of the covering of the roof (tiles, slates or felt) given. Walls are more difficult, as external decorative or weather-protecting finishes can hide indicators of the construction. It may be necessary to state what the construction appears to be—"The main walls appear to be of cavity construction, and are faced externally with rough cast render." The types of floors within the dwelling should be given (suspended timber, or solid floors), and the type(s) of windows (single glazed timber framed casements, double glazed metal framed vertically sliding sash, etc.).

2.50 Details of the rooms should be given. This should follow the inspection system; *i.e.* if the inspection started at the top floor, that floor should be described first—"The dwelling consists of two rooms and a combined bathroom and W.C. compartment to the first floor; and two rooms, a kitchen and an entrance hall (with staircase off) to the ground floor."

2.51 Finally details of the space and water heating systems should be given—"Space heating is by means of a solid fuel boiler providing heated water for circulation through radiators to each room and the first floor landing and ground floor entrance hall and passage. The boiler also provides for water heating."

Description of rooms, etc.

2.52 A standard system for identifying the sides of dwellings should be followed, and should be clearly stated on any inspection form, report or notice. This could be a simple statement—"The terms 'left' and 'right' refer to the left hand side and right hand side of the dwelling when inside and facing the front access door."

Using the front access door as a point of reference avoids problems in the case of dwellings in a large block which does not front onto a road.

2.53 Rooms should generally be described by reference to their position within the dwelling, and not by the use made of them at present. The present use of each room can be usefully indicated as well, but should not be the sole description. For example, "first floor front right (bed) room"; "ground floor rear left (living) room."

Where there are back additions, or side extensions, rooms can be distinguished by including "main" and "side extension." Staircases and passages should be described by reference to their position; for example, "ground/first staircase," "first floor landing and passage."

All kitchens, bathrooms and W.C. compartments should be described by reference to both the position within the dwelling and the use; for example, "ground floor back addition rear kitchen," "first floor main rear right bathroom."

2.54 Where it is necessary to describe a part of the structure within a particular room, this should be by reference to its position and, if appropriate, function. Walls should be described as "left flank wall," "front main wall," "rear internal wall" and "right party wall." Care should be taken with reveals to door and window openings, so that the terms "left" and "right" refer to the standardised reference as stated in the report.

Description of defects

Words such as "defective" should be avoided where possible, as they do not describe the problem that exists. Wherever possible, more specific descriptive words should be used, for example, "cracked," "rotting," "missing," "leaking," "likely to be dangerous," and "uneven." 2.55

An indication of the extent or effect of the defect being described may be useful. This may help to give a clear picture of the conditions, and assist in any assessment of the cost of remedial works necessary; it will also be a useful guide when assessing any changes or deterioration on a re-inspection. In the case of defects to floors, walls, or ceilings, this indication could be provided as a rough estimate of the area covered by a defect, and so the area to be treated by remedial works. In other cases it may be more difficult to fully assess the extent of remedial works (*e.g.* electrical wiring will require thorough checking by a competent electrical engineer before a full assessment can be given), but this should be stated.

The position could also be described in terms of the part of the structure affected. For example, "damp affected plaster to the right party wall, in particular to the area adjacent to the ceiling extending down about 150mm (an area of approximately 0.5 metre)."

Where a defect has damaged internal decorations, this should be described. For example, "damp stained and peeling wall paper, exposing damp affected plaster."

Where the effects of some defects or deficiencies are not apparent at the actual time of the inspection, but it is clear that they will recur this should be stated. 2.56

In other cases, it may not be possible to identify a defect, but the symptoms should be noted. Where there is spring or give to a suspended timber floor this may be as a result of defects to the joists, or it may be the result of previous settlement and shrinkage of timber. Where an inspection is made during dry weather, an eavesgutter may appear distorted and the adjacent wall surface stained (as if by water discharged from the distorted eavesgutter). In such cases, the symptom should be described as follows—"suspected defective timbers to the floor, in that the floor is springy," "suspected leaking and/or overflowing eavesgutter to the front main roof, in that the eavesgutter is distorted and the front main wall stained."

INSPECTIONS AND SURVEYS

Other information

2.57 Generally the floor area of each room, other than bathrooms, W.C. compartments and kitchens, should be estimated. This could be either by giving the estimated length and width, or by reference to the floor areas given in Table II in section 326(3) of the Housing Act 1985 (which deals with the permitted number standard for overcrowding). If the floor area is given by reference to Table II of section 326(3), a statement to that effect should be given in the report.

The floor area of a kitchen should be included where that room is also used for eating or living.

Actual measurement of the floor area will be necessary where it is suspected that overcrowding exists, or where details of the permitted number have been requested (under section 332(3) of the Housing Act 1985).

2.58 The facilities installed in kitchens, bathrooms and W.C. compartments should be recorded. This could include both the facilities provided by the landlord/owner, and those provided by the occupier.

Method of inspection

2.59 However the inspection is carried out, it should follow a set pattern or routine. This helps to ensure that no part of the dwelling is missed.

Politeness often dictates that the inspection commences within the dwelling (this avoids occupiers being concerned by someone standing outside making notes about their house). If the occupier wishes to show the inspector certain matters, then those should be seen first, but only as a superficial first step. After this, the inspection should follow the set pattern, for example, beginning at the top floor front left room, and working from top to bottom, left to right and front to back.

Each room should be inspected in detail, noting every obvious defect following the set pattern—ceiling, walls, floors, windows, door, and any facilities. The size of the room should be estimated (or measured). Even if an occupier has stated, for example, that a window doesn't open, it should be checked.

There may be furniture present in the room or dwelling, which cannot always be moved. Every effort should be made to check a suspected defect in detail, but if it is not possible, then a note should be made to that effect. For example, "The occupier stated that there is a large hole in the floor under the bed, but this could not be properly checked at the time of the inspection."

Where a ceiling, or wall has been covered (*e.g.* with polystyrene tiles or boarding) this should be noted, as the precise condition could not be properly assessed.

2.60 Having thoroughly inspected the first room, the inspection should proceed to the next and so on, passages and staircases being inspected after completing all the rooms on that floor and before proceeding to the next.

After completing the inspection of the whole of the interior (including, if necessary, any roof space and cellar), the exterior should be inspected. Again a set pattern or routine should be followed, although it is easier to inspect the rear of the dwelling first (because of access to a rear garden/yard), but from top to bottom carefully assessing each part of the structure. However, in many cases parts of the exterior are not visible from the outside (*e.g.* some roofs), or are more easily assessed from within the dwelling (*e.g.* back addition roofs are often visible from a first floor rear room) or an adjacent dwelling. Where a part cannot be properly checked, this should be stated.

Information on the occupation and ownership of the house should be noted. In the case of tenanted dwellings the details provided in a rent book should be checked and noted. This should provide details of the tenant's name, the start of the tenancy, the landlord's or agent's name and address, the rent, and rates payable. It should also contain the permitted number for the dwelling. The start of the tenancy should be checked with the occupier, and details of the number, ages and sexes of the household taken. **2.61**

Equipment for inspections

The equipment for an inspection may include the following— **2.62**

(a) Pens and pencils. While pens are preferable, pencils may be necessary for noting the condition of the exterior during rain.

(b) Notebook or inspection forms. The notebook or form may be needed at a court or public inquiry hearing as the only aide-memoire permitted, and any such notes must be made contemporaneously. The notebook or form should be retained safely.

(c) Camera (with spare films). Photographs of the front and rear elevation, and of particular defects at the time of the inspection may be useful. Cameras which produce instant pictures enable the result to be checked at the time, and, if necessary, a second attempt may be made to obtain a clear record; however, copies of instant pictures are relatively expensive. Details of where and when the film was developed and printed should be recorded.

(d) Torch (with spare batteries). This will be needed for checking roof spaces, and for checking some parts of rooms where lighting is poor.

(e) Tape measure, rule or measuring rod. These can be used for checking the floor areas of rooms and the area affected by a defect. Since most inspections are carried out by one person,

the equipment should be capable of being used by one person. A sonic measure can measure the distance between two points (in imperial or metric figures) and give a read-out of the area and volume.
- (f) Damp meter and accessories. Even if dampness is evident it should be confirmed by the use of some form of damp meter. The types and uses of damp meters are considered in more detail in Chapter 8.
- (g) Collapsible ladder for checking the condition of roof spaces and reaching other parts of the dwelling (either inside or outside). Although some occupiers may have ladders or stepladders, this cannot be relied on.
- (h) Mirror for checking the condition of awkward parts of the structure, for example, underfloor spaces, wall cavities and drains.
- (i) Sampling equipment. This should include sterile petri dishes for sampling possible mould growth, and sterile bottles for sampling water supplies.
- (j) Protective clothing. Disposable overalls may be necessary where a through inspection of areas such as roof spaces or cellars may be required, or where parts of the structure require investigation involving open-up.
- (k) Binoculars, monocular or telescope. These may be necessary for assessing the condition of roofs and chimney stacks.

Other equipment which may be needed is considered later.

Insurance and authorisation

2.63   There are three types of insurance cover required by anyone carrying out inspections—professional indemnity, public liability and loss, theft or damage of equipment.

Professional indemnity cover should provide protection against claims of professional negligence in relation to an inadequate assessment of the condition of the dwelling, or specifying, authorising or supervising the carrying out of works which were inadequate or inappropriate. Such claims may be made by an occupier or a landlord or owner, and could involve relatively minor matters (*e.g.* not noting, or not ensuring a remedy for, dampness) or the unnecessary loss of the occupier's home or the owner's building.

Public liability cover should provide protection for the inspector for accidental damage to an occupier's property (breaking an ornament or equipment) and for accidental damage to the structure (damaging a floor or ceiling).

Some of the equipment needed is relatively expensive, but can be easily lost, damaged or may be stolen. The inspector should be protected by adequate and specific insurance cover.

All representatives of a local authority should be provided with means of identification which enables the representative to be easily identified (both to gain access, and so that the occupier is aware of the name, designation and department of the representative) and clearly states the statutes and provisions and purposes for which the person is an authorised representative of the local authority. **2.64**

Evaluation and opinion

Intially, the condition of the dwelling should be compared with the basic public health criteria (see paras. 2.05–2.11), and evaluation in terms of the statutory standards should come later. There may be matters affecting the occupation of the dwelling which fall outside the present statutory standards, but which require comment and opinion from a public health view-point. To enable both forms of evaluation once the full detailed inspection has been carried out, additional comments on particular features or aspects of the dwelling, the site and the occupation and any other relevant matters should be included. These should include comments on the lay-out and design of the dwelling in terms of its suitability for occupation by any household. The process of inspection initially requires an examination of the separate parts of each room and of each part of the dwelling, it is only after completing the detailed examination that the dwelling can be considered as a whole. It may be that each individual part of the dwelling is satisfactory in isolation, but taken as a whole the dwelling is unsatisfactory. It may be that the layout of the dwelling, the disposition of facilities or rooms is such that there will be interference with the occupation of the dwelling. For example, there may be internal bad arrangement, with access to one bedroom only available through another, or with the arrangement of rooms on different floors, such that the use of the dwelling is made more difficult. **2.65**

The dwelling itself may be perfectly adequate for occupation, but its position within a building or the general environment around may make it unsuitable. A dwelling sited on the fourth floor of a building, with access only available via staircases will prevent the dwelling being suitable for households which include very young, old or disabled persons. The dwelling may be within a heavy industrial and commercial area with high levels of traffic, noise and atmospheric pollution which interfere with the use and occupation of the dwelling. The dwelling may be sited in an exceptionally exposed position, and although its design and construction would be satisfactory in a sheltered site, there have been no adaptations or alterations to take account of the exposure. The condition of the dwelling should be compared with that of others in the area.

INSPECTIONS AND SURVEYS

Any activities of the household which mitigate or compensate for defects in the dwelling should be recorded. The time of the year, the general weather conditions at the time of the inspection and for the period immediately prior to the inspection (which may affect the conditions) should be stated.

The provision for space heating can only be assessed after the whole of the dwelling has been thoroughly inspected. It should be assessed in terms of its suitability and capability to provide sufficient heat input for the whole of the dwelling, having regard to the layout and the design and construction of the dwelling. The thermal insulation provided by the structure can only be assessed after a complete inspection. It may be apparent that the space heating system and thermal insulation is such that the dwelling will be difficult or exceptionally difficult to heat adequately, and this should be stated.

The provision for ventilation should be assessed in terms of the individual parts of the dwelling, the dwelling as a whole, and the position of the dwelling. The fortuitous ventilation (via leakages around closed doors and windows) in a dwelling on a very exposed site may be excessive, and obvious from the details collected during the inspection.

2.66 On completion of the detailed inspection, and assessment of the dwelling as a whole, the inspector should consider the causes of the defects or likely explanations, for example, whether the disrepair is recent (resulting from the effects of severe weather conditions) or whether it is the result of inadequate maintenance over a long period. Where a structure has reached the end of its useful life, in spite of adequate maintenance, the report should make this clear.

2.67 Once the conditions have been evaluated, the relevant statutory standards should be considered. Each standard should be considered having regard to the desired outcome, the enforcement procedures and any implications for grant-aid.

Reports of inspections, etc.

2.68 Even though the inspection may have been carried out using a standardised form, and the result of the inspection has been the service of a notice, it may be necessary for a report to be prepared. This may be necessary where there is a court hearing either because of an appeal against the particular statutory action being taken or as part of the enforcement procedure, or where there is a public inquiry. Although a standardised inspection form may contain all the relevant information and comments, its layout will be geared towards the collection of the information at the time of the inspection. To provide a clear picture to the court or inquiry it will be necessary to prepare a report.

INSPECTION OF INDIVIDUAL DWELLINGS

Where there have been several inspections of the same dwelling over a period of time, which show changes in the conditions, a report combining the information collected at the different times will provide a clear indication of the conditions.

Examples of reports suggesting style and layout are given in Appendix 1.

6. Monitoring Structural Movement

"Tell-tales" are used as a means of checking whether there have been any changes in the width of cracks in buildings. Traditionally these consist of a strip of flat brittle material (usually glass), fixed by a dab of mortar (now usually epoxy resin adhesive) at each end across the crack (Fig. 1, p. 40). As the material is brittle, any movement associated with the crack will break it, either by tension as the crack widens, or by compression as the crack closes. 2.69

If one end of a traditional tell-tale becomes loose, it is useless and can be misleading if the loose fixing is not that obvious. To avoid this problem, and to be able to assess whether the crack is opening or closing a modification of the tell-tale can be used (Fig. 2). In this case two flat pieces of glass are positioned across the crack about 5 or 10mm apart, but each fixed at only one end, one on one side of the crack and the other the opposite side. A line is then drawn or painted across both pieces of glass. Any movement of the crack can then be observed by simply measuring the subsequent position of the lines on the glass. To avoid breakage, the glass can be replaced with strips of metal (although these will be subject to some thermal expansion and contraction). 2.70

Alternatively, two small metal discs can be fixed to opposite sides of the crack with epoxy resin adhesive (Fig. 3). The discs should be pre-marked with a cross, and the distance between the centre of the crosses measured and noted. Subsequent movement can be verified by measuring this distance. A similar method would be fixing two wood screws each side of the crack with the slots positioned vertically. (Care should be taken to avoid stressing or breaking the material by fixing the screws to close to the edges of the crack.) Again, the distance between the slots measured, and subsequent movement can be measured.

7. Non-Traditional House Construction

Introduction

There are many types of non-traditional constructional techniques used in housing. Although the inspection of dwellings built by such methods will vary little from the inspection of traditional forms of construction, the assessment of causes of defects can be more problematic. 2.71

Traditional construction is generally taken to mean those methods which use brickwork or stonework for the walls, and a timber roof

INSPECTIONS AND SURVEYS

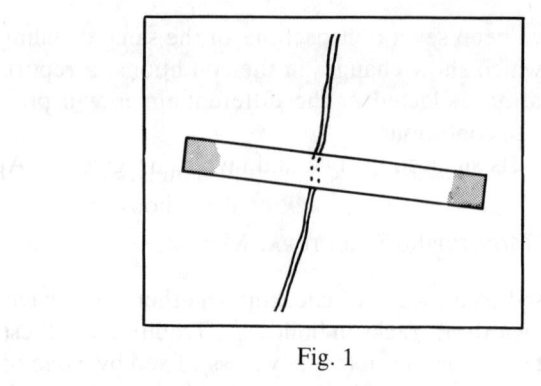

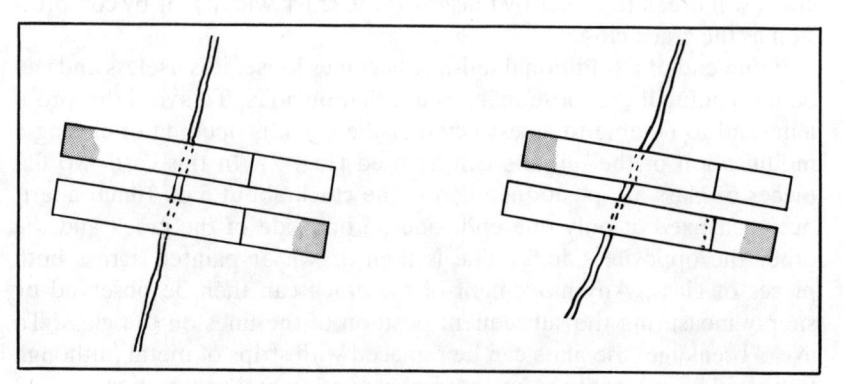

Fig. 1

Fig. 2

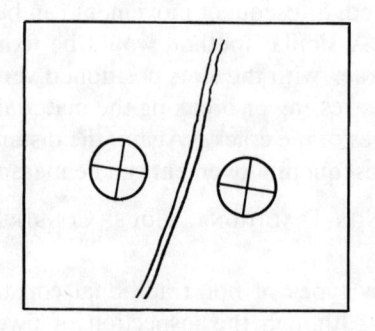

Fig. 3

construction covered with tiles or slates. The walls will be of solid or cavity construction, and floors may be solid or suspended timber. Non-traditional construction uses prefabricated components (either factory prefabricated, or prefabricated on site) and may include some traditional materials. Walls may be of concrete panels, steel, or timber. Although the majority of the non-traditional methods were developed since 1945, some were introduced as early as 1919.

2.72 Non-traditionally built houses can be difficult to identify, either because the components may be hidden behind cladding with traditional materials, or as there may have been renovation works including rendering or cladding of the exterior which may hide the more obvious clues. Identification of a non-traditional construction or material can be helped by measuring the thickness of the external walls, and by some internal features (such as support beams).

2.73 It is not possible in this work to give full and detailed descriptions of all the types of non-traditional and system building techniques and materials. However, there follow brief descriptions of some of the identifying features of the more common non-traditional systems. These details are not comprehensive, and experts with experience of non-traditional and system building techniques may be required for the assessment of their structure.

2.74 Several types of non-traditional construction systems have the general appearance of traditional houses, either because the walls are framed externally with render, or with brickwork cladding. These include Schindler and Hawksley S.G.S. and many timber-framed houses, which, because of the external brick facing, appear to be traditionally-built houses. Those faced externally with render include Parkinson, Winget, Whitson-Fairhurst, Unitroy and Underdown.

"No-fines" concrete

2.75 "No-fines" concrete has been used extensively since the early 1920s as a means of providing the structure of a wide variety of dwellings. It is a concrete composed of cement and coarse aggregate only, the fine aggregate (sand) is omitted so that there is a uniform distribution of voids throughout the mass of the concrete.

The open cellular structure is such that no-fines concrete is free-draining, and will allow water penetration. This means that the external faces must be finished with an effective water-proof render, and that openings must be properly weatherproofed. Where water gains entry into the concrete, it will drain downwards and may be trapped by any damp-proofing at floor level and above door and window openings. To prevent this water causing problems internally, the damp proof courses should slope towards the exterior and there should be weep-holes provided at the outer face.

Without these precautions, any water within the structure may appear as rising dampness internally, even in a flat well above ground floor. However, the cellular structure of no-fines concrete means that there is virtually no capillary attraction in concrete, and rising dampness cannot occur in the concrete itself (although it can still occur in the external rendering and internal plastering).

2.76 No-fines concrete is about two-thirds the weight of normal concrete, and has considerable benefits during the construction of buildings (lighter form-work being needed). Because of its cellular nature, no-fines provides better thermal insulation than normal concrete—a wall of 200mm thickness rendered and plastered giving similar thermal insulation to that of a solid brick wall of the same thickness.

Notes on features of some non-traditional houses

2.77 **Airy.** External walls are of reinforced concrete frame, clad externally with concrete shiplap panels. Roofs may be pitched and covered with tiles and with tile-hung gables, or flat with a tilted-up eaves soffit.

They are usually two storey semi-detached, although the system has been used for terraces and two storey blocks of flats.

2.78 **B.I.S.F. (British Iron and Steel Federation) houses.** These houses are of rolled steel frame wall construction, with external walls cement render on mesh to the ground floor and profiled sheet steel cladding to first floor level. Roofs are covered with corrugated asbestos cement sheeting, or corrugated sheet steel.

About 30,000 three-bedroom, semi-detached houses were built in England and Wales, and 1,500 terraced dwellings.

2.79 **Cornish unit houses.** The Type 1 house is of two distinct parts. The ground floor structure is made up of reinforced concrete columns, with reinforced concrete panels which slot between the columns in preformed grooves. The first floor and roof is a timber structure of a Mansard design, covered with tiles.

Although usually two storey semi-detached houses were built, there are also terraces and three storey blocks of flats.

2.80 The Type 2 house is visibly different, with larger reinforced concrete panels for the external wall cladding. Usually, both the ground and first storeys were of this post and panel construction, although the upper storey may be within a Mansard roof covered with tiles. The panels are again slotted into the reinforced concrete columns. The roofs are usually pitched and hipped and covered with tiles.

The Type 2 house may be found as bungalows, semi-detached house, terraces and two, three and four storey blocks of flats.

NON-TRADITIONAL HOUSE CONSTRUCTION

Reema. The walls are of large, storey height concrete panels, with a plain exposed aggregate external finish. Roofs are pitched, with or without hips. **2.81**

The method has been used for bungalows, semi-detached and terraced houses and medium and high rise blocks of flats.

Orlit. The walls are of precast reinforced concrete columns, faced externally with precast concrete slabs (approximately 400mm × 1,200mm or 400mm × 600mm). Roofs may be flat, or pitched with either hipped or gable ends). **2.82**

Usually semi-detached houses, but may be terraced or two storey blocks of flats.

Unity. This system uses storey height, precast columns, with external cladding and internal lining of concrete panels. The external cladding appears similar to blockwork laid with continuous vertical joints rather than any bonding. There may be recessed access doorways, and bay windows. Roofs are pitched, and may be hipped or with gables. **2.83**

Used for bungalows, semi-detached and terraced houses, and blocks of flats.

Woolaway. The construction is of storey height precast columns, with half-storey height concrete panels (about 1,200mm × 600mm wide) both internally and externally. However, externally the walls are faced with render. Roofs usually pitched with gable ends. **2.84**

Usually semi-detached houses, but may be bungalows, terraced houses and blocks of flats.

Boot. The walls are of precast reinforced concrete piers, with internal and external panels to form a cavity, and faced externally with render. Roofs usually pitched and hipped. **2.85**

May be found as either two storey semi-detached or terraced houses.

Wates. Walls are of precast reinforced concrete load-bearing panels. The vertical joints between the panels are designed so that they were filled with fine aggregate concrete and reinforcement to form columns which support and hold the structure together. There are string bonding units between the panels at first floor and eaves levels. Roofs usually pitched and hipped. **2.86**

Although usually two storey semi-detached houses, may be found as terraced houses and three storey blocks of flats.

Bison. The walls are of large (storey height) precast concrete panel construction. The system is used for medium and high rise blocks of flats. **2.87**

8. Specifications of Works

2.88 Specifications for notices must be carefully drafted. However, the phrasing of specifications for these purposes cannot be the same as those normally used, for example, by architects for new buildings, or the type of specifications used for grant-aided works (although once a notice has been served it may be that grant-aid is applied for and given, at which stage more exact specifications can be set). In the case of notices, although it is not always possible for the exact cause of any defect to be identified, any notices should outline the remedial works or steps in sufficient detail so as to make it quite clear what is to be achieved, while allowing the person carrying out the works some choice in the exact specification.

In addition, any notices served by the authority must be capable of enforcement, so that where works have been carried out, it is clear whether they have been carried out satisfactorily. There may also be some deterioration in the conditions at the dwelling between the time of the original inspection and the enforcement action. The phrasing of the specifications should be such that they will, generally, still be applicable at the time of the enforcement.

For example, if a notice merely states "repair the door," it cannot be effectively enforced. It is not clear what works are necessary, nor would it be clear whether any works that had been done had satisfactorily remedied the defect originally noted.

There should be a general statement on the standard and the practice to be followed in carrying out the works, so as to ensure that the proper materials, and good workmanship (including ensuring the making good of works disturbed) are used.

Some suggested examples of specifications illustrating the style and content required are given in Appendix 2.

9. House Condition Surveys

Introduction

2.89 The general duties imposed on local authorities—to cause an inspection of their district to be carried out from time to time so as to assess the need for action under the various provisions of the Housing Act 1985[20] and the Public Health Acts 1936 to 1969[21]—are probably most easily satisfied by conducting sample house condition surveys.

The general principle for such surveys was originally developed

---

[20] Housing Act 1985, s.605.
[21] Public Health Act 1936, s.91.

following recommendations of the Dennington Committee,[22] and from the National House Condition Survey first carried out in 1967. The result of that first survey indicated that 1.8 million dwellings were unfit for human habitation (which was twice the number previously "estimated" by local authorities, and showed a wider distribution of the unfit dwellings than had been supposed).

Initially, a sample house condition survey based on the English/Welsh National House Condition Surveys should be carried out covering the whole of the authority's district. This will provide information on local conditions for comparison with the national house condition statistics, giving an indication of any differences in type or scale of the housing condition problems in the authority's district. Subsequently, other house condition surveys can be carried out to provide more detailed information in respect of particular areas to assist in the selection of housing action, general improvement and clearance areas, or to assist in determining the priority to be given to, and most appropriate action to be taken in respect of, individual houses (*e.g.* where to concentrate efforts to ensure repairs and to deal with houses in multiple occupation).

Although there will be a large amount of information available to authorities which will give some indicators as to aspects of housing conditions (*e.g.* from census statistics, individual files, smoke control area action), such information does not provide an adequate basis for preparing a housing programme.

Sample house condition surveys are not geared towards providing information which could form the basis of any enforcement action, although obviously urgent problems can be referred for more detailed inspection and action. Such surveys are aimed at the collection of information for the general assessment of existing problems, and subsequently to assess the effectiveness of the authority's policies and programmes.

Whole area sample house condition surveys

In addition to being a means of satisfying the general statutory duty placed on authorities, a whole area house condition survey will provide a means of determining the housing policies and programmes of the authority. **2.90**

Any housing programme must take account of the local housing conditions, the appropriate actions to deal with those conditions and the availability of resources. In the longer term, a housing programme should be reassessed, for its effectiveness in dealing with the originally identified housing conditions, and to determine the need to re-direct any concentrated action.

---

[22] "Our Older Homes: a call for action" (1966) Ministry of Housing & Local Government.

INSPECTIONS AND SURVEYS

While a single house condition survey will provide information on which housing programmes and priorities can be based, it is only by carrying out succesive surveys at (say) five yearly intervals that the effectiveness of the programme and priorities can be assessed and, if necessary, resources re-directed.

2.91 Although an authority can enforce standards only where the dwellings are not owned and managed by the authority, the same standards (including the statutory standards) should be applied to all dwellings including those owned and managed by the authority. This will ensure that housing programmes and priorities are based on the condition of the total housing stock and needs of the district, and ensure that resources are concentrated or directed to deal with the most urgent and most unsatisfactory conditions irrespective of ownership and tenure.

Special house condition surveys

2.92 The whole area house condition surveys system can be adapted to enable surveys to be carried out either for a particular area within the authority's district, or for the collection of information on particular housing problems, for example, houses in multiple occupation, and houses requiring the installation of standard amenities.

The adaption of the forms, and the questions asked would depend on the particular needs of the survey.

Outline of sample house condition surveys

2.93 The general principles behind organising a sample house condition survey are the same whether it covers the whole of an authority's district or a particular area within that district. Choosing which area within a district should be based on the results of a district-wide survey. The outline given below is based on that described in Area Improvement Note No. 1.[23]

2.94 Although the principle of the sample house condition survey starts from a standard base enabling results to be compared to the national statistics, it is flexible enough to enable authorities to obtain information on particular or local problems. It is geared towards the assessment of the structural condition and the amenities of individual dwellings. Limited information about the occupation of dwellings is collected. A social survey can be carried out alongside the condition survey, but, because of the different skills required of an interviewer and that of a surveyor assessing house conditions, it is suggested that the two are not combined.

2.95 The aim of the house condition surveys is to provide information in a standardised form, and to provide a standardised assessment of

[23] "Sample house condition survey" (1971) H.M.S.O.

conditions, and it is necessary to ensure the surveyors involved apply the same standards and interpret those standards in the same way. To achieve this briefings and tutorials are necessary, and the maintenance of standard evaluation of conditions must be monitored.

The sample

2.96 The survey is based on a sample of 1,000 dwellings, irrespective of the total size of the authority's district. Because the survey is based on a sample, there will be errors, but these fall within set limits. Based on the sample, the results are given in terms of total numbers and percentages of the total number of dwellings in the district. For example, for a sample survey of 1,000 dwellings in a district of 10,000, the probable size of error can be calculated as follows—

No. of dwellings in category	Error range
100	plus or minus 60;
1,000	plus or minus 190;
5,000	plus or minus 320.

Any sampling technique has its limitations, and the information obtained must be carefully selected to ensure it provides only those conclusions which can be validly drawn from the sample. As numbers become smaller, the error range will increase, and may give totally misleading conclusions.

2.97 The sample for the survey must be drawn at random. The general principle is to avoid bias in the sample. Obtaining the sample fraction required could be based on the local Rating or Valuation List, or from the census. As the local Rating and Valuation lists will include non-domestic rateable units (which should not be included in the sample) the total size of the sample must be increased initially to allow for discarding of all non-residential units to obtain the required sample size (of 1,000 dwellings).

The principle for obtaining the sample is based on finding the sample fraction. For example, assuming the total rateable units in the district is 17,000, of which 13,500 are domestic and the remaining 3,500 are non-residential, the sample fraction would be 1,000/13,500 to give the required sample of 1,000. This gives a sample fraction of $\frac{1}{13}$, which, if applied throughout a list of the total number of rateable units of 17,000 will provide 1,307 units. Of this about 269 will be non-residential, and 1,038 residential, which can be reduced to the 1,000 required.

It is probable the sample will now be obtained from computer stored information. Whether it is from computer stored information or not, the first unit drawn must be taken at random by using a sample start number

INSPECTIONS AND SURVEYS

(this could be taken from a list of "random numbers" in a book on statistics, or by a simple alternative based on playing cards).[24]

2.98 Having obtained the list of sample units, all non-residential units should be discarded. Where there is any doubt as to whether the unit contains a dwelling (*e.g.* a public house, or a building which may have a residential caretaker) it should not be discarded. Once the list has been reduced to residential (and possible residential) units, it may need further reduction to obtain the final sample size. The discarding process should be the same as that adopted for extracting the initial sample from the list: *i.e.* working out the sample fraction to be discarded, obtaining a random start number and extracting the necessary number of units. Although the final sample number required is 1,000 dwellings, a small difference of say plus or minus 15 will have a negligible effect on the error range, and during the survey itself actual differences/changes will become apparent.

2.99 To maintain the random nature of the survey, each address should be given a consecutive serial number, and the first allocated to the first surveyor, the second to the second and so on. This may create difficulties in travel, and some compromise may be necessary. However, the aim should be to avoid one surveyor seeing a concentration of older dwellings, while another sees a concentration of new dwellings.

2.100 Finally, the sample for the survey should be split into two or more parts. This could be parts of equal size, so that one half of the survey is completed before the second started, giving some information and guide on the sort of results to be expected, and allowing for the possibility of adding/changing some of the information to be collected. Alternatively, the split could be unequal to allow a pilot survey to be run on (say) 100 dwellings, to show up any practical difficulties, or check the results and information collected.

Administrative arrangements

2.101 Before commencing a survey it will be necessary to inform the public generally that it is being undertaken, and to advise that any householder should not allow access to a surveyor before checking identification. In addition, the police, local newspapers and all local authority departments should be informed of the survey and of the identity of the surveyors. A central telephone number and address to receive outside enquiries should be given.

Letters should be sent to all the addresses in the sample, explaining

---

[24] For example—shuffle and cut a pack of cards and take the top card; where the sample interval required is between 1 and 9, take face value of the card (not counting Court cards or 10s); where the sample interval is 10 or over, the first card provides the first digit, the second the second and so on (where the constructed number exceeds the sample interval required, the procedure should be re-stated).

the purpose of the survey, asking for co-operation, and emphasising that access should not be allowed until the identity of the surveyor is checked.

Surveyors

2.102 Obviously, the number of surveyors required will depend on the size of the sample. On average, once the survey is underway, one surveyor can achieve an average daily rate of around 20 dwellings. Clearly this will depend on a number of factors: where there is a concentration of old dwellings in a relatively dilapidated condition, the daily rate will be lower than in an area of modern well maintained dwellings provided with all amenities; in rural areas, travel will decrease the daily rate.

However, assuming a rate of around 20 dwellings per day, the actual survey of 1,000 dwellings should take two surveyors about 5 to 6 weeks to complete.

2.103 The surveyors used should have some knowledge of building construction and experience of inspection or surveying. Local knowledge is not necessary, and may even introduce some bias into the assessment. Whatever the background, those selected should be prepared to fall in with the standardised and systematic approach necessary for the sample survey to provide as objective results as possible.

Briefing

2.104 Briefing and practice sessions are necessary to attempt to provide standardisation and to familiarise the surveyors with the forms to be used.

In addition to a general discussion on the background to the survey and the principles involved, detailed consideration will be necessary of the standards to be applied, the assessment of the scale of repair, and the description of rooms. There should be a practice run involving the surveying of 6 to 8 empty dwellings. This will highlight difficulties in form-filling, and will provide a basis for checking the bias of each surveyor.

The basic briefing and practice run should be followed-up by supervised field work on the survey proper, again checking for standardisation and form-filling.

Quality control

2.105 Throughout the survey it will be necessary to ensure standardisation of assessment and to limit errors in form-filling.

There are two simple methods to maintain standardised assessment. First by using a control surveyor who would be attached to each of the other surveyors for a day or more at different stages during the survey, and ensuring that the control surveyor sees a cross-section of the dwellings throughout the district. Both the control surveyor and the other surveyors would mark up separate forms at the same dwelling. The control surveyor is used as the base line, and the assessments made by the other surveyors adjusted up or down as necessary.

Second, each surveyor should re-visit a few dwellings already visited by another surveyor, and the results checked against the original. This would show differences in assessment which could be taken into account.

Such monitoring of the assessment made by surveyors will reveal errors in form-filling. In addition, each form should be checked on its return to the office. At this stage obvious errors can be corrected, or apparent anomalies checked while the surveyor's memory is still fresh.

2.106 The results can also be checked at various stages against other sources of information (*e.g.* census). This checking can only be in broad terms as the census data may be out of date, and will rely on different definitions. However, it can provide some guidance on the expected results from the survey on such figures as the number of dwellings, bathrooms, W.C. compartments, tenure and single or multiple occupation. In addition, as the original list of dwellings which formed the sample would have been drawn from the Valuation List or similar, it may be that some of the addresses have been demolished or changed from residential use, and corrections to the sample should be made during the survey and checked at the end.

Tabulation of results

2.107 The tabulation of the results will reflect the information collected and the needs of the authority. However, all the information collected need not be tabulated immediately, it could be that the initial information required was relatively simple, including the basic results, for example, the number unfit and repairable, the number unfit and not repairable, the number in disrepair, the number lacking standard amenities, the number in multiple occupation. After tabulation to this level, it could then be decided what additional information is required relating to each of those areas.

Tabulation can be carried out by hand or by computer (for which programs can be obtained, although some adaptation may be necessary to take account of the information required by the authority). Hand tabulation can be carried out while the survey is in progress.

Results

2.108 Generally, the percentage of the results obtained from the survey will be the same as for the district as a whole. For example, if 10 per cent. of the dwellings in the sample were found to be unfit, then 10 per cent. of the dwellings in the district will be unfit. There may need to be some minor adjustments to take account of, for example, the number of dwellings in the sample which were found to have been demolished.

2.109 As numbers will be required as well as dwellings, a multiplier will be required. This is basically obtained by reversing the process to obtain the sample fraction, but taking into account some minor corrections based on the findings of the survey. The minor corrections will take account of those dwellings found to be demolished, and the additional dwellings found where there were more than one in a rateable unit.

First there will be a total number of forms, one for each dwelling surveyed. To obtain the multiplier (which will be based on the total number of residential rateable units in the district) it is necessary to deduct from the total number of forms the additional dwellings found in single rateable units. For example, where 12 rateable units were each found to contain two dwellings (*i.e.* a total of 24 dwellings, and therefore 24 completed forms) and another 10 rateable units were found to contain three dwellings (*i.e.* 30 dwellings) the total number of forms should be reduced by the total number of extra dwellings (*i.e.* 12 + 20, a total of 32 extra dwellings).

The number of dwellings found demolished or otherwise untraceable should be added to the total number of completed forms, and the final figure divided into the total number of residential rateable units for the district, to give the multiplier. Results can then be expressed in terms of total numbers of dwellings in the district which are, for example, unfit by multiplying the number found unfit in the survey by the multiplier.

CHAPTER 3

HOUSING STANDARDS

3.01
1. Introduction	3.02
2. Statutory nuisances	3.08
3. Fitness for human habitation	3.19
4. Substantial disrepair	3.47
5. Interference with personal comfort	3.54
6. Standard amenities	3.60

1. INTRODUCTION

Standards enforceable by private individuals

3.02 The law can be invoked to remedy defects in housing in a wide variety of circumstances. In some cases the defect in a property may have caused direct physical injury to someone or damage to their possessions and may therefore give rise to a claim for damages against the person responsible for the maintenance of the building or the owner. Usually such claims will depend upon the status of the person seeking redress, such as a tenant, occupier or visitor to premises. Upon proof of the injury or damage suffered arising from the breach of a legal obligation, the courts can award damages to the injured party, and require remedial works to make good the breach. The basis for the legal claim will either be a breach of contract or the failure to abide by a reasonable standard of care.[1]

It is beyond the scope of this book to deal with the standards that the courts may enforce on behalf of individual tenants suing their landlords, and they are only briefly mentioned here for the sake of completeness. Detailed information and consideration of these standards are contained in other works, and those wanting more details should refer to them.[2]

3.03 The most common claims are those under section 11 of the Landlord and Tenant Act 1985, which implies into short leases a covenant by the landlord to maintain the structure and exterior of a dwelling in repair, and to keep the installations of gas, electricity, sanitation and heating in repair and proper working order. Perhaps a less utilised action is that claiming a breach of a duty of care owed to all persons who might reasonably be

---

[1] See further Arden and Partington, *Housing Law* (1983) Chaps. 15 and 16, pp. 639 *et seq.*
[2] *Ibid.*; also Luba, *Repairs: Tenants' Rights* (1986) and Martyn and Lloyd-Jones, *Housing Disrepair* (1985).

INTRODUCTION

expected to be affected by defects in the premises; for example, that imposed by section 4 of the Defective Premises Act 1972 (which extended the liabilities created under the Occupier's Liability Act 1957).

Relatively rare are claims relating to breaches of the duties to maintain dwellings fit for human habitation either as defined by statute or at common law. Such claims are rare because of the restricted circumstances in which the duties apply; the duty to maintain a dwelling fit as defined by section 10 of the Landlord and Tenant Act 1985 only applying to dwellings let at very low rents (*i.e.* £80 per annum in Inner London, and £52 per annum elsewhere),[3] and the duty to maintain a dwelling fit at common law applying to lettings for immediate occupation.[4] These two standards, however, are also relevant to enforcement procedures used by local authorities and are considered in some detail later in this chapter.

3.04 This book is concerned with those standards which local authorities can impose whether or not an individual occupier can be shown to have suffered some tangible injury or damage. Nevertheless, in a number of respects, the claims which an individual may be able to make against a landlord or owner of property, are of significance to local authority housing or environmental health officers.

In the first place, any notices served or action taken by a local authority officer may be evidence to support a tenant's claim for damages. There is no special privilege from disclosure to another interested party afforded to the reports of environmental health officers by the courts and there is therefore no reason why, upon payment of the costs of copying and administration, the report should not be made available to a tenant. In this respect the report is similar to the reports taken by the police following a road accident, which are frequently used to support (or reject) insurance claims. It is always open to a tenant to take out a witness summons against an environmental health officer who has inspected any property which is the subject of court proceedings.

Secondly, there are implications for a landlord arising from any report made to the landlord by an environmental health officer. The landlord's liability under section 11 of the Landlord and Tenant Act 1985 and the Defective Premises Act 1972 is dependent upon the landlord first having notice of the relevant defect. If the report contains allegations of disrepair, this will amount to notice for the purposes of section 11 of the Landlord and Tenant Act 1985,[5] and there seems no good reason why it would not also be sufficient notice for the purposes of the Defective Premises Act. Furthermore, if the landlord in question is the local

---

[3] Landlord and Tenant Act 1985, s.8.
[4] *Smith* v. *Marrable* (1843) 11 M & W 5; *Hart* v. *Windsor* (1844) 12 M & W 68.
[5] *McGreal* v. *Wake* (1984) 13 H.L.R. 109 and *Dinefwr Borough Council* v. *Jones* (1987) 19 H.L.R. 445.

HOUSING STANDARDS

authority itself, then any complaint by the tenant to an environmental health officer will be sufficient as notice upon which a claim may be based for breach of the implied covenant under the Landlord and Tenant Act 1985 or for breach of the landlord's duty of care under the Defective Premises Act 1972.[6]

Standards for the control of new buildings

3.05   All new buildings, including dwellings, are the subject of detailed regulations[7] concerning the general construction which are applied before the building is occupied during the process of construction. These regulations are enforced by building control officers and are outside the scope of this work, which is concerned only with the standards applicable to the existing housing stock. Nevertheless it does not necessarily follow that because a dwelling conforms to the building regulations, it will be up to the standards required by the Public Health and Housing Acts. In the vast majority of cases it is to be hoped that new houses will not fall below such standards once they are available for occupation. An example, however, of the possibility of a new home infringing the Housing Act 1985 would be a starter home with rooms of such small proportions that occupation by a family might amount to an offence under the overcrowding provisions in Part X of the Act.[8] Similarly it is not inconceivable that the amount of natural light, ventilation or the internal arrangement of a dwelling might be so far defective as to be unfit for human habitation.[9]

Standards applicable to existing dwellings

3.06   All housing is subject to legal regulations and standards determining the construction and the condition of the building. These standards are enforced regardless whether the occupier has suffered any loss or discomfort from the defect in the building, and in many cases can be enforced whether or not the occupier has made a complaint.

At some stage during or after the inspection of the dwelling, an evaluation of its condition in relation to the various standards must be made. In many instances the practice of environmental health officers may be to resolve the desired outcome of the inspection process in terms of a pragmatic view of the condition of the building, the needs of the occupier and even the availability and amount of any grant entitlement. In some cases this may amount to a prejudice in favour of a preferred procedure or policy, and the adoption of a particular standard before the conditions have been observed.

[6] *Dinefwr Borough Council* v. *Jones* (1987) 19 H.L.R. 445.
[7] Building Regulations 1985 (S.I. 1985 No. 1065) and Building (Inner London) Regulations 1985 (S.I. 1985 No. 1936).
[8] See Chap. 7.
[9] See paras. 3.24–3.44.

INTRODUCTION

In theory, the steps to be followed should be:

(a) the observation of the conditions (the inspection of the house or dwelling);
(b) a consideration of which standards the house or dwelling fails to satisfy;
(c) a consideration of the enforcement procedures and the results obtained by each of those procedures;
(d) a consideration of the needs and wishes of the occupier, and, secondarily, of the needs of the area and of the local authority; and
(e) an assessment of which of the available enforcement procedures will satisfy the needs of the occupier and of the area.

As a clear understanding and comparison of the standards is necessary before consideration of the relevant enforcement procedures, this chapter sets down the various standards in detail, together with any guidance and interpretations given by the courts. 3.07

It is important to note that each standard may use different terms or words to describe the same thing (*e.g.* "dwelling," "house," "dwelling-house" and "premises"). Each of the terms or words must be interpreted having regard to that particular standard, and guidance and interpretations given by the courts in respect of one standard may not be applicable to another.

2. STATUTORY NUISANCE—PUBLIC HEALTH ACT 1936

The term "statutory nuisance" is used in public health legislation to cover matters which "the health of the community requires to be dealt with speedily,"[10] and for which a summary procedure is necessary to remedy those matters. The main provisions are to be found in Part III of the Public Health Act 1936, which includes the definitions of situations and conditions which can constitute a statutory nuisance. Special procedures to dealing with statutory nuisances in certain circumstances are to be found in the Public Health (Recurring Nuisances) Act 1969 and section 76 at the Building Act 1984. 3.08

There are various specified situations and conditions defined as being statutory nuisances set out in section 92(1) of the 1936 Act. The most relevant to housing are: 3.09

"(a) any premises in such a state as to be prejudicial to health or a nuisance;"
"(c) any accumulation or deposit which is prejudicial to health or a nuisance; and

---

[10] *Halsbury's Laws* (4th ed.) Vol. 38, para. 401.

(d) any dust or effluvia caused by any trade, business, manufacture or process and [injurious or likely to cause injury to the public health or a nuisance]."[11]

The most common of these applicable to housing conditions is the general definition given in section 92(1)(*a*).

In interpreting this provision it is important to "keep close to the wording of the Act,"[12] and to look at each aspect of the definition, as well as the definition as a whole.

Types of accommodation to which the standard applies

3.10 It is clear from the definition that the standard applies to "premises." This term is defined as including "messuages, buildings, lands, easements and hereditaments of any tenure,"[13] and "land" is further defined as including "any interest in land and any easement or right in, to or over land."[13]

It is irrelevant whether the premises are occupied or whether any occupation is lawful. Empty premises can be in such a state as to be prejudicial to health,[14] and it has been accepted by a magistrates' court that premises occupied by squatters could be a statutory nuisance and the owner responsible for the condition.[15]

It is suggested that the only relevant circumstances are, (a) that the premises exist, and (b) their condition.

3.11 "Premises" can include a single room in a house (including the right of access and shared facilities used in association with that room), and an entire block of flats.[16]

Interpretation of the standard

3.12 Because the definition uses the phrase "premises in such a state," it is clear that it is the state of the premises as a whole that must be considered, not an individual defect or matter in isolation. A minor defect may not warrant the premises being classified a statutory nuisance; but a multiplicity of such defects could cause the premises to be "in such a state" as to be a statutory nuisance.

---

[11] The words in square brackets were substituted by the Local Government (Miscellaneous Provisions) Act 1982, s.26.
[12] Lord Wilberforce, in *Salford City Council* v. *McNally* [1975] 3 W.L.R. at 92.
[13] Public Health 1936, s.343.
[14] See *Lambeth London Borough Council* v. *Stubbs* (1980) 255 E.G. 789.
[15] *Gould* v. *Times Square Estates Ltd.* (unreported), Camberwell Green Magistrates' Court, noted in September 1975 issue of L.A.G. Bull. 247.
[16] *Birmingham District Council* v. *McMahon and Others* (1987) 19 H.L.R. 452.

3.13 It is the physical condition of the premises which is to be taken into account, and not the way those premises are used.[17] A clear example of the difference between the physical condition and the way the premises are used was given in the Divisional Court in *Greater London Council* v. *Tower Hamlets London Borough*.[18] Griffiths L.J., dealing with the responsibility for condensation, said:

> "If the construction of a building is so unusual that there has to be some special form of heating to combat condensation, it is reasonable that the landlord should be expected to instal items such as storage heaters to provide that warmth. Of course, if the tenant does not choose to use the facilities provided, he will have no cause for complaint if the result is that condensation makes the place uninhabitable."
>
> "A landlord is required to apply his mind to the necessity of ventilation and, if need be, to insulation and heating. The landlord must provide a combination of these factors to make a house habitable for the tenant. However, once the landlord has provided the facilities, the tenant must use them. If it is shown on any further inquiry into condensation in this flat that the landlord has done everything reasonable and the cause of the continuing condensation is that the tenant is unwilling to use the appliances or any reasonable alternative means of heating the flat, then the landlord cannot be held responsible for the ensuing state of the premises."[19]

3.14 The fact that the physical condition results from inherent defects, and that the premises were built to satisfy the building control legislation in force at the time and have been maintained to that standard (*i.e.* there is no breach of a repairing covenant) is irrelevant. The only relevant fact is the state of the premises as determined at the time of the assessment.[20]

3.15 The separation of the two limbs by the word "or" means that it is only necessary to show that the condition of the premises falls within one of the categories "prejudicial to health" or a "nuisance."[21]

3.16 The term "prejudicial to health" is defined in the Act as meaning "injurious, or likely to cause injury, to health."[22] This makes it clear that the likelihood or probability of injury is included as well as actual injury to health.

The term "health" is not defined in the Act. In ordinary language it

---

[17] *Metropolitan Asylum District Managers* v. *Hill* (1881) 6 App.Cas. 193, and *Fulham Vestry* v. *London City Council* [1897] 2 Q.B 76.
[18] (1983) 15 H.L.R. 57.
[19] *Ibid.* at 61.
[20] *Birmingham District Council* v. *Kelly and Others* (1985) 17 H.L.R. 572.
[21] *Betts* v. *Penge U.D.C.* [1942] 2 K.B. 154, and *Salford City Council* v. *McNally* [1975] 3 W.L.R. 87.
[22] Public Health Act 1936, s.343.

means "soundness of body,"[23] and it has been defined as "a state of complete physical, mental and social well-being and not merely the absence of disease or infirmity."[24] The courts have not given a clear interpretation of "health," but have tended towards a more restrictive view.

Lord Widgery C.J., in considering whether an accumulation of inert matter was prejudicial to health for the purposes of section 92(1)(c) of the Act, stated:

> "The words are obviously very wide, and one should hesitate, in construing the section in proceedings such as the present, to lay down boundaries which may in another case prove to be unsuitable. But I think that the underlying concept of the section is that that which it struck at is an accumulation of something which produces a threat to health in the sense of a threat of disease, vermin or the like."[25]

In contrast, in *R.* v. *Parlby*[26] (which dealt with housing conditions) it was held that the provisions were directed at situations where the premises are "decayed, dilapidated, dirty or out of order . . . where foul matter has been allowed to soak into walls or floors, or where they are so dilapidated as to be a source of danger to life and limb." Similarly, in *Malton Urban Sanitary Authority* v. *Malton Farmers Manure Co.*[27] (dealing with a smell emanating from accumulations) it was held that something was prejudicial to health because it "caused sick persons to become worse." In *Bennet* v. *Preston Borough Council*,[28] a more recent Crown Court case, the Judge took account of Lord Widgery's comments as noted above and held that unsafe electrical wiring could contribute to premises being prejudicial to health, if not from the threat of electric shocks and the possibility of fire, at least from the smoke that would result from the fire.

The Divisional Court has accepted, in several cases, that the presence of dampness caused by condensation, and associated mould growth can render premises prejudicial to health and so be a statutory nuisance.[29]

3.17 The term "nuisance" is not defined in the Act, but is to be given its common law interpretation.[30] It can be a private nuisance, such as

---

[23] *Shorter Oxford English Dictionary*.
[24] World Health Organisation, preamble to Constitution, 1952.
[25] *Coventry City Council* v. *Cartwright* [1975] 1 W.L.R. 845 at 849.
[26] (1889) 22 Q.B.D. 525.
[27] (1879) 4 Ex. D. 302.
[28] Preston Crown Court 1982, reported in *Environmental Health*, April 1983.
[29] *e.g. Dover District Council* v. *Farrar* (1980) 2 H.L.R. 32; *G.L.C.* v. *London Borough of Tower Hamlets* (1983) 15 H.L.R. 57 and *Birmingham District Council* v. *Kelly and Others* (1985) 17 H.L.R. 572.
[30] *National Coal Board* v. *Thorne* [1976] 1 W.L.R. 543, which relied on *Salford City Council* v. *McNally* [1975] 3 W.L.R. 87.

"interferences for a substantial length of time by owners or occupiers of property with the use and enjoyment of neighbouring property"[31]; or it can be a public nuisance, which has been expressed as "an act or omission which materially affects the material comfort and quality of life of a class of Her Majesty's subjects."[31]

Premises which comprise a part of a building and which are affected by a defect outside that part which interferes with the use and enjoyment of that part, will be affected by a private nuisance; an example of this would be a defective roof to a block of flats allowing water to penetrate into a flat—the roof not being a part of the flat affected. A public nuisance could be a leaking eavesgutter discharging water onto a public footpath, and so affecting the general public using that footpath.

Assessment of premises

3.18 The assessment of the state of the premises should be based on a comprehensive inspection of the premises. Whether or not premises are in such a state as to justify their classification as a statutory nuisance, should be decided with as much evidence as possible. Although a single individual defect or condition may be so significant as to make the premises as a whole a statutory nuisance, there may be other matters which contribute towards the overall state.

3. FITNESS FOR HUMAN HABITATION

3.19 There are at least two meanings of the term "fit for human habitation"—that at common law, and that defined by, and for the purposes of, the Housing Act 1985 and the Landlord and Tenant Act 1985.

Although the term "unfit for human habitation" has appeared in statutes since 1868,[32] prior to 1954[33] there was no statutory definition of "fit for human habitation." In many statutes, the phrase used was "in all respects reasonably fit for human habitation."[34] The common law standard of fitness for human habitation provided the basis of the interpretation of this latter phrase.

It is suggested that some guidance on the general approach to the interpretation of the present statutory standard of fitness may be drawn from the pre-1954 cases which considered the approach to deciding

---

[31] *National Coal Board* v. *Thorne* [1976] 1 W.L.R. 543 at 546.
[32] Artizans and Labourers Dwellings Act 1868.
[33] Housing Repairs and Rents Act 1954, s.9.
[34] *e.g.* Housing Act 1936, s.2; Housing, Town Planning etc. Act 1909, ss.14 and 15; and Housing of the Working Classes Act 1890, s.12.

HOUSING STANDARDS

whether a house was fit (either at common law or pre-1954 statute law), but not from those which dealt with the standard itself.

3.20 It should also be noted that the phrase "fit for human habitation" is used in the Public Health Act 1936,[35] and that the interpretation of the phrase for the purposes of that Act should be as described for fitness at common law (paras. 3.21–3.23)—the definition given in the Housing Act 1985 is specifically limited to that Act.[36]

Fitness at common law

3.21 At first it may seem that this is not a high standard, in that it is "a humble standard. It is only required that the place must be decently fit for human beings to live in."[37] And the house need only be in "good and tenantable repair."[38] However, bearing in mind that the standard is that of the "ordinary reasonable man,"[39] one of the major cases on the common law standard held that "if the state of repair of a house is such that by ordinary user damage may naturally be caused to the occupier, either in respect of personal injury to life or limb or injury to health, then the house is not in all respects reasonably fit for human habitation."[40]

This guidance suggests that the interpretation of the common law standard of fitness should be wide, so that this may well be a relatively high standard compared to others.

3.22 The important criteria for deciding whether a house is fit at common law are the effects of the defect or condition on the occupiers, which may include the risk of future danger. This approach is classically illustrated in *Summers* v. *Salford Corporation*,[41] in which Lord Atkin said:

> "In the present case the breaking of one sash cord necessarily involved the strong probability that its fellow cord, especially with the extra strain imposed on it, would also break, with the further certainty of danger to anyone handling the window at the time of the break and with the further certainty that until repair that window must either remain permanently closed or permanently open. Either event would prevent that room from being reasonably fit for occupation, and, as this room was one of only two bedrooms, it appears to me that until repair the whole house would be properly described as unfit for occupation."[42]

---

[35] s.94(2).
[36] s.604 stating "for any of the purposes of this Act."
[37] *Jones* v. *Geen* [1925] 1 K.B. 659.
[38] *Ibid.*
[39] *Hall* v. *Manchester Corporation* [1915] L.J. Ch. 732.
[40] *Morgan* v. *Liverpool Corporation* [1927] 2 K.B. 131, confirmed in *Summers* v. *Salford* [1943] A.C. 283.
[41] [1943] A.C. 283.
[42] *Ibid.* at 289.

This approach was supported by others in the same case, in particular Lord Russell of Killowen, who said that

> "One sash cord had been worn to breaking point and had in fact snapped . . . The sashcord on either side would normally be, and in fact was, in a precarious condition. The result of the state of affairs was that the window could not be put to its normal use, namely being opened and shut for the purpose of ventilation or cleaning without danger to the operator."[43]

Reinforcing the view that the effect of the defect is the all important factor, and whether the defect can be remedied cheaply and quickly is irrelevant, Lord Atkin also stated that the test of whether a house is unfit to live in "must not be measured by the magnitude of the repairs required. A burst or leaking pipe, a displaced slate or tile, a stopped drain, a rotten stair tread, may each of them until repair make a house unfit to live in, though each of them may be quickly and cheaply repaired."[44]

3.23 The wide range of the common law standard of fitness is demonstrated by some examples of matters which have been held to render a house unfit for human habitation:

(a) infestations of bugs[45];
(b) infestation with fleas (which drove the tenant and his wife from their bed)[46];
(c) defective drainage[47];
(d) infection of measles[48];
(e) falling ceiling plaster[49];
(f) infestation of rats (but not occasional visits by rats)[50];
(g) defective stairs[51] (but not defective common stairs, outside the premises let to the tenant)[52]; and
(h) insufficient water supply.[53]

Many of these matters could now be dealt with by the local authority under other legislation (*e.g.* Public Health Act 1936), but the condition could still render a house unfit at common law.

---

[43] *Summers* v. *Salford* [1943] A.C. 283 at 291.
[44] *Ibid.* at 288.
[45] *Smith* v. *Marrable* (1843) 11 M & W 5.
[46] *Thompson* v. *Arkell* (1949) 99 L.J. 597.
[47] *Wilson* v. *Finch Hatton* (1877) 2 Ex.D. 336.
[48] *e.g. Bird* v. *Lord Greville* (1844) C & E 317.
[49] *Sarson* v. *Roberts* [1895] 2 Q.B. 395.
[50] *Stanton* v. *Southwick* [1920] 2 K.B. 642.
[51] *Dunster* v. *Hollis* [1918] 2 K.B. 795.
[52] *McCarrick* v. *Liverpool Corporation* [1947] A.C. 219.
[53] *Chester* v. *Powell* (1885) 52 L.T. (N.S.) 722.

Statutory fitness

3.24 A statutory definition of the term "fit for human habitation" was first introduced in 1954,[54] and has only been amended once since.[55] The definition is now to be found in section 604 of the Housing Act 1985 and also in section 10 of the Landlord and Tenant Act 1985.[56]

3.25 It is suggested that the approach to the interpretation of the definition should be as described in para. 3.22, in relation to common law fitness, *i.e.* that the significant criteria is the effects of the defect or condition on the occupiers, including the risk of future danger, and whether a defect can be remedied cheaply and quickly is irrelevant.

However, the statutory definition of fitness for human habitation is specific about the matters which should be considered.

3.26 The definition in section 604(1) is:

> "In determining for any of the purposes of this Act whether premises are unfit for human habitation, regard shall be had to their condition in respect of the following matters—
> repair,
> stability,
> freedom from damp,
> internal arrangement,
> natural lighting,
> ventilation,
> water supply,
> drainage and sanitary conveniences,
> facilities for the preparation and cooking of food and for the disposal of waste water;
> and the premises shall be deemed to be unfit if, and only if, they are so far defective in one or more of those matters that they are not reasonably suitable for occupation in that condition."

Types of accommodation to which the standard applies

3.27 The standard can apply to residential accommodation of many types. The original definition of the standard of fitness for human habitation used the term "house,"[57] but on consolidation[58] the term "premises" was introduced into the definition. The reason for this change is not clear, and it is doubtful if it has affected significantly the application of

---

[54] Housing Repairs and Rents Act 1954, s.9.
[55] Housing Act 1969, s.71.
[56] Which relates to the implied covenant that houses let at low rents are to be fit for human habitation.
[57] See Housing Act 1957, s.4. It should also be noted that the otherwise identical definition of fitness in Landlord and Tenant Act 1985, s.10, retains the term "house."
[58] In the Housing Act 1985.

the standard, particularly as the provisions relating to enforcement refer to "houses"[59] except in certain specified situations.[60]

The term "premises" is not defined by the Housing Act 1985. However, the term "house" is defined as including "any yard, garden, outhouses and appurtenances belonging to the house or usually enjoyed with it."[61] This definition does not provide a clear indication of what exactly is a "house," but extends the term so as to include any associated land, buildings and amenities.

3.28 The courts have commented on the meaning of the term "house" in several cases, and in particular the Court of Appeal in *Quiltotex Co. v. Minister of Housing and Local Government*,[62] held that the definition in the Housing Acts is to be treated as an artificial extension of what is ordinarily understood by the word "house." Perhaps more helpful is the guidance given in *Critchell v. Lambeth Borough Council*,[63] when the court said that the word "house" should be interpreted as meaning "what is commonly called a house—that is a separate structure." However, this comment should not be taken to extremes; it is also clear that buildings and premises which are not commonly called houses can be considered such if the circumstances warrant it, and also that a terraced house (which is not necessarily a "separate structure") is certainly a "house."

3.29 It is suggested that the interpretation of the word "house" should be a question of fact and law, having regard to the particular time and to the context in which the word is used, and not being misled by any general term that may be used to describe the accommodation or premises. Provided that the interpretation is reasonable and justifiable, it is likely that the courts will not interfere.[64]

3.30 The courts have held various types of premises to be "houses" for particular purposes. These include:

(a) a common lodging-house: for the purposes of Part III of the Housing Act 1957 (now Part IX of the 1985 Act)[65];
(b) a common lodging-house: for the purposes of section 73 of the Housing Act 1964 (now section 379 of the 1985 Act)[66];
(c) a tenement, divided into separate dwellings, and which is a

---

[59] See Housing Act 1985, ss.189 and 264—paras. 5.80 and 5.104.
[60] *e.g.* Housing Act 1985, s.205 and s.264(7).
[61] Housing Act 1985, s.207.
[62] [1966] 1 Q.B. 704.
[63] [1957] 2 Q.B. 535.
[64] See in particular *Duke of Bedford v. Dawson* (1875) L.R. 20 Eq. 353; *Att.-Gen. v. Mutual Tontine Westminster Chambers Association Ltd.* (1876) 1 Ex.D. 469; *Re Bulter, Camberwell (Wingfield Mews) No. 2 Clearance Order 1936* [1939] 1 K.B. 570.
[65] *Re Ross and Leicester Corporation* (1932) 96 J.P. 459.
[66] *Silbers v. Southwark London Borough Council* (1977) 122 S.J. 128.

part of a larger building: for the purposes of Part III of the 1957 Act (now Part IX of the 1985 Act)[67];

(e) a building comprised of a dwelling and commercial premises: for the purposes of Part III of the 1957 Act (now Part IX of the 1985 Act) (however, the ratio of use for human habitation and other purposes may be relevant)[68];

(f) four houses altered so as to form a single building used as a hotel: for the purposes of the Rent Act 1968[69];

(g) unoccupied houses or rooms: for the purposes of Parts II and III of the 1957 Act (now Parts VI and IX of the 1985 Act)[70]; and

(h) a "hostel": for the purposes of sections 15 and 19 of the Housing Act 1961 (now sections 352 and 354 of the 1985 Act).[71]

It should be noted that each of these decisions deals with the interpretation of the word "house" in relation to the facts of the particular case and the legislation being applied.

In *Pollway Nominees Limited* v. *London Borough of Croydon*,[72] which dealt with the interpretation of the term "person having control,"[73] the case was argued on the basis that a purpose-built block of 42 flats was a "house" for the purposes of Part II of the 1957 Act (now Part VI of the 1985 Act). Lord Bridge commented that he was by no means prepared to accept that the block was a "house," but acknowledged that the House of Lords had heard no argument on the point and so refrained from expressing any opinion one way or another. Nonetheless, he did go on to state that "a building originally constructed as a single dwelling-house does not cease to be a 'house' under the Act if it is internally converted into a number of separate residential units . . ."

In *R.* v. *London Borough of Lambeth, ex p. Clayhope Properties Ltd.*,[74] Glidewell L.J., considering whether a flat in a purpose-built block of 20 dwellings was a "house" for the purposes of Part II of the 1957 Act, said that in his view "a flat is not a house within the meaning of Part II of the 1957 Act. A 'house' in its ordinary sense means a separate building. It may contain one dwelling, or more than one. Whether a

---

[67] *Quiltotex Co.* v. *Minister of Housing and Local Government* [1966] 1 Q.B. 704.

[68] *Premier Garage Co.* v. *Ilkeston Corp.* (1933) 97 J.P. 786; *Re Bainbridge, South Shields (D'Arcy Street) Compulsory Purchase Order 1937* [1939] 1 K.B. 500; *Re Butler, Camberwell (Wingfield Mews) No. 2 Clearance Order 1936* [1939] 1 K.B. 570, and *Annicola Investments Ltd.* v. *Minister of Housing and Local Government* [1968] 1 Q.B. 631.

[69] *Luganda* v. *Service Hotels Ltd.* [1969] 2 Ch. 209.

[70] *Robertson* v. *King* [1901] 2 K.B. 265; *Re South Shields Compulsory Purchase Order 1937* [1939] 1 All E.R. 419.

[71] *R.* v. *Camden Borough Council, ex p. Rowton (Camden Town) Ltd., The Times,* June 9, 1983.

[72] (1986) 18 H.L.R. 443.

[73] As defined by s.39(2) of the 1957 Act, now s.207 of the 1985 Act.

[74] (1987) 19 H.L.R. 426.

particular purpose-built block of flats is a 'house' for the purposes of Part II is a question of fact. In relation to this block I express no opinion; it may have to be tested later, or it may not."

3.31 It is also important to note that there is no requirement that the "premises" (or "house") must be occupied, provided that the definition of "premises" or "house" is satisfied, then the standard can be applied, and, unless it is being used for other purposes or its use for human habitation has been prohibited,[75] it is available for human habitation.

3.32 The 1985 Act states that the standard can be applied to "any part of a building which is used, or is suitable for use as, a dwelling."[76] It is now clear that individual self-contained flats within a purpose built block are not "houses," but parts of a "house."[77] In any event, it is clear that the provisions can be applied to a part of a building as well as to a whole building.

3.33 The Housing Act 1985 also states that the standard can be applied to "a hut, tent, caravan or other temporary or movable structure which is used for human habitation and which has been in the same enclosure for a period of two years next before the action is taken."[78] In this particular situation, the movable structure must be occupied at the time of the application of the standard. It should be noted that the requirement is that the movable structure should have been in the same enclosure, not necessarily in exactly the same position.

3.34 It should be noted that an "underground room" is specifically defined and that a specific standard applies to such rooms.[79]

Interpretation of the standard

3.35 Surprisingly, although the definition has been in the statutes since 1954, there have been no cases which have enabled the courts to comment or give guidance on the interpretation of it. The only guidance on the standard is that originally given in the Report of the Standards of Fitness Sub-Committee of the Central Housing Advisory Committee in 1966.[80] In that Report it was stated that the standard was "expressed in such broad terms that there have been doubts about the uniformity of interpretation."[81]

To attempt to remove that doubt, the Report set out explanatory notes, which were subsequently incorporated in a Ministerial Circular,[82]

---

[75] See Public Health Act 1936, Pt. III, paras. 5.44–5.45, and Housing Act 1985, ss.264–288.
[76] Housing Act 1985, s.205(*a*) and s.266(*a*).
[77] *R. v. Lambeth London Borough Council, ex p. Clayhope Properties Ltd.* (1987) 19 H.L.R. 426.
[78] 1985 Act, s.205(*b*) and s.264(7).
[79] *Ibid.* s.282.
[80] *Our Older Homes: A call for action*, Report of the Dennington Committee, para. 45.
[81] *Ibid.* para. 43.
[82] Ministry of Housing and Local Government Circular No. 69/67 (W.O. No. 61/67).

which commented that it was hoped that the explanatory notes "will be of help to officers concerned in inspecting and reporting on the fitness of houses, and authorities should consider taking the opportunity where it is appropriate of bringing them to the attention of owners."[83]

The Circular went on to point out "There should, however, be no suggestion that these explanatory notes can themselves provide a definitive or legal test as to what constitutes unfitness." The introductory paragraph to the notes also made it quite clear that the notes were intended as a guide, and that, although the matters listed in section 604 are exhaustive, the examples given were not exclusive.[84]

The Guidance Notes

3.36 *Repair*

"To be satisfactory, any part of the structure must function in the manner in which it was intended. Any disrepair that may exist in the house and its curtilage should not be a threat to the health of, or cause any serious inconvenience to the occupants. A multiplicity of items may well cause serious inconvenience.

Consideration must be given to the condition of all parts of the fabric of the house and to the fixtures normally provided by a landlord. It is not expected that disrepair of outbuildings, of boundary walls and of the surfaces of yards and paths will be sufficient, in the absence of defects in the house itself, to render it unfit but disrepair of these items should be taken into account in assessing the unfitness of the whole house.

The internal decorative condition of a house is largely dependent on the manner of occupation and should not, therefore, be taken into account. Although exterior painting is necessary for weather protection and is desirable from the point of view of amenity, lack of it does not by itself render a house unsuitable for occupation but it may well lead to serious disrepair of woodwork."[85]

This guidance suggests that the approach should be one of assessment of the function(s) of each part of the structure, together with the assessment of the effects of defects. Although the state of the internal decoration is not normally to be taken into account,[86] it can provide an indication of the effects of defects (*e.g.* the effect of rising dampness). All items of disrepair should be taken into account, as it is the overall effect of the condition of the whole house which must be assessed.

---

[83] Ministry of Housing and Local Government Circular No. 69/67 (W.O. No. 61/67) para. 2.
[84] *Ibid.* Appendix, para. 1.
[85] *Ibid.*
[86] But see *Ellis Copp & Co.* v. *Richmond-upon-Thames London Borough Council* (1978) 3 H.L.R. 55.

Stability 3.37

"Evidence of instability is only significant if it indicates the probability of further movement which would constitute a threat to the occupants of the house."[87]

The probability of further structural movement cannot always be assessed on a single inspection, and may require monitoring over a period of time (see paras. 2.69–2.70). Obviously, local knowledge and experience can provide useful background. For example, the incidence of mining in the area and the results of subsidence can provide an indication of whether further movement is likely. It should also be noted that settlement which has resulted in floors and walls being out of level will not, per se, make a house unfit; however, where previous movement has resulted in disrepair, it should be considered under the head "repair."

Dampness 3.38

"Any dampness should not be so extensive or so pervasive as to be a threat to the health of the occupants. Such items as a small patch of damp caused by defective pointing around window reveals or door jambs or by defective rain water pipes are due to disrepair rather than inherent dampness. Care must also be taken not to be misled by temporary condensation."[88]

The causes, assessment and effects of dampness are discussed in detail in Chapter 8.

Dampness is the visible effect of a defect. However, this explanatory note makes it clear that the cause of any dampness should be assessed. Unfortunately, this cannot always be done with certainty (remembering that the local authority does not necessarily have the power to open-up the structure to attempt to identify any cause(s)) and, the effect of a defective or missing damp proof course may be identical to a bridging of the cavity by rubble; and, once a part of the structure becomes affected by dampness it will increase the likelihood of condensation (that surface being cooled by the evaporation of the moisture, and its thermal insulation capabilities being reduced because of the dampness).[88a]

It has been suggested that the clear warning that "care must also be taken not to be misled by temporary condensation" should be taken to exclude condensation from consideration under section 604, as condensation is temporary, only occurring for part of the year. (On this basis, penetrating damp could be considered temporary, as it only occurs

---

[87] Ministry of Housing and Local Government Circular No. 69/67 (W.O. No. 61/67) Appendix.
[88] Ibid.
[88a] See, in particular, "Thermal Insulation of Buildings" (1971) H.M.S.O.

when it rains.) However, the difference between "temporary" and "permanent condensation" has been clearly explained as follows:

> "The risk of condensation . . . will depend on the structure of the building—for a wall of high thermal transmittance will always present a colder face to the air within the building than one which is well insulated—and also upon the amount of free water available. In unfavourable conditions the deposition of moisture may persist for long periods and for this reason is called 'permanent' condensation.
>
> In another set of conditions, namely, when a spell of cold weather is succeeded by warmer and damper weather, damp air from outside enters the building through the ordinary process of ventilation; the fabric of the building is still relatively cold, however, and consequently moisture again makes its appearance on the surface. As soon as the fabric gets warmed up to the new prevailing temperature, this condensation will disappear and for that reason it is conveniently described, in contradistinction to permanent condensation, as 'temporary' condensation."[89]

Persistent and extensive condensation can, therefore, be sufficient by itself to make a house unfit, and (although not argued before the court, and not that relevant to the case) the Court of Appeal would seem to support this submission.[90]

3.39 *Internal arrangement*

> "Internal bad arrangement is any feature which prohibits the safe or unhampered passage of the occupants in the dwelling, *e.g.* narrow, steep or winding staircases, absence of hand rails, inadequate landings outside bedrooms, ill defined changes in floor levels, a bedroom entered only through another bedroom, and also includes a w.c. opening directly from a living room or kitchen."[91]

This head was first introduced into the standard by section 71 of the Housing Act 1969. It is in many ways different from the other matters to be considered, as it requires a much more subjective approach. Occupiers of houses with steep staircases and with ill defined changes in floor levels are frequently unaware of those features (having become used to them). Those features may not interfere with the occupants, but may well interfere with the safe passage of visitors and new-comers to the house.

---

[89] "Post War Building Studies No. 1: House Construction" (1944) H.M.S.O.
[90] *Quick* v. *Taff-Ely Borough Council* (1985) 18 H.L.R. 66.
[91] Ministry of Housing and Local Government Circular No. 68/69 (W.O. No. 67/69), Appendix, para. 24, which quotes from the Dennington Report, para. 51.

Natural lighting 3.40

"There should be sufficient natural lighting in all rooms intended for sleeping, sitting or the consumption of prepared meals to enable domestic work to be done without the use of artificial light under good weather conditions."[92]

It is important to note that the explanatory notes make no reference to the size of the window, but only to whether there is sufficient light available through windows. The amount of light available through any window will depend on various factors, including:

(a) the orientation of that window, as a window facing north will provide light of a lower intensity (although with less variations) than one facing south;
(b) the size, as a large window will let in more light (however, this should be balanced against keeping the heat-loss through the window to a minimum);
(c) the shape of the window, as a wide shallow window will enable light to reach the width of the room easier than a narrow tall window, but a tall window will enable light to reach further back into the room;
(d) the position in relation to the shape of the room, as a window in an "L" shaped room may not enable light to effectively reach all parts; and
(e) whether there is any external obstruction which prevents light reaching the window.

There are no recommended standards for daylight in dwellings, and the traditional means for assessment has been first to consider the skyline visible from a central position of the room at about table height, and second a practical test of reading newsprint in different parts of the room with curtains fully drawn back and without the aid of artificial light. Such assessment can be supported with a light meter reading to confirm the findings.

Although the explanatory notes make no reference to kitchens or to staircases and passages, it is suggested that the natural lighting should also be assessed in those parts. The kitchen is the part of the dwelling where food will be prepared and cooked, and where cleanliness is of vital importance in maintaining hygiene, and thus where lighting must be adequate for those purposes. Staircases and passages because the adequate lighting is necessary to enable occupants to avoid obstructions (such as toys), and to help visitors avoid ill defined changes in floor levels.

---

[92] Ministry of Housing and Local Government Circular No. 69/67 (W.O. No. 61/67) Appendix.

HOUSING STANDARDS

3.41 *Ventilation*

"There should be adequate ventilation of all habitable rooms and working kitchens to the external air. For example, windows should be capable of being opened to such an extent that fresh air can readily circulate to all parts of the room.

Windows, satisfactory in themselves, may be made unsatisfactory by external obstructions."[93]

Since the production of the explanatory notes in 1966, considerable work has been done on the provision of ventilation. Research has shown that the optimum ventilation rate for a dwelling as a whole is between 0.5 and 1.0 air changes per hour,[94] and that such rates are fortuitously achieved by the leakages normally found around windows and doors[95] (other than those which have been effectively draught-proofed either at the time of manufacture or subsequently). In addition, the provision of an air brick or the presence of a flue to an open fire will increase that ventilation (without the opening of a window) to around 2.0 air changes per hour.

In addition to the optimum rates for the whole dwelling, there is a need to provide ventilation at times of high moisture production (*e.g.* cooking, washing and drying of clothes and bathing). It should be noted that natural ventilation by the opening of windows relies on wind speed and direction; where the opening is to windward, air will be forced into the dwelling rather than taking the moisture laden air out. In many cases, the provision of mechanical extraction ventilation is the only means of ensuring effective ventilation.

3.42 *Water supply*

"There must be an adequate and wholesome supply within the house. While one tap may be adequate, a polluted supply would, and an intermittent supply could alone be a sufficiently serious defect to render the house unfit."[96]

It is suggested that the supply must be both adequate and wholesome supply. It must be suitable for drinking, and a supply of tank water (as often found provided to dwellings within a house in multiple occupation) may not satisfy this requirement.

It should be noted that the term is not restricted, in the definition itself, to cold water, although the explanatory notes make that assumption. It has been held in a pre-1954 case (*i.e.* prior to the introduction of

---

[93] Ministry of Housing and Local Government Circular No. 69/67 (W.O. No. 61/67) Appendix.
[94] *e.g.* B.R.E. Current Paper 31/71—see Chap. 2, para. 2.19.
[95] B.R.E. News No. 55, Winter 1981, p. 8.
[96] Ministry of Housing and Local Government Circular No. 69/67 (W.O. No. 61/67) Appendix.

this standard) that the lack of an effective supply of hot water did not in itself warrant a house being classified as unfit for human habitation.[97] However, it is suggested that the availability of a supply of hot water for domestic purposes should be taken into account as a deficiency to be considered with any other defects and conditions.

Drainage and sanitary conveniences **3.43**

"There should be a readily accessible water closet for the exclusive use of the occupants of the dwelling in a properly lighted and ventilated compartment. (Where a shared water closet for single person dwellings has been approved by the local authority, it would not constitute a defect). The water closet and bath or shower (if any) should be connected to an efficient disposal system, *i.e.* a public sewerage system, septic tank or cesspool capable of dealing with the effluent.

There should be adequate means for the disposal of water from roof surfaces and yard pavings. Gutter and disposal pipes should be of a capacity capable of dealing with the normal discharge."[98]

The term "readily accessible" is not clear, and has been taken to mean that an outside W.C. compartment must be within a reasonable distance from the rear access door to the dwelling. However, it could also be argued that an outside W.C. compartment cannot, of itself, be held to be readily accessible, particularly at night or during wet and cold weather. Although it may be (at the present time) that an outside W.C. compartment would not be sufficient in isolation to render a dwelling unfit, it should be a factor taken into account.

Traditionally, the walls to many outside W.C. compartments were left unplastered. This practice left wall surfaces uneven and difficult to maintain in a clean and hygienic state, and as such should be considered a defect.

It will be noted that the explanatory notes include references to roof and yard drainage. However, a leaking eavesgutter or rain water fall pipe should be included under the "repair" head, but the lack of any such rain water goods would be included under this head.

Facilities for the preparation and cooking of food, and for the disposal of **3.44**
waste water

"There should be a sink, with an impervious surface, located beneath the piped water supply and connected to a suitable disposal system.

---

[97] *Daly* v. *Elstree Rural District Council* [1948] 2 All E.R. 13.
[98] Ministry of Housing and Local Government Circular No. 69/67 (W.O. No. 61/67) Appendix.

> There should be either a suitable fixed solid fuel or oil fired cooking appliance or provision for the installation of a gas or electric cooker."
>
> "Generally the disposition of these facilities should make the preparation and cooking of food capable of being carried out in a convenient and hygienic manner."[99]

The size and layout and the condition of the area where these facilities are provided is also relevant. Food cannot be prepared hygienically and conveniently in a small area, or where the walls and floor are uneven and incapable of being maintained clean. A similar approach should be taken to a kitchen in a dwelling as to any other food preparation room.

When originally introduced (in 1954) this head also referred to facilities for the storage of food, but this requirement was deleted in 1969. However, such provisions can still be required in dwellings if thought necessary.[1]

Application of the standard

3.45   Section 604 makes it quite clear that the "premises shall be deemed to be unfit if, and only if, they are so far defective in one or more of those matters that they are not reasonably suitable for occupation in that condition." When the standard was first introduced into statute,[2] the Ministerial guidance stated:

> "The absence of any statutory definition of unfitness . . . has created difficulties for local authorities in exercising their powers to require repairs to, and to secure the demolition of, unfit houses. The courts have given varying interpretations of unfitness and the reference to by-laws (directed to new buildings and containing requirements often inappropriate to existing houses) has caused further confusion.
>
> [The section] follows the definition recommended by a sub-committee of the Central Housing Advisory Committee in listing the matters to which regard must be had in deciding whether a house is fit or unfit for human habitation. It departs from the recommendations of the sub-committee in that it does not specify that a house is to be regarded as unfit solely because it is defective in one of these matters. Instead, it leaves the local authority to decide in the first place whether in view of the number or degree of the defects

---

[99] Ministry of Housing and Local Government Circular No. 69/67 (W.O.N. 61/67) Appendix.
[1] Public Health Act 1961, s.32(1); and in the case of houses in multiple occupation, Housing Act 1985, s.352.
[2] As Housing Repairs and Rents Act 1954, s.9.

the house is or is not reasonably suitable for occupation in that condition.

The purpose of the section is to make it clear what are the relevant matters (and the only relevant matters) to be considered in deciding whether a house is fit or not. It is so drafted that a decision that a house is unfit may be based either upon a major defect in one of the matters listed or upon an accumulation of smaller defects in two or more of them."[3]

This cumulative approach to the assessment of the condition of a house was confirmed in a case which considered the application of this standard (but not the standard itself).[4]   **3.46**

Revised fitness standard

At the time of writing, it is proposed that the present statutory definition of "fit for human habitation" given in section 604 of the 1985 Housing Act should be replaced by a revised fitness standard. The proposals were first mooted in the Green Paper "Home Improvement—A New Approach"[5] and although the detail of the standard has not been settled, the style and approach to be adopted have been made quite clear.   **3.46A**

The approach will follow that of the tolerable standard given in section 14 of the Housing (Scotland) Act 1974, but it would seem that the criteria listed are not so extensive as in that standard.

It would appear that the revised Fitness Standard will combine criteria dealing with the fabric and structure of the dwelling and the provision of some amenities (including personal washing facilities and hot water). It has also been suggested that it will exclude internal arrangement from the matters to be considered.   **3.46B**

The style proposed (based on the Scottish tolerable standard) will provide a check-list of the criteria rather than a list of matters which can be considered. This will have the major effect of preventing a decision that a dwelling fails the fitness standard because of an accumulation of minor defects in two or more of the criteria. Each criteria must be considered separately, and minor defects under one head which are not sufficient to justify failing the house under that head will have to be disregarded.

It has been suggested that this change in the style is an attempt to make it more objective. However, it will also lower the standard in areas such as repair even though it will raise it in respect of the amenities which should be provided.

---

[3] Ministry of Housing & Local Government Circular No. 55/54, Appendix II, paras. 35–37.
[4] *Wyse* v. *Secretary of State for the Environment and Another* [1984] J.P.L. 256.
[5] Cmnd. 9513, H.M.S.O. May 1985, paras. 61–65 and Annex II.

4. SUBSTANTIAL DISREPAIR: HOUSING ACT 1985, s.190(1)(a)

3.47 In some cases, a house may be in disrepair, but the effect of the conditions may not be such that the house is "so far defective" that it is "not reasonably suitable for occupation in that condition," *i.e.* the house is not unfit for human habitation.[6]

In such cases, section 190(1)(a) of the Housing Act 1985 states that where the local housing authority—"are satisfied that a house is in such a state of disrepair that, although not unfit for human habitation, substantial repairs are necessary to bring it up to a reasonable standard, having regard to its age, character and locality" they may act to ensure those repairs are carried out.

Types of accommodation to which the standard applies

3.48 It is clear from the provision that this standard applies to a "house." The Act also states that it can be applied to:

"(a) any part of a building which is used, or is suitable for use as, a dwelling, or
(b) a hut, tent, caravan or other temporary or movable structure which is used for human habitation and has been in the same enclosure for a period of two years next before action is taken."[7]

These three circumstances have been considered in detail in paras. 3.27–3.34 in relation to fitness for human habitation, and apply equally to this standard.

Interpretation of the standard

3.49 This standard was originally introduced in 1969[8] and relies on the same enforcement procedure available for dealing with houses unfit but capable of repair at reasonable cost.[9]

At the time of its introduction the provision was closely linked with a revision of the legislation relating to grants for repairs and improvement, and area improvement action, and was seen as "being an essential instrument in the furtherance of policies to save those houses which are worth saving, and to ensure that houses improved with the help of public money do not sink into unfitness through lack of repair."[10] However, it is now seen as being more widely available for arresting the deterioration of houses generally.

---

[6] Housing Act 1985, s.604; see paras. 3.24–3.46.
[7] *Ibid*. s.205.
[8] By Housing Act 1969, s.72, inserting the provision as s.9(1A) of the Housing Act 1957.
[9] Then Housing Act 1957, ss.9–16; now Housing Act 1985, Pt. VI—see paras. 5.65–5.151.
[10] Ministry of Housing & Local Government Circular No. 64/69, para. 16.

When introduced, it was said that while—   **3.50**

> "Ministers cannot authoritatively interpret the law, the view held is that substantial repairs . . . could reasonably be taken as including one or more large items, or a combination of smaller items that together are substantial. The section was not designed to provide for the rectification of minor defects that are bound to be present in nearly all houses after a time. Rather it is meant to deal with defects which have led to a cumulative deterioration in the property's fabric and fittings."[11]

Taking the approach suggested in respect of fitness for human habitation in paras. 3.22–3.25, it will be clear that there can exist matters of disrepair to the fabric and fittings of a house, the effect of which may not be serious at that particular time and which may not cause inconvenience to the occupants of the house, but if allowed to go unremedied, could lead to further deterioration which could affect the occupation. Examples of such disrepair could be open-jointed or perished brickwork, flaking external paintwork, rotting timber to window and door frames, and cracked plaster.   **3.51**

Care should be taken to differentiate between disrepair which is such as to make the house "so far defective" that it is "not reasonably suitable for occupation in that condition" (*i.e.* makes the house unfit for human habitation) and disrepair which is substantial. It is difficult to suggest any clear guide-lines and in many cases it may be academic as the action taken in either case will be the same—the service of a Notice requiring the necessary remedial works. Where it is necessary to differentiate, the decision should be based on a comprehensive assessment of the condition and the effects of that condition. Where the disrepair interferes with the occupation, it is more likely to be unfit.

Commenting on this standard and its associated enforcement procedure in *Hillbank Properties* v. *Hackney London Borough Council*,[12] Lord Denning said: **3.52**

> "It seems to me that the policy of Parliament was to make the owners of houses keep them in proper repair. Not only so as to keep up the stock of houses, but also to see that protected tenants should be able to have their houses properly kept up. It would be deplorable if there were no means of compelling owners of old houses to keep them in proper repair."

The standard is qualified by the phrase "age, character and locality" taken from common law. The interpretation of this phrase is based on a leading case on the standard of repair—*Proudfoot* v. *Hart*.[13] In this case   **3.53**

---

[11] Ministry of Housing and Local Government Circular No. 64/69 para. 17.
[12] [1978] Q.B. 998.
[13] (1890) 25 Q.B.D. 42.

it was said that the standard of repair of a house had to be determined having regard to the occupation of it by "a reasonable minded tenant of the class who would be likely to take it," and that therefore different standards would apply in Grosvenor Square and in Spitalfields.

Too often this is taken to mean that an amount of disrepair is acceptable or permissible in certain areas, but would not be acceptable in other areas. However, it is suggested that the phrase is intended to qualify the type of repairs and materials used in those repairs. It is suggested that neither Parliament nor the courts could have meant that a house (whether in Spitalfields or Grosvenor Square) can be in disrepair, but that the repairs to be carried out (rather than the amount of disrepair allowed to exist) must be appropriate having regard to the age, the character and the locality of the house.

In terms of age, a house built to conform with the building control legislation in force at the time of construction, should not be expected, structurally, to satisfy the current building control standards. For example, the replacement of a solid nine inch brick wall by a cavity wall cannot be said to be reasonable.

In terms of character and locality, a stone wall should be repaired with stone, and a brick wall with bricks; a slate roof should be repaired with slates, and a tiled roof with tiles.

5. INTERFERENCE WITH PERSONAL COMFORT: HOUSING ACT 1985, s.190(1)(*b*)

3.54 As with the preceding standard, there will be cases where there is some disrepair, but it is not substantial, and the effect of that disrepair is insufficient to make the house "not reasonably suitable for occupation in that condition." Where representations about the disrepair are made by an occupying tenant to the local housing authority, section 190(1)(*b*) of the Housing Act 1985 states that provided the authority "are satisfied . . . that a house is in such a state of disrepair that . . . its condition is such as to interfere materially with the personal comfort of the tenant" they may act to ensure those repairs are carried out.

Types of accommodation to which the standard applies

3.55 Again, it is clear from the provision that this standard applies to "houses," and the Act also states that it can be applied to both:

"(a) any part of a building which is used, or is suitable for use as, a dwelling, or
(b) a hut, tent, caravan or other temporary or movable structure which is used for human habitation and has been in the same

INTERFERENCE WITH PERSONAL COMFORT

enclosure for a period of two years next before action is taken."[14]

These three circumstances have been considered in detail in paras. 3.22–3.34 in relation to fitness for human habitation, and apply equally to this standard.

Interpretation of the standard

This standard was originally introduced by section 149 of the Housing Act 1980, which inserted section 9(1B) in the Housing Act 1957. As with the preceding standard, the provision relies on the same enforcement procedure available for dealing with houses unfit but capable of repair at reasonable cost.[15]   **3.56**

It was said that this provision was introduced to enable local authorities to deal with matters which had been previously dealt with under the statutory nuisance provisions of the Public Health Act 1936, but which it was thought could no longer be dealt with because of the decision of the Divisional Court in *National Coal Board* v. *Thorne*.[16]   **3.57**

However, it is clear that this case has been widely misunderstood, and did not impose restrictions on the interpretation of statutory nuisance, but merely required that matters must be properly categorised under those provisions (see paras. 3.12–3.17).

Nonetheless, this provision provides a useful alternative procedure, and completes the range of standards so that all types of disrepair in houses are covered by the Housing Act 1985—from disrepair such that the house should not be occupied in that condition, to disrepair which merely interferes with comfort.

It is suggested that the approach to the interpretation of this standard should be as described in relation to fitness for human habitation in para. 3.22. However, while it may be possible to decide that any disrepair is not substantial, and that the effect of that disrepair does not make the house unsuitable for occupation, it is perhaps more difficult to decide whether the disrepair interferes with the personal comfort of the tenant.   **3.58**

There is no definition or guidance given on either "interferes materially" or "personal comfort," and it should be noted that the application of the standard requires representation to be made by an occupying tenant. It is suggested that the approach should be to determine merely that the disrepair exists, and that there is prima facie evidence (which will be that of the tenant) that that disrepair interferes with comfort. It is also suggested that whether or not disrepair interferes with comfort cannot

---

[14] Housing Act 1985, s.205.
[15] See paras. 5.80–5.99.
[16] [1976] 1 W.L.R. 543.

be judged, for example, in terms of a young, healthy working man, and must be seen in terms of the occupying tenant making the representation. Disrepair which might not interfere with the comfort of a young, healthy working man (whose time in the house may be limited) could cause discomfort and difficulties to an elderly person or a young baby, and even be a danger to young children; as such, the disrepair would be seen as material interference with the comfort by the occupying tenant.

3.59 During the debate in Parliament on its introduction, the provision was said to have been drafted wide enough to cover electric wiring in "a poor or dangerous condition."[17] However, it is suggested that this example cannot be seen as providing guidance. Wiring in a poor or dangerous condition could be capable of making a house unsuitable for occupation, as it may be dangerous to use electric lights and equipment, and while the standard of fitness under section 604 of the 1985 Act does not require artificial lighting (or even electricity), if electric wiring is present its state of repair may contribute to the overall condition of the house and be one of the matters which leads to the conclusion that the house is unfit for human habitation. Also, it should be noted that electrical wiring in a dangerous state has been held to justify premises being classified as a statutory nuisance.[18]

6. STANDARD AMENITIES: HOUSING ACT 1985, s.508

3.60 This is a list of the amenities which every dwelling is expected to contain. To that extent it establishes a "standard" of minimum amenities. Grant-aid may (in specified circumstances) be available toward the cost of providing one or more of the amenities that may be missing in a dwelling, and the local housing authority has some discretion as to whether all of the amenities must be provided.

Types of accommodation to which the standard applies

3.61 The "standard" can be applied to two types of accommodation. The main type of accommodation is a "dwelling," which is defined, for these purposes, as—"a building or part of a building occupied or intended to be occupied as a separate dwelling, together with any yard, garden, outhouses and appurtenances belonging to it or usually enjoyed with it."[19]

It can also be applied to "houses in multiple occupation" and buildings deemed to be "houses in multiple occupation." For these purposes only,[20] a "house in multiple occupation" is defined as—"a house which is occupied by persons who do not form a single household, exclusive of

---

[17] Hansard, H.C., Vol. 985, col. 91.
[18] *Bennet* v. *Preston Borough Council* (1982) (unreported). See *Environmental Health*, April 1983.
[19] 1985 Act, ss.237 and 525.
[20] *Ibid.* s.525.

any part of the house which is occupied as a separate dwelling by persons who do form a single household." Buildings deemed to be "houses in multiple occupation" include buildings which comprise separate dwellings, at least two of which lack a sanitary convenience and personal washing facilities accessible only to those living in the dwelling[21]; buildings which comprise separate dwellings, at least two of which are occupied by persons who do not form a single household[22]; and tenement blocks,[23] in which one or more of the dwellings lack one or more of the standard amenities.[24]

Interpretation of the standard

3.62 The term "standard amenities" is specifically defined (with explanatory notes) by the 1985 Act[25] as:

> "A fixed bath or shower" and a "hot and cold water supply at a fixed bath or shower." Such a fixed bath or shower "shall be in a bathroom." However, if "it is not reasonably practicable for the fixed bath or shower to be in a bathroom, but it is reasonably practicable for it to be provided with a hot and cold water supply, it need not be in a bathroom but may be in any part of the dwelling which is not a bed room."
>
> "A wash hand basin" and a "hot and cold water supply at a wash hand basin."
>
> "A sink" and a "hot and cold water supply at a sink."
>
> "A water closet." Such a water closet "shall, if it is reasonably practicable, be in and accessible from within, the dwelling or, where the dwelling forms a part of a large building, in such a position in that building as to be readily accessible from the dwelling."

However, the explanatory notes in the section state that for the purposes of special grants in respect of a "house in multiple occupation," the bath or shower must be in a bathroom, and the qualification in respect of water closets does not apply.

3.63 Together with this list of standard amenities, the Act requires that dwellings being provided with the missing amenities must, on completion of the works involved, satisfy the "full standard" or the "reduced standard."[26] These terms are used to impose additional conditions in respect of dwellings in which the standard amenities are to be provided.

---

[21] 1985 Act, s.352(6).
[22] *Ibid.* s.374.
[23] *Ibid.* s.374(2).
[24] *Ibid.* s.374.
[25] *Ibid.* s.508.
[26] See *ibid.* s.209, para. 3.65.

HOUSING STANDARDS

3.64 The "full standard" is said to have been satisfied[27] if, after the works, the dwelling:

(a) has all the standard amenities for the exclusive use of its occupants;

(b) is in reasonable repair having regard to its age, character and the locality[28];

(c) satisfies any requirements made by the Secretary of State in respect of thermal insulation[29]; and

(d) is in all other respects fit for human habitation[30];

(e) has an expected life of 15 years.

3.65 The "reduced standard" is the full standard as reduced by the local housing authority deciding to dispense wholly or partially with any of the five requirements.[31] However, the authority cannot dispense with (a) above (*i.e.* the standard amenities) in the case of a dwelling which is (or is a part of) a house or building which is a house in multiple occupation[32] (or deemed to be such) and in respect of which a notice could be served requiring works to make that house or building fit for multiple occupation.[33]

3.66 As to the discretion available to the authority to dispense with the requirement in (d) above (para. 3.64) that the dwelling is in all other respects fit for human habitation, it is suggested that there is a difference between a dwelling which is not unfit for human habitation and a dwelling which is in all respects fit for human habitation.

There would appear to be three levels of "fitness for human habitation":

(a) unfit for human habitation, where the premises are so far defective having regard to the nine matters listed, that they are not reasonably suitable for occupation in that condition;

(b) not unfit, but not in all respects fit for human habitation, where the condition is such that they are not so far defective that they are not reasonably suitable for occupation; and

(c) in all respects fit for human habitation, where they are satisfactory having regard to all of the nine matters listed.

It is however, clear that the discretion available to the authority to

---

[27] 1985 Act, s.234.
[28] See comments on this phrase in respect of substantial disrepair—para. 3.53.
[29] Given in DoE Circular No. 21/80 (W.O. No. 42/80) as amended by Appendix E to DoE Circular No. 21/82 (W.O. No. 17/82), as O.35 W/m^{2o}C for roofs and the associated roof space and ceiling. This standard retained in force by virtue of Housing (Consequential Provisions) Act 1985, s.2.
[30] 1985 Act, s.604; see paras. 3.24–3.46.
[31] *Ibid.* s.234.
[32] Defined by the 1985 Act, s.345; see paras. 6.02–6.17.
[33] Under s.352 of the 1985 Act; see paras. 6.65–6.77.

dispense with the requirement in (d) above (para. 3.64) cannot be such as to enable the authority to permit a dwelling to be unfit for human habitation, as the authority is under a duty to take action in respect of such dwellings.[34]

Proposed target standard

As noted above (paras. 3.46A–3.46B), it has been proposed[35] that the present standard of fitness for human habitation will be amended so as to include the provision of some amenities. Although the details of the proposed revised fitness standard have not yet been settled, it would appear that the amenities at present listed as "standard amenities" will be part of that fitness standard. **3.66A**

To provide an upper standard for the purposes of improvement, it is proposed that there should be a target standard. This would include the requirement that the dwelling meets the fitness standard and also that other matters over and above that standard are provided.

---

[34] See *R.* v. *Kerrier District Council, ex p. Guppys (Bridport) Ltd.* (*No.* 1) (1976) 120 S.J. 646.
[35] Cmnd. 9513, H.M.S.O. (May 1985), Annex II.

CHAPTER 4

AUTHENTICATION AND SERVICE OF NOTICES

4.01
1. Informal notices — 4.02
2. Authentication of orders, notices, demands, etc. — 4.04
3. Service of notices, demands, etc. — 4.11
4. Identification of persons to be served — 4.17

1. INFORMAL NOTICES

4.02 Many local authorities or local housing authorities have adopted a practice of issuing information or intimation notices or warning letters prior to the service of the formal or statutory notice. This practice has no statutory force, and, the issuing of such informal notices or letters may result in additional (and unjustifiable) delays before the conditions are relieved or remedied. Once it has been decided that conditions require action, formal action should be taken without delay. Any unnecessary delays could lead to allegations of maladministration causing injustice to the occupants of the house, and perhaps to actions for negligence and (in some cases—notably where the means of escape from fire at a house in multiple occupation are inadequate) breach of statutory duty against the authority.

4.03 The practice may also cause a person receiving an informal notice to carry out works which they need not do, or for which they have no proper authority to do[1] (perhaps because the local authority served the wrong person with the notice).

2. AUTHENTICATION OF ORDERS, NOTICES, DEMANDS, ETC.

Format

4.04 Under the Housing Act 1985, the Public Health Acts 1936 to 1969, and the Building Act 1984 the Secretary of State has power to prescribe the format of notices, orders and demands.[2]

The format of documents such as notices has only been prescribed by the Secretary of State for the purposes of the Housing Act 1985. However, the prescribed forms for this Act require amendments, as they were originally issued in 1972, updated in 1974, 1975 and 1981, and have

---
[1] See *Harris* v. *Hickman* [1904] 1 K.B. 563 and *Thompson* v. *Hawse* (1895) 59 J.P. 580.
[2] 1985 Act, s.614; 1936 Act, s.283(2); and 1984 Act, s.92(2).

been retained in force by section 2 of the Housing (Consequential Provisions) Act 1985 but without being further amended.[3]

There is no prescribed format for notices and demands to be served under the Public Health Acts 1936 to 1969 or the Building Act 1984, but all such documents served by the local authority must be in writing.[4] **4.05**

Authentication

The provisions for the authentication of documents under the various Acts are inconsistent and it is necessary to ensure that in each case the correct officer signs the relevant document. **4.06**

All orders made by the local housing authority under the Housing Act 1985 must be under the seal of the authority and signed by the proper officer, and all notices, demands or other written documents served under that Act must be signed by the proper officer.[5] **4.07**

Notices, demands or other written documents served by the local authority under the Public Health Acts must be signed by the clerk to the council[6] or by the proper officer,[7] or the authority may authorise an officer to sign a particular class of documents.[8] **4.08**

Demands for the recovery of expenses served under the Public Health Acts may be signed by the chief finance officer to the council.[9]

Notices and demands served under the Building Act 1984 must be signed by the proper officer, or by an officer authorised to sign such documents or that particular document.[10] **4.09**

The signing of an order, notice, demand or other document may be by the signature of the officer or by means of a facsimile of the signature (however produced),[11] and may be signed "per pro" or "for and on behalf of . . . ".[12] An order, etc., not signed by the proper officer by one of these means will be invalid.[13] If a facsimile of an officer's signature is challenged, it may be necessary to establish that that officer had authorised the method of signing and the particular delegated user. **4.10**

---

[3] Housing (Prescribed Forms) Regulations 1972 (S.I. 1972 No. 228), as amended by the Housing (Prescribed Forms) (Amendment) Regulations 1974 (S.I. 1974 No. 1511), the Housing (Prescribed Forms) (Amendment) Regulations 1975 (S.I. 1975 No. 500), and the Housing (Prescribed Forms) (Amendment) Regulations 1981 (S.I. 1981 No. 1347); retained in force by Housing (Consequential Provisions) Act 1985, s.2.
[4] 1936 Act, s.283(1); 1984 Act, s.92(1).
[5] s.193 of and Sched. 22 to the Local Government Act 1972.
[6] 1936 Act, s.284(1).
[7] Sched. 29 to the Local Government Act 1972.
[8] 1936 Act, s.284(1).
[9] *Ibid.*
[10] 1984 Act, s.93.
[11] 1936 Act, s.284(2); 1984 Act, s.93(2).
[12] *Tennant* v. *London County Council* (1957) 121 J.P. 428, see also *Plymouth Corp.* v. *Hurrell* [1968] 1 Q.B. 455.
[13] *Graddage* v. *Haringey London Borough Council* [1975] 1 W.L.R. 241.

AUTHENTICATION AND SERVICE OF NOTICES

3. Service of Notices, Demands, Etc.

Service of notices, etc., by local housing authorities/local authorities

4.11 The service of notices, demands or other documents by a local housing authority or local authority must be carried out in accordance with the general provisions given under the Local Government Act 1972[14] and the specific provisions in the Housing Act 1985,[15] the Public Health Act 1936[16] and the Building Act 1984.[17] The provisions are all basically the same.

4.12 A document may be served by delivery to the addressee in person, or by leaving it at, or sending it by post (now normally recorded delivery post[18]), to the last known or usual residence of the addressee.

Where the document is to be served on an incorporated company or body, it must be delivered to the secretary or clerk of the company or body at the registered or principal office, or sent by post addressed to the secretary or clerk.

4.13 If it is not practicable, after reasonable enquiry, to obtain the name and/or address of the person to be served, the document can be properly served by addressing it to "the owner of . . . ," "the lessee of . . . ," "the occupier of . . . ," "the manager of . . . ," or "the person having control of . . . ," and naming the relevant premises, and by delivering it to some person on those premises.

If there is no person on the premises to whom it can be delivered, the document (or a copy of it) may be affixed to some conspicuous part of the premises. (What is a conspicuous part of the premises is a matter of fact.[19])

4.14 It should be noted that the Housing Act 1985 places a specific duty on local housing authorities to take reasonable steps to identify the person(s) to be served with any documents under the Act.[20] (As to power to demand information regarding occupiers and persons having an interest in any premises, see paras. 4.17–4.19.) However, any person having an estate or interest in any premises, may give notice to the local housing authority of their interest, and the authority must record the details given,[21] and this may provide the necessary information, or be a means of obtaining such information.

[14] s.233.
[15] s.617.
[16] s.285.
[17] s.94.
[18] Recorded Delivery Service Act 1962, s.1.
[19] *West Ham Corp.* v. *Thomas* [1908] 73 J.P. 65.
[20] s.617(1).
[21] 1985 Act, s.617(2). See also the general duty on landlords under Landlord and Tenant Act 1985, ss.1–7; and in respect of houses in multiple occupation the duties imposed by registration schemes and the making of management orders under Housing Act 1985, Pt. XI.

SERVICE OF NOTICES, DEMANDS, ETC.

Service of notices on local housing authorities/local authorities

4.15 Where notices or other documents are to be served on the local housing authority or local authority, they must be delivered to the clerk of the authority, or left at the office of the clerk with some person employed there, or addressed to the authority or their clerk and posted (by recorded delivery[22]) to the authority's office.[23]

4.16 Under the Public Health Acts, where a notice is required to be served on a specified officer of the local authority, it must be addressed to that officer and posted or delivered to that officer's office or residence.[24]

4. IDENTIFICATION OF PERSONS TO BE SERVED WITH ORDERS AND NOTICES

4.17 Various categories of persons having some interest in a house, dwelling or premises are defined in the Acts, and each is delegated some responsibility in relation to conditions that may exist. Therefore each (either separately, or jointly) may be subject to action taken by the local housing authority or local authority. Each category of person to whom responsibility is delegated is given in the appropriate paragraph in the text, but the procedure for the identification of such persons is dealt with below.

There are restrictions on anybody making enquiries of another, and local authorities are in this respect no different from anyone else. The basis for the following provisions lies in the duty to reply to the requests from the local authority.

4.18 Local housing authorities and local authorities are given a general power to demand information.[25] The authority may demand of any occupier, or any person who has an interest in the house, or any manager of the house, the name and address of any person known to the addressee to be an occupier, or to have an interest in the house or to be a manager of the house.

In addition to requiring the person served to supply such information, the demand must specify:

(a) the particular function and enactment for which the information is required;
(b) the address of the premises to which the demand relates; and
(c) a time (being not less than 14 days) within which the required information must be given.

---

[22] Local Government Act 1972, s.231.
[23] *Ibid.* s.231.
[24] 1936 Act, s.285.
[25] Local Government (Miscellaneous Provisions) Act 1976, s.16. A similar provision enabling local authorities/local housing authorities to demand information is contained in s.233 of the Local Government Act 1972. However, this provision does not allow a time limit to be specified within which the information must be given, and so makes enforcement difficult.

AUTHENTICATION AND SERVICE OF NOTICES

4.19 Failure to reply within the time specified, or to knowingly give false information is an offence. The maximum fine, on conviction, is not to exceed level 5 on the standard scale.[26]

---

[26] Criminal Justice Act 1982, s.37.

CHAPTER 5

ENFORCEMENT OF THE STANDARDS

1. Action to deal with statutory nuisances	5.02	**5.01**
2. Houses unfit for human habitation	5.65	
3. Houses in substantial disrepair and in disrepair which interferes with personal comfort	5.170	
4. Houses lacking standard amenities	5.202	

1. ACTION TO DEAL WITH STATUTORY NUISANCES

5.02   The following aspects of the procedure to deal with statutory nuisances are considered:

(i) the duty to deal with statutory nuisances;
(ii) the abatement notice;
(iii) the prohibition notice;
(iv) action for non-compliance with the notice;
(v) the court hearing;
(vi) the nuisance order;
(vii) enforcement of the nuisance order;
(viii) recovery of expenses;
(ix) statutory nuisances caused by two or more persons;
(x) injunctions for statutory nuisances;
(xi) speedy procedure for urgent statutory nuisances.

The duty to deal with statutory nuisances

5.03   As stated above[1] local authorities are under a general duty to ensure that their district is inspected from time to time to detect matters that should be dealt with as statutory nuisances.[2] However, the majority of conditions requiring such action probably come to the attention of the local authority by way of individual complaints from members of the public.

5.04   Once the authority becomes aware of the existence of a statutory nuisance, it is under a duty to take action to deal with it. This duty starts from the wording of section 93 of the 1936 Act which states: "Where a local authority are satisfied of the existence of a statutory nuisance, they shall serve a notice . . ."

---

[1] See Chap. 1, para. 1.05.
[2] Public Health Act 1936, s.91.

87

The imperative "shall" is used throughout the enforcement provisions in Part III of the 1936 Act. However, while the authority must take action, that action need not be restricted to proceeding under Part III of the 1936 Act, provided some legally recognisable action is taken that will achieve the speedy abatement of the conditions and prevent their recurrence. In *Nottingham City District Council* v. *Newton*,[3] Lord Widgery C.J. said:

> " . . . the fact that the imperative word 'shall' is used in that context does not mean that the local authority are bound to choose this method of dealing with the statutory nuisance in preference to any others which may be open to them."[4]

However, the choice is limited to procedures available under legislation (statutory action). Informal action is not an option.[5]

In circumstances where statutory action is being taken by the authority which will eventually remove the statutory nuisance, account must be taken of how quickly it will be effective. For example, a house in a clearance area[6] will eventually be demolished, but if that house is a statutory nuisance action may still be necessary to abate the conditions, although the works required may be of a temporary nature.[7]

The abatement notice

5.05   The procedure under Part III of the 1936 Act starts with the service of a notice, referred to in the Act as an "Abatement Notice."

Once the authority is satisfied of the existence of a statutory nuisance it must serve an abatement notice. This is to be addressed to and served on "the person by whose act, default or sufferance the nuisance arises or continues, or if that person cannot be found, on the owner or occupier of the premises on which the nuisance arises." However, "where the nuisance arises from any defect of a structural character, the notice shall be served on the owner of the premises."[8]

5.06   Although the local authority should attempt to identify the person on whom the notice should be served, this should be limited to reasonable inquiries, and should not be such as to cause unreasonable delay in abating the statutory nuisance. Delay should not exceed the 14 days allowed

---

[3] [1974] 1 W.L.R. 923.
[4] *Ibid.* at 927.
[5] See Chap. 4, paras. 4.02–4.03.
[6] Housing Act 1985, ss.289–298.
[7] *Salford City Council* v. *McNally* [1976] A.C. 379 (H.L. affirming [1975] 1 W.L.R. 365), and *Nottingham City D.C.* v. *Newton* [1974] 1 W.L.R. 923. See also s.328 of the 1936 Act.
[8] s.93.

for response to a notice requiring information.[9] If there is any doubt about responsibility for the conditions, the notice should be served on the owner or occupier.[10] Where the person responsible is identified but no longer has any interest in the premises, the notice can still be properly addressed to that person.[11]

It is suggested that the phrase "act, default or sufferance" is self-explanatory[12]: "act" means the doing of something which resulted in the conditions arising (including lawful action[13]); "default" has the opposite meaning—the failure to take action which would have prevented the conditions (including, but not limited to, the breach of repairing obligations[14]); and "sufferance" means allowing something to happen which resulted in the conditions. **5.07**

However, even if it was the act, default or sufferance of the occupier of the premises which resulted in a statutory nuisance caused by defects of a structural character, the notice must apparently still be served on the owner of the premises.[15] (The owner's remedy would appear to be a private action for damages against the person responsible after the abatement of the statutory nuisance.)

Action may still be taken by a local authority where the statutory nuisance is within their district but the cause of the conditions is in another district, (*e.g.* a common law nuisance—see Chapter 3, para. 3.17.[16] **5.08**

Where the person responsible for the statutory nuisance cannot be found, and it is inappropriate to serve the abatement notice on the occupier, the local authority may "themselves do forthwith what they consider necessary to abate the nuisance and prevent a recurrence thereof."[17] (As to the recovery of the authority's expenses in carrying out such works, see paras. 5.52–5.55 below.) **5.09**

"Owner"

The word "owner" is defined by the Act[18] as "the person for the time being receiving the rack-rent of the premises . . . whether on his own account or as agent or trustee for any other person, or who would so **5.10**

---

[9] Local Government (Miscellaneous Provisions) Act 1976, s.16. See Chap. 4, paras. 4.17–4.19.
[10] *Rhymney Iron Co.* v. *Gellingner D.C.* [1971] 1 K.B. 589.
[11] *Thompson* v. *Gibbon* (1841) 7 M. & W. 456.
[12] See *Dover D.C.* v. *Farrar* (1982) 2 H.L.R. 32 for an example of interpretation.
[13] *Riddell* v. *Spear* (1879) 43 J.P. 317.
[14] *e.g.* under s.11 of the Landlord and Tenant Act 1985. But see also *Birmingham D.C.* v. *Kelly* (1985) 17 H.L.R. 572.
[15] 1936 Act, s.93. See paras. 5.05 and 5.06 above.
[16] *Ibid.* s.98.
[17] *Ibid.* s.93.
[18] *Ibid.* s.343.

ENFORCEMENT OF THE STANDARDS

receive the same if those premises were let at a rack-rent"; and, " 'rack-rent in relation to any property means a rent which is not less than two-thirds of the rent at which the property might reasonably be expected to be let from year to year . . . deducting therefrom the probable average annual cost of repairs, insurance and other expenses (if any) necessary to maintain the same in a state to command such rent."

5.11 Interpretation of the term "owner" may be difficult in certain circumstances. It would seem clear that, in addition to the "owner" being the person normally understood as the owner, where there is a single lessee that lessee is also an owner (and will always be so if paying the freeholder less than the rack-rent[19]). The identification of the "owner" becomes more confused where there are lessees and sub-lessees.

5.12 In *Kensington B.C.* v. *Allen*,[20] which considered the interpretation of "owner" under the equivalent provisions of the Public Health Act 1875,[21] it was held that there where more than one person received an amount equal to or more than the rack-rent, once one person had been identified it was not necessary to look further. In this case a lessee sub-let at a rack-rent, and the sub-tenant further sub-let at a rent greater than the rack-rent. In *Truman, Banbury, Buxton & Co. Ltd.* v. *Kerslake*[22] the definition of "owner" was held relevant to the question of who had the power to let the premises at a rack-rent at the time. In this latter case, both the lease and sub-lease were at rents below the rack-rent, but the sub-lease was for almost the whole of the period of the lease, so that the sub-lessee was the only person able to let at a rack-rent.

5.13 A receiver appointed by the courts is not an agent of the owner, and so cannot be an "owner,"[23] and a person whose role is merely to pay a cheque supplied by a tenant into the landlord's bank account is not an "owner."[24]

Trustees can be "owners," even though they may not receive rent and have no beneficial interest in the premises,[25] but they will be liable only to the extent of the trust funds in their possession.[26]

It would also appear that a mortgagee or a second mortgagee in possession is an "owner."[27]

---

[19] *Wareham and Dale Ltd.* v. *Fyffe* (1910) 74 J.P. 249.
[20] [1926] 1 K.B. 576. See also para. 5.56 on action where statutory nuisance caused by two or more persons.
[21] s.4.
[22] (1894) 2 Q.B. 774.
[23] *Bacup Corp.* v. *Smith* (1890) 44 Ch.D. 359.
[24] *Bottomley* v. *Harrison* [1952] 1 All E.R. 369.
[25] *Bowditch* v. *Wakefield Local Board* (1871) L.R. 6 Q.B. 567 and *Re Barney, Harrison* v. *Barney* [1984] 3 Ch. 562.
[26] *Glossop Corp.* v. *Cooper* (1913) 136 L.T.N. 90. See also para. 5.53.
[27] *Tottenham L.B.* v. *Williamson* (1893) 57 J.P. 614.

ACTION TO DEAL WITH STATUTORY NUISANCES

Content of the abatement notice

The abatement notice must require the addressee to abate the statutory nuisance, and "to execute such works and take such steps as may be necessary for that purpose."[28] It should then clearly specify the works and/or steps the local authority considers necessary both to abate the statutory nuisance and to prevent its recurrence, and should state a time limit (or limits) within which those works and/or steps must be completed. **5.14**

It should be noted that the local authority is required to specify works and/or steps which will ensure not only the abatement of the statutory nuisance, but also the prevention of its recurrence. Unfortunately, many local authorities appear to regard this procedure as being limited to ensuring only temporary works, sufficient merely for the abatement of the conditions for a limited period. There would seem to be good reason, however, for the works and/or steps specified to prevent any recurrence of the condition during the life of the premises (assuming proper future maintenance). **5.15**

It may not always be possible clearly to identify the cause(s) of conditions (particularly in the case of dampness), because authorities have no power to carry out full investigations in premises they do not own, and so exact specification of the remedial works will not be possible. However, the notice should in such cases, specify thorough investigations and the carrying out of such works as are shown to be necessary to remedy the cause(s) of the conditions and to prevent their recurrence, and then to give examples of the possible works and/or steps and to state the result to be obtained.[29] (Suggestions for the phrasing of specifications to be used in abatement notices are given in Appendix 2.) **5.16**

In any event, care must be taken clearly to state the result to be achieved. Inadequately worded notices, which do not specify sufficient works and/or steps to ensure the abatement of the conditions and prevention of a recurrence may be invalid.[30]

The works specified need not be limited to mere repair (*i.e.* restoring the premises to its original state by complying with any repairing obligations[31]), but can include improvement and the remedying of inherent defects provided that such work is necessary for the abatement of the statutory nuisance and preventing its recurrence.[32] **5.17**

The prospective lifespan of the premises is also important, and the works and/or steps specified should take this into account. In cases

---

[28] 1936 Act, s.93.
[29] See *R. v. Fenny Stratford J.J., ex p. Watney Mann (Midlands) Ltd.* [1976] 1 W.L.R. 1101.
[30] *Whatling v. Rees* (1914) 84 L.J.K.B. 1122.
[31] *e.g.* s.11 of the Landlord and Tenant Act 1985.
[32] *Birmingham D.C. v. Kelly* (1985) 17 H.L.R. 572.

where the prospective lifespan is short, the works and/or steps should be of a temporary nature.[33]

5.18 Where the notice fails to state a time limit (or limits) for the completion of the works and/or steps, then a reasonable time limit is to be assumed.[34] This will cause obvious difficulties regarding enforcement of the notice.

The time limit given must be reasonable having regard to the nature and extent of the works and/or steps required, and an unreasonably short time limit may invalidate the notice.[35] As the conditions to be dealt with may include matters which are a threat to the health of the occupiers, it may be appropriate to divide the work and/or steps into phases or programmes, requiring some to be done promptly and others at a later date.[36]

5.19 Finally, as the overriding aim of the abatement notice is the removal of conditions which are a nuisance or a threat to health, the need to allow reasonable time limit(s) for the addressee to carry out the works required should be balanced against the need to ensure the protection of the health and safety of the occupants and others as quickly and as thoroughly as is reasonably practicable.

The prohibition notice

5.20 An abatement notice is only valid if it can be shown that the statutory nuisance existed at the time of service. In many cases, it may be obvious that a statutory nuisance has occurred, and, even though not present at the time of inspection, also obvious that it will recur. A typical example applicable to housing is dampness. This may be a result of the penetration of rain through the structure or a result of condensation. The former will result in a statutory nuisance whenever there is rainfall and for a period afterwards, but may not be present during long periods of dry weather. The latter will occur during the colder periods of the year, but not during the summer months.

5.21 In any circumstances where the statutory nuisance has occurred in the past, and will recur unless works and/or steps are carried out, the local authority may serve a prohibition notice.[37]

5.22 The person on whom the prohibition notice is served, and the content of it are identical to the requirements for an abatement notice[38] and are described above in paras. 5.14–5.19.

5.23 Provided that the authority is satisfied that the statutory nuisance is likely to recur, a prohibition notice can be served even if an abatement

---

[33] *Nottingham City D.C.* v. *Newton* [1974] 1 W.L.R. 923.
[34] *Thomas* v. *Nokes* (1894) 58 J.P. 672.
[35] *Bristol Corp.* v. *Sinnot* [1918] 1 Ch. 62.
[36] *Nottingham City D.C.* v. *Newton* [1974] 1 W.L.R. 923 at 929.
[37] Public Health (Recurring Nuisances) Act 1969, s.1.
[38] *Ibid.* s.1(1).

ACTION TO DEAL WITH STATUTORY NUISANCES

notice has already been served,[39] and even if the statutory nuisance has not recurred either since its first occurrence or since the service of the abatement notice.[40] Alternatively, both can be served together, either separately or as a single document containing the two notices.[41]

Once a prohibition notice has been served, it would appear that the requirement to prevent the recurrence of the statutory nuisance remains in force indefinitely.[42]

5.23A

Appeals against abatement or prohibition notices

There is no right of appeal against an abatement or a prohibition notice. This is unnecessary as the actions and decisions of the local authority and the content of the notice are reviewed by the magistrates' court at the hearing of an information for non-compliance with a notice.

5.24

Action for non-compliance with notices

Laying an information

Where there has not been full compliance with all the requirements of an abatement notice, or where the local authority is satisfied that the statutory nuisance, although abated, is likely to recur, the authority is required to start proceedings in the magistrates' court.[43] (This duty does not preclude the authority from following some other (speedier or more effective) solution to ensure the abatement and prevention of recurrence of the conditions[44]).

5.25

Similarly, where there has been a recurrence of the statutory nuisance after service of a prohibition notice, or non-compliance with the requirements of such a notice, the local authority may start proceedings in the magistrates' court.[45]

Proceedings in either case are criminal,[46] and are started by way of information.[47] On receipt of the information the court must[48] (unless it considers the proceedings improper or vexatious[49]) issue a summons against the person served with the notice.

5.26

It should be noted that at the time of the passing of the Act, Parliament considered it so important that the statutory nuisance should be

5.27

---

[39] Public Health (Recurring Nuisances) Act 1969, s.1(3).
[40] *Peaty* v. *Field* [1971] 1 W.L.R. 387.
[41] Public Health (Recurring Nuisances) Act 1969, s.1(4).
[42] *R.* v. *Birmingham J.J., ex p. Guppy, The Times*, Oct 8, 1987,—a case under the similar provisions of Control of Pollution Act 1974.
[43] Public Health Act 1936, s.94(1).
[44] *Nottingham City D.C.* v. *Newton* [1974] 1 W.L.R. 923. See para. 5.04 above.
[45] 1969 Act, s.2(1).
[46] *Northern Ireland Trailers* v. *County Borough of Preston* [1972] 1 W.L.R. 203.
[47] See ss.1 and 2 of the Magistrates' Courts Act 1980.
[48] 1936 Act, s.94(1).
[49] *R.* v. *Bros* (1901) 66 J.P. 54.

abated that it provided for circumstances where the person responsible for the statutory nuisance, and the owner and occupier could not be found. In such cases the local authority can still bring proceedings, and the court (if satisfied that a statutory nuisance exists or is likely to recur) may address the nuisance order to the local authority, so enabling the authority to carry out the necessary works.[50]

The court hearing

5.28 Criminal proceedings start by the alleged offence being put to the accused (*i.e.* the person served with the notice) and the taking of a plea.

5.29 Where a plea of not guilty is entered, the court must proceed to hear the case in detail and may fully review the actions and decision of the local authority.

5.30 The local authority, as the prosecution, has the right to make an opening speech introducing the case to the court, and should summarise the relevant statute and case law and the evidence which will form the basis of their case. (It should be noted that the local authority cannot make a closing speech at the end of the hearing, other than to argue points of law relevant to the evidence heard and to correct any mistakes of fact in the closing speech for the defence).

5.31 The prosecution should present evidence on all of the following points:

(a) The state of the premises on or about the date of service of the abatement or prohibition notice. This will be factual evidence based on the inspection[51] carried out by an officer of the local authority, but may be supported by evidence from an occupier (or other person) to give an indication of the state over a period of time.

(b) That the local authority was satisfied that on the date of the service of the abatement notice a statutory nuisance existed, or, in the case of a prohibition notice, that a statutory nuisance was likely to recur. (Evidence on whether the conditions were prejudicial to health can be presented by an environmental health officer.[52] It will be a matter of fact and law whether the conditions were a nuisance[53]).

(c) That the person on whom the notice was served was the person by whose act, default or sufferance the statutory nuisance arose or continued, and/or (where the conditions resulted from defects of a structural character) the owner of the premises.[54]

---

[50] 1936 Act, s.94(6), and s.2(2) of the 1969 Act.
[51] See Chap. 2 on inspection of dwellings.
[52] *Patel* v. *Methab* (1980) 5 H.L.R. 80.
[53] See Chap. 3, para. 3.17.
[54] 1936 Act, s.93 and s.1(1) of the 1969 Act. See paras. 5.05 and 5.07 above.

ACTION TO DEAL WITH STATUTORY NUISANCES

(d) That the notice was properly served and authenticated.[55]
(e) That the content of the notice was correct and clearly indicated the works and/or steps to be carried out and a time period (or programme) for their completion. Also that those works and/or steps were considered by the local authority necessary to abate the statutory nuisance and/or prevent any recurrence of it, and that the time period (or programme) was considered reasonable in all the circumstances.[56]
(f) The state of the premises on or about the date of the information. This should include details of any deterioration in the conditions and whether there had been any works and/or steps carried out.
(g) That the local authority was satisfied that on the date of the information a statutory nuisance existed or was likely to recur. In the case of proceedings in respect of non-compliance with a prohibition notice, that the local authority was satisfied that the statutory nuisance had recurred between the date of service of the notice and the date of the information.
(h) The state of the premises at the date of the hearing before the court. Again, this should include details of any deterioration in the conditions and whether there had been any works and/or steps carried out (either as required by the notice or as possible alternatives to the requirements).
(i) Whether the local authority was satisfied that a statutory nuisance existed at the date of the hearing or was likely to recur.

In many cases it may be advisable to encourage the magistrates to visit the premises themselves to see the conditions. **5.32**

The defence may attempt to cast doubt on the prosecution's evidence through cross examination and by presenting its own evidence to challenge the facts. It can question each stage of the prosecution's case, in particular questioning whether the local authority had sufficient evidence on which to base each of its decisions and actions, and whether those decisions were correct. **5.33**

Provided that the court is satisfied on the following matters, it must order the defendant to pay the local authority's reasonable costs incurred by the laying of the information and the taking of proceedings (including the hearing)[57]: **5.34**

(a) that the local authority had reasonable grounds on which to base its decisions throughout the various stages;
(b) that the premises were a statutory nuisance at the date of

---

[55] See Chap. 4.
[56] See para. 5.04 above.
[57] 1936 Act, s.94(3), and s.3(2) of the 1969 Act.

service of the abatement notice, or that the premises had been such prior to the service of the prohibition notice;
(c) that the notice was properly authenticated, and served;
(d) that the person served was the person responsible for the statutory nuisance; and
(e) in the case of an abatement notice, that the statutory nuisance existed or was likely to recur at the date of the information, or, in the case of a prohibition notice, that the statutory nuisance had recurred or that the notice had not been complied with and the statutory nuisance was likely to recur.

5.35 Costs may, therefore, be recovered by the prosecution in circumstances where works had been done and the statutory nuisance abated before the date of the hearing and was unlikely to recur, provided that it is shown that the statutory nuisance existed at the date the information was laid.

5.36 It should be noted that the court need not agree with all the requirements of the notice, but must find that the statutory nuisance existed at the relevant dates.

5.37 The court must make a nuisance order[58] and (as it will have found the defendant guilty of a criminal offence[59]) may impose a fine not exceeding level 4 on the standard scale[60] where it is satisfied that:

(a) in the case of an abatement notice, that either the statutory nuisance exists at the date of the hearing, or even though abated (for whatever reason) it is likely to recur; or
(b) in the case of a prohibition notice, that a statutory nuisance had recurred or the defendant had failed to comply with any requirement of the notice, and that the statutory nuisance is likely to recur.

5.38 In those cases where the person responsible for the statutory nuisance and the owner and occupier cannot be found,[61] and the court directs the nuisance order to the local authority, the local authority will be able to recover its costs subsequently.[62]

5.39 It is again important to note that it is the state of the premises which is the main aspect of the hearing and its possible (not necessarily actual) effect on any occupiers. That the premises are not (or were not) occupied is not relevant, and the re-housing of present occupiers does not abate the statutory nuisance[63] (this would be removal merely of the

[58] 1936 Act, s.94(2), and s.2(2) of the 1969 Act.
[59] *Coventry City Council* v. *Doyle* [1981] 1 W.L.R. 1325.
[60] Criminal Justice Act 1982, s.37.
[61] See para. 5.06 above.
[62] 1936 Act, s.96 and s.3(1) of the 1969 Act.
[63] *Lambeth L.B.C.* v. *Stubbs* [1980] J.P.L. 517.

present occupiers from the threat to health, rather than removal of the threat to health of any possible occupiers—which is the main intention of the provisions).

5.40 Where the accused pleads guilty to the alleged offence and admits to being responsible for the statutory nuisance, or, in the case of an abatement notice, admits that the statutory nuisance exists at the date of the hearing, or is likely to recur; or that the statutory nuisance has occurred since the service of a prohibition notice, or that the notice has not been complied with, the court must still review the facts of the case and determine what works and/or steps are necessary to abate the statutory nuisance and prevent its recurrence, and what time limit (or limits) should be set for the completion of those requirements. In such cases the court must award the prosecution its reasonable costs incurred in laying the information and taking the proceedings.[64]

5.41 In *Salford City Council* v. *McNally*,[65] Lord Wilberforce gave guidance on the task of magistrates, particularly relevant to determining whether a statutory nuisance exists at the date of the hearing:

> "They should, in the first place, keep close to the wording of the Act and ask themselves, after they have found the condition of the premises, the questions (*i*) is the state of the premises such as to be injurious or likely to cause injury to health, or (*ii*) is it a nuisance? . . . If he answers either question in the affirmative he must make a [nuisance] order, and he should, if possible, make this as specific as he can, rather than order in general terms to abate the statutory nuisance."[66]

The nuisance order

5.42 Any nuisance order made by the court must be framed in such a way as to ensure that the conditions which constitute the statutory nuisance are both abated and prevented from recurring, or that no one is affected by those conditions.

However, the court has a wide discretion in how to achieve the aims. In *Nottingham City D.C.* v. *Newton*,[67] Lord Widgery C.J. stated:

> "In my view the position of the justices as a matter of law was this: once they were satisfied that the house constituted a statutory nuisance they were bound to make a nuisance order under section 94 but they have within the framework of the section a considerable tolerance as regards the precise terms which the nuisance order shall take. It must be directed, of course, to the abatement of the

---

[64] 1936 Act, s.94(3), and s.3(2) of the 1969 Act.
[65] [1976] A.C. 379.
[66] *Ibid.* at 389.
[67] [1974] 1 W.L.R. 923.

ENFORCEMENT OF THE STANDARDS

nuisance, that is the purpose of the order, but the section makes it clear that the justices have a discretion as to whether to require the owner to do the whole of that work referred to in the abatement notice as opposed to only part of it. Further the section expressly gives a discretion in regard to the time within which the work has to be done, and in my judgment would certainly enable the justices to divide the work into phases or programmes requiring some to be done quickly and others to be done at a later time. . . . In deciding within that wide ambit of detailed discretion just what the terms of the nuisance order should be, I have no doubt it is the duty of the justices, as common sense dictates, to look at the whole circumstances of the case and to try to make an order which is in its terms sensible and just having regard to the entire prevailing situation."[68]

5.43   The court may be assisted by the original abatement and/or prohibition notice served by the local authority, and will have the details of the condition of the premises as at the date of the hearing (which may indicate that some of the works and/or steps required by the notice have been carried out, or that conditions have further deteriorated) in deciding what works are now necessary. It may also have had evidence from the defendant of alternative or more economical means of abating the statutory nuisance.

Where a nuisance order requires works to be done, it must specify those works as clearly and as unambiguously as possible.[69] It must also specify a time limit (or limits) for the completion of the works/steps.[70]

5.44   Where the court is satisfied that the statutory nuisance is such that the building is "unfit for human habitation"[71] the nuisance order may also prohibit the use of the building for human habitation[72] until such time as a magistrates' court[73] is satisfied that the building has been made fit and withdraws the prohibition. It should be noted that there is no duty on the court to impose a prohibition on the use of the premises for human habitation, and it is suggested that the decision should be related to the gravity of the conditions and, in particular, any threat to the health of

---

[68] [1974] 1 W.L.R. 923 at 929.
[69] See *R.* v. *Wheatley* (1885) 16 Q.B.D. 34; *Whatling* v. *Rees* (1940) 79 J.P. 209; *McGillivray* v. *Stephenson* [1950] 1 All E.R. 942 and *R.* v. *Fenny Stratford J.J.*, *ex p. Watney Mann (Midlands)* [1976] 1 W.L.R. 1101.
[70] 1936 Act, s.94(2), and as applied by s.2 of the 1969 Act.
[71] This phrase is not the same as that given in s.604 of the 1985 Housing Act (which is limited—"In determining for any of the purposes of this Act . . . " *i.e.* the Housing Act 1985 only). See interpretation of fitness at common law at Chap. 3, paras. 3.21–3.23.
[72] See n. 69 above.
[73] The Act states a magistrates' court, so making it clear that this need not be the court comprised of the same bench as made the nuisance order prohibiting the use for human habitation.

occupiers. This power is in addition (and not as an alternative) to specifying the works/steps necessary to abate the statutory nuisance.

A nuisance order prohibiting the use of a building for human habitation is not a "housing order" for the purposes of Part III of the Land Compensation Act 1973,[74] and there is no provision in the Public Health Acts 1936/69 to remove any protection that may be given by the Rent Act 1977. So, although tenants cannot use a building subject to such a nuisance order for human habitation without committing an offence, they are not "displaced" for the purposes of the Land Compensation Act 1973. However, such tenants may be "homeless" for the purposes of Part III of the Housing Act 1985. (See Chapter 9 on effects of persons displaced by enforcement action.)   5.45

Appeals against the nuisance order

In addition to the general right of appeal on a point of law to the divisional court,[75] there is a right of appeal by any "person aggrieved" by the making of any order of the magistrates' court to the Crown Court.[76] On the hearing of an appeal by the Crown Court, the relevant dates are those which were considered by the magistrates' court[77] although the Crown Court must take account of the condition of the premises at the date of the appeal for the purposes of making any nuisance order.   5.46

It would appear that this right of appeal to the Crown Court is available to any "person aggrieved" by the decision of the magistrates' court, and this would seem to include the prosecution (*i.e.*, the local authority) in addition to any defendant and any owner or any other person affected by the making of the order.

Enforcement of the nuisance order

It is an offence to fail, without "reasonable excuse," to comply with the requirements of a nuisance order or knowingly to contravene the requirements of the order.[78] The maximum penalty on conviction is a fine not exceeding level 5 on the standard scale,[79] and the court may impose an additional fine not exceeding £50 for each day on which the offence continues after conviction.[80]   5.47

Proceedings for such an offence would normally be taken by the local authority in the magistrates' court (although there is nothing to prevent

---

[74] Land Compensation Act 1973, s.39.
[75] This would be an appeal for judicial review of the magistrates' court decision, started by way of case stated.
[76] 1936 Act, s.301.
[77] *Northern Ireland Trailers* v. *County Borough of Preston* [1972] 1 W.L.R. 203.
[78] 1936 Act, s.95(1), and as applied by s.3(1) of the 1969 Act.
[79] Criminal Justice Act 1982, s.37.
[80] 1936 Act, s.297 enables the court to fix a further reasonable time for compliance with the nuisance order, and order that the daily penalty be imposed for failure at the expiry of that further time without the need to return to the court.

ENFORCEMENT OF THE STANDARDS

a "person aggrieved" by the conditions initiating the proceedings), and, being criminal proceedings, would be started by way of information.[81]

5.48 Although it has been held to be a "reasonable excuse" that the defendant had no right of access onto the premises where the statutory nuisance arose,[82] this cannot relate to a statutory nuisance under section 92(1)(*a*) of the 1936 Act resulting from defects of a structural character as an owner can make an application to a magistrates' court for an order requiring the occupier to permit works/steps to be carried out.[83]

The lack of sufficient finances (or credit facilities) is not a reasonable excuse.[84]

5.49 Without prejudice to the power of the local authority to start proceedings for failure to comply with the nuisance order, the authority may also carry out the requirements of the nuisance order.[85] As to recovery of cost incurred by the authority in carrying out the works, see para. 5.52 below.

5.50 Where a nuisance order is drafted in terms of a programme of works and/or steps (requiring some matters to be dealt with promptly and others less so) it will become clear a relatively short time after the making of the nuisance order whether it is being complied with, and it would not be necessary to wait the full period stated.

Right of appeal against conviction

5.51 There is a right of appeal to the Crown Court[86] against conviction for non-compliance with a nuisance order. However, it would not be possible on such an appeal to raise matters relating to the content of the nuisance order (on which see para. 5.46 above).

Recovery of expenses

5.52 Where a local authority have carried out the necessary works or steps to abate and/or prevent a recurrence of a statutory nuisance, it may recover the expenses reasonably incurred (together with any interest at a reasonable rate[87] from the date of service of the demand for payment).[88] The expenses are to be recovered from the person responsible for the statutory nuisance arising and/or continuing (*i.e.* the person to whom the nuisance order was directed), or the person who was the

---

[81] 1936 Act, s.296.
[82] See *R. v. Cumberland J.J., ex p. Trimble* (1877) 41 J.P. 454 and *Scarborough Corporation v. Scarborough Sanitary Authority* (1876) 1 Ex.D. 344; both relating to statutory nuisances defined by the predecessor of s.92(1)(*c*) of the 1936 Act.
[83] 1936 Act, s.289; see Chap. 1, para. 1.40.
[84] *Saddleworth U.D.C. v. Aggregate and Sand Ltd.* (1970) 114 S.J. 931.
[85] Public Health Act 1936, s.95(2) and as applied by s.3 of the Public Health (Recurring Nuisances) Act 1969.
[86] 1936 Act, s.301.
[87] *Ibid.* s.291(3).
[88] *Ibid.* s.96.

owner of the premises on which the statutory nuisance arose at the time the works were carried out or a subsequent owner.[89]

The expenses may be recovered as a civil debt[90] (in the county court, or, for amounts above £5,000, in the High Court), either as a single sum or by instalments (over a period not exceeding 30 years). The local authority may collect such instalments from a rent paying occupier of the premises (provided that each instalment does not exceed the rent payable) and the occupier is empowered to deduct the amount paid to the authority from the rent payable to the owner.[91]

5.53 Where the amount is being recovered from an "owner" who is an agent collecting rent for another person, that "owner's" liability is limited to the amount collected since service of the demand, and the authority is able to recover the whole amount or the remainder from the other person.[92]

Where more than one person was responsible for the statutory nuisance, the court may apportion the expenses between those persons as it deems fair and reasonable.[93]

5.54 Until recovered, the expenses incurred (together with the interest from the date of service of the demand) is a charge against the premises.[94] The local authority is also given the powers and remedies available under the Law of Property Act 1925 for the enforcement of such a charge as if they were mortgagees, including power of sale and lease and appointment of a receiver.[95]

5.55 It should be noted that if a local authority delays in carrying out the necessary works and/or steps to abate and prevent a recurrence of the statutory nuisance (particularly if the time taken to complete those works/steps exceeds the time limit(s) specified), the reasonableness of the expenses could be open to question.

Statutory nuisances caused by two or more persons

5.56 Local authorities are able to take action against any one or more of the persons responsible for a statutory nuisance arising and/or continuing, either separately or together,[96] and the death of any of the defendants proceeded against jointly does not prevent the proceedings continuing.[97]

This general power includes the service of an abatement and/or

---

[89] 1936 Act, s.291(1).
[90] *Ibid.* s.293.
[91] *Ibid.* s.291(2).
[92] *Ibid.* s.294.
[93] *Ibid.* s.96(2).
[94] *Ibid.* s.291(1).
[95] *Ibid.* s.291(4).
[96] *Ibid.* s.97(1) and as applied by s.3 of the 1969 Act.
[97] *Ibid.* s.97(2), and as applied by s.3 of the 1969 Act.

prohibition notice, and proceedings in the magistrates' court for non-compliance with such a notice. At a hearing for non-compliance with a notice, the court may direct the nuisance order to any one or more of the defendants, and may impose a fine on any one or more, and may apportion costs as it deems fair.

Where only one or some of the persons responsible have been proceeded against, they may recover a proportion of their costs (including any costs awarded against them—*i.e.* the prosecution's costs) and any fine, from others who can be shown to bear some responsibility for the conditions.[98]

Injunctions

5.57 A local authority may, if of the opinion that the standard procedure under Part III of the 1936 Act would provide an inadequate remedy, take proceedings in the High Court in their own name for an injunction to secure the abatement and prohibition of a statutory nuisance.[99] Such proceedings may be taken even though the authority itself has suffered no damage,[1] and may be taken even if an abatement notice has been served and a hearing for non-compliance is pending.[2]

However, this power is only available where the statutory nuisance exists at the commencement of the action (*i.e.* it does not appear available where the statutory nuisance has occurred and is likely to recur, but does not exist at present—the prohibition notice circumstances).

5.58 As an alternative, an authority has a general right to take proceedings for an injunction in the county court, where such action is necessary to promote or protect the interests of the inhabitants of the authority's district.[3]

Speedy procedure to deal with urgent statutory nuisances

5.59 Where a local authority is satisfied that premises are a statutory nuisance[4] and that unreasonable delay[5] would occur if the abatement notice procedure[6] was followed, the authority may choose to initiate the speedy procedure under section 76 of the Building Act 1984.[7]

---

[98] 1936 Act, s.97(3), and as applied by s.3 of the 1969 Act.
[99] *Ibid.* s.100.
[1] *Warwick R.D.C.* v. *Miller-Mead* [1962] Ch. 441.
[2] *L.B. of Hammersmith* v. *Magnum Automated Products Ltd.* [1978] 1 W.L.R. 50.
[3] Local Government Act 1972, s.222.
[4] 1936 Act, s.92(1)(*a*) see Chap. 3, paras. 3.08–3.18.
[5] In *Celcrest Properties Ltd.* v. *Hastings B.C.* (Ch.D. October 29, 1979; unreported) it was held that an estimated 11–12 weeks to ensure completion of necessary works under Part III of the 1936 Act procedure (compared with four weeks under this procedure) was unreasonable delay and justified the speedy procedure.
[6] 1936 Act, ss.93–98; see paras. 5.03–5.56 above.
[7] Previously s.26 of the Public Health Act 1961.

This speedy procedure is available[8] even where the premises are in such a condition as to require or justify action by the authority under Part IX of the Housing Act 1985,[9] but not as an alternative to the prohibition notice procedure.

5.60

The procedure is as follows:

5.61

(a) The authority serve a notice on the same person on whom they would have served an abatement notice.[10] The notice must state[11]:
   (i) that the authority is satisfied that the premises are a statutory nuisance as defined by section 92(1)(a) of the 1936 Act,
   (ii) the defects which require to be remedied, and
   (iii) that the authority intends to commence carrying out appropriate remedial works nine days after the date of service of the notice.
(b) The person served with the notice may serve on the local authority a counter-notice within seven days of the service of the notice.[12] Such a counter-notice must state that the person intends to remedy the defects specified in the original notice.
(c) The authority may carry out works to remedy the defective state only where;
   (i) no counter-notice has been served on the authority and the nine days have elapsed,[13] or
   (ii) where a counter-notice was served but the works did not begin within a reasonable time,[14] or
   (iii) where a counter-notice was served and works were begun but reasonable progress was not made.[15]

Nothing in this provision enables works to be carried out which would knowingly contravene a building preservation order under section 29 of the Town and Country Planning Act 1947.[16]

5.62

---

[8] s.76(7) of the 1984 Act.
[9] *i.e.* unfit for human habitation (having regard to s.604 of the Housing Act 1985: see Chap. 3, paras. 3.24–3.46), or although not unfit, requiring substantial repairs (see Chap. 3, paras. 3.47–3.53), or in a condition such as to interfere materially with the comfort of the occupying tenant (see Chap. 3, paras. 3.54–3.59)—ss.189–190 of the Housing Act 1985: (see Chap. 5, paras. 5.66–5.201).
[10] See s.93 of the 1936 Act: *i.e.* the person responsible for the statutory nuisance arising and/or continuing, or, where the statutory nuisance results from defects of a structural character, the owner—see paras. 5.05 and 5.07.
[11] 1984 Act, s.76(1).
[12] *Ibid.* s.76(3).
[13] *Ibid.* s.76(2).
[14] *Ibid.* s.76(3).
[15] *Ibid.*
[16] *Ibid.* s.76(6).

Recovery of expenses

5.63 Any expenses incurred by the local authority in carrying out remedial works can be recovered from the person served with the notice.[17]

However, the court can only order the recovery of expenses if it is satisfied that the works carried out were necessary to remedy the defective state and that there would have been unreasonable delay in following the standard procedure under Part III of the 1936 Act. Similarly, where a counter-notice was served but the local authority stepped in to carry out or complete the remedial works, if the delay in starting or the progress of the works was not unreasonable, the court cannot order the recovery of the authority's expenses.[18]

The court may also inquire as to whether any of the expenses should be borne (wholly or partly) by some person other than the person served with the original notice, and may apportion the costs as appears just. In such cases the court must be satisfied that such other person(s) had notice of the proceedings and an opportunity to be heard.[19]

5.64 The amount that may be recovered by the local authority is the expense incurred in carrying out the remedial works and any interest (at a reasonable rate) from the date of service of the demand. That amount, until recovered, can be made the subject of a charge on the premises, and the authority has all of the powers and remedies under the Law of Property Act 1925 as if they were mortgagees, including power of sale and lease and appointment of a receiver.[20]

2. ACTION TO DEAL WITH HOUSES UNFIT FOR HUMAN HABITATION

5.65 The following aspects of the procedure to deal with houses unfit for human habitation are dealt with:

(i) the duty to deal with houses unfit for human habitation;
(ii) "reasonable expense";
(iii) persons having control etc.;
(iv) repair notices requiring works to make house fit;
(v) procedure to deal with houses not capable of being made fit;
(vi) undertakings and demolition and closing orders;
(vii) purchase of condemned houses for temporary accommodation.

---

[17] 1984 Act, s.76(2).
[18] *Ibid.* s.76(4).
[19] *Ibid.* s.76(5).
[20] *Ibid.* s.107.

Duty to deal with houses unfit for human habitation

5.66 As stated above,[21] local housing authorities are under a general duty to ensure that their district is inspected from time to time so as to detect (*inter alia*) houses which are unfit for human habitation.[22] In addition the authority will receive complaints from occupiers regarding the condition of the accommodation they occupy.

Howsoever the authority becomes aware that a house is unfit for human habitation, it is under a duty to take action either to ensure that it is made fit or that it is no longer available for human habitation. This duty is made clear by the imperative wording of the legislation, and has been confirmed by the courts.[23]

5.67 Because action taken under the Housing Act provisions carries with it in addition direct and indirect benefits to owners such as grant–aid for works,[24] it would seem that these provisions should be given preference over and above others which do not carry with them similar benefits to owners.[25] However, the actual conditions will dictate the appropriate action, and the authority is not limited to proceeding only under one statute, but may proceed under two or more providing there is no conflict. In certain circumstances, although action may have to be taken to require that the house is made fit, this does not prevent urgent matters (which may form a part of the whole of the works included on the notice) being dealt with under section 76 of the Building Act 1984.[26]

5.68 Where a local housing authority is satisfied that a house is unfit for human habitation it must[27] serve a repair notice requiring the house to be rendered fit[28] unless the authority is satisfied that the house cannot be rendered fit at "reasonable expense."

Where the authority is satisfied that the house cannot be rendered fit at reasonable expense it must take action[29] to ensure that either:

(a) the house is rendered fit voluntarily, or
(b) the house is no longer available for human habitation.

The wording of the legislation makes it clear that the emphasis is towards requiring the house to be made fit, and only where it is not

---

[21] See Chap. 1, para. 1.05.
[22] As defined by s.604 of the 1985 Act—see Chap. 3, paras. 3.24–3.46.
[23] R. v. *Kerrier D.C., ex p. Guppys (Bridport) Ltd. (No. 1)* (1976) 120 S.J. 646. However, no action can be taken where an owner has submitted, and the authority has approved, proposals for re-development under ss.308–311 of the 1985 Act—see s.204 and s.308(3)(*a*) of the 1985 Act.
[24] *e.g.* mandatory grants under Part XV of the 1985 Act, and vacant possession resulting from a closing order.
[25] *e.g.* Pt. III of the Public Health Act 1936—see Chap. 5, paras. 5.02–5.64.
[26] See Chap. 5, paras. 5.59–5.64.
[27] R. v. *Kerrier D.C., ex p. Guppys (Bridport) Ltd. (No. 1)* (1976) 120 S.J. 646, and see n. 23 above.
[28] Under the 1985 Act, s.189.
[29] *Ibid*. ss.264–282.

possible to render the house fit at "reasonable expense" is the emphasis shifted towards preventing it remaining available for human habitation.

5.69 It is important to note that in certain circumstances the authority must enforce these provisions in respect of houses in their ownership. Where the local housing authority is the "person having control" of the house[30] (even if there are other "owners" and/or mortgagees), and that house is repairable at reasonable expense, a repair notice cannot be served. However, where a house is owned by the authority, but someone else is the "person having control" of the house, then the repair notice must be served.

Where a house which is unfit and not repairable at reasonable expense is not solely and exclusively owned and managed by the local housing authority, the second type of procedure must be followed. It is only in cases where the house is exclusively owned and managed by the authority that neither procedure is applicable.[31]

Reasonable expense

5.70 In deciding whether houses[32] are capable of being rendered fit at "reasonable expense," the authority must have regard to 'the estimated cost of the works necessary to render them so fit and the value which it is estimated they will have when the works are completed."[33]

This is an important stage in the process followed by the local housing authority in determining the appropriate action to be taken. Interpretation of the "formula" given in the Act has been the subject of several High Court cases, but no clear and straightforward equation has been provided. What is clear from the judgments is that the "formula" is not exclusive or limited, and that the courts will not interfere with a decision of an authority provided that decision was based on a reasonable approach and took proper account of the estimated cost of the works and value of the premises.

5.71 The following guidance on the matters to be taken into account and the outline of the equation to be used in determining "reasonable expense" can be drawn from the various court decisions:

(a) Estimated cost of the works

This is the estimated cost of the works actually specified in the repair notice. However, there are other costs to be added to and subtracted from that estimated cost.[34]

---

[30] 1985 Act, ss.207 and 302, see paras. 5.77–5.78 below.
[31] *R.* v. *Cardiff City Council, ex p. Cross* (1982) 1 H.L.R. 54, and affirmed on appeal (1982) 6 H.L.R. 6.
[32] Note that the term "house" is used in s.189, and "premises" is used in s.604 of the Act (the definition of fitness for human habitation).
[33] ss.206 and 321 of the 1985 Act.
[34] See, in particular, *Hillbank Properties* v. *Hackney L.B.C.* [1978] Q.B. 998, *Ellis Copp & Co. Ltd.* v. *Richmond upon Thames L.B.C.* (1976) 3 H.L.R. 55, *Kimsey* v. *L.B. of Barnet* (1976) 3 H.L.R. 45, *F.F.F. Estates Ltd.* v. *Hackney L.B.C.* [1981] Q.B. 503,

ACTION TO DEAL WITH HOUSES UNFIT FOR HUMAN HABITATION

Added to the estimated cost of the specified works should be a contingency sum to allow for any unforeseen works which may be identified as being necessary during the carrying out of the specified works, and also an amount to cover the cost of any works which will obviously be necessary even though not specified in the repair notice (*e.g.* the making good of internal decoration damaged either by the existing state of the premises or the specified works to be carried out to render the house fit[35]). Also to be added must be an estimate (if appropriate) of the loss of rent and the cost of providing (temporary) alternative accommodation for the occupants of the premises while the works are carried out. Finally, the interest that may be payable on the capital necessary to cover the cost of the works should be included.

To be subtracted from the total estimated amount must be the amount of any grant-aid payable toward the cost of the specified works (it should be assumed that such grant-aid will be applied for and accepted). Set against the cost of any interest payable on the capital should be the possible increase in rent that may result from the carrying out of the works.[36]

As a comparison, the estimated cost of the works should be deducted from the cost of demolition if that would be the possible alternative to rendering the house fit.[37]

(b) Estimated value of the house before works

Although this is not one of the factors stated in the Act,[38] it is a relevant factor to be included in the equation.

Where demolition of the house is not practical (*i.e.* it is a part of a larger structure, the centre house in a terrace providing support to others), it has been held in one case to have no value,[39] in another to have only a nominal value[40] (although it should be noted that the value was not a point argued before the court in this case), while in a third the house was given its "open market" value.[41] The practice of attaching a nil or nominal value is based on the fact that the alternative to rendering it fit would be a prevention of it being available for human habitation.[42]

In different circumstances the courts have also attached a value to a

---

London Housing and Commercial Properties Ltd. v. *Cowan* [1977] Q.B. 148, *Harrington* v. *Croydon Corp.* [1968] 1 Q.B. 856, and *Kenny* v. *Kingston upon Thames L.B.C.* (1983) 17 H.L.R. 344.

[35] *e.g.* works following from the landlord's repairing obligations, on which see *McGreal* v. *Wake* (1984) 13 H.L.R. 107 and *Bradley* v. *Chorley B.C.* (1985) 17 H.L.R. 305.

[36] The works (and other factors) may justify amending the rent registered under the Rent Act 1977.

[37] *Dudlow Estates* v. *Sefton M.B.C.* (1978) 3 H.L.R. 91.

[38] ss.206 and 321 of the 1985 Act.

[39] *Kimsey* v. *L.B. of Barnet* (1976) 3 H.L.R. 45.

[40] *Dudlow Estates* v. *Sefton M.B.C.* (1978) 3 H.L.R. 91.

[41] *Inworth Property Co. Ltd.* v. *Southwark L.B.C.* (1977) 3 H.L.R. 67.

[42] ss.264(4)(*b*) and 265 of the 1985 Act.

house before the works, but these cases have involved "reasonable expense" in relation to repair notices requiring works to a house not unfit for human habitation.[43] In such cases the immediate possibility of preventing the house being available for human habitation is not an option—although the courts have also recognised that the intention of Parliament was to arrest deterioration which might result in the only option being to prevent it being available for human habitation.[44]

(c) Estimated value of the house after works

This is to be the freehold and open market value of the house considered as a saleable asset, and the estimated amount a willing purchaser would pay a willing vendor. The security of any tenant (and the possibility of vacant possession occurring—perhaps because of the age of the present tenant or that it is occupied on a shorthold tenancy) must be taken into account as a factor affecting a willing purchaser.[45]

5.72 To summarise, it would seem that consideration of what is "reasonable expense" is to be based on the following outline equation taking account of the factors outlined above:

A comparison of ((a) + (b)) and (c).

i.e. (the estimated cost of the works) + (the estimated value of the house before works) compared to (the estimated value of the house after works).

Where ((a) + (b)) is less than (c) the house is capable of being rendered fit at reasonable expense.

Where ((a) + (b)) is greater than (c) the house may not be capable of being rendered fit at reasonable expense.

5.73 However, a local housing authority should also take account of housing and social policy issues,[46] such as Parliament's intention to ensure proper maintenance of houses and not to encourage or permit an owner to allow a house to deteriorate to such an extent that vacant possession would be inevitable following the prevention of it being available for human habitation. Taking account of such issues may mean that the

---

[43] *i.e.* repair notices under s.189 of the 1985 Act—see paras. 5.170–5.201. See, in particular, *Ellis Copp & Co. Ltd. v. Richard upon Thames L.B.C.* (1976) 3 H.L.R. 55.
[44] *Hillbank Properties Ltd. v. Hackney L.B.C.* [1978] Q.B. 998, *per* Lord Denning at 82.
[45] See, in particular, *Bacon v. Grimsby Corp.* [1950] 1 K.B. 272, *Harrington v. Croydon Corp.* [1968] 1 Q.B. 856, *Inworth Property Co. Ltd. v. Southwark L.B.C.* (1977) 3 H.L.R. 67, *Hillbank Properties Ltd. v. Hackney L.B.C.* [1978] Q.B. 998, *Dudlow Estates v. Sefton M.B.C.* (1978) 3 H.L.R. 91, *F.F.F. Estates Ltd. v. Hackney L.B.C.* [1981] Q.B. 503, *Phillips v. L.B. of Newham* (1982) 43 P. & C.R. 54, *R. v. L.B. of Ealing, ex p. Richardson* (1982) 4 H.L.R. 125 and *Kenny v. Kingston upon Thames L.B.C.* (1985) 17 H.L.R. 344.
[46] *R. v. Maldon D.C., ex p. Fisher* (1986) 18 H.L.R. 197, *Kenny v. Kingston upon Thames L.B.C.* (1985) 17 H.L.R. 344 and *Legg v. Leominster D.C.* (unrep. C.A. December 16, 1985).

authority decides that it is "unreasonable" not to require the necessary works. This would suggest that it may be possible to consider the costs that would be incurred by the local housing authority as a result of the house not being available for human habitation (such as the costs following from the authority's duties to ensure the re-housing of any displaced occupiers, and to award any home loss and disturbance payment[47]).

5.74 The courts have also commented that it may be relevant to take account of the financial position of the person required to carry out the works to render the house fit, particularly in the case of an owner-occupier.[48] However, it is not clear why this should be relevant since, in addition to any grant-aid,[49] a loan may be available from the authority to cover the owner's outstanding contribution[50] and, if the works were carried out by the authority,[51] the costs incurred could be left as a charge against the house to be recovered when the house changes hands.[52] Taking account of the housing and social policy issues, it is suggested that the financial standing of the person required to carry out the works should be treated as of little (if any) relevance.

5.75 Finally, it should be noted that the consideration of what is "reasonable expense" is an exercise carried out by the local housing authority without reference to any owner or person having control of the house (*i.e.* there is no duty on the authority to consult, nor is there any right to make representations at this stage). However, there is a right of appeal against the action taken by the authority as a consequence of its decision as to whether the house is capable of being rendered fit at reasonable expense.[53]

It should also be noted that this exercise need not involve obtaining detailed estimates[54] (although it would seem difficult to carry out it without them).

Person having control etc.

5.76 The action to be taken by the local housing authority is directed at the "person having control" of the house or premises. Other persons having an interest in the premises may generally be contacted in the case of houses repairable at reasonable expense, and must be contacted where

---

[47] Pt. III of the Land Compensation Act 1973.
[48] *Hillbank Properties Ltd.* v. *Hackney L.B.C.* [1978] Q.B. 998.
[49] *Harrington* v. *Croydon Corp.* [1968] 1 Q.B. 856 and *Kenny* v. *Kingston upon Thames L.B.C.* (1985) 17 H.L.R. 344.
[50] Pt. XIV of the 1985 Act.
[51] Under s.193 of the 1985 Act—see paras. 5.93–5.99.
[52] Sched. 10 to the 1985 Act.
[53] s.191 of the 1985 Act—see paras. 5.85–5.86, and s.269 of the 1985 Act—see paras. 5.119–5.123.
[54] *Bacon* v. *Grimsby Corp.* [1950] 1 K.B. 272.

the house is not repairable at reasonable expense. The interpretation of the relevant terms is dealt with below.

"Person having control"

5.77   The "person having control" of the house is defined as:

"the person who receives the rack-rent of the premises (that is to say, a rent which is not less than ⅔rds of the full net annual value of the premises), whether on his own account or as agent or trustee for another person, or who would so receive it if the [premises] were let at such a rack-rent."[55]

The most authoritative decision on the interpretation of this term, *Pollway Nominees Ltd.* v. *London Borough of Croydon*[56] made it quite clear that the "person having control" is the person (or body or collection of persons) who either

(a) receives the rack-rent; or
(b) is in a position to let the "house" at a rack-rent.

Where a freeholder has let the house on a long lease at less than the rack-rent, the leaseholder becomes the "person having control"—the freeholder does not receive a rack-rent, and cannot re-let the "house"; whereas the leaseholder is in a position to sub-let it at a rack-rent. In this case the authority had served a repair notice[57] on the freeholders requiring works, *inter alia*, to the roof and common parts to a purpose-built block of 42 flats, 32 of which were held on separate 99 year leases and 10 on a single 99 year lease, Pollway (the freeholders) retaining possession of the whole of the exterior and the common parts. The total ground rents received by Pollway was substantially less than the rack-rent. The House of Lords held that because the premises had been let at ground rents which totalled less than two-thirds of the full net annual value, the freeholders could not be held to be the "person having control."

5.78   The definition of "person having control" given in the Housing Act 1985 is similar that given to the term "owner" in the Public Health Act 1936,[58] and the interpretation of "owner" under that Act may give further assistance on the interpretation of "person having control" for the purposes of the Housing Act.

It has been held that where both the lease and sub-lease were at rents below the rack-rent, but the sub-lease was for almost the whole of the period of the lease, so that the sub-lessee was the only person able to let

---

[55] 1985 Act, ss.207 and 322. The word "premises" in square brackets was substituted by para. 10 of and Sched. 5 to the Housing and Planning Act 1986.
[56] (1986) 18 H.L.R. 443.
[57] Under s.9(1A) of the 1957 Act, now re-enacted as s.190(1)(*a*) of the 1985 Act.
[58] 1936 Act, s.343—see paras. 5.10–5.13.

at a rack-rent. Thus, the "owner" is the person who had the power to let the premises at a rack-rent at the time.[59]

A receiver appointed by the courts is not an agent of the owner, and so cannot be an "owner" as defined by the Public Health Acts,[60] and neither is a person whose role is merely to pay a cheque supplied by a tenant into the landlord's bank account.[61] Trustees can be "owners," even though they may not receive rent and have no beneficial interest in the premises,[62] but will be liable only to the extent of the trust funds in their possession.[63]

"Owner"

It is important to note that the term "owner" is defined by the 1985 Act separately from "person having control," and that "owner" for these purposes is not the same as "owner" for the purposes of the Public Health Acts 1936 to 1969 or the Building Act 1984.[64]   5.79

The Housing Act 1985 states that "owner":

> "(a) means a person (other than a mortgagee not in possession) who is for the time being entitled to dispose of the fee simple in the premises, whether in possession or reversion, and
> (b) includes also a person holding or entitled to the rents and profits of the premises under a lease of which the unexpired term exceeds three years."[65]

This definition would include a leaseholder where the lease has more than three years to run, as well as a freeholder.

The repair notice requiring works to render the house fit

Where the local housing authority is satisfied that a house is unfit for human habitation (unless satisfied that it is not repairable at reasonable expense) it must serve a repair notice.[66]   5.80

This repair notice must be in the prescribed format[67] and must require

---

[59] *Truman, Banbury, Buxton & Co.* v. *Kerslake* [1894] 2 Q.B. 774.
[60] *Bacup Corp* v. *Smith* (1890) 44 Ch. D. 359.
[61] *Bottomley* v. *Harrison* [1952] 1 All E.R. 369.
[62] *Bowditch* v. *Wakefield Local Board* (1871) L.R. 6 Q.B. 567 and *Re Barney, Harrison* v. *Barney* [1984] 3 Ch. 562.
[63] *Glossop Corp.* v. *Cooper* (1913) 136 L.T.N. 90.
[64] See s.343 of the 1936 Act and s.126 of the 1984 Act.
[65] ss.207 and 322 of the 1985 Act.
[66] s.189(1) of the 1985 Act. This is a mandatory duty—see *R.* v. *Kerrier D.C., ex p. Guppys (Bridport) Ltd. (No. 1)* (1976) 120 S.J. 646—however, no action can be taken where an owner has submitted, and the authority has approved, proposals for re-development under ss.308–311 of the 1985 Act—see ss.204 and 308(3)(*a*) of the 1985 Act.
[67] Form No. 2A with appropriate amendments, Housing (Prescribed Forms) Regulations 1972 (S.I. 1972 No. 228), as amended (S.I. 1974 No. 1511, S.I. 1975 No. 500 and S.I. 1981 No. 1347), and retained in force by s.2 of the Housing (Consequential Provisions) Act 1985.

ENFORCEMENT OF THE STANDARDS

the addressee to execute the works specified in the notice within the time period (being not less than 21 days) stated in the notice.[68] It must also state that the specified works are those which, in the authority's opinion, will render the house fit for human habitation.[69]

5.81   So far as possible, the notice should clearly state the works to be carried out[70] and should be sufficiently precise to form the basis of an estimate to be obtained from a builder.[71] As local housing authorities have limited powers to carry out investigations in houses or premises not in their possession, it may not always be possible to give an exact and detailed specification of the works necessary. In such cases the repair notice should require thorough investigations to be made and the carrying out of works found to be necessary as a result of such investigations that will achieve the stated results.[72]

The time period given cannot be less than 21 days and must be reasonable having regard to the extent of the works.[73] However, it should be noted that the repair notice does not become operative until 21 days from the date of service (except where there is an appeal against the notice),[74] and so the time limit set in the notice, which must be at least 21 days, does not start to run until 21 days after service—the minimum time from the date of service to the expiry date becomes 42 days.

5.82   The repair notice must be addressed to and served on the "person having control" of the house. The local housing authority, at its discretion, may also serve copies on any other person having an interest in the house.[75] Where owners not in receipt of rents and profits have notified the authority of their interest, the authority must serve them with a copy of the notice.[76] A periodic tenant, a fixed term tenant with less than three years to run, a tenant of part of the house and a statutory tenant would appear to be excluded from having a legal interest.[77] However, there is nothing to prevent the authority from supplying such tenants with a copy of the notice requiring works to their home, and it may assist tenants in obtaining or substantiating civil claims.[78]

It is important to note that it is only where the local housing authority

---

[68] 1985 Act, s.189(2)(*a*).
[69] *Ibid.* s.189(2)(*b*).
[70] *Canterbury City Council* v. *Bern* (1982) 44 P. & C.R. 178.
[71] *Cohen* v. *West Ham Corp.* [1933] Ch. 814.
[72] *Church of Our Lady of Hal* v. *Camden L.B.C.* (1980) 255 E.G. 991.
[73] See *Ryall* v. *Cubitt Heath* [1922] 1 K.B. 275.
[74] 1985 Act, s.189(4).
[75] *Ibid.* s.189(3).
[76] *Ibid.* s.202.
[77] *Keeves* v. *Dean* [1924] 1 K.B. 685, and *Brown* v. *Minister of Housing & Local Government* [1953] 1 W.L.R. 1370.
[78] The lack of involvement of the occupying tenant should be compared with the compulsory improvement procedure under Part VII of the 1985 Act, in particular the need to consider "housing arrangements" under ss.211(3) and 213 of the 1985 Act.

is the "person having control" of the house (either because the house is owned and managed exclusively by the authority, or because there are other owners and/or mortgagees but not having control of the house) that a repair notice cannot be served. Where a house is owned by the authority, but someone else is the "person having control" of the house, then the repair notice must be served.[79]

As to authentication and service of notices, and identification of the addressee, see Chapter 4.   5.83

Once a repair notice has been served the local housing authority cannot refuse an application for a repairs grant so far as it relates to works required by the notice and the works are necessary to comply with that notice.[80] It should be noted that the applicant for the grant need not be the "person having control" of the house, *i.e.* need not be the person to whom the notice was addressed.   5.84

Appeals against repair notice requiring house to be made fit

There is a right of appeal by a "person aggrieved" by the repair notice.[81] The appeal is to the county court, and must be made within 21 days from the date of service (but excluding the actual day of service[82]) of the notice.

A "person aggrieved" must be someone who has been subjected to a legal burden or deprived of a legal entitlement,[83] but otherwise need not be the addressee of the notice (*i.e* the "person having control" of the house).

It is important to note that if the repair notice is invalid (whether because there is some material defect or informality in the notice or it was addressed to or served on the wrong person), there is no need to appeal,[84] although the question of validity can be raised on appeal.[85]

There are no grounds for appeal given in the Act, and it would seem that any aspect of procedure from the decision that the house is unfit for human habitation to the service of the notice may be questioned,[86] but   5.86

---

[79] *R. v. Cardiff City Council, ex p. Cross* (1982) 1 H.L.R. 54, and affirmed on appeal (1982) 6 H.L.R. 6.
[80] s.494 of the 1985 Act.
[81] s.191(1) of the 1985 Act.
[82] *Stewart v. Chapman* [1951] 2 K.B. 792. It would appear that the county court does not have power to extend this statutory time period—*Honig v. Lewisham B.C.* (1958 unrep.) [122 J.P.J. 302]. However, see *Arieli v. Duke of Westminster* (1983) 269 E.G. 535 and *Johnson v. Duke of Westminster* (1984) 17 H.L.R. 136.
[83] See, in particular, the view given by James L.J. in *Ex p. Sidebotham* (1880) 14 Ch.D. 458 at 465, and also *R. v. Nottingham Quarter Sessions, ex p. Harlow* [1952] 2 Q.B. 601.
[84] *Pollway Nominees Ltd. v. L.B. of Croydon* [1986] 3 W.L.R. 277 and *Graddage v. L.B. of Haringey* [1975] 1 W.L.R. 241.
[85] *Elliott v. Brighton B.C.* (1981) 79 L.G.R. 506.
[86] See, in particular, *L.B. of Wandsworth v. Winder* [1985] A.C. 461, *Cocks v. Thanet D.C.* [1983] A.C. 286, *R. v. Hackney L.B.C., ex p. Teepee Estates (1956) Ltd.* (1967) 19 P. & C.R. 87.

ENFORCEMENT OF THE STANDARDS

not matters arising after the expiration of the notice (*i.e.* not matters relating to works in default or demands for payment[87]). As the appeal can cover all these aspects including reviewing the local housing authority's decisions, it would seem that this right of appeal to the county court is preferable to an application for judicial review.[88]

5.87 On hearing the appeal, the county court may make such an order as it thinks fit, either confirming (with or without variation) or quashing the notice.[89]

If requested to do so by the local housing authority at any time before judgment is entered,[90] the judge must include in the judgment a finding as to whether the house can or cannot be rendered fit at reasonable expense.[91] (This point is of particular importance because the power of the authority to purchase a house not repairable at reasonable expense can only arise after a finding.[92])

Where a question is raised on appeal relating to whether the house is capable of being rendered fit at reasonable expense, the court makes its determination at the time of the hearing of the appeal (*i.e.* it does not review the situation that existed at the time the authority made its decision, or the date of service of the notice[93]). A challenge on the issue of reasonable expense must be on a point of law, and the courts will not interfere with the decision of the authority provided that it was based on a reasonable approach and took account of all the relevant factors.[94]

5.88 It should be noted that once an appeal has been brought within the 21 days allowed, the repair notice is suspended and does not become operative (*i.e.* the time limit specified in the notice does not start to run[95]) until the county court confirms the notice (with or without variation) and no appeal is made to the Court of Appeal against that decision within four weeks.[96] If an appeal is brought against the decision of the county court, the notice remains suspended until the Court of Appeal confirms the notice (with or without variation).[97] Withdrawal of an appeal has the same effect as a decision confirming the notice.[98]

---

[87] Sched. 10, para. 6 deals with appeals against demands—see para. 5.99. See also *Elliott v. Brighton B.C.* (1981) 79 L.G.R. 506.
[88] But see *R. v. L.B. of Southwark, ex p. Lewis Levy Ltd.* (1983) 8 H.L.R. 1.
[89] s.191(2) of the 1985 Act.
[90] If requested after judgment is entered, the request is too late—see *Victoria Square Property Co. Ltd. v. Southwark L.B.C.* [1978] 1 W.L.R. 463.
[91] 1985 Act, s.191(3).
[92] *Ibid.* s.192—paras. 5.100–5.103 below.
[93] *Leslie Maurice & Co. Ltd. v. Willesden Corp.* [1953] 2 Q.B. 1.
[94] See paras. 5.70–5.75 above.
[95] See s.189(4) of the 1985 Act—paras. 5.80–5.81 above.
[96] ss.189(4) and 191(4)(*a*) of the 1985 Act. The four week period is given by R.S.C. Ord. 59, r. 19.
[97] 1985 Act, s.191(4)(*b*).
[98] *Ibid.* s.191(4).

Where the court confirms the repair notice (with or without variations), the authority can proceed to enforce the notice after the expiry of the specified time period.[99] **5.89**

If the repair notice is quashed and the judge finds that the house is not capable of being rendered fit at reasonable expense,[1] the authority must either:

(a) purchase the house by agreement or compulsorily[2]; or
(b) follow the procedure to ensure that the house is either made fit voluntarily, or is no longer available for human habitation.[3]

Where the repair notice is quashed without any finding on whether the house is capable of being rendered fit at reasonable expense (because of a failure by the authority to request such a finding), the authority must follow the procedure to ensure that the house is either made fit voluntarily, or is no longer available for human habitation.[3] However, where the court has quashed the notice because excessive works were required, the authority must re-assess the situation and, unless satisfied that the house is not capable of being rendered fit at reasonable expense, serve a second repair notice requiring a reduced amount of works.[4]

Lessee's right to recover part of costs incurred

Where a lessee carries out the works required by a repair notice (or where the cost is recovered from a lessee by the authority after carrying out works in default[5]), that person may recover part of the cost from the lessor by agreement, or as determined by the county court.[6] Where the county court is involved it must consider the terms of the lease, including the unexpired period of the lease and the rent payable.[7] **5.90**

Where the lessor is also a lessee, part of the cost paid to the sub-lessee can be recovered from the appropriate lessor.[8]

These provisions do not apply if a charging order is in force, or an application for such an order is being considered.[9]

---

[99] 1985 Act, ss.193–205—see paras. 5.93–5.97 below.
[1] *Ibid.* s.191(3)—see paras. 5.70–5.75 above.
[2] *Ibid.* s.192—see paras. 5.100–5.103 below.
[3] *Ibid.* ss.264–282—see paras. 5.104–5.169 below.
[4] See *Cochrane* v. *Chanctonbury R.D.C.* [1950] 2 All E.R. 1134.
[5] Under Sched. 10 to the 1985 Act—see paras. 5.93–5.99 below.
[6] 1985 Act, s.199.
[7] *Ibid.* s.199(2).
[8] *Ibid.* s.199(3).
[9] *Ibid.* s.199(4).

Charging orders

5.91 If the works required by a repair notice are carried out, the value of the house will have been increased. If the cost of carrying out the works was borne by one of the owners, that person may protect the expenditure by applying to the local housing authority for a charging order to be made.[10] The effect of such a charging order is to create a charge against the house equal to the amount of the cost incurred by the applicant (including the cost of the application), to produce an annuity payable over 30 years at a rate of 6 per cent.[11]

An application for such a charging order must include a certificate from the proper officer of the authority that the works have been satisfactorily carried out and accounts and vouchers in relation to the works,[12] and, if the application is approved, certified copies of the certificate, accounts, vouchers and charging order must be filed by the proper officer.[13]

Once made, the charging order takes priority over virtually all other existing or future charges, with only certain exceptions.[14]

Protection of rights of tenants and lessees

5.92 It may be that the repair notice was served on and enforced against a "person having control" of the house who is not responsible for the repairs under a lease, contract or covenant, or that the works required were carried out by an owner who was not the "person in control" of the house and who was not responsible for the repairs under such a lease, contract or covenant. Nothing in Part VI of the Act, or any action taken by the authority or by an owner in response to the authority's action, under this Part of the Act prejudices action for breach of obligations under such a lease, contract or covenant.[15]

Similarly, nothing in this Part of the Act, or any action taken by the authority or by an owner in response to the authority's action, under this Part of the Act prejudices a tenant's right to take action for breach of the landlord's repairing obligations (either expressed or implied).[16]

---

[10] 1985 Act, s.200(1). The Secretary of State has power to prescribe the format of charging orders (s.201(1) of the 1985 Act), but does not appear to have done so.
[11] *Ibid.* s.200(3) and (4). Different rates cannot be set to apportion the burden—see *Holborn and Frascati* v. *London County Council* (1916) 80 J.P. 225.
[12] *Ibid.* s.200(2).
[13] *Ibid.* s.200(6).
[14] *Ibid.* s.201(2).
[15] *Ibid.* s.203(1) and (2).
[16] *Ibid.* s.203(3). Such obligations include those implied by ss.10–11 of the Landlord and Tenant Act 1985—see *McGreal* v. *Wake* (1984) 13 H.L.R. 107.

ACTION TO DEAL WITH HOUSES UNFIT FOR HUMAN HABITATION

Enforcement of repair notice requiring house to be made fit

Where the works required by the repair notice have not been completed within the period specified in that notice[17] (or the period set for compliance after an appeal[18]), the local housing authority may carry out the required works themselves and recover the cost incurred.[19]   5.93

The use of the discretionary term "may" in the section makes it clear that the authority need not proceed to carry out the works, but nor should they adopt a fixed policy either that they will or will not carry out such works, since such a policy would be a fetter on the exercise of their discretion and vulnerable to challenge in the High Court.[20] It is suggested that the discretion is not one which would allow no action where the house is unfit at the expiry of the notice; rather it is a discretion as to the most appropriate action to deal with the condition of the house at that time. It may be that the majority of the works have been completed and only minor items remain—in which case it may be more appropriate to take action under other provisions to deal with those items[21]; it may be that no works have been carried out and conditions have deteriorated to such an extent that the house is no longer capable of being made fit at reasonable expense.   5.94

Once the notice has expired the authority must review the situation, and determine the appropriate action. Clearly, where the house is still unfit for human habitation, the authority must take some action (the Act does not contemplate a house being unfit and no action being taken by the authority[22]). In such cases the action must be either: 5.95

(a) the carrying out of works to render the house fit for human habitation, and recovery of the cost incurred; or
(b) action to ensure that the house is no longer available for human habitation.[23]

The action decided upon should be appropriate (having regard to the reasonable cost involved in making the house fit) at the time—*i.e.* at the expiry of the repair notice.

---

[17] *i.e.* the reasonable period for the completion of the works (being at least 21 days) from the date the notice becomes operative. See s.191 of the 1985 Act—paras. 5.80–5.81 above.
[18] See s.191(2) and (4) of the 1985 Act—paras. 5.85–5.89 above. Clearly the court on appeal may vary the time period set in the notice.
[19] s.193 of the 1985 Act.
[20] *Elliott* v. *Brighton B.C.* (1981) 79 L.G.R. 506.
[21] *e.g.* s.190 of the 1985 Act, Pt. III of the Public Health Act 1936, or s.76 of the Building Act 1984.
[22] If the house is unfit, action must be taken under s.189 or s.264 of the 1985 Act—see *R.* v. *Kerrier D.C., ex p. Guppys (Bridport) Ltd. (No.* 1) (1976) 120 S.J. 646. These duties would still apply even after a repairs notice has been served under s.189 and has expired.
[23] 1985 Act, ss.264–282—see paras. 5.104–5.169 below.

5.96 Where the authority decide to carry out the necessary work in default of the person having control of the house they may give written notice to that person and to any owner, stating their intention to do so.[24] It is deemed to constitute the offence of obstruction for an addressee of the notice of intention (or any workman or contractor employed by such a person) to attempt to carry out works at any time after seven days from the date of service of the notice of intention, and while there is any workman or contractor employed by the authority in the house. However, if it is shown that the works attempted were urgently necessary to obviate danger to occupants, there is no offence.[25]

Although the authority is not required to give notice of their intention to carry out the works, there is no offence without such notice being served. Nor would there be an offence even if notice of intention had been served, if the original repair notice was invalid.[26]

5.97 If, after receiving notice of the intended action, an occupier, owner, or person having control of premises prevents any officer, agent or workman of the authority from carrying the works, the authority may apply to a magistrates' court, and the court may, by order, require that person to permit the authority to do what is necessary.[27] Failure to comply with the court order is an offence, with a maximum penalty on conviction of a fine not exceeding £20 for each day on which the offence continues.[28]

5.98 Any expenses incurred by the local housing authority in carrying out the works, together with interest (at a reasonable rate determined by the authority) from the date when the demand for payment is served until it is settled, can be recovered by action in the county court or High Court (depending on the amount involved).[29]

The money is to be recovered from the person on whom the notice was served, unless:

(a) on appeal against the notice the court has directed that some other person(s) pay all or part of the cost of the works; or
(b) the person on whom the notice was served is an agent or trustee for another, in which case that person's liability is

---

[24] 1985 Act, s.194(1). Note that the authority must serve copies on owners who have notified the authority of their interest under s.202 of the Act. There is no prescribed format for such notice of intention, but it is suggested that suitable amendments could be made to Form No. 1 Housing (Prescribed Forms) Regulations 1972 (S.I. 1972 No. 228).
[25] *Ibid.* s.194(2). Obstruction is dealt with in s.198 of the Act—see Chap. 1, paras. 1.16–1.17.
[26] *Canterbury City Council* v. *Bern* (1982) 44 P. & C.R. 178.
[27] 1985 Act, s.195.
[28] *Ibid.* s.195(2).
[29] *Ibid.* Sched. 10.

limited to the amount that has been in her hands on behalf of the other person since the date of service of the demand.

In addition the local housing authority has the same powers and remedies for enforcement of the charge against the house under the Law of Property Act 1925, and the power, as if they were mortgagees by deed having powers of sale and lease, to accept the surrender of leases and to appoint a receiver. However, the power to appoint a receiver cannot be exercised until one month from the date the charge takes effect.[30]

5.99 There is a right of appeal against a demand for the recovery of expenses, available to any person aggrieved. Such appeal must be within the 21 days from date of service of the demand before it takes effect. On such appeal, no question may be raised which might have been raised on appeal against the repair notice.[31] No appeal is necessary where the demand relates to works carried out following an invalid repair notice.[32]

Purchase and repair of house found on appeal to be not capable of being made fit at reasonable expense

5.100 Where the result of an appeal against a repair notice is the quashing of the notice together with a finding by the judge that the house is not capable of being rendered fit at reasonable expense,[33] the authority may purchase the house.[34] It is important to note that this power is only available where the authority have requested the judge to make such a finding.[35]

5.101 If the authority cannot reach an agreement to purchase the house, they may submit a compulsory purchase order to the Secretary of State for confirmation, but must do so within six months of determination of the appeal or this procedure cannot be used.[36] The Secretary of State may accept an undertaking from an owner or mortgagee of the house that the works specified in the original repair notice will be carried out within a stated period, and only confirm the compulsory purchase order if such an undertaking is breached.[37]

5.102 If the authority purchase the house compulsorily, they must forthwith carry out the works specified in the original repair notice[38]—*i.e.* they

---

[30] 1985 Act, para. 7 of Sched. 10.
[31] *Ibid.* para. 6 of Sched. 10. As to appeals against repair notices, see s.191—paras. 5.85–5.89 above.
[32] *West Ham Corp. v. Benabo* [1934] 2 K.B. 253.
[33] s.191(2) and (3) of the 1985 Act—see paras. 5.70–5.75 above.
[34] s.192 of the 1985 Act.
[35] s.191(3) of the 1985 Act, see—*Victoria Square Property Co. Ltd. v. Southwark L.B.C.* [1978] 1 W.L.R. 463.
[36] 1985 Act, s.192(2).
[37] *Ibid.* s.192(3).
[38] *Ibid.* s.192(4).

must carry out the works specified as necessary to make the house fit for human habitation. Although this duty does not appear to apply if the house is purchased by agreement, it is clear that purchase of a house under this provision adds the house to the permanent housing stock of the authority,[39] and it should therefore be rendered fit for human habitation.

5.103 The procedure for, and consequences of, compulsory purchase under this provision are those given in Part XVII of the 1985 Act, and the purchase and repair costs would be taken from the Housing Revenue Account.

It is suggested that the amount to be paid for the house under this provision would be the estimated value of the house before the works as accepted by the court on the hearing of the appeal.[40]

Procedure to deal with houses unfit and not capable of being made fit at reasonable expense

The time and place notice

5.104 Where the authority is satisfied that a house is unfit for human habitation and is not capable of being rendered fit at reasonable expense it must serve a time and place notice.[41] Such a notice must also be served where the county court on appeal quashes a repair notice and gives a finding that the house is not capable of being made fit at reasonable expense and the authority decides not to purchase the house (see paras. 5.100–5.103).[42]

The time and place notice must be in the prescribed format,[43] and must state a time (being at least 21 days after the date of service) and a place when the condition of the house, any proposals for carrying out works and the future use of the house will be considered by the authority.[44]

The notice must be served on the "person having control" of the house,[45] any other owner of the house, and every mortgagee it has been

---

[39] *Victoria Square Property Co. Ltd.* v. *Southwark L.B.C.* [1978] 1 W.L.R. 463.
[40] See para. 5.71 on determining reasonable expense.
[41] s.264(1) of the 1985 Act. This is a mandatory duty—see *R.* v. *Kerrier D.C., ex p. Guppys (Bridport) Ltd. (No.* 1) (1976) 120 S.J. 646. However, no action can be taken where an owner has submitted, and the authority approved, proposals for re-development under ss.308–311 of the Act—see s.308(3)(*a*) of the 1985 Act.
[42] s.191(3) of the 1985 Act.
[43] Form No. 6 (or, where the action is being taken in respect of a part of a building, Form No. 12) with appropriate amendments, Housing (Prescribed Forms) Regulations 1972 (S.I. 1972 No. 228) as amended and retained in force by s.2 Housing (Consequential Provisions) Act 1985.
[44] s.264(1) of the 1985 Act.
[45] Defined at s.322 of the 1985 Act—see paras. 5.77–5.78 above.

ACTION TO DEAL WITH HOUSES UNFIT FOR HUMAN HABITATION

reasonably practicable to ascertain.[46] It should be noted that the time and place notice must be served, not only on the person having control, but also on owners and mortgagees.[47]

The authority is not required to serve the time and place notice on a periodic tenant, a tenant on a fixed term with less than three years unexpired, a statutory tenant or a tenant of a part of a house.[48] However, there is nothing to prevent the authority so doing, and it is good practice to consult such tenants about the future of their home and the effects of any decision made by the authority on that home.[49] **5.105**

It is important to note that where a house which is unfit and not repairable at reasonable expense, and which is not in the exclusive ownership and management of the local housing authority (*i.e.* some other person is an owner or mortgagee), whether or not the authority is the "person having control" of the house, this procedure must be followed.[50] **5.106**

Proposals from owners etc.

If any person who had to be served with a time and place notice (other than a tenant given a copy at the authority's discretion) intends to submit proposals for the carrying out of works to the house, written notification of the intention must be given to the authority within 21 days from the day of service of the notice, and a list of the proposed works (not a detailed specification) submitted within such reasonable time as the authority allow.[51] **5.107**

In the case of a repair notice, it is the authority who specify the works and state that those works will, in their opinion, make the house fit.[52] However, in this situation it is the proposer who has to provide the list of works, but the list must be such as to satisfy the authority that the house will be made fit. It is suggested that when the authority receives written notification of the intention to submit proposals, the authority should give (at least) details of the principal grounds on which it decided that the house was unfit.[53] **5.108**

---

[46] This would include action under s.16 of the Local Government (Miscellaneous Provisions) Act 1976—see Chap. 4, paras. 4.17–4.19.
[47] This is not so with a repair notice, see s.189(3) of the 1985 Act—see para. 5.82.
[48] See *Brown* v. *Minister of Housing & Local Government* [1953] 1 W.L.R. 1370.
[49] Compare with the procedure for compulsory improvement (Pt. VII of the 1985 Act) and the duty to consider "housing arrangements" under ss.211(3) and 213 of the 1985 Act.
[50] *R.* v. *Cardiff City Council, ex p. Cross* (1982) 1 H.L.R. 54, and affirmed on appeal (1982) 6 H.L.R. 6.
[51] s.264(3) of the 1985 Act.
[52] s.189(2) of the 1985 Act—see para. 5.80 above.
[53] The same format could be adopted as that for a notice of principal grounds as served under para. 4(2) of Sched. 22 to the 1985 Act on an objector to a C.P.O. s.264(2) of the 1985 Act.

The consideration by the authority

5.109 At the meeting specified in the time and place notice, any person who had to be served with such a notice (*i.e.* other than a tenant given a copy at the authority's discretion) is entitled to be heard.[54] At the authority's discretion, other persons (such as the tenant) can be heard.

The authority must not have decided the action to be taken prior to the meeting,[55] and their considerations of proposals for the carrying out of works cannot be determined without having regard to the reasonable expense involved.[56] It would appear that there is no reason why an owner or mortgagee making a proposal to carry out works should not apply for, and obtain, a grant under Part XV of the Act (although, as an undertaking is not the equivalent of a repair notice, there is no mandatory grant).

Undertakings and demolition and closing orders

The undertaking

5.110 After consultation the authority may, if it thinks fit, accept an undertaking from an owner or a mortgagee.[57] Such an undertaking may be for either of the following:

(a) the carrying out of works which will (in the authority's opinion) make the house fit within a specified period; or
(b) that the house will not be used for human habitation, until the house has been made fit to the satisfaction of the authority and the undertaking cancelled.

5.111 There is no set format for an undertaking, but clearly it should be in writing. In the case of an undertaking to carry out works (as in para. 5.110(a) above), it should list the works to be carried out, state that those works will (in the authority's opinion) render the house fit, and the period (which should be reasonable having regard to the nature and extent of the works) within which those works are to be completed.[58]

Where the intention is to carry out works, but such works would be so extensive and would result in the occupier being displaced, the appropriate undertaking would be that the house will not be used for human habitation (*i.e.* as in para. 5.110(b) above).

---

[54] s.264(2) of the 1985 Act.
[55] *Fletcher* v. *Ikeston Corp.* (1931) 96 J.P. 7.
[56] *Stidworthy* v. *Brixham U.D.C.* (1935) 2 L.J.C.C.R. 41 and *Coleman* v. *Dorchester R.D.C.* (1935) 2 L.J.C.C.R. 113.
[57] s.264(4) of the 1985 Act.
[58] *Johnson* v. *Leicester Corp.* [1934] 1 K.B. 638.

ACTION TO DEAL WITH HOUSES UNFIT FOR HUMAN HABITATION

5.112 Once an undertaking that the house will not be used for human habitation is accepted by the authority, it is an offence for any person knowingly to use, or permit the use of, the house for that purpose, carrying a maximum penalty, on conviction, of a fine not exceeding level 5 on the standard scale,[59] and a further fine not exceeding £5.00 for each day (or part of a day) on which the offence continues after conviction.[60]

5.113 As soon as an undertaking that the house will not be used for human habitation takes effect,[61] any protection given to a tenant by the Rent Acts is removed. However, such an undertaking is a "housing order or undertaking" for the purposes of Part III of the Land Compensation Act 1973,[62] and the occupier will be entitled to rehousing,[63] disturbance payment[64] and in certain circumstances home loss payment.[65]

5.114 There is no specific right of appeal against the authority's refusal to accept an undertaking, but there is a right of appeal against the action taken by the authority in consequence of their refusal.[66] (See paras. 5.119–5.123 and 5.140–5.143 below).

Demolition/closing orders
5.115 Where:

(a) no undertaking is offered;
(b) an undertaking is offered, but not accepted by the authority;
(c) an undertaking to carry out work is accepted, but the work is not completed within the time specified in the undertaking; or
(d) an undertaking not to use the house for human habitation, but is contravened;

the authority must forthwith[67] make a demolition or closing order in respect of the house.[68]

The authority must make a demolition order, unless the house is a listed building,[69] or demolition would be inappropriate because of the effect on another building[70] (*e.g.* where the house is in the centre of a terrace and gives support to others). In the case of action taken by the

---

[59] Criminal Justice Act 1982, s.37.
[60] 1985 Act, s.264(6).
[61] *Ibid.* s.264(5).
[62] Land Compensation Act 1973, s.29(7).
[63] *Ibid.* s.39.
[64] *Ibid.* s.37.
[65] *Ibid.* s.29.
[66] s.269 of the 1985 Act.
[67] *i.e.* within a reasonable time—*London Borough of Hillingdon* v. *Culter* [1968] 1 Q.B. 124.
[68] 1985 Act, s.265(1).
[69] *Ibid.* s.304(1).
[70] *Ibid.* s.265.

ENFORCEMENT OF THE STANDARDS

authority in respect of a part of a building or an underground room deemed to be unfit,[71] a closing order is the only option.[72]

The demolition order

5.116   A demolition order must be in the prescribed format,[73] and must state[74]:

(a) the premises to which it applies;
(b) a period (not less than 28 days from the date the order becomes operative[75]) within which those premises must be vacated; and
(c) a period (not less than six weeks from the date of vacation) within which the premises must be demolished.

5.117   Having made the demolition order, the authority must serve copies of it on the following persons[76]:

(a) the "person having control" of the premises[77];
(b) any other person who is an owner[77]; and
(c) every mortgagee whom it has been reasonably practicable to ascertain.[78]

No time is set within which the copies of the order must be served, and it is to be assumed that they must be served forthwith. As to identification of persons to be served, authentication and service of orders, see Chapter 4.

There is no requirement to serve a copy of the order on an occupier, but it is suggested that it is good practice to do so, and at that time additional information could be provided regarding the consequence of the order and the entitlement of the occupier to rehousing, disturbance and possibly home loss payments.[79]

---

[71] 1985 Act, s.282.
[72] *Ibid.* s.266.
[73] Form No. 7, with appropriate amendments, Housing (Prescribed Forms) Regulations 1972 (S.I. 1972 No. 228) as amended and retained in force by s.2 of the Housing (Consequential Provisions) Act 1985.
[74] s.267 of the 1985 Act.
[75] Although the time limit must be at least 28 days from the date the order becomes operative, the actual time within which the house must be vacated is 28 days from the service of the notice to quit served by the authority under s.270 of the 1985 Act. As the authority will not know if an appeal is to be brought until the 21st day after service of copies of the demolition order, a period longer than 28 days is sensible to avoid confusion.
[76] s.268 of the 1985 Act.
[77] Defined by s.322 of the 1985 Act—see paras. 5.77–5.78.
[78] Identifying such persons would include serving requisitions for information under s.16 of the Local Government (Miscellaneous Provisions) Act 1976—see Chap. 4, paras. 4.17–4.19.
[79] See Pt. III of the Land Compensation Act 1973.

ACTION TO DEAL WITH HOUSES UNFIT FOR HUMAN HABITATION

The order becomes operative 21 days from the date of service of copies of the order. However, where an appeal is brought within the 21 day period, the order is suspended and does not become operative until the appeal is determined.[80] **5.118**

Right of appeal against demolition orders

There is a right of appeal within 21 days of the date of service of the order[81] to the county court available to a "person aggrieved" by a demolition order.[82] A "person aggrieved" must be someone who has been subjected to a legal burden or deprived of some legal entitlement.[83] **5.119**

A person who is in occupation of the premises which are the subject of the demolition order and who has a lease or agreement with an unexpired term of three years or less is specifically excluded from a right of appeal.[84] Such a tenant who is not given a specific right of appeal could apply for judicial review of the authority's decision to make the order if it can be shown that they took account of matters which were irrelevant to this procedure, or failed to take account of a relevant matter.[85]

The correct action for a person aggrieved by the refusal of the authority to accept an undertaking either to carry out works to make the house fit, or not to use, or permit the use of, the house for human habitation is to appeal against the demolition order to the county court. **5.120**

The county court on appeal may make such order as it thinks fit, either confirming the order (with or without variation) or quashing it, and it may also accept from an appellant any undertaking that would have been accepted by the local housing authority at the meeting set by the time and place notice.[86] Provided that, where that appellant was served with a time and place notice[87] and the undertaking relates to the carrying out of works to make the house fit, the court may only accept the undertaking if written notification of the intention to submit proposals was given to the authority and a list of the proposed works submitted.[88] It is clear that the court could accept an undertaking (of either type) from a person who was not served with a time and place notice, **5.121**

---

[80] s.268(2) of the 1985 Act.
[81] This does not include the actual date of service—see *Stewart* v. *Chapman* [1951] 2 K.B. 792. It would appear that the county court does not have power to extend this statutory time period—*Honig* v. *Lewisham B.C.* (1958 unrep.) [122 J.P.J. 302]. However, see *Arieli* v. *Duke of Westminster* (1983) 269 E.G. 535 and *Johnson* v. *Duke of Westminster* (1984) 17 H.L.R. 136.
[82] s.269(1) of the 1985 Act.
[83] See, in particular, the view given by James L.J. in *Ex p. Sidebotham* (1880) 14 Ch.D. 458 at 465, and also *R.* v. *Nottingham Quarter Sessions, ex p. Harlow* [1952] 2 Q.B. 601.
[84] s.269(2) of the 1985 Act.
[85] *R.* v. *Ealing L.B., ex p. Richardson* (1982) 4 H.L.R. 125 and *Legg* v. *Leominster D.C.* (unrep. C.A., December 16, 1985).
[86] 1985 Act, s.269(3).
[87] *Ibid.* s.264—see paras. 5.104–5.106.
[88] *Ibid.* s.269(4).

provided that person has a right of appeal. Any undertaking accepted by the court has the same effect as one accepted by the authority.[89]

The extent of the variation available to the county court[90] is not clear. Variation would not include substituting a closing order, since this would amount to quashing the demolition order. To achieve this the court would have to quash the demolition order, leaving it to the authority to make a closing order.

It is clear, however, that the court must consider the facts as they exist at the time of the hearing of the appeal.[91]

5.122 Once an appeal has been brought the demolition order is suspended and does not become operative until the county court confirms the order (with or without variation) and no appeal is made to the Court of Appeal against that decision within four weeks.[92] If an appeal is brought against the decision of the county court, the order remains suspended until the Court of Appeal confirms the order.[93] Withdrawal of an appeal has the same effect as a decision confirming the order.[94]

5.123 Once the demolition order has become operative[95] (or on the determination of, withdrawal of, or end of a period allowed for, an appeal[96]), no further matter may be raised.[97]

Enforcement of a demolition order

5.124 As soon as the order becomes operative, the local housing authority must serve a notice to quit on the occupier or occupiers of the premises to which the order applies.[98]

This notice must be in the prescribed format,[99] and must state[1]:

---

[89] 1985 Act, s.269(5) of *ibid*. s.264(4), (5) and (6)—see paras. 5.110–5.114.

[90] In one case, it was held that the court could extend the time for the vacating of the house, to allow time for the occupiers to be rehoused—*Pocklington* v. *Melksham U.D.C.* [1964] 2 Q.B. 673. However, this case was prior to Pt. III of the Land Compensation Act 1973, when it was the responsibility of the landlord to re-house not the authority, and the authority would not be appealing against the order.

[91] *Leslie Maurice & Co. Ltd.* v. *Willesden Corp.* [1953] 2 Q.B. 1.

[92] s.268(2) and s.269(6) of the 1985 Act. The four week period is that given by R.S.C. Ord. 59, r. 19.

[93] s.269(6)(b) of the 1985 Act.

[94] s.269 of the 1985 Act.

[95] *i.e.* 21 days from the date of service—see para. 5.118.

[96] s.269(6) of the 1985 Act—see para. 5.119.

[97] s.268(2) of the 1985 Act.

[98] Although the provision does not state forthwith, service cannot be delayed—*R.* v. *Epsom and Ewell Corp., ex p. R.B. Property Investments (Eastern)* [1964] 1 W.L.R. 1060.

[99] Form No. 10, with appropriate amendments, Housing (Prescribed Forms) Regulations 1972, as amended and retained in force by s.2 of the Housing (Consequential Provisions) Act 1985.

[1] s.270(1) of the 1985 Act.

(a) the effect of the demolition order;
(b) the date by which the order requires the premises to be vacated[2]; and
(c) that the occupier(s) must vacate the premises before the date set in the order or before 28 days from the service of this notice to quit, which ever is the later.[3]

If there is an occupier still in occupation at the expiry of the time given for vacating the premises, an application may be made to the county court by the local housing authority or an owner,[4] and the court must order vacant possession within not less than two weeks and not more than four weeks.[5] **5.125**

If the action to obtain possession through the county court is taken by the local housing authority, it may recover its costs from any owner of the premises.[6]

Nothing in the Rent Acts prevents possession being obtained after service of this notice to quit.[7]

Once the date by which the premises must be vacated has passed (*i.e.* the date stated in the notice to quit served by the authority), it is an offence to enter, or to permit someone to enter, into occupation of the premises or a part of it. Such an offence carries a maximum penalty, on conviction, of a fine not exceeding level 5 on the standard scale,[8] and of a further fine not exceeding £5.00 for every day (or part) on which occupation continues after conviction.[9] **5.126**

It has been held that it is necessary to prove knowledge of the effect of a demolition order before conviction can be obtained for such an offence, and, that even though a demolition order has been registered in the Local Land Charges Register, the person entering into, or permitting, occupation is not deemed to have knowledge of the order or its effect.[10] It suggested that it is necessary for local housing authorities to issue a notice giving a clear explanation of the effects of a demolition order with replies to requests for searches of the Local Land Charges Register, and for such a notice to be posted in a conspicuous part of the premises subject to such an order as soon as they become vacant.

---

[2] See s.267(1) of the 1985 Act—para. 5.116.
[3] See n. 77 above.
[4] Note that the application may be made by any owner (see s.322 of the 1985 Act—para. 5.79).
[5] 1985 Act, s.270(2).
[6] *Ibid.* s.270(4).
[7] *Ibid.* s.270(3). Note, it is the service of the notice to quit which removes Rent Act protection, not the demolition order—*Marela* v. *Machorowski* [1953] 1 Q.B. 565.
[8] Criminal Justice Act 1982, s.37.
[9] 1985 Act, s.270(5).
[10] *Barber* v. *Shah* (1985) 17 H.L.R. 584.

ENFORCEMENT OF THE STANDARDS

Disinfestation of premises to be demolished

5.127 Special provision is made where it appears to the local housing authority that the premises to be demolished are infested with vermin, and it is necessary to disinfest the premises before demolition (to prevent the vermin seeking other harbourage after the demolition).[11]

The authority may, at any time between the date of making the demolition order and the date it becomes operative[12] serve a notice[13] on the owner(s) stating that the authority intends to cleanse the premises before demolition.

Once such a notice has been served, demolition cannot take place until after the authority has carried out the disinfestation and has issued a further notice[14] to that effect.[15] The authority may carry out the disinfestation as soon as the premises have been vacated. However, an owner can ensure that demolition proceeds without unnecessary delay by serving notice on the authority requiring the disinfestation to be carried out within 14 days of the receipt of that notice, and can demolish the premises at the end of that period, whether or not the authority has disinfested.[16]

5.128 It should be noted that service of a notice of intention to disinfest will mean that the period given for the demolition of the premises after it has been vacated starts to run from the date of the authority's notice that they have completed the disinfestation, or from the end of the 14 day period given by the owner's notice served on the authority.[17]

Power to permit reconstruction

5.129 Once a demolition order has become operative,[18] an owner[19] may submit proposals for the reconstruction, enlargement or improvement of the house (or buildings including the house) to the authority.[20] If the authority are satisfied that the result will be one or more houses fit for human habitation, they may extend the period set by the demolition

---

[11] s.273 of the 1985 Act.
[12] *i.e.* 21 days from the date of service (or determination of an appeal)—see para. 5.118.
[13] Form No. 8, with appropriate amendments, Housing (Prescribed Forms) Regulations 1972, as amended and retained in force by s.2 of the Housing (Consequential Provisions) Act 1985.
[14] Form No. 9, with appropriate amendments, Housing (Prescribed Forms) Regulations 1972, as amended and retained in force by s.2 of the Housing (Consequential Provisions) Act 1985.
[15] 1985 Act, s.273(2)(*b*).
[16] *Ibid.* s.273(3).
[17] *Ibid.* s.273(4).
[18] *i.e.* 21 days from the date of service (or determination of an appeal)—see para. 5.118.
[19] Or any other person the authority are satisfied can (or will be able to) put the proposals into effect—s.274(1)(*b*) of the 1985 Act.
[20] s.274(1) of the 1985 Act.

ACTION TO DEAL WITH HOUSES UNFIT FOR HUMAN HABITATION

order[21] within which the premises are to be demolished,[22] and must serve notice to that effect on every person having an interest in the house.[23]

The authority may further extend the time period (more than once, if necessary) provided that they are satisfied there is no unreasonable delay in starting or progressing with works,[24] and on every extension of the time period must serve notice on every person having an interest in the house.[25]

Once the works are completed to the satisfaction of the authority, they must revoke the demolition order, but this is without prejudice to future action under Part IX of the 1985 Act.[26]

There is no prescribed format for notification of the authority's extension of the time allowed for demolition, or for the revocation of the demolition order.

Where the authority has paid out any compensation in the form of well-maintained payment[27] or owner-occupier's or business supplement,[28] and the person who received the compensation is entitled to an interest in the house at the time the demolition order is revoked, the authority can recover that compensation by issuing a demand.[29] **5.130**

Substitution of closing order

Once a demolition order has become operative,[30] an owner (or any other person with an interest in the premises) may submit proposals to the authority for the use of the premises other than for human habitation. The authority, if it thinks fit, may determine the demolition order and substitute a closing order.[31] **5.131**

Copies of the notice determining the demolition order and copies of the closing order must be served on the following persons[32]:

(a) the "person having control" of the premises[33];
(b) any other person who is an owner[33]; and

---

[21] *i.e.* the period of at least six weeks from the date of vacation, or of service of the notice of completion of disinfestation—ss.267 and 273 of the 1985 Act respectively—see paras. 5.116 and 5.127.
[22] 1985 Act, s.274(2).
[23] *Ibid.* s.273(4).
[24] *Ibid.* s.274(3).
[25] *Ibid.* s.273(4).
[26] *Ibid.* s.274(5).
[27] *Ibid.* Sched. 23.
[28] *Ibid.* Sched. 24.
[29] *Ibid.* s.590.
[30] *i.e.* 21 days from the date of service (or determination of an appeal)—see para. 5.118.
[31] 1985 Act, s.275(1).
[32] *Ibid.* s.275(2).
[33] Defined by s.322 of the 1985 Act—see paras. 5.77–5.79.

(c) every mortgagee whom it has been reasonably practicable to ascertain.[34]

There is no prescribed format for notification of the authority's decision to determine the demolition order, but it is suggested that the closing order should follow the prescribed format with appropriate amendments.[35]

Buildings which become listed

5.132 Where premises in respect of which a demolition order has taken effect[36] become a listed building[37] prior to demolition,[38] the authority is required to determine the demolition order and instead make a closing order.[39]

The authority must serve notice that the demolition order has been determined[40] and a copy of the closing order[41] on the following persons[42]:

(a) the "person having control" of the premises[43];
(b) any other person who is an owner[43]; and
(c) every mortgagee whom it has been reasonably practicable to ascertain.[44]

5.133 Where a building is not yet listed, but is being considered for listing, the Secretary of State may notify the authority of that consideration, and the authority must act as if it was already listed.[45]

---

[34] Identifying such persons would include serving requisitions for information under s.16 of the Local Government (Miscellaneous Provisions) Act 1976—see Chap. 4, paras. 4.17–4.19.
[35] Form No. 14 Housing (Prescribed Forms) Regulations 1972, as amended and retained in force by s.2 of the Housing (Consequential Provisions) Act 1985.
[36] *i.e.* 21 days from the date of service (or determination of an appeal)—see para. 5.118.
[37] Under s.54 of the Town and Country Planning Act 1971—see s.303 of the 1985 Act.
[38] *i.e.* the period of at least six weeks from the date of vacation, or of service of the notice of completion of disinfestation—ss.267 and 273 of the 1985 Act respectively—see paras. 5.116–5.127.
[39] s.304(2) of the 1985 Act.
[40] There is no prescribed form for the notice.
[41] Form No. 3, with appropriate amendments, Housing (Prescribed Forms) Regulations 1972, as amended and retained in force by s.2 of the Housing (Consequential Provisions) Act 1985.
[42] s.304(2) of the 1985 Act, which refers back to s.268(1) of the Act.
[43] Defined by s.322 of the 1985 Act—see paras. 5.77–5.78.
[44] Identifying such persons would include serving requisitions for information under s.16 Local Government (Miscellaneous Provisions) Act 1976—see Chap. 4, paras. 4.17–4.19.
[45] 1985 Act, s.304(3).

ACTION TO DEAL WITH HOUSES UNFIT FOR HUMAN HABITATION

Demolition

After the premises have been vacated, the owner is required to demolish the premises within the time period stated in the order.[46] However, there is a right to apply for permission to reconstruct the house,[47] and a right to apply for a closing order to be substituted for the demolition order so as to allow the use of the premises for some purpose other than human habitation.[48] In addition, where the premises becomes a listed building[49] at any time between the making of the demolition order and before demolition has occurred, the authority must substitute a closing order.[50]   5.134

Assuming that no applications for either reconstruction or alternative use have been made and the premises have not become a listed building, and the premises have not been demolished, the local housing authority is required to carry out the demolition and sell the materials resulting from that demolition.[51] Although no time period is set within which the authority must demolish, it should be forthwith; however, any delay does not invalidate the demolition order.[52]

The authority can grant a single contract for the demolition of the premises and allow the contractor to keep or sell the materials.[53] But it must be noted that as the owner is not placed under a duty by the Act to remove the materials from the site, the actual cost of removal cannot be recovered by the authority and cannot be set against the amount raised on sale of the materials.[54]   5.135

Where the cost of demolition (excluding the site clearance) exceeds income from the sale of the materials, the authority may recover the outstanding amount from the owner, if necessary, by proceedings in the county court as a civil debt.[55] Where there is more than one owner, the court determines the amounts to be paid by each[56] having regard to their respective interests and obligations (particularly repairing obligations[57]).[58] If one owner settles the debt with the authority, that owner may recover from the other owner(s) such amount (if any) as the court determines.[59]   5.136

---

[46] See 1985 Act, s.267—para. 5.116.
[47] *Ibid.* s.274—see para. 5.129.
[48] *Ibid.* s.275—see para. 5.131.
[49] Under s.54 of the Town and Country Planning Act 1971—see s.303 of the 1985 Act.
[50] s.304 of the 1985 Act.
[51] s.271 of the 1985 Act.
[52] *Martin* v. *Downham R.D.C.* (1953) 51 L.G.R. 430.
[53] *London Borough of Hillingdon* v. *Culter* [1968] 1 Q.B. 124.
[54] *Wigan Corp.* v. *Hartley* [1963] C.L.Y. 1664.
[55] s.272(1) of the 1985 Act.
[56] s.272(2)(*a*) of the 1985 Act.
[57] *e.g.* under s.11 of the Landlord and Tenant Act 1985.
[58] 1985 Act, s.272(6).
[59] *Ibid.* s.272(2)(*b*).

ENFORCEMENT OF THE STANDARDS

Where income from the sale of the materials exceeds the cost of demolition (excluding the cost of clearing the site), the authority must pay that surplus over to the owner.[60] Where there is more than one owner, the amounts paid to each is as agreed between them; or, if they cannot agree, the authority is deemed to be a trustee,[61] and may pay the surplus into court,[62] leaving it to the owners to apply to court for a determination of how the amount should be divided up (the court must then take account of the respective interests and obligations[63]).

The closing order

5.137 A closing order must be in the prescribed format,[64] and must state[65]:

(a) the premises to which it applies; and
(b) that the use of those premises for any purpose not approved by the local housing authority is prohibited.

The authority may approve the use of the premises for any purpose (other than human habitation) and must not unreasonably withhold approval.[66]

5.138 Having made the closing order, the authority must serve copies of it on the following persons[67]:

(a) the "person having control" of the premises[68];
(b) any other person who is an owner[68]; and
(c) every mortgagee whom it has been reasonably practicable to ascertain.[69]

No time limit is set within which the copies of the order must be served, and it is to be assumed that they must be served forthwith.

As to identification of persons to be served, authentication and service of orders, see Chapter 4.

There is no requirement to serve a copy of the order on an occupier, but it is suggested that it is good practice to do so, and at the same time

---

[60] 1985 Act, s.272(3).
[61] *Ibid.* s.272(4).
[62] Under s.63 of the Trustee Act 1925. See County Court Rules 1981, Ord. 11.
[63] *e.g.* under s.11 of the Landlord and Tenant Act 1985 and s.272(6) of the 1985 Act.
[64] Form No. 14, with appropriate amendments, Housing (Prescribed Forms) Regulations 1972, as amended and retained in force by the Housing (Consequential Provisions) Act 1985, s.2.
[65] 1985 Act, s.267.
[66] *Ibid.* s.267(3).
[67] *Ibid.* s.268.
[68] Defined by s.322 of the 1985 Act—see paras. 5.77–5.79.
[69] Identifying such persons would include service of requisitions for information under the Local Government (Miscellaneous Provisions) Act 1976, s.16—see Chap. 4, paras. 4.17–4.19.

additional information could be provided regarding the consequences of the order and the entitlement of the occupier to rehousing, disturbance and possibly home loss payments.[70]

The order becomes operative 21 days from the date of service of copies of the order. However, where an appeal is brought within the 21 day period, the order is suspended and does not become operative until the appeal is determined.[71]   **5.139**

Right of appeal against closing orders

There are two separate rights of appeal available to the county court.   **5.140**

The first is a right of appeal by a "person aggrieved" by the local housing authority's refusal to approve the use of the premises for some purpose other than human habitation.[72] The appeal must be brought within 21 days of the date of the refusal. A "person aggrieved" must be someone who has been subjected to a legal burden or deprived of some legal entitlement.[73]

The second is a right of appeal within 21 days of the date of service of the order[74] to the county court against the closing order.[75] Again this right is available to a "person aggrieved"[76]; however, a person who is in occupation of premises the subject of the closing order, having a lease or agreement with an unexpired term of three years or less is specifically excluded from the right of appeal.[77] Such a tenant, not given a specific right of appeal, could apply for judicial review of the authority's decision to make the order if it can be shown that they took account of matters which were irrelevant to this procedure, or failed to take account of a relevant matter.[78]

The correct action for a person aggrieved by the refusal of the authority to accept an undertaking either to carry out works to make the house fit, or not to use, or permit the use of, the house for human habitation would be to appeal against the closing order to the county court.   **5.141**

The county court on appeal may make such order as it thinks fit, either confirming the order (with or without variation) or quashing it,   **5.142**

---

[70] See Pt. III of the Land Compensation Act 1973.
[71] s.268(2) of the 1985 Act.
[72] s.267(2) of the 1985 Act.
[73] See, in particular, the view given by James L.J. in *Ex p. Sidebotham* (1880) 14 Ch.D. 458 at 465, and also *R. v. Nottingham Quarter Sessions, ex p. Harlow* [1952] 2 Q.B. 601.
[74] This does not include the actual date of service—see *Stewart v. Chapman* [1951] 2 K.B. 792.
[75] s.269(1) of the 1985 Act.
[76] See *Ex p. Sidebotham* (1880) 14 Ch.D.458, *per* James L.J. at 465, and *R. v. Nottingham Quarter Sessions, ex p. Harlow* [1952] 2 Q.B. 601.
[77] s.269(2) of the 1985 Act.
[78] *R. v. Ealing L.B., ex p. Richardson* (1982) 4 H.L.R. 125, and *Legg v. Leominster D.C.* (unrep., C.A., December 16, 1985).

and it may also accept from an appellant any undertaking that could have been accepted by the local housing authority at the meeting set by the time and place notice.[79] Provided that where the appellant was served with a time and place notice[80] and the undertaking relates to the carrying out of works to make the house fit, the court may only accept the undertaking if written notification of the intention to submit proposals was given to the authority and a list of the proposed works submitted.[81] It is clear that the court could accept an undertaking (of either type) from a person who was not served with a time and place notice, provided that person has a right of appeal.

An undertaking accepted by the court has the same effect as one accepted by the authority.[82]

At the hearing of an appeal the court must consider the facts as they exist at that time.[83]

5.143 Once an appeal has been brought, the closing order is suspended and does not become operative until the county court confirms the order (with or without variation) and no appeal is made to the Court of Appeal against that decision within four weeks.[84] If an appeal is brought against the decision of the county court, the order remains suspended until the Court of Appeal confirms the order (with or without variation).[85] Withdrawal of an appeal has the same effect as a decision confirming the order.[86]

Once the closing order has become operative[87] (or on the determination of, withdrawal of, or end of a period allowed for, an appeal[88]), no further matter can be raised.[89]

Enforcement of a closing order

5.144 As soon as the order becomes operative, it is an offence for a person knowingly to use, or permit the use of, the premises in contravention of the order (*i.e.* use for human habitation or for a non-approved alternative use).[90] The maximum penalty on conviction of such an offence is a fine not exceeding level 5 on the standard scale,[91] and a further fine not

---

[79] 1985 Act, s.269(3).
[80] *Ibid.* s.264—see paras. 5.104–5.106.
[81] *Ibid.* s.269(4).
[82] *Ibid.* ss.269(5), 264(4), (5) and (6)—see paras. 5.110–5.113.
[83] *Leslie Maurice & Co. Ltd.* v. *Willesden Corp.* [1953] 2 Q.B. 1.
[84] *Ibid.* ss.268(2) and 269(6). The four week period is that given by R.S.C. Ord. 59, r. 19.
[85] *Ibid.* s.269(6)(*b*).
[86] *Ibid.* s.269.
[87] *i.e.* 21 days from the date of service—see para. 5.139.
[88] 1985 Act, s.269(6)—see para. 5.140.
[89] *Ibid.* s.268(2).
[90] *Ibid.* s.277.
[91] s.37 Criminal Justice Act 1982.

ACTION TO DEAL WITH HOUSES UNFIT FOR HUMAN HABITATION

exceeding £50 for each day (or part of a day) on which the offence continues after conviction.[92]

5.145 Once the order has become operative, nothing in the Rent Acts prevents the owner[93] obtaining possession. As occupiers are entitled to rehousing and to disturbance (and perhaps home loss) payments[94] as soon as the order has become operative, it should not be a problem for the owner to ensure that the premises are vacated. However, the Act does not provide for the authority to take proceedings for possession where an occupier is reluctant to vacate, and in such cases it must be left to the owner to proceed (and a prosecution of the occupier would seem vindictive in these circumstances).

5.146 It has been held that it is necessary to prove knowledge of the effect of a closing order before a conviction for such an offence can be obtained, and that even though a closing order will be registered in the Local Land Charges Register, it does not mean that the person entering into, or permitting, occupation has knowledge of the order or its effects.[95] (See comments in para. 5.126 above, on this point.)

Determination of a closing order

5.147 If the authority are satisfied that the premises subject to a closing order have been rendered fit for human habitation, they must terminate the order.[96] Where a part of the premises has been rendered fit for human habitation, the authority must determine the order so far as it relates to that particular part.

5.148 A "person aggrieved" by the authority's refusal to determine a closing order (either in respect of the whole or a part of the premises) has a right of appeal to the county court within 21 days of the refusal.[97] A "person aggrieved" must be someone who has been subjected to a legal burden or deprived of some legal entitlement.[98] However, a person in occupation of the premises (*i.e.* using the building for an approved purpose, and not using the premises for human habitation which use would be an offence[99]) under a lease with three years or less to run is specifically excluded from this right of appeal.[1]

---

[92] s.277 of the 1985 Act.
[93] Defined by s.322 of the 1985 Act—see para. 5.79. Note that possession is to be obtained by an "owner," and not the "person having control" of the house.
[94] Pt. III of the Land Compensation Act 1973.
[95] *Barber v. Shah* (1985) 17 H.L.R. 584.
[96] 1985 Act, s.278(1).
[97] *Ibid.* s.278(2).
[98] See, in particular, the view given by James L.J. in *Ex p. Sidebotham* (1880) 14 Ch.D. 458 at 465, and also *R. v. Nottingham Quarter Sessions, ex p. Harlow* [1952] 2 Q.B. 601.
[99] s.277 of the 1985 Act—see para. 5.144.
[1] 1985 Act, s.278(3).

ENFORCEMENT OF THE STANDARDS

5.149 Where the authority have paid out any compensation in the form of well-maintained payment[2] or owner-occupier's or business supplement,[3] and the person who received the compensation is entitled to an interest in the house at the time the closing order is determined, the authority is entitled to recover that compensation by issuing a demand.[4]

Substitution of demolition order

5.150 At any time after a closing order has become operative,[5] the authority may determine the closing order and substitute a demolition order.[6] If the authority decide to substitute a demolition order, the procedure to be followed is the same as if the authority had originally decided to make such a demolition order (including the rights of appeal).[7]

This power to substitute a demolition order is not available where the closing order was made in respect of the following[8]:

(a) a part of a building or an underground room[9]; or
(b) a listed building or a building which is being considered for listing after a demolition order became operative.[10]

Closing orders in respect of part of a building

5.151 A local housing authority can make a closing order in respect of either of the following[11]:

(a) a part of a building used, or suitable for use, as a dwelling;
(b) an "underground room"[12] which is deemed to be unfit.[13]

The procedure followed is the same as that for making a closing order in respect of the whole of the premises,[14] including the acceptance of undertakings, but (obviously) excluding demolition orders.

It is important to note that an underground room which is not deemed to be unfit for human habitation,[15] may still be unfit having regard to the standard of fitness applicable to all premises.[16]

---

[2] Under 1985 Act, Sched. 23.
[3] *Ibid.* Sched. 24.
[4] *Ibid.* s.590.
[5] *i.e.* 21 days from the date of service of a copy of the order, *ibid.* s.268—see para. 5.139.
[6] *Ibid.* s.279(1).
[7] *Ibid.* s.279(3); *ibid.* s.265 and ss.267–275—see paras. 5.115–5.126.
[8] *Ibid.* s.279(2).
[9] *Ibid.* s.266.
[10] *Ibid.* s.304—see paras. 5.132–5.133.
[11] *Ibid.* s.266.
[12] Defined by s.280 of the 1985 Act.
[13] s.282 of the 1985 Act.
[14] However, the prescribed format for the closing order is given as Form No. 13, with appropriate amendments, Housing (Prescribed Forms) Regulations 1972, as amended and retained in force by the Housing (Consequential Provisions) Act 1985, s.2.
[15] s.282 of the 1985 Act.
[16] s.604 of the 1985 Act—see Chap. 3, paras. 3.24–3.46.

ACTION TO DEAL WITH HOUSES UNFIT FOR HUMAN HABITATION

Security of unoccupied buildings

5.152 Provision is made in the Local Government (Miscellaneous Provisions) Act 1982[17] to enable local authorities[18] to take action to ensure that permanently or temporarily unoccupied buildings are secured and not a danger to public health. These provisions are available in respect of any building, but are dealt with here because of the relevance to premises which are the subject of a closing order.

5.153 Where it appears to a local authority[18] that any building in its area is unoccupied and is either—

(a) not effectively secured against unauthorised entry; or
(b) likely to become a danger to public health

the authority may carry out works to ensure the building is effectively secured against unauthorised entry and prevent it becoming a danger to public health.[19]

Before carrying out the works, the authority must serve a notice on every owner or occupier.[20] This notice must specify the works it intends to carry out[21] and state that the authority will commence the works after a period of 48 hours from the service of the notice.[22]

If the authority is of the opinion that the works must be carried out immediately, service of the notice is not a prerequisite to starting the works. In addition, service of the notice is not necessary where it is not reasonably practicable to ascertain the name and address of an owner or an occupier.[23]

Obviously, the authority should not delay unreasonably carrying out the works while attempting to identify owners or occupiers (particularly since the provision is intended to prevent problems arising, and delay may result in such problems). It is suggested that where some delay can be allowed, that delay should be limited to the 14 day period allowed for response to a requisition for information,[24] even where it is only possible to serve such a requisition by posting a copy on some conspicuous part of the building.[25]

5.154 Where a notice is served under these provisions, there is a right of appeal against the notice to the county court within 21 days of the

---

[17] At ss.29–32 of the 1982 Act.
[18] Defined by s.29(4) of the 1982 Act as a District or London Borough Council, or the Common Council for the City of London.
[19] 1982 Act, s.29(2).
[20] *Ibid*. s.29(3).
[21] *Ibid*. s.29(7).
[22] *Ibid*. s.29(9).
[23] *Ibid*. s.29(8).
[24] Local Government (Miscellaneous Provisions) Act 1976, s.16.
[25] Local Government Act 1972, s.233.

ENFORCEMENT OF THE STANDARDS

service of the notice.[26] As the time period before works may be commenced by the authority is 48 hours from service, it may be that the appeal is brought after works have commenced or been completed. If works are in progress at the time the appeal is brought, the authority must immediately stop the works and carry out no further works until determination of the appeal.[27]

An appeal may be brought by a person on whom the notice was served,[28] and must be on one or more of the following grounds[29]:

(a) that the works specified in the notice were not authorised by the provisions;
(b) that the works were unnecessary; or
(c) that it was unreasonable for the authority to undertake the works.

5.155 The court, on hearing the appeal, may make such order as it thinks fit, either confirming (with or without variation) or quashing the notice.[30] It may also make an order regarding the recovery of any expenses that have been, or will be, incurred by the authority in carrying out the works. If the court confirms the notice, the authority may proceed to complete the works specified in that notice.[31]

5.156 A right of entry is given to any person authorised by the local authority enabling that person to enter the building, any land appurtenant to the building and any other apparently unoccupied land which it is necessary to enter in order to carry out the works.[32]

5.157 Any expenses incurred by the authority in carrying out the works may be recovered from the addressee of the notice, or the person who would have received that notice if it had been served. The procedure for recovery of expenses is that provided by section 293 of the Public Health Act 1936,[33] and the court may apportion the expenses between the defendant and another, or may order a person other than the defendant to bear all the expenses.[34]

5.158 Although probably not applicable to a house subject to a closing order, there are additional provisions and qualifications relating to this procedure in respect of buildings on "operational" land owned by British Rail and certain statutory undertakers.[35]

---

[26] 1982 Act, s.31(1) and (2).
[27] *Ibid.* s.31(4) and (7).
[28] *Ibid.* s.31(1).
[29] *Ibid.* s.31(3).
[30] *Ibid.* s.31(5).
[31] *Ibid.* s.31(7).
[32] *Ibid.* s.29(10)—see Chap. 1, paras. 1.15–1.42 for powers of entry under other Acts.
[33] *i.e.* as a simple contract debt.
[34] s.29(13) of the 1982 Act.
[35] s.30 of the 1982 Act.

ACTION TO DEAL WITH HOUSES UNFIT FOR HUMAN HABITATION

Purchase of condemned house for use as temporary accommodation

Where a local housing authority is required to make a demolition or closing order[36] but it appears that the house is, or can be made, capable of providing accommodation of a standard adequate for the time being, the authority may purchase the house.[37] **5.159**

This alternative to demolition or closing is only available in respect of houses and not in respect of the following[38]:

(a) temporary or movable structures[39];
(b) parts of buildings used, or suitable for use as, a dwelling[40];
(c) "underground rooms"[41]; or
(d) a listed building, or a building being considered for listing.[42]

Where the authority decide to purchase the house under this provision, it must serve notice of its intention.[43] This notice must be in the prescribed form,[44] and is to be served on the same persons who would have received copies of the demolition or closing order,[45] that is the following persons[46]: **5.160**

(a) the "person having control" of the premises[47];
(b) any other person who is an owner[47]; and
(c) every mortgagee whom it has been reasonably practicable to ascertain.[48]

As to identification of persons to be served, authentication and service of notices, see Chapter 4.

There is no requirement to serve a copy of the notice on an occupier, but it is suggested that it is good practice to do so, and at the same time additional information could be provided regarding the consequences of the notice and the entitlement of the occupier to re-housing, disturbance and possibly home loss payments.[49]

---

[36] Under s.265 of the 1985 Act—see para. 5.104.
[37] s.300(1) of the 1985 Act.
[38] s.300(4) and (5) of the 1985 Act.
[39] Which may be subject to a demolition or closing order by virtue of s.264 of the 1985 Act—see Chap. 3, para. 3.33.
[40] s.266(*a*) of the 1985 Act.
[41] ss.266(*b*) and s.282, as defined by s.280 of the 1985 Act.
[42] 1985 Act, s.304(1).
[43] *Ibid.* s.300(2).
[44] Form No. 11, with appropriate amendments, Housing (Prescribed Forms) Regulations 1972, as amended and retained in force by the Housing (Consequential Provisions) Act 1985, s.2.
[45] s.300(2)(*a*) of the 1985 Act.
[46] s.268(1) of the 1985 Act.
[47] Defined by s.322 of the 1985 Act—see paras. 5.77–5.79.
[48] Identifying such persons would include service of requisitions for information under the Local Government (Miscellaneous Provisions) Act 1976, s.16—see Chap. 4, paras. 4.17–4.19.
[49] Under Pt. III of the Land Compensation Act 1973.

The notice becomes operative 21 days from the date of service. However, where an appeal is brought within the 21 day period, the notice is suspended and does not become operative until the appeal has been determined.[50]

Right of appeal against notice of intention to purchase

5.161   There is a right of appeal within 21 days of the date of service of the notice[51] to the county court available to a "person aggrieved" by the notice of intention.[52] A "person aggrieved" is someone who has been subjected to a legal burden or deprived of some legal entitlement.[53] However, a person who is in occupation of the premises the subject of the notice and who has a lease or agreement with an unexpired term of three years or less is specifically excluded from a right of appeal.[54] A tenant not given a specific right of appeal, could apply for judicial review of the authority's decision to make the order if it can be shown that they took account of matters which were irrelevant to this procedure, or failed to take account of a relevant matter.[55]

5.162   The correct action for a person aggrieved by the refusal of the authority to accept an undertaking either to carry out works to make the house fit, or not to use, or permit the use of, the house for human habitation would be to appeal against the notice of intention to purchase to the county court.

5.163   The county court on appeal may make such order as it thinks fit, either confirming the notice (with or without variation) or quashing it, and it may also accept from an appellant any undertaking that could have been accepted by the local housing authority at the meeting set by the time and place notice.[56] Provided that, where that appellant was served with a time and place notice[57] and the undertaking relates to the carrying out of works to make the house fit, the court may only accept the undertaking if written notification of the intention to submit proposals was given to the authority and a list of the proposed works submitted.[58] It is clear that the court could accept an undertaking (of either

---

[50] s.268(2) as applied by s.300(2)(*b*) of the 1985 Act.
[51] This does not include the actual day of service—see *Stewart* v. *Chapman* [1951] 2 K.B. 792. It would appear that the county court does not have power to extend this statutory time period—*Honig* v. *Lewisham B.C.* (1958, unrep.) [122 J.P.J. 302]. However, see *Arieli* v. *Duke of Westminster* (1983) 269 E.G. 535 and *Johnson* v. *Duke of Westminster* (1984) 17 H.L.R. 136.
[52] s.269(1) as applied by s.300(2)(*b*) of the 1985 Act.
[53] See, in particular, James L.J. in *Ex p. Sidebotham* (1880) 14 Ch.D. 458 at 465, and also *R.* v. *Nottingham Quarter Sessions, ex p. Harlow* [1952] 2 Q.B. 601.
[54] s.269(2) as applied by s.300(2)(*b*) of the 1985 Act.
[55] *R.* v. *Ealing L.B., ex p. Richardson* (1982) 4 H.L.R. 125 and *Legg* v. *Leominster D.C.* (unrep., C.A. December 16, 1985).
[56] s.269(3) as applied by s.300(2)(*b*) of the 1985 Act.
[57] s.264 of the 1985 Act—see paras. 5.104–5.106.
[58] s.269(4) as applied by s.300(2)(*b*) of the 1985 Act.

type) from a person who was not served with a time and place notice, provided that that person has a right of appeal. Any undertaking accepted by the court has the same effect as one accepted by the authority.[59]

The extent of the variation available to the county court is not clear. The court does not appear able to substitute a demolition or a closing order for the notice, however, presumably the court could quash the notice and not accept an undertaking where it was satisfied that the house was not "capable of providing accommodation of a standard adequate for the time being." It is clear that the court must consider the facts as they exist at the time of the appeal.[60]

5.164 Once an appeal has been brought the notice is suspended and does not become operative until the county court confirms it (with or without variation) and no appeal is made to the Court of Appeal against that decision within four weeks.[61] If an appeal is brought against the decision of the county court, the notice remains suspended until the Court of Appeal confirms it [62] Withdrawal of an appeal has the same effect as a decision confirming the notice.[63]

5.165 Once the notice has become operative[64] (or on the determination of, withdrawal of, or end of a period allowed for, an appeal[65]) the authority may purchase the house.[66] If they cannot reach an agreement to purchase, they may submit a compulsory purchase order to the Secretary of State for confirmation. The compensation payable for the house will be the value of the site cleared and available for development[67] (*i.e.* the site value—no value is to be attached to the house itself[68]). This does not exclude[69] well maintained payments,[70] and owner-occupier or business subsidies.[71]

5.166 It is important to note that this procedure is only available as an alternative to demolition or closing, and that the house acquired does not become part of the authority's permanent housing stock.[72]

---

[59] s.269(5) as applied by s.300(2)(*b*), and s.264(4), (5) and (6) of the 1985 Act—see paras. 5.110–5.114.
[60] *Leslie Maurice & Co. Ltd.* v. *Willesden Corp.* [1953] 2 Q.B. 1.
[61] ss.268(2) and 269(6) as applied by s.300(2)(*b*) of the 1985 Act. The four week period is that given by R.S.C. Ord. 59, r. 19.
[62] s.269(6)(*b*) as applied by s.300(2)(*b*) of the 1985 Act.
[63] s.269 as applied by s.300(2)(*b*) of the 1985 Act.
[64] *i.e.* 21 days from the date of service.
[65] s.269(6) as applied by s.300(2)(*b*) of the 1985 Act.
[66] 1985 Act, s.300(3).
[67] *Ibid.* s.585(1).
[68] This would support the view that an unfit house has no value when calculating reasonable expense—see *Kimsey* v. *L.B. of Barnet* (1976) 3 H.L.R. 45—see para. 5.71.
[69] 1985 Act, s.585(3).
[70] *Ibid.* Sched. 23.
[71] *Ibid.* Sched. 24.
[72] *Victoria Square Property Co. Ltd.* v. *Southwark L.B.C.* [1978] 1 W.L.R. 463.

5.167 The standard of accommodation the house is to be capable of providing must, necessarily, be less than the standard of fitness for human habitation,[73] since the procedure that led to purchase started from a decision that the house was unfit and not capable of being rendered fit at reasonable expense.[74] This is confirmed by the 1985 Act, which specifically excludes houses acquired by this procedure[75] from the covenant implied into any tenancy agreement that the house is fit for human habitation at the commencement of a letting and that the landlord will maintain its fitness.[76] Nevertheless it is clear that the house should not be a statutory nuisance.[77]

5.168 Having acquired a house under this procedure, the authority may carry out such works as may be necessary from time to time to maintain it capable of providing accommodation adequate for the time being.[78]

5.169 It should be noted that there is no provision under this procedure removing Rent Act protection from any occupiers (as there is under the demolition and closing order procedures[79]), and the notice of intention to purchase is not a "housing order" for the purposes of Part III of the Land Compensation Act 1973. This will mean that the local housing authority will take over as landlord on acquisition of the house. An occupier's entitlement to re-housing, disturbance and home loss payment may depend on the amount and nature of any works necessary to render the house capable of providing accommodation adequate for the time being, and whether an occupier will be displaced (either permanently or temporarily) as a consequence.

3. Action to Deal with Houses in Substantial Disrepair and Houses in Disrepair which Interferes with Personal Comfort

Introduction

5.170 The procedures for the service of notices, appeals and enforcement in respect of these two standards are the same, with the exception of how the procedure starts. The procedures are also similar to those relating to repair notices requiring works to render a house fit,[80] but with some important differences. For the sake of clarity, the different factors which start the procedures are considered first and separately, and the enforcement procedure for both standards considered afterwards and together.

---

[73] As defined by s.604 of the 1985 Act—see Chap. 3, paras. 3.24–3.46.
[74] s.264(1) of the 1985 Act—see paras. 5.70–5.75.
[75] s.302(c) of the 1985 Act.
[76] Landlord and Tenant Act 1985, s.8.
[77] As defined by s.92(1)(a) of the Public Health Act 1936—see Chap. 3, paras. 3.08–3.18 for definition, and Chap. 5, paras. 5.02–5.64 for procedure. See *Nottingham Corp.* v. *Newton* [1974] 1 W.L.R. 923 and *Salford City Council* v. *McNally* [1976] A.C. 379.
[78] s.302(b) of the 1985 Act.
[79] s.270(3) and s.276 of the 1985 Act—see paras. 5.125 and 5.145.
[80] s.189 and ss.191–208 of the 1985 Act—see paras. 5.80–5.99.

ACTION TO DEAL WITH HOUSES IN DISREPAIR

Because action taken under these provisions carries with it additional benefits to owners such as grant-aid for works,[81] it should be given preference over and above others procedures which do not carry with them similar benefits.[82] However, it is the actual conditions that will dictate the appropriate action, and the authority is not restricted to taking action only under one statute, but may proceed under two or more providing there is no conflict. In certain circumstances, it may be that action is taken to ensure that the house is brought up to a reasonable standard at the same time as some other more urgent matters are dealt with under section 76 of the Building Act 1984 (see paras. 5.59–5.64). **5.171**

The following aspects of the procedures are considered: **5.172**

(i) detection of houses in substantial disrepair;
(ii) representations that disrepair interferes with comfort;
(iii) reasonable expense;
(iv) repair notices requiring works;
(v) enforcement of repair notices.

Detection of houses in substantial disrepair

The general duty placed on local housing authorities to ensure that their district is inspected from time to time[83] includes the duty to determine whether action should be taken to deal with houses which are in such a state of disrepair that, although not unfit for human habitation, substantial repairs are necessary to bring those houses up to a reasonable standard, having regard to their age, character and locality.[84] In addition, the authority will receive complaints from occupiers regarding the condition of their accommodation. **5.173**

Once the authority becomes aware that a house is in substantial disrepair it may take action to ensure that it is brought up to a reasonable standard of repair. Although this is a discretionary power, the discretion must be exercised reasonably: it cannot be fettered by a fixed policy, and must be exercised with regard only to the particular relevant matters and so as to promote (not defeat) the objects of the provisions and procedure.[85] The authority, once aware that a house is in substantial disrepair, must consider whether it is appropriate to act under these provisions to ensure that the house is brought up to a reasonable standard in terms of the conditions of the house, and not (for example) in

---

[81] *i.e.* mandatory repairs grants under s.494 of the 1985 Act.
[82] *e.g.* Pt. III of the Public Health Act 1936—see Chap. 5, paras. 5.02–5.64.
[83] s.605 of the 1985 Act.
[84] s.190(1)(*a*) of the 1985 Act—see Chap. 3, paras. 3.47–3.53.
[85] See in particular, *Padfield* v. *Minister of Agriculture* [1968] A.C. 997, and *Associated Provincial Picture Houses* v. *Wednesbury Corp.* [1948] 1 K.B. 223.

ENFORCEMENT OF THE STANDARDS

terms of whether there are sufficient funds available to cover the possible costs of a repair grant.[86]

Lord Denning, in a case considering this provision[87] (as it was contained in the 1957 Housing Act[88]), commented[89] that:

> "It seems to me that the policy of Parliament was to make owners of houses keep them in proper repair. Not only so as to keep up the stock of houses, but also to see that protected tenants should be able to have their houses properly kept up. It would be deplorable if there were no means of compelling owners of old houses to keep them in proper repair: or if owners of old houses could let them fall into disrepair—as a means of evicting the tenants. Of course if the state of a house is so bad that it should be condemned—whoever was occupying it—then let it be demolished or closed or purchased. But if it is worth repairing, then it should be repaired, no matter whether it is occupied by a protected tenant or an unprotected tenant."

Representations that disrepair interferes with comfort

5.174 In addition to the local housing authority's duty to consider whether houses are unfit for human habitation or in substantial disrepair, they must also consider any representations made to them that the condition of a house is such as to interfere with the personal comfort of an occupying tenant.[90] This procedure is started by a representation made by an "occupying tenant" and not at the volition of the authority.

5.175 An "occupying tenant" is defined by the Act[91] to mean:

> "a person (other than an owner-occupier) who—
> (a) occupies or is entitled to occupy the dwelling as a lessee; or
> (b) is a statutory tenant of the dwelling[92];
> (c) occupies the dwelling as a residence under a restricted contract[93]; or
> (d) is employed in agriculture (as defined by section 17(1) of the Agricultural Wages Act 1948) and occupies or resides in the dwelling as part of his term of employment."

5.176 Since the representation may have to be proved on any appeal,[94] it is advisable for it to be made in writing. This could be in the form of a

---

[86] s.494 of the 1985 Act.
[87] *Hillbank Properties Ltd.* v. *Hackney L.B.C.* [1978] Q.B. 998.
[88] s.9(1A).
[89] *Hillbank Properties Ltd.* v. *Hackney L.B.C.* [1978] Q.B. 998 at 1009.
[90] s.190(1)(*b*) of the 1985 Act—see Chap. 3, paras. 3.54–3.59.
[91] s.207, referring to s.236(2) of the 1985 Act.
[92] *i.e.* under the Rent Act 1977 or Rent (Agriculture) Act 1976.
[93] *i.e.* within s.19 of the Rent Act 1977.
[94] Under s.191 of the 1985 Act—see paras. 5.187–5.192.

standardised representation, prepared by the authority for signing by the tenant. It should clearly state that the person making the representation is the occupying tenant, identify the items of disrepair and state that the disrepair interferes materially with the personal comfort of the tenant. Such a prepared representation may avoid the occupying tenant being called to give evidence at the hearing of an appeal.

Reasonable expense

Although not expressed in the legislation, the courts have held[95] that the authority must consider whether the works specified in a repair notice in respect of a house in substantial disrepair can be carried out at "reasonable expense."[96] It can also be taken to apply to repair notices in respect of disrepair which interferes with personal comfort, but, it is suggested that it is unlikely to be a relevant factor as the cost of the works is likely to be relatively small compared to the pre-works and post-works value of the house. **5.177**

Reasonable expense is discussed in detail in paras. 5.70–5.75. However, there are differences in some of the factors relating to reasonable expense for the purposes of these provisions. In particular the estimated value of the house before the works[97] will not be nil or nominal because before reaching the stage of considering "reasonable expense," the authority have determined initially that the house is not unfit for human habitation. In addition, since there is no alternative action available (*i.e.* there is no demolition or closing order procedure available), no account can be taken of the cost of demolition. **5.178**

It would seem that where the works required would involve unreasonable expense, the authorities only choice is to reduce the amount of works required by the repair notice (*i.e.* lower the standard to which the house will be brought as a result of the notice); it may be arguable that this in any case is a reasonable standard having regard to the age, character and locality required by the provision.

It should be remembered that the authority may take compulsory improvement action (described in paras. 5.202–5.269) at the same time as action under these provisions, which may affect the proportion of the costs allocated to works required by the repair notice. In addition, it is suggested that there is nothing to prevent the authority issuing a repair notice under these provisions after the completion of works required by a repair notice requiring the house to be made fit—although in such cases, careful consideration must be given to the programming of the works, so as to avoid unnecessary expense and disruption caused by

---

[95] See in particular, *Hillbank Properties Ltd.* v. *Hackney L.B.C.* [1978] Q.B. 998, and *Kenny* v. *Kingston upon Thames R.L.B.C.* (1985) 17 H.L.R. 344.
[96] s.206 of the 1985 Act.
[97] See para. 5.71.

undoing works done under one notice to carry out works required in the other.

Repair notices requiring works

5.179 The procedures to be followed in serving a repair notice to make good substantial disrepair or disrepair which interferes with personal comfort, and the rights of appeal and enforcement procedures are similar to those as for a repair notice requiring works to render a house fit,[98] but with appropriate differences. For the sake of clarity, the stages are set out below taking account of those differences.

5.180 (a) Where a local housing authority is satisfied that a house is in such a state of disrepair that, although not unfit for human habitation, substantial repairs are necessary to bring it up to a reasonable standard, having regard to its age, character and locality, it may serve a repair notice requiring the execution of the necessary works.[99]

(b) Where a local housing authority is satisfied, on receiving representation made by an occupying tenant, that a house is in such a state of disrepair that, although not unfit for human habitation, its condition is such as to interfere materially with the personal comfort of the occupying tenant, it may serve a repair notice requiring the execution of the necessary works.[1]

5.181 The action to be taken by the local housing authority in either case is directed at the "person having control"[2] of the house. Other persons having an interest in the house may be informed, but at the discretion of the authority. The interpretation of the relevant terms is dealt with in paras. 5.76–5.79 in respect of action to deal with houses unfit for human habitation.

5.182 Clearly either form of repair notice can be served in respect of a tenanted house, but a repair notice cannot be served in respect of disrepair which interferes with personal comfort in the case of an owner-occupied house. In addition, it is important to note that in certain circumstances, the authority can enforce these provisions in respect of houses in their ownership. Where the local housing authority is the "person having control" of the house[3] (even if there are other "owners" and/or mortgagees), and that house is in substantial disrepair and the works necessary to bring it up to a reasonable standard can be carried out at reasonable expense, a repair notice cannot be served. However,

---

[98] See paras. 5.80–5.99.
[99] 1985 Act, s.190(1)(*a*).
[1] *Ibid.* s.190(1)(*b*).
[2] *Ibid.* s.207.
[3] See paras. 5.77–5.78.

ACTION TO DEAL WITH HOUSES IN DISREPAIR

where a house is owned by the authority, but someone else is the "person having control" of the house, the repair notice can be served.[4]

5.183 The repair notice must be in the appropriate prescribed form[5] and must require the addressee to execute the works specified in the notice within the time period (being not less than 21 days) stated in the notice.[6]

So far as possible, the notice should clearly state the works to be carried out,[7] and should be precise enough to form the basis of an estimate to be obtained from a builder.[8] Since local housing authorities have limited powers to carry out investigations in houses not in their possession, it will not always be possible to give an exact and detailed specification of the works necessary. In such cases, it is suggested that the repair notice should require the carrying out of thorough investigations and the execution of any works found to be necessary to achieve the stated results.[9]

5.184 The time period given cannot be less than 21 days and must be reasonable having regard to the extent of the works.[10] It should be noted that the repair notice does not become operative until 21 days from the date of service (except where there is an appeal against the notice),[11] and so the time limit set out in the notice, which must be at least 21 days, does not start to run until 21 days after service—the minimum time from the date of service to the expiry date becomes a total of 42 days.

5.185 The repair notice must be addressed to and served on the "person having control" of the house. The local housing authority, at its discretion, may also serve copies on any other person having an interest in the house.[12] Where owners not in receipt of rents and profits have notified the authority of their interest, the authority must serve them with a copy of the notice.[13]

As to authentication and service of notices, and identification of the addressee, see Chapter 4.

A periodic tenant, a fixed term tenant with a lease of less than three years to run, a tenant of part of the house and a statutory tenant would

---

[4] *R.* v. *Cardiff City Council, ex p. Cross* (1982) 1 H.L.R. 54, and affirmed on appeal (1982) 6 H.L.R. 6.
[5] Form No. 2B (in respect of substantial disrepair) and Form No. 2C (in respect of disrepair interfering with personal comfort), with appropriate amendments, Housing (Prescribed Forms) Regulation 1972, as amended, and retained in force by s.2 of the Housing (Consequential Provisions) Act 1985.
[6] s.190(2) of the 1985 Act.
[7] *Canterbury City Council* v. *Bern* (1982) 44 P. & C.R. 178.
[8] *Cohen* v. *West Ham Corp.* [1933] Ch. 814.
[9] *Church of Our Lady of Hal* v. *Camden L.B.C.* (1980) 255 E.G. 991.
[10] See *Ryall* v. *Cubitt Heath* [1922] 1 K.B. 275.
[11] 1985 Act, s.190(4).
[12] *Ibid.* s.190(3) of the 1985 Act.
[13] *Ibid.* s.202.

appear to be excluded from having a legal interest.[14] However, the authority can supply such tenants with a copy of the notice requiring works to their home, and it may assist them in obtaining or substantiating civil claims for disrepair.[15]

5.186 Once a repair notice has been served the local housing authority cannot refuse an application for a repairs grant insofar as it relates to works required by the notice and works necessary to comply with that notice.[16] It should be noted that the applicant for the grant need not be the "person having control" of the house, *i.e.* need not be the addressee.

Appeals against repair notices

5.187 There is a right of appeal by a "person aggrieved" by the repair notice.[17] The appeal is to the county court, and must be made within 21 days from the date of service (but excluding the actual day of service[18]) of the notice.

A "person aggrieved" must be someone who has been subjected to a legal burden or deprived of a legal entitlement, but otherwise need not be the addressee of the notice (*i.e.* the "person having control" of the house).[19]

5.188 It is important to note that if the repair notice is invalid (whether because there is some material defect or informality in the notice or it was addressed to or served on the wrong person), there is no need to appeal,[20] although the question of validity can be raised on appeal.[21]

5.189 The grounds of appeal are not specified by the Act, and it would seem that any aspect of the process from the decision that the house is in disrepair to the service of the notice may be questioned,[22] but not matters arising after the expiration of the notice (*i.e.* not matters relating to works in default or demands for payment[23]). As the appeal can cover all

---

[14] *Keeves* v. *Dean* [1924] 1 K.B. 685 and *Brown* v. *Minister of Housing & Local Government* [1953] 1 W.L.R. 1370.

[15] *e.g.* breach of repairing obligations implied into certain tenancy agreements by the Landlord and Tenant Act 1985, s.11.

[16] s.494 of the 1985 Act.

[17] s.191(1) of the 1985 Act.

[18] *Stewart* v. *Chapman* [1951] 2 K.B. 792. It would appear that the county court does not have power to extend this statutory time period—see *Honig* v. *Lewisham B.C.* (1985 unrep.) [122 J.P.J. 302]. However, see *Arieli* v. *Duke of Westminster* (1983) 269 E.G. 535, and *Johnson* v. *Duke of Westminster* (1984) 17 H.L.R. 136.

[19] See in particular, the view given by James L.J. in *Ex p. Sidebotham* (1880) 14 Ch.D. 458 at 465, and also *R.* v. *Nottingham Quarter Sessions, ex p. Harlow* [1952] 2 Q.B. 601.

[20] *Pollway Nominees Ltd.* v. *L.B. of Croydon* (1985) 17 H.L.R. 503, and *Graddage* v. *L.B. of Haringey* [1975] 1 W.L.R. 241.

[21] *Elliott* v. *Brighton B.C.* (1981) 79 L.G.R. 506.

[22] See in particular, *L.B. of Wandsworth* v. *Winder* [1985] A.C. 461, *Cocks* v. *Thanet D.C.* [1983] A.C. 286, *R.* v. *Hackney L.B.C., ex p. Teepee Estates (1956) Ltd.* (1967) 19 P. & C.R. 87.

[23] Sched. 10, para. 6 deals with appeals against demands—see para. 5.201. See also *Elliott* v. *Brighton B.C.* (1981) 79 L.G.R. 506.

these aspects including a review of the local housing authority's decisions, it would seem that an appeal to the county court is more appropriate than an application for judicial review.[24]

Where a question is raised on appeal relating to whether the works are capable of being carried out at reasonable expense, the court makes its determination at the time of the hearing of the appeal (*i.e.* it does not review the situation that existed at the time the authority made its decision, or the date of service of the notice[25]). Any challenge on the issue of reasonable expense must be on a point of law, and the courts will not interfere with the decision of the authority provided that it was based on a reasonable approach and took account of all the relevant factors.[26]

On hearing the appeal, the county court may make such an order as it thinks fit, either confirming (with or without variation) or quashing the notice.[27]   **5.190**

Once an appeal has been brought within the 21 days allowed, the repair notice is suspended and does not become operative (*i.e.* the time limit specified in the notice does not start to run[28]) until the county court confirms the notice (with or without variation) and no appeal is made to the Court of Appeal against that decision within four weeks.[29] If an appeal is brought against the decision of the county court, the notice remains suspended until the Court of Appeal confirms the notice.[30]   **5.191**

Withdrawal of an appeal has the same effect as a decision confirming the notice.[31]

Where the result of an appeal is the confirmation of the repair notice, the authority can proceed to enforce the notice after the expiry of the specified time period.[32]   **5.192**

Lessee's right to recover part of costs incurred

Where a lessee carries out the works required by a repair notice (or where the cost is recovered from a lessee by the authority after carrying out works in default[33]), that lessee may recover part of the costs incurred from the lessor by agreement or as determined by the county court.[34] Where the county court is involved it must consider the terms of   **5.193**

---

[24] But see *R. v. L.B. of Southwark, ex p. Lewis Levy Ltd.* (1983) 8 H.L.R. 1.
[25] *Leslie Maurice & Co. Ltd. v. Willesden Corp.* [1953] 2 Q.B. 1.
[26] See paras. 5.70–5.75.
[27] 1985 Act, s.191(2).
[28] *Ibid.* s.190(4).
[29] *Ibid.* ss.190(4) and 191(4)(*a*). The four week period is given by R.S.C. Ord. 59, r. 9.
[30] *Ibid.* s.191(4)(*b*).
[31] *Ibid.* s.191(4).
[32] *Ibid.* ss.193–205—see paras. 5.196–5.201.
[33] *Ibid.* Sched. 10—see paras. 5.199–5.201.
[34] *Ibid.* s.199.

the lease, including the unexpired period of the lease and the rent payable.[35]

Where there are sub-leases and the lessor is also a lessee, part of the costs paid to the sub-lessee can be recovered from the appropriate lessor.[36]

These provisions do not apply if a charging order is in force, or an application for such an order is being considered.[37]

Charging orders

5.194   If the works required by a repair notice are carried out, the value of the house will have been increased. If the cost of carrying out the works was borne by one of the owners, that person may protect that expenditure by applying to the local housing authority for a charging order.[38]

The effect of such a charging order is to create a charge against the house equal to the amount of the costs incurred by the applicant (including the cost of the application), to produce an annuity payable over 30 years at a rate of 6 per cent.[39]

An application for such a charging order must include a certificate from the proper officer of the authority that the works have been satisfactorily carried out, accounts and vouchers in relation to the works,[40] and if the application is approved, certified copies of the certificate, accounts and vouchers and of the charging order must be filed by the proper officer.[41]

Once made, the charging order takes priority over virtually all other existing or future charges, with only certain exceptions.[42]

Protection of rights of tenants and lessees

5.195   It may be that the repair notice was served on and enforced against a "person having control" of the house who is not responsible for the repairs under a lease, contract or covenant, or that the works required were carried out by an owner who was not the "person in control" of the house and who was not responsible for the repairs under such a lease, contract or covenant. Anyone in such a position may take action for breach of obligations under such a lease, contract or covenant, and any

---

[35] 1985 Act, s.199(2).
[36] *Ibid.* s.199(3).
[37] *Ibid.* s.199(4).
[38] *Ibid.* s.200(1). The Secretary of State has power to prescribe the format of charging orders (s.201(1) of the 1985 Act), but does not appear to have done so.
[39] *Ibid.* s.200(3) and (4). Different rates cannot be set to apportion the burden—see *Holborn and Frascati* v. *London County Council* (1916) 80 J.P. 225.
[40] *Ibid.* s.200(2).
[41] *Ibid.* s.200(6).
[42] *Ibid.* s.201(2).

such action is not prejudiced by the procedure for enforcing a repairs notice.[43]

Similarly, nothing in Part VI of the Act, nor any action taken by the authority or owner in response to the authority's action under this Part of the Act, prejudices a tenant's right to take action for breach of the landlord's repairing obligations (either expressed or implied).[44]

Enforcement of repair notices

Where the works required by the repair notice have not been completed within the period specified in that notice[45] (or the period set for compliance after an appeal[46]), the local housing authority may carry out the required works themselves and recover the cost incurred.[47] **5.196**

The use of the discretionary term "may" in the section makes it clear that the authority need not proceed to carry out the works. However, they cannot fetter their decision in this regard by adopting a fixed policy either that they will or will not carry out such works.[48] It is suggested that the discretion is one which allows for a review of the situation so as to decide the most appropriate action to deal with the condition of the house at that time. It may be that the majority of the works have been completed and only minor items remain—in which case it would be more appropriate to take action under other provisions to deal with those items[49]; it may be that no works have been carried out and conditions have deteriorated to such an extent that the house is now unfit for human habitation.

Where the authority decide to carry out the necessary work in default of the person having control of the house, they may give written notice to that person, and to any owner, stating their intention to do so.[50] **5.197**

If, at any time after seven days from the date of service of the notice of intention and while there is any workman or contractor employed by the authority in the house, an addressee of the notice of intention (or any workman or contractor employed by such a person) attempts to carry out works it is deemed to constitute the offence of obstruction.

---

[43] 1985 Act, s.203(1) and (2).
[44] *Ibid.* s.203(3). Such obligations include those implied by ss.10–11 of the Landlord and Tenant Act 1985—see *McGreal* v. *Wake* (1984) 13 H.L.R. 107.
[45] *i.e.* the reasonable period for the completion of the works (being at least 21 days) from the date the notice becomes operative. See s.191 of the 1985 Act—para. 5.184.
[46] See s.191(2) and (4) of the 1985 Act—para. 5.191. Clearly the court on appeal may vary the time period set in the notice.
[47] s.193 of the 1985 Act.
[48] *Elliott* v. *Brighton B.C.* (1981) 79 L.G.R. 506.
[49] *e.g.* Pt. III of the Public Health Act 1936, or s.76 of the Building Act 1984.
[50] s.194(1) of the 1985 Act. Note that the authority must serve copies on owners who have notified the authority of their interest under s.202 of the Act. There is no prescribed form for such notice of intention, but it is suggested that suitable amendments could be made to Form No. 1 Housing (Prescribed Forms) Regulations 1972 (S.I. 1972 No. 228).

However, if it is shown that the works attempted to be carried out were urgently necessary to obviate danger to occupants, there is no offence.[51]

The authority is not required to give notice of their intention to carry out the works; however, no offence is committed unless such a notice has been served. Nor will there be any offence even if notice of intention had been served, if the original repair notice was invalid.[52]

5.198 If an occupier, owner, or person having control of premises prevents any officer, agent or workman of the authority from carrying out the works after receiving notice of the intended action, the authority may apply to a magistrates' court, and the court may order that person to permit the authority to do what is necessary.[53] Failure to comply with the court order is an offence, with a maximum penalty on conviction of a fine not exceeding £20 for each day on which the offence continues.[54]

5.199 Any expenses incurred by the local housing authority in carrying out the works, together with any interest (at a reasonable rate determined by the authority) from the date when the demand for payment is served until it is settled, can be recovered by an action in the county court or High Court (dependent on the amount involved).[55]

The money is to be recovered from the person on whom the notice was served, unless:

(a) following an appeal against the notice the court has directed that some other person(s) pay all or part of the cost of the works; or
(b) the person on whom the notice was served is an agent or trustee for the person in control; in such cases the liability of the agent or trustee is limited to the amount collected on behalf of the other person since the date of the service of the demand.

5.200 The local housing authority is given the same powers and remedies for the enforcement of the charge against the house, under the Law of Property Act 1925, and as if they were mortgagees by deed having powers of sale and lease, to accept the surrender of leases and to appoint a receiver. However, the power to appoint a receiver cannot be exercised until one month from the date the charge takes effect.[56]

5.201 There is a right of appeal against a demand for the recovery of expenses available to any person aggrieved. Such appeal must be within the 21 days from the date of service of the demand before it takes effect.

---

[51] s.194(2) of the 1985 Act. Obstruction is dealt with in s.198 of the Act—see Chap. 1, paras. 1.16–1.19.
[52] *Canterbury City Council* v. *Bern* [1981] J.P.L. 749.
[53] 1985 Act, s.195.
[54] *Ibid.* s.195(2).
[55] *Ibid.* Sched. 10.
[56] *Ibid.* para. 7, Sched. 10.

ACTION TO DEAL WITH HOUSES IN DISREPAIR

On such appeal, no question may be raised which might have been raised on appeal against the repair notice.[57]

No appeal is necessary where the demand relates to works carried out following an invalid repair notice.[58]

4. Houses Lacking Standard Amenities

In this part the following aspects of the compulsory improvement procedure are discussed: **5.202**

    (i) introduction;
    (ii) definitions;
    (iii) general conditions necessary for compulsory improvement;
    (iv) compulsory improvement in H.A.A.s and G.I.A.s;
    (v) compulsory improvement outside H.A.A.s and G.I.A.s;
    (vi) appeals, purchase notices, etc.;
    (vii) enforcement of improvement notices.

Introduction

The general duty placed on local housing authorities to ensure that their district is inspected from time to time[59] includes determining whether action should be taken on an area basis to ensure the improvement of the dwellings within that area,[60] including the provision of any missing standard amenities. Once an Improvement Area (either General Improvement or Housing Action Area) has been declared, the authority may take action to ensure that any missing amenities are provided.   **5.203**

There is no duty placed on authorities to consider taking action in respect of individual dwellings outside Improvement Areas which lack one or more of the standard amenities. An occupying tenant, however, can make representations to the authority requesting it uses its powers to ensure that the missing amenities are provided.

Thus there are two ways in which such action can be taken; in the case of a dwelling outside both a Housing Action Area[61] and a General Improvement Area,[62] the procedure must be started by representation from an "occupying tenant" requesting that the authority use the compulsory improvement procedure.[63] In the case of dwellings within an

---

[57] 1985 Act, para. 6, Sched. 10. As to appeals against repair notices, see s.191 of the Act—paras. 5.187–5.192.
[58] *West Ham Corp.* v. *Benabo* [1934] 2 K.B. 253.
[59] s.605 of the 1985 Act—see Chap. 1, para. 1.05.
[60] Under Pt. VIII of the 1985 Act.
[61] Declared under 1985 Act, s.239.
[62] Declared under *ibid.* s.253.
[63] 1985 Act, s.212.

area declared by the authority to be a Housing Action or General Improvement Area, the authority may decide to use the compulsory improvement procedure.[64]

5.204 There are initial differences between the two types of procedure but the final stage of enforcement is the same. Each procedure is considered separately until the final (and identical) enforcement stage.

Definitions for the purposes of compulsory improvement

5.205 The following definitions apply for the purposes of the compulsory improvement procedure—

"**Dwelling.**" This is "a building or part of a building occupied or intended to be occupied as a separate dwelling, together with any yard, garden, outhouses and appurtenances belonging to it or usually enjoyed with it."[65] Whether or not a building (or a part of it) is a dwelling is a matter to be determined in terms of the intention of the person having control of it at the time the question arises.[66]

"**Occupying tenant.**" This is defined by section 236 of the 1985 Act, and is dealt with in para. 5.175 above.

"**Owner-occupier.**" This means "the person who, as owner or as lessee under a long tenancy, occupies or is entitled to occupy the dwelling, and "owner-occupied" shall be construed accordingly."[67]

"**Owner.**" This is defined as "the person who otherwise than as a mortgagee in possession, is for the time being entitled to dispose of the fee simple in the dwelling."[67]

"**Long tenancy.**" This means a lease for a term exceeding 21 years, but excludes certain types of leases terminable by notice after death or marriage, and includes other specified types of short leases and extended leases.[68]

"**Person having control of a dwelling.**" This is defined as:
(a) if the dwelling is owner-occupied, the person having control of it is the owner-occupier;
(b) if there is an occupying tenant of the dwelling who is a person employed in agriculture (as defined by section 17(1) of the Agricultural Wages Act 1948) and who occupies or resides in the dwelling as part of the terms of his employment, the person

---

[64] 1985 Act, s.210.
[65] Ibid. s.237.
[66] R. v. Camden L.B.C., ex p. Comyn Ching & Co. (London) Ltd. (1984) 47 P. & C.R. 1417.
[67] 1985 Act, s.237.
[68] Ibid. s.237, referring to the Leasehold Reform Act 1967, s.3.

having control of the dwelling is the employer or other person by whose authority the occupying tenant occupies or resides in the dwelling;

(c) in any other case, the person having control of the dwelling is the person who is either the owner of it or the lessee of it under a long tenancy and whose interest in the dwelling is not in reversion on that of another person who has a long tenancy."[69]

"**Improvement.**" This includes "alteration and enlargement and, so far as also necessary to enable a dwelling to reach the full standard or the reduced standard, repair, and "improved" shall be construed accordingly."[70] This definition differentiates "improvement" in relation to compulsory improvement from the usual common law interpretation separating "repair" from "improvement." At common law "repair" means "restoration by renewal or replacement of subsidiary parts of the whole," while "improvement" involves providing something of different quality or kind from what are originally provided.[71]

"**Housing arrangements.**" This is defined as:

"(a) making provision for the housing of an occupying tenant of a dwelling and his household during the period when improvement works are being carried out, or after the completion of the works, or during that period and after completion of the works (and for any incidental or ancillary matters), and

(b) contained in a written agreement to which the occupying tenant and either his landlord or the local housing authority, or both, are parties."[72]

"Housing arrangements" are, therefore, alternative accommodation, either provided temporarily (while the works are in progress) or permanently, and the subject of a written agreement. The alternative accommodation could be provided by either the landlord or by the authority. The incidental and ancillary matters would include such arrangements as furniture storage, removal costs and the cost of the alternative accommodation. The requirement that the arrangements are put into a written agreement would enable the tenant to take action in the Courts for breach of contract if the arrangements are not fulfilled.

The terms "standard amenities," "full standard" and "reduced standard" are considered in Chapter 3, paras. 3.64–3.65.

---

[69] 1985 Act, s.236.
[70] *Ibid.* s.237.
[71] See, in particular, *Lurcott* v. *Wakely & Wheeler* [1911] 1 K.B. 905.
[72] 1985 Act, s.235.

ENFORCEMENT OF THE STANDARDS

General conditions necessary for compulsory improvement

5.206 Before either type of compulsory improvement action can be taken, the following general conditions regarding the particular dwelling must be satisfied[73]

(a) it must be without one or more of the standard amenities[74];
(b) it must be capable of improvement to the "full standard,"[75] or failing that the "reduced standard"[75] at "reasonable expense"[76]; and
(c) it must have been provided (by erection or conversion) before October 3, 1961.

Dwellings excluded from compulsory improvement procedure

5.207 The compulsory improvement procedure cannot be used in respect of dwellings controlled by the Crown or public or quasi-public authorities.[77]

However, action can be taken in respect of dwellings in which the Crown or a Duchy have an estate or interest if consent is given by them in respect of the particular dwelling[78]; but no action can be taken in respect of dwellings where the person having control is a public or quasi-public authority.[79]

Where the compulsory improvement procedure has started and either the Crown or a public or quasi-public authority subsequently obtains an estate or interest, or becomes the person having control (as appropriate), the procedure becomes void.[80]

Compulsory improvement in H.A.A.s and G.I.A.s

5.208 The procedure in Housing Action or General Improvement Areas is available at the discretion of the authority. Such discretion must be exercised reasonably and cannot be fettered by a fixed policy. It must be exercised having regard only to the particular relevant matters and so as to promote (not defeat) the objects of the provisions and procedure.[81] The authority, once aware that a house in such an area lacks one or more of the standard amenities, must consider whether it is appropriate to act under these provisions to ensure that the missing amenities are provided.[82]

---

[73] 1985 Act, s.209.
[74] *Ibid.* s.237, referring to s.508—see Chap. 3, paras. 3.60–3.66.
[75] *Ibid.* s.234—see Chap. 3, paras. 3.64–3.65.
[76] Not defined for these purposes, but see paras. 5.70–5.75.
[77] 1985 Act, s.232.
[78] *Ibid.* s.232(1).
[79] *Ibid.* s.232(2).
[80] *Ibid.* s.232(3) and (4).
[81] See, in particular, *Padfield* v. *Minister of Agriculture* [1968] A.C. 997, and *Associated Provincial Picture Houses* v. *Wednesbury Corp.* [1948] 1 K.B. 223.
[82] ss.474–482 of the 1985 Act.

The provisional notice

The authority may serve a provisional notice[83] if it appears to the authority that the dwelling is in either a H.A.A. or a G.I.A., and the general conditions for compulsory improvement are satisfied.[84]   **5.209**

However, the authority cannot serve such a provisional notice in respect of an owner-occupied[85] dwelling unless[86]:

(a) it appears that it is not reasonably practicable for another dwelling to be improved without affecting the owner-occupied dwelling; and
(b) the other dwelling is in the same building as, or adjacent to, the owner-occupied dwelling; and
(c) that other dwelling is either—
 (i) not owner-occupied, or
 (ii) there is an approved application for an improvement, intermediate, special or repairs grant.[87]

The provisional notice should be in the prescribed form,[88] and must be served on the person having control of the dwelling.[89] It must specify the following[90]:   **5.210**

(a) the works which the authority consider are required to ensure the dwelling is improved to the full or the reduced standard;
(b) a date (not less than 21 days from the date of service of the notice) and a time and a place at which the specified works, alternative works, housing arrangements and any other matters will be discussed.

So far as possible, the notice should clearly state the works considered by the authority to be necessary,[91] and should be precise enough to be used as the basis of an estimate to be obtained from a builder.[92] The time period cannot be less than 21 days from the date of service.[93]

As to authentication and service of notices, and identification of the addressees, see Chapter 4.

---

[83] s.210(1) of the 1985 Act.
[84] s.209 of the 1985 Act—see para. 5.206.
[85] See para. 5.205.
[86] s.210(2) of the 1985 Act.
[87] Improvement grants—ss.467–473; intermediate grants—ss.474–482; special grants—ss.483–490; and repairs grants—ss.491–498 of the 1985 Act.
[88] However, the prescribed forms require extensive amendments—Form No. 52 Housing (Prescribed Forms) Regulations 1972 (S.I. 1972 No. 228) as amended and retained in force by the Housing (Consequential Provisions) Act 1985, s.2.
[89] See para. 5.205.
[90] s.213(1) of the 1985 Act.
[91] *Canterbury City Council* v. *Bern* (1982) 44 P. & C.R. 178.
[92] *Cohen* v. *West Ham Corp.* [1933] Ch. 814.
[93] This does not include the actual date of service—*Stewart* v. *Chapman* [1951] 2 K.B. 792.

ENFORCEMENT OF THE STANDARDS

5.211 The authority is also required[94] to serve copies of the provisional notice, at least 21 days before the date set in the notice, on the following:

(a) any occupying tenant of the dwelling; and
(b) every other person known by the authority to be an owner, lessee or mortgagee of the dwelling.[95]

In addition, any person who has an estate or interest in the dwelling and who is not served with a copy of the notice, is entitled to obtain a copy by making an application in writing to the authority.[96]

Discussions on the proposals, etc.

5.212 At the meeting at the time and place set by the provisional notice, any person who was required to be served with the notice or a copy of it[97] is entitled to be heard by the authority.[98]

The authority must not have decided the action to be taken before the meeting,[99] and it must consider all the representations made (whether made before the meeting or at the meeting); in particular, it must consider representations concerning the nature of the works proposed by the authority in the provisional notice or concerning the housing arrangements.[1]

5.213 After considering the representations made, the authority may accept an undertaking from either the person having control or from any other person having an estate or interest in the dwelling.[2]

5.214 There is no right of appeal against an authority's refusal to accept an offered undertaking, and a person aggrieved by such a refusal should appeal against the improvement notice.[3]

The undertaking and housing arrangements

5.215 Before accepting any undertaking, the authority must be satisfied that the housing arrangements[4] are satisfactory or that no such arrangements are required.[5]

---

[94] s.213(2) of the 1985 Act.
[95] Identifying such persons would include service of requisitions for information under s.16 of the Local Government (Miscellaneous Provisions) Act 1976—see Chap. 4, paras. 4.17–4.19.
[96] s.226 of the 1985 Act.
[97] *i.e.* the person having control, the occupying tenant, any owner, any lessee, and any mortgagee—see para. 5.205.
[98] s.213(3) of the 1985 Act.
[99] *Fletcher v. Ilkeston Corp.* (1931) 96 J.P. 7.
[1] 1985 Act, s.213(4).
[2] *Ibid.* s.211(1).
[3] *Ibid.* s.217—see paras. 5.245–5.252.
[4] Defined by *ibid.* s.235—see para. 5.205.
[5] *Ibid.* s.211(3)(*a*).

5.216 In accepting an undertaking, the authority must be certain that the person offering the undertaking has a right to carry out the improvement works as against all other persons having an estate or interest in the dwelling.[5a] The undertaking must be for the improvement of the dwelling[6] to the full standard.[7] Where, however, the authority is of the opinion that it is not practicable to improve to the full standard at reasonable expense,[8] it may accept an undertaking for the improvement to a reduced standard.[9]

There is no set form for the undertaking, but it must be in writing, and must specify the works that will be carried out, and the period within which those works will be completed (being not more than nine months from the date of acceptance of the undertaking).[10] It must also contain the signed written consent of the occupying tenant agreeing to the carrying out of the specified works.[11]

It is implicit that the authority may, in writing, extend the time period specified in the undertaking for the completion of the works,[12] provided they are satisfied it is reasonable to do so.

5.217 If the authority accepts an undertaking, it must serve a notice of acceptance on the person who offered the undertaking,[13] and, at the same time, serve a copy of that notice[14] on the occupying tenant and on every other person known to the authority to be an owner, lessee or mortgagee of the dwelling. There is no prescribed form for the notice of acceptance.

5.218 Once an undertaking has been accepted, certain preliminary conditions and requirements in respect of an application for an intermediate grant under Part XV of the 1985 Act will not apply, provided that the application relates only to those works specified in the undertaking.[15]

5.219 If, after the acceptance of an undertaking, the dwelling ceases to be included in, or is excluded from a H.A.A. or a G.I.A. (as the case may be),[16] the dwelling is treated as if it were still within such an area, and the relevant compulsory improvement provisions continue to apply as if it was in such an area.[17]

[5a] 1985 Act, s.211(3)(*a*).
[6] *Ibid*. s.211(1).
[7] Defined by *ibid*. s.234—see Chap. 3, para. 3.64.
[8] Not defined by *ibid*. Pt. VII, but see paras. 5.70–5.74 for reasonable expense in relation to fitness for human habitation.
[9] Defined by *ibid*. s.234—see Chap. 3, para. 3.65.
[10] *Ibid*. s.211(2).
[11] *Ibid*. s.211(3)(*b*).
[12] *Ibid*. s.211(4)(*a*).
[13] *Ibid*. s.211(4).
[14] *Ibid*. s.211(6).
[15] *Ibid*. s.477.
[16] See ss.239, 241, 250 and 251 of the 1985 Act—H.A.A.s, and s.258 of the 1985 Act—G.I.A.s.
[17] 1985 Act, s.233.

ENFORCEMENT OF THE STANDARDS

Discharge of an undertaking

5.220 Where the authority considers that the general conditions for the service of an improvement notice are no longer met,[18] it must discharge the undertaking by serving notice of discharge on the person from whom the undertaking was accepted,[19] and copies of that notice[20] on the occupying tenant and on every other person known to the authority to be an owner, lessee or mortgagee of the dwelling.

The authority is also, at its discretion, able to discharge the undertaking at any time. Although it is not clearly stated, the change of circumstances which would enable the authority to exercise this discretion must be that the undertaking appears unlikely to be fulfilled.

The improvement notice—dwellings in H.A.A.s or G.I.A.s

5.221 Having accepted an undertaking, the authority cannot serve an improvement notice, unless[21]:

(a) the works specified in the undertaking are not completed within the stated time period (or extended period); or
(b) there has been a change of circumstances since the acceptance of the undertaking and it appears unlikely that the undertaking will be fulfilled.

However, an improvement notice cannot be served if more than six months has elapsed since the expiry of the time period stated in the undertaking (or the extended period) for the completion of the specified works.[22]

5.222 Where no undertaking was offered, or any offered undertaking was not accepted by the authority, an improvement notice may be served,[23] provided that it is served within nine months of the date of service of the provisional notice.[24]

5.223 In any event, the authority cannot have a fixed policy that they will (or will not) continue the compulsory improvement procedure, and before serving an improvement notice it must review the situation,[25] and can only take into account relevant matters which must include that the following conditions are satisfied,[26] that is:

---

[18] 1985 Act, s.209—see para. 5.206.
[19] *Ibid*. s.211(5).
[20] See ss.239, 241, 250 and 251 of the 1985 Act—H.A.A.s, and s.258 of the 1985 Act—G.I.A.s.
[21] 1985 Act, s.211(4) and s.214(1)(*b*).
[22] *Ibid*. s.214(3)(*b*).
[23] *Ibid*. s.214(1)(*a*).
[24] *Ibid*. s.214(3)(*a*).
[25] See *Elliott* v. *Brighton B.C.* (1981) 79 L.G.R. 506.
[26] 1985 Act, s.214(2).

(a) the dwelling is still in an Housing Action Area or a General Improvement Area[27];
(b) the general conditions are still being met[28];
(c) either—
   (i) the dwelling is not owner-occupied, or
   (ii) if it is owner-occupied, the conditions for service of a provisional notice still apply[29]; and
(d) the housing arrangements are satisfactory, or none are required (or the tenant has unreasonably refused such arrangements).[30]

5.224 The improvement notice is served[31] on the person having control of the dwelling,[32] and, at the same time copies must be served on[33] the occupying tenant, and on every other person known to the authority to be an owner, lessee or mortgagee.[34] Because of the timescale involved in the procedure, it may be that there will have been changes in those persons to be served with copies since the provisional notice, and authorities should check by serving requisitions for information.[35]

The improvement notice must be included in the local land charges register.[36]

5.225 The improvement notice must be in the prescribed form[37] and must[38]:

(a) specify the works required to improve the dwelling to the full standard (or the reduced standard);
(b) state the authority's estimate of the cost of carrying out those works; and
(c) require the addressee to carry out those works within 12 months from the date the notice becomes operative.

So far as possible, the notice should clearly state the works required,[39]

---

[27] Under Pt. VIII of the 1985 Act.
[28] 1985 Act, s.209—see para. 5.206.
[29] *Ibid.* s.210(2)—see para. 5.209.
[30] Defined by *ibid.* s.235—see para. 5.205.
[31] *Ibid.* s.214(4).
[32] Defined by *ibid.* s.236—see para. 5.205.
[33] *Ibid.* s.214(4).
[34] Defined by *ibid.* s.236—see para. 5.205.
[35] Local Government (Miscellaneous Provisions) Act 1976, s.16—see Chap. 4, paras. 4.17–4.19.
[36] s.214(5) of the 1985 Act.
[37] Form No. 56 (with appropriate amendments) Housing (Prescribed Forms) Regulations 1972 (S.I. 1972 No. 228) as amended and retained in force by the Housing (Consequential Provisions) Act 1985, s.2.
[38] s.216(1) of the 1985 Act.
[39] *Canterbury City Council* v. *Bern* (1982) 44 P. & C.R. 178.

and it should be enough to enable an estimate to be obtained from a builder.[40]

Although the works specified in the improvement notice need not be the same as in the provisional notice (the authority having been able to consider the representations made, and conditions perhaps having changed), where the provisional notice required improvement to the reduced standard, the improvement notice cannot require improvement to the full standard.[41]

The 12 month time period allowed for the completion of the works may be extended in writing from time to time by the authority.[42] Where the improvement notice requires works to improve the dwelling to the reduced standard, the authority may substitute a shorter period for completion as they consider appropriate.[43]

As to authentication and service of notices, and identification of the addressees, see Chapter 4.

5.226 The improvement notice does not become operative until six weeks from the date of service (except where there is an appeal against the notice),[44] and the time limit for completion of the works does not start to run until the notice has become operative.

5.227 Once an improvement notice has been served, if the dwelling ceases to be included in, or is excluded from a H.A.A. or a G.I.A. (as the case may be),[45] the notice remains effective and the dwelling is treated as if it were still within such an area, and the relevant compulsory improvement provisions continue to apply as if it was in such an area.[46]

Once an improvement notice has been served, certain preliminary conditions and requirements in respect of an application for an intermediate grant under Part XV of the 1985 Act will not apply, provided that the application relates only to those works specified in the notice.[47]

Withdrawal of improvement notice

5.228 At any time after serving an improvement notice (whether or not it has become operative), the authority may withdraw that notice by serving a notice of withdrawal on the person having control of the dwelling, and by sending copies of that notice of withdrawal to the occupier (if that is not the person having control) and to every other person known to the authority to be an owner, lessee or mortgagee.[48]

---

[40] *Cohen* v. *West Ham Corp.* [1933] Ch. 814.
[41] 1985 Act, s.216(2).
[42] *Ibid.* s.216(1)(*c*).
[43] *Ibid.* s.216(3).
[44] *Ibid.* ss.218(1) and 217(1).
[45] See ss.239, 241, 250 and 251 of the 1985 Act—H.A.A.s, and s.258 of the 1985 Act—G.I.A.s.
[46] 1985 Act, s.233.
[47] *Ibid.* s.477.
[48] *Ibid.* s.219.

Compulsory improvement outside H.A.A.s and G.I.A.s

In the case of dwellings outside a Housing Action or a General Improvement Area, the procedure must be started by representation made by the occupying tenant[49] and is not available at the volition of the authority.

5.229

Such representation must be made in writing,[50] and could be standardised and provided by the authority for signing by the tenant. In addition to stating that the person making the representation is the occupying tenant of the dwelling, it must state that[50]:

(a) the dwelling is outside any Housing Action Area and General Improvement Area[51];
(b) the dwelling lacks one or more of the standard amenities[52];
(c) the dwelling was provided (whether by erection or conversion) before October 3, 1961; and
(d) the tenant requests the authority to exercise its compulsory improvement powers.

On receipt of such representation, the authority must notify the person having control of the dwelling of the representation.[53] Such notification should be in the prescribed form.[54]

After considering the representations the local housing authority may serve a provisional notice, provided it is also satisfied that[55]:

5.230

(a) the representations were made by the occupying tenant;
(b) the general conditions for service of an improvement notice are met[56]; and
(c) the dwelling ought to be improved to the full standard (or the reduced standard)[57];
(d) it is unlikely that the dwelling will be improved to that standard unless the authority takes action.

In addition, the authority must be satisfied that the general conditions necessary for improvement action are met,[58] and that the dwelling is not controlled by the Crown or a public or quasi-public authority.[59]

---

[49] 1985 Act, s.236—see para. 5.205.
[50] *Ibid.* s.212(1).
[51] *Ibid.* Pt. VIII.
[52] *Ibid.* s.508—see Chap. 3, paras. 3.60–3.66.
[53] *Ibid.* s.212(2).
[54] However, the prescribed forms require extensive amendments—Form No. 53 Housing (Prescribed Forms) Regulations 1972 (S.I. 1972 No. 228) as amended and retained in force by the Housing (Consequential Provisions) Act 1985, s.2.
[55] 1985 Act, s.212(3).
[56] *Ibid.* s.209—see para. 5.206.
[57] *Ibid.* s.234—see Chap. 3, paras. 3.64–3.65.
[58] *Ibid.* s.209—see para. 5.206.
[59] *Ibid.* s.232—see para. 5.207.

ENFORCEMENT OF THE STANDARDS

5.231 Once this procedure has been started by the receipt of a representation, it can continue even though the occupying tenant quits the dwelling, or the dwelling is included in an area subsequently declared a H.A.A. or a G.I.A.[60]

5.232 If the authority decides not to serve a provisional notice it must notify the occupying tenant of that decision, and must give a written statement of the reasons for the decision.[61]

5.233 Although it is clear that the authority have a discretion as to whether to serve a provisional notice, even when all the criteria have been satisfied that discretion must be exercised reasonably; it cannot be fettered by a fixed policy, and must be exercised having regard only to the particular relevant matters and so as to promote (not defeat) the objects of the provisions and procedure.[62] It is suggested that the authority, once aware that a dwelling ought to be improved should consider whether it is appropriate to act under these provisions to ensure that it is improved after considering the condition of the dwelling.

The provisional notice

5.234 The provisional notice must be in the prescribed form,[63] and must be served on the person having control of the dwelling.[64] It must specify the following[65]:

(a) the works which the authority consider are required to ensure the dwelling is improved to the full or the reduced standard;

(b) a date (not less than 21 days from the date of service of the notice) and a time and a place at which the specified works, alternative works, housing arrangements and any other matters will be discussed.

So far as possible the notice should clearly state the works considered by the authority to be necessary,[66] and should be precise enough to form the basis of an estimate to be obtained from a builder.[67] The time period cannot be less than 21 days from the date of service.[68]

As to authentication and service of notices, and identification of the addressees, see Chapter 4.

---

[60] 1985 Act, s.212(4).
[61] *Ibid.* s.212(3).
[62] See, in particular, *Padfield* v. *Minister of Agriculture* [1968] A.C. 997, and *Associated Provinicial Picture Houses* v. *Wednesbury Corp.* [1948] 1 K.B. 223.
[63] However, the prescribed forms require extensive amendments—Form No. 54 Housing (Prescribed Forms) Regulations 1972 (S.I. 1972 No. 228) as amended and retained in force by Housing (Consequential Provisions) Act 1985, s.2.
[64] s.212(3) of the 1985 Act.
[65] s.213(1) of the 1985 Act.
[66] *Canterbury City Council* v. *Bern* (1982) 44 P. & C.R. 178.
[67] *Cohen* v. *West Ham Corp.* [1933] Ch. 814.
[68] This does not include the actual date of service—*Stewart* v. *Chapman* [1951] 2 K.B. 792.

The authority is also required[69] to serve copies of the provisional 5.235
notice, at least 21 days before the date set in the notice, on the following—

  (a) any occupying tenant of the dwelling; and
  (b) every other person known to the authority to be an owner, lessee or mortgagee of the dwelling.[70]

In addition, any person who has an estate or interest in the dwelling and who is not served with a copy of the notice, is entitled to obtain a copy by making an application in writing to the authority.[71]

Discussions on the proposals etc.

At the meeting at the time and place set by the provisional notice, any 5.236
person who was required to be served with the notice or a copy of it[72] is entitled to be heard by the authority.[73] The authority must not have decided the action to be taken before the meeting,[74] and it must consider all the representations made (whether made before the meeting or at the meeting); in particular, it must consider any representations about the nature of the works proposed by the authority in the provisional notice or any which concern the housing arrangements.[75]

There is no power for the authority to accept an undertaking from any 5.237
person proposing to improve the dwelling, as the Act clearly states[76] that the authority may take "any further steps authorised under the following provisions of this Part," but the provisions relating to undertakings[77] precede this section.

The improvement notice—dwellings outside H.A.A.s and G.I.A.s

After the discussions, the authority may serve an improvement 5.238
notice,[78] provided it is served within twelve months of the date that representations from the occupying tenant were received by the authority.[79]

Although the authority has discretion as to whether to proceed and serve the notice, it cannot have a fixed policy. It should review the

---

[69] s.213(2) of the 1985 Act.
[70] Identifying such persons would include service of requisitions for information under Local Government (Miscellaneous Provisions) Act 1976, s.16.
[71] s.226 of the 1985 Act.
[72] *i.e.* the person having control, the occupying tenant, any owner, any lessee and any mortgagee—see para. 5.205.
[73] s.213(3) of the 1985 Act.
[74] *Fletcher v. Ilkeston Corp.* (1931) 96 J.P. 7.
[75] 1985 Act, s.213(4).
[76] *Ibid.* s.212(4).
[77] *i.e. ibid.* s.211.
[78] *Ibid.* s.215(1).
[79] Made under s.212—see para. 5.229.

ENFORCEMENT OF THE STANDARDS

situation immediately prior to service,[80] taking account only of the relevant matters, which must include the following[81]:

(a) that the general conditions are still being met[82];
(b) that the dwelling ought to be improved to the full standard (or the reduced standard)[83];
(c) that it is unlikely that the dwelling will be improved to that standard unless the authority proceed; and
(d) that the housing arrangements are satisfactory, or that none are required (or the tenant has unreasonably refused such arrangements).[84]

5.239 The improvement notice is served[85] on the person having control of the dwelling,[86] and at the same time copies must be served on the occupying tenant, and on every other person known to the authority to be an owner, lessee or mortgagee.[87] Because of the timescale involved in the procedure, it may be that there will have been changes in those persons to be served with copies since the provisional notice, and authorities should check by serving requisitions for information.[88]

As to authentication and service of notices, and identification of the addressees, see Chapter 4.

5.240 The improvement notice must be in the prescribed form,[89] and must[90]:

(a) specify the works required to improve the dwelling to the full standard (or the reduced standard);
(b) state the authority's estimate of the cost of carrying out those works; and
(c) require the addressee to carry out those works within 12 months from the date the notice becomes operative.

So far as possible, the notice should clearly state the works required,[91] and they should be precise enough to enable an estimate to be obtained

---

[80] *Elliott* v. *Brighton B.C.* (1981) 79 L.G.R. 506.
[81] 1985 Act, s.215(2).
[82] *Ibid.* s.209—see para. 5.206.
[83] *Ibid.* s.234—see Chap. 3, paras. 3.64–3.65.
[84] *Ibid.* s.235—see para. 5.206.
[85] *Ibid.* s.215(1).
[86] *Ibid.* s.215(3)—see para. 5.205.
[87] *Ibid.* s.215(3).
[88] Local Government (Miscellaneous Provisions) Act 1976, s.16.
[89] However, the prescribed forms require extensive amendments—Form No. 57 Housing (Prescribed Forms) Regulations 1972 as amended and retained in force by the Housing (Consequential Provisions) Act 1985, s.2.
[90] s.216(1) of the 1985 Act.
[91] *Canterbury City Council* v. *Bern* (1982) 44 P. & C.R. 178.

from a builder.[92] Although the works specified in this improvement notice need not be the same as in the provisional notice (the authority having had the opportunity to consider the representations made, or conditions perhaps having changed), where the provisional notice required improvement to the reduced standard, the improvement notice cannot require improvement to the full standard.[93]

The 12 month time period allowed for the completion of the works may be extended in writing from time to time by the authority.[94] Where the improvement notice requires works to improve the dwelling to the reduced standard, the authority may substitute a shorter period for completion as they consider appropriate.[95]

5.241 The improvement notice does not become operative until six weeks from the date of service (except where there is an appeal against the notice),[96] and the time limit for completion of the works does not start to run until the notice has become operative.

The improvement notice must be included in the local land charges register.[97]

5.242 Even if the original occupying tenant quits the dwelling, or the dwelling is included within an area declared to be a Housing Action Area or a General Improvement Area,[98] the notice remains effective.[99]

5.243 Once an improvement notice has been served, certain preliminary conditions and requirements in respect of an application for an intermediate grant under Part XV of the 1985 Act will not apply, provided the application relates only to those works specified in the improvement notice.[1]

Withdrawal of improvement notice

4.244 At any time after serving an improvement notice (whether or not it has become operative), the authority may withdraw that notice by serving a notice of withdrawal on the person having control of the dwelling, and by sending copies of that notice of withdrawal to the occupier (if that is not the person having control) and to every other person known to the authority to be an owner, lessee or mortgagee.[2]

---

[92] *Cohen* v. *West Ham Corp.* [1933] Ch. 814.
[93] 1985 Act, s.216(2).
[94] *Ibid.* s.216(1)(c).
[95] *Ibid.* s.216(3).
[96] *Ibid.* s.218(1) and s.217(1).
[97] *Ibid.* s.215(4).
[98] See ss.239, 241, 250 and 251 of the 1985 Act—H.A.A.s, and s.258 of the 1985 Act—G.I.A.s.
[99] 1985 Act, s.212(4).
[1] *Ibid.* s.477.
[2] *Ibid.* s.219.

Appeals, purchase notices etc.

Appeals against either type of improvement notice

5.245 A right of appeal against either form of improvement notice is available to[3]:

(a) the person having control of the dwelling (*i.e.* the addressee);
(b) any occupying tenant of the dwelling;
(c) any other person having an estate or interest in the dwelling.

The appeal is to the county court, and must be made within six weeks of the date of service of the notice.[4]

5.246 The appeal must be brought on one or more of the following grounds[5]:

(a) that it is not practicable to comply with the notice at reasonable expense[6];
(b) that the authority have unreasonably refused to approve alternative works[7];
(c) that the works in the notice are unreasonable in character or extent;
(d) that the dwelling is within a Clearance Area,[8] and it would be unreasonable for the authority to require the works to be carried out;
(e) that the dwelling does not lack any of the standard amenities;
(f) that the notice requires improvement to the full standard, but the specified works are inadequate to attain that standard;
(g) that some person with an estate or interest in the dwelling other than the appellant will benefit from the works and should contribute toward the costs of carrying out the works[9];
(h) that the notice is invalid because the procedure prior to the service of the improvement notice was not complied with;
(i) that there is some informality, defect or error in, or in connection with, the notice.

---

[3] 1985 Act, s.217(1).
[4] *Ibid.* s.217(1). Note that the time does not include the actual date of service of the notice—*Stewart* v. *Chapman* [1951] 2 K.B. 792. It would appear that the county court does not have power to extend to this statutory time—*Honig* v. *Lewisham B.C.* (1958 unrep.) [122 J.P.J. 302]. However, see *Arieli* v. *Duke of Westminster* (1983) 269 E.G. 535 and *Johnson* v. *Duke of Westminster* (1984) 17 H.L.R. 136.
[5] s.217(2) of the 1985 Act.
[6] Reasonable expense is not defined for the purpose of compulsory improvement—but see paras. 5.70–5.75 in relation to unfitness. Note that improvement notice must state the authority's estimate of the cost of the works—see para. 5.240.
[7] This would include refusal to accept an undertaking offered if the dwelling is in a H.A.A. or G.I.A.—see paras. 5.213–5.214.
[8] See s.289 of the 1985 Act.
[9] This does not include a statutory tenant—see *Harrington* v. *Croydon Corp.* [1968] 1 Q.B. 856.

There are two additional grounds of appeal available: **5.247**

(a) An owner-occupier served with an improvement notice,[10] may appeal on the ground that the authority were wrong to consider that circumstances existed which enabled the notice to be served[11] (see para. 2.209).

(b) An occupying tenant may appeal[12] on the ground that the requirements as to housing arrangements are not satisfied. [13]

Although the validity of the notice can be raised on appeal to the county court, if the notice is invalid (whether because of some material defect or error in the procedure prior to the service, or in connection with the notice itself) it has been held that there is no need to appeal because the notice cannot be enforced[14]; however, it is probably advisable to appeal to the county court for confirmation that the notice is invalid and to show that the interests of the appellant have been substantially prejudiced. (See para. 5.249.) **5.248**

The powers of the court on appeal are limited to some extent by the Act, so that: **5.249**

(a) it cannot extend the period given for the completion of the works specified[15];

(b) it cannot substitute improvement to the full standard where the notice required improvement to the reduced standard[16];

(c) it cannot substitute improvement to the reduced standard where the notice required improvement to the full standard[17]; and

(d) in the case of an appeal based on the ground that the notice is invalid, the court must confirm the notice unless satisfied that the interests of the appellant have been substantially prejudiced.[18]

Otherwise, the court may make such order it thinks fit confirming (with or without variation) or quashing the notice,[19] and where the appeal is based on the ground that some other person will benefit from the works, it may make such order as it thinks fit requiring payment to be made by

---

[10] 1985 Act, s.217(3)(*a*).
[11] *Ibid.* s.210(2).
[12] *Ibid.* s.217(3)(*b*)—see para. 5.205.
[13] s.214(2)(*d*) in the case of dwellings in H.A.A.s or G.I.A.s or s.215(2)(*e*) in case of other dwellings—see paras. 5.215 and 5.238.
[14] *Pollway Nominees Ltd.* v. *L.B. of Croydon* [1986] 3 W.L.R. 277 and *Graddage* v. *L.B. of Haringey* [1975] 1 W.L.R. 241.
[15] 1985 Act, s.217(4)(*a*).
[16] *Ibid.* s.217(4)(*b*).
[17] *Ibid.* s.217(4)(*c*).
[18] *Ibid.* s.217(6)—see *De Rothschild* v. *Wing* [1967] 1 W.L.R. 470.
[19] *Ibid.* s.217(4).

the other person,[20] either to the appellant or to the authority if the works are carried out by the authority.[21]

5.250 Where a question is raised on appeal relating to reasonable expense, to whether the dwelling is within a Clearance Area, or to whether it lacks any of the standard amenities, the court will make its determination based on the circumstances at the time of the appeal. This appears anomalous since the court does not review the circumstances which existed at the time the authority made its decision, or the date of service of the notice.

5.251 It should be noted that, in the case of a dwelling within a H.A.A. or a G.I.A., the court is not able to accept an undertaking in place of the improvement notice—its option would be to quash the notice, or to substitute the contents of the undertaking for those in the notice. Also, since the court cannot substitute a requirement that the dwelling is improved to the full standard where the notice required improvement to the reduced standard, its option would be to quash the notice, leaving the authority to recommence the procedure by issuing a new provisional notice.[22] However, although the court cannot substitute the reduced standard for the full standard, the authority would only need to issue a new improvement notice.

5.252 Once an appeal has been brought within the six week period allowed, the improvement notice is suspended and does not become operative (*i.e.* the time limit for the completion of works does not start to run[23]) until the county court confirms the notice (with or without variation) and no appeal is made to the Court of Appeal against that decision within four weeks.[24] If an appeal is brought against the decision of the county court, the notice remains suspended until the Court of Appeal determines the appeal.[25]

Withdrawal of an appeal has the same effect as a decision confirming the notice or determining the appeal.[26]

Although the Act states that subject to the specified right of appeal, the improvement notice once operative is conclusive as to matters which could be raised on appeal,[27] this would not affect the right to apply to the Divisional Court for judicial review.[28]

---

[20] 1985 Act, s.217(5).
[21] See *ibid*. s.220—see paras. 5.264–5.269.
[22] See *ibid*. s.216(2)—see paras. 5.209–5.211.
[23] See *ibid*. s.216(1)(*c*)—see paras. 5.226 and 5.241.
[24] *Ibid*. s.218(1) and s.217(1). The for week period is given by R.S.C. Ord. 59, r. 19.
[25] *Ibid*. s.218(2).
[26] *Ibid*. s.218(3).
[27] *Ibid*. s.218(4).
[28] See *Pearlman* v. *Keepers & Governors of Harrow School* [1979] Q.B. 56 and *Meade* v. *Haringey L.B.C.* [1979] 1 W.L.R. 637. But, see also *Smith* v. *East Elloe R.D.C.* [1956] A.C. 736.

Rights of entry and protection from liability

5.253 Once an undertaking has been accepted in respect of the improvement of a dwelling in a H.A.A. or a G.I.A.,[29] or an improvement notice has been served in respect of any dwelling,[30] the person who gave the undertaking or the addressee of the notice (*i.e.* the person having control of the dwelling) has a right of entry to carry out the specified works. This right of entry is against any other person having an estate or interest in the dwelling as well as against the occupying tenant, although the tenant should be protected by the terms of the housing arrangements.[31]

5.254 A lessee carrying out the improvement works specified in an undertaking or an improvement notice cannot be made liable for reinstatement of the premises to the condition they were in prior to those works.[32]

Addressee's right to recover part of costs incurred

5.255 Where the person having control of the dwelling (the addressee of the improvement notice) intends to carry out the works required by the improvement notice and is of the opinion that some other person(s) will benefit from the works, that person may appeal to the county court within six weeks from the date of service of the notice, requesting the court to make an order requiring payment from that other person(s).[33]

Charging orders

5.256 If the works required by an improvement notice are carried out, the value of the house will have been increased. Where the cost of carrying out the works was borne by the person having control of the dwelling (the addressee of the notice), that person may protect his expenditure by applying to the local housing authority for a charging order.[34] This does not apply to the carrying out of works under an undertaking.

The effect of such a charging order is to create a charge against the house equal to the amount of the costs incurred by the applicant (including the cost of the application), to produce an annuity payable over 30 years at a rate of 6 per cent.[35]

An application for such a charging order must include a certificate from the proper officer of the authority that the works have been satisfactorily carried out and accounts and vouchers in relation to the works,[36] and, if the application is approved, certified copies of the

---

[29] Under s.211 of the 1985 Act—see para. 5.213.
[30] Under ss.214 or 215 of the 1985 Act—see paras. 5.221–5.227 and paras. 5.238–5.243.
[31] s.224 of the 1985 Act—see Chap. 1, para. 1.32
[32] 1985 Act, s.224(4).
[33] *Ibid.* s.217—see para. 5.268.
[34] *Ibid.* s.229(1).
[35] *Ibid.* s.229(3) and (4).
[36] *Ibid.* s.229(2).

certificate and accounts and vouchers and of the charging order must be filed by the proper officer.[37]

Once made, the charging order takes priority over virtually all other existing or future charges, with only certain exceptions.[38]

5.257 There is a right of appeal to the county court against a charging order available to a person aggrieved within 21 days of service of the notice of the order. Once such an appeal has been brought, the charging order is suspended until the appeal is determined or withdrawn.[39]

Loans to cover cost of improvement

5.258 A person who is liable to incur costs, either by carrying out the works specified in an undertaking or an improvement notice (whether as the addressee of the notice or as a person required to make a payment to the addressee) may apply to the local housing authority for a loan to meet those costs.[40]

This is a specific right to apply for a loan in respect of works required under the compulsory improvement procedure, and is in addition to the right to apply for grant-aid[41] and the general provisions relating to loans from local housing authorities.[42]

The application would be for a loan to cover the amount not covered by the grant. Such application must be made in writing and within three months of the date the undertaking was accepted, the improvement notice became operative or the payment under a court order was made (or such longer period as the authority, in writing, permits).[43]

The authority must be satisfied that the applicant can meet the obligations that will apply in respect of the loan,[44] and that the applicant has an interest in the dwelling either as a estate in fee simple absolute in possession, or an estate for a term of years which will not expire until after the final repayment on a loan.[45] In addition, the authority must be satisfied that based on a valuation made, the principal of the loan does not exceed the estimated amount that can be secured as a mortgage against the dwelling on completion of the works.[46] The authority may offer a loan of a lesser amount than that requested by the applicant.[47]

5.259 The contract for the loan must require proof of title, and must include the stipulation that an improvement or intermediate grant will become

---

[37] 1985 Act, s.229(6).
[38] *Ibid.* s.230.
[39] *Ibid.* s.299(5).
[40] *Ibid.* s.228(1).
[41] Under *ibid.* Pt. XV.
[42] Under *ibid.* Pt. XIV.
[43] *Ibid.* s.228(2).
[44] *Ibid.* s.228(3).
[45] *Ibid.* s.228(4)(*a*).
[46] *Ibid.* s.228(4)(*b*).
[47] *Ibid.* s.228(3).

payable for the whole cost of the specified works, or partly for those works and partly for some other expenditure or payment. It may also include such other reasonable terms as the authority thinks fit, and may provide for the loan to be paid by instalments as works progress.[48]

5.260 The Secretary of State has power to give directions as to the rate of interest payable on any loan offered (either generally or specifically in respect of a particular case) and also to give directions as to the time within which loans or parts of loans are to be repaid.[49]

The general provisions relating to loans under Part XIV of the Housing Act 1985 apply to loans made under this provision.

Execution of works by authority under agency agreement

5.261 The local housing authority has the power to enter into an agency agreement to carry out the works of improvement required under an undertaking or improvement notice on behalf of, and at the expense of, the person having control of the dwelling (or other person having an estate or interest in the dwelling as appropriate).[50] Such an agreement can be entered into at any time once the undertaking has been accepted or the improvement notice becomes operative. Acting under such an agreement, the authority has the same rights of entry as the person on whose behalf it acts.[51]

Purchase notices

5.262 At any time within six months from the date of an improvement notice becoming operative, persons having control of the dwelling may serve notice on the authority requiring the authority to purchase their interest in the dwelling.[52] Once such a notice requiring purchase has been served, the authority is deemed[53] to have been authorised compulsorily to purchase that interest,[54] and must proceed to acquire that interest.

The authority is deemed to have served a notice to treat[55] on the date of service of the notice requiring purchase and cannot act to withdraw

---

[48] 1985 Act, s.228(5) and (6).
[49] *Ibid.* s.228(7).
[50] *Ibid.* s.225(1).
[51] *Ibid.* s.225(2); see s.224 of the 1985 Act—para. 5.253 and Chap. 1, para. 1.32.
[52] *Ibid.* s.227(1).
[53] *Ibid.* s.227(2).
[54] As a part of the Pt. II of the 1985 Act, general housing accommodation stock, with all the powers available under that Part of the Act once the dwelling is acquired.
[55] A notice to treat normally indicates that the commencement of the compulsory purchase procedure after confirmation of a C.P.O. and initiates the compensation proceedings, prevents new interests in the land being created, and enables the authority to serve notice of entry to take possession—see the Acquisition of Land Act 1981, the Compulsory Purchase Act 1965, the Land Compensation Act 1961, and Pt. XVII of the Housing Act 1985.

ENFORCEMENT OF THE STANDARDS

the deemed notice to treat.[56] Within 21 days from the date of receipt of the notice requiring purchase, the authority is required to notify every other person known to be an owner, lessee, mortgagee and occupier of the dwelling of the receipt (and effects) of that notice.[57]

5.263 It is suggested that when the authority is considering whether to serve a provisional notice in respect of a dwelling outside a H.A.A. or a G.I.A.[58] or an improvement notice in respect of any dwelling,[59] no account should be taken of the possibility of receiving a notice requiring purchase.[60]

Enforcement of improvement notices

5.264 A local housing authority has power to carry out or complete the works specified in an improvement notice in any one of three specific circumstances as described below.[61]

(a) If, after the expiry of the time limit specified by the notice (or such longer period as the authority may have permitted in writing), the works specified in the notice have not been completed, the authority may step in and carry out or complete those works.[62]

(b) Where the authority receive written notice from the person having control of the dwelling for the time being, that the person is unable to or does not intend to complete the works. The authority may step in and carry out or complete those works.[63] Care should be taken that the reason for the person not being able to carry out or complete the works does not arise out of a lack of finance or credit due to ignorance of the availability of grant-aid[64] or the possibility of a loan to cover an amount over and above that covered by grant-aid.[65] Such written notice may be given at any time before the expiry of the time limit specified by the notice (or such longer period as the authority may have permitted in writing). Receipt of the notification enables

---

[56] 1985 Act, s.227(2)—see the Land Compensation Act 1961, s.31.
[57] *Ibid.* s.227(3).
[58] *Ibid.* s.212—see paras. 5.209–5.211.
[59] *Ibid.* ss.214 and 215—see paras. 5.221–5.227 and 5.238–5.243.
[60] See, in particular, *Padfield* v. *Minister of Agriculture* [1968] A.C. 997, and *Associated Provincial Picture Houses* v. *Wednesbury Corp.* [1948] 1 K.B. 223.
[61] 1985 Act, s.220.
[62] *Ibid.* s.220(1).
[63] *Ibid.* s.220(2).
[64] *Ibid.* s.228—see paras. 5.227 and 5.243.
[65] Under Pt. XV of the 1985 Act. Note also that the restriction imposed by the provisions of s.465(1) of the 1985 Act (preventing approval of an application for grant-aid toward the cost of works already begun unless the authority are satisfied there were good reasons for starting before approval) does not apply where these works are required by a statutory notice—s.465(2) of the 1985 Act.

the authority to step in before the expiry of the time limit specified by the notice (or such longer period as may have been permitted in writing), and to carry out or complete the works within that time limit.

(c) If, after six months from the date the notice became operative,[66] the authority have reason to believe that the person having control of the dwelling for the time being is not able to or does not intend to complete the works specified in the notice, the authority may serve a notice requiring that person to provide, within 21 days, evidence of their intentions in respect of the work. Where the authority are not satisfied by any response and remain unconvinced of the ability or intention to comply with the notice within any time limit specified, the authority may step in before the expiry of the time limit specified by the notice (or such longer period as may have been permitted in writing), and carry out or complete the works within that time limit.[67] Again care should be taken that the reason for the person not being able to carry out or complete the works is not because of a lack of finance or credit, resulting from ignorance of the availability of grant-aid[68] or the possibility of a loan to cover an amount over and above that covered by grant-aid.[69]

5.265 The use of the discretionary term "may" in the section makes it clear that the authority need not proceed to carry out the works, but they should not adopt a fixed policy either that they will or will not carry out such works.[70] It is suggested that the discretion is not one which would allow no action (unless the circumstances or conditions of the dwelling have changed so that the authority is no longer satisfied that the dwelling ought to be improved), but it is a discretion as to the most appropriate action to deal with the condition of the dwelling at that time. Once the notice has expired the authority must review the situation, and determine the appropriate action at that time.

5.266 It will be noted that in the circumstances described in (b) and (c) in para. 5.264 above, enabling the authority to carry out or complete the specified works, the authority is required to complete those works before the expiry of the time limit set by the notice (or as extended by the authority in writing). As the time limit specified by the notice may be extended by the authority without any formal application,[71] it would

---

[66] 1985 Act, s.218—see paras. 5.241 and 5.226.
[67] *Ibid*. s.220(4).
[68] *Ibid*. s.228—see paras. 5.227 and 5.243.
[69] See n. 68 above.
[70] *Elliott* v. *Brighton B.C.* (1981) 79 L.G.R. 506.
[71] 1985 Act, s.216(1)(*c*).

ENFORCEMENT OF THE STANDARDS

appear that the authority could provide itself with written extensions, and may have to do so to avoid non-compliance within the time limit being a ground of appeal against any demand for recovery of expenses.[72]

5.267 Where the authority decide to carry out the necessary work in default of the person having control of the dwelling they must, 21 days before beginning those works, give written notice of intention to the occupier of the dwelling, to the person having control, and to every other person known to be an owner, lessee or mortgagee of the dwelling.[73]

5.268 Any expenses incurred by the local housing authority in carrying out the works, together with any interest (at a reasonable rate determined by the authority) from the date when the demand for payment is served until it is settled, can be recovered by action in the county court or High Court (depending on the amount involved).[74]

The money is to be recovered from the person on whom the notice was served, unless:

(a) on an appeal against the notice the court has directed that some other person(s) pay all or part of the cost of the works (see para. 5.247, ground (g)); or

(b) the person on whom the notice was served is an agent or trustee for another, when that person's liability is limited to the amount that has been in his hands on behalf of the other person since the date of the service of the demand.

In addition, the local housing authority has the same powers and remedies for the enforcement of the charge against the house under the Law of Property Act 1925, and otherwise as if they were mortgagees by deed having powers of sale and lease, to accept the surrender of leases and to appoint a receiver. However, the power to appoint a receiver cannot be exercised until one month from the date the charge takes effect.[75]

5.269 There is a right of appeal against a demand for the recovery of expenses available to any person aggrieved. Such appeal must be within the 21 days from the date of service of the demand before it takes effect. On such appeal, no question may be raised which might have been raised on appeal against the improvement notice.[76] No appeal is necessary where the demand relates to works carried out following an invalid improvement notice.[77]

---

[72] 1985 Act, para. 6, Sched. 10.
[73] *Ibid.* s.220(4).
[74] *Ibid.* Sched. 10.
[75] *Ibid.* para. 7, Sched. 10.
[76] *Ibid.* para. 6, Sched. 10. Appeals against improvement notices—s.217 of the 1985 Act—paras. 5.245–5.252.
[77] *West Ham Corp.* v. *Benabo* [1934] 2 K.B. 253.

CHAPTER 6

HOUSES IN MULTIPLE OCCUPATION

The standards dealt with in Chapter 3 and the enforcement procedures **6.01**
discussed in Chapter 5 are generally applicable to all accommodation available or used for human habitation. However, recognising that the occupation of a single house by more than one household will create additional problems, there are separate and additional provisions relating to the control of standards in "houses in multiple occupation."

1. Definition of "house in multiple occupation"	6.02
2. Fitness for multiple occupation	6.18
3. Management of houses in multiple occupation	6.29
4. Means of escape in case of fire	6.57
5. Action to deal with houses unfit for multiple occupation	6.64
6. Management orders	6.92
7. Prosecution for offences under management regulations	6.102
8. Notices to require works to make good neglect	6.104
9. Action to ensure adequate means of escape from fire	6.112
10. Enforcement of notices	6.132
11. Reconnection or maintenance of services	6.142
12. Control orders	6.147

Definition of "house in multiple occupation"
The Housing Act 1985 defines a "house in multiple occupation" as: **6.02**

> "a house which is occupied by persons who do not form a single household."[1]

For the purposes of special grants,[2] the phrase "house in multiple occupation" only applies to the multi-occupied part of the house, and not necessarily to the whole of the "house." The phrase "house in multiple occupation" is defined by section 525 of the 1985 Act as:

> " . . . a house which is occupied by persons who do not form a single household, exclusive of any part of the house which is occupied as a separate dwelling by persons who form a single household".

---
[1] Housing Act 1985, s.345.
[2] *Ibid.* ss.483–490.

Historical background to the definition

6.03 Before the Housing Act 1969, the phrase used in statutes was "... a house which, or part of which, is let in lodgings, or which is occupied by members of more than one family."[3] The present definition was introduced by section 58 of the Housing Act 1969.

Prior to the Housing Act 1985, the term "house in multiple occupation" was not used in the statutory provisions relating to conditions and the associated enforcement procedures,[4] but the phrase came into common usage as a result of head-notes to the statutes.

6.04 The pre-1969 definition was of long standing, and had been the subject of frequent comment by the courts. In *Kyffin* v. *Simmons*[5] it was held that "a house which, or part of which, is let in lodgings, or which is occupied by members of more than one family" included an ordinary house, not specifically constructed to be let as separate dwellings, with a common staircase and rooms on each floor let to separate families; in *Okereke* v. *Borough of Brent*[6] it was held that it also included a house divided into self-contained dwellings, each of which occupied by a different family.

However, in *Weatheritt* v. *Cantley*[7] it was held that the phrase excluded buildings divided into separate tenements where each tenement was occupied by a separate family and in *Holm* v. *Royal Borough of Kensington and Chelsea*[8] the court held that a house occupied by members of the same family living as two separate households was also excluded.

The decision in the *Holm* case on the definition before the 1969 Act made it clear that the term "family" was not appropriate or relevant to determining whether a house was in "multiple occupation," and as a result the present definition was introduced (by section 58 of the Housing Act 1969), bringing within the scope of the enforcement provisions certain categories of house which the courts had previously excluded.

6.05 Some pre-1969 decisions of the Courts provide guidance (but *only* guidance) on the interpretation of the present description. In particular the decisions in *Kyffin* v. *Simmons*[9] and *Okereke* v *Borough of Brent*[10] still appear useful based as they are on the style of occupation rather than on an interpretation of the term "family," and substituting "household" would not affect the style of occupation.

---

[3] *e.g.* s.12 of the Housing Act 1961, and previously s.36 of the Housing Act 1936 and s.90 of the Public Health Act 1875.
[4] The only exception being s.129(1) of the Housing Act 1974 dealing with special grants.
[5] (1903) 67 J.P. 227.
[6] [1967] 1 Q.B. 42.
[7] [1901] 2 K.B. 285.
[8] [1968] 1 Q.B. 646.
[9] (1903) 67 J.P. 227.
[10] [1967] 1 Q.B. 42.

DEFINITION OF "HOUSE IN MULTIPLE OCCUPATION"

When the present definition was first introduced (by the 1969 Housing Act) the Ministry of Housing and Local Government issued a circular which included the following comments[11]: **6.06**

> "5. The old definition, which has been used in statutes for over one hundred years, has been criticised recently by local authorities. They have said that the old definition gives rise to difficulties in houses occupied by persons all claiming some family relationship where, nevertheless, it seemed likely that there were in fact several households sharing unsatisfactory and inadequate facilities.
>
> 6. Facilities required in a house depend to some extent not only on the number of persons living there, but on the extent to which they live as separate households. But there are many kinds of situation to be covered, and the new definition has therefore been framed in the terms—'a house which is occupied by persons who do not form a single household.' While it is not open to Ministers to give any authoritative interpretation of the law the view taken is that it is reasonable to regard the new definition as covering in particular:
>
>   (i) a house occupied by two or more households;
>   (ii) a house occupied by a number of persons where the relationship between the various individuals resident at any one time are so tenuous as to support the view that they can neither singly nor collectively be regarded as forming a single household; and
>   (iii) a house which is occupied by one main household together with varying numbers of individuals who do not form a part of that household. The principal example of this third situation is where a house is used for accommodating lodgers, although in certain circumstances an individual lodger might form part of a household.
>
> Where a house is occupied by a family or a single person and there are also one or two lodgers fully 'living in' as part of the family, they could be held to be part of one 'household'; but catering for lodgers on any substantial scale as a business enterprise is likely to constitute multiple occupation under the new definition. It would be a question to be decided on all the facts of a particular case."

Aspects of the description of an H.M.O.

In considering what type of premises fall within the definition of "house in multiple occupation", it is necessary to look at each aspect as well as the whole. **6.07**

"**House.**" A general consideration of the interpretation of the word "house" for the purposes of the Housing Act 1985 is given above (see Chapter 3, paragraph 3.27—3.31), and since the term is not specifically **6.08**

---

[11] Circular No.67/69 (W.O. No.66/69) September 4, 1969.

defined in Part XI of the 1985 Act, the general definition given by section 399 is applicable.

The guidance to local authorities on interpretation[12] first introduced in 1969 has now been re-issued,[13] and include the following comments on the term "house":

> "In *Reed* v. *Hastings Corporation* (1964) 62 L.G.R. 588 the Court of Appeal held that section 90 of the Housing Act 1957 [as amended, now section 358] applied to a large property, designed for human habitation and used as a holiday home for schoolchildren. Lord Justice Harman stated that 'house' in section 90 meant a structure built or adapted for use as a dwelling-house or for the purpose of human habitation. 'This structure . . . was always obviously a dwelling-house, and a dwelling-house it still is, in my view.'[14]
>
> In *Okereke* v. *Brent L.B.C.* [1967] 1 Q.B. 42 the Court of Appeal held that a house which had been converted into three separate self-contained dwellings, was a house within the meaning of section 15 of the Housing Act 1961 [now section 352]. Lord Justice Salmon said: 'the word "House" has no very precise meaning. There are many types of houses . . . The fact that some of these types of houses may be more likely than others to pass the requirements of the Housing Acts with flying colours does not make them any more or less houses. Once it is decided as a fact that a building is a house and there is evidence to support the decision, the question of law arises as to whether or not it is a type of house to which the relevant section of the Housing Act applies."[15]

6.09 In *R.* v. *Lambeth L.B.C., ex p. Clayhope Properties Ltd.*,[16] it was agreed by both parties that a purpose-built block of 20 flats was a "house" for the purposes of section 9(1A) of the Housing Act 1957 [now section 190(1)(*a*) of the 1985 Act], and the Court of Appeal commented that whether a particular block was a "house" was a question of fact (on which see the previous comments of Lord Justice Salmon, para. 6.08).

If a purpose-built block of flats is a "house" it will have far reaching implications. It is suggested that a purpose-built block of dwellings, if it is a "house", must be a "house in multiple occupation", because it will clearly be "occupied by persons not forming a single household"[16a] (see paras. 6.10—6.14 on "occupied" and "form a single household").

---

[12] Appendix A of Circular No.25/82 (W.O. No.41/82) October 25, 1982.
[13] D.o.E. Circular No.21/86 (W.O. No.23/86 and Home Office No.39/86) May 22, 1986, introducing the Memorandum on Overcrowding and Houses in Multiple Occupation.
[14] *Ibid.* para. 3.1.2.
[15] *Ibid.* para. 3.1.3.
[16] (1987) 283 E.G. 739, affirming (1986) 18 H.L.R. 541, Q.B.D.
[16a] This follows from the decision in *Berg* v. *Trafford B.C.* (1988) 20 H.L.R. 47.

DEFINITION OF "HOUSE IN MULTIPLE OCCUPATION"

"Occupied." Guidance in the circular issued by central government[17] includes the following:

6.10

> "In *Silbers* v. *Southwark London Borough Council* (1977) 76 L.G.R. 421 the Court of Appeal held that section 73(1) of the Housing Act 1964 [now section 379(1) of the 1985 Act] applied to a common lodging house. Lord Justice Cumming-Bruce said that there was no reason for restricting the word 'occupied' to mean occupied by exclusive possession rather than to give it the ordinary meaning of 'living in.'[18]"

The principle adopted by the Court of Appeal in the *Silbers* case was taken further in *Minford Properties* v. *L.B. of Hammersmith*,[19] the court holding that the term "occupied" related to a question of fact, and that a former tenant remaining in occupation pending the expiry of a suspended possession order still "occupied" the house.

6.11

It would also seem, however, that even when a house is completely empty, it may be possible to take action as though it were a "house occupied by persons who do not form a single household". In *R.* v. *Kerrier D.C., ex p. Guppys (Bridport) Ltd., (No. 2)*[20] the Court of Appeal held that an empty house was not a house in multiple occupation as defined by section 129 of the Housing Act 1974 [now section 525 of the 1985 Act]. Consequently they held that although notices under sections 15 and 16 of the Housing Act 1961 [now sections 352 and 366 of the 1985 Act] had already been served the house did not qualify for a mandatory special grant. However, Lawton L.J. explained that:

6.12

> "In my judgment on the evidence, at the relevant time the house was not in multiple occupation, whatever that term may mean. In so deciding, I must not be taken as deciding that, if a house is empty at the time when an application is made for a special grant, that fact by itself disqualifies the applicant. The reason why I say that I must not be taken as deciding that is this. It seems to me arguable that if an owner of a house in multiple occupation can only do the works by getting the occupiers out of possession and he intends to make the house available for multiple occupation when he has done the work, he does not disqualify himself by the mere fact that the house has been empty while he was doing the work."

In this particular case it was clear that the owners intended to alter the house to provide separate self-contained dwellings, and so take the

---

[17] Circular No. 67/69 (W.O. No. 66/69) September 4, 1969.
[18] Memorandum on Overcrowding and Houses in Multiple Occupation, para. 3.1.5.
[19] (1978) 247 E.G. 561, D.C.
[20] (1985) 17 H.L.R. 426.

building outside the definition of house in multiple occupation as given by section 129 of the 1974 Act [now section 525 of the 1985 Act].

On this basis, it is suggested that it is arguable that the intention of the owner is the relevant factor, not merely the question of whether the house is or was "occupied," or in use as a house in multiple occupation, and that this principle applies both for the purposes of special grants and the general provisions relating to standards in multi-occupied houses.

6.13 **"Form a single household."** Commenting on the interpretation of the term "form a single household" the guidance in the circular[20a] concentrates on the decision of the House of Lords in *Simmons* v. *Pizzey*.[21] This case dealt with a refuge for battered women which was subject to a direction under section 19 of the Housing Act 1961 [now section 354 of the 1985 Act]. The number of persons accommodated in the house exceeded the limits set by the direction, and part of the question considered by the House of Lords was whether or not those persons (at the relevant date some 75 women and children) could be said to form a single household. If they could, the house would not be in multiple occupation.

An important aspect of this decision is that there were factors relating to the style of occupation which, taken in isolation, could lead to the conclusion that the house was occupied by a single household. For example no one was allocated a part, or a room (or even a bed) in the house on any permanent basis, there was no concept of separate households and the general living arrangements were organised collectively, including the eating arrangements and general household management. Other factors affected the interpretation, including the number of residents and the absence of an intention that any of the women and children accommodated at the premises should live there permanently; it was a temporary place of refuge, with some leaving to find accommodation of their own, others returning to the houses they had left, and others arriving with little or no notice. It was these points that the House of Lords relied on in finding that the occupiers could not reasonably be held to be a single household.

The guidance[22] focuses on one judgment, and states—

> "Lord Hailsham said that both the expression 'household' and membership of it is a question of fact and degree. He took three factors into account in deciding that the establishment in question was beyond the limits of what could conceivably be called a single household:

[20a] Circular No. 67/69 (W.O. No. 66/69) September 4, 1969.
[21] [1979] A.C. 37.
[22] Circular No. 67/69 (W.O. No. 66/69) September 4, 1969.

DEFINITION OF "HOUSE IN MULTIPLE OCCUPATION"

(a) the size was beyond what in that area 'can ordinarily and reasonably be regarded as a single household';

(b) the fluctuating character of the resident population 'both as regards the fact and fluctuation and of the extent of it';

(c) a temporary place of refuge for fortuitous arrivals could not be regarded as ordinarily forming a household at all."[23]

As mentioned above (para. 6.10), in *Silbers* v. *Southwark L.B.C.*,[24] the Court of Appeal held that a house used as a hostel for women who stayed for varying periods of time and who lived in dormitories was occupied by persons who did not form a single household. It should be noted that this house was at one time registered under Part IX of the Public Health Act 1936 [now Part XII of the 1985 Act] as a common lodging-house, and that there had been no real change in the use or style of occupation of the house since that registration.

6.14

By contrast, in *Hackney London Borough* v. *Ezedinma*[25] the Divisional Court decided that a magistrates' court was entitled to conclude that eight persons, each let a separate room and sharing three kitchens, could be held to be living as three households. In this case however, May J. also stated that he did not find compelling evidence that the tenants did comprise three households, but it was a matter of fact and degree for the justices and he would not interfere with their finding. In his judgment, Griffiths L.J. stated that he had been persuaded that the word "household" could be construed so as to include a single person lodging in a single room. He doubted whether he would have concluded that the occupiers of this house were living as three households, but declined to interfere with the decision of the magistrates.

Buildings deemed to be houses in multiple occupation

6.15

In addition to buildings which are "houses" and which are occupied by persons who do not form a single household and are therefore "houses in multiple occupation," the legislation specifies certain categories of buildings used for human habitation which can be treated, to some extent, as if they are such houses.

Buildings which, although not a house, comprise separate dwellings, at least two of which lack a sanitary convenience and personal washing facilities accessible only to those living in the dwelling, are deemed to be houses in multiple occupation.[26]

However, a direction[27] to reduce the number of persons or households in occupation cannot be issued in respect of such a building and

---

[23] (1985) 274 E.G. 924.
[24] (1977) 76 L.G.R. 421.
[25] [1981] 3 All E.R. 438.
[26] Housing Act 1985, s.352(6).
[27] *Ibid.* s.354.

although a notice can be served requiring additional amenities and facilities[28] with regard to the existing numbers in occupation, such a notice cannot be served with regard to a smaller number than the number actually in occupation.[29]

6.16 Similarly, buildings which comprise separate dwellings at least two of which are occupied by persons who do not form a single household, are also deemed to be houses in multiple occupation.[30]

6.17 A "tenement block," in which one or more of the dwellings lack one or more of the standard amenities, is deemed to be a house in multiple occupation.[31] A "tenement block" is defined as:

" . . . a building or a part of a building which was constructed in the form of, and consists of two or more flats, that is to say, separate sets of premises, whether or not on the same floor, constructed for use for the purpose of a dwelling and forming part of a building from some other part of which they are divided horizontally".[32]

Such tenements are only deemed to be houses in multiple occupation for the purposes of the application and enforcement of standards of management.[33]

It should be noted that in respect of action taken after August 25, 1969 but before April 1, 1985, the standard amenities referred to are those defined by section 58 and Part I of Schedule 6 to the Housing Act 1974, and such standard amenities must have been absent at any time after August 25, 1969.[34] In respect of action taken after April 1, 1985, the standard amenities are those defined by section 508 of the 1985 Act (see Chapter 3, para. 3.62).

Fitness for multiple occupation

Historical background

6.18 Prior to November 24, 1961,[35] local authorities were able to require works at a "house let in lodgings"[36] to make the house suitable for the numbers of individuals and/or households at the house; in default of requiring works the authority could direct a reduction in the number of individuals or households at the house.

Action could be taken once the authority was satisfied that:

---

[28] Housing Act 1985, s.352.
[29] *Ibid.* s.352(2).
[30] *Ibid.* s.374.
[31] *Ibid.* s.374.
[32] *Ibid.* s.374(2).
[33] *Ibid.* ss.369–373.
[34] s.89 and Sched. 8, para. 29 of the Housing Act 1969.
[35] On the coming into force of the Housing Act 1961—see s.23(9) of the 1961 Act.
[36] Housing Act 1957, s.36.

"with respect to such matters as are specified in paragraphs (*d*) to (*h*) of subsection (1) of section four of [the Housing Act 1957] the premises are so far defective, having regard to the number of individuals or households, or both, accommodated for the time being on the premises, as to be not reasonably suitable for occupation by those individuals or households."[36a]

The matters listed in paragraphs (*d*) to (*h*) of section 4(1) of the 1957 Act were: natural lighting; ventilation; water supply; drainage and sanitary conveniences; and facilities for the storage, preparation and cooking of food and for the disposal of waste water.[37]

The provisions of section 36 of the 1957 Act were re-enacted in a strengthened and extended form by the 1961 Act,[38] giving a power to require works to make the house fit for the numbers of households and/or individuals occupying it, and a second power to limit the numbers in the house. When re-enacted the new provision specified the matters, rather than referring back to matters listed in the standard of fitness. These new provisions contained an extended version of matters (*d*) to (*h*) of section 4 of the 1957 Act.

6.19

The provisions of the 1961 Act are now re-enacted unchanged by sections 352 and 354–357 of the 1985 Act.

Relationship between fitness for human habitation and for multiple occupation

There is a close relationship between the standard of fitness for human habitation and that for multiple occupation. Nevertheless it is quite clear (and logical) that the standard of fitness for human habitation takes overall priority.

6.20

This relationship is made clear by references back to the standard of fitness for human habitation originally made in the standard of fitness for multiple occupation in the legislation (see the above paragraphs), and which (to some extent) still continues.

Approach in the application of both standards of fitness

The general approach to be followed in applying the standards is determined by the relationship considered above. Local housing authorities are required first to determine whether a house satisfies the standard of fitness for human habitation,[39] irrespective of the type or style of occupation of that house (and whether it is occupied). As a second stage, where a house is occupied by "persons who do not form a single household," the authority should determine whether that house satisfies the standard of fitness for multiple occupation. Finally the authority

6.21

[36a] Housing Act 1957, s.36.
[37] *Ibid*. s.4, now re-enacted as s.604 of the Housing Act 1985.
[38] ss.15 and 19 of the 1961 Act.
[39] See Chap. 3, paras. 3.24–3.46.

must determine whether each separately occupied part of a house in multiple occupation satisfies the standard of fitness for human habitation.[40]

This step-by-step approach looks at the whole house in terms of whether it should be used or be available for human habitation, and whether as a whole house it is fit for multiple occupation. Finally it requires consideration of whether the separate individual parts should be used or be available for human habitation. It should be noted that the standard of fitness for multiple occupation does not enable the condition of the fabric to be taken into account—disrepair, stability and dampness are matters included in the standard of fitness for human habitation, but are not necessary for consideration in terms of fitness for multiple occupation. Again, this fact follows on from the step-by-step approach.

General approach to the standard of fitness for multiple occupation

6.22 The general principles discussed above on the approach to the standard of fitness for human habitation apply equally to the standard of fitness for multiple occupation. That is to say it is the effect of the deficiency that is important, having regard to the multiple occupation of the house.[41]

6.23 The main difference between the two standards is that the standard for multiple occupation concentrates on the facilities and amenities available for the use of the numbers of individuals and/or household occupying the house. This means that the standard is to be considered from two different points—first, whether or not the house satisfies the standard having regard to the number occupying it and secondly, whether or not the house could satisfy the standard if the number in occupation were reduced.

Definition of fitness for multiple occupation

6.24 The provisions require the local housing authority to be of the opinion that the house is so far defective with respect to any of the matters listed, and having regard to the number of individuals and/or households accommodated at the house (or the reduced number specified by the authority), that the house is not reasonably suitable for occupation by those individuals and/or households in that condition.[42]

The matters listed in the Act are:

"natural and artificial lighting,
ventilation,
water supply,
personal washing facilities,

---

[40] See interpretation of "house," paras. 6.08–6.09 above.
[41] See Chap. 3, para. 3.22.
[42] s.352(1) of the 1985 Act.

drainage and sanitary conveniences,
facilities for the storage, preparation and cooking of food, and for the disposal of waste water, and
installations for space heating or for the use of space heating appliances."

Interpretation of the standard of fitness for multiple occupation

6.25 There has been no statutory or ministerial guidance on the interpretation of these matters, and on only one occasion have the courts had an opportunity to comment on them. In *McPhail* v. *Islington L.B.C.*,[43] the Court of Appeal held that the term "personal washing facilities" enabled a local authority to require the provision of a hot water supply.

However, the Institution of Environmental Health Officers (I.E.H.O.) has issued guidance,[44] which starts from the basis that within the broad statutory definition of house in multiple occupation[45] there will be a range of styles of occupation, and that different standards should be applied having regard to the style of occupation. The I.E.H.O. has determined six broad categories and provided a recommended standard for each. Briefly, the I.E.H.O. categories are:

Category A. Houses occupied as individual rooms, bedsits or flatlets which may have a number of rooms for exclusive occupation (not necessarily behind one door), with some sharing of amenities, each part being separately rented.

Category B. Houses occupied on a shared basis—for example, occupied by individuals who for certain activities live as a single household unit but for others do not. Usually, the house will be let to a defined group and not to the individuals.

Category C. Houses where "lodgers" are taken in, and meals are provided together with the main resident household. The individual lodgers would have another primary residence.

Category D. Houses generally referred to as "hostels," "guesthouses," "bed and breakfast accommodation," providing to some extent accommodation for people with no other permanent place of residence (as distinct from a hotel providing accommodation solely for visitors to the area who will have another primary residence).

Category E. Houses which are hostels and require registration under the Registered Homes Act 1984—for example, residential homes

---

[43] [1970] 2 Q.B. 197.
[44] *Environmental Health Professional Practice*, Vol. II, Chap. III, Houses in Multiple Occupation—Formulation and Implementation of Policy Including Standards; I.E.H.O. 1986.
[45] s.345 of the Housing Act 1985. See paras. 6.02–6.14 on interpretation.

providing board and personal care for persons in need of such care by reason of age, disablement, past or present dependence on alcohol or drugs, or past or present mental disorder.

Category F. Houses or buildings which by erection or conversion contain dwellings which are self-contained, and where each dwelling is provided with facilities and amenities behind an access door. There would be no shared amenities.[46]

6.26 The I.E.H.O. also recommends standards in respect of each category of house in multiple occupation for adoption and application by local housing authorities.[47] These recommended standards deal with requirements for each category under the following headings:

Space;
Natural lighting;
Artificial lighting;
Ventilation;
Water supply;
Personal washing facilities;
Drainage and sanitary conveniences;
Facilities for storage, preparation and cooking of food and for the disposal of waste water;
Space heating; and
Refuse storage and disposal.

The standards are comprehensive and specific, taking account of the different problems and requirements necessary to ensure that the house in multiple occupation satisfies the possible needs dictated by the style of multiple occupation.

Over-occupation of houses in multiple occupation

6.27 This is the second part of the approach to the fitness of the house for multiple occupation. As stated above (para. 6.23), the standard is to be considered from two different points—first, whether or not the house satisfies the standard having regard to the number occupying it, and secondly, whether or not the house could satisfy the standard if the number in occupation were reduced.

In many cases a house in multiple occupation may satisfy the standard of fitness for multiple occupation if the number in occupation were reduced. Alternatively, the provision of additional facilities and/or amenities may be possible if numbers were reduced (thereby providing space for those facilities or amenities). If it is determined that a

---

[46] Para. 3.04.02 of the *Environmental Health Professional Practice,* Vol. II, Chap. III; I.E.H.O. 1986.

[47] Appendix II of the *Environmental Health Professional Practice,* Vol. II, Chap. III; I.E.H.O. 1986.

reduction in number of occupants will render the house fit for multiple occupation by that reduced number, reduction is enforced by "natural wastage" (*i.e.* prohibiting re-letting of tenancies which become terminated (for whatever reason) until the number falls below the limit set).[48]

6.28 It is important to note the difference between this and the overcrowding provisions in the Housing Act 1985.[49] This provision is a part of the standard of fitness for multiple occupation and the number in occupation of the house is to be considered having regard to the matters listed in the standard of fitness for multiple occupation; the overcrowding standards relate only to the number of persons in relation to rooms (and the floor area of those rooms) available for sleeping.

Management of houses in multiple occupation

6.29 Because additional problems can occur in houses in multiple occupation, particularly in the common parts, for which tenants of individual parts have no overall responsibility, local housing authorities have been empowered to deal with unsatisfactory standards of management.

No detailed standards are set down, but the Housing (Management of Houses in Multiple Occupation) Regulations 1962[50] outlines the duties of the manager and the matters which the local housing authority can take into consideration.

6.30 The management regulations do not apply to a house in multiple occupation until the local housing authority make a management order.[51] Once the order has been made the duties and standards set out below must be complied with.

General duties of management

6.31 The "manager," if not a resident in the house, must make arrangements to ensure that obligations under the regulations are discharged effectively (including arrangements for adequate supervision of the house), and must inform any agent or trustee (through whom rents are received) that the management order has been made, and that the management regulations apply to the house, and explain the duties imposed on that person.[52]

6.32 The term "manager" is defined as "the person who is an owner or a lessee of the house and who, directly or through an agent or trustee, receives rents or other payments from persons who are tenants of parts of the house, or who are lodgers; and, where those rents or other

---

[48] ss.354–347 of the Housing Act 1985. See below, paras. 6.78–6.91.
[49] Part X of the Housing Act 1985—See Chap. 7.
[50] S.I. 1962 No.668. Made originally under s.13 of the Housing Act 1961 (now re-enacted as s.369 of the Housing Act 1985), retained in force by s.2 of the Housing (Consequential Provisions) Act 1985.
[51] Under s.370 of the 1985 Act.
[52] Housing (Management of Houses in Multiple Occupation) Regulations 1962, reg. 3.

payments are received through another person as his agent or trustee, includes that other person."[53]

"Rents" are defined as "rents or other payments from tenants of parts of a house, or from lodgers therein, and "the rents," in relation to a person who is an owner or lessee of a house or an agent or trustee through whom rents are received, means such rents or other payments as are received by, or through, that person."[53]

6.33 Where managers who collect rents for other persons become aware of breaches of the duties of management, they must take the necessary action or bring the matter to the attention of the owner or lessee who receives the rent. In addition, the local housing authority may make a complaint about the management of the house, requiring the agent or trustee to pass it on to the owner or lessee who receives the rents, and also requiring the agent to supply the local housing authority with the name and address of the owner or lessee.[54]

These duties placed on an agent or trustee receiving rents for an owner or lessee do not relieve that agent or trustee from any of the duties or obligations placed on managers by the regulations or from any liability for failure to comply with them.[54]

6.34 Without prejudice to their powers the local housing authority may make an arrangement with the manager as to how business between the authority and the manager will normally be conducted, and, where there is more than one manager, nominate one with whom the authority will normally conduct business.[55]

The duties of management

6.35 The management regulations outline the duties and obligations of the manager, and these are summarised below.

6.36 **Water Supply and Drainage.** All means of water supply and drainage must be maintained in a proper state of repair, clean and in good order. Particularly, tanks and cisterns must be covered and kept clean and in working order; and water fittings, including pipes, tanks, taps, baths, and waterclosets must be protected against damage by frost. The manager must not unreasonably interrupt the supply of water.[56]

6.37 **Gas and electricity supplies, and installations for lighting and heating.** Installations in common parts of the house for:

(a) the supply of gas and electricity;

---

[53] Housing (Management of Houses in Multiple Occupation) Regulations 1962, reg. 2.
[54] *Ibid.* reg. 3.
[55] *Ibid.* reg. 19.
[56] *Ibid.* reg. 4.

(b) lighting; and
(c) space and water heating,

must be maintained in repair and proper working order, and artificial lighting for common parts must be readily available for use as reasonably required by occupants. Again, the manager must not unreasonably interrupt the supply of gas or electricity to any occupier.[57]

Rooms and installations in common use. Excluding any installations an occupier is entitled to remove, the manager must ensure that: 6.38

(a) rooms in common use are maintained in a proper state of repair (including reasonable decorative repair), clean and in good order;
(b) sanitary conveniences, baths, sinks, wash hand basins, and installations for cooking or storing food which are in common use are maintained in a proper state of repair, clean and in good order; and
(c) kitchens, bathrooms, lavatories and wash houses which are in common use, and any installations in such rooms are maintained in a proper state of repair (including reasonable decorative repair), clean and in good order.[58]

Other parts of the house in common use. The following common parts must be maintained in a proper state of repair (including reasonable decorative repair), clean and in good order, and kept reasonably free from obstruction, that is: 6.39

(a) staircases, passageways and corridors;
(b) halls and lobbies;
(c) entrances to the house (including entrance doors, porches and entrance steps); and
(d) balconies.[59]

In particular, banisters and handrails must be maintained in good order and repair, and any missing must be replaced. Additional banisters and handrails must be provided where safety requires.[60]

A staircase, passageway or corridor is considered to be in common use if it gives access to a tenant's living accommodation, and which, although not itself in common use, opens directly off a common part and is not separate from that common part by a door.[61]

---

[57] Housing (Management of Houses in Multiple Occupation) Regulations 1962, reg. 5.
[58] *Ibid.* reg. 6.
[59] *Ibid.* reg. 7.
[60] *Ibid.* reg. 7(3).
[61] *Ibid.* reg. 7(2).

6.40 **Accommodation let to tenants or lodgers.** At the commencement of the letting of any "premises"[62] let after the management order was made, the manager must ensure that:

> (a) they are, internally, in a reasonable state of structural repair, and in a clean condition; and
> (b) the following installations within the "premises" are in a reasonable state of repair and proper working order—
> > (i) for the supply of water, gas and electricity,
> > (ii) for making use of those supplies (including space and water heating installations), and
> > (iii) for sanitation.[63]

6.41 In respect of "premises"[63a] already let on the date of the making of the management order, and all "premises" occupied while the management order remains in force, the manager, within a reasonable time, must take such steps as may be necessary to:

> (a) put and maintain them, internally, in a reasonable state of structural repair; and
> (b) put and maintain in a reasonable state of repair and proper working order the installations within the "premises" for:
> > (i) the supply of water, gas and electricity, and for sanitation (including basins, sinks, baths and sanitary conveniences, but excluding other fixtures, fittings and appliances), and
> > (ii) space and water heating.[64]

The manager is not, however, obliged to carry out repairs to anything which the tenant is entitled to remove from the "premises". Nor does the manager have to carry out repairs which have become necessary because of untenant-like activities of the tenant.[65]

6.42 **Windows and ventilation.** All windows and other means of ventilation in any part of the house occupied or used by any tenants or lodgers must be maintained in good order and repair. However, this does not require the manager to carry out repairs which become necessary after the date of the management order and result from untenant-like activities of that tenant or lodger.[66]

---

[62] "Premises" is defined by reg. 8(1) as "being a room or set of rooms in a part of any house to which the regulations apply."
[63] *Ibid.* reg. 8.
[63a] "Premises" is defined by reg. 8(1) as "being a room or set of rooms in a part of any house to which the regulations apply."
[64] *Ibid.* reg. 8(3) and (4).
[65] *Ibid.* reg. 8(4) and (5).
[66] *Ibid.* reg. 9.

MANAGEMENT OF HOUSES IN MULTIPLE OCCUPATION

Means of escape from fire. All the means of escape from fire including any escape apparatus must be put and maintained in proper repair and good order, and kept free from obstruction. The local housing authority may also require the manager to display notices with respect to the means of escape from fire (other than the normal exits).[67]   **6.43**

Miscellaneous parts of the house. The manager is also required to ensure that: **6.44**

    (a) outbuildings, yards, and other areas belonging to the house and in common use are put and kept in a proper state of repair, clean condition, and good order;

    (b) any garden belonging to the house and in common use is kept in a tidy condition;

    (c) boundary walls, fences and railings belonging to the house are kept and maintained in reasonable repair so as not to be dangerous; and

    (d) any part of the house not in use (including any part subject to a closing order) and any passage or staircase giving direct access to such parts, is kept reasonably clean and free from refuse and litter.[68]

Disposal of refuse and litter. The manager must also ensure that refuse and litter does not accumulate in the house or its curtilage, except in proper containers. In order to satisfy this requirement, the manager must: **6.45**

    (a) ensure that there are suitable and sufficient refuse and litter containers (unless such provision is made by the local authority); and

    (b) make such other arrangements as may be necessary for the disposal of refuse and litter from the house (having regard to the service provided by the local authority).[69]

General safety of the occupants. The regulations also specifically place a general duty of care on the manager to ensure that reasonable precautions are taken to protect tenants and lodgers (and their households) from injury as a result of structural conditions, having particular regard to the number of persons living there. Without prejudice to this general duty, the manager must ensure that: **6.46**

    (a) roofs and balconies are made safe or reasonable measures are taken to prevent access to them; and

    (b) such safeguards as may be necessary are provided to prevent

---

[67] Housing (Management of Houses in Multiple Occupation) Regulations 1962, reg. 10.
[68] *Ibid.* reg. 11.
[69] *Ibid.* reg. 12.

accidents involving windows on staircases and landings which have sills at or near floor level.[70]

Duties to provide information

6.47 In addition to dealing with the general conditions and maintenance of the house, the management regulations require information to be provided to the occupants and to the local housing authority.

6.48 **Information for occupants.** The manager must ensure that the following information, amended and updated as necessary, is displayed in a position readily accessible to the occupants of the house:

(a) a notice giving the name and address of each manager of the house and of the person who is agent or trustee for the receipt of rents;
(b) a copy of the management order which applies to the house;
(c) a copy of the management regulations; and
(d) if required and provided by the local housing authority, a notice[71] summarising the main provisions of the management regulations and the provisions of the Housing Acts dealing with failure to comply with the requirements of those regulations.[72]

6.49 **Information for the local housing authority.** Unless the local housing authority state otherwise, all the following information must be supplied to them in writing.[73]

6.50 The local housing authority may require the manager to provide, within a specified reasonable time, any of the following details in respect of the house (but where only part of the house is occupied by tenants or lodgers, only in respect of that part of the house):

(a) the number of individuals and households accommodated;
(b) the number of individuals in each household;
(c) and the purpose for which each room is being used.[74]

6.51 On service of a copy of the management order[75] on an owner or lessee, the local housing authority may require[76] the following information:

(a) the name and address of that person;

---

[70] Housing (Management of Houses in Multiple Occupation) Regulations 1962, reg. 13.
[71] A model form of notice was given in the Appendix to Ministry of Housing and Local Government Circular No.16/62 (now withdrawn, although the content of the notice is still relevant).
[72] Management Regulations 1962, reg. 14.
[73] *Ibid.* reg. 18(5)
[74] *Ibid.* reg. 15.
[75] s.370(3) of the 1985 Act. See para. 6.94.
[76] Management Regulations 1962, reg. 18(1).

MANAGEMENT OF HOUSES IN MULTIPLE OCCUPATION

(b) particulars of that person's estate or interest in the house;
(c) particulars of which parts of the house are let to tenants or lodgers from whom that person receives rents;
(d) the name and address of any agent or trustee through whom that person receives those rents.

The authority may also require[77] any person who has an estate or interest in the house to supply the following information within a stated reasonable time: **6.52**

(a) any of the information listed above;
(b) the name and address of any other person known to the addressee to be a manager of the house (including how that information came to be known); and
(c) if the addressee receives rents through an agent or trustee, whether that agent or trustee is authorised to deal with matters relating to the management of the house, and if so, to what extent.

An owner who appoints an agent or trustee to receive rents must forthwith notify the local housing authority of the appointment and of the name and address of the agent.[78] **6.53**

Anyone acquiring an estate or interest in the house is also required forthwith to notify the local housing authority, giving particulars of the estate or interest acquired, and any person who ceases to hold an estate or interest must notify the authority of this and, where the estate or interest has been sold or transferred to another, of the name and address of that person.[79] **6.54**

Duties of occupants

The management regulations also place duties on occupants of the house.[80] These include a general duty on all occupants to take reasonable care not to hinder or frustrate the manager in carrying out his duties under the regulations, and in particular, occupants must: **6.55**

(a) allow the manager, at all reasonable times, to enter their accommodation, for purposes connected with the manager's duties;
(b) on request, give the manager such information as may be reasonably required in connection with those duties;
(c) comply with any reasonable arrangements made by the manager for the storage and disposal of refuse and litter; and

---

[77] Management Regulations 1962, reg. 18(2).
[78] *Ibid.* reg. 18(3).
[79] *Ibid.* reg. 18(4).
[80] *Ibid.* reg. 16.

(d) take reasonable care to avoid damaging anything the manager is obliged to keep in repair.

Duties of the local authority

6.56 Local housing authorities are required to maintain a register of the names and addresses of managers of houses subject to the management regulations.[81] It must include details of whether or not those managers have an estate or interest in the house or have been appointed as agent or trustee through whom rents are received.

Where the information was provided by the person to whom the entry relates, the authority must take reasonable steps to bring the entry to that person's attention.

The authority must make available an entry in respect of a particular house at the request of a person who:

(a) has an interest in the house;
(b) has a prospective interest in the house;
(c) is a resident of the house; or
(d) is otherwise sufficiently concerned with the house.

Means of escape in case of fire at houses in multiple occupation

6.57 The need for ensuring adequate means of escape in case of fire at houses in multiple occupation is based on the following principles:

(a) that there are inherent risks of fire in any residential property because of the presence of solid fuel appliances, electrical equipment, gas equipment and the normal domestic activities of the occupiers; and
(b) that these inherent risks are increased by the multiple occupation of a house because each separately let part of the property will make use of its own heating, lighting and possibly cooking equipment.

6.58 Some reduction of the risk of fire starting may be achieved by ensuring the proper provision and maintenance of pipework and wiring for gas and electrical installations.[82] As there will always be an increased risk of fire at a multi-occupied house there is additional legislative provision to ensure that the spread of any fire is limited, and that there is means of escape available to occupants.

6.59 Unfortunately, at the time of writing there are no national standards for means of escape from fire at houses in multiple occupation; standards are determined locally by the fire authority for the area. While

---

[81] Management Regulations 1962, reg. 19.
[82] See ss.189–190, s.352 and ss.370–372 of the 1985 Act. See also paras. 6.37, 6.40–6.41, and 6.104–6.111.

some fire authorities[83] have produced a written code setting down the basis for the standards to be applied in their area, many have no such written code, and determine the means of escape necessary at a particular house after inspection by an officer.

Since 1981, the Home Office, Department of the Environment and Welsh Office, have been preparing a *Guide to Means of Escape and Related Fire Safety Measures in Certain Existing Houses in Multiple Occupation*. If and when this is issued it will provide a basis for national standards for means of escape. However, local housing authorities will still need to consult with the fire authority for the area for interpretation of this Guide.

Outlines of standards for means of escape based on the recommendation made by the Institution of Environmental Health Officers[84] and the comprehensive codes of practice issued by the Greater London Council Fire Brigade[85] are given in paras. 6.61—6.63 below. The draft of the Home Office Guide follows similar principles, differing only in the detail from the G.L.C. and I.E.H.O. recomendations. These recommendations and codes of practice aim to: **6.60**

(a) reduce the risk of fire occurring by ensuring that the house is properly adapted to the style of multiple occupation;
(b) provide for early detection of fires and early warning of occupants by smoke and heat detectors and a fire alarm system;
(c) provide some means of fighting a fire so as to give an opportunity of putting it out at an early stage limiting its spread;
(d) provide structural means to limit the spread of fire and smoke throughout the house and provide protected escape routes for the occupants by ensuring that:
  (i) separately let parts of the house are separated from each other by fire-resisting construction;
  (ii) any staircase is enclosed by fire-resisting construction to provide a protected staircase as an escape route, and also to limit the spread of fire and smoke by reducing the "chimney effect" of a staircase;
  (iii) any passage or corridor which provides access between escape routes is broken by self-closing smoke stop doors; and

---

[83] *e.g.* the Greater London Council Fire Brigade now the London Fire and Civil Defence Authority.
[84] Appendix III, *Environmental Health Professional Practice*, Vol. II, Chap. III, Houses in Multiple Occupation—Formulation and Implementation of Policy Including Standards; I.E.H.O. 1986.
[85] Code of Practice—Means of Escape in Case of Fire; 1974. Code of Practice—Means of Escape in Case of Fire: Houses in Multiple Occupation; 1978. Code of Practice—Means of Escape in Case of Fire: Houses in Multiple Occupation: Addendum in respect of Houses used as Hostels, Lodging Houses and Similar Establishments; 1981.

(iv) there is at least one escape route from the house to the street, either directly from the house or via another building;

(e) where the house comprises more than three storeys above ground level, the provision of secondary (alternative) means of escape by:

(i) an external staircase (not a ladder) accessible through a door;

(ii) an external balcony or walkway linking the house to adjacent premises; or

(iii) a connecting door (of one hour fire resisting construction) through a separating wall between two premises, with appropriate security devices (kick-through panels are not appropriate), and with rights of access written into the title deeds where the premises are in separate ownership.

See pages 199–201 for diagrams of examples of means of escape from fire.

Staircase and passages and corridors

6.61 Each staircase to the house should be protected and separated from each floor by partitions with doors at the top and base of each run of the staircase. The partitions should extend from floor to ceiling level of each floor, and be of material designated as providing a minimum of at least half an hour fire resistance. The doors should be of fire resisting construction,[86] hung on at least two metal hinges having a melting point of not less than 800 degrees celsius, and be set in a door frame which has stops of not less than 25mm. The doors should be made self-closing by a spring device which will hold the door firmly closed, and be free of any means of holding the door open (except an electro-magnetic device connected to the detection/alarm system).

The soffits of staircases, and parts of ceilings directly below any passage, staircase and designated escape route to the floor above should be of adequate fire resistance.

Corridors connecting one protected staircase with another should be broken by a self closing smoke stop door and frame which together will not collapse for at least half an hour, and which will resist the passage of flame and hot gases for not less than 20 minutes.[87]

Cupboards within a protected staircase or escape route must be of materials giving at least half hour fire resistance, and fitted with fire resisting self closing doors, or fire resisting doors kept locked shut when not in use (in which case they must be marked—"THESE DOORS TO BE KEPT LOCKED SHUT WHEN NOT IN USE" in 10mm. high plain letters).

Glazing within a protected staircase or escape route must be of fire

[86] To satisfy British Standard B.S. 476, Part 8; 1972.
[87] To satisfy B.S. 476, section 7, Part 20; 1972.

MEANS OF ESCAPE IN CASE OF FIRE AT HOUSES IN MULTIPLE OCCUPATION

Outline diagrams giving examples of means of escape

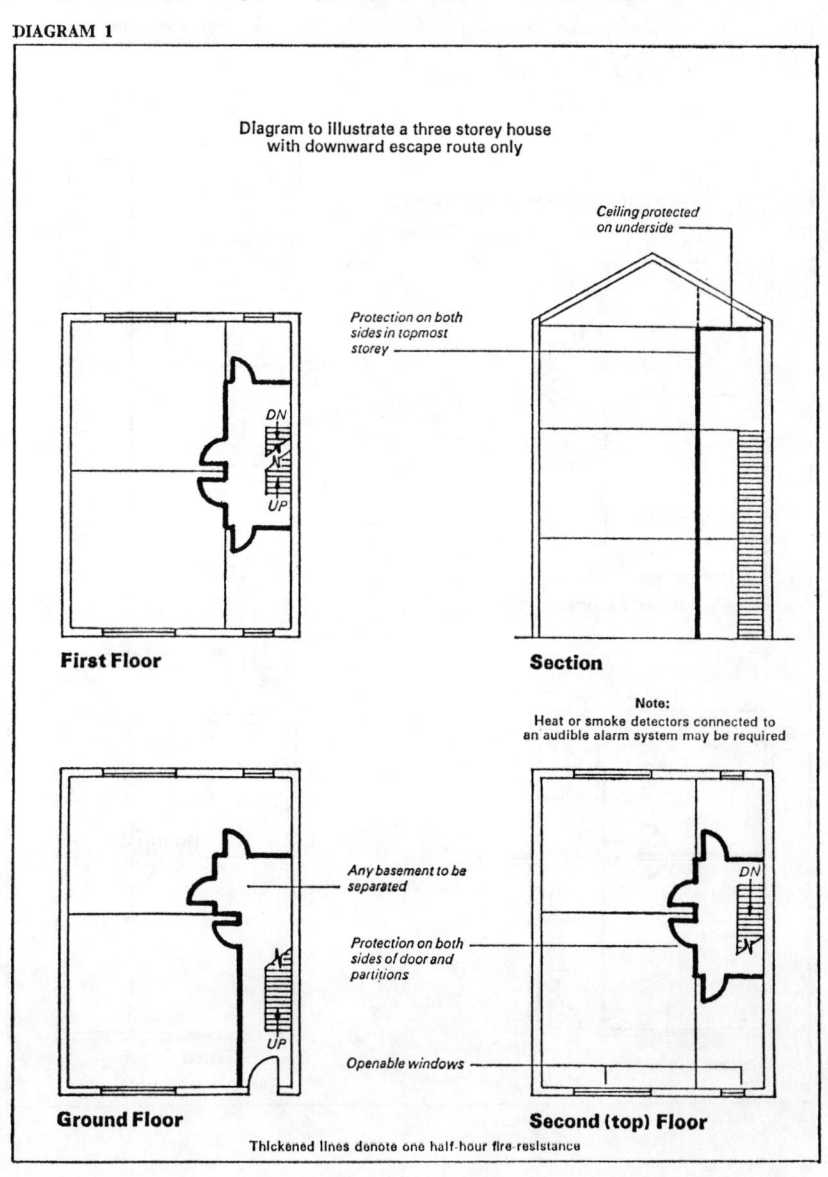

DIAGRAM 1

Diagram to illustrate a three storey house with downward escape route only

Ceiling protected on underside

Protection on both sides in topmost storey

First Floor

Section

Note:
Heat or smoke detectors connected to an audible alarm system may be required

Any basement to be separated

Protection on both sides of door and partitions

Openable windows

Ground Floor

Second (top) Floor

Thickened lines denote one half-hour fire-resistance

HOUSES IN MULTIPLE OCCUPATION

DIAGRAM 2

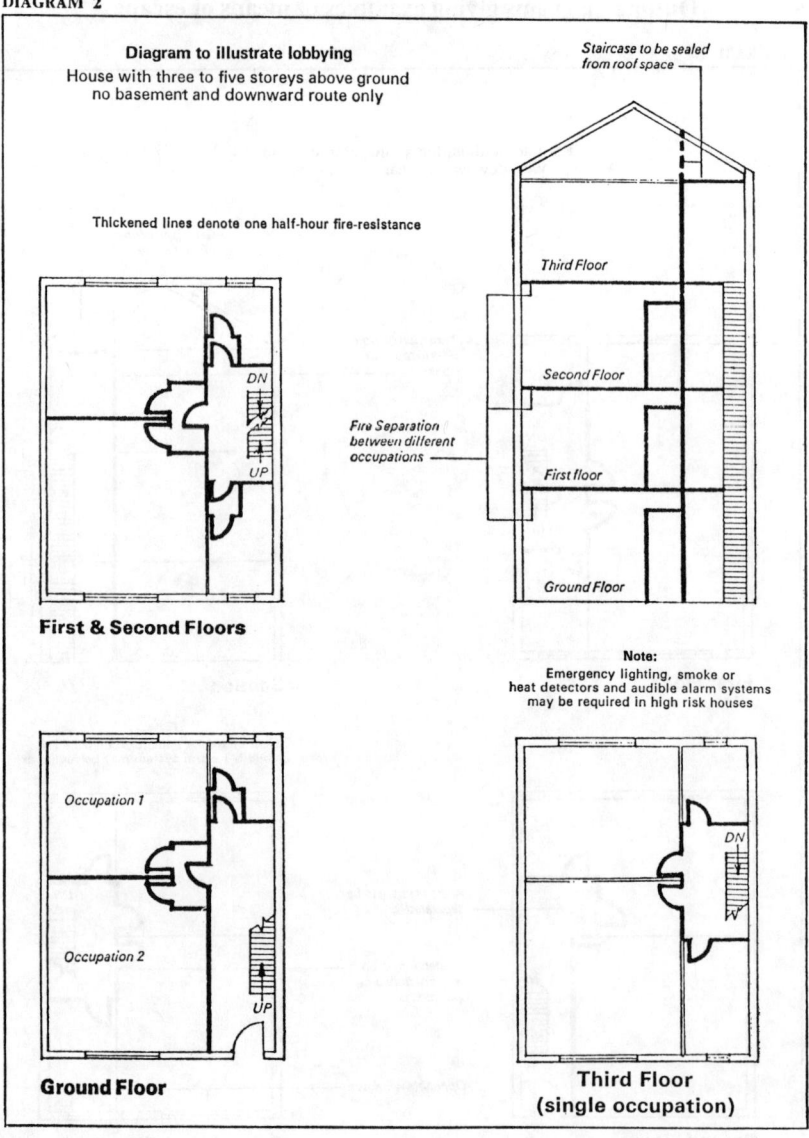

Diagram to illustrate lobbying
House with three to five storeys above ground
no basement and downward route only

Thickened lines denote one half-hour fire-resistance

Staircase to be sealed from roof space

Third Floor
Second Floor
First floor
Ground Floor

Fire Separation between different occupations

First & Second Floors

Ground Floor

Occupation 1
Occupation 2

Note:
Emergency lighting, smoke or heat detectors and audible alarm systems may be required in high risk houses

Third Floor
(single occupation)

MEANS OF ESCAPE IN CASE OF FIRE AT HOUSES IN MULTIPLE OCCUPATION

DIAGRAM 3

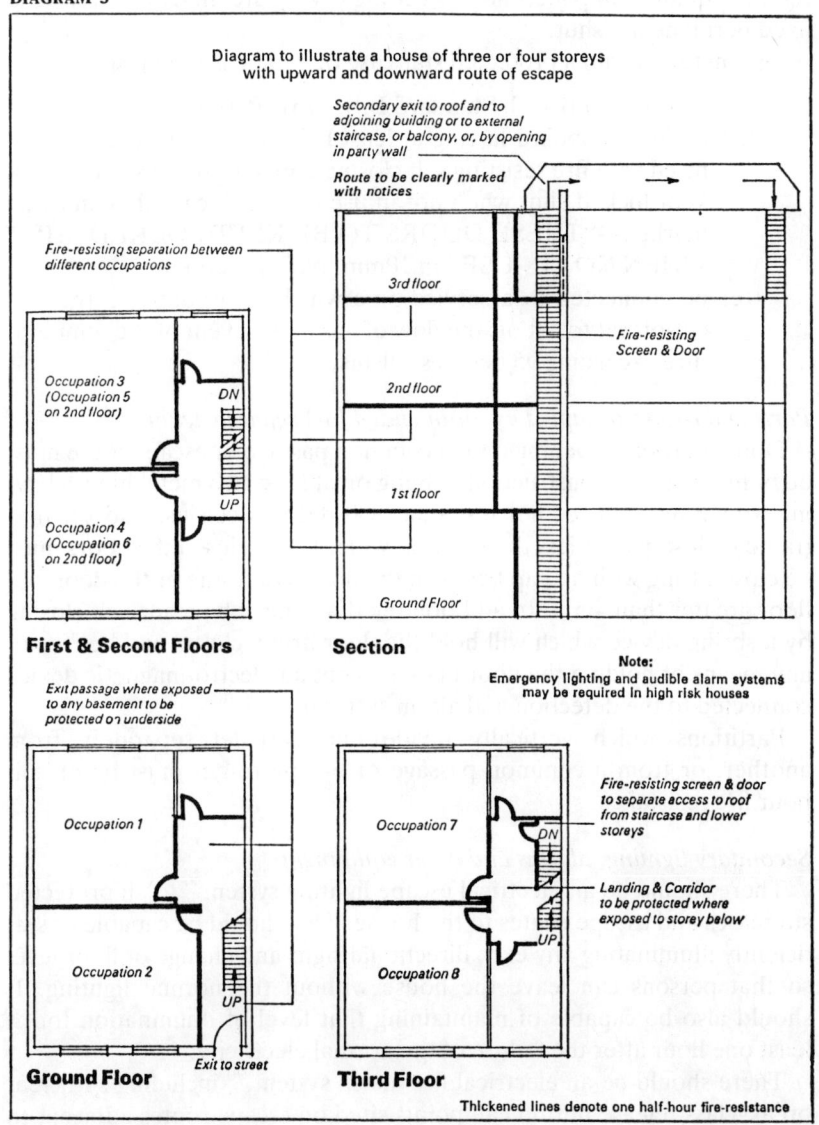

Diagram to illustrate a house of three or four storeys with upward and downward route of escape

First & Second Floors

Section

Ground Floor

Third Floor

Note: Emergency lighting and audible alarm systems may be required in high risk houses

Thickened lines denote one half-hour fire-resistance

Taken from *Environmental Health Professional Practice*, Vol. II, Chap. III, Houses in Multiple Occupation—Formulation and Implementation of Policy Including Standards, I.E.H.O. 1986.

resisting quality, in panels not exceeding 0.4 square metres in area, and fixed permanently shut.

Gas meters within a protected staircase or escape route must:

(a) conform to British Standard B.S. 4161, Part 3 (1968);
(b) be in a cupboard having at least half hour fire resistance, and fitted with fire resisting self closing doors, or fire resisting doors kept locked shut when not in use (in which case they must be marked—"THESE DOORS TO BE KEPT LOCKED SHUT WHEN NOT IN USE" in 10mm. plain letters); or
(c) be connected to a service pipe which incorporates a thermal cut-off set to cut off the flow of gas in the event of the temperature exceeding 95 degrees celsius.

Parts and rooms occupied as (or intended for) separate letting

6.62 Doors to rooms opening onto a common passage or escape route must be of fire resisting construction,[88] hung on at least two metal hinges having a melting point of not less than 800 degrees celsius, and set in a frame with stops not less than 25mm. wide. When closed the doors must be close-fitting with no gap between the door and frame or the door and floor greater than 4mm. In addition the doors must be made self closing by a spring device which will hold the door firmly closed and be free of any means of holding the door open (except an electro-magnetic device connected to the detection and alarm system).

Partitions which vertically divide one part let separately from another, or from a common passage or escape route, must be of half hour fire resistance.

Secondary lighting, alarms and other equipment

6.63 There should be an electrical escape lighting system[89] to all protected staircases and escape routes to the house. This should be capable of sufficiently illuminating any exit, directional signs and change of floor level so that persons can leave the house without the normal lighting. It should also be capable of maintaining that level of illumination for at least one hour after the failure of the normal electricity.

There should be an electrical fire alarm system,[90] including sufficient break-glass release button call points sited on escape routes adjacent to each of the downward flights of stairs to each floor level.

There should be smoke detectors[90] in circuit with the fire alarm system, and sited so as to detect smoke in protected staircases, escape routes, shared bathrooms and store rooms. In kitchens and boiler rooms heat detectors[90] should be fitted in lieu of smoke detectors.

---

[88] To satisfy British Standard B.S. 476, Part 8; 1972.
[89] To satisfy B.S. 5266, Part 1; 1975.
[90] To satisfy B.S. 5839, Part 1; 1980.

MEANS OF ESCAPE IN CASE OF FIRE AT HOUSES IN MULTIPLE OCCUPATION

There should be at least two telephones sited on the escape routes and readily available for calling the fire brigade and other emergency services.

There should be fire instruction notices throughout the house giving clear instructions for action to be taken in the event of a fire and the method of calling the fire brigade. In addition there should be notices giving clear indication (in 10mm. high plain letters) of the direction of escape routes and of alternative or secondary escape routes.

There should be hand appliances for the fighting of fires as follows:

(a) on escape routes adjacent to the staircase to each floor two water type extinguishers of a specification to satisfy the requirements of the fire authority;
(b) in kitchens one fire blanket;
(c) in boiler rooms, one nine litre foam extinguisher and two buckets of sand.

Each appliance should be inspected and certified every 12 months by an independent and competent person, and the certificate issued clearly displayed adjacent to the relevant appliance.

Action to deal with houses unfit for such multiple occupation

Where a local housing authority is of the opinion that a house is in multiple occupation and is unfit for such multiple occupation[91] it may: **6.64**

(a) serve a notice[92] requiring the carrying out of works necessary to render the house fit for that multiple occupation; or
(b) give a direction[93] specifying the maximum number to occupy the house; or
(c) serve a notice[94] requiring the carrying out of works necessary to render the house fit for multiple occupation by a reduced number, and specifying that number. (However, such a notice cannot be served in respect of a building deemed to be a house in multiple occupation[95].)

Notices requiring works to make a house fit for multiple occupation

Where the local housing authority serve a notice requiring works to render the house fit for multiple occupation, it must be of the opinion that the house is so far defective with respect to any of the matters listed in section 352(1) of the 1985 Act,[96] and having regard to the number of **6.65**

---

[91] See paras. 6.18–6.28.
[92] 1985 Act, s.352(2)(*a*).
[93] *Ibid.* s.354.
[94] *Ibid.* s.352(2)(*b*).
[95] *Ibid.* s.352(6), see paras. 6.15–6.17.
[96] See paras. 6.24–6.26.

individuals and/or households accommodated at the house (or the reduced number specified by the authority), that the house is not reasonably suitable for occupation by those individuals and/or households in that condition.

The matters to be considered are: natural and artificial lighting; ventilation; water supply; personal washing facilities; drainage and sanitary conveniences; facilities for the storage, preparation and cooking of food; and for the disposal of waste water; installations for space heating or for the use of space heating appliances.[97]

6.66 The notice must be in the prescribed form,[98] and must:

(a) specify the works which in the opinion of the local authority are necessary to render the house reasonably suitable for occupation by either the numbers of individuals and/or households accommodated at the house for the time being, or the reduced and specified number of individuals and/or households that the local authority are satisfied the house could accommodate after the completion of the works; and

(b) state a period (being not less than 21 days from the date of the service of the notice) within which the specified works must be completed.[99]

6.67 Where possible, the notice should specify the actual works to be carried out, and not merely state the effect or result to be obtained.[1]

The time period given for completion of the specified works must be reasonably sufficient having regard to the extent of those works,[2] but the authority may from time to time give written permission for an extension of the stated period.[3]

6.68 The notice must be addressed to and served[4] on—

(a) the "person having control of the house"[4a];
(b) any person to whom the house is let at a rack-rent; or
(c) any person who is an agent or trustee for a person to whom the house is let at a rack-rent, and who receives rents or payments from tenants or lodgers in the house.

The decision as to whom the notice should be addressed to and served on should be based on which of the persons is responsible for the multiple

---

[97] s.352(1) of the 1985 Act.
[98] No.37, Housing (Prescribed Forms) Regulations 1972 (S.I. 1972 No.228).
[99] s.352(4) of the 1985 Act.
[1] See *Canterbury CC* v. *Bern* (1982) 44 P. & C.R. 178.
[2] See 1985 Act, s.353(2)(*e*).
[3] *Ibid.* s.352(4).
[4] *Ibid.* s.352(3).
[4a] See Chap. 5, para. 5.77 on interpretation of this phrase.

ACTION TO DEAL WITH HOUSES UNFIT FOR MULTIPLE OCCUPATION

occupation, and in a position to be able either to reduce the numbers in occupation and/or to carry out the works considered necessary.[5]

Once notice under this provision has been served the local housing authority is required[6] to notify any other person known by the local authority to be an owner, lessee or mortgagee of the house that the notice has been served.[7]

Grant-aid for works

Once a notice under this provision has been served the local housing authority cannot refuse an application for a special grant towards the cost of the specified works, but the grant is only payable for those works relating to the provision of standard amenities and works associated with such provision.[8] **6.69**

Withdrawal of notice requiring works

A local housing authority may[9] withdraw a notice requiring works if they are satisfied that: **6.70**

(a) the number of individuals living at the house has been reduced to a level that makes the works unnecessary; and
(b) the number will be maintained at or below that level.

Satisfaction that the number of individuals at the house will be maintained at or below the reduced level may be, but need not be, based on the fact that the local housing authority have given a direction.[10]

Notification of the withdrawal of the notice must be in writing, and must be given to the person on whom the notice was served. Withdrawal of the notice does not prejudice the service of a subsequent notice under section 352 of the 1985 Act.[11] **6.71**

Appeals against a notice requiring works

A person on whom a notice requiring works to make a house fit for multiple occupation has been served has a right of appeal to the county court[12] within 21 days of the date of service of that notice (the authority may extend the 21 day period in writing[13]). **6.72**

---

[5] See Chap. 1, paras. 1.33–1.34 on the power of the courts to grant authority to carry out works.
[6] s.352(3) of the 1985 Act.
[7] Form No.49, Housing (Prescribed Forms) Regulations 1972 (S.I. 1972 No. 228).
[8] 1985 Act, s.486(1)(*a*).
[9] Under *ibid*. s.352(5).
[10] Under *ibid*. s.354.
[11] Under *ibid*. s.352(5).
[12] *Ibid*. s.353.
[13] *Ibid*. s.353(1).

6.73 The grounds for appeal are limited[14] to the following:

  (a) that the condition of the house did not justify the specified works;
  (b) that there has been some material informality, defect or error in, or in connection with, the notice[15];
  (c) that the local housing authority have unreasonably refused to approve alternative works, or that the specified works are otherwise unreasonable in character or extent, or are unnecessary;
  (d) that the time specified for the completion of the works is not reasonably sufficient[16];
  (e) that some other person is wholly or partly responsible for the condition of the house, or will benefit from the execution of the works, and so should bear all or part of the cost of carrying out the works; and
  (f) in the case of a notice requiring works for a reduced and specified number of individuals and/or households, that the number specified is unreasonably low.

6.73A It is suggested that the relevant date for considering whether the condition of the house justified the specified works (*i.e.*, ground (a) above) would be the date of the service of the notice, but the relevant date for considering the reasonableness *etc* of the works (*i.e.*, ground (c) above) would be the date of the hearing of the appeal.[16a]

6.74 If the appeal is founded on ground (e) above, the appellant should serve a copy of the notice of appeal on the person (or persons) alleged liable to bear all or part of the cost of the works. On the hearing of an appeal founded on this ground, the court may make such order as it thinks fit with respect to the payment to be made by the other person(s), or where the works have been carried out by the local housing authority, to be made to the authority.[17]

6.75 If on hearing the appeal, the court is satisfied that:

  (a) the number of individuals living at the house has been reduced to a level that makes the works unnecessary; and
  (b) the number will be maintained at or below that level,

it may revoke the notice, or may vary the works specified in the notice.[18]

---

[14] 1985 Act, s.353(2).
[15] The county court is required to dismiss an appeal if the informality, defect or error was not a material one—s.353(3) of the 1985 Act.
[16] s.352(4) of the 1985 Act enables the local housing authority to extend the time specified in the notice at least once.
[16a] *Berg* v. *Trafford B.C.* (1988) 20 H.L.R. 470.
[17] 1985 Act, s.353(5).
[18] *Ibid.* s.353(4).

ACTION TO DEAL WITH HOUSES UNFIT FOR MULTIPLE OCCUPATION

Satisfaction that the number of individuals at the house will be maintained at or below the reduced level may be, but need not be, based on the fact that the local authority have given a direction under section 354 of the 1985 Act.

Once an appeal has been lodged the time limit specified in the notice cannot be taken to have expired until 28 days (or such longer period as the court may lay down) from determination of the appeal.[19] Withdrawal of an appeal is deemed to be determination of that appeal.[20]   6.76

Enforcement of fitness notices

As to enforcement of notices requiring works to render a house fit for multiple occupation (including prosecution for non-compliance, carrying out works in default, continuing liability after expiry of the time limit and/or enforcement and recovery of local authority's expenses) see paras. 6.132–6.141 below.   6.77

Directions to limit the number in occupation

As an alternative to requiring works to render a house fit for multiple occupation by the number of individuals and/or households accommodated there for the time being, a local housing authority may (except in respect of a building deemed to be a house in multiple occupation[21]) give a direction under section 354(1) of the 1985 Act, either: 6.78

  (a) specifying the maximum number of individuals and/or households able to occupy the house in its existing condition[22]; or
  (b) in conjunction with a notice requiring works to make the house fit for multiple occupation[23] specifying the maximum number able to occupy the house after completion of the works specified by that notice.[24]

A direction can be given even if there is a previous direction which specified a higher number. (There appears to be no need to revoke the previous direction in such cases.)[25]

It is important to note that the numbers specified must be determined having regard to the matters set out in section 352(1) of the 1985 Act, and not having regard to the space available (*i.e.* a direction is not a means of reducing or preventing overcrowding, but of dealing with fitness for multiple occupation; overcrowding in general being dealt with   6.79

---

[19] 1985 Act, s.375(2).
[20] *Ibid.* s.399.
[21] By *ibid.* s.352(6).
[22] *Ibid.* s.354(7).
[23] Under *ibid.* s.354(2)(*b*).
[24] *Ibid.* s.354(6).
[25] *Ibid.* s.354(5).

by Part X of the 1985 Act, and in respect of houses in multiple occupation by sections 358–364 of the 1985 Act—see Chapter 7).

6.80 At least seven days prior to giving the direction, the local housing authority must[26] serve a notice of intention:

(a) on an owner of the house;
(b) on every person known to be a lessee of the house; and
(c) post a copy in some part of the house accessible to those living there.

The notice of intention must be in the prescribed form.[27]

6.81 Having served the notice of intention, the local housing authority must afford to any person served an opportunity to make representations in respect of the proposed direction.[28]

6.82 Not less than seven days after the date of service of the notice of intention, the local housing authority may give the direction, which must state the highest number of individuals, or households or both, able, in the opinion of the local housing authority, having regard to the matters set out in section 352(1) of the 1985 Act,[29] to occupy the house in its present condition, or in the condition after completion of the works specified in a notice under section 352(2)(b) of the 1985 Act.[30] The direction may specify separate limits (or numbers) for different parts of a house, where those parts are or are likely to be occupied by different persons.[31]

The direction must be in the prescribed form.[32]

6.83 Within seven days of the giving of the direction, the authority must[33]:

(a) serve a copy on an owner of the house;
(b) serve a copy on every person known to be a lessee of the house; and
(c) post a copy in some part of the house accessible to those living there.

6.84 Once the direction has been given it places a duty on the "occupier for the time being" not to permit the number of individuals or households occupying the house to increase above the limit(s) specified, and if that number already exceeds the limit(s) given, not to permit the number to increase further.[34]

---

[26] 1985 Act, s.354(3).
[27] Form No.39 Housing (Prescribed Forms) Regulations 1972 (S.I. 1972 No.228).
[28] s.354(3) of the 1985 Act.
[29] See paras. 6.24–6.26.
[30] s.354(6) and (7) of the 1985 Act.
[31] s.354(2) of the 1985 Act.
[32] Form No.40 Housing (Prescribed Forms) Regulations 1972 (S.I. 1972 No.228).
[33] 1985 Act, s.354(4).
[34] *Ibid.* s.355(1).

Knowingly failing to comply with this duty is an offence,[35] the maximum penalty on conviction being a fine not exceeding level 4 on the standard scale.[36]

In *L.B. of Hackney* v. *Ezedinma*,[37] the Divisional Court commented on the interpretation of the "occupier for the time being" and "household." A direction had been given by the local authority, setting the maximum number at 11 individuals or three households. Subsequently, Mr. Ezedinma (authorised by the owners to let out rooms) let three rooms on three separate occasions to three different persons. Before the magistrates' court it was argued that the occupiers did not each live as a separate household, but either as individuals (the total number being eight occupiers), or as three groups using the three available kitchens. The magistrates found that the local authority had not proved beyond reasonable doubt that there were more than three households, and also that Mr. Ezedinma was not the occupier for the time being, and so dismissed the informations. 6.85

On appeal the Divisional Court held that Mr. Ezedinma was the "occupier for the time being." It is suggested that this decision was based on Mr. Ezedinma being seen as the only person in possession of the whole house, the residents only having exclusive occupation of parts of the house and use of common parts.

The Divisional Court also held that whether the eight residents were living as three households was a matter of fact and degree, and the magistrates were entitled, on the evidence before them, to decide that the premises were not occupied by more than three households.

Griffiths L.J. stated that he had been persuaded that the term "household" could be construed to include a single person lodging in a single room.

There is no right of appeal against a direction; however, there is a right of appeal against a refusal to revoke or vary a direction (on which see para. 6.88). 6.86

Revocation and variation of directions

A local housing authority may revoke a direction, or may vary the direction to allow more people to be accommodated in the house.[38] A direction cannot be varied to lower a limit already given (this can be achieved, however, by the authority, at their own volition, issuing a new direction—see para. 6.78). 6.87

Such variation or revocation can be made at any time provided that:

---

[35] 1985 Act, s.355(2).
[36] Criminal Justice Act 1982, s.37.
[37] [1981] 3 All E.R. 438.
[38] s.357(1) of the 1985 Act.

(a) application has been made to the local housing authority by a person having an estate or interest in the house; and
(b) works have been carried out in the house; or there has been some other change of circumstances.

Where a local authority varies or revokes a direction, notification of the variation or revocation must be given in the prescribed form.[39]

Appeals against refusal to vary or revoke a direction

6.88 If a local housing authority either refuses an application to vary or revoke a direction, or fails to notify the applicant of its decision within 35 days of the date of application, the applicant has a right of appeal to the county court.[40]

The 35 day period allowed for notification of the local housing authority's decision, may be extended in writing by the applicant.

6.89 On hearing the appeal, the court has the power to revoke the direction or to vary it in any manner in which it might have been varied by the local housing authority.[41]

Information as to occupation of a house subject to a direction

6.90 At any time while a direction is in force a local housing authority may serve on the occupier of the house (or the occupier of part of the house) a requisition for information,[42] requiring all or any of the following details:

(a) the number of individuals living in the house (or part of the house);
(b) the number of families or households to which those individuals belong;
(c) the names of those individuals and of the heads of each family or household; and
(d) the rooms used by those individuals and the families or households respectively.

6.91 The requisition for information must be in the prescribed form.[43] The information required must be supplied in writing, and must be given to the local housing authority within seven days of service of the requisition. Failure to reply, or knowingly giving false information is an offence[44] carrying a fine on conviction not exceeding level 2 on the standard scale.[45]

---

[39] Form No.41, Housing (Prescribed Forms) Regulations 1972 (S.I. 1972 No.228).
[40] 1985 Act, s.357(2)
[41] *Ibid*. s.357(3).
[42] *Ibid*. s.356.
[43] Form No.42 Housing (Prescribed Forms) Regulations 1972 (S.I. 1972 No.228).
[44] s.356(2) of the 1985 Act.
[45] Criminal Justice Act 1982, s.37.

Management orders

6.92 A management order is simply an order applying the Housing (Management of Houses in Multiple Occupation) Regulations 1962 to a specified house. In this sense it is probably unique because regulations which require standards and practices in particular circumstances normally apply without any initial action being necessary by the enforcing agency.

Making a management order

6.93 A management order can be made if it appears to the local housing authority that[46]:

(a) the house in multiple occupation is in an unsatisfactory state in consequence of a failure to maintain proper standards of management; and
(b) it is necessary for the management regulations to apply to the house.

6.94 The order takes effect on the date it is made.[47]

It must be in the prescribed form.[48] The order itself is not addressed to an individual or body (because it relates to the house) but within seven days of the making of an order the local housing authority must[49]:

(a) serve a copy on an owner of the house;
(b) serve a copy on every person known to the local housing authority to be a lessee of the house; and
(c) post a copy in the house, in a position accessible to those living there.

The requirement to post a copy of the order in some part of the house accessible to the occupants is self-explanatory, its purpose being to inform the occupants that the order has been made.

The order must also be registered as a local land charge.[50]

Effect of a management order

6.95 The making of a management order applies the Housing (Management of Houses in Multiple Occupation) Regulations 1962[51] to the house until such time as the order is revoked. These Regulations were originally made under section 13 of the 1961 Act.[52] It should be noted that section 369 of the 1985 Act[53] gives a general power to the Secretary

---

[46] Housing Act 1985, s.370(1).
[47] Ibid. s.370(2).
[48] Form No.35 Housing (Prescribed Forms) Regulations 1972 (S.I. 1972, No.228).
[49] Housing Act 1985, s.370(3).
[50] Ibid. s.370(5).
[51] S.I. 1962 No.668, retained in force by s.2 of the Housing (Consequential Provisions) Act 1985.
[52] Now re-enacted as s.369 of the Housing Act 1985.
[53] As did s.13 of the Housing Act 1961.

HOUSES IN MULTIPLE OCCUPATION

of State to make regulations, and also (without prejudice to the general power) specifies various matters which may be dealt with by any regulations. The legislation also states[54] that these regulations may make different provision for different types of houses (although advantage of this has not yet been taken).

6.96 Once a management order has been made, it is an offence[55] for a person knowingly to contravene, or, without reasonable excuse to fail to comply with, any regulations applied by virtue of a management order. A person convicted of such an offence is liable to a fine not exceeding level 3 on the standard scale.[56]

In addition (and without prejudice to this general provision), the local housing authority may serve a notice requiring the carrying out of works to make good the neglect (see paras. 6.104–6.111).

Revocation of a management order

6.97 On receipt of an application from a person having an estate or interest in the house, the local housing authority may revoke the management order.[57] Where a local housing authority refuses to revoke the management order, the applicant has a right of appeal to the county court.[58]

There is similar right of appeal where an authority fails to notify the applicant of its decision within 35 days from the date of application (or such longer period as the applicant, in writing, allows).

Appeals

6.98 Appeals are made to the county court for the area. A management order remains effective even when there is an appeal lodged with the court.[59]

The rights of appeal given[60] are either against the making of the management order, or against the refusal (or the deemed refusal) to revoke the management order.

Appeals against the making of a management order

6.99 The right of appeal against the making of the order is available to any person on whom a copy of the management order was served, and to any other person who is a lessee of the house[61]; while this takes account of lessees who were not known to the local housing authority and therefore not served with a copy of the order, it would appear to exclude residents without any estate or interest in the house.

[54] At subs. 3.
[55] s.369(5) of the Housing Act 1985.
[56] Criminal Justice Act 1982, s.37.
[57] Housing Act 1985, s.370(4).
[58] *Ibid.* s.371(4).
[59] *Ibid.* s.371(3).
[60] *Ibid.* s.371.
[61] *Ibid.* s.371(1).

The only ground for an appeal is that the making of the order was unnecessary.

At the hearing the court must take account of the state of the house at the time the order was made, and also the state at the time of hearing the appeal.[62] However, the court must disregard any improvements made since the making of the order unless it is also satisfied that effective steps have been taken to ensure that the house will be kept in a satisfactory state in future. **6.100**

Where the court allows the appeal, it must revoke the management order.[63] Such revocation is without prejudice to the effects of the order prior to the court's decision, and without prejudice to the local housing authority's power to make a further order.

Appeals on refusal to revoke a management order

If, on hearing an appeal against the refusal (or deemed refusal) of the local housing authority to revoke a management order, the court is of the opinion that there has been a substantial change in circumstances since the making of the order, and also that it is in other respects just to do so, it may revoke the order. Again, this is without prejudice to the effects of the order prior to the court's decision, and without prejudice to the local housing authority's power to make a further order. **6.101**

Prosecution for offences under the management regulations

It is an offence[64] for a person either to knowingly contravene, or without reasonable excuse to fail to comply with, any of the requirements of the management regulations when applied to a house by a management order. A person convicted of such an offence is liable to a fine not exceeding level 3 on the standard scale.[65] **6.102**

The section is phrased so that it is an offence if it can be shown that the person, with or without actual knowledge of the condition of the house and/or the particular defects, without reasonable excuse failed to take appropriate action.[66] Therefore, it is only necessary to prove (beyond reasonable doubt) that:

(a) the conditions or defects existed at the house on the date of the alleged offence;
(b) that a management order had been properly made, copies served on the relevant persons and a copy posted in the house;
(c) that the accused is a person who is responsible for the conditions or defects which exist at the house; and

---

[62] 1985 Act, s.371(2).
[63] *Ibid.* s.371(3).
[64] *Ibid.* s.369(5).
[65] Criminal Justice Act 1982, s.37.
[66] See *City of Westminster* v. *Mavroghenis* (1984) 11 H.L.R. 56.

HOUSES IN MULTIPLE OCCUPATION

(d) that the accused, without reasonable excuse, failed to take appropriate action to remedy the conditions or defects.

6.103 Since the management regulations place duties on the manager, the occupants and the local authority, failure to satisfy those duties may be actionable as a breach of statutory duty.[67] In addition, the management regulations place duties on the local housing authority,[68] and an authority may "knowingly contravene or without reasonable excuse" fail to comply with those duties. Since the 1985 Act does not specify responsibility for enforcement,[69] a tenant or manager of a house subject to a management order may be a "person aggrieved"[70] by a failure to satisfy the duties and may take proceedings.

Notices to require works to make good neglect

6.104 Without prejudice to the power to prosecute for failure to comply with the requirements of the management regulations, a local housing authority may serve a notice specifying works to make good the neglect.[71] Such a notice may be served in respect of a house subject to a management order where, in the opinion of the authority, the condition of the house is defective (having regard to the requirements of the management regulations) because of neglect.

The notice may be served in respect of conditions that existed before the management order took effect,[72] and so can be served together with the copies of the management order.

6.105 The notice must be in the prescribed form,[73] and addressed to and served on the "person managing the house."[74] However, if it is not practicable after reasonable inquiry to ascertain the name and address of the person managing the house, the notice may be served properly by addressing it to the "manager of the house," naming the house to which the notice relates, and delivering it to some person at the house.[75]

It should also be noted that once a management order has taken effect,

(a) it is a duty of the manager to display a document in the house giving the name and address of the manager(s)[76]; and
(b) the local housing authority can require the name and address of an owner or lessee (which person would also be a

---

[67] See L.A.G. Bull., February 1978, p34.
[68] Management Regulations 1962, reg.17.
[69] s.369 of the Housing Act 1985.
[70] See in particular, *Att.-Gen. (Gambia)* v. *Pierre Sarr N'Jie* [1961] A.C. 617.
[71] Housing Act 1985, s.372.
[72] *Ibid.* s.372(1)(*b*).
[73] Form No.36 of the Housing (Prescribed Forms) Regulations 1972 (S.I. 1972 No.228).
[74] As defined by the Housing Act 1985, s.398(6).
[75] *Ibid.* s.372(2).
[76] Management Regulations 1962, reg. 14.

"manager") served with a copy of the management order, and of any other manager of the house.[77]

The notice must require the person managing the house to:

(a) carry out the works specified in the notice, being works which in the opinion of the local housing authority are necessary to make good the neglect[78]; and
(b) give a time limit (not less than 21 days for the service of the notice) for completion of the specified works.[79]

The period specified should be a reasonable period having regard to the works specified,[80] and the local housing authority may (from time to time) give written permission for an extension of the period specified.[81]

6.107 In addition to serving the notice on the person managing the house, the authority must inform any other person who is to their knowledge an owner, lessee or mortgagee of the house of the fact that such a notice has been served.[82] This notification must be in the prescribed form.[83]

Appeals against the notice to make good neglect

6.108 Any person who is served with a notice requiring works to make good neglect,[84] or is an owner, lessee or mortgagee of the house, has a right of appeal to a county court within 21 days of service of that notice[85] (or such longer period as the authority, in writing, allows).

The appeal may be on any of the following grounds[86]:

(a) that the condition of the house did not justify execution of the works specified in the notice;
(b) that there has been some material informality, defect or error in, or in connection with, the notice[87];
(c) that the local housing authority have unreasonably refused to approve alternative works, or that the specified works are otherwise unreasonable in character or extent, or are unnecessary[88];

---

[77] Management Regulations 1962, reg. 18.
[78] Housing Act 1985, s.372(1) and (3).
[79] *Ibid.* s.372(3).
[80] *Ibid.* s.373(2).
[81] *Ibid.* s.372(3).
[82] *Ibid.* s.372(4).
[83] Form No.49 of the Housing (Prescribed Forms) Regulations 1972 (S.I. 1972 No.228).
[84] Under the Housing Act 1985, s.372.
[85] *Ibid.* s.373(1).
[86] *Ibid.* s.373(2).
[87] The court must dismiss the appeal if the informality, defect or error was not a material one—*ibid.* s.373(3).
[88] The standard of works should be reasonable having regard to the age, character and prospective life of the house—on which see Chap. 3, para. 3.53.

HOUSES IN MULTIPLE OCCUPATION

(d) that the time specified for the completion of the works is not reasonably sufficient[89]; and

(e) that some other person is wholly or partly responsible for the condition of the house, or will benefit from execution of the works, and so should bear all or part of the cost of carrying out the works.

6.108A It is suggested that the relevant date for considering whether the condition of the house justified the specified works (*i.e.*, ground (a) above) would be the date of the service of the notice, but the relevant date for considering the reasonableness, etc., of the works (*i.e.*, ground (c) above) would be the date of hearing of the appeal.[89a]

6.109 If the appeal is founded on ground (e) above, the appellant must serve a copy of the notice of appeal on the person (or persons) whom it is alleged should bear all or part of the cost of the works. On hearing the appeal, the court may make such order as it thinks fit with respect to the payment to be made by the other person(s), or, where the works have been carried out by the local housing authority, to be made to the authority.[90]

6.110 Once an appeal has been lodged the time limit specified in the notice cannot be taken to have expired until 28 days (or such longer period as the court may set) from determination of the appeal.[91] Withdrawal of the appeal is deemed to be determination of that appeal.[92]

Enforcement of notices to make good neglect

6.111 As to enforcement of notices requiring works to make good neglect of proper standards of management (including prosecution for non-compliance, carrying out works in default, continuing liability after expiry of the time limit and/or enforcement and recovery of local housing authority's expenses) see paras. 6.132–6.141.

Means of escape from fire

6.112 Where a local housing authority becomes aware that a house in multiple occupation is not provided with such means of escape from fire as they consider necessary, they may (and in certain cases must[93]):

(a) serve a notice requiring provision of the necessary means of escape; or

(b) if the means of escape would be adequate if a part of the house

---

[89] Note that the authority can extend the time specified in the notice at least once—s.372(3) of the Housing Act 1985.
[89a] This follows from the decision in *Berg* v. *Trafford B.C.* (1988) 20 H.L.R. 47.
[90] Housing Act 1985, s.373(4).
[91] *Ibid.* s.375(2).
[92] *Ibid.* s.399.
[93] *Ibid.* s.365(1).

were not used, take action to ensure that the part in question is not used for human habitation; or

(c) take action to secure that a part is not used for human habitation, and serve a notice requiring the provision of necessary means of escape for the remainder of the house.

Before taking the appropriate action the authority must consult with the local fire authority.[94]

6.113 This provision is discretionary, except where the Secretary of State has made it a duty in respect of certain types of houses in multiple occupation.[95] The Secretary of State has specified[96] that local housing authorities must enforce the provision in houses of at least three storeys in which the combined floor area exceeds 500 square metres.[97]

Notices requiring adequate means of escape

6.114 A notice requiring works is served where the authority is of the opinion that the means of escape in case of fire are inadequate. The notice must be in the prescribed form,[98] addressed to and served on[99]:

(a) the "person having control of the house"[99a];
(b) any person to whom the house is let at a rack-rent; or
(c) any person who is an agent or trustee for a person to whom the house is let at a rack-rent, and who receives rents or payments from tenants or lodgers in the house.

The notice should be addressed to either the person responsible for the multiple occupation, who is, therefore, in a position to reduce the numbers in occupation, or the person who is able to carry out the works considered necessary[1] (which may be the same person).

6.115 The notice must[2]:

(a) specify the works which the local housing authority is satisfied are necessary to provide an adequate means of escape from fire;

---

[94] Housing Act 1985, s.365(3).
[95] *Ibid.* s.365(2).
[96] Housing (Means of Escape from Fire in Houses in Multiple Occupation) Order 1981 (S.I. 1981 No.1576).
[97] The term "storey" does not include any storey lying wholly or mainly below the floor level of the principal entrance to the house, but the combined floor area includes any such storey and any staircases.
[98] Form No.38, Housing (Prescribed Forms) Regulations 1972 (S.I. 1972 No.228), as amended by the Housing (Prescribed Forms) (Amendment Regulations) 1981 (S.I. 1981 No.1347).
[99] s.366(2) of the Housing Act 1985).
[99a] See Chap. 5, para. 5.77 on interpretation of this phrase.
[1] See Chap 1, paras. 1.33–1.34 on the power of courts to grant authority to carry out works.
[2] s.366(3) of the Housing Act 1985.

(b) require the person on whom the notice was served to carry out those works; and

(c) specify a period (being not less than 21 days from the date of service of the notice) for completion of the specified works.

So far as possible the notice should clearly specify the works required and not merely state the results to be achieved.[3]

6.116 The works specified must be reasonable having particular regard to the persons occupying the house. In *Kingston-upon-Hull D.C.* v. *University of Hull*,[4] a house was owned and managed by a non-profit-making body whose specific function was to provide accommodation for students, and it was held that the authority must have regard to the age and character of the students and to the level of supervision or management involved before determining what means of escape were reasonably necessary in all the circumstances. However, it is suggested that works necessary in houses providing general accommodation on the open market cannot provide any guarantee of the extent of supervision, nor that the occupants will be limited to a particular category (as in this case).

6.117 The authority may extend, if necessary more than once, the time period specified in the notice for completion of the works.[5]

6.118 The local housing authority must inform any other person known to be an owner, lessee or mortgagee of the house that a notice has been served,[6] and that notification must be in the prescribed form.[7]

Grant-aid for works

6.119 Once a notice under this provision has been served requiring the provision of adequate means of escape in case of fire, the local housing authority cannot refuse an application for a special grant towards the cost of the specified works.[8]

Appeals against a notice requiring provision of adequate means of escape

6.120 A person on whom a notice requiring works to provide adequate means of escape is served[9] has a right of appeal to the county court within 21 days of the date of service of that notice, or such longer period as the authority in writing allows.[10]

---

[3] See *Canterbury C.C.* v. *Bern* (1981) 44 P. & C.R. 178.
[4] L.A.G. Bull., August 1979, p.191.
[5] Housing Act 1985, s.366(3).
[6] *Ibid.* s.366(2).
[7] Form No.49, Housing (Prescribed Forms) Regulations 1972 (S.I. 1972 No.228).
[8] Housing Act 1985, s.486(1) (*b*).
[9] *Ibid.* s.366(2).
[10] *Ibid.* s.367(1).

Grounds for appeal are limited to the following[11]: 6.121

(a) that the notice is not justified by the terms of section 366 of the 1985 Act;
(b) that there has been some material informality, defect or error in, or in connection with, the notice[12];
(c) that the local housing authority have unreasonably refused to approve alternative works, or that the specified works are otherwise unreasonable in character or extent, or are unnecessary;
(d) that the time specified for completion of the works is not reasonably sufficient[13]; and
(e) that some other person is wholly or partly responsible for the condition of the house, or will benefit from the execution of the works, and so should bear all or part of the cost of carrying out the works.

In *Berg* v. *Trafford B.C.*,[14] the Court of Appeal held that on hearing an appeal founded on ground (a) above, the date when the notice was served is the relevant date for considering whether the notice was justified, even if a resolution authorising service was passed by the council or a committee before that date. 6.122

It was also held in *Berg* v. *Trafford B.C.*, that the date of the hearing is the relevant date for an appeal founded on ground (c) above (that the character and extent of the works was unreasonable or unnecessary). 6.123

The Court of Appeal went on to state that in such a case, the court should consider works required by the notice in terms of the physical characteristics of the house at that date, and that occupation of the house need not be relevant. This means that even if the house is no longer in multiple occupation at the date of the hearing, or the numbers in occupation have changed, the notice is still valid and may be enforced. However, where style of occupation has changed and is likely to remain changed, the courts will take this into account as a relevant factor. The court said that if a house is no longer multi-occupied at the relevant date the notice is not to be suspended (as was Trafford's practice), but it suggested that the authority might be entitled to extend the time period for compliance specified in the notice[15] (see para. 6.117).

---

[11] Housing Act 1985, s.367(2).
[12] The court must dismiss the appeal if the informality, defect or error was not a material one—s.367(3) of this Housing Act 1985.
[13] It should be noted that the local housing authority can extend the time specified in the notice at least once—Housing Act 1985, s.366(3).
[14] (1988) 20 H.L.R. 47.
[15] It should be noted that the local housing authority can extend the time specified in the notice at least once—Housing Act 1985, s.366(3).

6.124 If the appeal is founded on ground (e) above, the appellant should serve a copy of the notice of appeal on the person (or persons) alleged to be liable to bear all or part of the cost of the works. On the hearing of an appeal founded on this ground, the court may make such order as it thinks fit with respect to the payment to be made by the other person(s), or, where the works have been carried out by the local housing authority, to be made to the authority.[16]

6.125 Once an appeal has been lodged, the time limit specified in the notice cannot be taken to have expired until 28 days (or such longer period as the court may lay down) from determination of the appeal.[17] Withdrawal of an appeal is deemed to be determination of that appeal.[18]

Enforcement of notices requiring the provision of adequate means of escape

6.126 As to enforcement of notices requiring the provision of adequate means of escape from fire at houses in multiple occupation (including prosecution for non-compliance, carrying out works in default, continuing liability after expiry of the time limit and/or enforcement and recovery of local housing authority's expenses) see paras. 6.132–6.141 below.

Securing that a part of the house is not used

6.127 Where the local housing authority is satisfied that:

(a) the existing means of escape in case of fire would be adequate if a part of the house were not used for human habitation[19]; or

(b) the means of escape in case of fire could be made adequate if a part of the house were not used for human habitation,[20]

it may ensure that the part in question is not used for human habitation, and in the case of (b) serve a notice requiring the necessary works.[21]

6.128 In order to secure that a part of a house is not used for human habitation, the authority may either:

(a) after consultation with any owner or mortgagee, accept an undertaking that the part in question will not be used for human habitation without permission from the local housing authority[22]; or

---

[16] Housing Act 1985, s.367(4).
[17] *Ibid.* s.375(2)
[18] *Ibid.* s.399.
[19] *Ibid.* s.368(1).
[20] *Ibid.* s.366(1)(*b*).
[21] As under s.366 of the Housing Act 1985, except that the notice must be in the form prescribed by Form No.34, Housing (Prescribed Forms) Regulations 1972 (S.I. 1972 No.228) as amended by the Housing (Prescribed Forms) (Amendment) Regulations 1981 (S.I. 1981 No.1347).
[22] Housing Act 1985, s.368(2). Note that there is no prescribed form for an undertaking.

(b) make a closing order under Part IX of the 1985 Act[23] (see Chapter 5, paras. 5.137–5.146).

6.129 A local housing authority is not required to accept any undertaking offered.[24] Where an undertaking has been accepted and then contravened, the authority may substitute a closing order under Part IX of the 1985 Act[25] (see Chapter 5, paras. 5.137–5.146).

Once an undertaking has been accepted any protection given to an occupier by the Rent Act 1977 is lost.[26]

It is an offence for any person, knowing that an undertaking has been accepted, either to use, or to permit to be used, the relevant part of the house in contravention of the undertaking. The penalty on conviction is a fine not exceeding level 5 on the standard scale[27] and a further fine not exceeding £5 for every day or part of a day on which the offence continues after conviction.[28]

The effect and consequences of closing orders made under section 368 of the 1985 Act are the same as for closing orders made under Part IX of the 1985 Act (including offences Chapter 5, paras. 5.137–5.146, and rights to home loss and disturbance payments and alternative accommodation under Part III of the Land Compensation Act 1973—see Chapter 9, paras. 9.23–9.38), except that closing orders can only be determined[29] if the local housing authority is satisfied that the means of escape in case of fire will be adequate even if the relevant part of the house is available to be used for human habitation.[30]

Additional and alternative legislation relating to means of escape from fire

6.130 In addition to the provisions described above there are various statutory provisions which relate to means of escape from fire. These include:

(a) section 72 of the Building Act 1984, which applies to certain buildings (including flats, hotels and boarding houses) exceeding two storeys where the upper storey is over 20 feet above ground level;
(b) Part XII of the Housing Act 1985, which applies to common lodging-houses; and
(c) the Fire Precautions Act 1971, which applies to designated

---

[23] Housing Act 1985, s.368(4).
[24] *Ibid.* s.368(2) and (4).
[25] *Ibid.* s.368(4).
[26] *Ibid.* s.368(6).
[27] Criminal Justice Act 1982, s.37.
[28] Housing Act 1985, s.368(3).
[29] *Ibid.* s.278.
[30] *Ibid.* s.368(5).

types of premises (including hotels and boarding houses operating on a commercial basis).

6.131 Although in some cases the enforcing authority will not be the local housing authority (*e.g.* under the Fire Precautions Act 1971), it is important to note that the standards required will be similar if not the same. The standards set in each case will be based on the recommendations of the fire authority. Where action is taken in respect of one building under more than one statutory provision, it will be the superior provision that is effective (action under the inferior provisions being null and *ultra vires*), but such duplication is preferable to a lack of any action.

It should also be noted that the Fire Precautions Act 1971 can be used to prohibit premises being made available for the provision of sleeping accommodation.[31] It is suggested that this procedure should be directed at premises such as hotels where the residents have another, main, residence.

There is no provision in the 1971 Act removing Rent Act protection from occupiers, and no provision for compensation and rehousing (such as under the Land Compensation Act 1973).

Enforcement of notices

6.132 Where a notice:

(a) requiring works to render a house fit for multiple occupation under section 352 of the 1985 Act; or
(b) requiring works to make good neglect under section 372 of the 1985 Act; or
(c) requiring the provision of adequate means of escape in case of fire under section 365 of the 1985 Act;

has not been complied with within the time period specified (or, where there has been an appeal within 28 days, or such longer period as the court may lay down, from determination of the appeal), the local housing authority may:

(i) carry out the works specified or as amended by the court on appeal[32]; and/or[33]
(ii) prosecute the addressee for the offence of wilfully failing to comply with the notice.[34]

6.133 Choice of the appropriate action should be geared to ensuring the provision and maintenance of minimum standards. Prosecution by itself

---
[31] s.10 of the 1971 Act.
[32] Housing Act 1985, s.375(1).
[33] *Ibid.* s.376(5).
[34] *Ibid.* s.376(1).

ENFORCEMENT OF NOTICES

will not guarantee that the minimum standards will be attained or maintained.

Carrying out of works in default

6.134 Once the time period given in the notice has expired (or the 28 days, or such longer period as the court may have laid down, after determination of an appeal) the authority may carry out the works specified in the notice (or as varied by the court on an appeal).[35]

6.135 If at any time after the service of the notice the person on whom the notice was served notifies the authority in writing that they are unable to carry out the works, the authority may carry out specified works forthwith.[36] No indication is given regarding the reasons which may prevent a person served with the notice from being able to carry out the works, but it is suggested that an example may be where that person lacks sufficient financial resources or credit facilities to comply with the notice. However, it is suggested that this does not include the person who claims to be unable to gain entry in order to carry out the specified works, because the court has a power to order entry in such circumstances.[37]

6.136 Any expenses incurred by the local housing authority in carrying out the works, together with any interest (at a reasonable rate determined by the authority) from the date when the demand for payment is served until it is settled, can be recovered by action in the county court or the High Court (depending upon the amount involved).[38]

The money is to be recovered from the person on whom the notice was served, unless:

(a) on an appeal against the notice the court has directed that some other person(s) pay all or part of the cost of the works; or
(b) the person on whom the notice was served is an agent or trustee for another; that person's liability is limited to the amount that has been in his hands on behalf of the other person since the date of the service of the demand.

6.137 The local housing authority may also make application to the county court[39] and where the court is satisfied that:

(a) the expenses incurred by the local housing authority (together with any interest) are unlikely to be recovered;
(b) some person is profiting because of the works carried out in that they are receiving rents or other payments which they

---

[35] Housing Act 1985, s.375(1).
[36] *Ibid.* s.375(3).
[37] *Ibid.* s.377—see Chap. 1, paras. 1.33–1.34.
[38] *Ibid.* Sched. 10.
[39] *Ibid.* Sched. 10, para. 8.

would not have received if the numbers in the house had been limited to the appropriate number having regard to the condition of the house prior to the completion of the works; and

(c) that person has had proper notification of the local housing authority's application to the court;

it may make an order requiring that person to make such payment or payments as it thinks just.

6.138 The local housing authority also has the same powers and remedies for enforcement of the charge against the house under the Law of Property Act 1925, and otherwise as if they were mortgagees by deed having powers of sale and lease, to accept surrender of leases and to appoint a receiver.[40] However, the power to appoint a receiver cannot be exercised until one month from the date when the charge takes effect.

Offences for failure to comply with a notice

6.139 It is an offence for a person served with a notice:

(a) requiring works to render a house fit for multiple occupation under section 352 of the 1985 Act;
(b) requiring works to make good neglect under section 372 of the 1985 Act; or
(c) requiring the provision of adequate means of escape in case of fire under section 365 of the 1985 Act;

wilfully to fail to comply with the requirements of that notice.[41] The maximum penalty on conviction is a fine not exceeding level 4 on the standards scale.[42]

A continuing liability is imposed on the person served with a notice after conviction of the offence of wilfully failing to comply with a notice.[43] This continuing liability means that a subsequent offence is committed immediately after conviction of the first offence and so on until the notice has been complied with. The maximum penalty on conviction under this provision remains a fine not exceeding level 4 on the standard scale.[44]

The power of the local housing authority to carry out the specified works themselves is not affected by this continuing liability.[45]

6.140 Where an offence has been committed by a body corporate, and it can be shown that a director, manager, secretary, other similar officer of that body, or person purporting to act as such was also responsible, then

---

[40] Housing Act 1985, Sched. 10, para. 7.
[41] *Ibid.* s.376(1).
[42] s.37 of the Criminal Justice Act 1982.
[43] Housing Act 1985, s.376(2).
[44] s.37 of the Criminal Justice Act 1982.
[45] Housing Act 1985, s.376(5).

ENFORCEMENT OF NOTICES

both the body corporate and that person are deemed to be guilty of the offence, and can be proceeded against and punished accordingly.[46]

6.141 Where a person has notified the local housing authority in writing that they are unable to carry out the works (see para. 6.135), that person cannot be guilty of an offence under section 376(1) or section 376(2) of the 1985 Act.[47]

Reconnection or maintenance of supply of water, gas or electricity

6.142 At the written request of an occupier stating that the supply of water, gas or electricity has been, or is likely to be, disconnected because of the failure of the owner (or former owner) to make payment relating to that supply, a council may make such arrangements as it thinks fit to restore or continue the supply.[48]

6.143 For the purposes of these provisions:

(a) the term "council" means the district council, the London borough council or the common council[49]; and
(b) the term "owner" is "a person who . . . is entitled on his own behalf or as trustee or agent for another person to rent for the premises from the occupier of the premises"; and "former owner" is "a person who was so entitled to rent for the premises from the occupier of the premises".[50]

6.144 In a case where the supply is likely to be disconnected, and arrangements made by the council include payment of a sum owed by a person, the council may recover the sum (together with any interest, at a reasonable rate, from the date of the demand) from that person.[51] Where the supply has already been disconnected, and arrangements made by the council include a reconnection charge, the council may recover from the owner of the premises that amount (together with any interest at a reasonable rate, from the date of the demand, but less any amount recovered from an occupier—see para. 6.146).

6.145 Any demand to recover money under these provisions must[52]:

(a) be in writing;
(b) give details of the payment to which it relates; and
(c) state the rate of interest that will accrue from the date of the demand.

6.146 As an alternative, the council may recover payments made under these provisions by serving a notice on the occupier requiring that

---

[46] Housing Act 1985, s.613.
[47] Ibid. s.376(4).
[48] Local Government (Miscellaneous Provisions) Act 1976.
[49] Ibid. s.33(1).
[50] Ibid. s.33(5).
[51] Ibid. s.33(2).
[52] Ibid. s.33(4).

amounts equal to the rent are paid to the council. This procedure can only be used in cases where the owner had been responsible for making the payments.[52a]

Control orders

Introduction

6.147 During the late 1950s and early 1960s, there was considerable public outcry against the gross exploitation associated with some of the most unsatisfactory houses in multiple occupation. Press stories of harassment and illegal evictions and descriptions of appalling conditions became more numerous and explicit. It became clear that landlords could control large numbers of such houses, enjoying a large income and easily avoiding attempts by authorities to protect occupiers and control conditions. One such person whose activities as a landlord featured in some of the most sensational reports was Peter Rachman, whose name became synonymous with the worst forms of exploitation, harassment and slum conditions in multi-occupied houses.[53]

In response to the clear shortcomings of the legislation and the impotency of authorities, new provisions were introduced to try to increase protection for occupiers and strengthen local authorities' powers to ensure satisfactory standards.

One of the new provisions introduced was the control order procedure, intended to be used in cases where the living conditions were "so bad as to justify the exercise of this new power of summary intervention by the authority in the interest of the people living in the house".[54]

6.148 Simply, a control order allows an authority to take possession of a house for up to five years, and to do anything (short of selling the house) that needs to be done to bring the house to a satisfactory standard. The procedure is peremptory, and the liability of the authority to those dispossessed is strictly limited.

Unfortunately, to achieve this simple objective is legally complex and on a practical level the administrative co-ordination of the different departments within an authority necessary for the procedure can create its own difficulties.

Although it is to be hoped that the circumstances necessitating use of the control order procedure will rarely occur, when they do occur action should be taken without delay. The authority to make an order should be easily obtainable at any time; alternatively the authority to make an order should be delegated to an appropriate officer.[55] It is also suggested that, before a control order needs to be made, arrangements

[52a] Local Government (Miscellaneous Provisions) Act 1976, s.33(4).
[53] Green, *Rachman* (Hamlyn, 1981).
[54] Min. of H. & L.G. Circular No. 51/64, Appendix 1, para. 10.
[55] See Chap. 1, paras. 1.11–1.14 on delegation.

CONTROL ORDERS

are established to ensure co-ordination between various departments within the authority (or appropriate outside agencies—for example housing associations) involved in managing a house subject to a control order. Such departments may include environmental health, legal section, housing management, finance and technical services.

The following aspects of the control order provisions are considered below: **6.149**

(i) The making of a control order
(ii) The effect of a control order
(iii) Appeals against a control order
(iv) The management scheme
(v) Appeals against the management scheme
(vi) Accounts and compensation
(vii) Rights of entry
(viii) Revocation of a control order
(ix) Appeals against refusal to evoke a control order
(x) Effect of expiry or revocation of a control order
(xi) Compulsory purchase order after a control order

(i) The making of a control order
A local housing authority may make a control order in respect of a house in multiple occupation where they are satisfied that[56]: **6.150**

(a) (i) a notice has been, or could be, served under section 352 of the 1985 Act requiring works to make the house fit for the number of individuals or households in the house[57]; or
(ii) a management order under section 370 of the Act has been, or could be, made,[58] with or without a notice under section 372 requiring works to make good the neglect,[59] or
(iii) a direction has been, or could be, given under section 354 limiting the number of individuals or households who can be accommodated at the house[60]; and
(b) living conditions in the house are such that an order is necessary to protect the safety, welfare or health of the residents.

It is clear that the criteria in both (a) and (b) must be satisfied before an authority can invoke the control order procedure.

Whether or not the circumstances noted in (a) above are satisfied has been considered previously in this Chapter (see paras. 6.24–6.56). Perhaps surprisingly, the need for adequate means of escape in case of fire, **6.151**

---
[56] Housing Act 1985, s.379(1).
[57] *Ibid.* s.352 and see paras. 6.65–6.68.
[58] *Ibid.* ss.370–371 see paras. 6.93–6.96.
[59] *Ibid.* ss.373 and see paras. 6.104–6.107.
[60] *Ibid.* ss.354–357 and see paras. 6.78–6.83.

or action to ensure such means,[61] are not matters specifically mentioned, although it is suggested that the lack of adequate means of escape is a matter affecting the safety of residents. (See also paras. 6.157, 6.170, 6.184 and 6.189 which, *inter alia*, describe how the provision of such means of escape in case of fire can be ensured in the event of a control order being revoked on appeal, or by the authority itself.)

More difficult, however, is the assessment of factors which are not related to the physical condition of the house, but which threaten the safety, welfare or health of the residents. Guidance given by central government is not very helpful on this point:

> "In forming a picture of the living conditions the local housing authority would appear to be entitled to add such other evidence of the environment in which the residents live (*e.g.* noise, bad smells, rowdyism or other anti-social behaviour within the house) as is capable of being established by direct observation. It is important that—
> (i) in arriving at their judgment, the authority should not rely upon any rumour or hearsay but base its decision on reports of living conditions actually observed by responsible officers, or on other evidence of bad living conditions at the time of making the order which can be substantiated to its satisfaction and in any subsequent appeal proceedings; and
> (ii) the conditions are so bad as to necessitate summary intervention by the local authority as against the more orthodox means of control under the Public Health Acts and the 1985 Act."[62]

This advice seems to be over-cautious. It also implies that the life-style of residents should be a main consideration, whereas it is clearly the management and control of the house which must be the main concern of the authority, together with considerations such as whether the residents are being provided with proper accommodation and whether there are any conditions or circumstances which threaten their safety, welfare or health.

It was held in *R. v. L.B. of Southwark, ex p. Lewis Levy Ltd.*[63] that refusal to carry out works, and threats to close a hostel and evict the residents were proper facts to take into account in deciding whether to make a control order. In *R. v. Secretary of State for the Environment, ex p. R.B. of Kensington and Chelsea*,[64] considering a compulsory purchase order subsequent to a control order (see paras. 6.194–6.198), the

---

[61] Housing Act 1985, ss.365–368 and see para. 6.112.
[62] Memorandum to D.o.E. Circular No.12/86, para. 3.9.2, (W.O. No. 23/86). This is an edited version of the advice given in Circular 51/64, now withdrawn.
[63] (1983) 8 H.L.R. 1.
[64] (1987) 19 H.L.R. 161.

court commented on "proper housing accommodation." Taylor J.[65] said that if, "by reason of the landlord's conduct, a tenant is put in bodily fear, is harassed, threatened with eviction or exclusion, if essential services are not maintained, or the tenant's property is invaded and he is verbally abused, it would be a callous misuse of language to say that he was being provided with proper housing accommodation." It is suggested that these matters could be taken into account to justify the making of a control order.

The collection of evidence, "hearsay" and "rumour" is considered in Chapter 9, paras. 9.02–9.17.

6.152 The control order must be in the prescribed form,[66] must be properly authenticated (see Chapter 4, paras. 4.04–4.10), and must be registered as a local land charge.[67]

Although it need not do so, the authority may exclude from the control order (and so from the effect of the Order) any part of the house which is occupied by a person having an estate or interest in the whole house.[68]

6.153 A control order applies to the house, and as soon as possible after it has been made, the authority must[69]:

(a) post a copy of the order in some conspicuous part of the house, together with a notice explaining the rights and grounds of appeal against the order; and
(b) serve a copy of the control order, and a notice explaining the rights and grounds of appeal against the order, on—
  (i) any person known to be managing the house[70];
  (ii) any person known to have control of the house[70];
  (iii) any owner, lessee or mortgagee.[70]

There is a prescribed form for the notice explaining the right and grounds of appeal.[71]

(ii) The effects of the control order

6.154 A control order comes into force as soon as it is made, and as soon as practicable after making the order, the authority must enter the premises and take such immediate steps as they consider necessary to protect

---

[65] (1987) 19 H.L.R. 161 at 170.
[66] Form No. 50, with appropriate amendments, Housing (Prescribed Forms) Regulations 1972 as amended.
[67] Housing Act 1985, s.381(5).
[68] *Ibid.* s.380.
[69] *Ibid.* s.379(3).
[70] *Ibid.* s.398.
[71] Form No. 51, with appropriate amendments, Housing (Prescribed Forms) Regulations 1972 as amended.

the safety, welfare and health of the residents.[72] These steps may involve temporary works to remove conditions which are likely to be dangerous to the residents. It may be that the making of the control order itself will provide much of the protection required because it will dispossess those who previously managed and controlled the house.

6.155 As soon as the control order is made and for as long as it is in force, the authority has the right to possession and the right to do anything which someone with an estate or interest in the house could have done but for the order, and the authority will not generally incur any liability to those dispossessed persons.[73]

This right to possession does not affect the rights and liabilities of a person who occupies a part of the house under a lease or agreement but who has no estate or interest in the whole house, and such a lease or agreement continues.[74] Although the authority has the right to possession of the house, it will not become a part of their stock under Part II of the 1985 Act,[75] and the occupants will continue to enjoy any Rent Act protection that may have applied before the making of the order.[76] The authority may create interests in the house, but not tenancies or licences for fixed terms of more than one month or periodic tenancies on more than four weeks' notice.[77] However, such new interests do not automatically gain Rent Act protection.

6.156 If the house is subject to a lease giving the lessee an interest in the whole house (see para. 6.155 on other types of leases), either the lessor or lessee may apply to the county court for a variation or determination of the lease.[78]

The court must determine the lease if it is satisfied that[79]:

(a) if the lease were determined and the control order revoked, the lessor would be in a position, and is ready, to take whatever action the authority would have taken had the control order remained in force; and

(b) the authority would revoke the control order if the lease were determined.

The court may apply such terms and conditions to determination as it thinks fit, including the imposition of compensation or damages in respect of the lease[80] and the modification of provisions relating to the

---

[72] Housing Act 1985, s.379(2).
[73] *Ibid.* s.381(1)(*b*).
[74] *Ibid.* s.382.
[75] *Ibid.* s.381(6).
[76] *Ibid.* s.382(3) and (4).
[77] *Ibid.* s.381(1)(*c*) and (2).
[78] *Ibid.* s.391(1).
[79] *Ibid.* s.391(2).
[80] *Ibid.* s.391(3) and (4).

transfer back of the landlord's interest on revocation of the control order.[81]

Since the authority has possession and manages the house once the order has been made, it must make reasonable provision for insuring the house, including any part excluded from the order, against destruction or damage.[82]

6.157

Once the control order has been made, any notice, order or direction relating to the house ceases to have effect. This does not, however, remove criminal liability relating to the period while the notice, order or direction were effective before the control order was made, and the authority has the right to recover the cost of works previously carried out at its expense.[83]

6.158

The control order applies the provisions of the management regulations,[84] imposing duties on residents[85] and placing the authority under a duty to maintain proper standards of management in the house.[86] The authority must also take any action it would have required to be taken under any provisions of the 1985 Housing Act (not only those provisions relating to houses in multiple occupation).[87]

Although the authority is under this general duty to carry out works it would have required but for the order, where it becomes clear to the authority that the house, or a part of it, is unfit for human habitation and not capable of repair at reasonable expense, the procedure under sections 264–282 of the 1985 Act must be followed (see Chapter 5, paras. 5.104–5.169).[88]

In addition to transferring the right of possession of the house to the local housing authority, the control order also transfers to the authority the right to possession of furniture in any furnished letting.[89]

6.159

Where such furniture is owned by more than one person, any of them may apply to the county court for an adjustment of their rights and liabilities and the court may make such adjustment, with or without conditions, as it thinks fit.[90]

On the written application of the owner of the furniture, the authority

---

[81] Housing Act 1985, s.391(5) and see paras. 6.191–6.192 and Sched. 13, para. 15 on the effects of cessation of a control order.
[82] *Ibid.* s.385(1)(*c*) and (2).
[83] *Ibid.* s.381(4).
[84] Housing (Management of Houses in Multiple Occupation) Regulations 1962 (S.I. 1962 No. 668) (retained in force by the Housing (Consequential Provisions) Act 1985)—see paras. 6.29–6.56.
[85] Housing Act 1985, s.382(5).
[86] *Ibid.* s.385(1)(*a*).
[87] *Ibid.* s.385 (1)(*b*).
[88] *R.* v. *Cardiff C.C., ex p. Cross* (1982) 6 H.L.R. 1 C.A., affirming (1981) 1 H.L.R. 54.
[89] Housing Act 1985, s.383(1). The term "furniture" includes fittings and other articles, *ibid.* s.383(5).
[90] *Ibid.* s.383(3) and (4).

may renounce its right of possession by giving two weeks notice to the applicant.[91] Since this would mean that the owner could then remove that furniture, the authority is enabled to provide any furniture, fittings and conveniences to replace the furniture removed or otherwise necessary.[92]

(iii) Appeals against a control order

6.160 An appeal against the making of a control order may be made to the county court by:

(a) any person with an estate or interest in the house[93]; or
(b) any other person who is able to satisfy the court that he may have been prejudiced by the making of the order.[94]

The appeal can be brought at any time after the making of the order but before six weeks from the date the authority serve a copy of the management scheme.[95]

6.161 The grounds of appeal are set out in the Act, and are that[96]:

(a) the state or condition of the house did not justify the taking of any of the actions described in para. 6.150 (a) above;
(b) it was not necessary to make the control order to protect the safety, welfare or health of the residents;
(c) although it had not been done, it was reasonably practicable for the authority to have excluded from the order a part of the house occupied by the dispossessed proprietor;
(d) the control order was invalid because a requirement of the Act has not been complied with, or because there was some informality or defect in connection with the order.

Where the appeal is founded on ground (d), the court is required to confirm the order unless satisfied that the interests of the appellant have been substantially prejudiced.[97]

6.162 Although the Act states that subject to this right of appeal the control order is final and conclusive as to any matter which would have been raised on appeal, this would not seem to prevent an application for judicial review.[98]

6.163 Where the court decides to revoke the control order after hearing an appeal, it must consider[99] whether any of the actions listed in para.

---

[91] Housing Act 1985, s.383(2).
[92] *Ibid.* s.388.
[93] *Ibid.* s.384(1).
[94] *Ibid.* s.384(3).
[95] *Ibid.* s.384(2) and see paras. 6.174–6.177.
[96] *Ibid* s.384(1).
[97] *Ibid.* s.384(4).
[98] See in particular, *R. v. L.B. of Southward, ex p. Lewis Levy Ltd.* (1983) 8 H.L.R. 1.
[99] Sched. 13, para. 17(2).

6.150 (a) or the service of a notice under section 366 of the Act[1] requiring works to ensure adequate means of escape in case of fire, ought to be taken. If the court approves the taking of any of these actions there is no right of appeal available.

6.164 If at the time of a decision by the court to revoke the order the authority is carrying out works at the house which it could have required under any provision relating to public health or housing conditions, the court may postpone the revocation until those works are complete, provided that it is satisfied that the works are urgent and necessary to protect the safety, welfare or health of the residents or other persons.[2]

The court must fix a date for revocation of the order even if the authority is to appeal against the decision.[3] The court may also authorise the authority to create tenancies which expire or which can be terminated up to six months after the order has been revoked (thus giving the residents some protection).[4]

6.165 On revocation of an order by the county court, the authority is required to pay to the dispossessed proprietor the balances left from the income received after deducting its expenditure (other than capital expenditure) and any compensation payments already made. The court has power to increase the amount of the balances (to a maximum equal to the amount lost by the dispossessed proprietor as a result of the order) if it is satisfied the balances were low and having regard to the various standards applicable to the house, the numbers accommodated and the rents charged.[5]

6.166 The authority may apply to the court for approval of works carried out prior to revocation of the control order. Provided that such works were works that but for the order the authority could have required under any provision relating to public health or housing conditions, and that the works were urgently needed to protect the safety, welfare or health of residents or others, the court may approve recovery of reasonable expenses incurred by the authority.[6]

These reasonable expenses may then be deducted from the balances payable to the dispossessed proprietor, and any outstanding amount becomes a charge against the property. For the purposes of recovering such a charge, the authority has the same powers and remedies under the Law of Property Act 1925 and otherwise as if it was a mortgagee (except that a receiver cannot be appointed until one month after the date on which the charge takes effect).

---

[1] See paras. 6.114–6.118.
[2] Housing Act 1985, Sched. 13, para. 17(3).
[3] *Ibid.* para. 17(4).
[4] *Ibid.* para. 17(5).
[5] *Ibid.* para. 18.
[6] *Ibid.* para. 19.

6.167 An appellant who intends to appeal against a decision of the county court to confirm a control order, may apply to the court to direct that the cost of certain works should not be recoverable by the authority unless the order is confirmed on that further appeal.[7]

6.168 If on appeal against the decision of the county court to confirm the control order the court decides to revoke it, and the authority is carrying out works, revocation may be postponed until the works are complete. The court must be satisfied that the works are works which the authority could have required under any provision relating to public health or housing conditions, and that they are urgently needed to protect the safety, welfare or health of residents or other persons.[8]

(iv) The management scheme

6.169 Once the control order has been made, the local housing authority is required to prepare a management scheme.[9] This management scheme must contain[10]:

    (a) details of all works involving capital expenditure which the authority, but for the control order, would have required to be carried out at the house under any statutory provisions[11];
    (b) an estimate of the cost of such works;
    (c) the maximum number of individuals or households who should live in the house having regard to—
        (i) the matters set out in section 352 of the 1985 Act[12];
        (ii) the present condition of the house;
        (iii) the future condition as works progress; and
    (d) an estimate of the balance (called the surpluses on the revenue account) which will accrue from time to time, being the excess left from the income from residents less the compensation paid to the dispossessed proprietor and any expenditure not covered by (a) above.

6.170 The duty to prepare the management scheme must not delay the authority from carrying out any works at the house, whether such works are necessary to protect the safety, welfare or health of the residents, or otherwise,[13] and the authority may carry out any necessary works whether or not they are included in the management scheme[14] (the management scheme should include all works).

---

[7] Housing Act 1985, Sched. 13, para. 20(2).
[8] *Ibid.* para. 20(1).
[9] Housing Act 1985, s.386.
[10] *Ibid.* Part I of Sched. 13.
[11] This includes any provisions of the 1985 Act, the Public Health Acts and any other provisions relating to public health or housing conditions.
[12] See para. 6.24.
[13] See paras. 6.154 and 6.158.
[14] s.386(3) of the Housing Act 1985.

CONTROL ORDERS

Although once the control order is effective, management of the house will be transferred to the authority (or a body acting on its behalf), best practice would be for the environmental health department to specify all the works to be carried out at the house and to set maximum numbers in relation to the matters in section 352 of the Act, based on the standards and timetables that the department would have required but for the order.

6.171 The expenditure in para. 6.169(d) above will include the rates, etc., insurance premiums,[15] the cost of any furniture, etc.,[16] and the cost of providing temporary accommodation and of moving any residents to and from such accommodation.[17]

6.172 Within eight weeks of the date on which the control order was made, the authority must serve a copy of the management scheme on[18]:

(a) everyone served with a copy of the control order[19]; and
(b) any other person known to be a dispossessed proprietor, owner, lessee or mortgagee of the house.

6.173 The authority may vary the scheme at any time, provided that variation results in an increase to the surpluses on the revenue account (see para. 6.169 (d) above).[20]

On application by the authority or a person having an estate or interest in the house, the county court may review the surpluses on the revenue account in the scheme, and may vary the scheme (but not the works) and the surpluses on the revenue account for any period (including past periods).[21]

(v) Appeals against the management scheme

6.174 An appeal against the management scheme may be made to the county court by a person with an estate or interest in the house subject to the control order. The appeal must be brought within six weeks from the date of service of a copy of the scheme (see para. 6.172), or such longer period as the local housing authority, in writing, allows.[22]

6.175 Where an appeal is being brought against the scheme together with an appeal against the making of the control order under section 384 of the 1985 Act (see para. 6.160), the proceedings should be combined, and, if

---

[15] See para. 6.157.
[16] See para. 6.159.
[17] Housing Act 1985, Sched. 13, para. 2(3).
[18] *Ibid.* s.386(1).
[19] See para. 6.153.
[20] Housing Act 1985, Sched. 13, para. 5.
[21] *Ibid.* para. 6.
[22] *Ibid.* s.386(2) and Sched. 13, para. 3(1).

the court decides to revoke the control order, it is not to proceed with the appeal against the scheme.[23]

6.176 The grounds of appeal are set out in the Act; they are that[24]:

(a) having regard to the condition of the house and to other circumstances, any of the works specified in the scheme are unreasonable in character or extent, or are unnecessary;

(b) any of the works do not involve capital expenditure;

(c) as specified by the scheme, the number of individuals or households who should live in the house is unreasonably low;

(d) the estimate of the surpluses on the revenue account is unduly low because of assumptions made by the authority on matters within its control (*e.g.* that rents charged by the authority are too low).

6.177 The court may confirm or vary the management scheme as it thinks fit.[25]

(vi) Accounts and compensation

6.178 The authority must keep full accounts of the income and expenditure in respect of a house subject to a control order, and must allow the dispossessed proprietor and anyone with an estate or interest in the house reasonable facilities for inspecting, copying and verifying the accounts.[26]

The authority is specifically required to keep an account showing surpluses on the revenue account and capital expenditure relating to the management scheme.[27]

6.179 Compensation must be paid by the authority to the dispossessed proprietor for the period during which the control order is in force, and for the period during which the authority has the right to possession of any furniture.[28]

The method of calculation of compensation payable in respect of the house is set out in Part II of Schedule 13 to the 1985 Act, and disputes relating to calculation or, where more than one person qualifies for compensation, to the proportions payable, are to be resolved by the District Valuer. Compensation accrues on a daily basis and is payable quarterly beginning three months after the date on which the order was made.[29]

Compensation for furniture will be at a rate agreed between the parties or as determined by the local rent tribunal.

If there is a mortgage or charge relating to the house or furniture at

[23] Housing Act 1985, s.386(2) and Sched. 13, para. 3(4).
[24] *Ibid.* s.386(2) and para. 3(2).
[25] *Ibid.* s.386(2) and para. 3(2).
[26] Housing Act 1985, s.390(1).
[27] *Ibid.* Sched. 13, para. 4.
[28] *Ibid.* s.389(1).
[29] *Ibid.* s.389(2).

the time compensation is due, the mortgage or charge will attach to any compensation payable.[30]

(vii) Rights of entry
In addition to the general powers of entry described in Chapter 1 (see paras. 1.15—1.34), the local housing authority, and any representative authorised in writing by it, has a specific right to enter any part of the house subject to a control order. This power of entry enables the authority to survey and examine the house or to carry out works at all reasonable times. It extends to a part of the house excluded from the order provided that access is necessary for surveying, examining or carrying out works in the part subject to the order.[31]

6.180

Obstruction of a properly authorised person attempting to exercise this right to enter may be an offence.[32] Although there is no requirement to give notice prior to attempting to gain entry, it is advisable to do so, particularly where it is suspected that entry may be refused.

Where an authority gives notice of its intention to carry out works in a house subject to a control order, and an occupier of a part of the house prevents those works being carried out, a magistrates' court may order that occupier to permit the work to proceed.[33] Failure to comply with such an order may be an offence, carrying a maximum fine not exceeding level 3 on the standard scale,[34] and a further fine of up to £20.00 for each day (or part of a day) that the offence continues.[35]

6.181

The local housing authority must provide any reasonable facilities for inspecting and examining the house requested by the dispossessed proprietor.[36]

6.182

(viii) Revocation of a control order
At any time prior to the automatic expiry of a control order (*i.e.* five years from the date it was made—see para. 6.154) the authority may revoke an order on its own initiative, or on receipt of an application for revocation. In either case, the authority must give 21 days notice of its intention to revoke the order to the residents and to all known owners, lessees and mortgagees.[37]

6.183

Where a person applies to the authority for revocation and sets down the grounds on which the application is made, the authority, if it decides

---

[30] Housing Act 1985, s.389(3).
[31] *Ibid.* s.387(1), (2) and (3).
[32] *Ibid.* s.396.
[33] *Ibid.* s.387(4).
[34] Criminal Justice Act 1982, s.37.
[35] Housing Act 1985, s.387(5).
[36] *Ibid.* s.390(2).
[37] *Ibid.* s.392(2) and (3).

not to revoke the order, must give reasons for rejecting the application.[38]

6.184 Where the authority decides to revoke the order on its own initiative (but not where its decision follows an application) it may apply to the county court for approval to take any of the following steps[39]:

(a) service of a notice requiring works under section 352 (to make the house fit for multiple occupation), section 366 (to provide adequate means of escape in case of fire) or section 372 (to make good the results of bad management) of the 1985 Act[40];
(b) the giving of a direction under sections 354–357 of the 1985 Act[41]; or
(c) the making of a management order under section 370 of the 1985 Act.[42]

There is no right of appeal against a notice, direction or order issued with the approval of the court.[43]

(ix) Appeals against refusal to revoke a control order

6.185 Where a person makes an application to the authority for revocation of a control order (see para. 6.183), the applicant may appeal to the county court against that decision.[44] An appeal may also be made where the authority fails to inform the applicant of its decision within 42 days of the application (or such longer period as the applicant in writing allows).[45]

6.186 On such an appeal, the county court may revoke the order, and must revoke it if[46]:

(a) the appellant has an estate or interest in the house which, apart from the authority's rights resulting from the control order[47] and the rights of occupiers, would give him the right to possession of the house;
(b) the estate or interest was, when the control order came into force, subject to a lease which has since expired; and
(c) the appellant satisfies the court that, if the order is revoked, he is in a position to and intends to demolish or reconstruct the

---

[38] Housing Act 1985, s.392(4).
[39] *Ibid.* s.392(5).
[40] See paras. 6.65–6.68, 6.114–6.118 and 6.104–6.107 respectively.
[41] See paras. 6.78–6.86.
[42] See paras. 6.93–6.96.
[43] *Ibid.* s.392(5).
[44] Housing Act 1985, s.393(1)(*a*).
[45] *Ibid.* s.393(1)(*b*).
[46] *Ibid.* s.393(2).
[47] *Ibid.* s.381 and see para. 6.155.

house, or to carry out substantial construction work on the site.

If the court finds that although these criteria are not satisfied at the date of the hearing of the appeal but that they will be satisfied at a future date, it may determine to revoke the order on that future date.

If the appeal fails, a second appeal against the same control order cannot be made within six months of the determination of the first appeal without leave of the court. This requirement applies to any prospective appellant, not only to the original one.[48] **6.187**

Where at the date of the appeal the local housing authority is carrying out works detailed in the management scheme, it may represent to the court that immediate revocation of the order would unreasonably delay the completion of those works. If the court thinks fit, it may postpone revocation until those works are complete.[49] **6.188**

The court may also postpone revocation of the order until the time allowed for bringing an appeal against its decision has expired and any such appeal has been determined.[50]

When deciding to revoke the order on appeal the court may approve the taking of any of the actions listed in para. 6.184 (a), (b) and (c), and if it does so there is no right of appeal available against such action.[51] **6.189**

If there will be a charge due to the authority on appeal and revocation of the control order, the court may require that the appellant pays off the charge (or a part of it) before revocation.[52] **6.190**

The court also has power to authorise the authority to create tenancies which will expire or can be terminated up to six months after the order has been revoked (thus giving the residents some protection).[53]

(x) Effects on expiry or revocation of a control order

Unless revoked by the authority or by the county court on appeal, a control order is effective for a period of five years from the date it was made.[54] It would appear that the authority is not required to give any notice if the order is to expire naturally (by contrast with the case of revocation by the authority—see para. 6.183). **6.191**

On the date the control order ceases to have effect the rights, duties, and consequences flowing from the order also cease.[55] These rights and duties include the authority's right to possession of the house and any furniture, and its management duties and responsibilities (see paras. **6.192**

---

[48] Housing Act 1985, s.393(3).
[49] *Ibid.* s.393(4) and Sched 13, para. 21(2).
[50] *Ibid.* s.393(4) and para. 21(3).
[51] *Ibid.* s.393(4) and para. 21(4).
[52] *Ibid.* s.393(4) and para. 21(5).
[53] *Ibid.* s.393(4) and para. 21(6).
[54] *Ibid.* s.392(1).
[55] *Ibid.* s.394 and Sched. 13, para. 15.

6.154–6.159), and possession passes back to the dispossessed proprietor (or successor).

Any agreement creating rights of occupation made by the authority while the order was effective continues with the dispossessed proprietor substituted for the authority, but no liability to the landlord is imposed on a dispossessed proprietor who is a lessee (or imposed on a superior lessee) for anything done pursuant to the terms of such an agreement.

6.193 Except where the control order ceases to have effect following a compulsory purchase order (see paras. 6.194–6.198) or is revoked by the county court on appeal against the order (see paras. 6.160–6.168),[56] a final balance must be struck in the accounts on the date the order ceases to have effect. The authority has a charge against the house for any expenditure reasonably incurred under the management scheme which has not been met by the surpluses on the revenue account under that scheme. For the purposes of recovering such a charge the authority has the same powers and remedies under the Law of Property Act 1925 and otherwise as if it was a mortgagee (except that a receiver cannot be appointed until after one month from the date the charge takes effect).[57]

If there are proceedings to vary the management scheme pending on the date when the order ceases to have effect, those proceedings may continue (see para. 6.173). However, if the authority recovers a charge before such proceedings are determined, it must account for any amount recovered which the court decides ought not to have been recovered.[58]

(xi) Compulsory purchase order after a control order

6.194 Within 28 days of the making of a control order, a local housing authority may make a compulsory purchase order for the acquisition of a house under Part II of the 1985 Act.[59]

6.195 Where the authority makes a compulsory purchase order within the 28 days, the duty to prepare and serve a management scheme under section 386 of the Act (see paras. 6.169–6.173) is suspended until the authority has been notified of the Secretary of State's decision on the compulsory purchase order.[60] The time within which the authority must serve copies of the scheme (see para. 6.172) is eight weeks from either:

(a) the date the authority is notified of the Secretary of State's decision not to confirm the compulsory purchase order; or

(b) the date on which the compulsory purchase order becomes operative if the Secretary of State confirms it.

---

[56] Housing Act 1985, s.394 and Sched. 13, para. 16(6).
[57] *Ibid.* s.394 and para. 16.
[58] *Ibid.* s.394 and para. 16(5).
[59] *Ibid.* s.394 and para. 22 (see s.17 on power to C.P.O.).
[60] *Ibid.* s.394 and para. 23.

The preparation of the management scheme remains necessary even if the compulsory purchase order is confirmed as it enables the authority to recover the expenses it incurred between the date of the control order and the date of the notice of entry (see para. 6.196).

If the compulsory purchase order is confirmed, the control order ceases to have effect on the date the authority either[61]: **6.196**

(a) enters into a contract to purchase the house by agreement; or
(b) on the date the authority serves a notice of entry under section 11 of the Compulsory Purchase Act 1965, or a notice under section 583 of the 1985 Housing Act.

Once the control order ceases to have effect as described in para. 6.196, the authority must pay the dispossessed proprietor the balance which has accrued out of rents or other payments from residents less compensation payable to the dispossessed proprietor and all non-capital expenditure incurred by the authority while the control order was effective. **6.197**

The authority must serve a notice informing the dispossessed proprietor of the balances it proposes to pay and of the right to appeal to the county court.[62]

The dispossessed proprietor may appeal to the county court against the balances proposed to be paid by the local housing authority within 21 days of service of the notice (or such longer time as the authority, in writing, allows).

The court may increase the amount of the balances (to a maximum equal to the amount lost by the dispossessed proprietor as a result of the order) if it is satisfied that the balances were low, and having regard to the various standards applicable to the house, the numbers accommodated and the rents charged.[63]

The authority may recover capital expenditure incurred while the control order was effective by serving a notice on the dispossessed proprietor.[64] Such a notice must specify: **6.198**

(a) the works carried out which were works
  (i) the authority could, but for the control order, have required to be carried out under any provision relating to public health or housing conditions; and
  (ii) urgently needed at the time to protect the safety, welfare or health of the residents or other persons; and
(b) the right to appeal against the notice.

---

[61] Housing Act 1985, s.394 and Sched. 13, para. 24.
[62] Ibid. s.394 and para. 25(1) and (2).
[63] Ibid. s.394 and para. 25(3), (4) and (5).
[64] Ibid. s.394 and para. 26.

The dispossessed proprietor may appeal against the notice to the county court within 21 days of service of the notice (or such longer time as the authority, in writing, allows), and the court may confirm, vary or quash the notice.

Capital expenditure incurred as detailed in the notice may be deducted by the authority out of the balances payable to the dispossessed proprietor (as described in para. 6.197). Any outstanding amount may be deducted (together with any interest) from the compensation payable if the house is compulsorily acquired.

Chapter 7

OVERCROWDING

1. Historical background and introduction — 7.02   **7.01**
2. Standards applicable to all dwellings — 7.07
3. Definitions — 7.14
4. Offences — 7.20
5. Information — 7.31
6. Enforcement of overcrowding provisions — 7.39
7. Overcrowding in houses in multiple occupation — 7.48
8. Procedure for abating or preventing overcrowding in houses in multiple occupation — 7.52
9. Miscellaneous overcrowding provisions — 7.67

1. Historical Background and Introduction

The legislation aimed at controlling overcrowding in dwellings can be confusing. This is partly because the main standard and enforcement procedures are themselves confusing, and partly because there are also several non-statutory overcrowding standards some of which may be applied to the same accommodation. The principle standards are to be found in the Housing Act 1985 and deal with the number of persons who may sleep in the space available. This Chapter concentrates on these standards, but other standards exist for different purposes. For example, under sections 354 to 357 of the Housing Act 1985, the numbers in occupation of a house in multiple occupation can be limited having regard to the facilities available (on which see Chapter 6). Furthermore, the Registrar General adopts a different standard for the purposes of the national census.   **7.02**

Originally, overcrowding was dealt with under the Public Health Act 1875 as one of the matters defined as a statutory nuisance. No fixed standard was given in the Act, which merely stated: **7.03**

> "Any house or part of a house so overcrowded as to be dangerous or injurious to the health of the inmates, whether or not members of the same family . . . shall be deemed to be (a nuisance) liable to be dealt with summarily."[1]

It has been suggested that this provision was ineffective, and that action was only taken to deal with gross cases of overcrowding.[2] Perhaps

---

[1] Public Health Act 1875, s.91.
[2] See Swift, *Housing Administration* (2nd ed., 1938) Chap. 17.

to make the provisions more widely enforceable, specific standards were set down in the Housing Acts, and overcrowding in houses ceased to be a statutory nuisance. However, one overcrowding provision remains in the Public Health Act 1936, dealing with tents, vans sheds or similar structures which are overcrowded.[3]

7.04 The present standard was first introduced as sections 1 to 12 of, and the First Schedule to the Housing Act 1935, and has been re-enacted as Part X of the Housing Act 1985, despite the comment by the Minister of Health on its introduction in 1935,[4] that:

> "It is relevant to point out that this standard does not represent any ideal standard of housing, but the minimum which is in the view of Parliament tolerable while at the same time capable of early enforcement."

7.05 It would seem that when introduced, the standard was aimed at limiting the spread of disease by contact and by droplet infection, and by a desire to reduce what was seen as situations which might increase the chances of sexual abuse or promiscuity between the sexes within a household. The dual concerns are reflected in the two parts of the standard, one dealing with the total number of persons permitted within a dwelling, and the other with separation of the sexes.

However, the standards can only be applied to ensure that sufficient space and rooms were available to the household, and there is control over how a household decides to use that space.

7.06 Medical research carried out between 1920 and 1950 showed that there was a close relationship between many types of infection and overcrowding.[5] Other reports relate increases in airborne infections to poverty rather than overcrowding[6] (although overcrowding is one of the possible results of poverty), and to sanitation and hygiene.

More recently, the evidence relating to the effects of space availability recognises the need for space for purposes other than simply sleeping.

Psychiatric problems may result from inadequate space for privacy for individuals within the household, or for the play and recreation of children. In these respects the standards are inadequate, since they are directed only to sleeping. The World Health Organisation stated in 1972,[7] that the

> "Lack of privacy and of freedom of movement in the house as a

---

[3] Public Health Act 1936, s.268(2)(*a*).
[4] In Memoradum B "The Prevention and Abatement of Overcrowding" (October 1935).
[5] See in particular, Annual Report of the Chief Medical Officer of Health 1937, Ministry of Health; Britten R. (1942) 32 *American Journal of Public Health Reports* 195.
[6] See, in particular, Wright G.P. and Wright H.P. (1942) 42 *Journal of Hygiene* (Cambridge), 451.
[7] *Health Hazards of the Human Environment.*

consequence of overcrowding is considered as a cause of mental unrest. Shared and interconnected bedrooms with direct access, a family room where it is impossible to find a quiet place if so desired, windows and doors which do not permit visual privacy are typical of the deficiencies that may generate feelings of irritation, resentment, and frustration as a result of intrusions, interruptions and general interference."

The lack of play space for children has been recognised as repressing their development,[8] and the space generally available has been shown to be directly related to the mental health of women in particular.[9]

2. STANDARDS APPLICABLE TO ALL DWELLINGS

There are two principle standards, both of which must be satisfied by all dwellings. The first—the "room standard"—deals with separation of the sexes, directed at preventing "sexual overcrowding." The second—the "space standard"—is a standard of capacity, and deals with the amount of space available for sleeping within the dwelling, from which can be calculated for any dwelling a permitted number (a maximum number) of persons that may sleep it. **7.07**

The Housing Act 1985 defines the standards[10] as follows: **7.08**

> "A dwelling is overcrowded for the purposes of this Part (of the Act) when the number of persons sleeping in the dwelling is such as to contravene—
> (a) the standard specified in section 325 (the room standard), or
> (b) the standard specified in section 326 (the space standard)."

The "room standard"

The "room standard" is contravened "when the number of persons sleeping in the dwelling and the number of rooms available as sleeping accommodation is such that two persons of opposite sexes who are not living together as husband and wife must sleep in the same room."[11] **7.09**

For the purposes of this "room standard":

> "(a) children under the age of ten shall be left out of account, and
> (b) a room is available as sleeping accommodation if it is of a type

---

[8] "Families in Flats" (1967) 4 B.M.J. 382–386. "Families in High Rise Flats" (1982) B.M.J. 284–846. Mackintosh J.M., *Housing and Family Life* (1953).
[9] Gabe J. & Williams P. "Women, Housing and Mental Health" (Paper at "Unhealthy Housing: A Diagnosis" (Conference at University of Warwick, 1986.)).
[10] Housing Act 1985, s.324.
[11] *Ibid*. s.325(1).

normally used in the locality either as a bedroom or as a living room."[12]

The age limit set here is arbitrary and not based on a view of sexual maturity, as the 1985 Act also deals with separation of the sexes at eight years old in the case of the power of local housing authorities to make byelaws in respect of their own lodging-houses (s.23(3)), and 12 years old in the case of houses in multiple occupation (s.360(2)), see para. 7.59. In the case of common lodging-houses, the age for separation of the sexes is left to the discretion of the local housing authority (s.406), while in the case of canal boats the ages for separation of the sexes are 12 years for females and 14 years for males (Canal Boat Regulations 1878, reg. 8,[12a] retained in force by the Public Health (Control of Disease Act) 1984).

7.10 It must be noted that the "room standard" is only contravened when the number of persons and available rooms is such that sexual overcrowding is unavoidable; it is not contravened if the sleeping arrangements of the household could be re-organised to avoid the sexual overcrowding.

The "space standard"

7.11 The "space standard" is contravened "when the number of persons sleeping in a dwelling is in excess of the permitted number, having regard to the number and floor area of the rooms of the dwelling available as sleeping accommodation."[13]

For the purposes of this "space standard"—

"(a) no account shall be taken of a child under the age of one and a child aged one or over but under ten shall be reckoned as one-half of a unit, and

(b) a room is available as sleeping accommodation if it is of a type normally used in the locality as a living room or as a bedroom."[14]

7.12 The "permitted number" for a dwelling is the lower of the figures obtained by reference to both of the following tables based on those given in section 326(3) of the Housing Act 1985. In calculating the permitted number, no account is to be taken of rooms having a floor area of less than 50 sq. ft.[15]

---

[12] Housing Act 1985, s.325(2).
[12a] S.I. 1978 No. 1878.
[13] Housing Act 1985, s.326(1).
[14] *Ibid.* s.326(2).
[15] *Ibid.* s.326(3).

STANDARDS APPLICABLE TO ALL DWELLINGS

TABLE 1

Number of rooms	Number of persons
1	2
2	3
3	5
4	7.5
5 or more	2 for each room

TABLE 2

Floor area of room	Number of persons
110 sq. ft or more	2
90 sq. ft. or more but less than 110 sq. ft.	1.5
70 sq. ft. or more but less than 90 sq. ft.	1
50 sq. ft. or more but less than 70 sq. ft.	0.5

Measuring rooms

7.13 The Secretary of State may, by regulation, prescribe the manner by which the floor area of a room is to be ascertained.[16] The Regulations currently in force[17] state that:

(a) measurements are to be taken at floor level, and to the back of any projecting skirting boarding;
(b) to be excluded from the total floor area of a room is any part of the floor over which the ceiling height is less than five feet;
(c) to be included in the total floor area of a room is any part of the floor covered by fixed cupboards or chimney breasts; and
(d) to be included in the total floor area of a room is any part of the floor in any bay.

The powers of an authorised officer to enter premises are dealt with elsewhere (see Chapter 1), but if entry is to be made for the purpose of measuring rooms notice should be given in the prescribed form.[18]

3. Definitions

7.14 Before dealing with the enforcement of the standards, it is necessary to consider the interpretation of the provisions in Part X of the 1985 Act.

---

[16] Housing Act 1985, s.326(4).
[17] Housing Act (Overcrowding and Miscellaneous Forms) Regulations 1937 (S.R. and O. 1937 No. 80) retained in force (originally by s.191(4) of the Housing Act 1957) by s.2 of the Housing (Consequential Provisions) Act 1985.
[18] *Ibid.* Form A, (retained in force by s.2 of the Housing (Consequential Provisions) Act 1985).

7.15 "Dwelling" is defined[19] as "premises used or suitable for use as a separate dwelling."

This definition means that any building or part of a building used or suitable for use as a dwelling, including a single room with or without all the necessary facilities[20] (provided that the room satisfies the requirements set out in paras. 7.09 and 7.11), is included within the definition. This definition makes it clear that the principle overcrowding standards apply to all types of housing, including separately let parts of a house in multiple occupation (and thus the provisions relating to houses in multiple occupation described in paras. 7.52 to 7.66 are in addition to the principle standards). However, it would seem that where no exclusive right of occupation has been granted (as distinct from the right of access through parts of premises[21]) the premises will not be a "separate dwelling".[22] The decision as to whether a "dwelling" exists should be based on the particular circumstances of the case.[23]

"Room" is defined[24] as being available for sleeping accommodation "if it is of a type normally used in the locality either as a living room or as a bedroom." Thus, W.C. compartments and bathrooms would be excluded from being "room available for sleeping accommodation," but a kitchen/diner would probably be included.[25] However, a room which is unfit for human habitation does not count as a room[26] and, by extension, it would seem that a house which is unfit for human habitation would have a permitted number of nil.

7.16 "Agent" is defined[27] as "a person who collects rent in respect of the dwelling on behalf of the landlord, or who is authorised to do so."

"Landlord" is defined[28] as "the immediate landlord of an occupier of the dwelling." It will therefore include a tenant who sub-lets part of the premises as a dwelling to another person.[29]

"Owner" is defined[30] as:

---

[19] Housing Act 1985, s.343.
[20] See *Curl* v. *Angelo* [1948] 2 All E.R. 189.
[21] See, in particular, *James* v. *James* [1952] C.L.Y. 2948; *James* v. *Coleman* [1949] E.G.D. 122; *Trustees of the Waltham Abbey Baptist Church* v. *Stevens* (1950) E.G. 294; and *Hayward* v. *Marshall* [1952] 2 Q.B. 89.
[22] See, in particular, *Cole* v. *Harris* [1945] K.B. 474; *Winters* v. *Dance* [1949] L.J.R. 165; *Neale* v. *Del Soto* [1945] K.B. 144; *Sharpe* v. *Nicholls* (1945) 147 E.G. 177, and *Goodrich* v. *Paisner* [1957] A.C. 65.
[23] See in particular *Wright* v. *Howell* (1947) 92 S.J. 26; *Metropolitan Properties* v. *Barder* [1968] 1 W.L.R. 286, and *Anspach* v. *Chalton Steam Shipping Co. Ltd.* [1955] 2 Q.B. 21.
[24] Housing Act 1985, s.325(2)(*b*) and s.326(2)(*b*).
[25] See *Zaitzeff* v. *Olmi* (1952) 102 L.J. 416.
[26] *Patel* v. *Godal* [1979] 12 C.L.Y. 1620.
[27] Housing Act 1985, s.343.
[28] *Ibid*.
[29] s.343 gives additional meanings to the terms "agent" and "landlord" in the case of tied accommodation.
[30] Housing Act 1985, s.343.

DEFINITIONS

(a) "a person (other than a mortgagee not in possession) who is for the time being entitled to dispose of the fee simple, whether in possession or reversion"; and
(b) "includes also a person holding or entitled to the rents and profits of the premises under a lease of which the unexpired term exceeds three years."

The term "person" is not defined, but for the purposes of both the room standard and the space standard, a child under the age of one year is not counted as a person at all, and so far as the space standard is concerned, a child over the age of one year but under ten years is counted as one-half of a person[31] (see paras. 7.09 and 7.11).

7.17

The term "suitable alternative accommodation" is defined[32] in relation to the occupier of a dwelling as being a dwelling which satisfies the following conditions:

7.18

(a) the occupier and family can live in it without causing it to be overcrowded;
(b) it is certified by the local housing authority to be suitable to the needs of the occupier and family as respects security of tenure, proximity to place of work and otherwise, and to be suitable in relation to the means of the occupier; and
(c) where the dwelling belongs to the local housing authority, it is certified by the authority to be suitable to the needs of the occupier and family as respects accommodation.

The certification by the authority that a dwelling constitutes suitable alternative accommodation under (b) or (c) above, or that such accommodation is available must be by the appropriate prescribed form.[33]

Prior to April 1, 1986 (the coming into force of the Housing Act 1985), the definition of "suitable alternative accommodation" in the case where the dwelling belongs to the local authority ((c) in para. 7.18) was specific as to the number of "bedrooms" a dwelling should contain for certain sizes of families. This was based on definitions and advice in relation to overcrowding and slum clearance given in the 1930s, and became the so-called "bedroom standard," which was (and in some cases still is) used for determining the size of accommodation to be offered by authorities.

7.19

This was drawn to the attention of local authorities in 1936[34] as follows:

---

[31] Housing Act 1985, ss.325(2)(*a*) and 326(2)(*a*). See also *Zbytniewski* v. *Broughton* [1956] 2 Q.B: 673.
[32] Housing Act 1985, s.342.
[33] Forms G or H in the Housing Act (Overcrowding and Miscellaneous Forms) Regulations 1937 (S.R. and O. 1937 No. 80) (retained in force by s.2 of the Housing (Consequential Provisions) Act 1985).
[34] Ministry of Health Circular No. 1539, May 7, 1936.

"In planning their new houses the main consideration for the local authority to take into account is the provision of accommodation suitable and convenient for the type and size of family which will normally occupy it, and there should be no question of modifying an otherwise suitable plan merely for the purpose of increasing the number permitted by the overcrowding standard, *e.g.* the fact that a room of 110 feet in area would not be overcrowded under the Act of 1935 if occupied by two persons does not imply that this size is an adequate area for all bedrooms. The standard of occupation to be adopted for rehousing under the Act of 1935 is that laid down for slum clearance schemes, namely that specified in section 37 of the Act of 1930. This section provides that the local authority 'shall treat a house containing two bedrooms as providing accommodation for four persons; a house containing three bedrooms as providing accommodation for five persons; and a house containing four bedrooms as providing accommodation for seven persons.' It will be observed that this is not a complete standard of accommodation in as much as no mention is made of the size of the bedrooms and no indication of the standard for families consisting of more than seven persons, while it will be observed that in this section children count as whole persons whatever their age."

Unfortunately, this advice and guidance now seems to have been forgotten although it does not appear to have been withdrawn.

4. OFFENCES

Offences by the occupier

7.20 The occupier of a dwelling commits an offence by causing or permitting it to be overcrowded,[35] and is liable (on conviction) to a fine not exceeding level 1 on the standard scale, and to a further fine not exceeding £2 for each day on which the offence continues after conviction.[36]

7.21 Once an offence is committed, any security given by the Rent Act 1977 is removed,[37] and a county court must grant an application for possession. Persons displaced from their home as a result of such an application are not protected by Part III of the Land Compensation Act 1973, and have no rights to rehousing, home loss or disturbance payments. However, such persons may be protected under Part III of the Housing Act 1985 as "homeless." (As to the rights of persons displaced from their home see Chapter 9.)

---

[35] Housing Act 1985, s.327(1).
[36] *Ibid*. s.327(3) and Criminal Justice Act 1982, s.37.
[37] Rent Act 1977, s.101.

OFFENCES

7.22 There are, however, two situations in which no offence is committed:
1. Where[38]
   (a) the overcrowding has resulted from children passing the age of one or ten years (and so being counted as an additional one-half a person), and there has been no other change in the persons occupying the dwelling; and
   (b) the occupier applies to the local housing authority for suitable alternative accommodation.
   This exemption ceases to apply to the occupier in either of the following circumstances[39]:
      (i) where suitable alternative accommodation has been offered to the occupier, and the occupier fails to accept the offer; or
      (ii) suitable alternative accommodation is available to a person who is not a member of the occupier's family, and the occupier has failed to require that person's removal from the dwelling.
2. If the persons sleeping in an overcrowded dwelling include a member of the occupier's family who does not live at the dwelling, but is sleeping there temporarily.[40] (This exception obviously does not apply where the dwelling would be overcrowded even without the temporary visitor.)

Offences by the landlord

7.23 The landlord of a dwelling commits an offence by causing or permitting it to be overcrowded, and is deemed to have caused or permitted the dwelling to be overcrowded only in the following circumstances[41]:

(a) at the time of letting, the landlord (or representative) had reasonable cause to believe that the dwelling would become overcrowded so as to render the occupier guilty of an offence;
(b) at the time of letting, the landlord (or representative) failed to make inquiries of the occupier as to the number, age and sex of the persons who would be allowed to sleep in the dwelling;
(c) after receipt of a notice by the landlord (or agent) from the local housing authority[42] stating that the dwelling is overcrowded so as to render the occupier guilty of an offence, the

---

[38] Housing Act 1985, s.328(1) and (2).
[39] *Ibid.* s.328(3).
[40] *Ibid.* s.329.
[41] *Ibid.* s.331(1) and (2).
[42] Form C in the Housing Act (Overcrowding and Miscellaneous Forms) Regulations 1937 (S.R. and O. 1937 No. 80) (retained in force by s.2 of the Housing Consequential Provisions) Act 1985).

landlord failed to take steps to ensure the overcrowding was abated.

7.24 In the case of (c) above (in para. 7.23), the steps the landlord should take to ensure the overcrowding is abated can include, if necessary, action to obtain possession through the courts. Once an offence is being committed, either by the tenant or by the landlord (see paras. 7.20 and 7.23) any security given by the Rent Act 1977 is removed, and the court must grant possession.[43] (See also the comments in para. 7.20).

7.25 On conviction of the offence of causing or permitting overcrowding, a landlord is liable to a fine not exceeding level 1 on the standard scale, and to a further fine not exceeding £2 for each day on which the offence continues after conviction.[44]

7.26 Where the landlord is the local housing authority, a prosecution may be brought against the authority for an offence under these provisions, but only if the Attorney General gives consent.[45]

Licences to exceed the permitted number

7.27 On the application of an occupier (or intending occupier) of a dwelling, a local housing authority may grant a licence[46] authorising the occupier to allow an additional specified number[47] of persons to sleep in the dwelling over and above the permitted number for that dwelling. The authority may take account of exceptional circumstances (including seasonal increases in population, *e.g.* temporary workers such as fruit-pickers, and perhaps tourists), and also that it is expedient to issue a licence.[48] Such a licence must be in the prescribed format[49] and can be granted for any period (although it would seem that one month should be the minimum as revocation of a licence cannot be achieved within a shorter period—see para. 7.27) to a maximum period of 12 months.[50]

The licence can be issued unconditionally, or can impose conditions specified in the licence.[51] There is no indication of the type or range of conditions that may be imposed, but the prescribed form sets out "conditions" which are merely explanatory.

---

[43] Rent Act 1977, s.101. See also *Zbytniewski* v. *Broughton* [1956] 2 Q.B. 673, and *Buswell* v. *Goodwin* [1971] 1 W.L.R. 92.
[44] Housing Act 1985, s.331(3), and Criminal Justice Act 1982, s.37.
[45] *Ibid.* s.339(2).
[46] *Ibid.* s.330.
[47] *Ibid.* s.330(2).
[48] *Ibid.* s.330(2).
[49] *Ibid.* s.330(3), and Form E in the Housing Act (Overcrowding and Miscellaneous Forms) Regulations 1937 (S.R. and O. 1937 No. 80) (retained in force by s.2 of the Housing (Consequential Provisions) Act 1985).
[50] Housing Act 1985, s.330(5).
[51] *Ibid.* s.330(3).

OFFENCES

7.28 The authority may revoke the licence at their discretion and at any time, by giving notice in writing to the occupier[52] specifying when the licence is to cease (but not less than one month from the date of service of the notice).[53]

7.29 Copies of the licence and of any notice of revocation must be served by the authority on the landlord of the dwelling (if any) within seven days of the issuing or service of the original.[54]

7.30 So long as the licence remains in force, an occupier (and the landlord) will not commit the offence of contravening the "space standard" (see para. 7.11), provided that the number of persons sleeping at the dwelling does not exceed the total of the permitted number together with the additional number specified in the licence.

It should be noted that the licence can only relate to the "space standard" allowing the permitted number to be exceeded up to the specified additional number of persons, and cannot relate to allowing the "room standard" (see para. 7.09) to be contravened.

5. INFORMATION

7.31 The Act makes various requirements relating to the provision of information in respect of overcrowding. This includes information for occupiers about the legislation and the permitted number of their dwelling, the right to information from the local authority, and the duty to provide information to the authority.

Information for occupiers

7.32 It is the duty of a "landlord" to provide a rent book (or similar document) to every "tenant" of premises whose rent is "payable weekly" under the Landlord and Tenant Act 1985.[55]

For these purposes, the term "landlord" means the person who granted the tenancy (or that person's successor)[56] and "payable weekly" refers to how the rent is paid and not how it is calculated (*e.g.* where rent is calculated as an annual rent, but payable on a weekly basis, it would be "payable weekly"; but where rent is calculated as a weekly rent, but payable monthly, it would not be "payable weekly").

7.33 Every rent book or similar document so provided is required to contain:

---

[52] See Form F in the Housing Act (Overcrowding and Miscellaneous Forms) Regulations 1937 (S.R. and O. 1937 No. 80) (retained in force by s.2 of the Housing (Consequential Provisions) Act 1985).
[53] Housing Act 1985, s.330(4).
[54] *Ibid.* s.330(6).
[55] Landlord and Tenant Act 1985, s.4.
[56] *Ibid.* s.4(3).

(a) the name and address of the landlord[57];
(b) a summary of sections 324–331 of the Housing Act 1985 in the prescribed format[58]; and
(c) a statement of the permitted number for the dwelling.[59]

7.34 A "landlord" who fails to provide a rent book or provides one without details of her name and address commits an offence, and is liable (on conviction) to a fine not exceeding level 4 on the standard scale.[60]

If a rent book or similar document (including a type other than that required to be provided under the Landlord and Tenant Act 1985, *e.g.* a Giro payment book) used by or on behalf of a landlord (as defined by the Housing Act 1985—see para. 7.16) does not contain a summary of sections 324 to 331 of the Housing Act 1985 or does not contain a statement of the permitted number for the dwelling, the landlord commits an offence, and is liable (on conviction) to a fine not exceeding level 1 on the standard scale.[61]

7.35 Where, for the purpose of checking the information provided and the permitted number, an authorised officer of a local housing authority requires an occupier to produce a rent book (or similar document) which is in the occupier's custody, the occupier must do so or must produce it at the authority's offices within seven days. An occupier who fails to so produce the rent book commits an offence, and is liable (on conviction) to a fine not exceeding level 1 on the standard scale.[62]

Information and local housing authorities

7.36 Where an occupier (or landlord) of a dwelling applies to the local housing authority for a written statement of the permitted number for that dwelling, the authority must provide such a statement.[63] Although the authority is under a duty to respond to such an application, it does not appear to commit an offence if it fails to respond, but would be in breach of its statutory duty.

7.37 A local housing authority may, by notice, require an occupier to give, within 14 days of the authority's notice, a written statement of the number, ages and sexes of the persons sleeping in the dwelling.[64] Although the Act does not require such a notice to be in the prescribed

---

[57] Landlord and Tenant Act 1985, s.5.
[58] Housing Act 1985, s.332(1), and Pt. I of the Sched. to the Housing Act (Overcrowding and Miscellaneous Forms) Regulations 1937 (S.R. and O. 1937 No. 80) (retained in force by s.2 of the Housing (Consequential Provisions) Act 1985).
[59] Housing Act 1985, s.332(1).
[60] Land and Tenant Act 1985, s.7(1), and Criminal Justice Act 1982, s.37.
[61] Housing Act 1985, s.332(2), and Criminal Justice Act 1982, s.37.
[62] *Ibid.* s.336, and Criminal Justice Act 1982, s.37.
[63] *Ibid.* s.332(3).
[64] *Ibid.* s.335(1).

format, there is a form given.[65] It is suggested that the notice should be specific and state the 24 hour period for which the information is required, to avoid any confusion.

It is an offence for an occupier to fail to supply details within the 14 days, or to knowingly give false information, and the occupier would be liable (on conviction) to a fine not exceeding level 1 on the standard scale.[66]

7.38 A landlord of a dwelling (or her agent) is required to notify the local housing authority within seven days of the discovery of the dwelling being overcrowded.[67] It is an offence to fail to notify the authority within the seven days, carrying, on conviction, a penalty not exceeding level 1 on the standard scale.[68] However, no offence is committed where the overcrowding has already been notified to the authority, or has been brought to the landlord's (or agent's) attention by the authority, or is allowed by a licence issued by the authority.[69]

6. ENFORCEMENT OF THE OVERCROWDING PROVISIONS

Surveys

7.39 Where a local authority have information which suggests that there is a need to prepare a report on overcrowding in its district or a part of its district, it must[70]:

(a) cause an inspection to be made of the district (or the part of the district);
(b) prepare a report showing the results of the inspection, and the number of new dwellings required to abate the overcrowding identified;
(c) unless satisfied that the required new dwellings will be provided by other means, prepare proposals for the provision of those new dwellings; and
(d) submit the report on the inspection and any proposal for providing the new dwellings to the Secretary of State.

7.40 The Secretary of State can direct the authority to cause the inspection to be made and to submit the report and any necessary proposals, and may, after consulting the authority, set dates by which the authority must complete the various duties.[71]

---

[65] Form B in the Housing Act (Overcrowding and Miscellaneous Forms) Regulations 1937 (S.R. and O. 1937 No. 80) (retained in force by s.2 of the Housing (Consequential Provisions) Act 1985).
[66] Housing Act 1985, s.335(2).
[67] *Ibid*. s.333(1).
[68] *Ibid*. s.333(3), and Criminal Justice Act 1982, s.37.
[69] Housing Act 1985, s.333(2).
[70] *Ibid*. s.334(1).
[71] *Ibid*. s.334(1) and (2).

7.41 The duties described above should be considered together with the general duty on authorities to periodically review housing conditions in their district,[72] and the duty to periodically review the housing needs of the district.[73]

7.42 Advice and guidance on overcrowding surveys was given in some detail on the introduction of the overcrowding provisions in 1935.[74]

Basically, this guidance recommends that the survey be carried out in two parts. The first stage involving a preliminary house-to-house check to ascertain the number of households, the persons in those households, and the number of rooms occupied by the households. From this information, the dwellings could be categorised into:

(a) those definitely overcrowded (irrespective of room size);
(b) those possibly overcrowded depending on the size of the rooms within the relevant dwelling;
(c) those not overcrowded.

The second stage to be a detailed inspection (including measurement of rooms) but limited to those dwellings suspected of being overcrowded (those categorised in (b) above). The Circular also sets out standard survey forms to provide uniformity of the results.

Advice was also given in 1935 on the considerations and proposals to be made for the provision of any necessary new dwellings to relieve the overcrowding identified.[75]

General

7.43 It is the duty of the local housing authority to enforce the overcrowding provisions in Part X of the 1985 Housing Act,[76] and prosecutions for any of the offences (see paras. 7.20 to 7.25 and 7.34) may only be brought by such an authority.[77] However, where it is the local housing authority which has committed the offence, a prosecution may be brought against the authority with the consent of the Attorney General.[78]

In the case of an offence under the Landlord and Tenant Act 1985 in

---

[72] Housing Act 1985, s.605.
[73] Ibid. s.8, (see also *Re Havant and Waterloo Urban District Council Compulsory Purchase Order (No. 4)* [1951] 2 K.B. 779, which held that the needs of the district are not limited to the needs of those currently living within the authority's district).
[74] Memorandum B—"The Prevention and Abatement of Overcrowding"; Ministry of Health (October 1935).
[75] Memorandum C—"The Redevelopment of Overcrowded Areas"; Ministry of Health (October 1935).
[76] Housing Act 1985, s.339(1).
[77] Ibid. s.339(2)(*a*).
[78] Ibid. s.339(2)(*b*).

relation to the provision of a rent book (see para. 7.34) prosecutions may be taken by the local housing authority.[79]

Notices

Where a dwelling is overcrowded so as to render the occupier guilty of an offence (see paras. 7.20 to 7.22), the local housing authority may serve a notice on the occupier requiring that the overcrowding be abated within 14 days from the service of the notice.[80] The notice should be in the prescribed format.[81] **7.44**

If at any time within three months from the end of the 14-day period stated in the notice, the dwelling is occupied by the same occupier or a member of that occupier's family, and is overcrowded (so as to render the occupier guilty of an offence—see paras. 7.20 to 7.22), the authority may apply to the county court for possession. On such application (any protection given by the Rent Act 1977 being removed[82]), the court must order possession to be given to the landlord within a period not less than 14 or more than 28 days.[83] **7.45**

The expenses incurred by the authority in ensuring vacant possession for the landlord may be recovered from the landlord as an ordinary civil debt.[84]

Although not clearly set out in the legislation, the authority may also serve a notice[85] on the landlord stating that the dwelling is overcrowded in such circumstances as to render the occupier guilty of an offence (this does not mean that the occupier created or permitted the overcrowding, but just that the overcrowding exists—see paras. 7.20 to 7.22). **7.46**

On receipt of such a notice the landlord must take all necessary steps, including, if necessary, action to obtain possession through the courts (see paras. 7.23 and 7.24).

It is suggested that the enforcement procedures available should be used with caution, as the result may be homelessness, which, while having removed the public health problem of overcrowding, has created another (and perhaps more serious) problem. **7.47**

The best practice is, therefore, either preventative action to ensure suitable alternative accommodation is made available before an offence has been committed (or before statutory overcrowding has occurred),

---

[79] Landlord and Tenant Act 1985, s.34.
[80] Housing Act 1985, s.338(1).
[81] Form D in the Housing Act (Overcrowding and Miscellaneous Forms) Regulations 1937 (S.R. and O. 1937 No. 80 (retained in force by s.2 of the Housing (Consequential Provisions) Act) 1985).
[82] Rent Act 1977, s.101.
[83] Housing Act 1985, s.338(2).
[84] *Ibid*. s.338(3).
[85] Form C in the Housing Act (Overcrowding and Miscellaneous Forms) Regulations 1937 (S.R. and O. 1937 No. 80) (retained in force by s.2 of the Housing (Consequential Provisions) Act 1985).

or, where overcrowding has occurred, the issuing of a licence until such alternative accommodation is available.

7. Overcrowding in Houses in Multiple Occupation

7.48 Additional (discretionary) provisions are available to local housing authorities to deal with overcrowding in houses in multiple occupation. These provisions were introduced by section 12 of the Housing Repairs and Rents Act 1954, and enabled an authority to set maximum numbers of persons who could sleep in a multi-occupied house, and to prevent sexual overcrowding.

The provisions were re-enacted as section 90 of the Housing Act 1957, and then replaced by provisions introduced by section 146 of the Housing Act 1980. These provisions have now been re-enacted by the Housing Act 1985 as sections 358 to 364.

7.49 The present provisions provide for two alternative remedies for overcrowding in houses in multiple occupation, both based on the service of a notice stating the maximum number of persons to be allowed to sleep in the house (or specified parts of the house). The first makes it an immediate offence to allow persons to sleep in the house (or part of the house) in excess of the stated maximum. The second makes it an offence to allow new residents to sleep in the house (or part) if that would mean the stated maximum would be exceeded.

7.50 It is important that these provisions are distinguished from those dealing with over-occupation in houses in multiple occupation. These overcrowding provisions deal with the number of persons who may sleep in the house (or a part of it) having regard to the space available, and also with separation of the sexes in sleeping accommodation. The over-occupation provisions in sections 354 to 357 of the 1985 Act (see paras. 6.78 to 6.91) deal with the number of persons or households who may occupy the house (or a part of it) having regard to the facilities available within the house.

Definitions

7.51 For the purposes of these overcrowding provisions:

1. The term "house in multiple occupation" is considered in detail in paras. 6.02 to 6.17.
2. The term "person having an estate or interest" in the house includes a statutory tenant within the meaning of the Rent Act 1977 or Rent (Agriculture) Act 1976.[86]
3. The "person managing" the house means the person who receives rents or payments from tenants of parts of the

---
[86] Housing Act 1985, ss.398 and 622.

8. PROCEDURE FOR ABATING OR PREVENTING OVERCROWDING IN HOUSES IN MULTIPLE OCCUPATION

7.52 If it appears to a local housing authority that a house in multiple occupation either is accommodating at present, or is likely to accommodate in the future, an excessive number of persons having regard to the rooms available, the authority may take action under these provisions.[88]

Notice of intention

7.53 The procedure is initiated by the authority giving notice of their intention to take action under these provisions. This notice of intention must be in writing (there is no form prescribed at present), and the authority must:

(a) send it to—
   (i) the person who is the occupier of the house[88a]; and
   (ii) any person apparently managing the premises; and
(b) ensure, so far as is reasonably possible, that every person living in the house is informed of their intention to take action.[89]

The taking of steps to inform all the residents could include sending each resident a copy, or posting a copy of the notice of intention in some conspicuous part of the house.

7.54 All persons given notice of the authority's intention, or residents notified of the authority's intention, must be allowed to make representation to the authority regarding the proposed action.[90]

Overcrowding notice

7.55 Not less than seven days after the service of the notice of intention the authority may serve an overcrowding notice on[91]:

(a) the occupier of the house;
(b) any person managing the premises; or
(c) both the occupier and the person managing the premises.

The person who appears to be responsible for controlling the number of persons sleeping (or likely to sleep) in the house should be the addressee of the notice.

---

[87] Housing Act 1985, s.398.
[88] *Ibid.* s.358(1).
[88a] See *Hackney B.C.* v. *Ezedinma* [1981] 3 All E.R. 438, on interpretation of this phrase—see also Chap. 6, para. 6.85.
[89] Housing Act 1985, s.358(2).
[90] *Ibid.*
[91] *Ibid.* s.358(1).

7.56 The overcrowding notice must[92]:

    (a) specify each room in the house;
    (b) specify in respect of each of those rooms—
        (i) the maximum number of persons who may sleep there at any one time; or
        (ii) a special maximum applicable where some or all of the occupants are under a specified age; or
        (iii) that the room is unsuitable for use as sleeping accommodation.

(The age to be specified in relation to (b)(ii) is left to the discretion of the authority, but see para. 7.59.)

7.57 In addition, the overcrowding notice must require the addressee to refrain from either[93]:

    (a) (i) knowingly permitting the number given for a room to be exceeded; and
        (ii) knowingly permitting such a number of persons to sleep in the house so that the only way to avoid "sexual overcrowding" is to ignore the requirements of the overcrowding notice.[94]

    or

    (b) knowingly to allow "new residents" into the house resulting in either of the offences given in (a) above.[95]

7.58 An overcrowding notice becomes operative 21 days from the date of service, unless there is an appeal against the notice (see para. 7.65).[96]

7.59 For these purposes "sexual overcrowding" occurs when two persons over the age of twelve years and of opposite sexes, not living together as husband and wife are forced (because of the number of persons in the house) to share a room to avoid exceeding the maxima set by the overcrowding notice.[97]

This should be compared to the age limits for sexual overcrowding in the principle overcrowding provisions as described in para. 7.09.

7.60 A "new resident" is anyone not living in the house immediately prior to the date of the overcrowding notice.[98] This wide definition would seem to mean that a child born after the date of an overcrowding notice would be a "new resident."

---

[92] Housing Act 1985, s.359(1).
[93] *Ibid*. s.359(2).
[94] *Ibid*. s.360(1).
[95] *Ibid*. s.361(1).
[96] *Ibid*. s.358(3).
[97] *Ibid*. s.360(2) and s.361(2).
[98] *Ibid*. s.361(1).

PROCEDURE FOR ABATING OR PREVENTING OVERCROWDING

An overcrowding notice which requires the addressee to refrain from allowing new residents into the house (as described in (b) in para. 7.57 may, at any time, be withdrawn and replaced by an overcrowding notice relating to existing residents (as described in (a) in para. 7.57).[99] **7.61**

Information as to numbers

At any time after the service of an overcrowding notice, the local housing authority may serve a requisition for information on the occupier.[1] Such a requisition can require the occupier to provide a written statement of all or any of the following within seven days of the service of the requisition: **7.62**

(a) the number of individuals sleeping in any part of the premises;
(b) the number of families or households to which those individuals belong;
(c) the names of the individuals, and the heads of each of the families or households;
(d) the respective rooms used by the individuals and families or households.

Offences

It is an offence for a person to contravene the requirements of an overcrowding notice. Anyone who does so, is liable (on conviction) to a fine not exceeding level 4 on the standard scale.[2] **7.63**

It is also an offence for the addressee not to reply to a requisition for information, or to knowingly give false information. A person convicted of such an offence is liable to a fine not exceeding level 2 on the standard scale.[3]

Revocation or variation of an overcrowding notice

On the application of a person having an estate or interest in the house, the local housing authority may[4]: **7.64**

(a) revoke the overcrowding notice;
(b) vary the contents of the overcrowding notice so as to allow more persons to be accommodated in the house.

Appeals

A person aggrieved by an overcrowding notice may appeal, within 21 days of the service of the notice to the county court. On appeal, the county court may confirm, quash or vary the overcrowding notice.[5] **7.65**

---

[99] Housing Act 1985, s.359(2).
[1] *Ibid.* s.364.
[2] *Ibid.* s.358(4), and Criminal Justice Act 1982, s.37.
[3] Housing Act 1985, s.364(2) and Criminal Justice Act 1982, s.37.
[4] *Ibid.* s.363(1).
[5] *Ibid.* s.362(1).

Once such an appeal has been brought, the overcrowding notice is suspended and does not become operative until the county court confirms the notice (with or without variation) and no appeal is made to the Court of Appeal against that decision within four weeks.[6] If an appeal is brought against the decision of the county court, the notice remains suspended until the Court of Appeal confirms the notice (with or without variation).[7] Withdrawal of an appeal has the same effect as a decision confirming the notice.

7.66 If the authority refuse an application by a person with an estate or interest in the house for revocation or variation of the overcrowding notice (para. 7.64), or fail to notify the applicant of their decision within 35 days of the application (or longer if the applicant so allows) the applicant may appeal to the county court.[8] On hearing such an appeal, the county court may make any decision the authority may have made.[9]

9. MISCELLANEOUS OVERCROWDING PROVISIONS

Overcrowding in temporary and moveable dwellings

7.67 A tent, van, shed or similar structure used for human habitation and which is so overcrowded as to be "prejudicial to the health of the inmates" is a statutory nuisance for the purposes of Part III of the Public Health Act 1936.[10]

For the interpretation of "prejudicial to health" see Chapter 3, para. 3.16, and for the procedure to ensure the abatement of overcrowding which is a statutory nuisance see Chapter 5, paras. 5.05–6.64.

Other provisions relating to overcrowding

7.68 There are some other provisions which relate to the number of persons permitted to sleep in premises, including:

(a) power to make byelaws as to common lodging-houses (Housing Act 1985, s.406)[11];

(b) power to make byelaws as to accommodation for persons temporarily engaged in hop, fruit or vegetable picking (Public Health Act 1936, s.270)[12];

(c) duty of the Secretary of State to make regulations as to canal

---

[6] Housing Act 1985, s.362(2)(*a*). The 4 week period is that given by R.S.C. Ord. 59, r. 19.
[7] *Ibid*. s.362(2)(*b*).
[8] *Ibid*. s.363(2).
[9] *Ibid*. s.363(3).
[10] Public Health Act 1936, s.268(2).
[11] Although authorities have power to make such byelaws, the model byelaws have remained unaltered since 1938, and the DoE in Circular 12/86 (W.O. No. 23/86) recommends that authorities use their powers under Pt. XI of the 1985 Act instead (see Chap. 6).
[12] Model byelaws are available, although outdated.

boats (Public Health (Control of Disease) Act 1984, s.49)[13]; and

(d) power of local housing authority to make byelaws for the management, use and regulation of houses owned and managed by the authority (Housing Act 1985, s.23).

---

[13] Canal Boat Regulations 1878 to 1931, as amended.

Chapter 8

DAMPNESS

8.01
1. Definition of "dampness"	8.03
2. Direct physical damage dampness	8.07
3. Threats to health resulting from dampness	8.20
4. Sources of dampness	8.34
5. Measurement for dampness in the fabric	8.84
6. Measurements for relative humidity and condensation	8.95
7. Sampling possible mould growth	8.97
8. Investigation of sources of dampness	8.103
9. Investigation of condensation	8.108

Introduction

8.02 Dampness in dwellings is one of the more serious problems encountered, in that its effect on the health of the occupiers may be difficult to isolate and diagnose. It is also problematic in that it is often difficult to assess the source or cause of the dampness and determine the appropriate remedial measures. It is, therefore, helpful to attempt a definition of dampness and its causes, before considering any remedial steps.

1. Definition of "Dampness"

8.03 Water is naturally present in many of the materials used in buildings, and provided that the amount remains within certain limits (dependent on the particular material) it presents no problems. It is when the amount of water exceeds the upper limit that problems can occur, and it is this excess water content that is usually termed "dampness."

Water vapour (a gas) is present in the air. Kept within certain limits it will cause no problems.

8.04 Water is held in building materials in several ways. First, it will be chemically combined within materials such as concrete and plaster. Water is used in the process of mixing plaster and concrete (in an average sized house the amount used may be well in excess of 2,000 litres), and during the drying out and curing period most of this water will evaporate out of the materials. The period may be as long as 12 months, although not all the water will evaporate out because a small quantity will have become chemically bonded within the material.

Second, all porous materials used in buildings will exchange moisture

DEFINITION OF "DAMPNESS"

with the air and other materials immediately adjacent. Vapour pressure ensures that a balance in moisture levels is maintained by forcing vapour from high pressure areas to low pressure areas. As a result moisture from air containing relatively large amounts of water vapour will be forced into bricks, plaster and timber (for example) which are relatively dry; moisture can also pass from those materials into air which is relatively dry. The amount of moisture a material is capable of holding depends on the material. For example, in a relatively moist but not "damp" atmosphere, the Building Research Establishment state that bricks will have a moisture content of 1.5 per cent. to 2.5 per cent.; plaster around 1 per cent.; and wood around 11 per cent. However, if the moisture content of the materials is increased (for example, by an external source of water), moisture will gradually be forced from the material into the atmosphere until a balance has been reached. Provided that the amount of moisture introduced is not too great, and that the air is capable of holding the additional moisture without problems (or that the air is replaced with drier air), there will be no "damp" problems. However, if moisture continues to be introduced into the materials, those materials will not dry out.

As these porous materials are never truly dry (*i.e.* there is always some moisture present in addition to any chemically bound water), their normal state is generally referred to as "air-dry." Sometimes materials are contaminated with inorganic salts and the normal "air-dry" balance will be disrupted. The materials will continue to take in moisture from the air (even if that air is of low relative humidity), and can become visibly "damp." These inorganic salts are termed hygroscopic, because of their affinity for water.

Third, all porous materials are riddled with very fine hair-like pores or capillaries. Unlike larger holes found in free-draining materials, these pores or capillaries are so small that the surface tension of water becomes strong enough to draw water up the capillaries against the force of gravity, with the same effect as a wick or blotting paper. This "capillary attraction" enables materials such as bricks and concrete to draw water out of the soil surrounding foundations to heights well above ground level. In practice, for various reasons including the fact that evaporation may remove moisture as quickly as it can be replaced by the slow speed of the capillary attraction, this height may be up to 1 metre above ground level; higher still where evaporation is prevented. Capillary attraction is the cause of rising dampness.

Finally, the same capillary attraction will cause water to travel from one side of a material to the other, causing (for example) rain water to pass quickly through hair-line cracks in a rendered wall where, once inside, the water cannot readily evaporate outwards and may cause problems internally. Larger holes will more obviously allow water to penetrate through from the outside to affect the interior of a building. Such holes may be a result of disrepair, or ineffective weather-proofing detailing at joints between materials (*e.g.* joints between window frames and the reveals to the wall opening). Again, once the water has penetrated, capillary attraction will draw the water further into the structure to act as a sort of reservoir affecting the interior.

8.05 Although it interacts with and affects the amount of moisture held within the structure of the building, it is easier to discuss the moisture content of the atmosphere within a building separately. But it must be remembered that moisture in the structure may be a result of high moisture content of the air and not come from an external source.

The amount of water vapour that a given volume of air can hold will depend on the temperature of that air—the warmer the air, the greater the amount of water vapour it is capable of holding. "Relative humidity" is the ratio between the amount of water vapour held by the air and the maximum amount of water vapour which the air at that temperature is capable of holding.

"Relative humidity" is an important method of measurement in assessing whether or not "damp" air is the cause of any damp problems. However, it must be remembered that air within a room will not be at the same temperature throughout that room, and that relative humidity will vary with the temperature. There will be both an air temperature and a relative humidity spectrum in a room, the air temperature being affected by heat sources and points where heat is conducted away, so that the capability of air to hold water vapour will vary from point to point, being greater where the temperature is higher and lower where the air is at its coldest.

In winter the air temperature in a living room will be highest close to a heat source within the room, and lowest immediately adjacent to a window. The amount of water vapour does not change since it is the capability of the air to hold water vapour which is affected by the temperature levels and which changes the relative humidity. Condensation may occur on cold surfaces where the air temperature has been reduced. It can occur on a larger scale throughout a dwelling, affecting the colder rooms even though there may have been no moisture produced in those rooms. Vapour pressure (expressed in millibars) operates irrespective of air temperature differences; and this vapour pressure will balance out areas of high and low pressure by forcing vapour from high pressure areas (*e.g.* kitchens during cooking and clothes washing) to low pressure areas (*e.g.* bedrooms during the day).

The relative humidity of the atmosphere within a dwelling should be between 30 per cent. and 70 per cent. If it persistently exceeds 70 per cent. at any point within the dwelling, "damp" problems will occur. At this stage, however, the dampness will not be visible. Visible dampness

DEFINITION OF "DAMPNESS"

(condensation) occurs when the ratio of the amount of water vapour is equal to or exceeds the amount needed to saturate the air at that particular temperature. For example, 180 cubic metres of air at 15 degrees celsius is capable of holding 1.6 litres of water vapour. If that amount of water vapour is present and held by that volume of air, it is at 100 per cent. relative humidity at 15 degrees celsius. Raising the temperature of that volume of air to 20 degrees celsius will increase the amount of water vapour it is capable of holding to 2.2 litres, and assuming that the amount of water vapour remains at 1.6 litres, the relative humidity would become 75 per cent. at 20 degrees celsius. Reducing the temperature of that volume of air to 10 degrees celsius will reduce the amount of water vapour it is capable of holding to 1.1 litre, but if the amount of water vapour remains at 1.6 litres, the air must give up 0.5 litres in the form of actual water—the air will have passed below its "dew point" (the temperature at which moisture starts to form, *i.e.* 100 per cent. r.h.) and condensation will have occurred.

From the above it can be seen that "dampness" is the presence of excess moisture, and that "dampness" (as a problem) actually occurs before it is visible or can be felt. **8.06**

2. Direct Physical Damage from Dampness

Dampness can cause the physical deterioration of some materials used in construction, including the rusting of metals, perishing of plaster and swelling and warping of timber. **8.07**

Dampness can increase the rusting of iron-based metals, including the reinforcement of concrete, wall-ties and metal wall cladding. In addition to rust weakening the metal (which can result in the failure of that metal component), rusted metal expands. The pressure created by expanding rusted metal can cause spalling of concrete and the opening-up of mortar joints in cavity walls. This rusting of iron-based metals can occur whether or not there is a "dampness" problem, and merely because of moisture present in the atmosphere. It is therefore necessary to ensure that all iron-based metal components used in construction are properly protected against moisture (even normal levels of atmospheric moisture). Dampness problems will, however, increase the rate of rusting and deterioration.

Where dampness has been present over a long period and there has been continuing evaporation and replacement of the moisture, it can cause perishing of plaster and concrete. This has an effect similar to weathering, but more rapid. The surface of perished plaster and concrete may become loose and dust off and may become gritty and uneven. Perished plaster may become soft and flaky. It may also lose its key with the wall surface and become "blown" and unkeyed. In the case of ceilings, the additional weight of water in the plaster may cause it to soften, sag and crack. These effects of dampness are usually obvious, and it is also obvious whether the material has been damaged to such an extent that replacement is necessary once the source of the dampness has been remedied.

Timber (particularly soft wood) which is continually affected by dampness, or is alternatively damp and then dry, will warp and distort. Unprotected timber will swell and shrink as the moisture content rises and falls. This swelling and shrinking particularly affects external doors and windows, which when swollen can be difficult to open and close, and when shrunk will be ill fitting and allow draughts. Usually, damp penetration into the timber can be prevented by painting or sealing, but there may be a route for moisture from another part of the structure into an unprotected surface of the timber, for example, rising dampness through a wall may enter into the unprotected face of a door lining and frame, and water penetration through a wall may enter the unprotected face of a timber window frame.

Salt contamination caused by dampness

8.08 The penetration of moisture through the structure, either by capillary attraction from the soil or by penetration through some building materials, can result in the deposition of salts on the surface of the damp affected wall. In some cases this salt contamination of the surface merely damages decorations and is unsightly; in other cases it can become the cause of dampness to a wall or floor.

Water in the soil contains many different materials including soluble nitrate and chloride salts. Such salts can be held in solution in the water and carried through the structure of walls and floors by rising dampness, and, as the moisture evaporates from the surface of the wall or floor, the salts will be left behind. The salt solution will be very weak, and the amounts deposited on the surface will be minute, but, where the rising dampness has continued over many years, the quantity can become significant. As salts are left behind by the evaporation of the moisture from the damp affected material, salts will become concentrated on, and close to, the surface, and at the boundaries of the damp affected area—most densely in wallpaper and the surface finishing coat of plaster and in smaller amounts in the wall itself.

Nitrate salts are a result of the decay of organic matter, and are naturally present in the soil. They can also be introduced into the soil or into building materials by fertilizers or by animal contamination (particularly of unprotected sand). Small quantities of chloride salts may be found in some building materials (particularly some inadequately washed sands from coastal areas), but they are found in larger quantities in the soil. Both salts are hygroscopic, and will absorb moisture from the atmosphere. Even when the original source of the dampness has been remedied, the presence of hygroscopic salts can keep a surface damp, and the only remedy will be replacement of the salt-infected material.

Certain types of solid floor construction contain magnesium chloride, and, if they lack a damp proof membrane, these chloride salts may be taken into adjacent wall plaster by rising dampness.

8.09 Hygroscopic salts may be deposited by dampness penetrating through a chimney flue and stack. These will have been dissolved from the soot deposited within the flue. They often include ammonium sulphates and may be associated with brown staining.

8.10 Other salts, including carbonates and sulphates, may be deposited on the surface as a result of the drying out of new building work or as a result of dampness from rain penetration. These salts are naturally present in building materials, and will have been dissolved within the structure and left behind by evaporation of moisture. They are rarely hygroscopic, and are referred to as efflorescent salts. Deposits of efflorescent salts can usually be removed by brushing and should not require replacement of the affected material.

Fungal and insect damage to damp affected timber

8.11 Damp affected timber is more likely to be affected by fungal and wood boring insect attack. The moisture content of most timbers within a building should be between 10 per cent. (in well heated and properly ventilated areas) and 20 per cent. (in areas such as roof spaces and sub-floor spaces). The fungi which will attack and decay timber require a moisture content in excess of 18 per cent. Even the slightest problem of dampness can provide ideal conditions to enable such fungi to become established, and, unfortunately, the timber most likely to be attacked is that hidden from everyday sight.

Spores of the timber attacking fungi are always present in the air, and once deposited on the surface of timber with a suitable moisture content, can quickly germinate and become established. Provided that the moisture content is kept below 18 per cent. and there is no surface film of water deposited by condensation, the fungi cannot germinate.

8.12 Perhaps the most serious of the timber attacking fungi is the so-called dry rot fungus—*Serpula lacrymans*.[1] This is a member of the *Basidiomycotina* group of fungi. The main body of the fungus is a mass of mycelial strands which spread through the timber and can grow for several metres across non-nutrient environments (*e.g.* brickwork and plaster). It feeds by releasing enzymes into the timber which "digest" it into

---

[1] On dry and other wood rots see Bravery, Berry, Carey & Cooper, "Recognising Wood Rot and Insect Damage in Buildings," B.R.E. 1987.

simple solution nutrients which are then absorbed by the fungus. Although the spores require timber with a moisture content of at least 20 per cent. to initiate growth, once established it can continue to degrade timbers with a lower moisture content because of its ability to exude water from the hyphae (hence the name *lacrymans*). This means that once the fungus has become established it can spread rapidly and that merely removing the source of dampness will not necessary prevent further growth or kill the fungus. After the fungus has become well established, it will produce and form a fruitbody releasing spores for dispersal by air movement. The number of spores released is such that in a house with an active fruitbody in the cellar there were found to be concentrations of 75,000 spores per cubic metre of air; and, in a room two floors above (without any fruitbodies) there were 16,000 spores per cubic metre.[2]

8.13 The presence of *Serpulas lacrymans* requires not only the remedying of the source of dampness, but the cutting out and destruction of all obviously infected timber and at least 450mm. of apparently uninfected adjacent timber, and the thorough treatment of all timber and other parts of the structure with a water-based fungicide.[2a] It is necessary to carry out a full and detailed survey of all timbers within the structure, and to ensure that it is all properly protected against dampness and that there is adequate ventilation (particularly of the sub-floor and roof spaces). Because of the risk of re-infection by spores remaining in the building, and the re-establishment of growth by retaining any infected timber, it is important that thorough treatment with a preservative of all retained timber is carried out and only preservative-treated replacement timber used. In addition, there should be subsequent re-inspection of the building.

8.14 Other timber attacking fungi (including *Coniophora puteana*, the cellar fungus; *Phellinus contiguus*, *Asterostroma spp.* and *Donkioporia expansa*, the white rots; *Pleurotus ostreatus*, the oyster fungus; and *Paxillus panuoides*, brown rot) may require slightly higher moisture contents in the timber, and are certainly more easily stopped by the removal of the source of dampness. However, it is still necessary to cut out and destroy all infected timber, and to give precautionary treatment with a fungicide.[3]

8.15 Care must be taken in assessing the type of any fungi affecting timber, as some cause no damage to the timber, and remedial treatment may

---

[2] Maunsell J., "Sensitisation risks from inhalation of fungal spores" *Laryngol Otol*, 1954:68 765–775.

[2a] Caution must be exercised in the type and amount of fungicide used, as some are known to contain chemicals which can affect the health of the user and of occupants after use—see in particular *Roof* magazine May/June 1987, pp. 13–15 and *The Observer*, January 24, 1988.

[3] On dry and other wood rots see n. 1 above.

not involve the replacement of timber. Such fungi include *Myxomycetes* (slime moulds), and *Coprinus spp.*, *Peaziza spp.* and *Pyronema domesticum* (which are more often found on damp plaster and brickwork, but may be found on damp timber).

8.16 It should be remembered that any fungi will also produce spores, and that those spores may be responsible for causing or aggravating respiratory conditions including rhinitis, asthma and alveolitis, particularly when the concentration of spores will be high in an enclosed space such as a dwelling.[4] As such, any treatment carried out to remove fungal growth must be done with proper regard to the safety of those carrying out the work and the occupants of the dwelling. (Allegic reactions to fungal spores are discussed below at paras. 9.30–9.31.)

8.17 Although wood boring insects may attack any timber (other than that which is impregnated with an insecticide), they have a preference for damp timber, and some have a predilection for timber infected by fungi. The death watch beetle (*Xestobium rufovillosum*) attacks only hard woods which have been infected by fungi, but it is necessary to carry out treatment to remove the dampness, the fungus attacking the timber and the insect.

Although the common furniture beetle (*Anobium punctatum*) will attack air-dry timber with moisture content well below 20 per cent., the normal life cycle of about three years from egg to adult beetle can be reduced to as little as one year in persistently damp timber. In addition to insecticidal treatment and replacement of weakened timber, it is necessary to carry out a thorough survey to ensure that there is no dampness and that there is sufficient ventilation of all timber.

8.18 Some insects attack only well-rotted or decayed timber, and treatment need only involve removal of weakened timbers and the wood rot—it is not necessary to use insecticides. Examples of such insects include *Euophryum confine* and *Pentarthrum huttoni* (wood boring weevils) *Nacerdes melanura* (wharf borer beetle) and *Tenebrio mollitor* (mealworm beetle).

There are other insects which will apparently attack timber, for which no, or only minimal, treatment is necessary. These include *Ernobius mollis* (bark borer beetle) and *Cerambycidae spp.* (forest longhorn beetle) for which only the removal of bark is needed, and the *Buprestidae spp.* (jewel beetle) for which no treatment is required.[5]

8.19 Identification of beetles can be carried out by public analysts, or specialists including the British Museum and the Medical Entomology Centre at the University of Cambridge.

---

[4] "Mould Fungal Spores" 1985, I.E.H.O. Professional Practice Vol. I, Chap. II.
[5] On wood-attacking insects generally see above n. 1 "Recognising Wood Rot and Insect Damage in Buildings".

3. Threats to Health Resulting from Dampness

8.20 The presence of dampness (particularly damp air, in the sense of high relative humidity levels above 70 per cent.) can affect health in various ways. It can reduce the ambient temperature, it can provide favourable conditions for dramatic increases in the mite population and for mould fungal growth, and it may enable pathogenic organisms to remain viable for longer periods in the air and in dust. It will also interfere with the body's natural cooling mechanism which relies on evaporation, and it is based on this interference that it has been suggested that the upper relative humidity limit from the standpoint of health should be 60 per cent.[6]

The thermal insulation capabilities of the structure are reduced by the presence of dampness. Water is a good conductor of heat, and will reduce the thermal insulation provided by most materials used in building. This increases the fabric heat loss and so either reduces surface and air temperatures within the building or increases the cost of maintaining reasonable temperatures. In addition, the latent heat required to evaporate moisture from damp surfaces (*i.e.* the heat required to change liquid water into vapour) further cools the internal surfaces.

The presence of dampness in the building fabric or atmosphere will also result in damp clothing and bedding. Both will reduce the insulation they are intended to provide, and will provide favourable conditions for mites and moulds. They will also mean that occupiers will need greater amounts of heat input to feel warm.

8.21 The most serious threats to health are probably those from mites and mould fungal spores. These are considered in some detail below.

Mites

8.22 In terms of species and numbers, mites are a part of what is probably one of the largest groups in the animal kingdom, but a group whose importance is often underrated. They belong to the class *Arachnida*, of which there are about nine orders generally recognised, including spiders and scorpions. The most troublesome kinds (as pests and nuisances) are the mites and ticks of the order *Acari*.

Mites are generally small in size (many barely visible to the naked eye, being typically up to about 0.5mm. in length), have eight legs in the adult stage, and a body which lacks the segmentation found in insects and which is covered with numerous outstanding bristles.

As a group, mites are diverse in their food choice and habitats. Some feed on plants, some scavenge, some are predators (feeding on other

---

[6] See Goromosov, "The Physiological Basis of Health Standards for Dwellings" 1968, W.H.O.

mites or small arthropods), some are parasites living internally or externally on their hosts, while others feed on small mould fungi. Of particular economic importance in commercial food premises (but also found in domestic larders) are those mites which cause considerable damage to stored food, including the flour mite (*Acarus siro*), the cheese mite (*Tyrophagus casei*), and the dried fruit mite (*Carpoglyphus lactis*).

Of the parasitic mites, probably the best known is the itch mite (*Sarcoptes scabiei*) which is responsible for scabies in man. Other parasitic mites may attack man in the absence of their preferred host, including *Dermanyssus gallinae* (a common parasite of wild birds in temperate climates) and *Cheyletiella yasguri* (which infests dogs and cats).[7]

Both mites and house dust have been recognised as sources of allergens responsible for rhinitis and asthma since around 1922. But it was in 1964 that it was shown that house dust contained several species of mites, and in particular *Dermatophagoides pteronyssinus*.[8] This mite has been found world wide in house dust, and has been shown to possess potent allergens, not only in itself, but also in its excretory and secretory products (including cast skins, faeces and portions of dead mites). More recently, the house mite (*Glycyphagus domesticus*), which is a common inhabitant of dwellings, has also been shown to be a source of allergens.[9]

8.23

D. pteronyssinus is present in virtually every dwelling, feeding on the shed human skin scales present in house dust. It is most abundant on mattresses and in bedding. *G. domesticus*, also found in almost all dwellings, feeds on the moulds growing on damp wallpaper, furnishings, and on foodstuffs.

8.24

Both mites (and others commonly found in house dust) require a relatively moist environment in which to live. Optimum conditions for development are around 23 to 25 degrees celsius and relative humidities of between 80 and 90 per cent. Neither mite appears to develop at or below relative humidities of 60 per cent. It is well established that the mites are far more numerous in the dust from damp houses, than in dry houses.

In a study carried out in 1968, it was shown that the number of airborne mites (and mite debris) increased during such activities as bedmaking. Since allergic reactions result from inhalation of the mites or mite debris, such an increase in numbers could be the cause of asthma and rhinitis attacks. But the study also noted that this increase in the

8.25

---

[7] See Alexander, *Arthropods and Human Skin*, Springer-Verlag 1984.
[8] Maunsell, Wraith and Cunnington "Mites and House Dust Allergy in Bronchial Asthma" (1968) The Lancet 1267.
[9] Cunnington, "Allergy to Mites in House Dust and the Domestic Environment" (1908) 6 R.S.H. 229.

number of airborne mites and mite debris could be counteracted by regular vacuum-cleaning of the mattress and bedding. However, in a subsequent controlled trial (reported in 1980), attempts were made to reduce the mite population of mattresses and bedding by following strict anti-mite measures, including the thorough weekly vacuuming of mattresses, laundering and airing of bedding, and replacement of feather pillows by pillows with synthetic fillings. These anti-mite measures failed to produce significant effects on the mite population on the mattresses and bedding, or to give any notable relief to occupants suffering from mite-sensitive asthma, particularly where the dwelling was affected by dampness. This study concluded that in damp houses anti-mite measures appeared to have little effect, while in dry houses the bedding contained few mites anyway, making the anti-mite measures unnecessary.[10]

8.26   House dust mites and house mites (and perhaps other mites commonly found in house dust) are important agents of allergic respiratory diseases. It would seem that the most effective control measure to limit the size of the population of these mites, and so reduce the likelihood of allergic respiratory diseases caused by inhalation of the mites and of mite debris, is to prevent favourable conditions for their development by preventing or remedying dampness in dwellings. Other measures to try to control or limit the mite population will have only a very temporary, if any, beneficial affect.

Mould fungal spores

8.27   Mould is a term generally used to describe fungi having a mycelium—*i.e.* a network of individual microscopic filaments called *hyphae*, which grow only at the tips, branching periodically, to spread over and through the material on which the mould fungi grow and feed. Fungi lack chlorophyll, and obtain all their nutrients from their surroundings, without the need for light. Although they can be parasitic, the term "mould" is primarily used to describe the saprophytic fungi which grow on foodstuffs and dead organic material.

8.28   Mould fungi obtain nutrients (mainly sugars, starches and cellulose) by releasing enzymes into the substrate to "digest" it and form simple soluble nutrients to be absorbed by the fungi. These saprophytic fungi can cause food spoilage (sometimes producing potent mycotoxins including *aflatoxins*, which cause liver cancers in animals and are suspected of causing them in man), others cause wood rot (*e.g. Serpula*

---

[10] Burr *et al.*, "Effects of Anti-Mite Measures on Children with Mite-Sensitive Asthma", *Thorax*, 1980, 35:7:506; Burr *et al.*, "Effects of a Change to Mite-Free Bedding on Children with Mite-Sensitive Asthma" *Thorax*, 1980, 35:7:513.

THREATS TO HEALTH RESULTING FROM DAMPNESS

lacrymans), or grow on leather and fabrics. They may also grow on surfaces in dwellings, obtaining nutrients from organic materials in paper, paste and paint, and from surface contaminants present in even the cleanest of dwellings. The most common mould fungi found in dwellings include *Penicillium*, *Cladosporium*, *Mucor*, *Stemphylium*, *Aspergillus* and *Pullularia spp.*

Reproduction is by both sexual and asexual means, resulting in the production of spores for dispersal by various methods. Asexual reproduction is by division from a budding or swelling hypha; sexual reproduction involves the fusion of nuclei and often the production of distinctive fruitbodies. Dispersal of spores may be by a variety of means, but of particular importance to their effect on health is that relying on air movement (by far the commonest method).

The air almost always contains fungal spores, number and type depending on the time of day, the weather, the season and the geographical location.[11]

8.29 In dwellings, the food necessary for spore germination and growth of fungi is readily available, and temperature ranges are ideal. The most variable factor is the availability of moisture. For practical purposes, germination of mould spores requires atmospheric relative humidities from 70 per cent. to 100 per cent., depending on the species; and although some mould fungi can grow very slowly at relative humidities of down to 65 per cent., 70 per cent. is the lowest limit for growth for most mould fungi. Moisture is also required for mould growth, although the requirements of different species vary widely.

8.30 Fungal spores, including those from moulds and from timber attacking fungi, can have serious effects on health. The spores of many fungi are proven allergens which can sensitise the mucus membranes of the respiratory tract similarly to pollen. While fungal spores may not be such potent allergens as pollen, they are present in the air for longer periods and in larger numbers, particularly in the confined space of a dwelling, which will lead to high concentrations and greater periods of exposure.

The size of a spore (varying between one micron to over 100 microns) will affect how far into the respiratory tract it will penetrate before being deposited, and so determine the part of the respiratory tract that may be affected by the allergic reaction. When breathing through the nose, spores greater than ten microns will be trapped in the nasal passages, spores between about ten and four microns will be deposited in the bronchi and bronchioles, while those spores smaller than four microns

---

[11] Deacon, *Introduction to Modern Mycology* (1984) "Mould Fungal Spores" (1985) I.E.H.O. Professional Practice Series Vol. I, Chap. II.

will penetrate into the alveoli. Breathing through the mouth will allow larger spores to reach the trachea and bronchi.

8.31 Sensitivity to spores is acquired by exposure to them in sufficient quantities, or over a long enough period. It is estimated that between 10 per cent. and 20 per cent. of the population are atopic, having a constitutional predisposition to becoming sensitised by exposure to the concentrations of spores normally found in the atmosphere (*i.e.* 50–100,000 spores per cubic metre of air). Such atopic persons often become sensitised at an early age. The other 80 to 90 per cent. of the population (the non-atopic) can still become sensitised, but, because they are not predisposed, sensitisation requires longer periods of exposure and may require higher concentrations of spores. Non-atopic persons tend to become sensitised later in life. Once sensitised, further contact with the spores (even at relatively low concentrations) will produce an allergic response. It should also be noted that fungal spores can attack compromised persons, for example those suffering from diabetes and leukaemia, and those on immunosuppressant drugs.

8.32 In addition to the threat to physical health, the additional work involved in cleaning and redecorating, and reluctance to invite friends and relatives into the home will have a detrimental affect on the mental health of the occupiers.

8.33 It is not possible to prevent the fungal spores from being present in the atmosphere but it is possible to change the environment within a dwelling so as to limit or prevent spore germination and mould growth. As room temperatures within a dwelling which are required for health and comfort for the human occupants are also ideal for fungal growth and the sources of nutrients for growth are readily available it is the moisture levels within the dwelling which should be controlled so as to avoid conditions favourable for spore germination and future fungal growth.

4. Sources of Dampness

8.34 The effective remedy for dampness is dependent upon accurate diagnosis of its source. The principal sources of dampness in a dwelling can be conveniently summarised as follows:

(a) water used in the construction process;
(b) rising dampness;
(c) dampness penetrating through the fabric of the building;
(d) dampness from traumatic defects (*i.e.* burst pipes or overflowing tanks);
(e) condensation in roof spaces, flues and sub-floor spaces; and
(f) atmospheric moisture from the biological and domestic activities of the occupiers.

Each category is considered briefly, together with an outline of remedial measures necessary. The assessment and diagnosis of dampness is dealt with in more detail below (at para. 8.103). **8.35**

Water used in the construction process

Most of the large volume of water used in the construction of a house must be dried out to enable final internal finishing and decorating, and to avoid possible health risks from the dampness and from any mould growth. Inadequate natural ventilation during this period may result in relative humidity levels above 70 per cent., enabling mould growth to become established. Natural drying-out is most difficult in those parts where air movement is slow (*e.g.* unventilated cupboards). **8.36**

The drying out process may be speeded-up artificially, but this may cause other problems, (plaster and concrete cracking and losing its key, warping and distorting of timber). **8.37**

Artificially speeding of the drying out process can be achieved by increasing the heat.[12] However, care should be taken during this process to maintain a balance between heating, ventilation and, if necessary, dehumidification:

(a) Heat and ventilation. Decreasing ventilation (to conserve heat) will increase water vapour in the air within the building, and may lead to high relative humidity levels and/or actual condensation, as surface temperatures will initially remain low. Without adequate ventilation, mould growth can be a problem.

(b) Heat and dehumidifiers with no ventilation. Dehumidifiers will remove moisture from the air, but ventilation must be then reduced as far as possible, because ventilation will introduce moisture from outside to be removed by the dehumidifiers. Heat should also be provided, because dehumidifiers are more efficient at high temperatures.

Drying out is slowed down by occupation of the building, which introduces moisture through the normal biological and domestic activities of any household, reduces the ventilation levels and increases the heat input. The process is more difficult in winter, and problems are less likely if the process starts in spring or summer. **8.39**

Dampness problems from this source usually occur in new buildings or buildings where there has been recent plastering, concreting or brickwork. Inquiries about any such works will assist in distinguishing **8.40**

---

[12] B.R.E. Digest 163.

dampness from this source from condensation, which, in old buildings may be similar in appearance.

Rising dampness

8.41   To prevent capillary attraction drawing water from the soil up through the walls and solid floors it is necessary to include non-porous barriers (damp proof courses and membranes) in those parts of the structure.

Most houses built before 1920 were not provided with damp proof courses or membranes. To prevent rising dampness in such houses, damp proof courses must be provided. This can be achieved by cutting out bricks or mortar and inserting a physical barrier such as dense engineering bricks, or plastic sheeting; by injecting chemical repellants based on silicone or aluminium stearate which block or line the pores of the material to prevent capillary action; or by electro-osmotic systems, which interfere with the electric potential found in damp walls to stop the upward flow of moisture in the material. In solid floors it is necessary to take up and re-form the floor, incorporating a damp proof membrane.

8.42   The problem can be hidden (rather than cured) by "dry-lining" the affected walls. This is usually achieved by a false plaster-board wall fixed to battens over the affected walls. The space behind the false wall must be ventilated to prevent damp air between the plaster-board and the original wall surface allowing mould, fungus or insects to become established. This does not prevent the rising dampness, but provides a dry internal finish. ("Dry-lining" is different from the provision of insulation to the internal surfaces of external walls, and the two should not be confused. (See paras. 8.113–8.115 on thermal insulation as a treatment for condensation.)

An alternative to "dry-lining" is the use of corrugated bitumen lathing fixed to the original wall surface, and plastered on the internal face. The lathing acts as a vertical damp proof course and protects the internal plaster finish. However, unless ventilation is provided through the corrugations between the original wall and the lathing, the dampness will tend to rise further up the wall and become apparent above the treated area.

As a short-term solution, affected walls can be re-plastered using a rendering mix incorporating a water-proofing compound. Again this merely acts as a vertical damp proof course, but the dampness may rise above the treated area.

8.43   Houses built since 1920 should have been provided with damp proof courses and membranes, but these can sometimes fail. The damp proof course may be incorrectly positioned in a wall, or may not connect with a damp proof membrane in a floor, and moisture will by-pass the course

SOURCES OF DAMPNESS

or membrane. Soil or other materials against the outer surface of a wall can provide a route for moisture to by-pass the damp proof course. Mortar or building rubble can bridge the cavity of a cavity wall, again providing a route for moisture.

It is necessary to identify the cause (or causes) of the rising dampness in such cases, and to carry out appropriate remedial works. Where the cause cannot be properly identified, it may be necessary to provide a new damp proof course either by insertion or injection of a chemical.

8.44 Rising dampness over a period of time is likely to lead to hygroscopic salts migrating into the internal plaster finish. These salts may remain after the original source of the dampness has been removed, and will absorb moisture directly from the atmosphere (even at low relative humidity levels). However, the presence of these salts will usually inhibit the germination and growth of fungal spores. Where rising dampness has been a problem for some years, it is necessary to remove the existing plaster (even if not obviously contaminated) and to re-plaster using plaster which incorporates a salt inhibitor.

8.45 Rising dampness will also affect solid floors in direct contact with the soil unless there is an effective damp proof membrane. Such a membrane should extend over the whole area of the floor and connect with the damp proof courses to the walls. Many solid floors are provided with an impervious finish, for example thermo-plastic tiles (particularly in kitchens and bathrooms).

Such impervious finishes act as a second damp proof membrane, and the screed immediately below the surface finish may be damper than air-dry. This results from the very slow movement of water vapour from the floor below the damp proof membrane to the screed (forced through by vapour pressure, as virtually all so-called damp proofing materials will allow some vapour penetration), and the evaporation of that water vapour from the floor surface being slowed by the impervious finish. This will be exacerbated if the impervious surface finish has been laid before the screed had completely dried out. Provided that the amount of moisture in the screed is not so great that it causes the tiles to bubble and lift, or causes dampness in any timber in contact with the floor (*e.g.* skirting boards), and provided that moisture is not rising up the plaster to walls (which should stop short of the floor surface), there is no real problem.

8.46 Where there is a problem, the floor screed must be removed and a damp proof membrane provided (*e.g.* polythene sheeting or bitumen) and properly connected to any damp proof course to walls and a new screed laid.

8.47 At one time some timber floors were constructed with battens or joists resting directly on the soil. Such floors rot and collapse, although there is often no warning of the collapse. Such floors should be replaced, either with a suspended timber floor provided with a sub-floor space and adequate ventilation and air movement, or with a solid floor incorporating a damp proof membrane.

8.48 All timber floors must be protected from dampness by a damp proof course (although it is possible, but not advisable, to use timber impregnated with a preservative if it comes in contact with the soil), and adequate sub-floor ventilation and air movement to ensure that the timber remains air-dry. Where a dampness problem in a suspended timber floor is identified, in addition to any other remedial work it is necessary to ensure adequate ventilation and air movement within the sub-floor space.

Dampness penetrating the fabric of the building

8.49 Dampness may penetrate the structure because of defects in weatherproofing. These may be inherent defects, or disrepair caused by a lack of proper and adequate maintenance.

8.50 Chimney stacks are particularly exposed to the weather, both being high and having four exposed sides and a top. Defects in weather-proofing of the cap will allow water to penetrate into the stack and soak down into the roof space or lower still. In older houses the junction of the roof covering the stack is often inadequately protected by cement fillets, which readily crack and are unable to move with the roof covering. Where the junction is protected with metal flashings, these may be inadequately dressed to the stack and roof covering and allow water to be blown through joints.

Parapet walls are (like chimney stacks) particularly exposed, and must be provided with a proper coping to throw off the water, and a damp proof course.

8.51 Displaced tiles or slates will allow easy access for water, and roofs with a shallow pitch and covered with tiles may allow water through when there are high winds from a particular direction.

Most flat roofs require more maintenance than pitched roofs but, unfortunately, they rarely receive that extra attention. The covering of flat roofs must be able to remain effective despite the expansion and contraction that will occur because of the heating effect of the sun and cooling effect of the night.

8.52 Some solid walls in older houses may have been built from high porosity bricks, unable to withstand driving rain. Failure of the pointing will retain rain water and may allow it to soak through the wall rather than drain safely down the outer face. Hair-line cracking of render (which provides not only a decorative finish but also the weather protection of porous walls) will both draw water in by capillary attraction, and prevent its evaporation outwards. This lateral penetration of dampness through walls usually affects the wall facing the prevailing moisture laden wind (normally from the south west).

Where a damp proof course is provided, but is less than 150mm. above the adjacent ground level, rain may splash back to soak the wall above (particularly where the adjacent ground is paved).

The weakest point in any wall is where that wall is broken by a door or window opening. The joint between wall and frame must be properly weather proofed to prevent water penetration around the frame. Window sills must be sound and should throw water off and away from the wall, and be provided with a throating to prevent water running along the underside into the wall. Door openings must be provided with a weather protecting threshold, and perhaps a weather board fitted to the door itself, to prevent rain being driven under the floor.

The main function of a cavity wall is to prevent direct penetration of water through the wall. Rain will be able to penetrate through the usual 112mm. thick outer leaf, but should not be able to cross the cavity, and so will run down the inner face of the outer leaf to damp proof course level, where there should be weep-holes (unfilled vertical joints between bricks) to allow it to drain safely out. Where there are mortar droppings on the cavity wall-ties or rubble and debris accumulated at the bottom of the cavity, there is a route across for the moisture. A route provided by mortar droppings will result in isolated damp spots on the inner face of the wall; a route provided by debris at the base of the cavity will result in an effect similar to rising dampness. The tops of door and window openings in cavity walls must be protected by an effective damp proof course to drain the water outwards.

Defective rainwater goods (*e.g.* eavesgutters and rain-water fall pipes) can be the cause of considerable localised dampness. The rainwater goods collect water which has run off a roof, and, if defective, may be the source of large quantities of water which can quickly soak a wall, wash away pointing and wear away brickwork. Although there may be signs of the effect of water leaking or overflowing from rain water goods (either in the form of cleaner areas of the wall where the water has washed away surface dirt, or efflorescent stains), the most appropriate time for examination of their effectiveness is during heavy rain. **8.53**

Having identified the cause of damp penetration, the appropriate remedial works should be carried out to provide adequate weather protection. **8.54**

Dampness from traumatic defects

Water pipes, storage tanks, sanitary equipment and drainage and waste pipes are all present in dwellings. All must be properly installed, maintained and protected against frost to prevent leakage. Dampness from such defects may be mistaken for rain penetration where, for example, there is dampness to a ceiling from a slowly leaking pipe or **8.55** tank. It may be necessary to carry out a check of all pipework and water storage tanks, particularly those in places which are not easily accessible. All facilities and pipe work should be checked while water is in the facility or passing through the pipes. Hair-line cracks in wash hand basins and wc basins can allow water through to soak the floor (in addition to being unhygienic and insanitary).

8.56 Although not a traumatic defect, inadequately sealed joints between sink/drainer units, wash hand basins and baths and the adjacent wall surfaces will allow water accidentally splashed to run behind the fitting and soak the wall and perhaps the floor.

8.57 Having identified the defect, appropriate remedial works should be carried out including (if necessary) provision of adequate protection against damage by frost. In the event of a major pipe-burst it is important to remove excess water as quickly as possible.

Condensation in roof spaces, flues and sub-floor spaces

8.58 Water vapour produced in the warm air of a dwelling will be forced (by vapour pressure) through ceilings and spaces around loft access covers into the roof space. All roof spaces are relatively cooler than the actual living space below, and where there is insulation to the upper surface of the top floor ceiling, will be considerably cooler. The result is that air within the roof space will be at a higher relative humidity, and there is an increased likelihood of condensation occurring (particularly where the under-tile felting is of an impermeable plastic sheeting). As the roof space is an area which is not regularly observed, condensation may pass unnoticed for sometime, soaking roof timbers, dripping onto any insulation and damaging the ceiling.

Problems of condensation (and mould and fungal growth within the roof space) are easily distinguished from problems of penetration. Condensation will be spread throughout the roof space, with the exception of areas close to chimney stacks (particularly those serving solid fuel heating appliances), and any dripping of water may be spread over the whole of the roof space area, whereas penetrating dampness will be localised and associated with an obvious defect or at a point of weakness (*e.g.* around the chimney stack where it penetrates the roof covering).

The most effective solution in the case of pitched roofs is the provision of adequate ventilation and air movement within the roof space. There is no need to keep the roof space at a higher temperature than outside (although there must be proper and adequate insulation of all water pipes and tanks within the roof space), and, provided that the air movement is adequate, there will be no damage to stored household goods and furniture. Limiting the amount of water vapour reaching the roof space will also assist in reducing the possibility of problems, and can be achieved by providing a vapour check (*e.g.* polythene sheeting) under any insulation and by providing a seal to the access cover and an effective seal around any pipes penetrating the ceiling.

8.59 With flat roofs the problem is usually one of condensation on the underside of the roof or of interstitial condensation (occurring within the structure of the roof) since the waterproof roof covering will act as a vapour check. Condensation occurring on the ceiling (underside of the roof) should be easily distinguished from penetration because of the more generalised spread of the dampness. Interstitial condensation, however, will be apparent only when the roof fails, or is opened-up.

The remedy is to provide an effective vapour check on the dwelling side of any insulation, to prevent (as far as possible) any water vapour reaching the cooler parts of the roof structure.

8.60 A product of the combustion of all fuels (with the exception of electricity—which is not burnt as other fuels are) is water vapour. This results from the combination of hydrogen present in the fuel with oxygen from the air, and, in the case of solid fuels, from the evaporation of water held by the fuel. The water vapour is carried by the flue gases up the flue. Provided that the temperature of the flue gases remains fairly high, the water vapour (along with all the other flue gases) will be discharged into the atmosphere from the chimney. However, modern solid fuel appliances are highly efficient, making available for space and water heating as much as possible of the heat from the combustion process, with the result that the flue gases are at a relatively low temperature. Often the temperature of flue gases from modern appliances will be such that the water vapour will condense out before the gases reach the outside.

Water condensing out of the flue gases will run down the flue and may penetrate through walls to cause dampness in the living space. This water will dissolve salts on the inside of the flue, and deposit them on the surface of plaster. These salts will include sulphates (from sulphur in the fuels) which will damage plaster and cement mortar causing it to perish and crumble. The salts will also be hygroscopic and cause brown staining of brickwork, plaster and decorations, resulting in dampness even after a flue has become disused.

Condensation can also occur in disused flues where warm moist air from rooms enters an old flue and may be cooled to below the dew-point.

Flues should be lined with materials which prevent any water being able to penetrate into the walls to affect the living space. Such lining may also provide some insulation which will help to keep flue gases above the dew-point.

8.61 There will be water vapour in the atmosphere of sub-floor spaces below suspended timber ground floors. This water vapour comes mainly from evaporation of moisture from the soil (even where there is oversite concrete, rarely provided with a damp proof membrane) and from those parts of the walls below the damp proof courses. The water vapour will be taken in by floor timbers, which can easily reach moisture levels above 18 per cent. and so enable timber attacking fungi to become established. Although actual condensation in sub-floor space is rare, high water vapour levels will be a problem.

The moisture level of floor timbers can be kept below 18 per cent. by providing proper and adequate ventilation and maintaining sufficient air movement within the sub-floor space.

Atmospheric moisture from biological and domestic activities

8.62 Once a dwelling is occupied, moisture will be generated through the normal biological and domestic activities of the occupiers, that is from activities such as breathing, cooking, personal washing, and clothes washing and drying. Obviously, the amount of moisture generated will vary with the number of persons in the household, their ages and life-style, but it has been estimated that the amount of moisture generated by a typical four person household will be between 10 and 20 litres every 24 hours.

Since the function of any house is to provide for human habitation, its design and construction and the space heating and ventilation systems provided should be able to prevent that moisture generated by the household resulting in relative humidity levels persistently above 70 per cent. and condensation (other than for occasional short periods of an hour or so).

The atmospheric balance

8.63 There are four main and interrelated factors which affect the occurrence of high relative humidity and condensation[13]:

(a) provision for space heating, and the use made of it;
(b) provision for ventilation, and the use made of it;
(c) thermal capacity, response and insulation of the structure; and
(d) the amount of moisture generated within a dwelling.

It is the relationship between these four factors which is important, but it is necessary to consider each factor separately to appreciate the manner in which they interract.

(a) Space heating

8.64 The space heating system must be capable of raising temperatures throughout the dwelling to reasonable levels and to maintaining such levels. Whether the system is capable of achieving this will depend on the size and capacity of the system itself, the size (*i.e.* the cubic capacity)

---

[13] See—British Standard B.S.5250:1975, and "Remedies for Condensation and Mould in Traditional Dwellings," B.R.E. 1985.

and layout of the dwelling, the thermal insulation of the fabric of the dwelling, and the thermal capacity and thermal response of the materials used in the construction of the dwelling.

The temperature levels that should be attainable when the outdoor temperature is 0 degrees celsius are as follows:

(i) a minimum of 21 degrees celsius for the living room and bathroom;
(ii) a minimum of 18 degrees celsius for the kitchen and bedrooms; and
(iii) a minimum of 16 degrees celsius for circulation areas.

Obviously the size of the dwelling will affect the amount of heat input required to attain and maintain these temperatures, but the system must also be capable of distributing heat input. If all of the heat input required for a dwelling is provided at one point only, the dwelling cannot be properly heated throughout, and a system which quickly provides local warmth for the occupiers may leave some parts of the room and some parts of the dwelling relatively cold.

Distribution of heat throughout the whole of the dwelling will be affected by the layout of the dwelling. Where the dwelling is on two floors, with bedrooms above living rooms and kitchens, there will be some heat gain from the lower floor rooms (assuming adequate levels of insulation); but where the dwelling is on one floor, there will be little heat gain from other rooms within the dwelling (even if there may be some heat gain from another dwelling, it should not be assumed).

Provided that the indoor temperature is higher than the outdoor temperature, heat will be lost through the fabric of the structure. The space heating system must be able to provide sufficient heat input both to raise the indoor temperature and to compensate for heat lost through the fabric. Thermal insulation of the fabric will determine the amount of heat lost—the greater the insulation, the lower the heat loss, and therefore the less heat input required both to raise and to maintain temperatures. **8.65**

The thermal capacity and response of the fabric of the structure, and the position of any high insulating layer will affect the type of heating system. Where the fabric of the structure has a high thermal capacity and is slow to react to temprature changes, the heating system should be able to provide low levels of heat input for relatively long periods (this will also utilise the heat storage capabilities of the structure).

Various types of heating system will be unsuitable for dwellings constructed from materials of high thermal capacity and slow response. Where the heating system heats the air first and relies on that heated air to raise the temperature of the structure, there will be a considerable period where the temperature difference between the air and the structure will be great (*i.e.* there is a considerable period when conditions are ideal for condensation to occur). Similarly any system which allows the occupants to feel warm and comfortable before the structure can react to the change in temperature (*e.g.* small high temperature radiant heaters) will mean that heat input is reduced too soon, again before the structure has been able to react, (creating conditions ideal for condensation). Particularly appropriate for such structures are systems which use heated water circulating through radiators, because they are slow to react (the radiators staying warm after the heating system has been turned off) and the occupants feel the temperature change more gradually. With systems that provide low levels of heat input over relatively long periods, or are themselves relatively slow to react, supplementary means of "topping-up" should be provided to give occupants a means of quickly warming themselves. (It should be noted that such systems are generally more likely to avoid conditions ideal for condensation and mould growth than systems which provide the same total amount of heat input over short periods.)

Where the majority of thermal insulation is concentrated in a layer on the inner face of the fabric, there will be a quick thermal response. In such dwellings the heating system can be one which reacts quickly, because there will be little difference between air and surface temperatures.

8.66 Any system provided should also be of an appropriate type having regard to the external conditions and to the position of the dwelling. This is particularly relevant to systems using a fuel which requires a flue that may be affected by wind speed and direction.

8.67 Generally, the heating system should be based on the system of calculations provided in British Standard B.S. 5449, Part I, 1977, which takes into account these various factors.

8.68 Obviously, once a properly designed and appropriate heating system of adequate size and capacity is provided, the occupier must make proper use of it. As such, the system should be one which is capable of being easily operated and controlled, and the amount of supervision and involvement required should be considered. It would be inappropriate to provide a system, otherwise totally suitable having regard to the dwelling, which is labour intensive where an occupier is unlikely or unable to provide sufficient involvement (perhaps because of physical disability). In addition, where the heating system is of adequate size and capacity, but the cost of operating it is high (perhaps because of the amount of heat loss through the fabric) it may be beyond the financial means of the occupier to attain and maintain the temperature levels.

8.69 It should be noted that an electric socket outlet is not a part of the heating system. An electric socket outlet is a supply of energy which can be used to run a variety of appliances, including lights, televisions, radios and heaters. It can also be used for a variety of types of heaters, including radiant bar heaters, fan heaters, oil-filled radiators and convector heaters, some of which may be inappropriate for the particular dwelling.

8.70 Flueless heaters fuelled by gas or oil will discharge water vapour (which is a product of combustion) into the atmosphere within the dwelling. While such heaters will not be the cause of condensation, they may add that additional amount of water vapour which tips the balance in the case of dwellings only just capable of coping with the water vapour produced by the household. It should be noted that the amount of water vapour emitted by such heaters has been accepted as part of the total moisture generated by a typical household since at least 1977 (*i.e.* 4kW of heat input for five hours in a 24 hour period). Such heaters, however, should be unnecessary if the provision for space heating is properly designed and appropriate.

(b) Ventilation

8.71 The provision for ventilation of a dwelling must be adequate to ensure the replacement of vitiated air and the removal of moisture laden air, while keeping heat loss to a minimum and avoiding draughts. Ventilation rates of 0.5 to 1.0 air changes per hour throughout the whole dwelling are ideal for these purposes. Rates above this increase the heat input required, reduce the air temperature generally and cool structural surfaces. Fortuitous ventilation rates of around 0.7 air changes per hour will be obtained by infiltration and leakages around closed windows and doors (except where excessive draught-proofing has sealed all possible sources of such ventilation). Flues to open fire-places and fitted gas fires, and air bricks increase the overall ventilation rates to at least 2.0 air changes per hour.

Although ventilation rates for the dwelling as a whole should be between 0.5–1.0 air changes per hour, in those areas where high moisture producing activities will be carried out (*i.e.* the kitchen and the bathroom) higher ventilation rates will be required during those activities (*e.g.* during cooking, clothes washing and drying, and bathing). These higher ventilation rates at times of high moisture production will reduce overall relative humidity levels. It should be remembered that natural ventilation relies on wind speed and direction, and may result in the moisture laden air in these areas being forced further into the dwelling (even around closed internal doors), rather than being quickly and safely taken outside. Ideally, the higher ventilation rates should be provided by mechanical extract ventilation, which will ensure that moisture laden air is quickly removed from these areas.

8.72 The means of providing ventilation to the dwelling generally should be both controllable and effective. In many dwellings, the only means of providing ventilation is by opening large windows which will result in excessive and uncontrolled ventilation, particularly in cold periods of the year and where the dwelling is in an exposed position. If this is the only provision for ventilation it will discourage occupiers from ventilating adequately, if at all. Such provision may mean that ventilation cannot be provided while the dwelling is unoccupied, because of the lack of adequate security. Trickle type ventilating slots with shutters will be more effective and controllable, and more likely to be used. Any ventilators should be sited so as to avoid draughts, which generally means at a high level but within easy reach of occupants.

8.73 Extractor fans in kitchens and bathrooms should be capable of providing an extraction rate of about 80 litres per second, and must be properly positioned. They should be sited close to the point where moisture producing activities will be carried out; above or nearly above the cooking facilities and also close to the sink. They should be as close as possible to ceiling level, at least above the height of the top of doors, and distant from any point where air will be drawn into the room from outside (so as to avoid immediate extraction of incoming air).

Ideally, such fans should be connected to a humidity sensitive switch sited on an internal wall remote from the fan. Such a switch avoids the occupants having to decide when the fan should be operated (*i.e.* when the relative humidity has exceeded 65 per cent.). The switch should be on an internal wall so that it is able accurately to sense water vapour in the atmosphere generally, and it should be remote from the fan and incoming air to avoid being affected by the cooling effect of the air streams.

8.74 The domestic activity producing the highest moisture emission is clothes drying, which will be carried out indoors during bad weather. As important as the amount of moisture produced is the time period within which it is produced; five litres of water vapour will be produced by drying 3kg. dry weight of clothes. If this is produced over a 24 hour period the ventilation rate could be relatively low to ensure it is extracted from the dwelling, but if it is produced within 30 minutes (by a tumble drier, for example) the ventilation rate during that time must be high. Ideally, provision should be made for direct venting of the moisture laden air produced by clothes drying to the external air. Where a clothes drying cupboard is provided, this can be by means of simple air vents, one at low level allowing air from within the dwelling into the cupboard and one at high level venting to the outside. Provision should also be made for direct venting of tumble driers to the external air (a vent for connecting the flexible ducting from the drier).

(c) Thermal insulation

8.75 Thermal insulation of the dwelling relates to the ability of the fabric to conduct heat from one side to the other to compensate for differences in temperature. The thermal insulation capability of parts of the fabric is usually given in terms of the thermal transmittance coefficient (or "U value"), which is the quantity of heat (in Watts) conducted through a square metre of the structure per degree temperature difference between the inside and outside, expressed in $W/m^{2\circ}C$. As the U value is an expression of the amount of heat conducted through the fabric, the higher the U value, the greater the heat loss and therefore the lower the thermal insulation capability.

Thermal insulation of a dwelling should be sufficient to minimise heat loss and avoid relatively cold surfaces which might induce condensation. It also has a direct relationship to the space heating sytem, affecting the type of system, the size and the amount of heat input required. Obviously the provision of adequate thermal insulation only reduces the amount of heat loss through the fabric, and heat must still be provided and properly distributed within the dwelling.

8.76 Present minimum thermal insulation standards for new dwellings in England and Wales[14] require maximum U values of 0.6 $W/m^{2\circ}C$ for walls, and 0.35 $W/m^{2\circ}C$ for roofs (including the associated ceiling). As the part of the fabric which allows the greatest heat loss is the glazed window area, present standards limit the amount of single glazed window area to 12 per cent. of the total perimeter wall area of the dwelling, or 24 per cent. for double glazed window area. These are minimum figures, and where a dwelling is in a particularly exposed position they will be inadequate.

The Royal Institute of British Architects and the Institute of Housing regard these standards as inadequate and suggest that U values of 0.4 $W/m^{2\circ}C$ and 0.23 $W/m^{2\circ}C$ respectively would be more appropriate.[15]

8.77 The design and construction of a dwelling should not only meet the overall insulation values, but should also avoid cold-bridges (*i.e.* features which conduct heat more readily through the structure than other parts). Such features will be found at corners formed by two external walls, and at the junctions of solid floors or ceilings with external walls, where the surface temperature may be as much as 5 degrees celsius lower than adjacent areas. These particular cold-bridges are a result of a greater external surface area compared with the internal surface area, the external surface losing the same amount of heat but taking it from a reduced internal surface area. Cold-bridges may also be found where the cavity of a wall is closed, and particularly where it is closed with a material which has a higher U value and/or is of a denser material than other parts of the wall (*e.g.* at window and door openings, particularly where there is a dense concrete lintel to the opening).

---

[14] Building Regulations 1985 (S.I. 1985 No. 1065).
[15] *Homes for the Future* (1983) I.o.H. and R.I.B.A.

(d) Moisture production

8.78 Many of the day-to-day biological and domestic activities carried out by a household will result in moisture being emitted into the atmosphere within a dwelling. The amounts emitted will vary depending on the number of persons in the household, the amount of time spent within the dwelling, and the activities carried out in the dwelling.

Where the household includes very young children, considerably more clothes washing and drying will be carried out than in a household with older children. Where no (or very little) clothes washing and drying is carried out, there will be considerably less moisture produced.

It is now accepted that the amount of moisture produced will vary within a characteristic range, and a table giving an indication of the range is set out below.

Range of typical moisture emission rates—four person household

Source	Moisture emission per 24 hours (litres)
Everday sources of moisture –	
4 persons asleep for 8 hours	1.0–2.0
2 persons active for 16 hours	1.5–3.0
Cooking	
(*e.g.* by gas for 3 hours)	2.0–4.0
Bathing, dish washing, etc	
(estimated)	0.5–1.0
Normal daily total	5.0–10.0
Additional irregular sources–	
Washing clothes	
(estimated)	0.5–1.0
Drying clothes	
(*e.g.* unvented tumble driers)	3.0–7.5
Flueless oil or gas heater	
(*e.g.* 4kW for 5 hours)	1.0–2.0
Possible daily total	10.0–20.0

(Based on the information given in British Standard B.S.5250:1975 and B.R.E. Digest No. 297, May 1985).

Differences in these moisture emission rates will obviously vary, but the variations are surprisingly small. Even in the case of a single person household many of the moisture producing activities may remain much the same, and only in an extreme case will the emissions be as low as 4.5 litres (assuming only minimal activities within the dwelling) and will generally be around 10.0 litres. With larger households, the increase will be mainly in the area of the amount emitted by the number of persons, with less of an increase in the other areas. These figures acknowledge that clothes will be dried indoors during bad weather, and that the moisture produced may not be vented directly to the external air.

8.79 The amount of moisture emitted into the dwelling by a flueless gas or oil heater and by a gas cooker (which is also a flueless appliance) is not a major source of water vapour, and alternative means of heating and cooking will provide only a slight reduction in the overall moisture emission rates. The amount of moisture emitted by the combustion of the different oils and gas to produce one kilowatt of heat is—

    Paraffin – 0.098 litres; Butane – 0.113 litres;
    Propane – 0.118 litres; North Sea Gas – 0.146 litres.

8.80 The main moisture producing activities of cooking and clothes drying will tend to be carried out in the kitchen. It is not reasonable or practicable to expect that these activities should not be carried out, or should be reduced. However, the provision of proper and effective means of ventilation or of means of extracting water vapour from the atmosphere can dramatically reduce the overall amount of moisture.

As described above (see para. 8.71), effective ventilation to ensure that the moisture laden air is quickly taken out of the dwelling is difficult (if possible) by natural means. However, if an extractor fan (with a humidity sensitive switch) is provided in the kitchen, and if clothes drying equipment or facilities are vented directly to the outside, most of the moisture produced will be quickly taken out of the dwelling, giving a possible reduction in the total water vapour in the dwelling of between 5.0 and 11.5 litres of water vapour.

8.81 Dehumidifiers can provide an alternative means of reducing overall amounts of water vapour within the atmosphere of a dwelling. Dehumidifiers are not a means of ventilation. Ventilation will therefore still be necessary, but should be kept to a minimum while a dehumidifier is in use, to prevent additional moisture being brought into the dwelling from outside. Dehumidifiers operate by cooling the air to below its dew-point and collecting the moisture which condenses out. The drier and cooler air is then heated and returned to the room. Since heat is produced by condensing water vapour, dehumidifiers can provide up to 30 per cent. more heat than would be provided by the energy (electricity) used.

The performance of a dehumidifier is affected by the temperature and moisture content of air, operating best in higher temperatures and with high moisture levels. A dehumidifier should be sited in warm moist areas with minimum ventilation, and not in the cooler parts of a dwelling distant from moisture producing activities (which may be the parts most affected by condensation and associated mould growth). Except where the dehumidifier is provided only for a temporary period (*e.g.* to assist in the drying out of new wall plaster), the water collecting tank should be plumbed into a waste pipe. Small dehumidifiers will provide a small reduction in the overall moisture content, but will not be effective in dealing with high moisture production over short time periods.

Extractor fans will result in a minor amount of heat loss (because air taken out of the dwelling will be warm and replacement air cool), but they are generally cheaper to provide and install, more effective in dealing with short periods of high moisture production, and probably more reliable.

Summary

8.82–
8.83

It is an imbalance in the relationship between the four factors of heating, ventilation, insulation and moisture production that can cause problems of dampness, resulting in excessive relative humidity levels or condensation. Excessive moisture production by the occupying household is rare, but the amount of moisture produced may tip the balance when the design and construction of the dwelling is such that it is only just capable of coping without dampness problems.

Probably the most common imbalance is in respect of provision for thermal insulation and for space heating. While provision for ventilation may be not ideal, it is rarely the main cause of problems, and may help to balance out the deficiencies of insulation and heating.

5. Measurement for Dampness in the Fabric

8.84 Because "dampness" occurs before it can be detected visibly or by touch, accurate measurement of the amount of "dampness" is essential. There are several methods which can be used, some which can be carried out during a general inspection and others which are appropriate for more detailed diagnosis in complicated cases.

Laboratory measurement

8.85 This method measures the water content of samples of material, and the presence of hygroscopic salts in the material. It is used to give an indication as to whether a wall is affected by rising dampness or dampness from penetration, and for providing evidence of the possible presence of hygroscopic salts, whether or not there is dampness from any other source.

Samples of material from the wall are taken using a low–speed drill with a masonry bit (approx. 9mm. diameter), the first 10mm. or so being rejected and the spoil collected in a small stopped bottle. Samples should be taken at various depths into the wall so that the moisture content at those depths can be assessed. Provided that the drill bit is sharp, the speed very slow and the material not too hard, the amount of heat produced by drilling should be insufficient to have any significant effect on the accuracy of the measurement.

Samples should be taken at various points suspected of being affected by dampness, and also at a point not so suspected. Sample points should start close to floor level and continue to a level above any obvious "tidemark," and at least one point well above the obviously affected area. Samples should be taken both in brickwork and in mortar joints. Details of each sample and the point from which it was taken should be accurately recorded.

The procedure for measuring the moisture content and the hygroscopic moisture content is as follows: **8.86**

(a) A small amount of the sample is placed in a previously weighed petri dish and weighed immediately. This weight (less the weight of the dish) gives the weight of the sample as taken from the structure (weight A).
(b) The petri dish with sample is put into a container with a relative humidity of 75 per cent., which is then sealed. (A 75 per cent. relative humidity is easily obtained by using a saturated solution of common salt inside the container.)
(c) After at least 16 hours (overnight) the sample is reweighed. This (less the weight of the dish) gives the weight of the sample with the water absorbed from the air of the container by any hygroscopic salts (weight B).
(d) The sample is then dried in an oven at about 100 degrees celsius for approximately 1 hour, then removed and covered and allowed to cool. Once cool, the sample is reweighed to give (less the weight of the dish) the dry weight of the sample (weight C).

The percentage moisture content is given by dividing the difference between the original weight of the sample (A) and the dry weight (C) by the original weight (A), and multiplying by 100 ($\frac{A-C}{A} \times 100$).

The percentage hygroscopic moisture content is given by dividing the difference between the weight of the sample with any absorbed water (B) and the dry weight (C) by original weight (A), and multiplying by 100 ($\frac{B-C}{A} \times 100$).

If the percentage hygroscopic moisture content is not required (because rising dampness is not suspected), stages (b) and (c) can be omitted.

8.87 A comparison of the hygroscopic moisture content with the moisture content gives an indication of the cause of dampness at the point of the sample. For example, where hygroscopic moisture content is higher than moisture content it indicates that dampness comes from the air rather than another source; where the moisture content is higher, dampness comes from a source other than the air. Where the interior of the wall is found to be dry with high hygroscopic moisture content from samples close to the surface, this suggests that any dampness is a result of salt contamination. High moisture content throughout the wall (perhaps with low hygroscopic moisture content) indicates that rain penetration is the most likely cause. Dampness damage with low moisture and hygroscopic moisture contents suggests either condensation or irregular rain penetration.

Carbide meter method

8.88 This is a method which can be used on site to produce the same results as in the laboratory, and is based on the reaction between calcium carbide and water which will produce acetylene gas under pressure.

(a) Samples are collected as described above (para. 8.85) for the laboratory method.
(b) A measured amount of the sample is placed into the carbide meter (a pressure container with calibrated gauge), a measured amount of calcium carbide powder added, and the container sealed.
(c) The meter is shaken and as the calcium carbide reacts with water in the sample, acetylene gas is produced creating pressure within the container.
(d) The pressure gauge on the container is calibrated to give a direct reading of the moisture content based on the standard weight of the sample.

8.89 To obtain the hygroscopic moisture content, a measured amount of the sample is placed in a container with a relative humidity of 75 per cent. (as described above for the laboratory method). This sample is then placed into the carbide meter with calcium carbide and the pressure reading taken.

The interpretation of the results obtained using the carbide meter is as given for the laboratory method.

Moisture meters

8.90 During general inspections the most practical method of assessing moisture levels is by use of a moisture meter. While these meters do not give laboratory-accurate results, they will provide information which, together with visual assessment, can be used to indicate quickly the extent of any dampness problem and the most probable main source of the moisture.

Moisture meters rely on measuring the effect of the presence of water on the amount of electricity conducted between two probes, or the effect the presence of water has on a di-electric field.

8.91 Conductance meters rely on the fact that many materials used in construction (including wood, brick and concrete) will not conduct electricity when they are dry, but the presence of free water (*i.e.* not chemically bound water) in those materials will allow electricity to be conducted through them, the amount of electricity conducted increasing with the amount of water present. The free water actually dissolves minute amounts of substances in the material to become a very weak electrolyte. Since the amount of free water will increase the amount of electricity the material can conduct, a measurement of the amount of electricity conducted gives an indication of the amount of free water present, *i.e.* an indication of the "dampness" of the material.

Di-electric field (or capacitance) meters measure the ratio of an electrical field created by two plates, one negatively and the other positively charged, to the potential difference. This measurement will depend on various factors including the material within the electrical field. A dry brick wall will increase electrical capacitance by a very small amount, but the presence of free water will increase the capacitance, again in relation to the amount of free water present.

8.92 Both types of meter can be used for taking surface moisture readings. They should be used to check for dampness generally, and to plot "contours" by taking readings at regular intervals over the area suspected of being damp, the "contours" joining points of equal readings. This will establish the area mainly affected and indicate whether there is a sudden change from damp to dry (suggesting rising dampness) or a gradual change (suggesting penetration or a traumatic source).

8.93 It is important to note that the different types of meter and different meters of the same type may be calibrated with different scales which are not be capable of comparison. Any assessment of dampness in a dwelling should be carried out with the same meter.

Some meters give readings on a relative (arbitrary) scale of 0–100, the figures only providing a means of determining different levels of "dampness" and not readings of moisture content. Some meters have different scales for different materials, and other meters give readings on a wood moisture (or wood moisture equivalent—W.M.E.) scale, which is a (relatively accurate) reading of the moisture content of wood, and can be used as a relative (arbitrary) scale for other materials.

8.94 Although readings will be affected by the presence of hygroscopic salts, probably the most popular of the two types of meter for assessing dampness in buildings is the conductance meter. Such meters are available with accessories to enable readings to be taken within the fabric of the building, to check for hygroscopic salts, and for taking spot readings of surface temperatures, relative humidity and air temperatures.

Readings can be taken within the fabric using a conductance meter with probes which are insulated except for the tips, and so remain unaffected by surface dampness (and will be unaffected by hygroscopic salts—there being none, or negligible amounts, within the fabric), and so give readings of the dampness present at a depth. High surface readings with low readings within the fabric suggest either condensation or hygroscopic salts. High readings on the surface and within the fabric suggest sources of dampness other than condensation.

6. Measurements for Relative Humidity and Condensation

8.95 To be able to assess whether there are "damp" problems caused by high relative humidity levels or actual condensation it may be necessary to take several measurements of:

(a) internal and external air temperatures;
(b) internal surface temperatures; and
(c) internal and external relative humidities.

Ideally, measurements should be taken over a period of time, but this is rarely practicable. It is usual to take spot readings, but the limitations of these readings must be appreciated. Air and surface temperatures and relative humidities constantly change during the day and night and are affected by heat input, sunlight and domestic activities. There will also be an air temperature and relative humidity spectrum within a room at any one time. However, provided that these limitations are recognised, readings can provide an indication as to whether high relative humidity or condensation is likely to be or is already a cause of problems.

8.96 Spot readings of the air temperature can be taken using the dry bulb thermometer in a whirling hygrometer, or with a battery powered electric digital thermometer.

Air temperature can be monitored over a period of time using a thermograph. Inside, the thermograph must be properly and carefully sited so as to be unaffected by radiation from heat sources and sunlight (as well as in a position where it is unlikely to be knocked). Outside, it should be protected from sun, rain and damage, while being able to monitor the air temperature.

To obtain the air temperature range, daily readings can be taken with a maximum/minimum thermometer (the time at which the readings are taken should be taken into account).

Surface temperatures can easily be taken using a battery powered electric digital thermometer with a probe which can be pressed onto the surface to be measured.

Relative humidity readings can be obtained using a whirling hygrometer. This consists of two thermometers, one with an ordinary dry bulb and the other with a bulb kept moist by a covering of wet muslin. The hygrometer is whirled for a short while, and readings are then taken. This is repeated until the same reading is obtained on consecutive occasions from the wet thermometer. From the wet and dry bulb temperature readings the relative humidity and moisture content of the air can be found by reference to psychrometric tables.

Direct relative humidity readings can be obtained with a battery powered digital thermo-hygrometer.

Recording hygrometers and thermo-hygrographs are available for monitoring the relative humidity and the air temperature and relative humidity over a period. These must be carefully and properly calibrated, used and positioned to provide effective results.

7. Sampling Possible Mould Growth

Where it is necessary to take samples of materials suspected of being infected by mould growth to establish the presence of mould, and for identification of the type (or types) of any mould, the following procedure should be adopted. The procedure is relatively straightforward, because it is only necessary to minimise the possibility of contaminating the sample, and to maintain the sample as near as possible to the state in which it was taken. **8.97**

The following equipment is necessary: **8.98**

(a) sterile petri dishes (either plastic or glass);
(b) scalpel;
(c) labels;
(d) sellotape; and
(e) insulated container.

Using a scalpel, a small area of the mould infected surface should be removed (an area of around 25mm. x 25 mm.) and placed into a sterile petri dish. **8.99**

If the sample is to be taken from a surface covered with wall paper, the paper should be lifted from the surface. If the sample is to be taken from a painted surface, the paint should be carefully flayed from the surface with the scalpel, or the possible mould lifted from the surface by pressing the adhesive side of wide sellotape onto the surface and carefully lifting it off (bringing with it any mould and spores).

The sample should be placed in the petri dish, and the dish covered, sealed and clearly labelled with the date of the sample, and address of the premises and the position of the surface from which the sample was taken.

8.100 To prevent continuing growth (particularly of any spores or mould that may have been introduced at the time of sampling) the sample should be stored in an insulated container as soon as possible. If delivery of the sample to the analyst is to be delayed for any reason, the sample should be stored in a refrigerator until delivery is possible.

8.101 The analyst should be instructed to examine the sample and to report on the following:

(a) the type, or types, of any moulds present in the sample;
(b) the size of the spores of any mould(s) identified; and
(c) any other relevant matters.

It is not strictly necessary to ask the analyst to comment on any diseases that may be caused by any moulds identified, since this can be obtained from other sources once the other information has been provided.

8.102 On receipt of the analyst's report, arrangements should be made for the occupiers of the infected premises to be tested for allergic reactions to the spores of the identified mould(s). The tests should include an examination, lung function tests, skin tests and radio allergosorbent tests. Arrangements for the tests should be made through the local allergy clinic or through the community physician.

8. Investigation of Source of Dampness—General

8.103 Where there is no obvious source of dampness (*e.g.* missing slates or tiles, soil piled up against an outside wall) it may be necessary to carry out investigations to obtain indications of the most likely source and to eliminate the least likely or impossible sources. However, it may not be possible to identify clearly the source of dampness without opening-up the structure, but to justify doing so it may be necessary to isolate the most probable sources. Every investigation will differ and will depend on the extent of the dampness problem and the degree of difficulty in isolating the cause and suggesting the appropriate remedial works. The suggestions given below are intended to provide guidance on the sort of details which may be necessary in some cases, but will not be necessary or appropriate for every case.

8.104 Initially, a general inspection should be carried out. This may need to include noting details of the external air temperature and weather conditions on the day and immediately prior to the inspection. Having noted the areas affected by dampness during the general inspection, it may be necessary to carry out a more detailed investigation, including, for example, plotting the damp affected areas using a moisture meter to give "contours" to show details of the dampest areas. This may provide sufficient information to be able to identify the source (or main source) of the dampness.

Before proceeding with further investigations of the structure, additional information could be obtained by interviewing the occupants. This should include obtaining details of when the dampness is most obvious, whether there is any relationship between the dampness and weather conditions (*e.g.* an area only appears damp after rain, or is relatively unaffected by rain but the dampness is more apparent during colder periods of the year), and when the area was last decorated.

Where condensation is considered a possibility, spot readings of air temperature and relative humidity, and surface temperature readings of both affected and unaffected areas of external walls and ceilings can be taken.

8.105 As a guide, to attempt to exclude dampness passing through the fabric (either as rising or as penetrating dampness) it may be necessary to check moisture levels within the fabric. Initially, this can be carried out using a conductance moisture meter and deep-wall probes (probes approximately 200mm. in length and insulated except for the tips). The procedure is as follows:

(a) note surface moisture readings using the surveying probes;
(b) drill two holes into the wall at the same point. The holes should be approximately 50mm. apart, and about 10mm. in depth. Note moisture readings using the deep-wall probes; and
(c) drill the holes deeper (at least once), and note moisture readings again.

(Since plaster is usually between 10–15mm. thick, readings taken at depths greater than 20mm. will be readings beyond the plaster coat of moisture levels within the wall fabric.)

If the results of such readings show that the fabric of the wall is not damp, the cause is most likely to be condensation, contamination of the plaster with hygroscopic salts, or dampness rising up the plaster coat from the floor or from below a damp proof course. If the readings in the wall fabric are as high or higher than surface readings, the main source of dampness is probably through the fabric.

8.106 To determine whether there is any hygroscopic salt contamination, samples of wall paper and plaster scrapings can be taken for analysis.

Samples of wall-paper should be taken using a scalpel (or similar sharp knife), and should consist of a small area of wallpaper (about 30–40mm. square) carefully removed from at least one point at the maximum height of the damp affected area. Samples of wall plaster should be taken from similar points (the maximum height of the damp affected area) and should consist of scrapings from the surface, not more than 1–2mm. in depth. Control samples should also be taken from obviously unaffected areas. Each sample should be placed into a container (*e.g.* a petri dish), and the container sealed and clearly labelled. Full details of the dwelling, the room, the wall and the position the sample was taken from should be carefully recorded.

The analyst should be asked to examine each sample for the presence of chloride and nitrate salts, and to give details of the amount of each present (weight:weight). It is important to note that a quantitative measurement of these salts can be misinterpreted. Because the position of the point at which the sample was taken and the depth of any plaster scrapings will affect the amount of salts present, the quantity found will not give a clue to the amount of and duration of rising dampness. The information is required for guidance and to give some comparison between the samples taken. The presence of any measureable quantity of nitrates and chlorides indicates contamination of the plaster, and the presence of nitrates indicates that contamination is from an organic source.

8.107 Further investigations, if necessary, may involve the exposing of the cavity of a cavity wall to check the position and condition of any damp proof course and its relationship with any damp proof membrane to a floor, and the state of the cavity, particularly whether there is any debris in the base of the cavity or mortar droppings on wall-ties which may provide a route across the cavity. As an alternative to opening up the structure, holes (approximately 20mm. diameter) can be drilled and the condition of the cavity checked using a borescope.

9. Investigation of Condensation

8.108 As with investigations for any source of dampness, where condensation is the obvious cause but further investigations are necessary to establish the remedial works necessary, these investigations should concentrate on the most likely problem areas. The least likely explanation is that the moisture produced by the household is excessive. The investigation of condensation should be thorough and detailed, and should be based on the following. As stated in relation to the investigation of dampness generally, each case will differ and the investigations carried out should be determined by the extent of the problem and the degree of difficulty in isolating the cause of the condensation and suggesting the appropriate remedial works. The suggestions given below are intended to provide guidance on the type of investigations which may be necessary in some cases, but may not be necessary or appropriate for every case.

8.109 Condensation is most prevalent during the colder periods of the year, between October and April. It is during this period when most complaints are made, and it is during this period when any investigations should be carried out (investigations at other times may be totally misleading, and any technical measurements taken are likely to be meaningless).

The position, orientation, design, layout and construction of the dwelling and of the building should be checked, particular attention being paid to features which may make the dwelling prone to problems of condensation.

The following list gives an indication of the range of possible factors which may need to be considered in complex cases involving condensation. **8.110**

External

General details regarding the construction and design of dwelling and building, for example construction materials, terraced/detached/flat/bungalow, flat or pitched roof, obvious system-built.
Exposure of building and of dwelling.
Orientation of building and dwelling.
Prevailing wind, and geographical features likely to affect weather and exposure of dwelling.
Whether the design includes features susceptible to condensation, (*e.g.* exposed undersides to solid floors, projecting floor/ceiling slabs to form balconies).
Whether there is an obviously large single glazed window area to dwelling.
Details of wind direction at the time of investigation, weather conditions, air temperature and relative humidity.

Internal

Room
Position in dwelling and use of room.
Type and position of any heating provision (both fixed and any supplementary provided by occupant).
Type and position of provision for ventilation.
Facilities present (*e.g.* sinks, water supplies, cookers, washing machines, clothes driers).
Floor area and ceiling height.
Details of activities at the time (*e.g.* cooking, clothes drying), and whether heating and ventilation are in use.
Air temperature.
Relative humidity.

Ceiling
Whether separates from another dwelling, another floor, balcony or from roof space (if any).

Materials and construction (if possible).
Any obvious cold-bridges.
Position of damp/mould, and its relationship to other features (*e.g.* window openings, walls, air bricks).
Details of decorative finish and when it was last decorated.
Whether (and when) there has been any cleaning or treatment of mould.
Surface temperature.
Surface moisture readings (on and under any paper).

Walls
Whether affected walls are internal, party or external.
In the case of an external wall, the compass direction faced.
In the case of internal and party walls, details of use of the other side.
Material and type of construction (if possible).
Measured thickness of wall (if possible).
Measured area of wall.
Measured glazed window area.
Whether the wall is obviously dry-lined.
Any obvious cold-bridges.
Position of damp/mould, and its relationship to other features (*e.g.* window openings, floors, ceilings, air bricks).
Details of decorative finish and when it was last decorated.
Whether (and when) there has been cleaning or treatment of mould.
Surface temperature.
Surface moisture readings (on and under any wall paper).

Floor
Whether it separates from another dwelling, another floor, or has an exposed under-side.
Materials and construction (if possible), and surface finish (*e.g.* thermoplastic tiles).
Any obvious cold-bridges.
Position of any damp, and the relationship to other features.
Details of any floor covering.
Whether the floor surface has been recently washed.
Surface temperature.

Windows
Position and orientation of opening.
Type of window frame and material.
Single or double glazed.
Size of window opening.
Type of opening light.

Whether the glazing is affected by condensation.
Whether the frame is affected by mould or damp (take readings).
Position of any damp/mould on reveals.
Surface moisture readings of reveals.
Whether internal sill/window board is affected by mould or damp (take readings).

General
Details of provision for space heating—system, fuel, rooms supplied with heat, size/capacity of system.
Details of provision for ventilation.
Depth and condition of any loft insulation.

Occupation details

Since condensation will be affected by the size and day-to-day activities of the household (these may reduce the more obvious effects of condensation, or may mean that condensation occurs in one dwelling, but not in another identical dwelling) it may be necessary to obtain information on the activities of the household. 8.111

The range of matters it may be necessary to consider include the following:

General
The number and age of everyone who normally lives at the dwelling.
Details of who normally goes out to work, school or college, and which of them (if any) returns at lunchtime.

Cooking
Details of equipment used (*e.g.* gas, electric and/or micro-wave).
Average number of meals cooked per day.

Clothes washing
Details of equipment used (*e.g.* twin tub, automatic, or none).
Average number of times per week equipment used.
Are clothes washed by hand, if so, how often?
Are clothes ever boiled, if so how often?
Is a laundrette used for clothes washing, if so how often?

Clothes drying
Details of equipment used (*e.g.* tumble dryer, spin dryer, convector dryer).
Average number of times used per week.
If a tumble dryer, is it used with a vent?
Is a laundrette used for drying clothes, if so how often?

Personal washing
Average number of baths per week for household.

Heating
Details of when and for how long the heating system is used each day.
Details of when and for how long any supplementary heaters are used each day.
Details of any flueless gas or oil heaters, and the amount of fuel used per week.

Ventilation
If there are any extractor fans, how often are they used?
If there are any ventilators fitted to walls or windows, how often are they opened?
How often, for how long (on average) and which windows are opened each day?

Miscellaneous
Details of all electrical equipment and appliances.
Details of all gas equipment and appliances.
Details of gas and electric and other fuel bills.

Remedial works for condensation

8.112   Only after the results of any appropriate investigation have been collected and considered can the most likely problem areas be identified, and remedial steps considered.

This evaluation should include the adequacy of the thermal insulation and space heating system, the use made of the space heating system, the effectiveness of the provision for ventilation, and the use made of the ventilation system.

Insulation and heating

8.113   These two factors should be considered together. In the case of any dwelling affected by condensation, a sufficient amount of heat input (properly distributed throughout the dwelling) is required to reduce the probability and possibility of condensation occurring, and the space heating system must be capable of providing that heat input at a reasonable cost and a cost within the means of the occupier. The amount of thermal insulation determines the fabric heat loss from the dwelling and so (together with the volume of the dwelling) directly affects the amount of heat input required. The amount of thermal insulation also affects the internal surface temperatures—the less thermal insulation, the lower the internal surfaces temperature and the greater the likelihood of condensation occurring.

INVESTIGATION OF CONDENSATION

The design and layout of the dwelling will also affect the remedial measures that will be necessary. In the case of a dwelling on two floors, there will be some heat gain from the lower floor, and improving the insulation may mean that more of the heat normally provided within the dwelling is retained, making the upper floor warmer. However, in the case of a dwelling on one floor, increasing the thermal insulation of bedrooms will not raise the temperatures, and it may be necessary to both improve the insulation and provide additional means of heating. **8.114**

Detailed calculations of fabric heat loss based on the temperatures within each room are usually unnecessary to determine the remedial works. For general guidance it is usually sufficient to compare the effect of increasing the thermal insulation, to estimate the cost of providing that insulation and to consider the cost benefits (in terms of the reduction in heating costs). Similarly, it should be unnecessary to carry out detailed calculations to check the capacity of a heating system (which, if they are necessary, should be based on the design temperature difference between inside and outside). **8.115**

Ventilation and moisture control

Measurement of ventilation rates is complex and will vary depending on the particular climatic conditions at the time. Generally, it should be unnecessary to attempt actual measurement of the rates, and a general assessment of the provision for ventilation and the use made of it should be sufficient to determine whether alternative provision is needed to ensure control of moisture levels within the dwelling. **8.116**

CHAPTER 9

OTHER MATTERS: EVIDENCE, COUNCIL HOUSES, COMPENSATION

9.01
1. Evidence — 9.02
2. Procedure for sub-standard council houses — 9.18
3. Obligations to occupiers displaced — 9.23

1. EVIDENCE

Introduction

9.02 A burden borne by all those entrusted with the enforcement of legal standards is that ultimately, if their powers are to have effect at all, they must appear in court to justify their actions. Environmental health officers may therefore be called upon to appear before public inquiries, and the magistrates', county or even Crown courts to give evidence. They may, infrequently, be required to give evidence in an inquest or the High Court, although the issues with which they deal are only likely to be heard in the High Court on appeal from the lower courts, in which case all the evidence will be dealt with by documents and their oral evidence will not be required.

9.03 The presentation of evidence in any court involves two separate considerations for "professional" witnesses. First, there are the practical issues concerning the gathering and explanation of facts and opinions, and secondly, the implications of legal rules imposed by the individual courts for defining which facts and opinions are admissible. In many instances, such as an appeal against the service of a notice, the question of whether or not the matter will be heard before a court is outside the control of the officer, and all decisions should therefore be taken on the basis that the officer *may* be called to account before the court. Consequently there is a need for an acquaintance with the principles of admissibility of evidence to support the decisions of the officer. In all cases where legal proceedings seem likely, it is advisable to discuss the relevant evidence and law with the legal department well in advance.

The principles of evidence

9.04 To non-lawyers, the idiosyncracies of lawyers' decisions on what may be produced in evidence can be intimidating. The issues can also be complex for the lawyer, and it is no part of this book to expound the detailed rules of evidence,[1] but in order to assist environmental health officers who may be unfamiliar with the courts, a brief outline is given of some of the basic principles, together with some more detailed examples.

The rules of procedure and evidence differ from court to court. The criminal courts (the magistrates' court and Crown Court) have more stringent rules than the civil courts (the county court and High Court), whereas public inquiries may be even more informal. The legal departments of local authorities should be consulted in any difficult case. **9.05**

Most cases upon which environmental health officers will be called to give evidence in housing matters are likely to involve challenges to the accuracy or correctness of one or more of the following:

(a) the administrative procedure followed;
(b) the condition of the dwelling;
(c) the enforcement procedure adopted; and
(d) the expert opinion relied upon.

The common form of trial in this country is adversarial, which means that one party is given the responsibility of establishing (proving) to the satisfaction of the court that their case is to be preferred on the evidence presented. This responsibility is called the burden of proof, and in the civil courts, a party will be successful if the facts can be established to the satisfaction of the court "on the balance of probabilities." In the criminal courts the prosecution will have to establish the facts of the case to a higher standard; the prosecution must prove the case "beyond reasonable doubt." **9.06**

Public inquiries and inquests are inquisitorial and there is, therefore, not the same emphasis upon one party having to establish a particular case. The inspector or coroner asks questions of all witnesses and arrives at a conclusion on the basis of reviewing all the evidence.

An opposing lawyer, particularly in the adversarial process, may strive to exploit any weakness in a case, and the only safeguard is thorough preparation.

Most cases will only involve one or two disputed issues and will contain a large amount of common agreement. It will save the court time and individual officers work, if likely areas of dispute can be clarified before the hearing. For example, challenges to the authority of a notice may be relatively unusual. An officer should nevertheless be aware of any relevant decisions taken by the council in relation to the issue and

---

[1] Publications on the Law of Evidence which officers may find useful for further explanation include *Cross on Evidence* (6th ed., 1985) and *Phipson on Evidence* (13th ed., 1984). Useful guidance is also to be found in *Stones' Justices' Manual* (Latham and Richman (eds.)) (for magistrates courts) and the *County Court Practice* (Gregory (ed.)) (annually).

be ready to supply a copy of relevant minutes of council proceedings if challenged. It is also important to ensure that an officer's evidence relates to the relevant dates required by the legislation. Thus, for example, it will be necessary to show in a statutory nuisance case that the nuisance existed at the time of service of the notice *and* at the date of the hearing.[2]

9.07 A firm knowledge of the legislation under which the officer purports to act is also necessary. The court will be interested to know about an officer's application of a particular legal standard to the condition of the dwelling that becomes the subject of the proceedings. The courts are interested in the witness's observations of the condition of premises as a background to the formulation of a professional opinion of the appropriate action. It will not be necessary for the officer to give evidence of the law which is for the court to establish. Law reports and statutes will be acknowledged by the courts without the need for them to be proved in evidence. It is wise, however, in an area of law where the officer may have more knowledge than some lawyers, to ensure that copies of the relevant statutory provisions, cases and ministerial circulars are available for the court and the opposing side.

The expert witness

9.08 Environmental health officers will be treated as expert witnesses. Their training and formal qualification places them in a better position than lay people to make judgments and form opinions. In order to be treated as an expert witness an officer should inform the court of their role and qualifications. Strictly, it is not the passing of exams or the obtaining of specific qualifications that give an individual the status of expert witness, but their knowledge and experience of the relevant subject. For example, the courts have held that an amateur hand writing enthusiast, could nevertheless be "expert," since he had studied the subject and accumulated experience of analysis.[3]

9.09 The status of expert witness carries with it the possibility of giving evidence of opinion, normally denied to other witnesses. It will enable the expert to be present in court to hear all the evidence and comment upon it, although permission to remain in court should be obtained before the court hears any evidence. The expert status will only extend to matters within the officer's special knowledge and it will not necessarily be accepted that an environmental health officer is, for example, an expert in heat transference technology and microbiology. Their expertise in matters of health and housing will be accepted, and officers should be acquainted with the relevant research and reports, for example, those from the Building Research Establishment and the Institution of Environmental Health Officers.

---

[2] See above para. 5.31.
[3] *R. v. Silverlock* [1894] 2 Q.B. 766.

Most cases can be expected to focus on the officer's appraisal of the fabric of the house (a factual issue) and the expert judgment that those conditions amount to an infringement of the standard required by the legislation. While it is a question of fact ultimately to be determined by the court whether or not the particular state of a building, for example, is "prejudicial to health," an officer's opinion based upon appraisal of the defects and knowledge of medical research will be admitted as evidence that it is prejudicial to health and, in the absence of any challenge or other evidence to the contrary, will be conclusive.[4]

The hearsay evidence rule

The primary principle of the admissibility of evidence is relevance, but not all relevant evidence is admissible in the courts. A major limitation is that the courts tend to reject any "second hand" evidence as "hearsay." The hearsay rule is commonly stated thus: "an assertion other than one made by a person while giving oral evidence in the proceedings is inadmissible of any fact asserted."[5] The rule, however, has many exceptions and can be intimidating or confusing to any but the most frequent visitors to the courts.

One of the exceptions particularly relevant to environmental health officers is that evidence of opinion, which they give as an expert, may be based upon hearsay. The most obvious example is that any scientific knowledge relating to, say, the effect of dampness upon health will have been gained from reading the research of others. It is not necessary to call the particular researcher, nor is it necessary to produce a particular article or book in the court. An officer's general expertise and knowledge of such work will suffice, subject to their being able to answer any challenges to their knowledge based upon contrary research opinion.

Another example illustrates the difficulties of hearsay evidence. An officer is told by an occupant that a wall was damp in December but not in June. In evidence the officer can repeat the statement made by the occupier as information upon which the officer concluded that the dampness was condensation; but that does not mean that it will be accepted as evidence that the wall was damp in December or at any time, because it is hearsay. To prove the latter the occupier would have to be called, or some other evidence such as the officer's own observations would have to be produced in court.

The best practice to ensure that the courts will accept a particular item in evidence is to review all the facts and allegations upon which the case depends and to call as a witness the person who observed a particular condition, or heard an alleged threat, for example, from a landlord, to give evidence in person. Similarly it will not be possible for an officer to

9.10

9.11

9.12

9.13

---

[4] *Patel* v. *Methab* (1981) 5 H.L.R. 78.
[5] *Cross on Evidence, op. cit.*, Chap. XV, p. 454.

submit a written report in evidence without attending court and testifying in person. A report written by that officer can then be produced.

On occasions the report of another expert, such as a heating engineer or structural surveyor, may be relevant to a case. Whilst an officer is at liberty to comment in evidence upon such a report, the person who made that report must herself be called as a witness if the contents of the report are to be admitted.

9.14 Where the law requires only that a power should be exercised reasonably (for example in the making of a management order on a house in multiple occupation[6]), officers are entitled to rely upon the statements of others without necessarily obtaining direct evidence for themselves. The position was succinctly put by McCullough J. in a case involving the legislation concerning homeless persons (now Part III of the Housing Act 1985), when he stated that:

> "there was nothing in the [Homeless Persons] Act which requires a local authority to act as if it were a court of law and to ignore hearsay evidence, or which obliges them to confirm by direct evidence that which they are told by way of hearsay. They are required to act reasonably. If, having consulted a number of people who would reasonably be expected to be in a position to give accurate information, they come to a conclusion,"

that a particular incident or condition occurred, they are entitled to act on such information.[7]

A control order may only be made when the authority decides that "the living conditions in a house are such that, for the protection of the safety, welfare or health of the people living in the house, it is necessary."[8] The guidance given by the Department of the Environment cautions that an:

> "authority should not rely on any rumour or hearsay but base its decision on reports of living conditions actually observed by responsible officers, or other evidence of bad living conditions at the time of making the order which can be substantiated to its satisfaction in any subsequent appeal proceedings".

The need to act quickly, however, in the "designedly peremptory"[9] situations envisaged for the procedure should not be overlooked. Reports by responsible people are sufficient for a decision to make a control order and the making of the order should not be delayed unnecessarily in order to obtain direct evidence, which can later be obtained, if

---

[6] ss.370–372 of the Housing Act 1985—see Chap. 6, paras. 6.92–6.96.
[7] See Chap. 6, para. 6.150.
[8] D.O.E. Circular No. 12/86 (Home Office No. 39/86, W.O. No. 23/86) para. 3.9.2.
[9] Ministry of Housing and Local Government Circular No. 51/64, para. 5, now withdrawn by D.O.E. Circular No. 12/86.

necessary after the making of the order and before any appeal proceedings.

9.15 Most cases with which environmental health officers are concerned will be based upon the observation of physical conditions, and officers should conduct their investigations on the basis that they are assembling evidence which may ultimately have to be presented to the court. Clear records should therefore be made at the time when the information is collected. Whilst it may be some time after the inspection that a formal report is written,[10] notes made at the time of an inspection may be used in the witness box to refresh the officer's memory. Accurate labelling and recording of samples is necessary.[11] Photographs, polaroid or otherwise, can be a useful record of temporary conditions.

On rare occasions, such as the investigation of conditions prior to the making of a control order, it may be advisable to obtain a written and signed statement from a potential witness. If possible this should be taken at the time and officers would be well advised to carry with them on such occasions blank forms to be completed on the spot. This is particularly helpful in situations involving harassment, when efforts might otherwise be made to encourage a victim to withdraw any allegation. Such a statement cannot be used as evidence in any subsequent proceedings when it will be necessary to call the witness in person, but it can be a valuable aid to support a witness who may otherwise be vulnerable to threats.

9.16 The court's preference for the best evidence extends to the requirement to produce the original of any document, although if it has been lost, a copy may be admissible upon proof that the original is lost and that the copy is a true copy of it. Copies of many public records are also admissible.[12]

9.17 Photographs are admissible as evidence, subject to their authentication, which in civil cases can usually be agreed before the trial. In criminal cases it is not necessary to call the photographer as a witness, since there is provision for uncontested evidence to be dealt with by a written statement.[13]

2. PROCEDURE—SUBSTANDARD COUNCIL HOUSES

9.18 While the statutory standards dealt with in this book relate to all dwellings, those standards cannot be enforced where the dwelling is owned and managed by the local housing authority. This was made clear by the Court of Appeal in *R. v. Cardiff City Council ex p. Cross*,[14] in which it was held that it was not possible for an authority to serve a

---

[10] See Chap. 2, para. 2.68.
[11] See, for example, Chap. 8, paras. 8.99 and 8.106.
[12] See *Cross on Evidence,* above n. 1, Chap. XX, p.607
[13] Criminal Justice Act 1967, s.9.
[14] (1982) 6 H.L.R. 1, affirming (1981) 1 H.L.R. 54.

notice under section 9(1) or section 16(1) of the Housing Act 1957 [now section 189 and section 264(1) of the 1985 Act] in respect of a house in the sole ownership of, and managed by, itself.

9.19 In 1984, during the passage of the Housing and Building Control Bill[15] through the House of Lords, Baroness Vickers pointed out that this decision meant that while tenants of private landlords were protected by the public health and housing legislation, tenants of local authorities were not so protected. To try to overcome this disparity, she proposed that a new clause should be added to the Bill.

Lord Skelmersdale, on behalf of the government, stated that he was unconvinced that the proposed clause was necessary. He said "any secure tenant can already go to his landlord and complain about the unsatisfactory condition of his dwelling. In most cases, such landlords have duties under section 32 of the 1961 Housing Act to keep in repair the exterior and structure of their properties and to maintain the installations for various basic services. If a landlord who has been notified fails to remedy a defect, then the tenant can pursue his case through the courts by exercising his right to ask for specific performance of a repair under section 125(1) of the 1974 Housing Act. Obviously, this will happen only in extreme cases as most public sector landlords are only too keen to keep their properties up to standard."[16]

(Section 32 Housing Act 1961 and section 125(1) of the 1974 Act are now section 11 and section 17(1) of the Landlord and Tenant Act 1985 respectively.)

He also said that a statement would be included on the problems in a Department of the Environment Circular, and Baroness Vickers agreed to withdraw her suggested new clause.

9.20 Advice was subsequently issued[17] which suggests that authorities should:

> "introduce and publish arrangements whereby, if a council tenant seeks the help of the Environmental Health Officer about the condition of his dwelling in which in the opinion of the Officer is such that would otherwise necessitate action under the 1957 Act, the Officer shall notify the Chief Housing Officer who should ensure that the necessary remedial works are carried out within a reasonable time."

Although the circular only refers to the Housing Act 1957, it is suggested that any procedure adopted by an authority should cover all legislative provisions.

---

[15] Now consolidated into the Housing Act 1985 and the Building Act 1984.
[16] Hansard, col. 816, April 5, 1984.
[17] D.o.E Circular No.21/84 (W.O. No.42/84), para. 117.

Based on the advice in the circular, the Institution of Environmental Health Officers suggested the following procedure. **9.21**

(a) Complaint received by environmental health department.
(b) Inspection made by environmental health officer.
(c) Service of the equivalent of the appropriate notice on the director of housing/housing manager.
(d) The "notice" should include the same details as would normally be included, *e.g.* the Act and provision, the works required, the time within which those works should be completed, the appropriate sanction, and the action that will be taken by the committee instead of that sanction, and any "rights of appeal."
(e) A copy of the "notice" should also be sent to the tenant, and the service of the notice reported to the relevant committee (as would be the equivalent notice).
(f) If the "notice" is not complied with, the sanction procedure should be instigated, and the tenant so advised.
(g) In a case where a closing or demolition order would have been appropriate, the equivalent of a time and place notice should be served, and the meeting held, between representatives of the housing department the environmental health department and the legal section. The meeting should be exactly the same as a normal time and place meeting.

Obviously, any sanctions will be of limited effect and cannot be enforced in the courts, but the very least should be a formal report to a specifically constituted sub-committee (not the committee normally reported to by either the environmental health or the housing department). If the report is accepted by that sub-committee, it should be reported to a full council together with a reprimand. Similarly, any "appeal" procedure should be to a sub-committee. **9.22**

It is also suggested that, together with a copy of the "notice," tenants should be advised of their rights, for example, to take action under section 99 of the Public Health Act 1936 or under section 11 of the Landlord and Tenant Act 1985, and be advised to contact a solicitor for further advice, information and assistance.

3. Obligations to Occupiers Displaced

There are several enforcement procedures which will displace the occupying household from their home including: **9.23**

(a) where a house is unfit for human habitation[18] and not capable

---
[18] Housing Act 1985, s.264—see Chap. 3, paras. 3.24–3.46.

of repair at reasonable expense and the authority accept an undertaking not to use it for human habitation,[19] or make a demolition or closing order[20];

(b) where the housing arrangements[21] associated with the compulsory improvement procedure[22] consist of the permanent rehousing of the occupying household; and

(c) where the authority accept an undertaking or make a closing order in respect of part of a house in multiple occupation[23] to ensure that the means of escape in case of fire are adequate for the house.

In these cases, the authority is under a duty to ensure that the displaced household is re-housed, and the occupier qualifies for compensation toward the cost of moving and may qualify for compensation for the loss of the home. The obligation and the rights to compensation are discussed in paras. 9.25–9.38.

9.24 There are other enforcement procedures, however, which result in the displacement of the occupying household, but for which there is no specific protection or rights to compensation. These include:

(a) where premises are a statutory nuisance[24] and the magistrates' court, being satisfied that the premises are unfit for human habitation, make a nuisance order prohibiting use for human habitation[25]; and

(b) where an occupier is guilty of causing or permitting a dwelling to be overcrowded and the landlord or the authority obtain possession to abate that overcrowding.[26]

In these cases, the displaced occupiers are "homeless," and the authority may be obliged to provide housing accommodation or advice under their general duties to homeless persons.[27] Obligations to the homeless are outside the scope of this book, and reference should be made to other works.[28]

It should be noted that the service of a direction to ensure the reduction of numbers in a house in multiple occupation having regard to the facilities available, and the service of an overcrowding notice to reduce

---

[19] Housing Act 1985, s.264(4)(*b*)—see Chap. 5, paras. 5.110–5.114.
[20] *Ibid.* s.265—see Chap. 5, paras. 5.115–5.150.
[21] *Ibid.* s.235—see Chap. 5, para. 5.205.
[22] *Ibid.* Pt. VII—see Chap. 5, paras. 5.202–5.269.
[23] *Ibid.* s.368—see Chap. 6, paras. 6.127–6.129.
[24] Public Health Act 1936, s.92(1)(*a*)—see Chap. 3, paras. 3.08–3.18.
[25] *Ibid.* s.94(2)—see Chap. 5, paras. 5.44–5.45.
[26] Housing Act 1985, s.331(2)(*c*) or s.338(1)—see Chap. 7, paras. 7.23–7.24 and 7.45.
[27] *Ibid.* Pt. III.
[28] *e.g.* Arden & Partington, *Housing Law* (1983), Arden, *Manual of Housing Law* (3rd ed. 1986) and Hughes, *Public Sector Housing Law* (1987).

numbers in a house having regard to the space available, will not displace existing occupants, but rely on a reduction occurring as existing occupants move out of their own accord and prevent new residents moving in until the number has been reduced to below the limits set.

Obligation to ensure re-housing

The obligation to secure re-housing arises in certain specified circumstances where the occupying household is displaced and "suitable alternative residential accommodation on reasonable terms" is not otherwise available.[29]

9.25

The term "suitable alternative residential accommodation on reasonable terms" is not defined, but guidance may be obtained from decisions by the courts on similar terms used in the Rent Acts[30] and on the definition given to a similar term in respect of the overcrowding provisions of the 1985 Housing Act.[31]

The phrasing of the obligation suggests that the authority need not provide the accommodation itself, but may make arrangements for the provision of that accommodation (*e.g.* the authority may have an agreement with a housing association enabling the authority to allocate accommodation managed by that association).

There are four specified circumstances which trigger the authority's obligation. These are:

9.26

(a) Where the occupying household is displaced by the acquisition of land by an authority possessing compulsory purchase powers.[32] It is clear that the acquisition may be made either by agreement or compulsorily, provided that the authority has the power to acquire compulsorily. Such displacement could be caused by an authority other than the local housing authority, but the obligation to secure re-housing will usually fall to the local housing authority.[33] In certain circumstances, however, the obligation will be on the authority exercising the power, for example, a Development Corporation, Commission for New Towns, or the Development Board for Rural Wales.[34]

(b) Displacement caused by the making or acceptance of a

---

[29] s.39(1) of the Land Compensation Act 1973.
[30] For a discussion on the interpretation under the Rent Acts see Arden & Partington, *Housing Law* (1983), and Megarry, *The Rent Acts* (1967).
[31] s.342 of the Housing Act 1985—see Chap. 7, para. 7.18.
[32] Land Compensation Act 1973, s.39(1)(*a*).
[33] *Ibid.* s.39(7). Where the re-housing authority is not the authority causing the displacement, the displacing authority is required to compensate the re-housing authority by s.42.
[34] *Ibid.* s.39(8)

OTHER MATTERS: EVIDENCE, COUNCIL HOUSES, COMPENSATION

"housing order" or "undertaking."[35] For these purposes, a "housing order" is[36]:
  (i) a demolition or closing order in respect of a house (or part) unfit for human habitation[37];
  (ii) a closing order in respect of part of a house in multiple occupation[38]; or
  (iii) an obstructive building order.[39]
  And an "undertaking" is[40] one accepted in lieu of—
  (iv) an improvement notice in respect of a dwelling in a Housing Action or General Improvement Area[41]; and
  (v) a demolition or closing order as mentioned in (i) or (ii).
(c) Displacement caused by the "improvement" of buildings or the "redevelopment" of land previously acquired for such improvement or redevelopment by an authority possessing compulsory purchase powers.[42] In this context, "improvement" includes enlargement or alteration and "redevelopment" includes change of use.[43] The improvement or redevelopment need not be carried out by the authority, provided that it was originally acquired by that authority for such improvement or redevelopment.[44]
(d) Permanent displacement resulting from the service of an improvement notice.[45] No obligation arises where the displacement is temporary during the carrying out of works,[46] or if the displaced occupier chooses not to return after the works.[47]

9.27 No obligation is owed to a displaced occupier where:

(a) the acquisition of the land by the authority (as in para. 9.26(a))

---

[35] Land Compensation Act 1973, s.39(1)(*b*).
[36] *Ibid.* s.39(9), referring to s.29(7A) inserted by Sched. 2, para. 23 to the Housing (Consequential Provisions) Act 1985.
[37] Housing Act 1985, s.265—see Chap.5, paras. 5.115–5.150.
[38] *Ibid.* s.368—see Chap. 6, paras. 6.127–6.129.
[39] *Ibid.* ss.283–288.
[40] Land Compensation Act 1973, s.39(9), referring to s.29(7A) inserted by Sched. 2, para. 23 of the Housing (Consequential Provisions) Act 1985.
[41] Housing Act 1985, s.211—see Chap.5, paras. 5.208–5.228.
[42] Land Compensation Act 1973, s.39(1)(*c*).
[43] *Ibid.* s.29(7A) inserted by the Housing (Consequential Provisions) Act 1985, Sched. 2, para. 23.
[44] *G.L.C.* v. *Holmes* [1986] Q.B. 989.
[45] ss.214 and 215 of the Housing Act 1985—see Chap. 5, paras. 5.221–5.227 and 5.238–5.243.
[46] This would still amount to "housing arrangements" which the authority is required to be satisfied are adequate—see Chap. 5, para. 5.205.
[47] s.39(6A) of the Land Compensation Act 1973, inserted by s.130 and Sched. 13 to the Housing Act 1974.

is a result of a blight notice served by the occupier under section 192 of the Town and Country Planning Act 1971[48];
(b) the occupier is a trespasser or has been allowed to occupy the building pending its demolition or improvement[49];
(c) the occupier has been advanced money for the purpose of obtaining alternative accommodation[50];
(d) in the case of para. 9.26(a) or (c), the occupier was not residing at the accommodation at the time of the publication of the notice of the compulsory purchase order before confirmation, or the date of the publication of a Bill (*i.e.* special or local Act), or the date of an agreement to purchase[51]; and
(e) in the case of para. 9.26(b) or (d), the occupier was not residing at the accommodation at the date the order was made, the notice served or the undertaking accepted.[51]

Disturbance payments

9.28 An occupier displaced as a result of one of the circumstances noted in para. 9.26 or as result of the "improvement" or "redevelopment" carried out by a registered housing association[52] on land it had previously acquired, is entitled to a disturbance payment.[53] In this context "improvement" includes enlargement or alteration and "redevelopment" includes change of use.[54]

9.29 The disturbance payment is to cover the "reasonable expenses of the person entitled to the payment in removing from the land from which he was displaced."[55]

The assessment will depend on the particular case and its merits and circumstances. In *Glasgow Corp.* v. *Anderson*[56] it was said that it should cover "not only the immediate expenses of the physical transfer of furniture and fittings but also those reasonable expenses which could be shown to flow from, and be incurred as a natural and direct consequence of the necessity to remove from the old house and set in the new . . ." And, that there was "no reason to think that, in particular appropriate cases, the cost of such operations as redecoration or even rewiring a house or part of a house might not be included."

9.30 Where the person is displaced from a dwelling which has been structurally modified to meet the special needs of a disabled person (even if

---

[48] Land Compensation Act 1973, s.39(2).
[49] *Ibid.* s.39(3) as amended by s.130 of and Sched. 13 to the Housing Act 1974.
[50] *Ibid.* s.39(5).
[51] *Ibid.* s.39(6).
[52] Registered under the Housing Association Act 1985.
[53] Land Compensation Act 1973, s.37(1).
[54] *Ibid.* s.37(9) referring to s.29(7A) as inserted by Sched. 2, para. 23 to the Housing (Consequential Provisions) Act 1985.
[55] s.38(1)(*a*) of the Land Compensation Act 1973.
[56] (1970) S.L.T. 225.

that person is not the applicant) and assistance would be received under section 29 of the National Assistance Act 1948 for making those modifications, the reasonable cost of making comparable modifications to the new dwelling are added to the removal costs.[57]

Compensation may be paid to cover the loss of any trade or business if that was carried on at the land from which the person was displaced.[58]

Any dispute as to the amount of a disturbance payment is to be referred to and settled by the Lands Tribunal.[59]

9.31 The authority responsible for making the disturbance payment is the authority making the acquisition, the order, accepting the undertaking, serving the notice or carrying out the improvement or redevelopment, or the housing association carrying out the improvement or redevelopment.[60]

9.32 To qualify for a disturbance payment, the person must have been in lawful possession of the land at the relevant time, which is as noted in para. 9.26(d) and (e).[61] Lawful possession in this context appears to include a weekly tenancy,[62] but not a lodger or person merely having a right of occupation (a licence).

A person is displaced in certain circumstances even if no notice to treat has been served.[63]

Where the person displaced will be entitled to other compensation under any other Acts or an owner-occupier's supplement there will be no entitlement to a disturbance payment.[64]

Home loss payment

9.33 In addition to the disturbance payment as compensation toward the costs involved in removing, a displaced occupier may be entitled to a home loss payment, which, as the name implies, is intended as compensation towards the loss of the home.

9.34 There are various criteria which must be satisfied for a displaced occupier to qualify for a home loss payment. The displacement must have occurred on or after October 17, 1972,[65] and must be as a result of one of the following:

(a) the compulsory acquisition of an interest in the dwelling.[66]
This circumstance is not satisfied if the occupier gives up

---

[57] Land Compensation Act 1973, s.38(3).
[58] *Ibid.* s.38(1)(*b*) and (2).
[59] *Ibid.* s.38(4).
[60] *Ibid.* s.37(1).
[61] *Ibid.* s.37(3).
[62] *Newey* v. *Liverpool C.C.* (1982) 14 H.L.R. 73.
[63] Land Compensation Act 1973, s.37(1)(*a*).
[64] *Ibid.* s.37(2)(*b*) and (*c*).
[65] *Ibid.* s.29(9).
[66] *Ibid.* s.29(1)(*a*).

possession prior to the authority being authorised to acquire an interest in the dwelling, but once authorisation has been given, it is not necessary for the occupier to be required to give up possession.[67]

(b) The making of a "housing order" or the acceptance of an "undertaking."[68] For these purposes a "housing order" is[69]:

   (i) a demolition or closing order in respect of a house (or part) unfit for human habitation[70];

   (ii) a closing order in respect of part of a house in multiple occupation[71]; or

   (iii) an obstructive building order.[72]

   And an "undertaking" is[73] one accepted in lieu of—

   (iv) an improvement notice in respect of a dwelling in a Housing Action or General Improvement Area[74]; and

   (v) a demolition or closing order as mentioned in (i) or (ii).

   In the case of an undertaking accepted in lieu of an improvement notice, the displacement must be permanent and not temporary while works are in progress (even if the occupier decides not to return to the improved dwelling).[75]

(c) Permanent displacement resulting from the service of an improvement notice.[76] Again the displacement must be permanent and not temporary during the carrying out of works.[77]

(d) Displacement caused by the "improvement" of buildings or the "redevelopment" of land previously acquired for such improvement or redevelopment by an authority possessing compulsory purchase powers.[78] In this context, "improvement" includes enlargement or alteration and "development"

---

[67] Land Compensation Act 1973, s.29(3).
[68] *Ibid.* s.29(1)(*b*).
[69] *Ibid.* s.29(7A), inserted by Sched. 2, para. 23 to the Housing (Consequential Provisions) Act 1985.
[70] Housing Act 1985, s.265—see Chap. 5, paras. 5.115–5.150.
[71] *Ibid.* s.368—see Chap. 6, paras. 6.127–6.129.
[72] *Ibid.* ss.283–288.
[73] Land Compensation Act 1973, s.29(7A), inserted by Sched. 2, para. 23 to the Housing (Consequential Provisions) Act 1985.
[74] Housing Act 1985, s.211—see Chap. 5, para. 5.208–5.229.
[75] Land Compensation Act 1973, s.29(3A), inserted by s.130 of and Sched. 13 to the Housing Act 1974. In *R.* v. *Islington L.B.C., ex p. Casale* (1985) 18 H.L.R. 146, it was held that although extensive improvement and alteration had been carried out (involving a reduction of the internal area, the loss of two bedrooms and a change of address as the access door was removed to another street) the dwelling was still the same dwelling and there was no displacement.
[76] Land Compensation Act 1973, s.29(1)(*b*) as amended by s.130 of and Sched. 13 to the Housing Act 1974.
[77] *Ibid.* s.29(3A) inserted by s.130 of and Sched. 13 to the Housing Act 1974, and see note 62 above.
[78] *Ibid.* s.29(1)(*c*) as amended by s.130 of and Sched. 13 to the Housing Act 1974.

OTHER MATTERS: EVIDENCE, COUNCIL HOUSES, COMPENSATION

includes change of use.[79] The improvement or redevelopment need not be carried out by the authority, provided that it was originally acquired by that authority for such improvement or redevelopment.[80]

(e) Displacement caused by the "improvement" or "redevelopment" carried out by a registered housing association[81] on land it had previously acquired.[82] In this context, "improvement" includes enlargement or alteration and "redevelopment" includes change of use.[83]

9.35 In addition, the occupier must have occupied the whole (or a substantial part) of the dwelling as his sole or main residence for at least five years prior to displacement.[84] Occupying or residing successively in different "dwellings" in the same building counts as occupying the same dwelling; and "dwelling" means a room or rooms not constructed or structurally adapted for use as a separate dwelling.[85]

For the five year qualifying period, the occupier must have had an interest or right to occupy the dwelling.[86] Such interest or right would be any legal interest, a statutory tenancy, a restricted contract, or a right of occupation under a contract of employment.[87] However, where the occupier has such an interest or right at the time of displacement, and resided at the dwelling as a spouse or child of a person with such a right or interest and succeeded that person, that period of residence is counted.[88]

9.36 The amount of a home loss payment is currently three times the rateable value of the dwelling, but not less than £150 and not more than £1,500.[89]

A home loss payment must be claimed by the person entitled to it, and such claim must be made in writing and with such information as the responsible authority reasonably requires to satisfy itself that the claimant is entitled to the payment.[90] The claim may be made at any

---

[79] Land Compensation Act 1973, s.29(7A), inserted by Sched. 2, para. 23 to the Housing (Consequential Provisions) Act 1985.
[80] *G.L.C.* v. *Holmes* (1985) 18 H.L.R. 131.
[81] Registered under the Housing Association Act 1985.
[82] s.29(1)(*d*) of the Land Compensation Act 1973, added by Sched. 5 to the Housing Rents and Subsidies Act 1975 and amended by s.156 of and Sched. 23 to the Rent Act 1977, and the Housing (Consequential Provisions) Act 1985.
[83] s.29(7A) of the Land Compensation Act 1973 as inserted by Sched. 2, para. 23 to the Housing (Consequential Provisions) Act 1985.
[84] Land Compensation Act 1973, s.29(2).
[85] *Ibid.* s.32(5).
[86] *Ibid.* s.29(2)(*b*).
[87] *Ibid.* s.29(4).
[88] *Ibid.* s.32(3).
[89] *Ibid.* s.30(1). The multiplier and the limits may be altered by the Secretary of State by order—*ibid.* s.30(2).
[90] *Ibid.* s.32(1).

time within six years from the date of displacement,[91] and must be paid within three months of the date of the claim.[92]

The home loss payment is to be claimed from, and paid by, the authority (or housing association) responsible for the action which caused the displacement (see para. 9.34).[93] **9.37**

Other compensation

There are other forms of compensation that an occupier may be entitled to as a result of action taken by the local housing authority. These are outside the scope of this book, but include well-maintained payments in respect of the maintenance of an unfit dwelling acquired by the authority,[94] and compensation orders,[95] in respect of premises which are a statutory nuisance and where a magistrates' court makes a conviction. **9.38**

---

[91] Land Compensation Act 1973, s.32(1), as amended by s.114 of the Local Government Planning and Land Act 1980.
[92] *Ibid.* s.32(2).
[93] *Ibid.* s.29(1), as amended by s.130 of and Sched. 13 to the Housing Act 1974.
[94] See the Housing (Payments for Well Maintained Houses) Order 1982 (S.I. 1982 No. 1112).
[95] s.35 of the Powers of Criminal Courts Act 1973.

APPENDIX 1

EXAMPLE INSPECTION REPORTS

The following reports are given as examples to suggest style, content and layout.

REPORT ON INSPECTION OF NO.15 CHADWICK HOUSE,
NASSAU TERRACE, SIMONSTON

Inspector	J. Snow
Date of inspection	December 4, 1986
Tenant	Mr & Mrs A. T. Enant
Landlord	Maxwell Sweet, 22 Old Street, Simonston
Tenancy commenced	March 17, 1979
Rent	£23.17 p.w. (excl.)
Rates	£10.23 p.w.
Household consists of	The tenants and their daughter (aged 3 years—born 03/09/1985)
Equivalent number	2.0 persons
Permitted number	Given in the rent book as 5.0 persons

N.B.—For the purposes of this report:
The terms "left" and "right" refer to the left hand side and right hand side of the dwelling when inside and facing the front access door. Room sizes are estimates (unless otherwise stated) based on the figures given in Table II of section 326(3) of the Housing Act 1985.

General description

The premises known as Chadwick House, Nassau Terrace, Simonston, is a purpose-built eight storey block of 44 double level dwellings (maisonettes).

Access to the individual dwellings is by way of common staircases in attached turrets to each flank end of the block, giving access onto open-sided balconies to the second, fourth, and sixth floors to the front of the block. The front main wall to the block faces approximately north-west. The construction of the block is non-traditional, and appears to include "no-fines" concrete, and also dense reinforced concrete (particularly for cross walls and floor/ceiling slabs). The roof to the block is flat and covered with felt. The front and rear main walls are faced externally with render, although under-window panels to the rear walls are faced with brickwork. The exposed areas of the flank walls are faced externally with brickwork. The walls to the staircase turrets are faced

APPENDIX I

externally with render. Windows to the block are single glazed, metal framed casements. The access balconies are formed by a projection of about one metre of the concrete floor/ceiling slabs. There are also private balconies to the lower floors of 33 of the maisonettes (those on the second/third, fourth/fifth and sixth/seventh floors) all with access from the main living rooms. Refuse disposal is by means of chutes, with disposal points in the access turret to the left flank end, at common landings, provided with hoppers.

No. 15 Chadwick House is a double level dwelling (maisonette) sited on the sixth and seventh floors and centrally. It consists of two (bed) rooms, a combined bathroom and W.C. compartment to the upper floor; and a (living) room (with a small private balcony to the rear), a kitchen/diner and an entrance hall (with staircase off) to the lower floor.

Space heating provision consists of electric elements set in the floor to the lower floor rear (living) room and the lower floor passage, and an electric radiant bar heater to the lower floor rear (living) room. Water heating is by means of electric immersion heaters. Clothes drying facilities consist of an electrically heated cabinet to the lower floor front left kitchen, the cabinet vented to the kitchen at low level and to the external air (by ducting) at high level.

Details of inspection—Internal

Upper floor front right bathroom
  Facilities
           wash hand basin, with hot and cold water thereto; bath, with hot and cold water thereto; and W.C. basin, with low level flushing cistern thereto.
  Defects:
  1. Slight mould spotting to the surface of the polystyrene tiles to the ceiling, in particular to the area adjacent to the front main wall.
  2. Slight mould growth to the surfaces of the window frames.
  3. Inadequately sealed joint between the wash hand basin and the adjacent wall surface, with a gap (of about 25mm) between the ceramic tile splash-back and the wash hand basin.
  4. Loose ceramic tile to the splash-back to the wash hand basin.
  5. Inadequately sealed joint between the bath and the adjacent wall surfaces, in particular the sealant is cracked and part missing.
  6. Missing ceramic tile to the boxing between the bath and the front main wall surface.
  7. Peeling wall paper to the right party wall, exposing uneven plaster to that wall.
  8. Damp affected plaster to the front main wall generally.
  9. Mould growth to the surface of the front main wall, in particular concentrated to an area close to the ceiling.
  10. Ill fitting plywood cover to the service ducting to the left internal wall, in particular with gaps around the pipes leading into the service ducting.

N.B. The ceiling was covered with polystyrene tiles and its condition could not be properly assessed.

EXAMPLE INSPECTION REPORTS

Upper floor front left (bed) room
Size—over 110 sq. ft.
Defects:

11. Damp affected plaster to the window reveals.
12. Damp affected plaster to the front main wall, generally.

N.B. It appeared that the front main wall had been lined internally.

Upper floor rear (bed) room
Size—over 110 sq. ft.
Defects:

13. Fracture to the joint between the rear main wall and the left party wall.
14. Fracture and loose plaster in the joint between the left party wall and the ceiling, and onto the left party wall close to the rear main wall.
15. Cracked plaster at joint between the front internal wall and the left party wall.
16. Missing plaster to the rear main wall, in particular to an area above the window opening.
17. Cracked putty pointing to the window glazing.
18. Hair-line cracking to the plaster to the reveals to the window opening, extending onto the rear main wall.

N.B. It appeared that the rear main wall had been lined internally. It was noted that there was a portable electric convector heater to this room. There was evidence that mould growth had been cleaned off the surfaces of the rear main wall and the right party wall (adjacent to the rear main).

Upper floor landing and lower/upper staircase
No obvious defects.

Lower floor entrance hall
Defects:

19. Damp and perished plaster to the left internal wall, concentrated in the area of adjacent to the floor and extending up about one metre.
20. Damp and perished plaster to the right party wall, in particular to the area adjacent to the floor.
21. Unsealed, unprimed and unpainted timber repairs to the frame to the front access door.
22. Damp affected plaster to the front main wall to the cupboard containing the electricity meter.
23. Peeling wall paper to the right internal wall and front internal wall (the walls forming the electricity meter cupboard), exposing damp and perished plaster to those walls, in particular to the area adjacent to the floor.
24. Unhung door to the gas meter cupboard to the left internal wall.
25. Cracked and bulging and damp affected plaster to the ceiling, in particular to the area adjacent to the front access door.

APPENDIX I

26. Slight mould spotting to the surface to the ceiling, in particular to the area adjacent to the front access door.
27. Area of missing plaster skim to the left reveal to the front access door opening, exposing damp and perished plaster to that reveal.
28. Damp and perished plaster to the reveals to the front access door opening generally.
29. Cracked and loose plaster to the right reveal to the front access door opening.
30. Damp and perished plaster to the right internal wall below the staircase.
31. Damp affected plaster to the understairs soffit.
32. Damp affected plaster to the rear internal wall, in particular to the area adjacent to the floor and extending up about 450mm.
33. Rotting timber to the skirting board to the walls to the entrance hall generally.

Lower floor front left kitchen/diner
Facilities

   stainless steel sink/drainer unit, with hot and cold water thereto; and gas cooking facilities.

Defects:

34. Peeling plastic surface to the worktop adjacent to the sink/drainer unit.
35. Inadequately sealed joint between the sink/drainer unit and the adjacent wall surface.
36. Uneven and bulging ceramic tiles to the splash-back to the sink/drainer unit and worktop.
37. Damp and perished plaster to the front main wall, generally.
38. Damp and perished plaster to the reveals to the window opening.
39. Damp affected plaster to the ceiling, in particular to the area adjacent to the front main wall.
40. Damp affected plaster to the left party wall, generally.
41. Damp affected plaster to the rear internal wall, in particular to the area adjacent to the floor and extending up about one metre.
42. Damp affected plaster to the right internal wall, concentrated to the area adjacent to the floor.
43. Missing cover to the top ventilator to the front store cupboard.
44. Damp affected plaster to the walls to the front store cupboard, in particular to the areas adjacent to the floor and extending up about one metre.
45. Rotting timber to the skirting boarding to the walls generally.

Lower floor rear (living) room
Size—over 110 sq. ft.
Defects:

46. Damp and perished plaster to the front internal wall, in particular to the area adjacent to the floor and extending up about 500mm.

EXAMPLE INSPECTION REPORTS

47. Broken thermo-plastic tiles to the floor, exposing damp affected concrete to the floor.
48. Damp affected plaster to the rear main wall, in particular to the area adjacent to the door opening to the rear private balcony.
49. Rotting timber to the skirting boarding to the front internal wall.

Miscellaneous

50. The wiring to the electrical installations to the dwelling appear likely to be dangerous, and should be checked in accordance with the Regulations of the Institution of Electrical Engineers.

External

Defects:

51. Hair-line cracking to the render to the front main wall to the dwelling generally.
52. Open joints between the reveals and the window sub-frames to the upper floor front left window opening and the lower floor left window opening.
53. Open joints between the reveals and the frame to the front access door to the dwelling.
54. Cracked putty pointing to the window glazing to the front elevation generally.

N.B. The condition of the roof above this dwelling could not be inspected at this time.

Comments on conditions noted at No. 15 Chadwick House

At the time of this inspection the weather was mild (the temperature between 11° and 13°C), and cloudy with sunny periods, with a light to moderate wind from the south-west.

The presence of dampness was confirmed using a Protimeter Diagnostic Mark III.

In addition to disrepair resulting from a lack of proper and adequate maintenance, the main problems are those of condensation and mould growth directly related to the design and construction of the block.

In my opinion, these problems result from the following deficiencies:

(a) the lack of adequate thermal insulation provided by the fabric of the block;
(b) the presence of cold-bridges in the design and construction of the block;
(c) the lack of a properly designed and appropriate space heating system to this dwelling;
(d) the lack of a properly designed ventilation system to the dwelling; and
(e) the exposed position of the block and dwelling, which exacerbates the other deficiencies.

The fabric of the block does not appear capable of providing adequate thermal insulation. This will mean that heat introduced into the dwelling can readily

APPENDIX I

escape through the fabric while leaving internal surfaces relatively cold. Warm, moisture laden air coming into contact with such surfaces will be cooled, increasing the relative humidity of that air. If the relative humidity exceeds 70 per cent., mould growth can become established. If the air is cooled to below its dew-point, it will give up some of the water vapour in the form of condensation, which, in addition to allowing mould spore germination and mould growth to occur, may cause damage to the structure of the block.

The design and construction of the block also incorporates cold bridges (points at which heat is more readily conducted through the structure). At such points, the surface temperature will be lower than that of adjacent areas. Examples of such cold-bridges are the floor/ceiling slabs where they are extended to form the access balconies to the front elevation, and the private balconies to the rear elevation; these act like fins on a radiator, exposing a large surface area which will quickly dissipate heat from the floor/ceiling slabs.

This dwelling also lacks a properly designed and appropriate space heating system capable of economically raising temperatures throughout the dwelling to reasonable levels, and of maintaining such levels. Because of this deficiency, parts of the dwelling will remain unheated and relatively cold. Warm, moisture laden air migrating to these parts will be cooled, thus raising its relative humidity.

Although the dwelling is provided with means for natural ventilation, it lacks a properly designed ventilation system capable of ensuring that moisture laden air is quickly and safely taken out of the dwelling from those areas where moisture production will be high (*i.e.* the kitchen and the bathroom). Natural ventilation relies on wind speed and direction, and frequently results in excessive ventilation which cools surfaces and wastes heat. In addition, where the opening is to windward, the moisture laden air will be forced further into the dwelling (even around closed doors).

These deficiencies are exacerbated by the exposed position of the block and this dwelling, which will increase the ventilation heat loss through leakages around closed windows and doors and the natural ventilation provided by opened windows and will further increase the heat loss through the fabric.

Because of inadequate thermal insulation provided by the fabric of the block, inadequate provision for space heating, and the exposed position of the block and this dwelling, I am of the opinion that the dwelling will be expensive and exceptionally difficult to heat adequately.

It is clear that the evidence of dampness resulting from condensation and the associated mould growth is related to the design and construction of the block including the cold-bridges. It is also apparent that the problems have been occurring for some time, and have (to some extent) been recognised by the landlord. This recognition has resulted in attempts having been made to alleviate the problems by lining the internal surfaces of some external walls to increase the thermal insulation. However, this lining has not been carried out adequately, in that:

    (a) the materials used have been of an inadequate standard;
    (b) the lining lacks a vapour check to reduce the possibility of interstitial condensation; and

(c) the amount of insulation provided has been insufficient to reduce the thermal transmittance coefficients to adequate levels.

In any event, merely increasing the thermal insulation of the fabric will only reduce the rate of heat lost through the fabric; it is still necessary to make provision to enable adequate levels of heat to be provided within the dwelling, to ensure that heat is properly distributed throughout the dwelling and to provide for an effective means of ensuring that moisture levels can be reduced and maintained at low levels.

A second problem is that the design, construction and repair of the block is such that water can penetrate through the fabric. Having penetrated into the "no-fines" concrete, the moisture is able to drain down to the relatively impervious dense concrete floor/ceiling slabs. As the moisture is not able to drain away, it rises up (by capillary action) the plaster of walls internally, giving the appearance of rising dampness at those levels.

To bring the dwelling to a satisfactory condition it is necessary to:

(i) carry out properly appropriate works to remedy the defects noted to the dwelling;
(ii) investigate thoroughly and identify the source of water penetration into the dwelling, and to carry out appropriate works to prevent any recurrence of that penetration;
(iii) increase the thermal insulation of the fabric of the block and this dwelling to adequate levels;
(iv) provide and maintain proper and adequate space heating facilities to the dwelling, such facilities to be capable of economically heating the whole of the dwelling; and
(v) install and maintain extractor fans (connected to humidity sensitive switches) to the kitchens and the bathrooms of the dwelling.

The condition of the dwelling known as No. 15 Chadwick House, Nassau Terrace, Simonston is such that I am satisfied that it is prejudicial to health, and therefore a statutory nuisance as defined by section 92(1)(a) of the Public Health Act 1936.

Having regard to the matters set out in section 604 of the Housing Act 1985, I am also satisfied that the dwelling known as No. 15 Chadwick House, Nassau Terrace, Simonston, should be declared unfit for human habitation under that Act.

Having regard to the age, character and locality, and to the possible prospective life of the dwelling known as No. 15 Chadwick House, Nassau Terrace, Simonston, I am of the opinion that the landlord is in breach of the repairing covenant that may be implied into the tenancy agreement by section 11 of the Landlord and Tenant Act 1985.

I am also of the opinion that the landlord is in breach of the duty of care owed by virtue of section 4 of the Defective Premises Act 1972.

It is suggested that the landlord is asked to provide the following information:

(a) the date of construction of the block, or the date of acquisition;
(b) full details of the design and construction of the block and dwelling, if known;

APPENDIX I

(c) details of the works of thermal insulation carried out; and
(d) details of any works proposed to be carried out to the dwelling and the block.

J. Snow F.I.E.H., F.R.S.H.

The following part report is given to suggest a layout for a report on re-inspection.

REPORT ON RE-INSPECTION OF NO. 15 CHADWICK HOUSE, NASSAU TERRACE, SIMONSTON

Inspector F. Green
Date of re-inspection March 12, 1987
Tenant Mr & Mrs A. T. Enant
Landlord Maxwell Sweet, 22 Old Street, Simonston

N.B.—This re-inspection was based on the conditions as noted in the report on inspection dated December 4, 1986 and carried out by J. Snow F.I.E.H., F.R.S.H.

Details of inspection (December 4, 1986)	**Details of re-inspection** (March 12, 1987)

Internal

Upper floor front right bathroom

1. Slight mould spotting to the surface of the polystyrene tiles to the ceiling, in particular to the area adjacent to the front main wall. — Still present.
2. Slight mould growth to the surfaces of the window frames. — Still present.
3. Inadequately sealed joint between the wash hand basin and the adjacent wall surface, with a gap (of about 25 mm) between the ceramic tile splash-back and the wash hand basin. — Still present.
4. Loose ceramic tile to the splash-back to the wash hand basin. — Still present.

EXAMPLE INSPECTION REPORTS

5. Inadequately sealed joint between the bath and the adjacent wall surfaces; in particular the sealant is cracked and part missing.   Still present.
6. Missing ceramic tile to the boxing between the bath and the front main wall surface.   Still present.
7. Peeling wall paper to the right party wall, exposing uneven plaster to that wall.   Still present.
8. Damp affected plaster to the front main wall generally.   Still present.
9. Mould growth to the surface of the front main wall, in particular concentrated in an area close to the ceiling.   Still present, but now to the surface of the wall generally.
   9a. Mould growth to the surface of the right party wall, in particular to the area adjacent to the front main wall.
10. Ill fitting plywood cover to the service ducting to the left internal wall, in particular with gaps around the pipes leading into the service ducting.   Still present.

Upper floor front left (bed) room

11. Damp affected plaster to the window reveals.   Still present.
12. Damp affected plaster to the front main wall, generally.   Still present.
    12a. Mould growth to the surface of the window reveals.
    12b. Mould growth to the surface of the front main wall generally.
    12c. Mould growth to the surface of the ceiling, in particular to the area adjacent to the front main wall.

Comments and conclusions

At the time of this re-inspection the weather was cold (the temperature about 2°C), and dry, but with a strong wind from the north-east.

The presence of dampness was confirmed using a Protimeter Diagnostic Mark III.

Based on the conditions noted during this re-inspection I would support the comments and conclusions made in the report of inspection dated December 4, 1986. In particular:

APPENDIX I

(a) that there is disrepair resulting from a lack of proper and adequate general and specific maintenance;
(b) that the design and construction of the block is such that the dwelling is unable to cope with the water vapour produced through the normal biological and domestic activities of the household without high relative humidity levels or actual condensation occurring, particularly during the colder periods of the year; and
(c) that the design, construction and repair of the block is such that water can penetrate through the fabric, and, as the moisture is not able to drain away, it rises up the plaster of walls internally giving the appearance of rising dampness at levels well above ground floor.

Based on this re-inspection, I am of the opinion that the condition of the dwelling has deteriorated since the inspection of December 4, 1986.

The condition of the dwelling known as No. 15 Chadwick House, Nassau Terrace, Simonston is such that I am satisfied that it is still prejudicial to health, and therefore a statutory nuisance as defined by section 92(1)(a) of the Public Health Act 1936.

Having regard to the matters set out in section 604 of the Housing Act 1985, I am also satisfied that the dwelling known as No. 15 Chadwick House, Nassau Terrace, Simonston should still be declared unfit for human habitation under that Act.

Having regard to the age, character and locality, and to the possible prospective life of the dwelling known as No. 15 Chadwick House, Nassau Terrace, Simonston, I am of the opinion that the landlord remains in breach of the repairing covenant that may be implied into the tenancy agreement by section 11 of the Landlord and Tenant Act 1985.

I am also of the opinion that the landlord remains in breach of the duty of care owed by virtue of section 4 of the Defective Premises Act 1972.

Included in the comments and conclusions to the report on inspection was the recommendation that the landlord should be asked to provide certain information. To date, that information has not been provided.

F. Green F.I.E.H., F.R.S.H

Appendix 2

EXAMPLE SPECIFICATIONS

These examples are given to illustrate the style and content of specifications for notices. The first is a suggested general statement on practice, standards and materials for inclusion in every notice.

General

Properly make good all work (including internal decorative work) disturbed during the carrying out of the specified works. All rubbish and spillage occasioned during the carrying out of the specified works, whether internally or externally, to be properly and thoroughly cleared and carted away.

Unless otherwise specified, materials used in the carrying out of the specified works must be materials which have been tested, licensed, certified or approved by an independent third party (*e.g.* the British Board of Agrément, and the British Standards Institution).

And, unless otherwise specified, the practice followed in the carrying out of the specified works must be in accordance with the latest relevant Codes of Practice issued by an independent third party (*e.g.*, the British Standards Institution and the Specification for the Improvement, Repair and Rehabilitation of Property as published by the Institution of Environmental Health Officers). And, all work to be carried out by or under the close supervision of experienced tradesmen, skilled in the particular type of work.

Where appropriate, the necessary applications must be made for Building Regulation approval, and nothing in this notice shall be taken as implying such approval.

All work to be executed in the most careful and efficient manner to cause as little inconvenience as possible to the occupier and to adjoining occupiers and to the public. All necessary precautions must be taken to prevent damage to the existing structure and to the decorations both internally and externally. Temporary screens, temporary roofs and dust sheets must be provided where necessary to protect the existing structure, decorations, furniture and effects.

Any hazardous materials, toxic substances, or solvents used must be properly transported and stored and contained and labelled in accordance with the requirements of current relevant British Standards and Codes of Practice and regulations.

Internal

Ceilings

Dampness from unidentified source
Thoroughly investigate the source of the dampness to the ceiling, and carry out such works as may be necessary to prevent a recurrence of the dampness.

And, hack off any damp affected plaster to the ceiling, and properly re-plaster, using good quality plaster-board and set with good quality plaster floated off to a smooth and even finish flush with the adjacent plaster.

Provide ceiling

Provide a ceiling, and for that purpose properly fix plaster-boarding, scrimming the joints and edges, and properly skim the ceiling with plaster floated off to a smooth and even finish.

Take down and replaster

Take down the existing ceiling, and properly fix new plaster-boarding, scrimming the joints and edges, and properly skim the ceiling with plaster floated off to a smooth and even finish.

Cracked, loose and uneven

Hack off the cracked and loose and uneven plaster to the ceiling and properly re-plaster the stripped areas using good quality plaster-board and set with good quality plaster floated off to a smooth and even finish flush with the adjacent areas.

Doors

Disrepair to front access door/frame

Thoroughly overhaul the front access door and door frame, carrying out such works as may be necessary to ensure that the door is capable of being readily opened and securely closed, and that when closed is close-fitting to the frame.

Disrepair to internal door frame

Thoroughly overhaul the door frame, cutting out the broken or otherwise defective timber and properly splicing in new sound timber and sealing and making good the joints, and carrying out such other works as may be necessary to ensure that the door is capable of being readily opened and closed, and that when closed is close-fitting to the frame.

Renew internal door

Provide and properly hang a new door to the door frame, and provide and properly fit door furniture to the new door. And, carry out such works as may be necessary to ensure that the door is capable of being readily opened and closed, and that when closed is close-fitting to the frame and stop.

Windows

Disrepair to traditional sash window frame

Thoroughly overhaul the window sashes and frame, cutting out any rotted or broken or otherwise defective timber and properly splicing in new sound timber, renewing any broken or worn or otherwise defective sash cords, cutting out any cracked or holed glazing and properly re-glazing using good quality glass and putty, and carrying out such other works as may be necessary to ensure that the sashes are capable of being readily opened and securely closed.

Disrepair to timber casement window frame

Thoroughly overhaul the timber casement window frame and opening lights, cutting out any rotted or broken or otherwise defective timber and properly

EXAMPLE SPECIFICATIONS

splicing in new sound timber, renewing any broken or otherwise defective hinges and stay-bars, cutting out any cracked or holed glazing and properly re-glazing using good quality glass and putty, and carrying out such other works as may be necessary to ensure that the opening lights are capable of being readily opened and securely closed.

Disrepair to metal casement window frame

Thoroughly overhaul the metal casement window frame and opening lights, renewing any broken or otherwise defective hinges and stay-bars, cutting out any cracked or holed glazing and properly re-glazing using good quality glass and putty, and carrying out such other works as may be necessary to ensure that the opening lights are capable of being readily opened and securely closed.

Broken glazing

Cut out the broken glazing to the side hung opening light to the window, and properly re-glaze using good quality glass of appropriate thickness and type and good quality putty or glazing beading.

Electricity

Electric wiring requires thorough checking

The wiring to the electrical installations to the dwelling to be inspected by a competent electrical engineer in accordance with the requirements of the regulations of the Institution of Electrical Engineers, and any works found to be necessary so as to satisfy the said regulations to be carried out.

Inappropriate siting of electricity supply head

To prevent access to the electricity supply head and distribution board by young children, properly re-position the supply head and distribution board, or contain the supply head and distribution board within a properly constructed and secure cupboard.

Facilities

Inadequately sealed joint between wash hand basin and wall

Thoroughly rake out the joint between the wash hand basin and the adjacent wall surface, and, using good quality materials, properly seal and make water-tight the joint.

Provide wash hand basin

Provide and properly install a wash hand basin. Such wash hand basin to be securely fixed and the joint between the basin and the adjacent wall surface effectively sealed and made water-tight. And, provide a ceramic tile splash-back to the adjacent wall surface, and for that purpose provide and properly fix ceramic tiles to that wall, and properly grout the joints between the tiles to leave the splash-back to a smooth and even and impervious finish. And, provide and maintain a supply of hot water and a supply of cold water to taps fitted to the wash hand basin, such works to be carried out having regard to the requirements of the local water authority. And, properly connect the said wash hand basin to a trapped waste pipe of suitable material, such waste pipe to be properly clipped and supported and to be so designed as to be capable of safely carrying away the waste water from the wash hand basin into the drainage system.

Renew existing wash hand basin

Take out the existing wash hand basin, and provide and properly and securely fit a good quality new wash hand basin. And, properly connect the said basin to a trapped waste pipe of good quality, capable of safely carrying the waste water and discharging it in a proper manner into an existing drainage inlet. And, provide and fit good quality taps to the basin, and properly connect the taps to the hot and cold water supplies. And, properly seal and make water-tight the joint between the wash hand basin and the adjacent wall surface.

Leaking waste pipe to wash hand basin

Take out the existing waste pipe serving the wash hand basin, and provide a new trapped waste pipe of a suitable material. And, properly connect the waste pipe to the wash hand basin and to the existing soil and ventilation pipe. And, provide and properly fix sufficient clips adequately to support the waste pipe, and leave the waste pipe in such condition as to be capable of safely carrying away the waste water from the said basin and discharging it into the drainage system.

Provide sink/drainer unit

Provide and properly install a sink/drainer unit and cupboard to the kitchen. Such sink/drainer unit and cupboard to be securely fixed and the joint between the unit and any adjacent wall surface effectively sealed and made water-tight. And, provide a ceramic tile splash-back to any adjacent wall surface, and for that purpose provide and properly fix ceramic tiles to that surface, and properly grout the joints between the tiles so as to leave a smooth and even and impervious finish to the splash-back. And, provide and maintain a supply of hot water and a supply of cold water to taps fitted to the sink/drainer unit, such works to be carried out having regard to the requirements of the local water authority. And, properly connect the said sink/drainer unit to a trapped waste pipe of suitable material, such waste pipe to be properly clipped and supported and to be so designed as to be capable of safely carrying away the waste water from the sink/drainer unit into the drainage system.

Mould growth

Mould growth to walls and ceiling

Carefully remove all traces of mould growth from the surface of the walls and ceiling to the room, and strip off any decorative finish to the infected areas. And, thoroughly cleanse the stripped areas using a one-to-four solution of domestic bleach in slightly soapy water. And, thoroughly sterilise the cleansed areas using a toxic wash of quaternary ammonium compounds (or other equally effective and approved material), carefully following the supplier's instructions.

Walls

Dampness from unknown source

Thoroughly investigate the source of dampness to the wall, and carry out such works as may be necessary to prevent a recurrence of the dampness.

And, for that purpose open-up the wall to expose the cavity, and clear out any rubble or debris found, and renew any defective damp proof course, and ensure that any damp proof course properly joins with any damp proof membrane, and carry out any other appropriate works found to be necessary. And, properly re-instate the wall, and hack off the damp affected plaster to the wall, and properly re-plaster the stripped areas, using good quality plaster floated off to a smooth and even finish, flush with the adjacent areas.

Provide plaster to unplastered walls
Thoroughly prepare and key the wall surfaces and, using good quality materials, properly plaster and skim, floating off to a smooth and even finish.

Uneven wall plaster
Hack off the uneven plaster to the wall, and properly re-plaster the stripped areas, using good quality plaster floated off to a smooth and even finish flush with the adjacent areas.

Fractured internal wall
Thoroughly investigate the cause of the fracture to the left internal wall, and carry out such works as may be necessary to prevent further structural movement of the wall. And, thoroughly rake out the fracture, removing all loose plaster and debris. And, using good quality materials, properly fill and make good the fracture, leaving the repaired areas to a smooth and even finish flush with the adjacent areas.

Floors

Uneven solid floor
Take up the existing uneven solid floor. And, properly reconstruct the floor, and for that purpose provide a 100mm consolidated hardcore base blinded with 25m of sand, and provide a damp proof membrane of 1000 gauge polythene sheeting turned up 175mm on all edges, and cover with 100mm of concrete. The floor to be finished with a sand and cement screeding and thermo-plastic tiles laid to a smooth and even and impervious surface.

Unsafe suspended timber floor
Properly reconstruct the unsafe suspended floor. And for that purpose, take out all rotted or broken or otherwise defective timbers to the floor and properly renew using new and sound and properly seasoned timber. And, properly lay and fix timber boarding to the floor, and carry out such other works as may be necessary to leave the floor sound and even and in good order.

Thermal Insulation

Provide additional thermal insulation to walls and ceiling
Carry out such works as may be necessary to ensure that the nominal thermal transmittance coefficient of the external walls to the dwelling is reduced to a maximum of 0·6 watts per square metre per degree Celcius, and that the nominal thermal transmittance coefficient of the roofs (including the associated

ceilings) is reduced to a maximum of 0·35 watts per square metre per degree Celsius.

Provide external insulation to walls

Carry out works to ensure that the thermal transmittance coefficient of the external walls of the dwelling is reduced to a maximum of 0·6 watts per square metre per degree Celsius, and for that purpose—

To the external surfaces of the external walls and of the reveals to the window openings, and of return walls to balconies, properly apply insulation in the form of expanded polystyrene boards. Such boards to be of an appropriate quality, and of an appropriate thickness, and to be provided with a grooved face as a key for render.

The insulation boards to be fixed to the external surfaces of the walls and reveals by means of mushroom–headed expanding mechanical fixing pins, and the joints between the boards to be closely butt-jointed.

And, provide and properly fit proprietary window sills, copings for balconies and insulation stop-ends as necessary.

And, properly render the whole of the outer grooved face of the insulated boards with a water-proof render in a two coat work to a total thickness of at least 25mm.

And, properly make good all works disturbed, refixing as necessary all external pipework.

Or, properly carry out alternative and appropriate works of insulation to the external surfaces of the external walls and of the reveals to the window openings, and of return walls to balconies, effectively to reduce the thermal transmittance coefficient to the stated maximum level.

Provide internal insulation to walls

Carry out works to ensure that the thermal transmittance coefficient of the external walls is reduced to a maximum of 0·6 watts per square metre per degree Celsius, and for that purpose—

Properly line the internal surface of the external walls to the dwelling and of the reveals to any window and external door opening, using plaster-board and rigid gas-filled polyurethane board. Such plaster-board to be of at least 9mm thickness, and such polyurethane board to be of at least 20mm thickness. The plaster-board to be fixed to timber battens and noggins, and the polyurethane board to fill the spaces between the battens and noggins.

The timber grounds and battens and noggins to be vacuum pressure impregnated with preservative. The battens to be at least 50mm wide by 20mm thick and to be at 400mm centres and set on a ground of appropriate size, the noggins to be positioned as necessary to provide support to all edges of the laminated insulation board. The ground and battens and the noggins to be fixed to the walls by means of rust resistant nails, and to be separated from the surface of the walls by strips of 1,000 gauge polythene sheeting or of bitumen felt as protection from any dampness in the walls.

The polyurethane board to be carefully fitted to fill closely all of the spaces between the battens and noggins and grounds to the whole of the area to be dry-lined.

EXAMPLE SPECIFICATIONS

A vapour check to be provided to reduce the possibility of interstitial condensation. The vapour check to be of 1,000 gauge polythene sheeting fixed to the battens and noggins over the polyurethane board to the whole of the area to be lined. The jointing of the sheeting to be only at battens or noggins, and to be an overlap of at least 50mm.

The plaster-board to be fixed to the battens and noggins over the polythene vapour check using 12 S.W.G. galvanised clout nails at 50mm centres and set back at least 15mm from the edge of the board. Joints between boards and between boards and walls or ceilings to be properly scrimmed with 90mm wide hessian or jute scrim and sealed. Any external angles to be properly protected with proprietary corner protection.

The whole of the lined area to be skimmed with a coat of at least 5mm thick good quality plaster, floated off to a smooth and even finish, and to be properly made good at junctions with internal walls and ceilings and window and door frames.

And, properly refit and make good the old skirting boarding to the walls and architraving and to window and door openings, or, provide and properly fit new skirting boarding and architraving as necessary. And, provide and properly fit as necessary new internal window boards to any window openings. And, properly refix or reposition and refix all electric socket outlets and electric light switches ensuring that the covers to the switches and sockets are above the finished surface of the plaster skim coat.

Or, properly carry out alternative and appropriate works of insulation to the internal surfaces of the external walls and of the reveals to the window openings, effectively to reduce the thermal transmittance coefficient to the stated maximum level.

Ventilation

Provide extractor fans

Provide and properly fit electrically operated extractor fans, one to the kitchen and one to the bathroom. Such fans to be capable of providing the respective rooms with at least three and not more than 18 air changes per hour. The fans to be sited in the window or an external wall and as close to the ceiling as possible. Each fan to be connected to a humidity sensitive switch, such switch to be properly positioned remote from the fan (on an internal wall) and set so as to operate the respective fan when the relative humidity of that room reaches 65 per cent. at a temperature of 20°C, and also to be connected to a manually operated switch.

Space heating

Provide adequate space heating system

Make proper and appropriate provision for space heating based upon the calculations in British Standard B.S. 5449 Part I of 1977, and for that purpose provide and properly install a space heating system throughout the whole of the dwelling, or provide and properly install separate space heating units to each room and to the circulation areas. And, ensure that the said space heating facilities are of an appropriate type having regard to the construction of the dwelling, and are capable of economically raising temperatures throughout the dwelling to the following levels and of maintaining such levels, that is to say a minimum of 21° to the living room and to the bathroom, a minimum of 18°C to the kitchen and to the bedrooms, and a minimum of 16°C to the circulation areas.

External

Roofs

Overhaul
Thoroughly overhaul the roofs to the dwelling, including the associated flashings and fillets, and carry out such works as may be necessary to ensure that the roofs and flashings and fillets are left in a sound and water-tight condition.

Suspected defective roof timbers
Strip the whole of the tiles from the main roof, setting aside for re-use all sound tiles and thoroughly examine the roof timbers, removing all rotted or otherwise defective timbers and renew using new and well seasoned timber. And, properly re-cover the roof, using good quality materials matched to the original, and carrying out such works as may be necessary to leave the roof in a sound and water-tight condition.

Uneven felt to flat roof
Strip the whole of the felt from the back addition roof, and thoroughly examine the roof timbers. And, cut out any timbers found to be defective, and properly renew using new and sound and well seasoned timbers. And, properly re-felt the roof using good quality materials, properly jointed to the adjacent wall and finished at the eaves. And, properly re-form the flashing to the joint to the adjacent wall. And, finish the roof with surface dressing, and leave the roof in a sound and water-tight condition.

Rainwater goods

Misaligned eavesgutter
Thoroughly overhaul and re-align or renew the eavesgutter serving the front main roof, leaving the eavesgutter capable of safely carrying away the water from the roof and discharging it into the existing rainwater fall pipe.

Re-position rainwater pipe
Properly reposition and securely fix the rainwater fall pipe to the front main wall, ensuring that the pipe discharges in a proper manner into a drainage inlet.

Drainage

Relay gulley
Take out the existing gulley to the rear yard, and properly relay the drain and gulley so that the gulley is positioned correctly to receive the drainage from the

sink to the ground floor rear kitchen. And, properly back-fill and cover the drain, and re-form the yard surface.

Short waste pipe

Properly extend the existing short waste pipe serving the sink to the ground floor rear kitchen, ensuring that the said waste pipe discharges in a proper manner into the existing drainage system.

Leaking joints to soil/vent pipe

Rake out the existing joints to the soil and ventilation pipe to the rear main wall, and, using good quality materials, properly seal and make air-tight the joints.

Walls

Defective render

Hack off the areas of cracked and broken or otherwise defective render to the rear main wall. And, in a two coat work of appropriate thickness, properly re-render the stripped areas using good quality materials, thoroughly keyed to the wall and finished to match the existing.

Fractured

Hack off the render to the front main wall adjacent to the fracture, and thoroughly examine the exposed brickwork. And, cut out all fractured, perished or otherwise defective bricks, and effectively stitch and renew the brickwork using new sound bricks and good cement mortar. And, in a two coat work of appropriate thickness, properly re-render the stripped areas using good quality materials, thoroughly keyed to the wall and finished to match the existing.

Windows

Rotted timber sub-frame

Cut out the rotted timber from the sub-frame to the window frame to the ground floor front (living) room, and properly splice in new sound timber, sealing and making good the joints.

Cracked sill

Thoroughly rake out the crack to the concrete sill to the ground floor rear kitchen window opening, removing all debris. And, properly fill and make good the crack, leaving the sill in a sound condition.

Or, cut out the existing cracked sill, and, using good quality materials, properly re-form the sill ensuring that it is capable of draining surface water away from the window opening and that it is provided with a throating to the underside.

Cracked putty pointing

Cut out the cracked or otherwise defective putty pointing to the window glazing to the dwelling generally, and, using good quality putty, properly re-point the glazing, leaving the same safe and water-tight.

External paintwork

Flaking

Thoroughly rub-down the surfaces to the external timber to the dwelling generally, removing all flaking paintwork, and, thoroughly cleanse and prepare the surfaces. And properly stop and prime the surfaces, and apply at least one under-coat and one top-coat of good quality paint.

Yards and garden walls

Uneven yard surface

Take up the existing uneven rear yard surface. And, on a base of 150mm of well rammed hard-core, properly re-surface the yard with a suitable hard and impervious material laid to a smooth and even finish, and provided with such falls as may be necessary to ensure the drainage of surface water to existing drainage inlets.

Cracked retaining wall

Take down the cracked and leaning stonework retaining wall to the rear yard. And, properly rebuild the wall using good quality stonework (or other suitable materials) set in good quality cement mortar, and rake out and repoint the joints with good quality cement mortar and leave the wall sound and safe.

Broken fences

Remove any existing broken and part missing fencing to the front garden. And, provide and properly and securely fix new fence posts, and fix fencing of suitable material, leaving the fence sound and safe.

Houses in multiple occupation—fire precautions

Separate basement from ground floor

Carry out such works as may be necessary to ensure that the whole of the basement floor is properly separated from the ground floor by means of a partition and door positioned at the top of the basement/ground staircase. The said partition to be constructed of materials which are designated as providing a minimum fire resistance of not less than one half hour. The said door to be of fire resisting construction to comply with British Standard B.S. 476 Part 8 1972, and to be hung on at least two metal hinges having a melting point of not less than 800°C, and to be set in a door frame which has stops of not less than 25mm, and is made self-closing by means of a spring device which will hold the door firmly closed, and is free of any device or means of holding the door open (except an electro-magnetic device connected to the detection/alarm system). The said partition and door, together to be so constructed to provide a minimum fire resistance of not less than one half hour.

And, carry out such works as may be necessary to ensure that those parts of the ceilings and staircase soffits to the basement floor which are directly below any passage, any staircase and any designated escape route to the ground floor are of adequate fire resistance. In any case where such ceilings and staircase soffits are of sound lath and plaster or of defective plaster-boarding, take down the existing ceiling and provide new ceiling by means of plaster-boarding of not less than 4.5mm thickness or other suitable and approved material, and scrim the joints and edges, and properly skim the ceiling with plaster floated off to a smooth and even finish.

Provide internal escape route

Carry out such works as may be necessary to ensure that each of the staircases between each of the floors throughout the house is properly protected and separated from each floor by means of a properly constructed partition and a door at the top of each such staircase run and a door at the base of each such staircase run. The said partition to extend from the floor level to the ceiling level of each floor, and to be constructed of materials which are designated as providing a minimum fire resistance of not less than one half hour. Each of the said doors to be of fire resisting construction to comply with British Standard B.S. 476 Part 8 1972, and to be hung on at least two metal hinges having a melting point of not less than 800°C, and to be set in a door frame which has stops of not less than 25mm, and is made self-closing by means of a spring device which will hold the door firmly closed, and is free of any device or means of holding the door open (except an electro-magnetic device connected to the detection/alarm system). Each of the said partitions together with the associated doors, to be so constructed to provide a minimum fire resistance of not less than one half hour.

And, carry out such works as may be necessary to ensure that the soffits to each of the staircases throughout the house, and those parts of the ceilings to each floor within the house which are directly below any passage, any staircase and any designated escape route to the floor above are of adequate fire resistance. In any case where such ceilings and staircase soffits are of sound lath and plaster or of defective plaster-boarding, take down the existing ceiling and provide new ceiling by means of plaster-boarding of not less than 4.5mm thickness or other suitable and approved material, and scrim the joints and edges, and properly skim the ceiling with plaster floated off to a smooth and even finish.

And, carry out such works as may be necessary to ensure that any cupboard within a protected staircase or within an escape route is properly constructed of materials having a standard of fire resistance of not less than one half hour, and is fitted with fire resisting and self closing doors, or fire resisting doors which are kept locked shut when not in use. In the case of doors which are not self closing, the doors are to be marked with a permanent notice of 10mm high plain letters stating "THESE DOORS TO BE KEPT LOCKED SHUT WHEN NOT IN USE."

And, carry out such works as may be necessary to ensure that all glazing within a protected staircase or within an escape route is of fire resisting quality, and that the panels of such glazing do not exceed 0s34 square metres in area, and that all such glazed panels are fixed permanently shut.

And, ensure that all protected staircases and all escape routes to the house are maintained free of any gas or electrical cooking or heating appliances.

And, ensure that any gas meter within a protected staircase or escape route:

(a) conforms to British Standard B.S. 4161 Part 3 of 1968 in respect of the construction of the meter; or
(b) is housed within a cupboard constructed of materials having a standard of fire resistance of not less than one half hour, and which is fitted with fire resisting and self closing doors, or fire resisting doors which

APPENDIX 2

are kept locked shut when not in use and marked with a permanent notice in 10mm high plain letters stating "THESE DOORS TO BE KEPT LOCKED SHUT WHEN NOT IN USE";

or

(c) is connected to a service pipe which incorporates a thermal cut-off device set to cut off the flow of gas in the event of the temperature exceeding 95°C.

Protect doors to individual lettings

Carry out such works as may be necessary to ensure that each and every door to any room within the house which opens onto a common passage or escape route is a fire resisting and a self closing door, that is to say that each such door:

(a) is of fire resisting construction to comply with British Standard B.S. 476 Part 8 of 1972; and

(b) is hung on at least two metal hinges which have a melting point of not less than 800°C; and

(c) is set in a door frame which has stops which are not less than 25mm wide and is so hung and adjusted that when closed the door is close-fitting to the frame and stop, with no gap between the door and frame and between the door and floor greater than 4mm; and

(d) is made self closing by means of a spring device which will hold the door firmly closed; and

(e) is free of any device or means of holding the door open, except an electro-magnetic device connected to the detection and alarm system.

Provide escape lighting

Provide and properly install and maintain an electrical system of escape lighting to all protected staircases and escape routes to the house. Such escape lighting system to be capable of sufficiently illuminating any exit and any directional signs and any changes of floor levels, to enable persons to leave the house without the assistance of normal lighting. And such system of escape lighting to be capable of maintaining that level of illumination for not less than one hour from the time of the failure of the normal electricity system, and generally to be in accordance with the requirements of British Standard B.S. Part 1 of 1975.

Provide fire alarm system

Provide and properly install and maintain an electrical fire alarm system to the house. Such fire alarm system to include break glass release button call points of sufficient number and sited in any escape route to the house at points adjacent to each of the downward flights of stairs to each floor level, and generally to be in accordance with the requirements of British Standard B.S. 5839 Part 1 of 1980.

And, provide and properly install and maintain smoke detectors to the house. Such smoke detectors to be in circuit with the electrical fire alarm system, and to be so sited to be capable of detecting effectively the presence of smoke in all protected staircases and in all escape routes and in all shared bathrooms and in all store rooms. In all kitchens and in all boiler rooms within the house, heat

EXAMPLE SPECIFICATIONS

detectors are to be provided and properly installed and maintained in lieu of smoke detectors, and such heat detectors are to be in circuit with the electrical fire alarm system. Generally, such smoke and heat detectors are to be in accordance with the requirements of British Standard B.S. 5839 Part 1 of 1980.

Provide telephone

Provide and properly install and maintain a telephone or telephones connected to the British Telecom telephone system. Such telephone or telephones to be sited in escape routes to be readily available for calling the fire brigade and other emergency services.

Provide fire instruction notices

Provide and properly fix and maintain fire instruction notices throughout the house. Such fire instruction notices to give clear instructions of the action to be taken in the event of a fire, and the method of calling the fire brigade. In addition to the fire instruction notices, provide and properly fix notices giving clear indication in plain lettering of not less than 10mm height, of the direction of escape routes and of alternative or secondary escape routes.

Provide fire extinguishers

Provide and properly maintain throughout the house hand appliances for the fighting of fires. Such appliances to be of the following type:

(a) in each of the escape routes and positioned adjacent to the staircase on each floor, two water type extinguishers of a specification to satisfy the requirements of the fire authority; and
(b) in each kitchen to the house, one fire blanket; and
(c) in each boiler room to the house, one nine litre foam extinguisher and two buckets of sand.

And, each such hand appliance provided for the fighting of fires to be inspected and certified at least once every 12 months by an independent and competent person, and the certificate issued clearly displayed adjacent to the relevant appliance.

APPENDIX 3

CHARACTERISTICS OF SOURCES OF DAMPNESS

The assessment of the main cause of dampness affecting any dwelling is based on a thorough investigation of the dwelling to check for the presence of various characteristics which will help to identify the main cause of the dampness. Once the main cause has been identified, further investigations may be necessary to determine the remedial works and/or steps necessary to prevent any recurrence.

Some of the characteristics of construction damp are:

    (i) Appears relatively soon after occupation following construction, rehabilitation or conversion works.
    (ii) Efflorescent salts (white) on the affected surfaces.
    (iii) Unrelated to weather conditions, although may become more quickly apparent during colder weather.
    (iv) Mould growth may be present, particularly in areas where air movement slow (cupboards, etc).

Some of the characteristics of rising dampness are:

    (i) Affected areas to ground floor level and walls only and usually concentrated from floor level to about 1 metre above (but may be higher, and may be affected by water-proofing compounds in plaster).
    (ii) Mould growth unlikely to be present, because of the inhibiting affect of salts.
    (iii) Skirting boarding affected by dampness.
    (iv) Upper limit of affected area clearly and sharply defined ("tidemark" effect), with change from damp to dry within 20–30mm.
    (v) Affected areas tend to be damper in humid weather, drier in dry weather, because of the absorption of atmospheric moisture by the hygroscopic salts, but otherwise unaffected by weather or time of year.
    (vi) The presence of hygroscopic salts, particularly nitrates, identified by analysis of surface scrapings and wall paper.
    (vii) Dampness present within the fabric of the wall.

Some of the characteristics of hygroscopic salt contamination are:

    (i) Dampness still present after source of dampness has been remedied.
    (ii) Mould not normally present.

CHARACTERISTICS OF SOURCES OF DAMPNESS

- (iii) Affected areas tend to be damper in humid weather, drier in dry weather, because of the absorption of atmospheric moisture by the hygroscopic salts, but otherwise unaffected by weather or time of year.
- (iv) The presence of hygroscopic salts, particularly nitrates, identified by analysis of surface scrapings and wall paper.
- (v) Dampness not present in the fabric of the wall.

Some of the characteristics of penetrating dampness are:

- (i) Can affect ceilings as well as walls and not limited to any floor level.
- (ii) Usually can be directly associated with a defect externally (*e.g.* slipped or missing slates, leaking eavesgutters), or at weakest points of structure (*e.g.* below and to sides of window and door openings).
- (iii) May be concentrated in spots on external cavity walls.
- (iv) Obviously directly related to rainfall.
- (v) Mould may be present, but limited to damp affected areas which may not be room corners and cupboards.
- vi) Nitrate hygroscopic salts not present, and other hygroscopic salts not usually found.
- (vii) Dampness present within the fabric of the wall, often high levels within the fabric and lower at the surface.

Some of the characteristics of traumatic dampness are:

- (i) Dampness usually very localised, and sometimes amount of dampness very high.
- (ii) Not associated with changes in weather conditions, but may follow warmer weather immediately after extreme cold.
- (iii) Mould growth may be present.
- (iv) Hygroscopic and efflorescent salts not present.

Some of the characteristics of condensation are:

- (i) Concentrated on surfaces likely to be colder than others, *e.g.* corners and junction of external walls, above window and door openings, at junction of walls with solid floor, and where ceiling below balcony.
- (ii) Most apparent during colder periods of year, from October to April, but not otherwise related to weather.
- (iii) Often affects room without heat source and with more than one external surface, and with walls facing prevailing wind.
- (iv) Mould growth present, usually spreading beyond visibly damp affected areas.

APPENDIX 3

(v) Damp affected areas not clearly defined, a gradual change from damp to dry.
(vi) Skirting boarding usually dry.
(vii) Hygroscopic salts not present.
(viii) No (or considerably less) dampness within the fabric.

APPENDIX 4

SOME REFERENCE MATERIAL AND ADDRESSES

Reference books, etc

Bassett, *Environmental Health Procedures* (2nd ed., 1987, H. K. Lewis & Co.)
Arden, *Manual of Housing Law* (3rd ed., 1987, Sweet & Maxwell)
Martyn & Lloyd-Jones, *Housing Disrepair* (1985, Longman)
Luba, *Repairs: Tenants' Rights*; (1986, Legal Action Group)
Hughes, *Public Sector Housing Law* (2nd ed., 1987, Butterworths)
Bassett & Davies, *Environmental Health* (15th ed., 1981, H. K. Lewis & Co.)
Arden & Partington, *Housing Law* (1983, Sweet & Maxwell)
Encyclopedia of Housing Law and Practice (Sweet & Maxwell)
Encyclopedia of Environmental Health Law and Practice (Sweet & Maxwell)
Cross, *Evidence* (6th ed., 1985, Butterworths)
Woodfall's Landlord and Tenant (Sweet & Maxwell)
Hill and Redman's Law of Landlord and Tenant (Butterworths)
Collins, *Hypothermia—the facts* (1983, Oxford University Press)
Turiel, *Indoor Air Quality and Human Health* (1985, Stanford University Press, California)
Housing Law Reports (bimonthly) (Sweet & Maxwell)
The County Court Practice (Butterworths)
The Supreme Court Practice (Sweet & Maxwell)
Stone's Justices' Manual (Butterworths)
Phipson, *Evidence* (13th ed., 1984)
CIBS Guide (CIBS) (in particular, Chapter A3)
Environmental Health Professional Practice Series (Institution of Environmental Health Officers)
Defects Action Sheets (Building Research Establishment) (about 8–10 per annum)
House's Guide to the Construction Industry (House Information Services Ltd.)
Housing Year Book (Institute of Housing)

Magazines

Roof (Shelter) (bimonthly)
Environmental Health (Institution of Environmental Health Officers) (monthly)

APPENDIX 4

Environmental Health News (Institution of Environmental Health Officers) (weekly)
Housing (Institute of Housing) (monthly)
Inside Housing (Institute of Housing) (weekly)
Estates Gazette (Estates Gazette) (weekly)
Legal Action (Legal Action Group) (monthly)
Journal of the Royal Society of Health (Royal Society of Health) (bimonthly)

Addresses

Institution of Environmental Health Officers;
Chadwick House
Rushworth Street
London SW1
Tel: 01–928 6006

Institute of Housing;
9 White Lion Street
London N1
Tel: 01–837 4280

Royal Society of Health;
38A St George's Drive
London SW1
Tel: 01–630 0121

Royal Institute of Chartered Surveyors;
12 Great George Street
London SW1

The Institution of Structural Engineers;
11 Upper Belgrave Street
London SW1

Royal Institute of British Architects;
66 Portland Place
London W1

Institution of Electrical Engineers;
Savoy Place
London WC2

British Board of Agrément;
P.O. Box 195
Bucknalls Lane
Garston
Watford WD2 7NG

SOME REFERENCE MATERIAL AND ADDRESSES

Building Research Establishment;
Garston
Watford WD2 7JR

Chartered Institution of Building Services;
222 Balham High Road
London SW12

Building Standards Institute;
2 Park Street
London WC1

Shelter;
88 Old Street
London EC1

Legal Action Group;
242 Pentonville Road
London N1

INDEX

abatement notice,
  appeal against, 5.24
  content of, 5.14—5.19
  non-compliance with, action for,
    court hearing, 5.28—5.41
    laying information, 5.25—5.27
  owner, meaning, 5.10—51.3
  service of, 5.05—5.09
acari — *see* **mites**
acarus siro — *see* **mites**
access,
  door — *see* **door**
  multiple occupation, house in, 6.39
  safe, 2.28
accident,
  protection against, 2.08
accommodation,
  bed and breakfast, 6.25
  human habitation, fitness for — *see*
    human habitation
  local housing authority, general duties of,
    1.06
  statutory nuisance, application of
    standard, 3.10—3.11
  suitable alternative, meaning, 7.18—7.19
accounts,
  control order, 6.178—6.179
action area — *see* **housing action area**
addresses,
  list of, App. 4
administration,
  house condition survey, 2.101
aflatoxins — *see* **dampness**
age,
  house, of,
    effect on standard of repair, 3.53
  person, of,
    overcrowding of room, 7.09
agency agreement,
  works, execution by authority under,
    5.261
agent,
  meaning, 7.16
air,
  moisture content, 8.04
Airey,
  non-traditional construction, 2.77
alarm,
  fire, 6.63

allergic respiratory disease — *see*
  respiratory disease
alveolitis,
  fungal damage giving rise to, 8.16
amenity,
  space, access to, 2.28
  standard,
    accommodation to which applicable,
      3.61
    compulsory improvement — *see*
      compulsory improvement
    fixed bath, 3.62
    fixed shower, 3.62
    full, 3.63, 3.64
    interpretation of standard, 3.62—3.66
    meaning, 3.62
    minimum, 3.60
    proposed target standard, 3.66A
    reduced, 3.63, 3.65
    sink, 3.62
    wash hand basin, 3.62
    water closet, 3.62
anobium punctatum — *see* **dampness**
appeal,
  abatement notice, against, 5.24
  control order, against,
    grounds of, 6.161
    refusal to revoke, 6.185—6.190
    revocation after hearing, 6.163—6.166
    works in progress, effect of, 6.168
  conviction, against, 5.51
  demolition order, against, 5.119—5.123
  fire, notice requiring adequate means of
    escape, 6.120—6.125
  improvement notice, against, 5.245—
    5.252
  intention to purchase, notice of, against,
    5.161—5.169
  management scheme, against, 6.174—
    6.177
  multiple occupation, order in respect of
    — *see* **multiple occupation, house in**
  nuisance order, against, 5.46
  overcrowding notice, against, 7.65—7.66
  prohibition notice, against, 5.24
  repair notice, against, 5.85—5.89,
    5.100—5.103
arachnida — *see* **mites**
area improvement,
  general — *see* **general improvement area**

353

INDEX

area improvement—*cont.*
  housing — *see* **housing action area**
  local housing authority, general duties of, 1.05
artificial lighting — *see* **lighting**
aspergillus — *see* **dampness**
assessment,
  housing conditions, of, 2.02—2.04
  premises, of, 3.18
asterostroma spp. — *see* **dampness**
asthma,
  fungal damage giving rise to, 8.16
  mites responsible for, 8.23
atmosphere,
  balance, 8.63
  biological activities, moisture from, 8.62—8.83
  domestic activities, moisture from, 8.62—8.83
authentication,
  demand, of, 4.06—4.10
  document, of, 4.06—4.10
  notice, of, 4.06—4.10
  order, of, 4.06—4.10
authorisation,
  representative of local authority, of, 2.64

B.I.S.F. — *see* **British Iron and Steel Federation**
balcony,
  multiple occupation, house in, 6.39
bark borer beetle — *see* **dampness**
basidiomycotina — *see* **dampness**
basin,
  w.c. — *see* **w.c. compartment**
  wash hand, as standard amenity, 3.62
bath,
  fixed, as standard amenity, 3.62
bathroom,
  conditions, 2.17
  facilities, 2.37
  fixed bath, 3.62
  fixed shower, 3.62
  moisture production, 8.78
  standard amenity, 3.62
  ventilation, 2.19
  wall surface, 2.32
  wash hand basin, 3.62
  waste water, 2.29
bed and breakfast accommodation,
  multiple occupation, house in, 6.25
bedroom standard,
  overcrowding, 7.19
bedsit,
  multiple occupation, house in, 6.25
beetle — *see* **dampness**
biological activities,
  atmospheric moisture from, 8.62—8.83

bird,
  mites infesting, 8.22
bison,
  non-traditional construction, 2.87
boot,
  non-traditional construction, 2.85
briefing,
  housing condition survey, 2.104
British Iron and Steel Federation,
  non-traditional construction, 2.78
British Museum,
  beetles, indentification of, 8.19
British Rail,
  operational land owned by, 5.158
brown rot — *see* **dampness**
bugs,
  infestation of, 3.23
building,
  demolition — *see* **demolition**
  fabric of, dampness penetrating — *see* **dampness**
  listing of, 5.132—5.133
  meaning, 2.03
  multiple occupation, house in, deemed to be, 6.15—6.17
  new, standards for control of, 3.05
  part of, closing order in respect of, 5.151
  unoccupied, security of, 5.152—5.153
buprestidae spp. — *see* **dampness**
butane,
  moisture emission, 8.79

Cambridge University,
  beetles, identification of, 8.19
caravan,
  human habitation, fitness for, 3.33
  overcrowding in, 7.67
  personal comfort, interference with, 3.55
  substantial disrepair, in, 3.48
carpoglyphus lactis — *see* **mites**
cat,
  mites infesting, 8.22
ceiling,
  condensation, investigation of, 8.110
  defects, 2.34
  falling plaster, 3.23
cellar fungus — *see* **dampness**
cerambycidae spp. — *see* **dampness**
character,
  repair, effect on standard of, 3.53
charging order,
  human habitation, unfitness for, 5.91
  improvement notice, 5.256—5.257
  personal comfort, interference with, 5.194
  substantial disrepair, house in, 5.194
cheese mite — *see* **mites**
cheyletiella yasguri — *see* **mites**

INDEX

child,
  home, effect of, 2.04
  physical injury, causes of, 2.15
chimney,
  flue, condensation in, 8.60
  stack, defect in, 2.26
cladosporium — *see* **dampness**
clearance — *see* **slum clearance**
closing order,
  appeal against, right of, 5.140—5.143, 5.154—5.155
  British Rail, operational land owned by, 5.158
  circumstances giving rise to, 5.115
  demolition order, substitution of, 5.150
  determination of, 5.147—5.149
  enforcement, 5.144—5.146
  entry, right of, 5.156
  expenses, 5.157
  format, 5.137
  part of building in respect of, 5.151
  service of, 5.138—5.139
  statutory undertaker, land owned by, 5.158
  unoccupied building, security of, 5.152—5.153
clothes,
  condensation, investigation of, 8.111
  drying, 2.36, 2.39
  moisture production, 8.78
  washing, 2.36
code of practice,
  fire, means of escape in case of, 6.60
comfort — *see* **personal comfort**
committee,
  delegation of functions to, 1.11—1.14
common law,
  human habitation, fitness for, 3.21—3.23
compensation,
  control order, 6.178—6.179
  disturbance payment, 9.28—9.32
  home loss payment, 9.33—9.37
  other, 9.38
compulsory improvement,
  dwelling, 5.207
    exclusion from procedure, 5.207
    meaning, 5.205
    person having control of, meaning, 5.205
  general conditions necessary for, 5.206
  general improvement area, in — *see* **general improvement area**
  generally, 5.202—5.204
  housing action area, in — *see* **housing action area**
  housing arrangements, meaning, 5.205
  improvement notice,
    appeal against, 5.245—5.252
    charging order, 5.256—5.257

compulsory improvement—*cont.*
  improvement notice—*cont.*
    costs incurred, addressee's right to recover part of, 5.255
    demand for recovery of expenses, appeal against, 5.269
    enforcement of, 5.264—5.269
    entry, rights of, 5.253—5.254
    loans to cover costs, 5.258—5.260
    purchase notice, service of, 5.262—5.263
    service of, 5.238—5.243
    withdrawal of, 5.244
    works, execution by authority under agency agreement, 5.261
  long tenancy, meaning, 5.205
  owner, meaning, 5.205
  owner-occupier, meaning, 5.205
  provisional notice,
    copies, 5.235
    discussion on proposals, 5.236—5.237
    format, 5.234
    service of, 5.230.5.233
    representation, 5.229
compulsory purchase order,
  control order, after, 6.194—6.198
  displacement of occupier — *see* **occupier**
concrete,
  no-fines, 2.25, 2.75—2.76
condemned house,
  purchase of, 5.159—5.169
condensation,
  flue, in, 8.60
  investigation of,
    external, 8.110
    generally, 8.108—8.110
    internal, 8.110
    occupation details, 8.111
  measurement for, 8.95—8.96
  remedial works for, 8.112—8.116
  roof space, in, 8.58—8.59
  sub-floor space, in, 8.61
conditions,
  assessment of, 2.02—2.04
  bathroom, 2.17
  compulsory improvement, necessary for, 5.206
  health effects of — *see* **health**
  kitchen, 2.17
  local housing authority, general duties of, 1.06
  statutory nuisance, 3.09
  see also **house condition survey**
coniophora puteana — *see* **dampness**
construction,
  condensation, investigation of, 8.110
  legionella, spread of, 2.12
  non-traditional — *see* **non-traditional construction**

355

INDEX

construction—*cont.*
  process, water used in, 8.36—8.40
  traditional, 2.71
contagion,
  protection against, 2.08
contract,
  demolition, for, 5.135
control,
  order,
    accounts, 6.178—6.179
    appeal against, 6.160—6.168
    background to, 6.147—6.149
    compensation, 6.178—6.179
    compulsory purchase order after, 6.194—6.198
    effects of, 6.154—6.159
    entry, rights of, 6.180—6.182
    expiry, effects of, 6.191—6.193
    making of, 6.150—6.153
    management scheme,
      appeal against, 6.174—6.177
      preparation of, 6.169—6.173
    revocation,
      application for, 6.183—6.184
      effects of, 6.191—6.193
      refusal to revoke, appeal against, 6.185—6.190
  person having, 5.76—5.79
cooking,
  condensation, investigation of, 8.111
  facilities for, 3.44
  moisture production, 8.78
coprinus spp. — *see* **dampness**
Cornish unit house,
  type 1, 2.79
  type 2, 2.80
corridor,
  fire, means of escape in case of, 6.61
  multiple occupation, house in, 6.39
council house,
  compulsory improvement procedure, exclusion from, 5.207
  human habitation, fitness for, 5.69, 5.106
  sub-standard, procedure on, 9.18—9.22
court,
  evidence,
    expert witness, 9.03, 9.08—9.10
    generally, 9.02—9.03
    hearsay, rule of, 9.11—9.17
    principles of, 9.04—9.07
  local authority, challenge to action taken by, 2.41
  non-compliance with notice, action for, 5.28—5.41
  nuisance order, power to make, 5.42—5.45
Crown property,
  compulsory improvement procedure, exclusion from, 5.207

damage for dampness — *see* **dampness**
damp proof course,
  defects, 2.25
dampness,
  causes of, 2.16
  condensation,
    flue, in, 8.60
    investigation of,
      external, 8.110
      generally, 8.108—8.110
      internal, 8.110
      occupation details, 8.111
    measurement for, 8.95—8.96
    remedial works, 8.112—8.116
    roof space, in, 8.58—8.59
    sub-floor space, in, 8.61
  damp proof course,
    effect of, 2.25
    provision of, 8.41, 8.43, 8.48
  direct physical damage from, 8.07—8.19
  dry-lining,
    alternative to, 8.42
    provision of, 8.42
  effect of, 2.16
  fabric of building,
    measurement for,
      carbide meter method, 8.88—8.89
      generally, 8.84
      laboratory, 8.85—8.87
      moisture meter, 8.90—8.94
    penetration of, 8.49—8.54
  generally, 8.02
  human habitation, fitness for, 3.38
  meaning, 8.03—8.06
  membrane, provision of, 8.41, 8.43, 8.46
  mites, health threat resulting from — *see* **mites**
  mould fungal spores,
    aflatoxins, 8.28
    aspergillus, 8.28
    cladosporium, 8.28
    food,
      germination, for, 8.29
      spoilage, 8.28
    growth,
      generally, 8.28
      sampling of, 8.97—8.102
    health, effect on, 8.30—8.33
    liver cancer, as cause of, 8.28
    meaning, 8.27
    mucor, 8.28
    penicillium, 8.28
    prevention of, 8.33
    pullularia spp.8.28
    reproduction, 8.28
    sensitivity to, 8.31
    serpula lacrymans, 8.28
    size, 8.30
    stemphylium, 8.28

356

INDEX

dampness—*cont.*
  mould fungal spores—*cont.*
    wood rot, as cause of, 8.28
  relative humidity,
    meaning, 8.05
    measurement for, 8.95—8.96
    measurement of, 8.05
  rising, 8.41—8.48
  salt,
    contamination caused by, 8.08—8.10
    efflorescent, 8.10
    hygroscopic, 8.08, 8.09
  sources of,
    atmospheric balance, 8.63
    biological activities, from, 8.62—8.83
    characteristics of, App. 3
    condensation,
      flue, in, 8.60
      roof space, in, 8.58—8.59
      sub-floor space, in, 8.61
    construction process, water used in, 8.36—8.40
    domestic activities, from, 8.62—8.83
    fabric of building, penetration of, 8.49—8.54
    investigation of, 8.103—8.107
    moisture production, 8.78—8.81
    rising dampness, 8.41—8.48
    space heating, 8.64—8.70
    summary of, 8.34—8.35
    thermal insulation, 8.75—8.77
    traumatic defect, from, 8.55—8.57
    ventilation, 8.71—8.74
  spores,
    mould fungal, 8.27—8.33
    presence of, 8.11
    re-infection by, 8.13
    respiratory conditions, aggravation of, 8.16
  thermal insulation,
    effect on, 8.20—8.21
    source of dampness, as, 8.75—8.77
  timber,
    fungal damage,
      asterostroma spp., 8.14
      basidiomycotina, 8.12
      brown rot, 8.14
      cellar fungus, 8.14
      coniophora puteana, 8.14
      coprinus spp., 8.15
      donkioporia expansa, 8.14
      dry rot, 8.12—8.13
      moisture content, 8.11
      myxomycetes, 8.15
      oyster fungus, 8.14
      paxillus panuoides, 8.14
      peaziza spp., 8.15
      phellinus contiguus, 8.14
      pleurotus ostreatus, 8.14

dampness—*cont.*
  timber—*cont.*
    fungal damage—*cont.*
      pyronema domesticum, 8.15
      respiratory conditions, aggravation of, 8.16
      serpula lacrymans, 8.12—8.13
      slime mould, 8.15
      spores,
        presence of, 8.11
        re-infection by, 8.13
        respiratory conditions, aggravation of, 8.16
      white rot, 8.14
    insect damage,
      anobium punctatum, 8.17
      bark borer beetle, 8.18
      buprestidae spp., 8.18
      cerambycidae spp., 8.18
      death watch beetle, 8.17
      ernobius mollis, 8.18
      euophryum confine, 8.18
      forest longhorn beetle, 8.18
      furniture beetle, 8.17
      identification of beetles, 8.19
      jewel beetle, 8.18
      mealworm beetle, 8.18
      nacerdes melanura, 8.18
      pentarthrum huttoni, 8.18
      tenebrio mollitor, 8.18
      wharf borer beetle, 8.18
      wood boring weevils, 8.18
      xestobium rufovillosum, 8.17
    shrinking, 8.07
    swelling, 8.07
    unprotected, 8.07
  water vapour, 8.03—8.06
death watch beetle — *see* **dampness**
defects,
  access, 2.28
  ceiling, 2.34
  description of, 2.55—2.56
  doors,
    external, 2.30
    internal, 2.33
  eavesgutter, 2.27
  electric wiring, 2.14
  floors, 2.31
  foundations, 2.24
  gas pipework, 2.14
  health, effect on, 2.23—2.35
  roof, 2.26
  traumatic, dampness from, 8.55—8.57
  walls,
    external, 2.25
    internal, 2.32
  waste water, 2.29
  window, 2.35

INDEX

dehumidifier,
 heat and, 8.37
delegation of functions,
 local authority, by, 1.11—1.14
 local housing authority, by, 1.11—1.14
demand,
 authentication, 4.06—4.10
 format, 4.04—4.05
 service of, 4.11—4.16
 signing of, 4.10
demolition,
 contract for, 5.135
 cost of, 5.136
 order,
  appeal against, right of, 5.119—5.123
  building which becomes listed, 5.132—5.133
  circumstances giving rise to, 5.115
  closing order, substitution of, 5.131
  disinfestation of premises, 5.127—5.128
  enforcement, 5.124—5.126
  format, 5.116
  reconstruction, power to permit, 5.129—5.130
  service of, 5.117—5.118
  substitution of, 5.150
 time period, 5.134
Dennington Committee recommendations, 2.89
 see also **house condition survey**
dermanyssus gallinae — *see* **mites**
dermatophagoides pteronyssinus — *see* **mites**
direction,
 multiple occupation, as to — *see* **multiple occupation, house in**
disease,
 cause of, 2.05
disinfection — *see* **infestation**
displaced occupier — *see* **occupier**
disrepair — *see* **substantial repair**
disturbance payment,
 occupier displaced, obligations to, 9.28—9.32
document,
 authentication, 4.06—4.10
 format of, 4.04—4.05
 service of, 4.11—4.16
 signing of, 4.10
dog,
 mites infesting, 8.22
domestic activities,
 atmospheric moisture from, 8.62—8.83
donkioporia expansa — *see* **dampness**
door,
 external, 2.30
 fire, limit on spread of, 2.33
 handle, 2.30

door—*cont.*
 internal, 2.33
 lock, 2.30
drainage,
 human habitation,
  fitness for, 3.43
  house unfit for, 3.23
 multiple occupation, house in, 6.24, 6.26
 surface water, of, 2.28
 waste water, of, 2.29
dried fruit mite — *see* **mites**
dry rot fungus — *see* **dampness**
dry-lining,
 alternative to, 8.42
 provision of, 8.42
dust,
 mites contained in, 8.23—8.26
dwelling,
 assessment of, 2.02—2.04
 compulsory improvement — *see* **compulsory improvement**
 description of, 2.47—2.51
 existing, standards applicable to, 3.06—3.07
 inspection of,
  authorisation, 2.64
  equipment for, 2.62
  evaluation, 2.65—2.67
  form,
   basic information recorded, 2.44, 2.45
   defects, description of, 2.55—2.56
   description, 2.47—2.51
   multiple occupation, house in, 2.46
   other information, 2.57—2.58
   room, description of, 2.52—2.54
   use of, 2.43
  general aim, 2.40
  insurance, 2.63
  legal considerations, 2.41
  method, 2.59—2.61
  opinion, 2.65—2.67
  practical considerations, 2.42
  report, 2.68
 interior of, effect on well-being of occupant, 2.22
 interpretation of term, 3.07
 meaning, 2.03, 5.205, 7.15
 moveable, overcrowding in, 7.67
 new, standards for control of, 3.05
 person having control of, meaning, 5.205
 self-contained, 6.25
 temporary, overcrowding in, 7.67
dwelling-house,
 interpretation of term, 3.07

eavesgutter,
 blocked, 2.27
 dampness caused by, 8.53

INDEX

eavesgutter—*cont.*
  distorted, 2.27
  leaking, 2.27
  purpose, 2.27
electricity,
  defective wiring, 2.14
  multiple occupation, house in,
    maintenance, 6.142—6.146
    management, 6.37
    reconnection, 6.142—6.146
  space heating—*see* **space heating**
enforcement,
  closing order, of, 5.144—5.146
  compulsory improvement—*see*
    compulsory improvement
  demolition order, of, 5.124—5.126
  entry, powers of—*see* **entry, powers of**
  fire, notice requiring adequate means of escape, 6.126
  human habitation, house unfit for—*see*
    human habitation
  improvement notice, of, 5.264—5.269
  local housing authority, general duties of, 1.09
  multiple occupation—*see* **multiple occupation, house in**
  nuisance order, of, 5.47—5.50
  overcrowding—*see* **overcrowding**
  personal comfort, interference with—*see* **personal comfort**
  private individual, by, 3.02—3.04
  repair notice, of, 5.93—5.99
  statutory nuisance—*see* **nuisance**
  substantial disrepair—*see* **substantial disrepair**
entrance—*see* **access**
entry, powers of,
  closing order, 5.156
  control order, 6.180—6.182
  improvement notice,
    enforcement, 5.253—5.254
    obstruction, 1.19
    offence, 1.19
    other persons, powers of, 1.27—1.28
    purposes for which granted, 1.18—1.19
    statutory provisions, 1.15
    works, power to carry out, 1.32
  local authority officer, powers of, 1.21—1.23, 1.36—1.37
  multiple occupation, house in,
    obstruction, 1.23
    offence, 1.23
    officer, by, 1.21—1.23
    statutory provisions, 1.15
    warrant issued by magistrate, by, 1.21, 1.24—1.25
    works, power to carry out, 1.33—1.34
  obstruction,
    generally, 1.41—1.42

entry, powers of—*cont.*
  obstruction—*cont.*
    improvement notice, 1.19
    multiple occupation, house in, 1.23
    overcrowding, 1.26
    repair notice, 1.17
    slum clearance, 1.20
  overcrowding,
    obstruction, 1.26
    purposes, 1.26
  owner, power of, 1.40
  repair notice,
    obstruction, 1.17
    offence, 1.17
    purposes for which given, 1.16
    statutory provisions, 1.15
    works, power to carry out, 1.29—1.31
  slum clearance,
    obstruction, 1.20
    offence, 1.20
    purposes, 1.20
  statutory provisions, 1.15, 1.35
  warrant, 1.21, 1.24—1.25, 1.38—1.39
equipment,
  damage of, insurance, 2.63
  fire, in case of, 6.63
  inspection of dwelling, for, 2.62
ernobius mollis—*see* **dampness**
euophryum confine—*see* **dampness**
evaluation,
  dwelling, inspection of, 2.65—2.67
evidence,
  expert witness, 9.03, 9.08—9.10
  generally, 9.02—9.03
  hearsay, rule of, 9.11—9.17
  principles of, 9.04—9.07
expenses,
  human habitation, house unfit for, action to deal with, 5.70—5.75
  recovery of,
    abatement notice, 5.52—5.55
    closing order, 5.157
    prohibition notice, 5.52—5.55
    urgent statutory nuisance, 6.53—5.64

fabric of building,
  dampness in—*see* **dampness**
facilities,
  bathroom, 2.37
  kitchen, 2.36
  space heating, 2.38
  ventilation, 2.39
  w.c. compartment, 2.37
fire,
  door helps to limit spread of, 2.33
  means of escape in case of,
    additional legislation, 6.130—6.131
    adequate, notice requiring,
      appeal against, 6.120—6.125

INDEX

fire—*cont.*
  means of escape in case of—*cont.*
    adequate, notice requiring—*cont.*
      enforcement, 6.126
      grant-aid for works, 6.119
      service of, 6.114—6.118
    alarm, 6.63
    alternative legislation, 6.130—6.131
    codes of practice, 6.60
    corridor, 6.61
    examples, outline diagrams of, 6.63
    legislation, 6.130—6.131
    national standards, 6.59—6.60
    other equipment, 6.63
    passage, 6.61
    principles, 6.57
    provision of, 6.112—6.113
    recommendations, 6.60
    risk, reduction of, 6.58
    secondary lighting, 6.63
    securing that part of house is not used, 6.127—6.129
    separate letting,
      parts occupied as, 6.62
      room occupied as, 6.62
    staircase, 6.61

fitness,
  human habitation, for—*see* **human habitation**
  multiple occupation—*see* **multiple occupation, house in**

flatlet,
  multiple occupation, house in, 6.25

fleas,
  infestation with, 3.23

floor,
  condensation, investigation of, 8.110
  defects, 2.31
  sub-floor space, condensation in, 8.61

flour mite—*see* **mites**

flue,
  condensation in, 8.60

food,
  cooking, facilities for, 3.44
  mites, 8.22
  mould fungal spores,
    effect of, 8.28
    germination, 8.29
  multiple occupation, house in, 6.24, 6.26
  preparation, facilities for, 3.44

forest longhorn beetle—*see* **dampness**

form,
  dwelling, inspection of—*see* **dwelling**

format,
  closing order, of, 5.137
  demand, of, 4.04—4.05
  demolition order, of, 5.116
  notice, of, 4.04—4.05
  order, of, 4.04

foundations,
  failure of, 2.24
  purpose, 2.24

functions—*see* **delegation of functions**

fungal damage to timber—*see* **dampness**

furniture beetle—*see* **dampness**

gas,
  defective pipework, 2.14
  heater, moisture production, 8.78—8.79
  multiple occupation, house in,
    management, 6.37
    reconnection, 6.142—6.146
  North Sea, moisture emission, 8.79

general improvement area,
  compulsory improvement in,
    generally, 5.208
  improvement notice,
    service of, 5.221—5.227
    withdrawal of, 5.228
  proposals, discussions on, 5.212—5.214
  provisional notice, 5.209—5.211
  undertaking,
    discharge of, 5.220
    housing arrangements and, 5.215—5.219
  entry, powers of, 1.18

glycyphagus domesticus—*see* **mites**

grant,
  fire, means of escape in case of, 6.119
  multiple occupation, house in, 6.69

Greater London Council,
  fire, means of escape in case of, 6.60

guest-house,
  multiple occupation, fitness for, 6.25

habitation—*see* **human habitation**

hall,
  multiple occupation, house in, 6.39

health,
  dampness, threat resulting from—*see* **dampness**
  defect, effect of, 2.23—2.35
  factors affecting,
    bathroom, 2.17
    dampness—*see* **dampness**
    electric wiring, 2.14
    gas pipework, 2.12
    income, 2.12
    interior of dwelling, 2.22
    kitchen, 2.17
    lighting, 2.20
    noise, 2.21
    physical injury, 2.15
    residential area, 2.22
    space heating, 2.18
    thermal insulation, 2.18
    unemployment, 2.12

INDEX

health—*cont.*
  factors affecting—*cont.*
    ventilation, 2.19
    water, 2.13
    work experience, 2.12
  housing, relationship with, 2.05, 2.12
  meaning, 3.16
  mental — *see* **mental health**
  mites, threat from — *see* **mites**
  occupier, comparison of good and bad areas, 2.12
  prejudicial to, meaning, 3.16
  rehousing, effect of, 2.12
healthful housing,
  basic principles,
    accident, protection against, 2.08
    contagion, protection against, 2.08
    generally, 2.07
    physiological needs, 2.08
    psychological needs, 2.08
  guidelines, 2.05—2.11
  meaning, 2.10
  need for, 2.06
heating — *see* **space heating**
home,
  child health, effect on, 2.04
  loss payment, 9.33—9.37
  meaning, 2.03
  physical attributes, 2.03
Home Office,
  fire, means of escape in case of, 6.60
hostel,
  multiple occupation, fitness for, 6.25
house,
  condemned, purchase of, 5.159—5.169
  condition survey — *see* **house condition survey**
  construction, non-traditional methods, 2.09
  dust, mites contained in, 8.23—8.26
  human habitation, fitness for — *see* **human habitation**
  interpretation of term, 3.07
  local housing authority, owned by — *see* **council house**
  meaning, 2.03, 3.27—3.32, 6.08—6.09
  multiple occupation, in — *see* **multiple occupation, house in**
  personal comfort, interference with — *see* **personal comfort**
  shared basis, occupied on, 6.25
  substantial disrepair — *see* **substantial disrepair**
  see also **dwelling**
house condition survey,
  administrative arrangements, 2.101
  local authority, general duties of, 2.89
  quality control, 2.105—2.106

house condition survey—*cont.*
  results,
    multiplier, 2.109
    percentage, 2.108
    quality control, 2.106
    tabulation of, 2.107
  sample,
    computer stored information, obtained from, 2.97
    consecutive serial number, 2.99
    discarding process, 2.98
    errors, 2.96
    general principle, 2.89
    outline, 2.93—2.109
    principle for obtaining, 2.97
    split of, 2.100
    whole area, 2.90—2.91
  special, 2.92
  surveyor,
    briefing, 2.104
    knowledge, 2.103
    number of, 2.102
household,
  expectations of, 2.03
  form single, meaning, 6.13—6.14
housing,
  accommodation — *see* **accommodation**
  action area — *see* **housing action area**
  arrangements, meaning, 5.205
  conditions — *see* **conditions**
  enforcement procedures — *see* **enforcement**
  function, principles underlying, 2.02
  health, relationship with, 2.05, 2.12
  healthful — *see* **healthful housing**
  local authority — *see* **local housing authority**
  multiple occupation — *see* **multiple occupation, house in**
  non-traditional construction — *see* **non-traditional construction**
  order,
    home loss payment, 9.34
    meaning, 9.26, 9.34
    re-housing, obligation to ensure, 9.26
  overcrowding — *see* **overcrowding**
  standards — *see* **standards**
  statutory nuisance — *see* **nuisance**
housing action area,
  compulsory improvement in,
    generally, 5.208
    improvement notice,
      service of, 5.221—5.227
      withdrawal of, 5.228
    proposals, discussions on, 5.212—5.214
    provisional notice, 5.209—5.211
    undertaking,
      discharge of, 5.220

INDEX

housing action area—*cont.*
  compulsory improvement in—*cont.*
    undertaking—*cont.*
      housing arrangements and, 5.215—5.219
  entry, powers of, 1.18
human habitation,
  fitness for,
    accommodation to which applicable, 3.27—3.34
    common law, 3.21—3.23
    guidance notes,
      dampness, 3.38
      drainage, 3.43
      food, facilities for preparation of, 3.44
      internal arrangement, 3.39
      natural lighting, 3.40
      repair, 3.36
      sanitary convenience, 3.43
      stability, 3.37
      ventilation, 3.41
      waste water, disposal of, 3.44
      water supply, 3.42
    interpretation of standard, 3.35
    meaning, 3.19—3.20
    multiple occupation, fitness for, relationship with, 6.20
    revised fitness standard, 3.46A
    statutory fitness, 3.24—3.26
  unfitness for,
    action to deal with, generally, 5.65
    closing order,
      appeal against, right of, 5.140—5.143, 5.154—5.155
      British Rail, operational land owned by, 5.158
      circumstances giving rise to, 5.115
      demolition order, substitution of, 5.150
      determination of, 5.147—5.149
      enforcement, 5.144—5.146
      entry, right of, 5.156
      expenses, recovery of, 5.157
      format, 5.137
      part of building, in respect of, 5.151
      service of, 5.138—5.139
      statutory undertaker, land owned by, 5.158
      unoccupied building, security of, 5.152—5.153
    condemned house, purchase of,
      appeal against notice, right of, 5,161—5.169
      notice of intention, service of, 5.159—5.160
    demolition order,
      appeal against, right of, 5.119—5.123

human habitation—*cont.*
  unfitness for—*cont.*
    demolition order—*cont.*
      building which becomes listed, 5.132—5.133
      circumstances giving rise to, 5.115
      closing order, substitution of, 5.131
      demolition,
        contract for, 5.135
        cost of, 5.136
        time period, 5.134
      disinfestation of premises, 5.127—5.128
      enforcement, 5.124—5.126
      format, 5.116
      reconstruction, power to permit, 5.129—5.130
      service of, 5.117—5.118
      substitution of, 5.150
    duty to deal with, 5.66—5.69
    examples, 3.23
    person having control, 5.76—5.79
    reasonable expense,
      estimated costs of works, 5.71
      estimated value of house,
        after works, 5.72—5.75
        before works, 5.71
      generally, 5.70
    repair notice,
      appeal against, 5.85—5.89, 5.100—5.103
      charging order, 5.91
      costs incurred, lessee's right to recover part of, 5.90
      enforcement of, 5.93—5.99
      lessee,
        costs incurred, right to recover part of, 5.90
        protection of rights of, 5.92
      service of, 5.80—5.84
      tenant, protection of rights of, 5.92
      time and place notice,
        authority, consideration by, 5.109
        owner, proposal from, 5.107—5.108
        service of, 5.104—5.106
      undertaking, 5.110—5.114
humidity — *see* **dampness**
hut,
  human habitation, fitness for, 3.33
  personal comfort, interference with, 3.55
  substantial disrepair, in, 3.48
hygrometer,
  air temperature, measurement of, 8.96

I.E.H.O. — *see* **Institution of Environmental Health Officers**
improvement,
  area — *see* **area improvement**

INDEX

improvement—*cont.*
  compulsory — *see* **compulsory improvement**
  displacement of occupier caused by — *see* **occupier**
  meaning, 5.205
  notice,
    appeal against, 5.245—5.252
    charging order, 5.256—5.257
    costs incurred, addressee's right to recover part of, 5.255
    enforcement of, 5.264—5.269
    entry, powers of,
      obstruction, 1.19
      offence, 1.19
      other persons, powers of, 1.27—1.28
      purposes for which granted, 1.18—1.19
      statutory provisions, 1.15
      works, to carry out, 1.32
    entry, rights of, 5.253—5.254
    general improvement area, in,
      service of, 5.221—5.227
      withdrawal of, 5.228
    housing action area, in,
      service of, 5.221—5.227
      withdrawal of, 5.228
    liability, protection from, 5.253—5.254
    loan to cover costs, 5.258—5.260
    purchase notice, 5.262—5.263
    service of, 5.238—5.243
    withdrawal of, 5.244
    works, execution by authority under agency agreement, 5.261

income,
  health, effect on, 2.12

indemnity,
  insurance, 2.63

individual — *see* **private individual**

infestation,
  bugs, with, 3.23
  disinfestation, 5.127—5.128
  fleas, with, 3.23
  rats, with, 3.23

informal notice,
  issue of, 4.02—4.03

information,
  dwelling, inspection of — *see* **dwelling**
  local authority, general power to demand, 4.18
  local housing authority, general power to demand, 4.18
  multiple occupation, house in,
    local housing authority, for, 6.49—6.56
    occupant, for, 6.48
  offence, 4.19
  overcrowding, as to — *see* **overcrowding**

injunction,
  statutory nuisance,
    abatement of, 5.57—5.58
    prohibition of, 5.57—5.58

injury — *see* **physical injury**

inquiry — *see* **public inquiry**

insect damage to timber — *see* **dampness**

inspection,
  condensation, of,
    external, 8.110
    generally, 8.108—8.110
    internal, 8.111
    occupation details, 8.111
  dampness, sources of, 8.103—8.107
  defects, effect of, 2.23—2.35
  dwelling, of — *see* **dwelling**
  facilities,
    bathroom, 2.37
    kitchen, 2.36
    space heating, 2.38
    ventilation, 2.39
    w.c. compartment, 2.37
  from time to time, meaning, 1.10
  healthful housing — *see* **healthful housing**
  house condition survey — *see* **house condition survey**
  individual dwelling, of — *see* **dwelling**
  local housing authority, duties of, 1.05, 1.08
  non-traditional construction — *see* **non-traditional construction**
  principles of, 2.02—2.04
  report, example of, App. 1
  structural movement, monitoring of, 2.69—2.70
  works, specification of, 2.88

Institute of Housing,
  thermal insulation standards, 8.76

Institute of Environmental Health Officers,
  fire, means of escape in case of, 6.60
  multiple occupation, standards of fitness for, 6.25, 6.26

insulation — *see* **thermal insulation**

insurance,
  dwelling, inspection of, 2.63
  equipment, damage to, 2.63
  loss, 2.63
  professional indemnity, 2.63
  public liability, 2.63
  theft, 2.63

interference with personal comfort — *see* **personal comfort**

internal arrangement,
  condensation, investigation of, 8.110
  human habitation, fitness for, 3.39

intimation notice,
  issue of, 4.02

investigation — *see* **inspection**

itch mite — *see* **mites**

INDEX

jewel beetle — *see* **dampness**
justice of peace — *see* **magistrate**

kitchen,
  clothes washing and drying, 2.36
  conditions, 2.17
  cooking, 3.44
  facilities, 2.36
  food preparation, 3.44
  moisture production, 8.78, 8.80
  ventilation, 2.19
  wall surface, 2.32

laboratory,
  dampness in fabric, measurement for, 8.85—8.87
land,
  meaning, 3.10
landlord,
  meaning, 7.16
  overcrowding — *see* **overcrowding**
  standards, enforcement of, 3.02—3.04
lavatory — *see* **w.c. compartment**
legionella,
  spread of, 2.12
lessee,
  repair notice,
    costs incurred, right to recover part of, 5.90
    protection of rights of, 5.92
letter,
  warning, issue of, 4.02
liability,
  improvement works, protection from, 5.253—5.254
  insurance, 2.63
licence,
  permitted number, as to, 7.27—7.30
lighting,
  artificial,
    multiple occupation, house in, 6.24, 6.26
    need for, 2.20
  natural,
    advantages of, 2.20
    human habitation, fitness for, 3.40
    multiple occupation, house in, 6.24, 6.26
  secondary, in case of fire, 6.63
listed building,
  demolition, becoming prior to, 5.132—5.133
litter,
  multiple occupation, house in, 6.45
loan,
  improvement, to cover cost of, 5.258—5.260
lobby,
  multiple occupation, house in, 6.39

local authority,
  committee, 1.11—1.14
  delegation of functions, 1.11—1.14
  demand,
    service by, 4.11—4.14
    service on, 4.15—4.16
  document,
    service by, 4.11—4.14
    service on, 4.15—4.16
  information, general power to demand, 4.18
  meaning, 1.02, 1.04
  notice,
    service by, 4.11—4.14
    service on, 4.15—4.16
  officer — *see* **officer**
  order,
    service by, 4.11—4.14
    service on, 4.15—4.16
  other, delegation of functions to, 1.11—1.14
  sub-committee, 1.11—1.14
local government,
  local authority — *see* **local authority**
  local housing authority — *see* **local housing authority**
local housing authority,
  committee, 1.11—1.14
  delegation of functions, 1.11—1.14
  demand,
    service by, 4.11—4.14
    service on, 4.15—4.16
  document,
    service by, 4.11—4.14
    service on, 4.15—4.16
  entry, powers of — *see* **entry, powers of**
  general duties,
    accommodation, 1.06
    area improvement, 1.05
    conditions, 1.06
    enforcement, 1.09
    from time to time, meaning, 1.10
    inspection, 1.05, 1.08
    multiple occupation, house in, 1.05
    overcrowding, 1.07
    repair notice, 1.05
    slum clearance, 1.05
    statutory nuisance, 1.08
  house owned by — *see* **council house**
  information,
    general power to demand, 4.18
    multiple occupation, house in, 6.49—6.56
  meaning, 1.02, 1.03
  notice,
    service by, 4.11—4.14
    service on, 4.15—4.16
  officer — *see* **officer**

INDEX

local housing authority—*cont.*
  order,
    service by, 4.11—4.14
    service on, 4.15—4.16
  other, delegation of functions to, 1.11—1.14
  overcrowding, duty as to — *see* **overcrowding**
  sub-committee, 1.14—1.14
locality,
  repair, effect of standard of, 3.53
lodger,
  multiple occupation, house in, 6.25, 6.40—6.41
loss,
  equipment, of,
    home loss payment, 9.33—9.37
  insurance, 2.63

magistrate,
  entry, warrant issued in respect of,
    conditions, 1.39
    grounds for, 1.38
    multiple occupation, house in, 1.21, 1.24—1.25
maintenance,
  electricity, of, 6.142—6.146
  gas, of, 6.142—6.146
  water supply, of, 6.142—6.146
management,
  multiple occupation — *see* **multiple occupation, house in**
  scheme,
    appeal against, 6.174—6.177
    preparation of, 6.169—6.173
mealworm beetle — *see* **dampness**
measles,
  infection of, 3.23
Medical Entomology Centre, Cambridge University,
  beetles, identification of, 8.19
mental health,
  mould fungal spores, effect of, 8.32
  noise, effect of, 2.21
meter,
  capacitance, 8.91
  carbide, 8.88—8.89
  conductance, 8.91, 8.94
  di-electric field, 8.91
  hygroscopic salt, presence of, 8.94
  moisture, 8.90—8.94
  readings, 8.93—8.94
mites,
  allergic reactions, 8.23, 8.25—8.26
  environment, 8.24
  food choice, 8.22
  habitat, 8.22
  inhalation of, 8.25, 8.26
  scabies, responsibility for, 8.22

mites—*cont.*
  size, 8.22
  types of,
    acari, 8.22
    acarus siro, 8.22
    arachnida, 8.22
    carpoglyphus lactis, 8.22
    cheese mite, 8.22
    cheyletiella yasguri, 8.22
    dermanyssus gallinae, 8.22
    dermatophagoides pteronyssinus, 8.23, 8.24
    dried fruit mite, 8.22
    flour mite, 8.22
    glycyphagus domesticus, 8.23, 8.24
    itch mite, 8.22
    sarcoptes scabiei, 8.22
    tyrophagus casei, 8.22
  see also **dampness**
moisture,
  biological activities, from, 8.62—8.83
  domestic activities, from, 8.62—8.83
  everyday sources, 8.78
  meter, 8.90, 8.94
  production, 8.78—8.81
  removal, 8.116
  see also **dampness**
monitoring — *see* **inspection**
mortgagee,
  owner, as, 5.13
mould — *see* **dampness**
moveable dwelling,
  overcrowding in, 7.67
movement — *see* **structural movement**
mucor — *see* **dampness**
multiple occupation, house in,
  aspects of description, 6.07—6.14
  building deemed to be, 6.15—6.17
  control order — *see* **control**
  electricity supply,
    maintenance, 6.142—6.146
    management, 6.37
    reconnection, 6.142—6.146
  enforcement of notice,
    action, 6.132—6.133
    offence for failure to comply, 6.139—6.141
    works carried out in default, 6.134—6.138
  entry, powers of,
    obstruction, 1.23
    offence, 1.23
    officer, by, 1.21—1.23
    statutory provisions, 1.15
    warrant issued by magistrate, 1.21, 1.24—1.25
    works, to carry out, 1.33—1.34
  fire, means of escape in case of,
    additional legislation, 6.130—6.131

INDEX

multiple occupation, house in—*cont.*
  fire, means of escape in case of—*cont.*
    adequate, notice requiring,
      appeal against, 6.120—6.125
      enforcement, 6.126
      grant-aid for works, 6.119
      service of, 6.114—6.118
    alarm, 6.63
    alternative legislation, 6.130—6.131
    codes of practice, 6.60
    corridor, 6.61
    examples, outline diagrams of, 6.63
    legislation, 6.130—6.131
    national standards, 6.59—6.60
    other equipment, 6.63
    passage, 6.61
    principles, 6.57
    provision of, 6.112—6.113
    recommendations, 6.60
    risk, reduction of, 6.58
    secondary lighting, 6.63
    securing that part of house is not used, 6.127—6.129
    separate letting,
      parts occupied as, 6.62
      room occupied as, 6.62
    staircase, 6.61
  fitness,
    both standards, application of, 6.21
    general approach to, 6.22—6.23
    historical background, 6.18—6.19
    human habitation, fitness for, relationship with, 6.20
    interpretation of standard, 6.25—6.26
    meaning, 6.24
  form single household, meaning, 6.13—6.14
  gas supply,
    management, 6.37
    reconnection, 6.142—6.146
  generally, 6.01
  historical background to definition, 6.03—6.06
  house, meaning, 6.08—6.09
  local housing authority, general duties of, 1.05
  management,
    duties of,
      common use,
        installation in, 6.38
        other parts in, 6.39
        room in, 6.38
      drainage, 6.36
      electricity supply, 6.37
      fire, means of escape from, 6.43
      gas supply, 6.37
      heating, 6.37

multiple occupation, house in—*cont.*
  management—*cont.*
    duties of—*cont.*
      information, provision of,
        local housing authority, for, 6.49—6.54
        occupant, for, 6.48
      lighting, 6.37
      litter, disposal of, 6.45
      local authority, duty of, 6.56
      miscellaneous parts of house, 6.44
      occupant,
        duties of, 6.55
        general safety of, 6.46
      refuse, disposal of, 6.45
      tenant, accommodation let to, 6.40—6.41
      ventilation, 6.42
      water supply, 6.36
      windows, 6.42
    electricity supply, 6.37
    gas supply, 6.37
    general duties, 6.31—6.34
    generally, 6.29—6.30
    manager, meaning, 6.31—6.32
    order,
      appeal, 6.98—6.101
      effect of, 6.95—6.96
      making, 6.93—6.94
      meaning, 6.92
      revocation, 6.97
    regulations, prosecution of offence under, 6.102—6.103
    rent, meaning, 6.32
    water supply, 6.36
  meaning, 6.02
  neglect, notice to make good,
    appeal against, 6.108—6.110
    enforcement, 6.111
    service of, 6.104—6.107
  occupied, meaning, 6.10—6.12
  overcrowding—*see* **overcrowding**
  tenement block, 6.17
  unfitness,
    action to deal with, generally, 6.64
    number in occupation, direction to limit,
      appeal, 6.88—6.89
      generally, 6.78—6.86
      information as to, 6.90—6.91
      revocation, 6.87
      variation, 6.87
    works to make house fit,
      grant-aid, 6.69
      notice of,
        appeal against, 6.72—6.76
        enforcement, 6.77
        service of, 6.65—6.68
        withdrawal of, 6.70—6.71

INDEX

multiple occupation, house in—*cont.*
  water supply,
    maintenance, 6.142—6.146
    management, 6.36
    reconnection, 6.142—6.146
myxomycetes—*see* **dampness**

nacerdes melanura—*see* **dampness**
national house condition survey
  recommendations, 2.89
  see also **house condition survey**
natural lighting—*see* **lighting**
neglect,
  notice to make good—*see* **multiple occupation, house in**
new building,
  standards for control of, 3.05
new resident,
  meaning, 7.60
no-fines concrete,
  external wall, 2.25
  non-traditional construction, 2.75—2.76
noise,
  external environment, from, 2.21
  mental health, effect on, 2.21
  physical injury, cause of, 2.21
non-traditional construction,
  basic technical considerations, 2.09
  identification of, 2.72
  no-fines concrete, 2.75—2.76
  types of,
    Airey, 2.77
    bison, 2.87
    boot, 2.85
    British Iron and Steel Federation, 2.78
    Cornish unit, 2.79—2.80
    generally, 2.71—2.74
    orlit, 2.82
    reema, 2.81
    unity, 2.83
    Wates, 2.86
    woolaway, 2.84
North Sea gas,
  moisture emission, 8.79
notice,
  abatement—*see* **abatement notice**
  authentication, 4.06—4.10
  format, 4.04—4.05
  identification of person to be served with, 4.17—4.19
  improvement—*see* **improvement**
  informal, 4.02—4.03
  intimation, 4.02
  overcrowding—*see* **overcrowding**
  prohibition—*see* **prohibition notice**
  repair—*see* **repair**
  service of, 4.11—4.14, 4.15—4.16
  signing of, 4.10
  specification, example of, App. 2

notice—*cont.*
  time and place—*see* **time and place notice**
  works, specification of, 2.88
nuisance,
  meaning, 3.17
  order,
    appeal against, 5.46
    conviction, right of appeal against, 5.51
    court, power of, 5.42—5.45
    enforcement, 5.47—5.51
  private, meaning, 3.17
  public, meaning, 3.17
  statutory,
    abatement notice,
      appeal against, 5.24
      content of, 5.14—5.19
      non-compliance with, action for,
        court hearing, 5.28—5.41
        laying information, 5.25—5.27
      owner, meaning, 5.10—5.13
      service of, 5.05—5.09
    conditions applicable to, 3.09
    duty to deal with, 5.03—5.04
    expenses, recovery of, 5.52—5.55
    injunction, 5.57—5.58
    land, meaning, 3.10
    local housing authority, general duties of, 1.08
    meaning, 3.08—3.09
    non-compliance with notice, action for,
      court hearing, 5.28—5.41
      laying information, 5.25—5.27
    nuisance order,
      appeal against, 5.46
      conviction, right of appeal against, 5.51
      court, made by, 5.42—5.45
      enforcement, 5.47—5.51
    overcrowding—*see* **overcrowding**
    premises,
      assessment of, 3.18
      meaning, 3.10—3.11
      physical condition of, 3.12—3.17
    procedure to deal with, generally, 5.02
    prohibition notice,
      appeal against, 5.24
      non-compliance with, action for,
        court hearing, 5.28—5.41
        laying information, 5.25—5.27
      service of, 5.20—5.23A
    situations applicable to, 3.09
    two or more persons, caused by, 5.56
    urgent,
      expenses, recovery of, 5.63—5.64
      speedy procedure to deal with, 5.59—5.64

obstruction—*see* **entry, powers of**

INDEX

occupant,
  interior of dwelling, effect of, 2.22
  multiple occupation, house in,
    general safety, 6.46—6.47
    information, 6.48
  residential area, effect of, 2.22
occupation,
  condensation, investigation of, 8.111
  multiple — *see* **multiple occupation, house in**
  over-occupation — *see* **overcrowding**
occupied,
  meaning, 6.10—6.12
occupier,
  displaced,
    disturbance payment, 9.28—9.32
    home loss payment, 9.33—9.37
    obligations to, 9.23—9.38
    other compensation, 9.38
    re-housing, obligation to ensure, 9.25—9.27
  good and bad areas compared, 2.12
  overcrowding — *see* **overcrowding**
offence,
  entry, powers of,
    improvement notice, 1.19
    multiple occupation, house in, 1.23
    overcrowding, 1.26
    repair notice, 1.17
    slum clearance, 1.20
  information, disclosure of, 4.19
  management regulations, under, 6.102—6.103
  multiple occupation, house in,
    enforcement, 6.139—6.141
    entry, powers of, 1.23
    notice, failure to comply with, 6.139—6.141
  overcrowding — *see* **overcrowding**
officer,
  authorisation, 2.64
  delegation of functions to, 1.11—1.14
  dwelling, assessment of, 2.03
  entry, powers of,
    multiple occupation, house in, 1.21—1.23
    persons who may accompany, 1.37
    purposes, 1.36
    slum clearance, 1.20
oil heater,
  moisture production, 8.78—8.79
opinion,
  dwelling, inspection of, 2.65—2.67
order,
  authentication, 4.06—4.10
  closing — *see* **closing order**
  compulsory purchase, after control order, 6.194—6.198
  control — *see* **control**

order—*cont.*
  demolition — *see* **demolition**
  format, 4.04—4.05
  housing — *see* **housing**
  identification of person to be served with, 4.17—4.19
  nuisance — *see* **nuisance**
  service of, 4.11—4.14, 4.15—4.16
  signing of, 4.10
orlit,
  non-traditional construction, 2.82
overcrowding,
  agent, meaning, 7.16
  definitions, 7.14—7.19
  dwelling, meaning, 7.15
  enforcement,
    notice, 7.44—7.47
    prosecution of offence, 7.43
    survey, 7.39—7.42
  entry, powers of,
    obstruction, 1.26
    offence, 1.26
    purposes, 1.26
    statutory provisions, 1.15
  historical background, 7.02—7.06
  information,
    duty to provide, 7.31
    local housing authority, duty of, 7.36—7.38
    occupier, for, 7.32—7.35
  landlord,
    meaning, 7.16, 7.32
    offence by, 7.23—7.26
    rent book, provision of, 7.32—7.35
  local housing authority, general duties of, 1.07
  moveable dwelling, in, 7.67
  multiple occupation, house in,
    fitness, 6.27—6.28
    local housing authority, action by,
      generally, 7.52
      notice of intention, 7.53—7.54
    overcrowding notice,
      appeal, 7.65—7.66
      contents, 7.56
      numbers, information as to, 7.62
      offence, 7.63
      revocation, 7.64
      service of, 7.55—7.61
      variation, 7.64
  new resident, meaning, 7.60
  notice,
    appeal, 7.65—7.66
    contents, 7.56
    numbers, information as to, 7.62
    offence, 7.63
    revocation, 7.64
    service of, 7.55—7.61
    variation, 7.64

INDEX

overcrowding—*cont.*
  offence,
    landlord, by, 7.23—7.26
    notice, as to, 7.63
    occupier, by, 7.20—7.22
  other provisions relating to, 7.68
  owner, meaning, 7.16
  permitted number, licence to exceed, 7.27—7.30
  person, meaning, 7.17
  room,
    meaning, 7.15
    measurement of, 7.13
    standard, 7.09—7.10
  sexual, 7.09—7.10, 7.59
  shed, in, 7.67
  standards,
    generally, 7.07—7.08
    meaning, 7.08
    room, 7.09—7.10
    space, 7.11—7.13
  suitable alternative accommodation, meaning, 7.18—7.19
  temporary dwelling, in, 7.67
  tent, in, 7.67
  van, in, 7.67

owner,
  entry, power of, 1.40
  meaning, 5.10—5.13, 5.79, 5.205, 7.16
  mortgagee as, 5.13
  receiver cannot be, 5.13
  time and place notice, proposals as to, 5.107—5.108
  trustee as, 5.13

owner-occupier,
  meaning, 5.205

oyster fungus — *see* **dampness**

paraffin,
  moisture emission, 8.79

passage,
  fire, means of escape in case of, 6.61
  multiple occupation, house in, 6.39

paxillus panuoides — *see* **dampness**
peaziza spp. — *see* **dampness**
penicillium — *see* **dampness**
pentarthrum huttoni — *see* **dampness**

person,
  meaning, 7.17

personal comfort,
  interference with,
    accommodation to which applicable, 3.55
    action to deal with, generally, 5.170—5.172
    interpretation of standard, 3.56—3.59
    meaning, 3.54
    reasonable expense, 5.177—5.178

personal comfort—*cont.*
  interference with—*cont.*
    repair notice,
      appeal against, 5.187—5.192
      charging order, 5.194
      enforcement, 5.196—5.201
      lessee,
        costs incurred, right to recover part of, 5.193
        protection of rights of, 5.195
      service of, 5.179—5.186
      tenant, protection of rights of, 5.195
    representations as to, 5.174—5.176
  meaning, 3.58

personal washing facilities,
  condensation, investigation of, 8.111
  multiple occupation, house in, 6.24, 6.26

phellinus contiguus — *see* **dampness**

physical injury,
  causes of, 2.15
  noise, effect of, 2.21

physiological needs,
  healthful housing, basic principles of, 2.08

pipework,
  gas, 2.14
  rain waterfall, 2.27
  water, metal used for, 2.13

place — *see* **time and place notice**
pleurotus ostreatus — *see* **dampness**

premises,
  assessment of, 3.18
  disinfestation of, 5.127—5.128
  human habitation, fitness for — *see* **human habitation**
  in such a state, meaning, 3.12
  interpretation of terrm, 3.07
  meaning, 3.10—3.11
  physical condition of, 3.12—3.17

private individual,
  standards, enforcement of, 3.02—3.04

private nuisance,
  meaning, 3.17

prohibition notice,
  appeal against, 5.24
  non-compliance with, action for,
    court hearing, 5.28—5.41
    laying information, 5.25—5.27
  service of, 5.20—5.23A

propane,
  moisture emission, 8.79

provisional notice,
  compulsory improvement procedure, 5.209—5.211, 5.234—5.235

psychological needs,
  healthful housing, basic principles of, 2.08

INDEX

public inquiry,
evidence,
expert witness, 9.03, 9.08—9.10
generally, 9.02—9.03
hearsay, rule of, 9.11—9.17
principles of, 9.04—9.07
local authority, challenge to action taken by, 2.41
public nuisance,
meaning, 3.17
pullularia spp. — *see* **dampness**
purchase notice,
improvement notice, following, 5.262—5.263
pyronema domesticum — *see* **dampness**

quality control,
housing condition survey, 2.105—2.106

rainwater — *see* **water**
rats,
infestation of, 3.23
re-housing,
displaced occupier, obligation to ensure, 9.25—9.27
receiver,
owner, cannot be, 5.13
reconnection,
electricity, of, 6.142—6.146
gas, of, 6.142—6.146
water supply, of, 6.142—6.146
reconstruction,
power to permit, 5.129—5.130
recovery of expenses — *see* **expenses**
reema,
non-traditional construction, 2.81
reference material,
books, App. 4
magazines, App. 4
refuse disposal,
multiple occupation, house in, 6.26, 6.45
rehousing,
health, effect on, 2.12
relative humidity — *see* **dampness**
remedial works — *see* **works**
render,
defects, 2.25
repair,
human habitation, fitness for, 3.36
notice,
appeal against, 5.85—5.89, 5.100—5.103
charging order, 5.91
costs incurred, lessee's right to recover part of, 5.90
enforcement of, 5.93—5.99
entry, powers of,
obstruction, 1.17
offence, 1.17

repair—*cont.*
notice—*cont.*
entry, powers of—*cont.*
purposes for which given, 1.16
statutory provisions, 1.15
works, to carry out, 1.29—1.31
lessee,
costs incurred, right to recover part of, 5.90
protection of rights of, 5.92
local housing authority, general duty of, 1.05
personal comfort, interference with — *see* **personal comfort**
service of, 5.80—5.84
substantial disrepair, house in — *see* **substantial disrepair**
tenant, protection of rights of, 5.92
report,
dwelling, inspection of, 2.68
inspection, example of, App. 1
resident,
new, meaning, 7.60
residential area,
well-being of occupant, effect on, 2.22
residential home,
multiple occupation, fitness for, 6.25
respiratory disease,
fungal damage giving rise to, 8.16
mites responsible for, 8.23, 8.25—8.26
mould fungal spores,
caused by, 8.30
sampling of, 8.102
results,
housing condition survey — *see* **house condition survey**
rhinitis,
fungal damage giving rise to, 8.16
mites responsible for, 8.23
roof,
chimney stack, 2.26
condensation in, 8.58—8.59
construction, 2.26
covering, 2.26
flat, 2.26
room,
condensation, investigation of, 8.110
description of, 2.52—2.54
meaning, 7.15
multiple occupation, house in, 6.25
overcrowding,
measurement of, 7.13
standard, 7.09—7.10
underground, 3.34
rot — *see* **dampness**
Royal Institute of British Architects,
thermal insulation standards, 8.76

370

INDEX

safety,
    multiple occupation, house in, 6.46—6.47
salt,
    dampness, contamination caused by, 8.08—8.10
    efflorescent, 8.10
    hygroscopic, 8.08, 8.09, 8.94
sample house condition survey — *see* **house condition survey**
sanitation,
    sanitary idea, development of, 2.05
    water closet — *see* **w.c. compartment**
sarcoptes scabiei — *see* **mites**
scabies,
    mites responsible for, 8.22
security,
    unoccupied building, of, 5.152—5.153
serpula lacrymans — *see* **dampness**
sexual overcrowding,
    multiple occupation, house in, 7.59
    prevention of, 7.09—7.10
shed,
    overcrowding in, 7.67
shower,
    fixed, as standard amenity, 3.62
sink,
    standard amenity, as, 3.62
slime mould — *see* **dampness**
slum clearance,
    entry, powers of,
        obstruction, 1.20
        offence, 1.20
        purposes, 1.20
        statutory provisions, 1.15
    local housing authority, general duties of, 1.05
sources of dampness — *see* **dampness**
space,
    multiple occupation, house in, 6.26
    overcrowding, 7.11—7.13
space heating,
    atmospheric balance, effect on, 8.64—8.70
    condensation,
        investigation of, 8.111
        remedial works, 8.113—8.115
    multiple occupation, house in, 6.24, 6.26
    open fire, 2.38
    provision for, 2.38
    radiator, 2.38
    solid fuel, 2.38
    thermal environment, effect on, 2.18
specification,
    example, App. 2
    works, of, 2.88
spores — *see* **dampness**
stability,
    human habitation, fitness for, 3.37

stairs,
    defective, 3.23
    fire, means of escape in case of, 6.61
    multiple occupation, house in, 6.39
standard amenity — *see* **amenity**
standards,
    discretionary nature of, 2.02
    entry, powers of — *see* **entry, powers of**
    existing dwelling, applicable to, 3.06—3.07
    human habitation, fitness for — *see* **human habitation**
    multiple occupation — *see* **multiple occupation, house in**
    new building, control of, 3.05
    overcrowding — *see* **overcrowding**
    personal comfort, interference with,
        accommodation to which applicable, 3.55
        interpretation of standard, 3.56—3.59
        meaning, 3.54
    private individual, enforcement by, 3.02—3.04
    standard amenity,
        accommodation to which applicable, 3.61
        full standard, 3.63, 3.64
        human habitation, fitness for, 3.66
        interpretation of standard, 3.62—3.66
        meaning, 3.62
        minimum, establishment of, 3.60
        proposed target standard, 3.66A
        reduced standard, 3.63, 3.65
    statutory nuisance — *see* **nuisance**
    substantial disrepair,
        accommodation to which applicable, 3.48
        interpretation of standard, 3.49—3.53
        meaning, 3.47
    thermal insulation, 8.76
statutory nuisance — *see* **nuisance**
statutory undertaker,
    operational land owned by, 5.158
stemphylium — *see* **dampness**
structural movement,
    metal discs, use of, 2.70
    monitoring of, 2.69—2.70
    tell-tale, use of, 2.69—2.70
sub-committee,
    delegation of functions to, 1.11—1.14
substantial disrepair,
    accommodation to which applicable, 3.48
    action to deal with, generally, 5.170—5.172
    age, 3.53
    character, 3.53
    detection of house in, 5.173
    interpretation of standard, 3.49—3.53
    locality, 3.53

INDEX

substantial disrepair—*cont.*
  meaning, 3.47
  reasonable expense, 5.177—5.178
  repair notice,
    appeal against, 5.187—5.192
    charging order, 5.194
    enforcement, 5.196—5.201
    lessee,
      costs incurred, right to recover part of, 5.193
      protection of rights of, 5.195
    service of, 5.179—5.186
    tenant, protection of rights of, 5.195
survey,
  from time to time, meaning, 1.10
  house condition — *see* **house condition survey**
  overcrowding provisions, enforcement of, 7.39—7.42

tell-tale,
  structural movement, monitoring of, 2.69—2.70
temporary dwelling,
  overcrowding in, 7.67
tenancy,
  long, meaning, 5.205
tenant,
  multiple occupation, house in, management of, 6.40—6.41
  repair notice, protection of rights of, 5.92
  standards, enforcement of, 3.02—3.04
tenebrio mollitor — *see* **dampness**
tenement block,
  meaning, 6.17
  multiple occupation, house in, deemed to be, 6.17
tent,
  human habitation, fitness for, 3.33
  overcrowding in, 7.67
  personal comfort, interference with, 3.55
  substantial disrepair, in, 3.48
theft of equipment,
  insurance, 2.63
thermal insulation,
  atmospheric balance, effect on, 8.75—8.77
  condensation, remedial works for, 8.113—8.115
  dampness, presence of, 8.20—8.21
  external noise, from, 2.21
  standards, 8.76
  thermal environment, effect on, 2.18
  thermal transmittance coefficient, 8.75
thermo-hygrometer,
  relative humidity, measurement of, 8.96
thermograph,
  air temperature, monitoring of, 8.96

thermometer,
  air temperature, measurement of, 8.96
timber — *see* **dampness**
time and place notice,
  authority, consideration by, 5.109
  owner, proposal from, 5.107—5.108
  service of, 5.104—5.106
trustee,
  owner, as, 5.13
tyrophagus casei — *see* **mites**

undertaking,
  compulsory improvement procedure, 5.215—5.220
  human habitation, house unfit for, 5.110—5.114
unemployment,
  health, effect on, 2.12
unfitness,
  human habitation, for — *see* **human habitation**
unity,
  non-traditional construction, 2.83
unoccupied building,
  security of, 5.152—5.153
urgent statutory nuisance — *see* **nuisance**

van,
  overcrowding in, 7.67
ventilation,
  air changes, 2.19
  atmospheric balance, effect on, 8.71—8.74
  bathroom, 2.19
  clothes drying, 2.36, 2.39
  condensation,
    investigation of, 8.111
    remedial works, 8.116
  heat and, 8.37
  human habitation, fitness for, 3.41
  kitchen, 2.19
  multiple occupation, house in, 6.24, 6.26, 6.42
  natural, 2.39
  provision for, 2.39
  sewerage system, 2.29

w.c. compartment,
  basin, 2.37
  conditions, 2.17
  multiple occupation, house in, 6.24, 6.26
  sewerage system, 2.29
  standard amenity, as, 3.62
  wall surface, 2.32
  see also **bathroom**
wall,
  cavity, function of, 8.52
  condensation, investigation of, 8.110
  damp proof course, 2.25

372

INDEX

wall—*cont.*
  external, 2.25
  internal, 2.32
  render, 2.25
  skirting board, 2.32
  window sill, 2.25
warning letter,
  issue of, 4.02
warrant,
  entry, powers of,
    conditions, 1.39
    grounds for, 1.38
    multiple occupation, house in, 1.21, 1.24—1.25
washing facilities—*see* **personal washing facilities**
waste water—*see* **water**
water,
  construction process, used in, 8.36—8.40
  contamination, 2.13
  fall pipe, 2.27, 8.53
  pipe, metal used for, 2.13
  supply,
    adequacy of, 3.42
    insufficient, 3.23
    multiple occupation, house in,
      maintenance, 6.142—6.146
      management, 6.36
      reconnection, 6.142—6.146
      standards, 6.24, 6.26
    wholesome, whether, 3.42
  waste,
    defect, effect of, 2.29
    multiple occupation, house in, 6.24, 6.26
  see also **dampness**
Wates,
  non-traditional construction, 2.86

weevil—*see* **dampness**
wharf borer beetle—*see* **dampness**
white rot—*see* **dampness**
window,
  condensation, investigation of, 8.110
  multiple occupation, house in,
    management of, 6.42
  opening light, 2.35
  purpose, 2.35
  sill, 2.25
witness,
  expert, 9.03, 9.08—9.10
wood—*see* **dampness**
wood boring weevil—*see* **dampness**
woolaway,
  non-traditional construction, 2.84
work experience,
  health, effect on, 2.12
works,
  agency agreement, execution by authority under, 5.261
  condensation, for, 8.112—8.116
  entry to carry out,
    improvement notice, 1.32
    multiple occupation, house in, 1.33—1.34
    repair notice, 1.29—1.31
  human habitation, house unfit for,
    estimated cost, 5.71
    estimated value after, 5.72—5.75
    estimated value before, 5.71
  multiple occupation, house in—*see* **multiple occupation, house in**
  specification of, 2.88
World Health Organisation,
  healthful housing, meaning, 2.10

xestobium rufovillosum—*see* **dampness**